Format design by Nancy H. Dale

First edition

Library of Congress
Catalogue Card Number: 60-5451

Manufactured in the
United States of America
Van Rees Press • New York

The author and the publisher wish to thank the following for their
kind permission to quote their materials: J. M. Dent & Sons Ltd.,
The Nigger of the Narcissus, by Joseph Conrad; Harcourt, Brace
and Company, *The American Songbag,* compiled by Carl Sandburg; W. W. Norton & Company, Inc., *Songs of American Sailormen,* by Joanna C. Colcord; Oxford University Press, Inc., *Aaron
Copland,* by Arthur Berger, *Singing Family of the Cumberlands,*
by Jean Ritchie; Theodore Presser Company, *One Hundred English
Folksongs,* by Cecil Sharp, Copyright 1916; The Viking Press, Inc.,
The Grapes of Wrath, by John Steinbeck.

Folksingers and
Folksongs in America

FOLKSINGERS AND FOLKSONGS IN AMERICA

A handbook of biography, bibliograph and discography by

RAY M. LAWLE

Illustrated from paintings
Thomas Hart Benton and
others, and from designs in
Steuben Glass

DUELL, SLOAN AND PEARCE New Yo

To the Memory of

My Great-Uncle } Jimmy Blair

Maker of Country Fiddles and a
Natural-Born Musician

Preface

BEFORE the critics get their shootin' irons primed and pointed my way, let me hasten to explain the title of this book. The word "folksingers" in the title is used in its broadest sense— meaning anyone who sings folksongs as a regular practice, either for pleasure or for profit. Many of the singers presented here are not traditional singers but are singers of folksongs: the point is further clarified in the Prologue and in the short biographies. Another point: the "in America" of the title means only the United States and parts of Canada, not South of the Border.

So extensive have become the activities of folksinging, of folksong collecting and recording in our time, and so rich is the field for both singer and collector, that I believe it will prove useful and, perhaps, entertaining to present an over-all picture of the field. A brief Prologue attempts some clarification of terms and problems. Book One presents brief biographies of about 225 singers. Some of these who have attained national, and even international, reputations by their performance in folksong literature, in fact, who have made a career as balladeers, I have discussed in a reasonably full account. Others are presented briefly, either because their folksong activity seemed minor or my information about them was scanty.

Interlude I offers a brief discussion of folk-music instruments, suggesting something of their history, structure, and current use.

The Library of Congress, Music Division, *Check-List of Recorded Songs in the English Language in the Archive of American Folk Song* (to July, 1940), as well as many other sources, throws much light on the use and popularity of folk instruments.

The annotated bibliography offered in Book Two, though not definitive, is intended to give an accurate and popular description of the major, and indeed many minor, collections of American ballads and folksongs, and to present a brief description of some important archives. Some background works of one kind or another are added for good measure. It is hoped that the annotations will be useful to teachers, librarians, researchers, or others wanting specific information on collections.

Questions of provenience of particular ballads and folksongs, their line of ancestry and their many variant forms, have been left to the more scholarly minded. Much has been done on these problems and much remains to be done. But the purpose in Book Two has been to group the collections, to describe them, to make some observations, and to draw a few comparisons, so that anyone interested in American folksong may have a bird's-eye view of the field. Since the American field alone is extensive, I have arbitrarily excluded British and other nationalities. There is bound to be overlapping in many areas—for instance, in sea songs and ballads—but this does not affect the major plan of classification.

Interlude II presents two related but often differing interests in folklore activities: folklore societies and folk festivals. These two aspects of folklore, related but often separated—the one mainly scholarly and the other mainly popular—show increasing activity in our complex American cultural heritage.

Book Three is an attempt to give a reasonably complete listing, with song titles, of long-playing records of folksongs, one group presented alphabetically by singers' names, another group by album titles. A limited check list of song titles is given for further reference, and the method of developing this list is discussed in Book Three.

The present study is intended to throw a little candlelight rather than a brilliant fluorescence on an exceedingly fascinating and varied field: the collecting and singing of ballads and folksongs. Indeed, with a few carefully selected background books, an anthology of representative folksongs and ballads, a double handful of carefully chosen records, and a good player, this study may very well serve as a popular reference text.

Readers are invited to send me comment or criticism, corrections or additions. Being of a sanguine turn of mind, I like to think that further editions are in the offing. Most surely, as time passes, there will be further collections, new singers, and more recordings, for folksong is living musical literature.

R. M. L.

Junior College of Kansas City
3845 McGee Street
Kansas City 11, Missouri

Acknowledgments

A REFERENCE work like FOLKSINGERS AND FOLKSONGS IN AMERICA could not be written without the help of many people and many published sources, and it is a pleasure to acknowledge my indebtedness.

Book One is built largely out of the factual detail given me directly by the more than two hundred singers who have so willingly cooperated in filling out questionnaires, answering letters, submitting to interviews, and, in various ways, putting facts at my disposal. I thank them all for their generous and friendly aid. Often, in the biographical sketches, for liveliness and color I prefer to let the singers speak for themselves. Some who have given far more than the usual courtesies required should be mentioned here for special thanks: John Allison, Hélène Baillargeon, Bobby Barnes, Robert and Evelyne Beers, Bill Bonyun, Oscar Brand, the late Charles F. Bryan, Loman Cansler, Paul Clayton, Kathy Dagel, Bob Duncan, Richard Dyer-Bennet, Sam Eskin, Dr. Patrick Gainer, Dr. Shep Ginandes, Terry Golden, Anne Grimes, Cisco Houston, Max Hunter, E. G. Huntington, Burl and Helen Ives, Gene Jemison, Buell Kazee, Barry Kornfeld, Adolph and Augusta Kukler, May Kennedy McCord, Brownie (Dr. Norman L.) McNeil, Alan Mills, Absie Morrison, Jim and Carmen Murray, John Jacob and Rena Niles, Joan O'Bryant, Mary O'Hara, the Ritchie family (especially Jean), Ruth Rubin, Pete Seeger, Fred M. Smith, Win Stracke, Pick Temple, Ross Whitmire, and Hally Wood (Gordon).

Printed sources used in preparing the Prologue and Interludes I and II, as well as other portions of the text, have been acknowledged by footnotes. Some persons and titles should have further specific mention here. Issues of the *Journal of American Folklore* have furnished numerous references of one kind or another, and Charles Haywood's monumental *Bibliography* has proved indispensable. I have drawn freely on standard histories of music and musical instruments, and these are mentioned in footnotes. For details on folklore societies I am indebted to Professor Wayland D. Hand and the *Journal of American Folklore*. For permission to use Thomas Eakins' "Cowboy Singing," I am indebted to the Metropolitan Museum of Art; for "Swing Low Sweet Chariot," to the City Art Museum, St. Louis; for the painting "Casey Jones," to Fred Ludekens and *Esquire* magazine; for many courtesies, to Thomas Hart and Rita Benton; and for permission to use Benton paintings, I am indebted to the Bentons and to various owners of Benton works.

Book Three is based largely on the catalogues of many recording companies. I am especially grateful to the following record makers for materials and information: Audio-Fidelity, Capitol, Cavalier, Columbia, Decca, Dyer-Bennet, Elektra, Folkways, Judson, London, Lyrichord, RCA Victor, Rebel, Riverside, Stinson, Topic, Tradition, Vanguard, Verve, Westminster. Two general record catalogues, *The Long Player* and *Schwann's Long Playing Record Catalog*, have been combed for numerous details.

I would be less than grateful if I did not mention the many libraries that have had a share in this work: the Junior College Library and the Public Library of Kansas City, Missouri; the University Libraries of Kansas and Missouri; the Public Library of St. Louis, Missouri; the Library of Lincoln University, Jefferson City, Missouri. I am especially grateful for the inter-library loan service, which has made it possible for me to use books from all parts of the country without the expense of travel and time. My thanks are due also to G. Schirmer, Inc., New York, for the loan of sets of "The American Folk-Song Series."

I cannot begin to name all who have been helpful in one way or another, but I wish to mention a few: Archie Green, San Francisco, for the loan of many books; Norman E. Pierce, San Francisco; Ben Gray Lumpkin of the University of Colorado; Otto Rayburn and Vance Randolph of Eureka Springs, Arkansas; Lewis Nordyke of Amarillo, Texas; Duncan Emrich, formerly of the Library of Congress, Music Division; Mrs. Rae Korson, Reference Librarian, Archive of American Folk Song, Library of Congress; my colleagues Dean Miles G. Blim, Assistant Dean Howard N. Monnett, Dr. Arthur

N. Wilkins, and John M. Gazda, all of the Junior College; and the following Junior College students who have assisted in clerical services: Ernest Z. Adelman, Mrs. Kent McMillen, Deanna Nunn, Sharon Tunnell, Mrs. Nelson Whipkey; and the Dean's secretary, Mrs. Dollie Button Heisler. Dr. Wilkins and Miss Florence Trotter have done me inestimable service in reading proof.

Further, I am grateful to the publisher, Mr. Charles A. Pearce of Duell, Sloan and Pearce, for helpful suggestions and encouraging letters during the later stages of preparing this book.

Finally, I wish to thank my wife, Mrs. Hazel Kesler Lawless, for clerical help, encouragement, and unending patience over long years of work.

However much assistance I may have had from any of the above-named persons, printed sources, or institutions—and they have given much—I hasten to absolve them from responsibility for errors and shortcomings in the pages that follow.

RAY M. LAWLESS

Contents

Preface   vii

Acknowledgments   xi

List of Illustrations   xvii

PROLOGUE

CHAPTER 1: Some Problems and Definitions   3

CHAPTER 2: Folksong and the Fine Arts   12

BOOK ONE An alphabetical presentation of singers of ballads and folksongs

CHAPTER 3: The Singers, A to C   29

CHAPTER 4: The Singers, D to G   73

CHAPTER 5: The Singers, H to K   107

CHAPTER 6: The Singers, L to M   138

CHAPTER 7: The Singers, N to R   173

CHAPTER 8: The Singers, S to Z (with Supplement)   204

INTERLUDE I

CHAPTER 9:   Folk-Music Instruments   247

BOOK TWO   Collections of ballads and folksongs

CHAPTER 10: The Collecting of Ballads and Folksongs   271
CHAPTER 11: "The Big Ten" Among Collectors   275
CHAPTER 12: Other Major Collections   297
CHAPTER 13: Compilations Designed for Singing   326
CHAPTER 14: Minor Compilations and Curiosities   360
CHAPTER 15: Archives and Bibliographical Items   393
CHAPTER 16: Supplemental Section of Background Books   410

INTERLUDE II

CHAPTER 17: Folklore Societies and Folk Festivals   433

BOOK THREE   Folksong Titles and Discography

CHAPTER 18: A Check List of Folksong Titles   451
CHAPTER 19: Long-Playing Records of Individual
             Singers   485
CHAPTER 20: Long-Playing Records of Choral or Other
             Groups, Instrumentals, etc.   586

Index of Names and Subjects   631
Title Index   644
Index of Long-Playing Records   655

Illustrations

following page 206

"The Music Lesson," by Thomas Hart Benton

"Home on the Range" commemorative plaque

"Home on the Range" birthplace

"The Jealous Lover of Lone Green Valley," by Thomas Hart Benton

"The Wreck of the Old 97," by Thomas Hart Benton

"Jesse James Train Robbery," by Thomas Hart Benton

"Swing Low Sweet Chariot," by John McCrady

"Cowboy Singing," from the White House piano

"New England Barn Dance," from the White House piano

"Ceremonial Chant of the American Indians," from the White House piano

"Negro Cotton-Picker," from the White House piano

The White House piano

"The Virginia Reel," from the White House piano

"Casey Jones," by Fred Ludekens

following page 430

"Cowboy Singing," by Thomas Eakins

Steuben glass: "Stephen Foster Bowl"

Steuben glass: "Prairie Smoke"

Steuben glass: "The Western Group"

Steuben glass: "The American Ballad Series"

"Sourwood Mountain," by Thomas Hart Benton

Anne Grimes with folk-music instruments

A group of Schwarzer zithers

Jethro Amburgey making a dulcimer and Homer Ledford playing a dulcimer

Lon Jordan demonstrates a method of fiddling

Nemonie Balfour playing the lute

Ruth Tyler playing a primitive Ozark dulcimer

Prologue

CHAPTER 1

Some Problems
and Definitions

HALF a century and more ago, many students of folksong, looking regretfully toward the past and uncertainly toward the future, noted that ballads and folksongs were something that had had their day. Old people knew many old songs, but the old people were passing. Young folks were singing different songs learned from the gramophone, phonograph, tin-pan alley, or the music hall. The English collector, Cecil J. Sharp, rarely collected from anyone under sixty. He felt that folksinging would soon be extinct, that no one born after 1840 could be a folksinger.[1] The great Francis James Child in the late nineteenth century barely touched the oral sources for his great collection. Even as late as 1922, Louise Pound, editing a book of ballads and songs, noted that their singing had gone out of fashion, that rural entertainment had been changed by the new mechanical devices.[2]

Growing urban life seemed less conducive to folksinging than rural life had been in an earlier day. With easier and faster means of travel, with telephones and other mechanical devices of communication, regional areas were gradually losing their isolation and hence tended to draw away from the past. It was supposed that folksongs and folksinging were on the way out, except as an antiquarian hobby, as new times brought new interests.

But folksongs—a part of our culture for centuries past—and folksingers—a healthy tribe despite our vast mechanization—have a stubborn existence not easily ignored nor soon forgotten. As we

3

think, therefore, of singers and songs and collectors, we find the resurgence of folksong in our generation to be one of the minor miracles of a highly industrialized society. Reasons for this resurgence are numerous and somewhat complex, but not far to seek.

Two world wars have made Americans more and more aware of their cultural resources, among which is the great wealth of folksong, inherited and native-born. Realizing that times change, collectors began salvaging the oral songs. They discovered, often, more than they expected. Folksingers, finding their songs were taken seriously, began remembering more and more; hence, the collecting and publishing of folksongs have brought them—the songs and the singers—to public attention. Both popular and serious composers turned to folksongs as a new source of inspiration for new compositions. This fact has led to confusion as to what a folksong is and what use should be made of it. Some facts which at first tended to destroy folksinging were the very factors that helped to preserve it: canned music, for instance, instead of replacing folk music, offered a means of popularizing it and of preserving it. This fact also has led to confusion in the public mind as to what a folksong is.

Another fact, no doubt, has contributed to the resurgence of folksong. Though the folksong is relatively simple and is thought of as primitive music, its intrinsic beauty and universal appeal have given it a standing as genuine art. A highly trained singer no longer condescends in presenting a folksong even on the most formal program, and certainly no composer, of whatever ability, apologizes for using a folk tune for a new composition. Indeed, such a fact may enhance his composition.

The question, then, is not how soon will American folksong become extinct, but rather what form or forms it will take in survival. It will survive in the many recordings that have been made. The Archive of American Folk Song in the Library of Congress now has more than 40,000 pieces of recorded folk music, some of which are available to the public on nonbreakable records. Besides this vast store, there are state and regional archives.[3] In a recent 176-page catalogue issued by the Library of Congress, titled *A List of American Folksongs Currently Available on Records*,[4] there are listed 1,500 recorded folksongs made by two dozen commercial companies. "At the time of compilation of this list," the introductory note states, "all the records were available for purchase." This catalogue does not include hundreds of private pressings of folksongs, known to many record collectors. Ben Gray Lumpkin's *Folksongs on Records*,[5] which lists around 4,000 titles, indicates that many of the records were out of print when the booklet was published in 1950.

Folksong will survive, if silently, in the many book collections that have been made, most of them in the present century. It will survive, in one way and another, in many art forms—drama, opera, symphony, choral or instrumental arrangements, painting, the plastic arts, etc. It will survive in the singing of many professional artists, from the lowliest to the most sophisticated and highly trained. It will survive, let us hope, on the lips of the common people, the unconscious artists, though their lives and interests change in a swiftly changing world.

In the pages ahead it is hoped that the reader will become more conscious of this survival as he learns about many singers, representative of many types in our society, about certain uses made of folksong as it develops into other art, about the many fine collections available in many libraries, about the numerous recordings, and about other activities which manifest the persistent aliveness of this area in our culture.

Before dipping into the main courses served up in the pages ahead, it may be helpful to clarify certain terms by definition. For example, what is a folksong? What is a folksinger? It is pretty generally understood what a *ballad* is—a song that tells a story or, to say it another way, a story told in song. And when we say *traditional ballad*, we mean one that has come down from the past, has lost its individual authorship, shows evidence of variation in content by the existence of more than one version, is compact and concise in narrative, and usually has repetition and refrain.

But a *folksong* * is not so easily defined. A ballad is a folksong, but a folksong is not a ballad unless it tells a story. Folksong, then, has come to be the inclusive word, covering many varieties of music of the common people, and present-day collectors are likely to use it in this all-inclusive sense.† For instance, the *shanty* (or *chantey*), a sailor's work song of the sea, is a folksong. A *spiritual* is a religious folksong. The *blues*, a predominantly melancholy type of jazz, may be a folksong. And there are folksongs of every occupation—railroading, war, canal life, mining, herding cattle, domestic life, robbery and badman activities, slum life, pioneering, and so on. But the specific characteristics of a genuine, *traditional folksong* (or *folk tune*, for it may be instrumental) are these: it is "music that has

---

* Throughout this book, unless I am quoting, I use the spelling *folksong* and *folksinger*. Collectors and other users vary from *folk song* to *folk-song* to *folksong.*

† For example: Arnold's *Folksongs of Alabama;* Barbeau and Sapir's *Folk Songs of French Canada;* Cox's *Folk-Songs of the South;* Morris's *Folksongs of Florida;* Randolph's *Ozark Folksongs;* Sharp's *English Folk Songs from the Southern Appalachians;* White's *American Negro Folk-Songs.*

been submitted to the process of oral transmission: it is the product
of evolution and is dependent on the circumstances of continuity,
variation, and selection." [6]

Many songs called folksongs are written in imitation of the folksong; so many, in fact, that dictionaries include this idea among
the definitions. But the careful scholar insists on "oral transmission,
continuity, variation, selection." The folksong is to be distinguished
from the *art song*, which is the work of a known composer of standard musical training and which exists by print (and copyright) and
usually does not circulate orally or show variation. Sometimes, too,
we think of the art song as showing more subtlety and sophistication,
though this is not necessarily true. The folksong is further to be
distinguished from the *popular song*, which may be a current hit
for a time, but has neither variation nor continuity, and circulates
by sheet music and recordings. Nor are the so-called country-style
and Western-style songs (often neither country nor Western) to be
mistaken for folksongs. They are varieties of popular song. In the
course of time any of these, either art or popular songs, could become folksongs (e.g., "Silent Night" or "Home on the Range"), just
as sometimes a folksong sails out into the vast sea of popular song
(e.g., "On Top of Old Smoky" or "Shenandoah"). As an instance
of how the popular song becomes a folksong, let us look for a
moment at "Home on the Range."

"Home on the Range," adopted in 1947 as the official state song
of Kansas, was first picked up as a folksong in 1908 by John A.
Lomax in a mesquite grove back of a saloon in San Antonio, Texas.
Many years later Lomax wrote about collecting the song,[7] which
he first reprinted in 1910.[8] His informant was an old Negro who
had been a camp cook many years before along the old Chisholm
Trail. The song was apparently known all over the Midwest,[9]
though it did not come to national attention until the early 1930's.
Then questions of authorship arose and various claims were made.
Kirke Mechem, for many years secretary of the Kansas State Historical Society, assembled the evidence and established beyond
question that a Dr. Brewster Higley wrote the words in 1873 and
a Mr. Daniel E. Kelley composed the music for "Home on the
Range." [10] Higley and Kelley lived on neighboring farm claims in
Smith County, Kansas, not far from Smith Center.

The most fascinating account to date about "Home on the Range"
is that told by Missouri-born author Homer Croy. The song haunted
him, and he was determined to run it down, or, to use his phrase,
"look it up." It proved no easy task, but like a good reporter he
stayed on the scent and got his information. Among other things

he learned that Dr. Higley had taken a claim in central Kansas and worked as a pioneer doctor; that the cabin where he had lived was used as a henhouse (when Homer Croy saw it); that the song was first played by an orchestra led by Cal Harlan, who died in 1938, aged eighty-nine, and who "had played and sung it more than a thousand times"; that the song had many variants, and people all over the Solomon Valley knew it and used it at dances and play parties; that Dr. Higley moved to Shawnee, Oklahoma, where he died in 1911, also at the age of eighty-nine. Homer Croy visited Dr. Higley's son, grandson, and great-grandson at Shawnee and went with the grandson to the cemetery and stood in reverent awe looking at the grave of a man who had given him and others so much pleasure.[11]

On July 22, 1954, the pioneer log cabin where Dr. Higley lived when he composed the song—the log cabin Homer Croy was shocked to find used as a henhouse—was dedicated as a state shrine. A marble plaque affixed to the rude structure marks the birthplace of "Home on the Range," first titled "My Western Home."[12] In its eighty-odd years, the song, in true folksong fashion, has seen many changes, both in melody and words; but the changes, though numerous, are not great enough to obscure the original words and beautiful melody. The song has established itself in the hearts of the people all over the nation and has been carried by many Americans to all parts of the world—by many who never saw the song in print and had no thought who the author or composer might be. Thus does a folksong develop from a known, popular composition.

Something should be said at this point about the *hillbilly song* or *tune*, another type not to be confused with folksong. The term hillbilly is not native to the hill country, but in effect is a humorous and contemptuous term applied by some uninformed city folk to people in the back country. Though the hillbilly song may draw extensively on folksong materials, it is scarcely more than a travesty on the true folksong. Such a song, to be sure, sometimes attains wide currency in the popular field, but obviously that does not make it a folksong, for it lacks the specific characteristics mentioned earlier. Furthermore, it lacks the dignity, seriousness, even earthiness, of the genuine folksong.

And what is a *folksinger?* Again we have a term, widely used, not easily defined. It might be supposed that anyone who sings folksongs is a folksinger. A good many persons who have recently turned to singing folksongs—because such singing is now popular and lucrative, and because they love the songs—are commonly called folksingers. But this use is inexact, most dictionaries to the contrary.

A person who sings operatic arias is not necessarily an opera singer. Many persons can and do sing ballads and folksongs who are not to be designated folksingers in the exact sense, even though the Merriam-Webster unabridged dictionary records that a folksinger is "a singer or writer of folk songs." In the strict sense of the word, a *folksinger* is one who has grown up in an environment where traditional folksongs are a part of his upbringing, where he learns the songs orally and not from books or recordings, and where he is not even aware, at least in his early years, that he is singing folksongs. Such a person may become a professional singer, but he is still a folksinger when he sings a folksong. The point is, he must have grown up in the tradition, have known the songs as a part of his family or community culture.

Singing of the kind mentioned above is usually simple and unaffected, though it is sometimes complicated and stylized. Cecil Sharp, describing the manner of singing which he often encountered, especially among older singers, says: "Traditionally folksongs are sung not only without gestures, but with the greatest restraint in the matter of expression; indeed, the folksinger will usually close his eyes and observe an impassive demeanor throughout his performance." [13] Sharp considered this method extraordinarily effective. Vance Randolph, famous collector in the Ozarks, and other collectors have noted the same stylized manner.

But the traditional folksinger has no monopoly on the singing of folksongs. What about the multitude of other persons, trained and untrained, who sing folksongs and sing them well or ill? The fact is, there are many good singers of folksongs without the traditional background. In short, just about everybody today sings them, or uses them in some way, whether in the home, in school, in serious music composition, or otherwise. Oscar Brand, no mean singer himself and a young man with a clever pen, wrote in the *Saturday Review* (December 12, 1953): "The traditional song has infiltrated into every pore of the body of American music." And somewhat earlier he had written me that "everybody is a folksinger if you wait around long enough"—meaning that all of us know some traditional songs, though we may not have thought of them as folksongs.

In Book One, which follows immediately after this Prologue, are presented brief biographies of a gallery of singers, only a small sampling of the many thousands who sing folksongs in our time. Some of these are folksingers with the traditional background; others are singers of folksongs. All of them, it is hoped, are effective and sympathetic interpreters of our traditional music. Here are people from all walks of life, all levels of society—teachers and university professors, housewives, vagabonds, professional entertainers, camp and festival workers, miners and construction workers, radio personalities, collectors and researchers, record collectors and writers, actors, artists, and farmers. Their common bond is the love of folksongs and the love of singing them. No attempt has been made to group or classify them other than alphabetically, but the brief biographical sketches will generally tell the reader whether they are traditional folksingers or just good singers of folksongs, and the length of the sketches will suggest their relative importance. They are the people, and unnumbered others like them, who make folksong a living art in our day. May their tribe increase!

To get a fair idea of the countless numbers who sing folksongs, one need only examine some of the major collections. For instance, 163 persons contributed folk ballads, and a much larger number contributed folksongs, to the *Frank C. Brown Collection of North Carolina Folklore* (1952); some 250 persons contributed to *Ballads and Songs* (1940) collected by the Missouri Folklore Society; 53 persons contributed three or more songs each to Gardner and Chickering's *Ballads and Songs of Southern Michigan* (1939); over a period of eight years, beginning in 1949, approximately 200 persons contributed songs to the Arkansas Folklore Archive; about 50 persons contributed to Arnold's *Folksongs of Alabama* (1950), a relatively small collection; more than 450 persons contributed to Randolph's *Ozark Folksongs* (1946-50); and literally thousands of names appear in the Library of Congress Archive of American Folk Song check list. Yes, just about "everybody is a folksinger if you wait around long enough." The problem here, then, is to present a good, if small, sampling of the many thousands who sing folksongs in our time.

In Book Two, after the collections were examined and the annotations prepared, * a major problem was to devise a classification or grouping that will make this part of the study usable. Obviously the work of certain collectors stands out as distinctive and significant in the field. I have chosen ten of these collectors as top performers and designated them "the big ten." The choice hinges in part on the time devoted to collecting (usually twenty years or more), in part on the wealth of material brought to light, and in part on the high quality and effectiveness of the editorial work brought to bear on the materials.

In addition to the top ten, there are many major collections that show a considerable body of material set forth in a scholarly manner. Often these are only slightly below the first group in the matter of

---

* Unless otherwise indicated, I have read or examined all the works that have gone into the annotated bibliography.

years, wealth of material, and editorial work; for instance, the work of John Harrington Cox, Arthur Kyle Davis, Jr., and Mellinger E. Henry. Further, it seemed clear in examining the books that many collections were brought into being for the purpose of singing folksongs and ballads. Many in Chapter 13, then, are compilations with not only the tunes but with tunes set into piano arrangements. Such procedure has emphasized that ballad and folksong texts are not properly to be separated from the music; in short, that text and tune are parts of an organic whole, that the texts are living literature only in the singing of them. This emphasis is evident in such works as Schirmer's "American Folk-Song Series," Sandburg's *American Songbag*, Fowke and Johnston's *Canadian Folk Songs*, and the many fine volumes of spirituals.

In Chapter 14 of Book Two, the reader will find some curiosities and some minor collections that seemed to belong nowhere else, but for one reason or another called for inclusion in the bibliography. This section makes no pretense to completeness: there are scores and hundreds of minor collections and, I have no doubt, a whole parcel of curiosities that might be listed. (Here is a task for a meticulous and thorough bibliographer!)

In Chapter 15 of Book Two I have included materials that will help the indefatigable reader to pursue the subject without limit: bibliographical sources, the greatest being Charles Haywood's *Bibliography of North American Folklore and Folksong* (1951), and discussion of many of the archives, the most extensive being the Library of Congress Archive of American Folk Song. Much valuable discussion in the ballad and folksong field and related areas, of course, has been printed over the years. (Consider the seventy-two volumes of the *Journal of American Folklore*.) A supplemental list of works, obviously incomplete but very useful, has been added for further reading. Some of these, like Ritchie's *Singing Family* or Lomax's *Adventures of a Ballad Hunter*, are good popular reading; and some, like Wells's *Ballad Tree* or Jackson's *White Spirituals*, are definitely for the scholarly minded. Some, to be sure, like Gard's *Chisholm Trail* or Thompson's *Body, Boots and Britches* or Randolph's *Ozark Superstitions*, happily reach the general reader and are both popular and scholarly. The point is, the field is rich and varied: the alert and curious prospector will find no end of wealth.

Book Three attacks another problem of interest to lovers of ballads and folksongs—the recordings of the songs. The purpose in Book Three is to give a reasonably complete listing of long-playing folksong records during the decade 1948-58. With new stereo tapes and other audio developments now in process, it appears that the period mentioned may come to be considered the "golden decade" of the long-play. Thus it may be useful to present a catalogue of folksong records of this era. Since Ben Gray Lumpkin's *Folksongs on Records* (Denver, 1950), the *International Catalogue of Recorded Folk Music* (London, 1954), and *A List of American Folksongs Currently on Records* (Washington, D.C., 1953) do a reasonably effective listing of the 78 rpm recordings, I have attempted a listing only of the long-plays.

Along with the record listings, I offer a limited listing of the titles of folksongs, particularly those that appear on the long-playing records. The method of choosing the title list and the cross-indexing are explained in Book Three.

FOOTNOTES TO CHAPTER 1

[1] *English Folk Song: Some Conclusions* (London: Methuen & Co., Ltd., 1907), pp. 107, 109. After his collecting in America, he modified this view somewhat.

[2] *American Ballads and Songs* (New York: Charles Scribner's Sons, 1922), pp. xvi-xvii.

[3] See Book Two, Bibliography, Section 5.

[4] Published in 1953, and available for 60 cents from the Superintendent of Documents.

[5] For further description of Lumpkin's work, see Book Two, Bibliography, Section 5.

[6] Such a definition has been reached by the International Folk Music Council, according to Maud Karpeles, in the 1954 preface to *English Folk Song: Some Conclusions*, by C. J. Sharp.

[7] In the *Southwest Review*, XXI, 3 ff. (1945). Told again by John A. and Alan Lomax, *Folk Song: U.S.A.* (New York: Duell, Sloan & Pearce, Inc., 1947), pp. 196-98.

[8] In *Cowboy Songs and Other Frontier Ballads* (New York: Sturgis & Walton Company, 1910), pp. 39-43.

[9] As a boy, I heard it in the Cherokee Strip in the early 1900's. My father and grandfather had homesteaded a few miles east of the old Chisholm Trail.

[10] *The Kansas State Historical Quarterly*, XVII, 313-39 (November, 1949).

[11] Summarized from pp. 164-80 of Homer Croy's *Corn Country* (New York: Duell, Sloan & Pearce, Inc., 1947), one of the "American Folkways" volumes edited by Erskine Caldwell. See Book Two, Bibliography, for further titles.

[12] Reported in the Kansas City *Times*, Monday, July 26, 1954.

[13] Preface, *One Hundred English Folk Songs* (Boston: Oliver Ditson Company, 1916).

CHAPTER 2

Folksong and the Fine Arts *

THE story of how extensively the materials of folksong—and other kinds of folklore, for that matter—have been used in the fine arts has not yet been chronicled, and it is not within the scope of this book to tell that story fully. So extensive is the field that it requires a separate volume for anything like adequate treatment. Rather, I wish to point to some examples as indicative of what has been done and what may be done in the future.

No painter in America has done more to illuminate folksong ideas than Thomas Hart Benton (1889-). In the 1920's, he "began exploring the 'back country' of America by foot, bus, and train, searching out American subject matter." [1] In that decade, and more fully in the 1930's, he made drawings and paintings of scores of subjects using folk materials. Among these may be mentioned "Lonesome Road" (1927), a title from a well-known folk lyric; "Jealous Lover of Lone Green Valley" (1931), a direct portrayal of one of the universal ballad themes; "Wreck of the Old 97," a railroad ballad theme; "Sourwood Mountain," a nonsense and play-party song; and many folk subjects in his several murals: more especially his portrayal of the Jesse James and Frankie and Johnny stories in his social-history mural (1936) in the state capitol at Jefferson City, Missouri.

Palmer Hayden (1893-), a student in New York and Paris art

* The expression *fine arts* is used here in its broader meaning, to include painting, drama, opera, ballet, music, etc.

schools and a native of Wide Water, Virginia, in the 1930's did a series of twelve oil paintings covering the life of that "steel-drivin' man," John Henry, the subject of many ballads and the Negro folk-hero of the Big Bend Tunnel in West Virginia.[2] John McCrady (1911-   ), native of Mississippi and at present a teacher and practicing artist in New Orleans, in 1937 painted a large canvas of the famous spiritual, "Swing Low Sweet Chariot." [3] The canvas depicts a lonely cottage on a darkened landscape. Through the open door one sees a person near death surrounded by mourners, and above the cottage a chariot and band of angels, with old Satan in the scene contending for the departing spirit. In the mid-1940's, *Esquire* magazine commissioned the California artist Fred Ludekens to do a Casey Jones painting. For his canvas Ludekens chose the dramatic moment when

> Casey pulled up within two miles of the place
> Number Four stared him right in the face,
> He turned to the fireman, said, "Boy, you better jump,
> 'Cause there's two locomotives that's a-goin' to bump." [4]

Nor should we overlook a much earlier work: Thomas Eakins' justly famous painting called "Cowboy Singing" (1888). Eakins (1844-1916), frequently a realistic painter of man in action, spent the summer of 1887 on a cattle ranch in Dakota Territory, sharing the life of the ranch hands in their work and play, "joining in their songs accompanied by banjo or mouth organ." He had gone to the West just in time to catch the genuine picturesqueness of the cowboy's life, for soon that life would disappear. The terrible winter of 1888-89 killed off whole herds of cattle, and the homesteaders were making a relentless march into the unfenced plains. Plow, barbed wire, and statehood would soon alter the whole picture. Eakins' portrayal scarcely suggests the twentieth-century glamorized, slick Westerner. His cowboy is rough and rugged, with shaggy beard and unkempt hair under a broad-brimmed hat. He wears a tan leather jacket, a red bandanna, and somewhat heavy ill-fitting chaps over awkward boots. As he sits on an old chair strumming his five-string banjo, he gives out with some lonesome tune familiar to the cowboys and now, no doubt, collected in many a version in the published records. "Cowboy Singing," drawn from the living man in action, at once suggests the true spirit of the old West and the actual singing of a genuine folksong.[5]

In the field of drama, a number of interesting examples make use of folk-music materials. In 1930, John Huston made a dramatic stage version of the bawdy ballad, "Frankie and Johnny" (see Book Two).

In the same year, Marc Connelly's famous Biblical folk-play, *The Green Pastures*, utilizing many well-known Negro spirituals, began its long run on Broadway and eventually saw production in the major cities of the country. Roark Bradford, whose collection of Negro stories called *Ol' Man Adam an' His Chillun* was the basis of *The Green Pastures*, wrote a prose work about John Henry in 1931, which he developed into a three-act musical play and published in 1939. First production of *John Henry* starred the singer-actor Paul Robeson. In Bradford's version, John Henry is not the "steel-drivin' man" of many ballad versions, but a "cotton roller," i.e., one who piled bales of cotton on steamboats (see Book Two).

Some incidental use is made of folksongs in one of the plays for a Negro theater done by Randolph Edmonds, entitled *The Land of Cotton*. The play, begun in 1935 when Edmonds was a student at the Yale School of Drama, was first produced in March, 1941, at the People's Community Theatre of New Orleans, and it was published the next year.[6] It is a four-act tragic drama in which the share-croppers, white and Negro, attempt to organize to save themselves from squalor and starvation. Such songs as "Water Boy," "Keep Your Hand on the Plow," and—near the end, at the funeral of one who has died of starvation—the beautiful spiritual, "Steal Away to Jesus," and others lend emotional content to a moving drama.

Down in Oklahoma in the 1920's, a promising university student was beginning to see the possibilities of folk material in drama. Lynn Riggs (1899-1954) had already written *The Primitives, Sump'n Like Wings*, and *Big Lake*—all using folk story, speech, and song—before he developed the highly significant and successful *Green Grow the Lilacs* (1931). This regional play of six scenes, set in the Indian Territory of 1900, weaves into the plot no fewer than a dozen folksongs. In the published version, Riggs states in a preface that it was his intention to recapture "the great range of mood which has characterized the old folk songs and ballads I used to hear in my Oklahoma childhood."[7] And, as nearly everybody knows, *Green Grow the Lilacs* was the regional play from which Rodgers and Hammerstein created their *Oklahoma!*, a musical play that began an all-time record run in 1943.

Since many works of opera and ballet, especially in recent years, have used folk and folksong materials, one may incline to the belief that this kind of artistic creation is a modern phenomenon. It is well to remember that the first opera in English to be based in part on ballad or folksong materials was the satirical and highly successful *The Beggar's Opera* by John Gay written in 1728.[8] It contains over sixty airs, most of them old ballad tunes.

But to mention some more recent works. Vienna-born Kurt Weill in his American folk-opera, *Down in the Valley* (1948), weaves into the score, sometimes quoting directly, half a dozen folksongs familiar to many: "Sourwood Mountain," "Little Black Train," "Lonesome Dove," and "Hop Up, My Ladies"; and, of course, the title song gives the score its basic theme. Eusebia Simpson Hunkins' *Smoky Mountain* (1954), based on Appalachian folksongs, has seen more than a hundred performances.[9] An operatic work by the late Charles Faulkner Bryan titled *Singin' Billy* had its première in Nashville, Tennessee, in 1952 with a full student cast and orchestra from Peabody College and Vanderbilt University, the composer conducting. William Walker, leading figure in the opera and in real life the author of *The Southern Harmony*, was a teacher of rural singing schools and, according to George Pullen Jackson, great authority on spiritual folksongs, *Singin' Billy* was among "the first to tap this 'spiritual song' wellspring of our national lore and to transform it into musical drama."[10] Other recent folk operatic works are Benjamin Britten's *Paul Bunyan* (1941) and Aaron Copland's *The Tender Land* (1954).

And most popular of all in this field, and most originally conceived and created, is George Gershwin's *Porgy and Bess*, first produced by the Theatre Guild in 1935 and revived in the 1950's with phenomenal, world-wide success. Though Gershwin seemed at no time to quote directly any of the Negro songs or spirituals, such numbers as "Summertime," "My Man's Gone Now," "Leavin' fo' de Promis' Lan'," "Oh I Can't Sit Down," "Oh Doctor Jesus," "I'm on My Way," and others somehow impress the listener with their genuine folk character.[11]

In the ballet of recent years, a surprising number of works have been based on folksong and folk story. At once the music of Aaron Copland (1900-   ) comes to mind: *Billy the Kid* (1938), *Rodeo* (1942), *Appalachian Spring* (1944). In the first, he makes use of such cowboy tunes as "Old Grandad," "Good-by Old Paint," "Git Along Little Dogies," "The Dying Cowboy," and "The Old Chisholm Trail"; in the second, he uses "If He'd Be a Buckaroo by His Trade," "Sis Joe," and the square-dance tune, "Bonyparte"; and in the third, the beautiful old Shaker tune, "The Gift to Be Simple."[12] What Thomas Hart Benton has done with folklore and folksong in painting, Aaron Copland has done in ballet and symphonic composition. Like Benton, he uses the material freely, sometimes quoting and sometimes suggesting, and the result is a composition of original genius. As a recent critic has pointed out: "In his treatment of folk music Copland has grasped with extraordinary success its precise and essential curve both where he quotes directly and where he creates original tunes along traditional lines of folksong. . . . One of his special devices in transforming a folksong is to make it broad or tender when it has been slight or frivolous originally." [13]

Brief mention, if only for the sake of variety, should be made of three or four other works: the ballet suite, *Opus Americana No. 2,* of the French-American composer Darius Milhaud (1892-   ); the one-act American frolic (singing and dancing), *Sourwood Mountain,* based on American folksongs and fiddle tunes, by Pierson Underwood and Lawrence Perry; the recent work of the New York City Ballet Company in such productions as *Western Symphony* (1955) and *Square Dance* (1957). Among the songs in the former are "Red River Valley," "Oh Dem Golden Slippers," and "Good Night Ladies"; in the latter, traditional tunes, as well as the music of Corelli, form the musical basis. These works were performed with marked success in New York and elsewhere under the director-choreographer George Balanchine.

When we turn to the area of straight musical composition with folksong base—from piano to full orchestra—the works are infinitely more numerous and varied than in the areas of painting, drama, opera, and ballet. Charles Haywood in his invaluable *Bibliography of North American Folklore and Folksong* (New York: Greenberg, 1951) lists hundreds of these compositions. Almost every composer of this century, not to mention earlier ones, has tried his hand in the area. Piano compositions are too numerous to mention in this limited discussion, and orchestral suites and symphonies are numbered in the scores. One might begin by naming Dvořák's symphony, *From the New World* (1893), parts of which were based on Afro-American songs. Somewhat earlier (1891-92), Edward MacDowell had drawn freely on American-Indian music for his *Indian Suite,* opus 48, first performed by the Boston Symphony in 1896. And English composer Frederick Delius had used an old Negro melody for *Appalachia, Variations on an Old Slave Song,* a symphonic piece for full orchestra, first performed in Elberfeld, Germany, in 1905.

But to move somewhat closer to the present. In 1928, Lamar Stringfield was awarded a Pulitzer Prize for *Suite in Southern Mountains,* a work built around folk melodies.[14] William Grant Still in the 1920's and 30's composed symphonic works strongly based on Negro folklore and folksong, among them the symphonic poem, *Darker America* (1924), a melodic suite known as *From the Black Belt* (1926), an orchestral work called *Log Cabin Ballads* (1927), a four-movement *Afro-American Symphony* (1930), and a tone poem for piano and orchestra titled *Kaintuck'* (1935).[15]

Folksong base for orchestral compositions has become a habit with such current composers as Roy Harris, David Guion, Elie Siegmeister, Morton Gould, John Powell, and Aaron Copland. Mention of a few titles will illustrate. Roy Harris: *When Johnny Comes Marching Home* (1935), a two-part overture; his well-known *Folk Song Symphony* (1939); a free improvisation for symphony called *Blow the Man Down;* and his *Cumberland Concerto* (1951), premièred by the Cincinnati Symphony. David Guion: *Turkey in the Straw*, arranged for flute, piano, and strings; *Arkansas Traveler;* and his justly famous *Home on the Range.*[16] The best-known work of Elie Siegmeister is *Ozark Set* (1943), a full-orchestra piece requiring fifteen minutes to perform. Siegmeister also wrote and conducted the music for *Sing Out, Sweet Land* for the Theatre Guild in 1944, and was organizer and conductor of the *American Ballad Singers* in the 1940's.

Morton Gould: *Spirituals for Orchestra* (1941), a suite in five movements; some smaller orchestrations such as *Home on the Range, Swing Low Sweet Chariot, Go Down, Moses, When Johnny Comes Marching Home* (1942), and *Hill Billy.* John Powell, composer-pianist of Richmond, Virginia, has done much with folk themes: *Rhapsodie Nègre* (1919); *At the Fair*, a suite of sketches using Southern tunes; *In Old Virginia* (1921), an overture using country dance tunes; and *Virginia Symphony*, composed in 1937 but not premièred until 1951.

Ballet music of Copland has already been discussed briefly, but mention should be made of some of his other symphonic work: *Saga of the Prairies* (1937); a short orchestral work titled *John Henry* (1940); *A Lincoln Portrait* (1942), in three main sections. Julia Smith, a recent critic of Copland, in discussing his periods of development, assigns great importance to his Third Style or American Folksong Period (1934-55) and devotes half her book to these twenty years.[17]

To round out this discussion of "folksong to symphony," one should at least call attention to Tom Scott's *From the Sacred Harp* (1946); George Kleinsinger's *A Western Rhapsody*, based on cowboy folksongs; Harl McDonald's *Legend of the Arkansas Traveler* (1946); Charles F. Bryan's *White Spiritual Symphony* (1952) and *Birmingham Suite* (1953); Otto Luening's *Wisconsin Suite* (1954), based on songs remembered from childhood and premièred by the N.B.C. Symphony; Marcel G. Frank's *Arkansas Traveler* (1955), a new arrangement of variations on an old tune and premièred by the Kansas City Philharmonic; Wesley Gragson's *John Henry Suite;* Wayne Barlow's *The Winter's Passed* (1940), from the folk melody of "Black Is the Color of My True Love's Hair"; and Douglas Moore's *Village Street* (1942). These last three works stem from the Eastman School of Music, where, under the leadership of Howard Hanson, so much has been done in recent years to stimulate American composers and performers to develop music from native sources.[18]

In concluding this chapter on folksong and the fine arts, I wish to offer two unusual examples of the use of folk-music themes in the plastic, visual arts. The first of these is the series of decorations on the White House piano located in the East Room. On the concave-curved side panel of this beautiful concert grand Steinway * there are five scenes, done in finest metallic gold leaf, depicting phases of elementary American music. The designs were executed by Dunbar Beck, of the Steinway staff of artists and craftsmen.†

The central and largest of the five scenes shows a group of figures doing the Virginia Reel, a country dance of early origin. Immediately to the right of this scene (as one faces the curved panel) is shown "the Negro cotton-picker bursting forth into song" as a seated figure claps and sings. Farther to the right is a group of American Indians in a ceremonial chant and dance around an open fire. Another scene, immediately to the left of the Virginia Reel group, portrays the lone cowboy strumming a guitar and "singing beneath the prairie stars." The scene farthest to the left shows the New England Barn Dance, four figures swinging to the tune scraped out by the old fiddler as he calls the turns of the set. The use of such scenes on the chief official piano of the nation indicates the importance of elementary music, that is, of folk music, in the cultural life of our country.[19]

The second unusual example of the use of folk-music themes in the plastic, visual arts is the work done in Steuben Glass designing. Distinguished American sculptor Sidney Waugh, an associate designer for Steuben, and Steuben's staff of artists and craftsmen have created works of such exquisite design and striking beauty as almost to defy description. Using the method of copper-wheel engraving on hand-fashioned glass objects of a pure, colorless, transparent crystal,[20] Waugh and his associates have made, relative to folksong, a number of remarkable *objets d'art.*

* In 1938, this piano was presented to the nation by Theodore E. Steinway, president of Steinway and Sons, and was accepted by Franklin D. Roosevelt "for the nation." This was the second piano to be presented to the nation by the Steinway firm. Shortly after the turn of the century, during Theodore Roosevelt's administration, it had presented a beautiful instrument of baroque design, now a treasured relic in the Smithsonian Institution.

† The gold leaf was applied to the outside of the case and then shaded by hand by Mr. Beck. Then, for protection, the whole case was sealed with lacquer.

A first group consists of eleven pieces known as the American Ballad Series, begun in 1939 and completed in 1942. A large center bowl, nine inches in diameter, has four vivid intaglios representing four steps in our country's growth: Exploration, Colonization, Independence, and Expansion. Two lesser bowls, 7½ inches in diameter, have three intaglios each, one bowl representing Trade and Commerce, the other, Transportation. Four covered urns, each 11¾ inches high, have vividly engraved scenes representing Industry, The Arts, Agriculture, and The Sciences. Four cigarette jars, each 5½ inches high, present four typical American figures, each figure the subject of many a ballad or folksong: Trapper, Cowboy, Pioneer, and Indian. These small jars are exquisite jewels of unexcelled workmanship and fine design.

In 1946, Sidney Waugh created a design which in many respects is one of the most strikingly original of all his work relating to folksong: the large shallow plate called Prairie Smoke engraved with three intaglios depicting episodes in the lives of notorious American outlaws. One scene portrays Billy the Kid (William H. Bonney), who at the age of twelve shot his first man. Another scene portrays Wild Bill Hickok in his encounter with the ruthless McCanles gang of cattle rustlers; he is reported to have killed nine of them in this bloody battle. The third scene is the critical moment in the life of Jesse James when he stood on a chair to dust or straighten a picture and

> Robert Ford came along like a thief in the night
> An' he laid poor Jesse in his grave.

These scenes are the very essence of spirited, lawless action. As one looks down on them, engraved in intaglio on the underside of the plate, the effect is that of rich and ominous shadows. As one critic has written: "These Waugh designs ... are more pictorial, more tightly drawn, than his earlier conceptions. Their reduction in scale conveys the impression of a miniaturist, rather than a sculptor, working in glass." [21]

Another design by Sidney Waugh is the Stephen Foster Bowl, completed in 1947.[22] The main body of the bowl, which has an over-all height of 13½ inches, rises from a high inverted base. Five of Foster's well-known songs are represented in the intaglios: "Jeannie with the Light Brown Hair," "Ring de Banjo," "The Glendie Burke," "Old Folks at Home," and "Old Black Joe." Prominence of the banjo in the engravings suggests also "Oh Susanna," which truly became an American folksong through oral transmission, adoption by the folk, loss of the composer's name, and alteration in transmission. It was a song much used by the Forty-Niners and in the Westward Movement generally.*

Another creation in Steuben Glass, designed by Bruce Moore, distinguished American animal sculptor, should be mentioned here. This is the series of three crystal bowls called The Western Group, done in 1952. The largest of the three, a covered bowl thirteen inches high and called The Plains, shows the great herd led by "a mighty bison," with a buzzard floating "ominously overhead." The meager vegetation of cactus and sagebrush is overshadowed in turn by rain, sun, and thunderhead. One side bowl, called The Woodland, shows three groups of animals: American elk (wapiti), grizzly bear, and bushy-tailed raccoons. The other side bowl, called The Prairie, shows "a coyote howling at the moon, a colony of prairie dogs, and pronghorn antelopes." The portrayal of these American animals, all famous in history and legend and song, and the strikingly native designs by Sidney Waugh, show how thoroughly the artists have identified themselves with the American scene, how their works richly contribute to the beauty and understanding of American legend and folksong.[23]

The several examples discussed briefly in this chapter—paintings by Thomas Hart Benton and others, dramas by Lynn Riggs and others, operas by George Gershwin and Kurt Weill and others, ballet and symphonic works by Aaron Copland and Roy Harris and others, and the exquisite examples in the plastic and visual arts—all suggest the great things accomplished, as well as the future possibilities, in the fine arts, as creative minds turn more and more to native folk materials.

A famous writer in a famous preface once said it was his aim "to arrest, for the space of a breath, the hands busy about the work of the earth, and compel men entranced by the sight of distant goals to glance for a moment at the surrounding vision of form and color, of sunshine and shadow...." † It is my purpose in the present volume to have the reader glance for a moment at the surrounding vision of folksong. Let him delve into the rich volumes, let him listen to the songs, let him contemplate the art works that suggest some of the form and color, the sunshine and shadow of man's ephemeral journey on earth; so that, for the space of a breath, he will pause to con-

---

* It should be pointed out that most of Foster's songs, composed mainly for the minstrel stage, however popular they became, are not folksongs in the strict sense, though they are often so designated.

† Joseph Conrad, Preface, The Nigger of the "Narcissus" (New York: Doubleday, Page & Co., 1914). Used by permission of the publishers, J. M. Dent & Sons, Ltd.

template and comprehend, be it ever so little, the life and love, the labor and laughter, the song and sorrow of man as he walks the shining earth.

~~~~~~~~

FOOTNOTES TO CHAPTER 2

1 From the catalogue, *Thomas Hart Benton, a Retrospective Exhibition* (Lawrence, Kansas: University of Kansas Museum of Art, 1958). Growing up in southwest Missouri, he had already explored an interesting corner of America.

2 These paintings are now at the Harmon Foundation in New York City.

3 Owned by the City Art Museum, St. Louis, Missouri.

4 Lomax, *Folk Song: U.S.A.* (New York: Duell, Sloan and Pearce, Inc., 1947), p. 269.

5 Facts drawn in part from the pamphlet, *The Metropolitan Museum of Art Miniatures, Album M* (New York: The Metropolitan Museum of Art, 1949). The original Eakins water color, measuring 18 by 14 inches, hangs in the Metropolitan Museum.

6 *The Land of Cotton and Other Plays,* by Randolph Edmonds (Washington, D.C.: The Associated Publishers, Inc., 1942).

7 In 1954, the Limited Editions Club and the University of Oklahoma Press produced a sumptuous edition of *Green Grow the Lilacs* with illustrations by Thomas Hart Benton.

8 *Types of English Drama, 1660-1780*, ed. by David H. Stevens (New York: Ginn and Co., 1923). *The Beggar's Opera* was by all odds the most popular eighteenth-century drama, and its popularity continued down into the nineteenth century, with successful revivals in the twentieth. Well-known ballad airs include "London Is a Fine Town," "Over the Hills and Far Away," "Bonny Dundee," "Chevy Chase," and "Greensleeves."

9 *Journal of American Folklore Supplement*, April, 1956.

10 *Tennessee Folklore Society Bulletin*, XVIII, 55 (June, 1952).

11 George Gershwin enjoyed the collaboration not only of his lyric-writing brother Ira but of Dorothy and DuBose Heyward, authors of the original *Porgy and Bess* play, which in turn was based on Heyward's first novel, *Porgy* (1924). DuBose Heyward (1885-1940) was an authority on Negro life in Charleston, South Carolina, and a special student of Negro songs and spirituals.

12 *The Victor Book of Ballets and Ballet Music,* by Robert Lawrence (New York: Simon and Schuster, Inc., 1950), pp. 40-42.

13 *Aaron Copland,* by Arthur Berger (New York: Oxford University Press, 1953), pp. 57, 60.

14 *Southern Folklore Quarterly*, XI, 101 (March, 1947).

15 From Verna Arvey's biographical sketch of William Grant Still in *Twelve Negro Spirituals* (New York: Handy Bros. Music Co., Inc., 1937).

16 *Our American Music,* by John Tasker Howard (Third Edition, New York: Thomas Y. Crowell Co., 1954), pp. 588-89.

[17] *Aaron Copland: His Work and Contribution to American Music* (New York: E. P. Dutton & Co., Inc., 1955). Copland's ballet and symphonic works have been published by Boosey and Hawkes.

[18] A whole chapter could be devoted to the Eastman School of Music and its widespread influence, especially in the artistic development of native music. Space forbids.

In the discussion of folksong and symphony, as in other matters, I have drawn freely on Charles Haywood's *Bibliography* for titles; the usefulness of his great work can scarcely be over-emphasized.

[19] Pictures and factual details of the White House piano have been furnished by courtesy of Steinway and Sons, and are used here with their kind permission.

[20] *Steuben Glass,* Second, Revised and Enlarged Edition, by James S. Plaut (New York: H. Bittner & Company, 1951), p. 5: "In 1932, a chemical formula for pure crystal, achieved without discoloration, was realized at Corning." Plaut further states, p. 21: "Steuben is singularly fortunate in possessing a metal which, for transparency, luster, and colorlessness has no peer in the annals of glassmaking."

[21] *Ibid.,* p. 26.

[22] *Ibid.,* plate 68.

[23] Factual details and pictures have been supplied by Steuben Glass, New York City, and are used with their kind permission.

BOOK ONE

An alphabetical presentation
of singers of ballads and
folksongs

"Long ago man sang. While he was making language, first learning words and
giving names to things, he sang in that
dim misted time. Come war, come peace,
he will go on singing."

—CARL SANDBURG:
New American Songbag

ALPHABETICAL LIST OF SINGERS
DISCUSSED IN BOOK ONE

Adams, Derrol S.
Allison, John
Archer, Frances, and
  Gile, Beverly
Arkin, Alan
Bailey, Jay
Baillargeon, Hélène
Bair, Fred
Ball, E. C. and Orra
Barker, Horton
Barnes, Bobby
Barry, Margaret
Beers, Robert and Evelyne
Belafonte, Harry
Bender, Bill
Benton, Jessie
Bikel, Theodore
Boette, Marie
Bonyun, Bill
Boswell, George W.
Boyle, Mary Ella M.
Brand, Oscar
Briscoe, Mrs. Mary
Broonzy, Big Bill
Bryan, Charles F.
Buckley, Bruce
Burnett, W. H.
Byrne, Jerry
Cahn, Rolf
Cameron, Isla

Campbell, Booth
Cansler, Loman
Chalmers, Keith
Chase, Dorothy
Churchill, Stuart
Clark, Edgar Rogie
Clark, Keith
Clauson, William
Clayborn, James R. and
  Garland K.
Clayton, Paul
Cobos, Rubén
Colby, Fred W.
Coltman, Bob
Copeland, Dave
Cornett, Banjo Bill
Creswell, Grace
Crisp, Rufus
Dagel, Kathy
Dane, Barbara
Danufsky, Dr. Philip G.
Darling, Erik
Davis, Reverend Gary
Davis Family, The T. M.
Dehr, Rich
Deller, Alfred
Devoll, Dick
Diard, Marion
Duncan, Bob
Dyer-Bennet, Richard

Elliott, Bill
Elliott, Jack and June
Eskin, Sam
Faier, Billy
Filiatrault (see: Quatuor)
Flowers, Robert E. Lee
Foster, Pat
Fuller, Jesse
Gainer, Dr. Patrick W.
Gibson, Bob
Gile (see: Archer)
Ginandes, Dr. Shep
Glazer, Joe
Glazer, Tom
Golden, Terry
Gooding, Cynthia
Greer, Dr. and Mrs. I. G.
Gregory, Frosia
Grimes, Anne
Grise, Dr. George C.
Guthrie, Woody
Hall, Kenneth Martin
Hamilton, Frank
Hammontree, Doney
Hayes, Roland
Haynes, Valerie
Hays, Lee
Hellerman, Fred
Hickerson, Joe
High, Fred
Hillhouse, Mrs. Cora
Hilton, L. M.
Hinton, Sam
Holland, Lori
Holt, Will
House, Wallace
Houston, Cisco
Hunter, Max
Huntington, E. G. and Emily
Hurd, Peter
Isaacson, Dan
Ives, Burl
Jacob (see: Quatuor)

Jarrett, Merrick
Jemison, Gene
Kazee, Buell H.
Kincaid, Bradley
King, Marty
Kornfeld, Barry
Kossoy Twins, Ellen and Irene
Kukler, Mr. and Mrs. Adolph
Kunitz, Charlene
Lamarre (see: Quatuor)
Langstaff, John
Leadbelly (Huddie Ledbetter)
Lee, Archie
Lee, Katie
Lloyd, A. L.
Lomax, Alan
Long, Mrs. Maud
Loudermilk, Romaine H.
Lunsford, Bascom Lamar
MacColl, Ewan
McCord, May Kennedy
McCurdy, Ed
McNeil, Brownie
Marais, Josef and Miranda
The Marcottes, Will and Jean
The Mechau Family
    Paula, Vanni, Dorik,
    Duna, Michael
Mickelsen, Erik
Mills, Alan
Mitchell, Merlin
Mobley, Pleaz W.
Moon, Colonel Jacob R. and
    Winnifred
Morris, Jimmy
Morrison, Absie S.
Moser, Artus M.
Murai, Jean
Murray, Carmen and Jim, Jr.
Neal, Ruth
Nickerson, Camille L.
Niles, John Jacob
Nye, Hermes

O'Bryant, Joan
O'Hara, Mary
Okun, Milt
Oldfather, Charles H., Jr.
Oster, Dr. Harry
Paley, Tom
Peacock, Kenneth
Pennington, John B.
Powell, Desmond
Quatuor Alouette, Le
Reed, Jared
Reed, Susan
Ritchies, The Singing
   Abigail, Balis, Edna, Jason,
   Jean, Jewell, May, Una
Roberts, Robin
Robinson, Earl
Robinson, Frank V.
Ross, Bob
Roth, Herbert
Rubin, Ruth
Saletan, Anthony
Sandburg, Carl
Scammell, A. R.
Schlamme, Martha
Scott, Molly
Scott, Tom
Seeger, Pete
Sellers, Brother John
Silverman, Jerry
Smith, Fred M.

Smith, Winifred
Starr, Mary Agnes
Stekert, Ellen
Stone, Eleanor
Stracke, Win
Sturgill, Virgil L.
Summers, Andrew Rowan
Tarwater, Rebecca
Tate Family, The Charles
Temple, Pick
Terry, Sonny
Thomsen, Paul
Trottier (see: Quatuor)
Tyler, Ruth H.
Usher, Alex (Mrs.)
Van Wey, Adelaide
Vincent, Jenny Wells
Warner, Frank
Weissman, Dick
West, Harry and Jeanie
White, Josh
Whitmire, Mr. & Mrs. Ross C.
Wilder, Dick
Williams, Betty Vaiden
Williams, Cratis
Wilson, Stan
Wood, Hally
Wood, Theodore, Jr.
Yarbrough, Glenn
Zeitlin, David

CHAPTER 3

The Singers,
A to C

DERROL S. ADAMS

Derrol S. Adams, itinerant singer and worker without a permanent address, was born in Portland, Oregon, in 1925. He reports that his early schooling was "all over Oregon and Washington," since his father was an engineer, and the family "moved around a lot." Derrol had four years of training in an art school, but took no degree.

Adams is not a traditional singer, though he was singing ballads and folksongs from the age of nine or ten. As a small boy he played the mouth harp (harmonica). He has learned folksongs all over the Northwest and when he was in the military service. The banjo is his favorite instrument now, and he has performed on many an occasion in the Northwest, particularly in Oregon, Washington, Idaho, and California. Though not now married, he is the father of four children: Scotty, Marky, Deborah, and Gregorio.

JOHN ALLISON

"Back when I began," writes John Allison, "there was little public acceptance of ballad singers and collectors." Outside of Carl Sandburg, John Jacob Niles, Dr. I. G. Greer, Ross Whitmire, and a few other old-time collectors and singers in this study, John Allison predates them all and considers himself "a sort of senior member in this ballad-singing fraternity which has, during the past dozen years, grown to large proportions."

John was born in Englewood, New Jersey, in 1893. He attended

29

the Englewood and Lawrenceville schools and had a year of study in Bonn, Germany. His parents were musical people but not professionals. The nucleus of John's collection was based on his "father's memory of ballads and songs heard by him along the Hudson River." John's grandfather Allison was a boatman on the river for a generation, from 1825 to 1860—the great canal era.

Allison's activity as a folksinger began in 1927, when he, a friend, and Mrs. Allison formed a trio called "The Jubileers" (later known as "The American Folk Singers") and gave folksong shows on various New York City radio stations and at various clubs. Their first public appearance, in 1927, was at the Women's University Club. Allison has been collecting and singing ever since. His copyrighted material has appeared in the Ben Botkin books (see Book Two, Bibliography) and other publications. In the early 1940's, he made recordings (78 rpm) for RCA Victor and Keynote, and recently he has done LP's for Ficker Records * (see Book Three). All his work—programs, records, publications—have been favorably reviewed.

John Allison was married in 1925 to Lucy Dodsworth. They had one daughter, Joan Allison (McGee), born in 1926. Joan sang folksongs with her parents for a number of years (1938-45) before her marriage. (The McGees are now the parents of four children.) In 1953, John Allison made a second marriage, this time to Eleanor Wilcox. As to other activities, Mr. Allison writes: "I have over a period of 30 years been a landscape painter, with one-man exhibits in New York galleries, at the National Academy of Design, the Pennsylvania Academy in Philadelphia and elsewhere." For one who considers himself semi-retired, John Allison has enough doing for two busy lives.

FRANCES ARCHER AND BEVERLY GILE

In Archer and Gile, soprano and contralto respectively, we have one of several excellent singing teams discussed in this book.† Like Marais and Miranda (q.v.), their repertoire of songs and ballads is international. Frances Archer was born in Corpus Christi, Texas, went through high school there, and then attended the University of Texas at Austin. Beverly Gile was born in Los Angeles and attended the Beverly Hills High School.

---

* Some new ballads by Allison, to be released by Ficker, are called *Spaceway Ballads*—in which he takes the position of the imaginary ballad collector in the middle of the twenty-first century, 2050.

† Others: Marais and Miranda, Robert and Evelyne Beers, Jim and Carmen Murray, Harry and Jeanie West.

Both young women learned folksongs from "hearing folksingers, professional and non-professional." No doubt they have looked into a few books, too. Frances' mother is an amateur singer, though not of folksongs. Beverly's mother is a musician and teaches piano in Beverly Hills.

The young women gave their first recital at the Beverly Hills Women's Club in 1951. Since that date they have given an average of eighty concerts a year. They have sung in forty-eight states, in the provinces of Ontario and Quebec, and in Mexico. Their 1958-59 season included the Maritime Provinces of Canada. They present traditional songs from some fifteen countries in as many as thirteen languages. They are partial, however, to "lonesome tunes" of the South, and Miss Archer is especially fond of Negro spirituals.

During 1955-57, they collected folksongs in Kentucky. Also, while on tour, like other singers of folk materials, they are constantly adding more songs. Their artistic presentations—Miss Gile does the guitar arrangements—have been published by Walt Disney Music Company. They have appeared on radio and television and have made recordings (see Book Three). Favorable press notices have been frequent in such papers as the New York *Times* (October 8, 1955, and December 9, 1957), Los Angeles *Examiner* (May 11, 1955), and *Billboard* (December 23, 1957). Neither Miss Archer nor Miss Gile is married but, at the time of this writing, Beverly Gile was reported to be engaged.

ALAN ARKIN

Brooklyn-born in 1934, Alan Arkin went through the New York City public schools, has attended Los Angeles City College and Bennington College in Vermont but has taken no degrees. Alan has learned folksongs from books, records, and family. He writes: "My parents sing all sorts of music around the house, including folk music."

Though Alan has done much singing of folksongs in his travels—fifteen states, the Canadian provinces of Quebec and Ontario, France, England, Germany, and Switzerland—he does not consider singing his main forte. "My main contributions," he writes, "are in the arranging and writing end, rather than performing. My background and associations with folk music have enriched my own songs very much."

Besides many songs, Alan has written the background music to two plays, and for two years he did arranging for the Tarriers. At present he is teaching "basic theory and folk guitar," doing some acting, and studying music with the idea of becoming a serious composer. He has recorded for Elektra, Vanguard, and others (see Book Three).

Alan Arkin was married to Jeremy Yaffe on December 14, 1955. They have a son, Adam, born August 19, 1956.

JAY BAILEY

Born on January 24, 1935, at Cordell, Oklahoma, Jay Bailey is one of the young singers who have developed unusual artistry with the banjo. He attended grade school in Cordell, a private high school in St. Louis, Missouri, and enrolled at the University of Oklahoma in 1953, receiving a Bachelor of Arts in Letters in 1957.

Jay has learned a lot of old songs from his family, particularly from his grandmother. (Cordell is located in bleak western Oklahoma prairie country in the Arapaho and Kiowa Indian Reservations, but Jay hasn't begun to collect Indian music—yet!) He has learned much from recordings and books, but especially from singers, among them Pete Seeger. He dates his serious interest in ballad and folk music from his days at the university. After graduation, he acquired a tape recorder and began collecting.

Jay's public performance is not extensive as yet, though he has appeared before civic groups, in 1957 at the National Folk Festival in Oklahoma City, and three times (1957-58-59) at the Ozark Folk Festival. Since he expects to be called for a stretch in the Army, he hasn't settled in an occupation. In the meantime he keeps his fingers limber on the banjo.

HÉLÈNE BAILLARGEON

Folksinging in Canada, as in the United States, has changed much with the continuing industrialization of our society. Though many of the old ways and old singers are now gone, there are still many singers and much singing of folksongs. One may regret the loss of traditional ways and singers, but one may also rejoice that the fine old songs are kept alive in other ways. In Canada, as in the States, folksongs enliven many a radio program.

Among current Canadian singers, one of the most interesting and, according to numerous reports,[1] most effective is Hélène Baillargeon of Beauce County in Québec Province. Mlle Baillargeon was born August 28, 1916, in Saint-Martin de la Beauce, P. Q., Canada. Her early training was with the French nuns in Saint-Martin and then at the Académie du Bon-Pasteur, at Saint-George de Beauce. Later she attended Laval University, studying courses in social service and German but not taking a degree. Though she has known and loved folksongs all her life, she has had considerable classical training in music, having studied a year with Mme Franz Rupp in New York and for some time with the folklorist Alfred LaLiberté in Montréal. She sings German lieder, arias from Bach cantatas, and Wagnerian roles.

For relaxation from heavier roles, however, Mlle Baillargeon turned to folksongs, for which she has a natural gift. As a child she had learned many songs from the country people in Beauce County, as she accompanied her father on his rounds to the many farms he owned in that region.[2] Her first public performance as a singer was at the age of eighteen in Saint-George de Beauce. For the past ten or twelve years she has devoted her time more intensively to folksinging. Though she has done some collecting herself among country people, in her folksong work she has received much help from her distinguished friend, Dr. Marius Barbeau, foremost folklorist of Canada and folksong collector for the National Museum in Ottawa.[3]

Mlle Baillargeon's folksong activities are limited in some degree by her family interests. As she herself has said, "I made a choice. My husband and children come first—the time left is for folksongs." In 1944, she was married to André Côté, a lawyer. They are the parents of three lovely and lively children—Pierre (1945), François (1948), and Louise (1950), all of whom are learning folksongs in the ideal way: at their mother's knee! The Côté home is a gay and happy one, for everybody loves to sing, at work and at play.

Hélène Baillargeon has given a number of concerts, approximately fifty at various times and places in the province of Québec, but her chief work in folksong has been on the radio. On the French network she sings French folksongs on the program, "Le Réveil Rural," a weekly coast-to-coast broadcast to the farm communities. She is also on the English network with singer Alan Mills (q.v.) and the Art Morrow Singers. Again with Mills, accompanied by guitarist Gilbert Lacombe, she sings in the International Service of Radio-Canada for a program beamed to Mexico, Central and South America.[4]

Obviously, Mme Hélène Baillargeon Côté is a colorful personality, a successful homemaker and happy mother, a popular radio and television artist, and an authentic transmitter of Canada's wealth of wonderful folksong.[5]

FRED BAIR

The curious seeker is likely to find singers of folksongs in almost any stratum of society or in any profession. For example, down in Florida there's a city planner who for many years has sung folksongs, not professionally but for the love of singing them. Fred Bair, whose imposing title is "Head of Community Planning and Industrial Development Division, Florida State Improvement Commission, Tallahassee," was born in New York City in 1915. His schooling was in various communities—Colorado Springs, Shaker Heights (Ohio), Oberlin College, and finally a Bachelor of Arts degree from the University of Chicago.

Bair reports that he learned folksongs in the Kentucky mountains, the Southwest and Far West, and from New York to Florida and on to Kumamoto, Japan. And he's been singing them for over twenty years, though never professionally. "I have sat around with mountaineers, Indians, traders, cowboys, miscellaneous good guys and others whenever possible and sung with them often and occasionally at them" in a dozen or more states and in Japan. To quote him further on his amateur status as a singer: "With a group of kindred spirits I will sing as long as the night lasts. Three beers in me and I will pluck out chords with fingers nimble and flexible as garter snakes in a grass fire—chords that never were before and never will be again, and many of them never should have been, but it seemed a good idea at the time. I will sing on the beach or sing in the mountains, sing in a bar or at the sunny end of a haystack. But I will not be introduced and announced and play the selections on the program into a microphone, with or without commercials." Well, it's people like Fred Bair who help to keep folksongs alive!

And Fred's tribe is increasing. He was married to Margaret Hudgen in 1945. They are the parents of two sons aged fourteen and twelve, and a daughter aged seven, all of them much interested in working at folksongs with their singing father. So the busy city planner, plagued with trying to solve parking, zoning, and other metropolitan problems, can turn to folksongs for release and relaxation.

E. C. AND ORRA BALL

E. C. Ball was born October 1, 1914, at Rugby, Virginia, where he attended schools through the ninth grade and where he has lived all his life. He has known ballads all his life, learning chiefly from his mother. His public singing has continued over a period of more than thirty years, beginning in 1927 at an old-fashioned square dance.

Mr. Ball uses both guitar and banjo accompaniment and, like most folksingers, does his own arrangements. He also does some composing of ballads in the folk manner, as well as novelty and gospel songs. E. C. Ball was married to Orra Rudy on April 29, 1933, who also sings folksongs and works with him in many performances. She is versatile with folk instruments, too, playing the guitar, accordion, banjo, and mandolin.

The Balls have performed in the five states of Virginia, West Virginia, North Carolina, Kentucky, and Tennessee. Mr. Ball says the number of their performances runs into the hundreds, "maybe thousands." They perform in high schools and colleges, at folk festivals; and he has done recordings for the Library of Congress Archive (AAFS nos. 3 and 8). Since 1950, Mr. Ball has worked for radio station WBOB at Galax, Virginia. His regular occupation is bus driver, farmer, and singer.

HORTON BARKER

Horton Barker was born in Tennessee, August 23, 1889, into a folksinging family. His mother taught him folksongs, and he learned others from schoolmates. He received both elementary and high-school training at Staunton, Virginia.

Barker's first public appearance as a folksinger was at the White Top Mountain Folk Festival in August, 1933. White Top (see under "Folk Festivals" in Interlude II) has been one of the most important festivals in the revival and preservation of folksinging in the Appalachian area. Festivals began there in 1931.

Barker, who specializes in Anglo-American ballads, has performed hundreds of times in six different states in the Appalachian area. He has made recordings for the Library of Congress Archive (AAFS nos. 1 and 33), but has never commercialized his singing. Now retired, he says his chief activity is "just singing folk ballads." He does not use instrumental accompaniment.

BOBBY BARNES

Bobby (Henry) Barnes, native Texan and in recent years an enthusiastic Ozarkian, has known folksongs a long time through family tradition and by association with mountain singers. One of Bobby's great-grandfathers moved with his family from Virginia to Kentucky and then down into Tennessee. Her grandfather, Dr. John Calvin Denton, born and reared near Nashville, could "play the fiddle like anything" when she knew him as an old man. Another great-grandfather lived in the Ozarks on the White River for some time before migrating to Texas. His son John Henry, who was Bobby's paternal grandfather, and her father sang many old hymns, lullabies, and traditional songs—all of which we now know as folksongs.

Bobby was born January 8, 1907, near Waco, Texas; was graduated from the Waco High School; and studied music at Baylor University. In her late teens she was married to Wilmer Barnes.

They lived for many years in Waco, where Mr. Barnes operated a radio shop and Mrs. Barnes continued her musical interests, becoming prominent in many musical affairs of the city. During World War II, when Mr. Barnes was a communications technician at Waco Army Air Field, Bobby Barnes sang for ill veterans (especially in mental therapy) at the Waco Veterans Hospital. It was at this time that she took to the zither, a small instrument convenient to carry along. Now, in singing folksongs, she uses the zither exclusively.

The Barneses moved to Mountainburg, Arkansas, in 1951, and from this date onward Bobby developed a more intensive interest in folk music. Many of the songs she sings have come directly from the mountain people, though she has also studied the collections diligently. She sings the songs much as she finds them and does not try to "dress them up," believing that genuineness is better revealed in a simple presentation.

Bobby Barnes has done a good deal of folksinging in the past ten years, in all having given more than a hundred performances, major and minor. She performed at the Arkansas Folklore Society, Fayetteville, in June, 1951, and again in June, 1952. In September, 1951, she sang in a movie and TV show for N.B.C. called "Let's Go Visiting." In July, 1952, she sang folksongs at the Silver Strike Jubilee in Siloam Springs, Arkansas. She represented Arkansas at the National Folk Festival in St. Louis in May, 1952, singing ballads to the accompaniment of her zither. At Waco in March, 1953, she sang folksongs at the Texas Federation of Music Clubs, and also at the All-Florida Folk Festival held at White Springs in May, 1953.

In recent years Bobby Barnes has been regularly on the program of the Ozark Folk Festival, held each October in Eureka Springs, Arkansas. The Barneses moved to Eureka Springs early in 1954. They had no children. After Wilmer Barnes died there in May, 1955, Bobby returned to Waco, continuing her folksong activities as before. She is now chairman of the Folk Music Division, Texas Federation of Music Clubs.

MARGARET BARRY

Famous as a folksinger in Ireland and England and now tape-recorded for American records, Margaret Barry * is a traditional Irish street singer. She was born on January 1, 1917, in Cork, Ireland,

* Margaret Barry and a few others from the British Isles are included in this study because their records have become well known in America. Since much folksinging is international, it is sometimes difficult to stop at national boundaries.

where she grew up and received her elementary and secondary education.

Margaret learned songs from her parents and other singers, and has been singing all her life. At the age of fourteen she began singing professionally at Macroom, a village on the River Lee in County Cork. She uses the five-string banjo and improvises her accompaniments. She has recorded for Topic and Riverside Records (see Book Three).

Margaret was married in 1934 to Patrick Barry, a laborer. They have a daughter, Nora, born in 1936. A letter from London makes this further comment about her singing: "Margaret Barry earns her living by singing in public houses, i.e., licensed British taverns in London, performing on practically every night of the week in various pubs in company with Michael Gorman, a traditional Irish fiddler.... In addition to making records, they have broadcast and appeared on TV."

FIDDLER BEERS AND MRS. FIDDLER

The Montana Beers, Robert and Evelyne, or Fiddler Beers and Mrs. Fiddler as they like to be called, are among the husband-and-wife teams * who have made an artistic career from the world of folksong. Their contribution is a unique one, particularly in their use of folk music developed in a program titled "Fiddle Tunes and Rockin' Chair Songs." (These latter are composed popular ballads which, over a period of time, have acquired a folk flavor.)

The two Beers have led an interesting and colorful life, before as well as after their teaming up for a musical career. Robert Harlan Beers was born in a mining area near Clearfield, Pennsylvania, on October 1, 1920. He began schooling in the area and, when he was nine, the family moved to Joliet, Illinois, where he completed grade school. In 1935, the family moved to suburban St. Louis, where Robert attended the Kirkwood High School. In 1940, he entered the School of Music at Northwestern University and, following a three-year interruption because of the war, graduated in 1947 with a Bachelor of Music in Education.

Evelyne Christine Sauer (later changed to Andresen, her mother's name) was born on May 3, 1925, in Chicago and began her schooling there. Her mother was an excellent though untutored singer, who knew much light classical music and some folksongs from her Danish background. The Andresen grandparents had a profound

* Other such teams discussed in this book are Dr. and Mrs. I. G. Greer, Mr. and Mrs. Adolph Kukler, Josef Marais and Miranda, Jim and Carmen Murray, Harry and Jeanie West.

influence on Evelyne and gave her a basic appreciation for music, as well as considerable training. Evelyne is a lyric soprano, a natural-born singer with little formal training. Her family moved to St. Louis, and there in high school she had many opportunities to sing. By 1940, when she was fifteen, she had become a church soloist. In 1943, Robert Beers heard the young church soloist sing the beautiful spiritual, "Sweet Little Jesus Boy," and made occasion to meet her. Their common interests in music led to their marriage in 1944 and the beginning of a career that has given them a life of artistic adventure.

Robert had learned the violin first "by ear" from his grandfather and later from skilled teachers. He was concertmaster of his high-school orchestra, a member of the St. Louis Symphony while still in high school, and he made hundreds of solo appearances in schools, churches, other meetings, and on radio. Evelyne became a member of the Kirkwood Choral Society, which performed periodically with the St. Louis Symphony. In 1945, the Beers went to Chicago, where their daughter Martha Christine was born in December, 1945. Then, after Robert's music studies were completed at Northwestern in 1947, the Beers made the break that really opened a new musical career for them. They went "out West," to the big country, and plunged into a life still close to pioneering and the old mining days, and still rich in folk music.

Robert Beers now looked back to a time when his maternal grand-father, George Sullivan, an old-time fiddler who had retired to North Freedom, Wisconsin, began teaching him many old fiddle tunes. These old tunes took on a new quality of importance and became the basis of an "Old-Time Fiddler" sketch done for the acting group known as the Judith Mountain Players. Evelyne was a member of this acting group, and had been one of the four original members of the Virginia City (Montana) Players. From this sketch began Beers' career as America's Only Concert Fiddler. (He uses his grandfather Sullivan's old violin.)

Another instrument Robert Beers uses is the psaltery, a stringed instrument, forerunner of the piano. Robert's description is as follows: "This psaltery was made in Minneapolis in 1890, and is the one we use in our concerts. It is about the size of a virginal, standing on four stout legs, is 46 inches in length, 20 inches wide, with a soundbox 8 inches deep. I pluck the strings with the fingers and get a full range of harmonies in about six keys." He accompanies Evelyne's singing of folksongs.

So the Beers have developed into professional folk artists. Robert is concerned as an artist to make better known the fine old fiddle

tunes and to develop them for concert work. The Beers have uncovered a good deal of folk material in Montana and Wyoming,
and are on the lookout constantly for more songs and tunes. They
have performed in over twenty states, in Mexico and South America,
and their performances run into the hundreds. Robert played as
concertmaster in the Billings, Montana, Symphony from 1951 to
1955. It was then that the Beers began giving joint recitals, particularly of folk music, or of music based on folk materials. Their
concert work has been favorably reviewed in many papers and
journals, and they have appeared at many festivals, including the
Ozark Folk Festival (1957 and 1958) and the National Folk Festival
in Oklahoma City (1957). Their present base of operations is the
Spear T Ranch near Lewistown, Montana.

HARRY BELAFONTE

The meteoric rise of Harry Belafonte in the popular entertainment
world is a typically American success story. No singing star has more
clearly exemplified the rags-to-riches legend so well beloved in the
world of romance and so dear to the American public. For as recently
as 1949 Belafonte was working in New York's garment center at a
modest salary in order to support his growing family; six years later,
his annual earnings, not counting record royalties, passed the quarter-
million mark.[6]

Harry George Belafonte, Jr., was born March 1, 1927,[7] in New
York City of a Jamaican mother and a Martinique father. As a child,
he was taken back to Jamaica in the British West Indies. There he
received his elementary education and there he first became aware
of folk music. He returned to New York City in 1940 to enter George
Washington High School, graduating in 1944. After two years in the
Navy, he entered college at Hampton Institute, Hampton, Virginia,
but did not graduate.

Though he had known some folksongs from early childhood in
the West Indies, Belafonte began his entertainment career in the
field of drama. He joined the American Negro Theatre and studied
at the Drama Workshop in New York City. Though this work was
much to his liking, it offered little outlet for singing, and he needed
more income to support his family. Giving up his theater work in
1949, he attained moderate success as a "pop" singer, but found
such work unsatisfactory and, in his judgment, "artistically shallow."
Again, Belafonte's career came to a critical turn. With two friends
he opened a small restaurant in Greenwich Village and, in leisure
hours, rediscovered an immense satisfaction in singing folksongs
informally among friends. At the insistence of friends, late in 1950

40   SINGERS OF BALLADS AND FOLKSONGS

he decided to return to show business. This time his mind was made up: he would sing ballads and folksongs, but with a difference.

The "difference" that Harry Belafonte brought to the singing of folksongs was his ability as an actor. He began an intensive study of the field, first digging into the wealth of the Library of Congress Archive, then doing his own collecting by tape recorder as he traveled in the United States, Mexico, and the West Indies, from 1950 on. Teaming up with an expert guitarist, Millard Thomas, he built an acting-singing program of American folksongs, in time extending his repertoire to include Irish, Caribbean, South American, and Hebrew songs.

From the time of his debut as an actor-singer at the Village Vanguard in October, 1951, his success was assured. His talents were soon in demand throughout the land, from the Cocoanut Grove in Los Angeles to the Empire Room and the Starlight Roof of the Waldorf-Astoria and the Copacabana in New York. He was the first Negro to play the Empire Room of Chicago's Palmer House. He has performed in practically every state in the Union and in Canada. By late 1959, RCA Victor had released twenty-one EP and LP albums, some of which had an advance sale of over 50,000. His motion-picture performances include *Carmen Jones, Island in the Sun,* and *Odds Against Tomorrow.* Since then Belafonte has formed his own motion-picture company, Harbel, to produce films utilizing creative Negro talents. In 1955, he starred in the Paul Gregory musical show, *Three for Tonight.* In June, 1956, his one-man show broke the attendance record of New York's outdoor concert arena, Lewisohn Stadium. The following month, in Los Angeles, his show called "A Night with Belafonte" drew record crowds at the Greek Theatre. He played a starring role in the nation-wide tour of the musical drama, *Sing, Man, Sing,* and he has done guest-star stints on many a TV show. In October, 1956, the Catholic Interracial Council gave him the James J. Hoey Award for Interracial Justice. And so he has moved swiftly, from one success to another. Havana, Cuba, and London, England, saw and heard him in 1957, and he has had bookings in all the foreign hotels of the Conrad Hilton chain.[8]

How shall we account for the phenomenal success of this young man? Good management is part of the answer, but only a part. Exuberant youthfulness and a handsome face and figure are another part of the answer, but only a part. The real answer is that Harry Belafonte is a gifted, dedicated artist with a remarkable dramatic ability, a flair for showmanship, and a tremendous belief in what he does.* Every song he sings—and most of them are folksongs—becomes a new work of art in his singing. His gestures, his expressive intonations, his understanding of the historical and social content of a song, his sense of the comic and the tragic—all these combine to captivate not only his youthful admirers but the sharp-eared critics and lovers of serious art. In a setting of fine guitar music, with a background of orchestrations and choral accompaniments (written by Belafonte), the songs come through with a conviction, a sincerity, and a strange beauty none can deny.

While at Hampton Institute, Belafonte met Marguerite Byrd, who was studying for a master's degree in psychology. Later, she became a teacher and child psychologist in New York City. She and Harry Belafonte were married in June, 1948. They are the parents of two daughters: Adrienne, born May 27, 1949, and Shari, born September 22, 1954. With all his sensational success, Belafonte remains a modest man, serious and hard-working in his art, with great love for children. Until recently he lived modestly in a New York suburb. He and Marguerite Byrd were divorced early in 1957, and on March 8, 1957, he was married to Julie Robinson, a dancer in the Katherine Dunham troupe.[9] They have a son, David.

BILL BENDER

William Bender, Jr., now a captain in the United States Air Force Reserve, was born in New York City on August 1, 1916. His early education, elementary and high school, was in the Mamaroneck, New York, public schools. After a year at Wesleyan University in Connecticut and two years at the University of Colorado, he left college and did not return until 1946. He was married to Jeanne E. Lewis in 1943. In 1947, he took a Bachelor of Arts degree, *cum laude,* at the University of Colorado.

Bill Bender has been singing folksongs for some twenty years. His first paid public performance was somewhat accidental: on a night in February, 1936, he filled in at radio station WFAS, White Plains, New York, when the act originally scheduled became stalled in a snowdrift. Bender has picked up ballads for many years, from old and new books, and from many people here and there. He says he doesn't read music to speak of, but he adapts the tunes until they become singable for him.

Bender has performed in eight or ten states, and during the war in Japan and Korea, and in Britain over the B.B.C. He saw Army

---

* It is significant that one of his favorite singers is Mahalia Jackson, interpreter of spirituals and gospel songs.

service in World War II and in the Korean War. In the late 1940's, he did a series of American and Spanish-American songs for the Voice of America. Throughout 1951 he was the officer in charge of the radio combat reporters of the Far East Air Forces. Since 1951 Bender has been on the broadcasting staff of radio station WUOM, University of Michigan, Ann Arbor.

Bender accompanies himself on the Spanish guitar and has made recordings of frontier and cowboy ballads under Asch and Stinson labels. Ben Gray Lumpkin, authority on folksong records, speaks of his singing as "vigorous and pleasant." [10] Another critic speaks of his cowboy songs as done in a sort of "genuine easy Westernism." [11] His early recordings are now collector's items.

JESSIE BENTON

People say it isn't easy being the child of a famous father, but Jessie Benton seems to be doing all right. She was born in Kansas City, Missouri, in 1939, the second child of Thomas Hart Benton and Rita Piacenza Benton. Jessie attended Sunset Hill School in Kansas City and, after graduation in 1957, entered Radcliffe College, class of 1961.

Mrs. Benton is an excellent guitarist, Tom Benton played the harmonica for many years, and Jessie's brother Tom P. is a flutist and writer. Over the years the Bentons have been hosts to people in all walks of life—artists, students, writers, actors, educators, serious musicians, and even singers of folksongs. Among these last are such names as Burl Ives, Carl Sandburg, Pete Seeger, and John Jacob Niles. To put it another way, Jessie Benton has grown up in the world of art and music, including folksong, and has been deeply influenced by family and friends. Many of Tom Benton's paintings have grown out of the folklore—sometimes more narrowly out of the folksong—of America (see Prologue for further comment). Jessie, like other singers, has learned also from books and recordings.

Jessie Benton began her public performances in the summer of 1956 on Martha's Vineyard. This summer work continued and was accelerated in the summer of 1958. For her weekly appearances at a supper club she received a tidy sum which added materially to her Radcliffe College budget. Besides the Martha's Vineyard performances, she has performed in New York, Connecticut, and Missouri. Jessie is skillful with the guitar, having been tutored by her mother, and her high clear soprano is well suited to the mood and the melody of many a folksong. After college days are over, there is strong indication that she may become a professional folksinger.

THEODORE BIKEL

Actor Theodore Bikel has known folksongs all his life, even before, he says, "I could speak properly." He was born on May 2, 1924, in Vienna, Austria, where he grew up and received his schooling. Two of his eight years in Israel he spent in an agricultural college, and he also studied at the Habimah Seminary of Actors. In 1946, he entered the Royal Academy of Dramatic Art in London and received a degree (R.A.D.A.) in 1948.

Bikel learned folksongs from his parents, aunts and uncles, and "from just about everybody," and he was singing them publicly from the time he was seven years old. He has sung in many parts of the world, in a dozen or more languages, including the British Isles, France, Spain, Austria, Yugoslavia, Greece, Israel, and "at least half of the United States." The number of his appearances, he estimates, would reach "a good seven hundred." For accompaniment he likes the guitar, but also uses harmonica and khalil.*

Since Bikel is also composer and actor, his singing never comes off as a simple, objective presentation of a folksong. Every song, through his musical skill and vibrant personality, becomes a work of art. Asked if he cared to name a few favorites among folksongs, he replied: "It cannot be done, for it varies with the mood of the evening. As of the moment [it was July, 1958] gypsy music is the favorite." A prominent actor on the American stage in recent seasons, Theodore Bikel has taken time out to record many folksongs (see Book Three).

MARIE BOETTE

Miss Marie Boette, musician, teacher, and student, has known folksongs all her life and has been singing them publicly for over fifteen years. She was born July 27, 1895, in Parkersburg, West Virginia; attended schools there, graduating from Parkersburg High School; and has lived there much of her life. She took a Bachelor of Science degree in music education at New York University in 1934, a master's degree at Ohio University in 1942,[12] and for distinguished service to music was granted an honorary Doctor of Music degree by Davis and Elkins College in 1954.

Miss Boette knew German folksongs from her parents' singing, but she has learned British and American folksongs from "those who had them handed down from one generation to another in the West Virginia hills." She collected all her materials (songs with

* The Israeli recorder, sometimes spelled *chalil*.

tunes) in Upshur, Lewis, Nicholas, Cabell, Wirt, and Wood counties
and surrounding areas. Her collecting interest was stimulated when
she was associate professor of music for eleven years (1935-47) at
West Virginia Wesleyan College, Buckhannon, West Virginia.

Miss Boette has given over a hundred performances of folksongs
in several states—Ohio, West Virginia, Pennsylvania, and Kentucky.
For accompaniment she uses the rebec, autoharp, and sometimes the
zither. (She also owns a samisen and a dulcimer.) She has made
recordings, both on tape and records, for her own use. Besides this
deep and lifelong interest in folk music, Miss Boette has written
some worship songs and chants, and has done arrangements for
piano and pipe organ. At present she is organist and minister of
music at the First Presbyterian Church in her native city of Parkersburg.

BILL BONYUN

Brooklyn-born Bill Bonyun has been taking folk music seriously
for a long time and, in recent years, has been putting it to good
use in the schoolroom. Born on April 15, 1911, he was educated
in the Brooklyn, Summit (New Jersey), and Silver Bay (New York)
public schools. Beyond high school, Bill has picked up a pair of
degrees—A.B. and A.M.—after study at several universities: Wesleyan at Middletown, Connecticut, University of North Carolina,
and Columbia University.

Though Bill Bonyun's parents were not folk musicians, he looks
and often acts like a true-born Yankee brought up in the tradition
of folksong. This may be because his windswept beard makes him
look like a clipper captain, but the real reason is that he has learned
a lot of folksongs from neighbors in Maine, where he farmed from
1940 on. Later, his store of songs was augmented by other singer-
friends like Dyer-Bennet (q.v.) and Frank Warner (q.v.). And,
of course, he's learned many songs from the books, too.

A decade ago (1949), Bill began singing folksongs to school-
children, at an elementary school in Holbrook, Long Island. He
considers this the serious beginning of his "principal objective," to
teach the "social sciences through ballads and folksongs." Now, he
goes from one elementary school to another, in various parts of New
York and New England, spending a day in each school, presenting
songs and legends and having the pupils take part in the stories.

In 1955, Bill Bonyun began a special project: "During the late
spring, summer, and early autumn months, he sings on the green
at Old Sturbridge Village, a restoration village of 1800, located in
Sturbridge, Massachusetts, where he meets children and parents

from all over the United States." * This project has proved to be successful and highly entertaining. Now, also, Bill and friends have projected a series of recordings (see Book Three) to be used in schools. Bill also did the sound track for *Life* magazine's documentary film called *Hands That Built America.*

Assisting Bill Bonyun in his many activities—"she is the musician in the family," he says—is his wife, Gene Benedict. They were married in March, 1941, and are the parents of two sons, Stephen Benedict and William Archibald. The family home is in Brookhaven, New York, but there aren't many days of the year one would find Bill Bonyun there—he's likely to be off with his guitar on a singing jaunt somewhere, or on the trail of another legend or folksong!

GEORGE W. BOSWELL

George Boswell—teacher, singer, and collector—was born March 29, 1919, in Nashville, Tennessee, where he received his formal education. There he attended the Clemons School, David Lipscomb (junior) College (1935-37), Vanderbilt University (B.A. in 1941 and M.A. in 1948), and took a Ph.D. degree at George Peabody College for Teachers in 1951.

Dr. Boswell's father sang in choruses when he was a young man, and his mother sings and plays the piano. They were not folksingers, however, and their son George makes no claim to being a traditional singer, since his interest in folksinging did not begin until he was about thirty. In 1949, he began a serious collecting of folksongs in Tennessee, and he learned to sing folksongs from his many informants (over 150), especially from Dr. George P. Jackson, Donald Davidson, and Charles F. Bryan. He first performed, with guitar, about 1950 at Cookeville for the Tennessee Folklore Society. He has performed in three different states and has presented, including radio programs, over thirty recitals.

At present Dr. Boswell's collecting is considerably more important than his singing. Over the past half-dozen years he has collected about seven hundred variants of approximately four hundred folksongs in middle Tennessee. Some of these he has taken on tape and wire recording, but many in his collection he has notated immediately from the singers. Frequently Mrs. Boswell took down the words in shorthand as he carefully recorded the tunes, phonetically copying dialectal pronunciation and actual changes in meter signature, neutral tones, melodic variants, etc. In his collection are a good many instrumental (fiddle) tunes. His large collection of folksongs and

* *The Christian Science Monitor,* September 20, 1958.

fiddle tunes is unpublished, as of the present, but it is obvious that he has the making of an excellent two- or three-volume study.

George W. Boswell was married to Rose Emily Hall on August 21, 1951. They have two children: Jonathan Hall, born in 1952, and Rebecca Elizabeth, born in 1953. They live at Clarksville, Tennessee, where Dr. Boswell is a member of the English department at Austin Peay State College.

MARY ELLA M. BOYLE

Mary Ella Morris was born in 1931 in Tulsa, Oklahoma, where she received both her grammar-school and high-school education. Then she went East to Mount Holyoke College, South Hadley, Massachusetts, and took a Bachelor of Arts degree in 1952. She also studied one summer at the University of Colorado.

Though Mary Ella is an amateur in the singing of folksongs, she has known music and folksongs most of her life, for her family is a musical one. Much of her knowledge of folksinging and folksongs, however, has come from native singers in Oklahoma and elsewhere, from some trained artists, and from her study of the collections of folksongs. Her performing interest developed when she was a student at Mount Holyoke, and it has been growing over the past half-dozen years.

Mary Ella uses the autoharp for accompaniment and, like many singers of folksongs, works out her own arrangements. In recent years she has given recitals, two or three dozen of them, in Oklahoma and Massachusetts; and she has performed with the Mount Holyoke Glee Club in New York City and elsewhere when the club has been on tour.

Mary Ella Morris was married to Christopher George Boyle in December, 1951. They are the parents of two girls: Catherine, born in 1952, and Anne, born in 1954. Mr. Boyle is an English instructor at the St. Andrew's Episcopal School at Middletown, New Jersey, where the Boyles now live. With two small children to care for, Mrs. Boyle's folksong activities are limited, but her enthusiasm is genuine and her knowledge is growing.

OSCAR BRAND

The researcher would hunt a long time to find anyone, among the people in folksong activities today, more articulate or witty or better informed than Oscar Brand. Performer and emcee, organizer and director, historian and folklorist, book reviewer and commentator, he is alert to all the growing interests in folksong and its uses in our time.

Oscar Brand was born February 7, 1920, on a wheat farm near Winnipeg, Canada, of parents who were singers, as were his grandparents. His first schooling was in Winnipeg, but when he was seven the family moved to Minneapolis, then to Chicago, and finally on to New York City. When the family moved to Brooklyn, a final long stretch got Oscar through Erasmus Hall High School in 1937. For two years he worked as an itinerant farm hand (with banjo) before going on to college. In 1942, he took a Bachelor of Arts degree at Brooklyn College, majoring in abnormal psychology. World War II interrupted his further study. He worked in and around New York City in Army hospitals, using folksongs in psychiatric and psychological therapy. Leaving the Army in 1945, he became a professional folksinger, finding it, he said, "easier than working for a living."

Oscar Brand is a man of many talents. For about a year he went on tour as a singer with Herb Shriner. Late in 1945, he started his "Folk Song Festival" on station WNYC, which ran for nearly a decade and featured every singer of folksongs passing through the big city. Early in his career he graduated from the tenor banjo to the twelve-string guitar, which he plays with vigor and gusto. He is the author and composer of "A Guy Is a Guy," at one time a number-one song on the hit parade which sold over a million records for Columbia. About this composition he writes: "I cleaned it up from an old dirty song I was appalled by while serving in the Medical Corps." At various times he has appeared on most of the networks—in "Americana" for Firestone, on the "Kate Smith Hour," in Norman Corwin's documentary series, in the Dr. Christian show, to mention a few. He wrote scripts for the State Department for use on the "Voice of America." Agnes DeMille chose him to write the lyrics and act as technical adviser on her CBS-TV "Gold Rush." * He writes reviews and critical articles for the *Saturday Review* [13] and other journals.

The biographer is hard put to it to keep up with Oscar Brand; he has done so much and moved so fast. He does (or his records are doing) the cowboy commercials for Cheerios on the Wyatt Earp telecast. He has done singing and acting in films for Ford, Encyclopaedia Britannica, Allied Chemical Company, Cinevision, Remington Arms, and others. He has won citations at the Venice and Edinburgh International Folk Music Festivals.

In 1957, Oscar Brand brought out his first book, *Singing Holidays* (see Book Two, Chapter 13), and he has others in the making: *Old Bangum Would A-Hunting Go,* a story based on a motion

* From an undated brochure on Brand.

picture he wrote for Harlequin Films, is coming soon; his series of "Bawdy Songs and Backroom Ballads" (see Book Three, recordings) will be issued as a song book by Matador Music, with illustrations by Irving Sloane and arrangements by Robert Abramson. He was making 78 rpm records before the long-playing ones were born, and now his long-playing records make an impressive listing (see Book Three).

Brand has given folksong recitals at Carnegie Hall, Town Hall, and the Academy of Music in New York City, and in numerous schools, colleges, and halls all across the land—in fact, in all the states and in Canada. The number of his recitals runs far beyond the thousand mark: like the many songs he sings, he no longer knows the count. "By now," he writes, "I have learned so many songs I despair of singing half of my repertoire before I die."

With all his many activities, Oscar Brand somehow finds time for friends and family. His work as director of folk music for New York City's municipal station, WNYC, begun in 1945, has brought him in touch with hundreds of singers. He probably knows more singers of folksongs than any other man in the business, unless it be Alan Lomax. Tall and lanky, easy and affable, he is a master showman, and a man who carries his much learning lightly.

Oscar Brand made an early marriage that did not work out. But he is now happily married (on May 10, 1955) to the former ballet dancer, Rubyan Saber. Rubyan's dancing activities included the Radio City Ballet Corps, the part of Jeannie in *Brigadoon* and others. "When we married," writes Mr. Brand, "she stopped working, but she paints and housewifes—which is considerable work in itself." Obviously, since now they have a daughter, Jeannie, "named for Jean Ritchie, her godmother." And Rubyan helps Mr. Brand in his many broadcasting and recording activities.

Knowing all the activity Oscar Brand goes through day in and day out, one wonders if, after all, being a professional folksinger is "easier than working for a living." Not easier surely, but fascinating and exciting to this restless, colorful, and witty member of the big-city folksinging tribe. A recent letter from Oscar, packed with information on his daily round and his many projects in the making, concludes with this light touch: "Now I'll get up off the couch and go back to work." Psychiatric therapy still intrigues him!

MARY BRISCOE

Mrs. Mary (High) Briscoe, sister of Fred High (*q.v.*), was born March 30, 1875, on Indian Creek, near the place where Fred High's canning factory was located at High, Arkansas. Her early schooling was at the old Antioch schoolhouse about eighteen miles east of Eureka Springs. As children did much farm work in that early day, no one got more than three months' schooling in any one year.

Mary High learned folksongs very early in her family, as soon as she could hum a tune. She can't recall a time when she hasn't sung the old songs, and she knows many of them, all learned orally, of course. Formerly she preferred the love songs, but now, she says, "I love old-time religious songs best." Reminiscing about her singing, she said, "I could write a whole book on songs, for I have sung lots of them."

Most of Mrs. Briscoe's singing has been done along with the everyday duties of running a household, for she was married early and raised a large family. Publicly she has sung at the Arkansas Folklore Society meetings in Fayetteville, the Ozark Folk Festival in Eureka Springs, and some twenty of her songs have been tape-recorded for the University of Arkansas Folklore Archives.[14] She has also, at various times, sung folksongs in Missouri, Colorado, Oklahoma, and the old Indian Territory.

Mary High was first married in 1892, at seventeen, to Ben Casey, and years later to Sol Briscoe. She has had eleven children, nine of whom are still living. Commenting on her limited travels, Mrs. Briscoe said: "Oh, I'm just an old hill billie." Even so, she is a woman of keen mind and homely wit, and she has a tremendous memory for the old songs.

BIG BILL BROONZY

Like the meteoric career of Leadbelly (*q.v.*), though perhaps more limited and less spectacular, the career of Big Bill Broonzy developed into something fabulous. For Broonzy, like Leadbelly, rose from the most obscure beginnings to world-wide fame.

William Lee Broonzy was born on June 26, 1893,[15] into a large family—he had five sisters and three brothers—on a farm at Scott, Mississippi. What limited schooling he had was obtained after the family had moved to Arkansas. But there was always much singing in the big family, and Big Bill learned many songs, particularly from his father and from an uncle, Jerry Belcher. He recalled his first public performance in a church at Scott Crossing, Arkansas, in 1903, and he sang ballads and blues publicly till the day he died—August 15, 1958.

Most of his life Big Bill had farmed and sung, the former down in Arkansas and the latter just about all over the world. He sang in every state in the Union and in many foreign countries—Canada,

England, Australia, Holland, Belgium, Spain, Algeria, Italy, Germany, France. His first Carnegie Hall performance was in 1938. According to his count, he had recorded more than two hundred blues (his specialty) and over eighty other folksongs. Recordings have been done by Mercury, Columbia, RCA Victor, and others in the United States, and some recordings were done in Paris and elsewhere abroad.* Sales of his records long ago passed the quarter-million mark. Big Bill played the violin, but his special instrument was the guitar, on which his playing has been called fabulous because of the variety of effects he got in his accompaniments.

Big Bill Broonzy was first married in 1916 to Guitrue Embria in Pine Bluff, Arkansas. A second marriage was in 1941 in Texas, to Rosie Syphen. He was the father of five children. In his later years Mr. Broonzy made his home in Chicago, where he was a well-known figure at the Blue Note and other night clubs. Perhaps no singer of folk blues was better known or more widely traveled than Big Bill Broonzy. But time and again he went back to Arkansas, away from the noisy "city of the big shoulders" to the peace and quiet of hills and woods. His death in 1958 was an irreparable loss to the world of folksong.

CHARLES FAULKNER BRYAN

On August 7, 1955, when sudden death cut short the career of Charlie Bryan, the world of folksong lost one of its most active, sympathetic, gifted, and friendly interpreters. He was a man free "from pose and affectation of any sort, and his genuine interest in all sorts and conditions of people ... endeared him to a host of friends and admirers." [16]

Charles Faulkner Bryan, who sang ballads and folksongs, he wrote, "as far back as I remember," [17] was born on July 26, 1911, near McMinnville, Warren County, Tennessee. He received his early schooling, both grammar and high school, at McMinnville. At nineteen, he entered the Nashville Conservatory of Music, from which he was graduated with a Bachelor of Music degree in 1934. During this period of study, he organized and conducted for two seasons the Nashville Junior Concert Orchestra; also, he served as arranger and soloist at radio station WSM. From 1935 to 1939, he headed the department of music at the Tennessee Polytechnic Institute at

---

* See Book Three, Discography, for a listing of some of his long-playing records. Incidentally, it was Win Stracke (q.v.) who made the suggestion to Hugues Parnassié that Big Bill would make a hit with European audiences, and Win's prophecy proved to be the making of Big Bill's European fame.

Cookeville, from which institution he received a Bachelor of Science degree in 1939.

The next year he became a teaching fellow at George Peabody College for Teachers in Nashville. It was here that he came under the influence of the late George Pullen Jackson (q.v.), eminent folksong authority and our country's leading collector of spiritual folksongs. Bryan traveled with Jackson's Old Harp Singers, and his interest in folksong matters was renewed and intensified by this experience. In the spring of 1940 he was granted a master's degree at Peabody, and soon thereafter was named state supervisor of the Federal Music Project for Tennessee. Later he was to head this work for the whole Southern area, and in 1942 he was named regional consultant for the Office of Civilian Defense.

At the end of World War II, Charlie Bryan entered Yale University for a year of study with the composer Paul Hindemith. In 1945, he received a Guggenheim Fellowship and devoted the year 1946 to composing. Much was accomplished in that year, but the major orchestral and choral work was a secular folk cantata entitled *The Bell Witch*, premièred in Carnegie Hall, New York, Robert Shaw conducting. His interests and activities continued to broaden. In 1947, he joined the Peabody faculty as teacher of voice, theory, and choral music. For five seasons he directed the Peabody summer operas.

From 1946 on, the number of his compositions and arrangements begins to look impressive. Other orchestral compositions include *Cumberland Interlude, 1790*, for small orchestra and alto solo; [18] *White Spiritual Symphony*,[19] first performed by the Cincinnati Symphony, Eugene Goossens conducting; *Birmingham Suite*, an original symphonic work performed in March, 1953, by the Birmingham Symphony, Arthur Bennett Lipkin conducting. Two stage works, one a musical folk play, *Strangers in This World* (performing time, two hours), and the other an opera, *Singin' Billy*, in two acts (performing time, two and a half hours), make extensive use of folksong materials. The text for the first of these was done by Brainerd Chaney, and the libretto for the second by Donald Davidson. *Singin' Billy*, based on the *Sacred Harp* tradition, uses a number of old songs: "Wondrous Love," "Promised Land," "Jerusalem," and "Evening Shade."

Besides these larger works,[20] he made many solo, as well as three- and four-part arrangements, of songs, most of which are folksongs, such as "Charlottown," "I Have a Mother in the Heavens," "See Me Cross the Water," "Skip-to-M'Lou," "Amazing Grace," "Old Joe

Clark," and others. (Many of these are published by J. Fischer & Bro.) In collaboration with George Pullen Jackson, he prepared and published (C. C. Birchard and Co., Boston) *American Folk Music for High Schools and Other Choral Groups*, a collection of twenty-five songs.

Though Charlie Bryan had traveled widely and studied deeply, he never got far away from his folksong background, and he never wished to. Through his knowledge and sincere love of the old songs, he did much to improve the attitude of the public toward our native folk music.* His great-grandmother, not to mention many nearer relatives, was a folksinger. He learned much from aunts and uncles (and, no doubt, cousins!) and from many singers in the region he knew so well. From about 1935 on, he became a serious collector of both folksongs and folk instruments. He was particularly intrigued with the Appalachian Mountain dulcimer, on the origin and history of which he was working at the time of his death,[21] and on which he was an accomplished performer. He had given hundreds of performances—how many he would not even make a guess—in at least seventeen states.

In 1952, Charles F. Bryan was appointed music master at the new Indian Springs School for Boys at Helena, Alabama, a position that gave him further opportunity for composing and collecting. He was elected a member of the American Society of Composers, Authors, and Publishers (ASCAP) and for many years was active in the Tennessee Folklore Society, serving that body as president for two terms (1949 and 1950). He spent the summer of 1954 in Europe searching for origins of the dulcimer.

Charles Faulkner Bryan was married to Edith Hillis in 1936. Their two children are Betty Lynn, born in 1941, and Charles, born in 1947. The family shared his work and enthusiasm in the realm of music. They and the folksong world are richer for the life of this beloved teacher, composer, performer; they and the world are poorer for his untimely passing.

BRUCE BUCKLEY

Among the young performers of folksongs with a serious scholarly interest in folklore is Bruce Buckley. This book of sketches includes others with similar scholarly interests,† and thus the world of folk-

---

* Louis Nicholas' article, mentioned above, stresses this.

† See, among others, the sketches on George Boswell, Loman Cansler, Paul Clayton, Bob Duncan, Dr. Patrick Gainer, Anne Grimes, Joe Hickerson, Sam Hinton, Alan Lomax, Brownie McNeil, J. J. Niles, Jean Ritchie, Ruth Rubin, Ellen Stekert, Frank Warner, and Hally Wood.

song can be viewed from many angles and approached in different ways.

Bruce Buckley was born on April 28, 1928, in Portsmouth, Ohio, where he received his education through high school. He spent one year at the University of Missouri (1945-46), then enrolled at Miami University, Oxford, Ohio, taking a Bachelor of Arts degree in 1949. After a session in an Episcopal theological seminary, he again enrolled at Miami and took a master's degree in folklore in 1952. From Miami, Buckley went to Indiana University, where he is pursuing his studies toward a doctorate in folklore and where he is production supervisor of the Audio-Visual Center.

Bruce has learned folk music from his family, for his parents are musicians and singers, especially of country and Western songs. His father plays the mandolin. Bruce has also learned from books and records, and since 1951 he has done a good deal of collecting, especially in southern Ohio, Indiana, Kentucky, and Illinois.* In 1949, he became an active performer. He uses the guitar and dulcimer, and sometimes sings unaccompanied. Recitals and performances in a dozen states, from Massachusetts to Colorado, number close to two hundred, not including over one hundred TV shows and perhaps one hundred and fifty on radio. He is a member of The Settlers, a folksinging trio giving performances in the Midwest. (Joe Hickerson and Ellen Stekert are the other two.)

Mr. Buckley recorded a group of *Ohio Valley Ballads* for Folkways (see Book Three) in 1955, and has other recordings in the making. His work has been favorably reviewed in the *Journal of American Folklore* (1957), *Midwest Folklore* (1957), and the Indianapolis *Star* (June 19, 1955).

Bruce Buckley was married to Patricia Lee Morrison, painter, in 1951. They have a son, Morrison Bruce, born January 1, 1955.

W. H. BURNETT

Born at Pettigrew, Arkansas, in 1907, W. H. Burnett has known folksongs all his life, having learned them at home, mainly from his mother. He obtained his schooling in Madison County, and has lived in northeast Arkansas all his life. Though he does not perform much in public, on two occasions at least (1954 and 1955) he was persuaded to sing at the annual meetings of the Arkansas Folklore Society in Fayetteville. Ordinarily he doesn't use an instrument when he sings, but he is something of an expert with the mandolin.

W. H. Burnett was married in 1930, and has one daughter, Dorothy

* *Midwest Folklore*, III (Spring 1953), 5-18.

Fay, born in 1935. Mr. Burnett's regular occupation is that of night patrolman at the University of Arkansas in Fayetteville.

JERRY BYRNE

Jerry Byrne was born in Pennsylvania on June 28, 1888. He received practically no formal education, but his parents were folksingers and taught him many songs. He has sung these songs for as long as he can remember, in fact, for over sixty years. If his memory is correct, he made his first public appearance as a singer about 1896 at a home-talent show in Hazleton, Pennsylvania.

In his more than half a century as a coal miner, Mr. Byrne has collected a good many songs, though he has never published any. His interest has been in singing them. He uses a guitar for accompaniment and does his own musical arrangements. Over the years he has given many folksong recitals, in at least sixteen states, "too many to recall," he writes. In 1946, at Bucks Run, Pennsylvania, he made recordings for the Library of Congress Archive of American Folk Song (AAFS nos. 77 and 79) under the supervision of Mr. George Korson, noted authority on Pennsylvania folklore. Jerry Byrne has a fine baritone voice and, in addition to folksongs, has sung in church choirs for well over thirty-five years.

Jerry Byrne and Catherine Carter were married in 1914. They are the parents of eight living children, all grown; and they have a lively troop of grandchildren. After fifty-three years in the anthracite mines, Mr. Byrne retired to Harrisburg, Pennsylvania. To occupy his time, he works as a custodian, and he continues to sing the songs he loves and has known these many years.

ROLF CAHN

A good many people have taken to singing folksongs as a hobby or, frequently, as a job. A notable instance of this is Rolf Cahn, who pays high tribute to Pete Seeger, "the first really inspiring performer" he had heard. Cahn was born in Düsseldorf, Germany, on August 14, 1924, and was brought to America in his early years. His grade- and high-school years were spent in Detroit where, he reports, "all pre-college schooling was very conservative." He attended Wayne University, Detroit, and received a Bachelor of Arts degree in 1948.

Rolf Cahn's parents, who were brought up in the tradition of grand opera, sing German folksongs and ballads, but Rolf learned his folksongs from singers like himself. His serious interest began about 1946. He has traveled a great deal, having been in forty-two of the fifty states, and he served with the United States Army in Europe during World War II. Much of his singing has been in California. He has given programs on FM radio station KPFA in Berkeley, California, and during 1953-54 in San Francisco he had a children's program of recording and singing called "Come Sing with Me." He uses the Spanish guitar, and sometimes the banjo, and is adept at performing all kinds of folk music—spirituals, occupational songs, ballads of the pioneers, flamenco, blues, etc. He was once married and has a son Nicky, born in 1949. He reports that his occupation is "full time in folk music."

A news item in *Caravan* (June-July, 1959) reported that Mr. Cahn had gone to New England to establish "a teaching practice in the Boston area."

ISLA CAMERON

Scotland-born actress Isla Cameron has known ballads all her life and has been singing them professionally about ten years. She was born on March 5, 1930, at Blairgowrie, Perthshire, Scotland; went to school at Newcastle-upon-Tyne and won scholarships for special study in commercial subjects. Then she studied costume design at Kings College, Newcastle, and acting for a short while at the Royal Academy of Dramatic Art.

Isla learned many songs from her mother, who "knew a lot of tunes but not many words." She learned from others, too, especially from Ewan MacColl (*q.v.*), who encouraged her and taught her many songs. She reports that a maternal uncle "can sing ballads but won't." Miss Cameron sometimes uses guitar "but sings most songs unaccompanied." She has collected in the British Isles, not for the purpose of publishing, but "mainly to enlarge my own repertoire and find out more about people who sing and preserve songs."

Isla Cameron has given hundreds of folksong recitals in the British Isles—"I don't keep count and usually sing whenever I'm asked"—and in Paris at L'Abbaye, "a folksong club run by two American actors, Gordon Heath and Lee Payant." She doesn't especially like making records but has done a few, some for H.M.V. in London and others for Tradition Records in New York. Her main occupation is acting, and she makes her home in London.

BOOTH CAMPBELL

Down in the Ozarks, Booth Campbell and his folksinging have become legendary. For more than three quarters of a century he sang the old songs, to the accompaniment of guitar or homemade banjo (one he made over forty years ago), and he never went far away from his beloved hills. William Booth Campbell was born on March 21, 1872, at Boonesboro, now Cane Hill, Arkansas. This village, too small for most maps, was his permanent address for well over eighty years. There as a boy he received a country-school education. There on December 27, 1900, he was married to Maude Oates. And it was there his three children were born and grew up. In due time they attended the University of Arkansas, from which they were all graduated.

Booth Campbell sang folksongs for so long that he could scarcely recall when or where he learned a particular song. His father and mother were singers, one aunt was a music teacher, and a cousin taught him a goodly number of songs. Beyond that his repertoire grew like that of any other folksinger—from hearing others sing. He reports that his public performances began, that is, the "first of any moment," at the National Folk Festival in St. Louis in 1934. After that he sang many times at the National Festival, at the Ozark Folk Festival in Eureka Springs, Arkansas, from its beginning in 1948, at the Arkansas Folklore Society meetings in Fayetteville, and on numerous other occasions. He recorded for the Archive of American Folk Song, Library of Congress, and about two dozen of his songs have been tape-recorded for the Archive of Songs of the Arkansas Folklore Society.

One of his favorites at festivals was the "Good Old Rebel," which Vance Randolph persuaded him to record in 1942 for the Library of Congress. At that time he said to Randolph, "It don't seem hardly right for a fellow to go around singing songs agin the Government what with the war and all." [22] When, in 1954, C.B.S. filmed and recorded the TV picture in the Ozarks called *The Search*, Booth Campbell was a star performer, though he played and sang from a hospital bed.

Except for one trip some years ago to California, he was never far from home. One might say, however, paraphrasing Thoreau, that he had traveled a long way in the Ozarks. His work kept him in the hills, mostly at farming. In earlier years he was a house painter and paper-hanger. He had offers to go on the radio but preferred not to commercialize his singing. On this point, one comment shows his independence of spirit: "I refused to pay them fellers in New York anything to join their union just to sing on the radio." [23] Well into his eighties, he sang, as always, only for the love of singing.

On May 17, 1956, William Booth Campbell died in his eighty-fifth year, not far from where he was born. [24]

LOMAN CANSLER

Loman Cansler was born on September 6, 1924, on a farm near Long Lane, Dallas County, Missouri, about fifty miles northeast of Springfield. He attended Northview Rural School in Dallas County, finishing the eighth grade. He did not attend regular high school, but did some studies while in the Navy. After taking the GED tests, he entered the University of Missouri in 1946. He received a Bachelor of Science degree in 1949 and a master's degree in education in 1950. In addition, he has done some work at Colorado University and the University of Kansas City.

Loman has known folksongs since early childhood. He learned from his parents, from his maternal grandparents especially, and from neighbors and friends. In his teens, he and his brother Richard sang at pie suppers and other gatherings, but only later did Loman know the songs were called folksongs. His first formal appearance, with guitar, dates from 1949, when he sang at a church-sponsored retreat at Kaiser, Missouri, near the Lake of the Ozarks. He has sung in churches, at civic clubs, at Hull House Camp (Waukegan, Illinois), and "most of all to American history and other social-science classes."

Loman has done serious collecting for a number of years, during the summers particularly, in both Missouri and Illinois. Some of his songs and comments have been published in the *Southern Folklore Quarterly* (September, 1954, and June, 1956), *Rayburn's Ozark Guide* (Summer 1958), and in the bulletin of the *Missouri Council of Social Studies* (October, 1955). He has something over four hundred songs on tape (not all different songs) and has made a special study of sources of many of them. Folkways Records released his first long-playing record in July, 1959 (see Book Three).

After his studies at Missouri, Loman taught for two years at Fayette, Missouri. On June 12, 1952, he was married to Laura June McElwain, and they moved to the Greater Kansas City area that summer. They are the parents of three children: Philip Trent, born November 3, 1953; Joel Ethan, born November 19, 1954; and Myra Annette, born August 21, 1956. Since 1952, Mr. Cansler has been a teacher of American history and counselor at North Kansas City High School, North Kansas City, Missouri.

KEITH CHALMERS

Keith Chalmers, actor, singer, and community worker, was born February 13, 1917, in Fitchburg, Massachusetts. He grew up in Holyoke, receiving his early schooling there at Lovering School and

Highland Grammar School. The family moved to St. Petersburg, Florida, and Keith went through high school there. He attended Swarthmore College in Pennsylvania, graduating at twenty with a Bachelor of Arts degree. Later, he studied in the School of Drama at Yale and also did graduate work at the University of Pennsylvania.

Though Chalmers does not come from a family of folksingers, he has an impressive musical background. His mother is a singing teacher and church soloist; his father is a nonprofessional singer of minstrel songs and music-hall ballads. Chalmers plays the piano and flute, as well as the guitar. His incentive for folksinging came from John Jacob Niles' visits to Swarthmore.

For fifteen years now, Chalmers has been singing folksongs; he gave his first full-length program on December 14, 1948, for the Tuesday Nighters Club of the Methodist Church in Rutherford, New Jersey. Since then, he has given over a hundred recitals in many states, from Portland, Maine, to St. Petersburg, Florida. Like other singers, he gathers many songs in his travels, and his repertoire includes songs of sailors, cowboys, pioneers, railroaders, rivermen, loggers, hillfolk. In fact, his lecture-recitals include all kinds. He has created programs for children, schools, clubs, and churches, one of his favorite recitals being "Religious Folksong in America."

Chalmers accompanies himself on a beautiful antique Spanish guitar.[25] In World War II, as a member of the 38th Division Band, he performed in a number of soldier shows in the South Pacific area, using folk materials in some of these shows. Besides his singing, he has done considerable acting in summer theater groups, and he is the director of the Community Drama Group in St. Petersburg, Florida. Like others who, after growing up, have learned to love the old songs of America, he helps to keep alive this tradition of fine folk music.

DOROTHY CHASE

Dorothy Chase, born in Newton, Massachusetts, doesn't really consider herself a folksinger. But she and her husband, Charles Chase, a teacher in California, maintain a "Folk Music Center" in Claremont, California. They handle folksong records, children's records, folk-music instruments and repairs, and Dorothy teaches banjo and guitar.

Mrs. Chase has learned folk music from friends, especially from Bess Lomax Hawes, as well as from books and records. Even so, she doesn't care to do much performing: "I'm no performer—I just about *die* when I sing for the Brownies!"

Charles and Dorothy were married in 1938, and they are the

parents of four daughters—Susan (1941), Joanne (1942), Ellen (1947), and Sarah (1955).

STUART CHURCHILL

Northwest Kansas was the native stamping ground of one who became a distinguished singer and arranger of folksongs on the popular "Fred Waring Show." Stuart Churchill was born at the village of Long Island, located on Prairie Dog Creek in Phillips County, Kansas, January 15, 1907. His early schooling was done at St. Francis, a town on the Republican River in Cheyenne County, Kansas. His mother, a piano teacher, gave him his first musical training. After graduating from high school in 1925, he enrolled at the University of Michigan, majoring in music. During his undergraduate days, "Stu," as he was affectionately known, was a member of the university band and symphony orchestra, playing drums in the former and bassoon in the latter. Besides these university activities, he earned expense money by playing drums in Ann Arbor theaters and in "singing for his supper" at a restaurant.

Stuart's big chance came in his senior year at Michigan, when Fred Waring visited the campus and offered him a job with the Pennsylvanians. A few weeks after graduation, Stu joined Waring's group at the Chicago Theatre in July, 1929, and soon became one of Waring's most versatile musicians. Besides his ability to play six or eight instruments, he performed as tenor soloist and was a competent arranger. After seven years with the Pennsylvanians, Churchill became a free-lance radio artist, doing work for Sealtest, Old Gold, Swift, Corn Products, Woodbury, and others. In 1937, he was again with Fred Waring, in concert and recording work, until he left to join the United States Army.

This was March, 1942, and a turning point in Churchill's life. Stu was assigned to the Army's Special Services and immediately began rehearsals with the famous soldier show, *This Is the Army*. For over two years he toured with the *Army* show throughout the United States, and Hollywood put it on the screen—one of the most successful movies of the war. The troupe also appeared in Canada, the British Isles, Africa, India, various countries of continental Europe, Australia, and in many of the Pacific Islands.

Given his background, it might be supposed that Stuart Churchill was a ballad singer from his youth up. Such is not the fact, however, nor were his parents folk musicians or singers. Though he may have heard ballads in his youth—as who has not?—his folksong interest developed during World War II. At Camp Upton, one of his tentmates was folksinger Burl Ives. He learned much from Burl, bought himself a guitar, and became thereafter a collector and singer of folksongs, developing a repertoire of several hundred songs. After his around-the-world three-year stretch in the Army, Churchill rejoined Fred Waring's Pennsylvanians in 1945, under General Electric sponsorship, as arranger and singer of folksong literature. With his special training in music, his particular interest has been choral and orchestral arrangements.[26] This time he remained with Waring for seven years, and in these years listeners anticipated with delight his solo appearances with guitar in many a fine ballad. Songs and ballads from this period have been recorded by RCA Victor and Decca companies. Beginning in 1947, Churchill taught music for several summers in the "Waring Workshop" at Shawnee, Pennsylvania.

Churchill left the Waring organization in 1952, and from 1952 to 1956 had a private studio in New York City, teaching voice and piano. Earlier, he had taken a Bachelor of Science degree in music education at Columbia University. During 1956-57, he taught music in the elementary schools at Caldwell, New Jersey, and completed work for a master's degree at Columbia. Stuart Churchill was married to Audrey Schneider in 1943. They have a daughter, Linda, born October 13, 1946.

EDGAR ROGIE CLARK

Among the unusual and versatile workers in the folksong field, few have done more than Edgar Rogie Clark—singer, composer, lecturer, author, and scholarly folklorist. Clark was born in Atlanta, Georgia, in 1915, the son of an itinerant Baptist minister. His love of Negro music no doubt was strengthened in his early years, when his father's duties took the family to out-of-the-way places in the back country. But it was not until he was in high school, and after his parents had died, that Clark decided to make a career of music.

Clark acquired his pre-college training at the Atlanta University Laboratory School, after which he attended Clark College in Atlanta, graduating in 1935 with a Bachelor of Arts degree. In college, he earned his living by giving recitals, for he had a gifted tenor voice of bell-like quality. He added to his musical education by periodic study at the Chicago Musical College, the Juilliard School, and Tanglewood. Later, in 1942, he took a Master of Arts degree at Columbia University.

Though Clark's training is mainly in classical music and though he worked first as a concert singer, he has made Afro-American folklore and folk music his special field of study. He had learned folksongs from listening in early youth, and he has continued to learn them by field trips. These journeys have taken him to various parts of the United States, Jamaica, Haiti, and Trinidad. He did a good deal of folksinging while working at inter-cultural education in New York City in the early 1940's, but his first formal recital of folksongs was given at the Art Center in Salt Lake City in 1943.

Clark was granted a Ford Foundation Faculty Fellowship for the year 1952-53 to continue his folklore studies. The following year, he received the John Hay Whitney Fellowship. From these studies has come a book entitled *The Black Bard, A Review of Negro Folk Music*. During the past dozen or fifteen years, besides his regular teaching duties and many lecture-recitals interpreting Afro-American folk music, he has done considerable publishing. No fewer than fifteen essays, many of them on folklore subjects, have appeared in such magazines as *The Journal of Negro Education, The Opportunity Magazine, The Music Journal, The Survey, Phylon Magazine, Negro History Bulletin,* and the *Journal of American Folklore.* He has made several LP recordings (see Book Three), one of the chief being *The John Henry Legend.* Many arrangements for Negro folksongs and spirituals have come from his pen, some for women's voices, some for mixed voices. And he has edited a collection of Negro American folksongs titled *Copper Sun* (1957).

Mr. Clark is a founder of the International Council of Negro Folklore, a member of ASCAP, and was teacher and head of the department of music, Jackson College, Jackson, Mississippi, later at Central State College, Wilberforce, Ohio. He was once married, but is now separated, and has one son, Rogie, Jr., born in 1942.

KEITH CLARK

The particular contribution of Keith Clark to ballad lore is to write and sing historical incidents of his region in ballad form,* set them to traditional or composed ballad tunes, and thus enliven his work as teacher and recreation director. What a wonderful way to make the past come alive!

Keith was born in 1921 in Wheaton, Illinois. He attended grade school in Madison, Wisconsin, and high school at the Wheaton Community High School. He holds a Bachelor of Science degree (1943) and a Master of Science in education (1948) from the University of Illinois. Then, in 1949, he completed a Master of Arts at the Bread Loaf School, Middlebury College, Vermont. It was this last school experience that aroused his interest in ballad singing and composing.

Keith Clark has presented some five hundred performances of his

* Folkways Records recently (1958) released an album of these literary ballads, composed and sung by Keith Clark, under the title, *Ballads of LaSalle County, Illinois* (FA 2080).

composed ballads, as well as of traditional ballads, in half a dozen states, including appearances at the Bread Loaf School in Vermont, the Southern Illinois Folk Festival at Carbondale, the Illinois Historical Society, and the National Folk Festival in Oklahoma City (1957). For accompaniment he uses a guitar, sometimes a banjo. Keith is also interested in other kinds of public performance. To let him speak for himself: "I have a Barn Theatre in my back yard . . . and we have a summer theatre group that presents musicals. I also like to have folk singers perform; we have had concerts by Pete Seeger, Earl Robinson, Bob Gibson, Odetta, Fiddler Beers—either in the Barn or at the high school."

In 1942, Keith Clark was married to Harriet Sorenson, and they are the parents of four sons: Keith II (May 5, 1944), Christopher (May 21, 1947), Robin (October 25, 1949), and Jonathan (March 24, 1952). Mr. Clark is a teacher of English at the Ottawa Township High School and recreation director for the city of Ottawa, Illinois.

WILLIAM CLAUSON

American-born of Swedish ancestry, William Clauson is one of the most promising folksingers on the scene today. He was born on May 2, 1930, at Ashtabula, Ohio, and soon thereafter was taken to his grandparents' home in Sweden. He got his first schooling at Viskafors, Sweden, but was brought back to America at the age of seven. His schooling continued in Cleveland, Ohio, in Oakland, California, and in Los Angeles, where he finished high school.

From his earliest memories William Clauson has known and sung folksongs. His mother is a nonprofessional singer of folksongs and ballads, his grandfather taught him much Swedish folklore in the early years, and a "couple of aunts that reside in Sweden" are singers of folksongs. His first "public folksong recital" occurred on shipboard when he entertained with Swedish folksongs while returning to America in 1937.

From that early age of seven onward he has, in a sense, become an international folksinger, for he sings in many languages besides English—Swedish, French, Spanish, German, Italian. His singing in the States has taken him from New York to Oregon and California; he has toured Canada, Mexico, Denmark, Sweden, and England. Everywhere he is received with enthusiasm by critics, musicians, and the general public. Tenor Richard Crooks spoke of his having an "engaging concert manner" and a beautiful tenor voice. Carl Sandburg found him irresistible, a most colorful and versatile singer and accomplished guitarist. The Stockholm *Daily News* (September 16, 1954) called him a master of his art. The London *Times* (September 25, 1954) described his guitar accompaniments as "evocative and varied" and his songs as "full of interest and delight." In a later comment the *Times* (May 23, 1954) praised his "mellifluous lyrical tenor voice" and his "strong but entirely sympathetic" personality.

Clauson is a master of the guitar, which he uses in concert, but he also plays the banjo, mandolin, and lute. Like all folksingers, he frequently makes his own arrangements and sometimes composes songs in the folk idiom. And like many folksingers, too, he collects ballads and folksongs along the way. He has a sizable collection (not published) gathered in Mexico, South America, the British Isles, and the Scandinavian countries. In addition, he has made many recordings (see Book Three). To mention a few: he did an "Educational Series" (Bowmar Records of Los Angeles) of twenty-five songs in many languages of many peoples; he recorded Spanish carols for the Spanish Music Center of New York City; he did the sea shanties for the RCA Victor album of *20,000 Leagues Under the Sea*.

William Clauson, skilled in languages, an accomplished musician with a beautiful voice, is a professional balladeer and guitarist on the threshold of a brilliant career.

JAMES R. AND GARLAND K. CLAYBORN

The Clayborn brothers are two country musicians and folksingers who have spent most of their lives in their native county of Carroll, Arkansas. James was born on March 26, 1899, and Garland on April 2, 1900. Their formal education did not go beyond the grade school at Gap, Arkansas.

The Clayborns have known folk music for more than a half century, having learned it from their parents, friends, and neighbors. James's special instrument is the banjo and Garland's is the fiddle, but Garland also knows the mandolin, guitar, and piano. All their lives they have added to their repertoire but have not published or recorded. In the best tradition of the Ozarks, they are truly skilled country musicians. In the main, their performing has been in the Arkansas hills, though James has performed in Kansas, Oklahoma, and as far west as California. At the Ozark Folk Festival, Eureka Springs, Arkansas, in mid-October, 1958, they gave a fine exhibition of fiddle and banjo tunes.

Both James and Garland Clayborn have been married (James a second time in 1950), and each has two children. The children of James are George M., born September 8, 1919, and Mary Lou (now Mrs. Powell), born March 6, 1929. The children of Garland are Audy Blaine, born December 7, 1929, and Orba Wayne, born April

15, 1933. The Clayborns live at the village of Green Forest, Arkansas. James works as a carpenter and stonemason. Garland has long been a teacher of instrumental music—violin, guitar, mandolin, and piano.

PAUL CLAYTON

Among the younger (under thirty) scholar-performers in the folksong field, none is more active and articulate, or more authentic, than Paul Clayton. He is rightly referred to as "America's most recorded young folksinger." Clayton was born on March 3, 1933, in the onetime great whaling capital of the East Coast, New Bedford, Massachusetts. Because of family travels, his grammar schooling varied from New Bedford to places in New Hampshire and Florida. After completing four years of high school at New Bedford, he attended the University of Virginia, took a Bachelor of Arts degree and, a year later, a Master of Arts.

Paul's parents knew some traditional music. His mother played the piano and his father the banjo. One grandfather, for many years an outfitter to whaling and fishing vessels, was apparently a strong influence in Paul's early years. "Other relatives, aunts and great-aunts are singers," he writes, "but none of the family seems to have been as deeply interested in [folk] music as I am." After the family influences, Paul discovered records by such singers as Leadbelly, Niles, Sandburg, and, at age eleven, he "got a guitar and started learning songs."

When he was fifteen, Paul Clayton began his first series of folk-song radio programs, in New Bedford, a fifteen-minute weekly program written, announced, and performed by himself. This series began in April, 1948, and his singing activities have had a steady increase since that time. Eventually he did radio programs and regular concerts in Ontario, Quebec, and Prince Edward Island, and he has performed in about half of the states "from California to Massachusetts and Illinois to Louisiana." Abroad, he performed in several countries, such as England (for the B.B.C.), Italy, France, Germany, and others.

A second major interest with Mr. Clayton is his collecting, pursued actively since 1951, in particular his delving into out-of-the-way places and documents and coming up with different versions of the old songs. This has enriched both his singing and his writing. The Public Library and the Whaling Museum of New Bedford—incidentally, two of the finest on whaling anywhere in the world—have yielded him much new-old material. He has collected elsewhere in New England, as well as in Canada, and one time went on an extensive collecting tour of Virginia, North Carolina, and Kentucky.

He writes a vivid account of this experience in a long article titled "Ballad Collecting in the Cumberlands." * It should be pointed out that Clayton, in his academic studies, worked under the tutelage of the distinguished folklorist and archivist, Professor Arthur Kyle Davis, Jr., of the University of Virginia.

At the beginning, this account referred to Paul Clayton as "America's most recorded young folksinger." His first record was made in the summer of 1954. Besides his recordings for the B.B.C., the Library of Congress Archive, and the Helen Hartness Flanders Ballad Collection at Middlebury, Vermont, in the past seven years Clayton has recorded nearly three hundred songs on commercial LP recordings under the following labels: Stinson, Riverside, Tradition, Elektra, and Folkways (see Book Three for details). His professional folksinging, making records, appearances in concert and on TV, etc., have given him his main support since he began graduate study in folklore. In his singing he generally uses the guitar, sometimes the three-string dulcimer, and sometimes no accompaniment. Both Clayton's singing and his collecting have been favorably reviewed in popular and scholarly journals.†

As a performing folksinger, Paul Clayton feels certain obligations to his materials and to his audiences. He writes: "A professional folksinger working with public audiences ought to present the best text and tune. Therefore I feel free to collect texts and use the best tune I know, except when I am doing a record aimed at scholars where the text and tune, even if fragmentary, are presented as collected." That sounds like a sensible attitude.

SEÑOR RUBÉN COBOS

Rubén Cobos, born in Piedras Negras, Coahuila, Mexico, has known folksongs all his life, having learned them from the people of Mexico and New Mexico. His early schooling was in his native town and later schooling in San Antonio, Texas. Finally, he completed his secondary training at the Menaul (Presbyterian) School in Albuquerque, New Mexico.

Cobos obtained his higher education at the University of New Mexico, at Stanford University, and at Mexico's Instituto de Investigaciones Esteticas. He holds a bachelor's and a master's degree and

* The University of Virginia Magazine, I (Spring 1956), 20-37. On a later trip in the same states, with Diane Hamilton and Liam Clancy, he collected instrumental music of the southern Appalachians. (See Tradition Record TLP-1007.)

† See, for example, various numbers since 1954 of the Journal of American Folklore, Western Folklore, New York Folklore Quarterly, Tennessee Folklore Bulletin, etc.; also, the Washington Evening Star for June 21, 1958.

is completing his doctorate at the University of New Mexico. His special field of investigation is the New Mexican Indita ballads, that is, the folksongs that have developed from Spanish and Mexican sources. He has made a considerable collection of these ballads in the mountain villages of New Mexico. According to Señor Cobos, these songs fall into three main groups: folksongs of Spanish provenience, New Mexican Hispanic folksongs of Mexican origin, and local New Mexican Hispanic folksongs.

Though he has always been singing folksongs, Señor Cobos made his formal debut in his teens at the Menaul School Auditorium in 1932. Since 1944, he has been at the University of New Mexico, where he is assistant professor of modern languages and where he has charge of training the New Mexico Folk Singers. This group has given many recitals and has performed frequently at national folk festivals, held in St. Louis and other cities. Cobos has also presented recitals in Mexico and Texas. Like most Spanish singers, he uses the guitar.

Señor Cobos was married in 1936 to Rita Sanchez, but they are now divorced. They have three children: Evelia, born in 1937; Irving, born in 1940; and Helene, born in 1942. Cobos is a leading folksinger and folklorist of New Mexico.

FRED W. COLBY

Since he doesn't sing professionally and has "never given what you might call a recital," Fred Colby makes no pretense of being a folksinger. But over the years he has picked up a good many songs and ballads and, with his five-string banjo, entertains friends and civic groups as the occasion arises.

Fred W. Colby was born December 21, 1895, at Fairmount, Tennessee. During boyhood he attended a one-room school with the dignified name of the Fairmount Academy. He entered the University of Tennessee in 1914, taking a Bachelor of Science degree in agriculture a few years later. His work has continued in that field: he is a specialist with the University of Tennessee Agricultural Extension Service.

Colby learned folksongs—he's been singing them since his early teens—from his grandparents, neighbors, and other rural people he has known in his university extension work. He has never collected in any serious way, but he apparently remembers a good many songs. On occasion, newspapers such as the Washington *Post* and Nashville *Tennessean* have given favorable notice to his singing. He is married to Lillian Lowe, and their permanent home is near Signal Mountain, Tennessee.

BOB COLTMAN

Though born in New Rochelle, New York, on November 17, 1937, Robert Coltman has been educated in Pennsylvania and New Hampshire. His first two years of schooling were at the Buckingham (Pennsylvania) Friends School, the next three in one-room country schools, and the next three of lower school he was back at the Friends School. He completed high school in Newton, Pennsylvania, and entered Dartmouth College in 1955 with the class of 1959.

Bob's family were not folksingers, but he has learned folk music from many sources—books, recordings old and new, folksinging friends like Bill Bonyun (q.v.) and Harrison Taylor, groups in Cambridge, Massachusetts, and Philadelphia, and many singers in the southern Appalachians. His main instrument is the five-string banjo, but he also uses the six- and twelve-string guitar. And like other versatile performers, he does very well with the dulcimer, mandolin, fiddle, or harmonica.

Bob's public performance of folksongs with guitar began when he was in eighth grade at the Buckingham Friends School, and his interest has not waned since. He has performed in about a dozen different states, and in the summers of 1954 and 1955 he went on a singing-collecting tour of the Appalachian region, especially in Virginia, West Virginia, Kentucky, Tennessee, and North Carolina. His memory is well stocked with hundreds of songs, and he is developing into a professional folksinger.

Not a little of the interest and enthusiasm of Bob and others in singing folksongs can be attributed to activities at various Eastern colleges and universities. Serious folksong study in such schools as Cornell, Vassar, Smith, Wellesley, and others has stimulated and developed many an individual singer as well as folksinging groups. For instance, in the spring of 1958, Dartmouth College held a "Folk Singers Hootenanny" * at which some two thousand enthusiasts from New England enjoyed hearing themselves and one another sing folksongs, all of them more or less amateurs. Bob Coltman has grown up in this environment.

DAVE COPELAND

Dave Copeland, a student at Pomona College, class of 1960, was born on April 1, 1937, in Long Beach, California. He went through the Long Beach public schools, including the Woodrow Wilson High School. Then with his parents he went to Athens, Greece, where his

---

* Defined in *Webster's New World Dictionary* (1957) as "a meeting of folk singers, especially for public entertainment."

father, an officer in the Navy, was stationed for two years. This sojourn may account for his working toward a major in classical languages at Pomona.

The chief musical influence in Dave's life comes from his maternal grandfather, an accomplished musician who has played the cello and bass in chamber-music groups and in the Long Beach Symphony —"an old-time theatre musician," Dave calls him. But as for folk music, Dave is largely self-taught. At the age of ten he began playing the guitar and has recently taken to the five-string banjo. He has learned songs from books, recordings, and many people.

Dave has had his own radio show over Pomona's station KSPC-FM, and he has sung with the Pomona College Glee Club in its annual tours of the Bay area. As yet he has not broken into the big-time TV or night-club circuits with his folksongs. He sings now and then for church and club groups. He plans to become a teacher and intends to continue his folk music as a side line. An excellent idea, for trained teachers are much in demand, and skilled amateur singers of folksongs are always good company!

BANJO BILL CORNETT

Bill Cornett—banjoist, folksinger, farmer, and country storekeeper —was born in Hindman, Kentucky, July 2, 1890. His formal education ended with the eighth grade. But his folk-music activity, which began when he was a very small boy, has continued for about sixty years. He learned folksongs from his mother and his grandfather. His first performance was at Christmastime in 1895, in the courthouse at Hindman, Kentucky.

Besides knowing an almost indeterminable number of old ballads, he has himself composed and sung a goodly number on local subjects: one about a double murder in a neighboring county, another about a disastrous hotel fire in Hazard, Kentucky, and another—one of his favorites—about a drunken driver who ran over and killed his own small son.[27] Bill Cornett has sung and played in fourteen states, has been on many radio and other programs, including the National Folk Festival in St. Louis. Known widely as Banjo Bill, he also plays the guitar and fiddle.

Bill Cornett was married to Malissa Combs on October 25, 1913. They have ten children, all born at Hindman and all grown now. Six of the children are graduates of Morehead (Kentucky) State Teachers College. One daughter, Mrs. Lake Cornett Cooper, has taught mathematics at the University of Kentucky and is completing a doctorate in mathematics.[28] Bill would like to get more of his songs on records, or perhaps someday publish a book of ballads he has collected. But, he reports, "It took all my earnings to raise and school my children."

During the summer of 1955 Bill Cornett made a successful venture into politics: he was elected to the state legislature from his district, winning by 589 votes. (Once earlier he had been defeated for the same post.) He has sung and played folk music for so many years that a session in the legislature will not greatly change his musical life.

GRACE CRESWELL

Though Nashville, Tennessee, is often called the nation's hillbilly capital, it is worth mention also as the home of some genuine folk-singers—none more authentic than Grace Creswell. Born Grace Weaver on October 11, 1919, in the Glen Alpine Community of Tennessee, her family had lived in the Tennessee Valley for seven generations and farmed the land now inundated by the Tennessee Valley Authority. Since Glen Alpine was just a cove and post office, Grace Weaver got her high-school education in the small town of Clinton, Tennessee.

In some ways, however, the family heritage was more important than any schooling. And among the Weavers and the Wallaces (her maternal grandparents), singing was a natural activity. Grace learned from many members of her family—her mother, brothers, sisters, aunts, and grandparents. Her memory goes back to the age of three, when she sang "Wondrous Love" at a church gathering, and she has been singing ever since.

After Clinton the family moved to Knoxville, Tennessee, where her father worked as a carpenter. In 1940, Grace Weaver married George Creswell. They moved to Chicago for a time, then back to Tennessee, in Nashville, where they now live. They have two children: Cindy, born in 1943, and Dick, born in 1948. Grace Creswell's first public, full program of folksongs dates from 1951, when she gave a recital at Western Kentucky State College at Bowling Green. Karl Kershaw, Tennessee painter, is credited with "discovering" her folk-singing talents. As he was doing her portrait and noticing that she appeared strangely sad, he asked her to sing. To his surprise, she gave forth with some folksongs, sad but genuinely beautiful. So began her public career.

Most members of her family had played some musical instrument, and Mrs. Creswell plays the dulcimer, autoharp, and guitar. The first she uses mostly at home, the others on trips. And like most good folksingers, she often sings without accompaniment. Grace Creswell doesn't compose music and she is not a collector, though occasionally people give her old songs she hadn't known. Her accompaniments are simple but adequate for her rich contralto voice. Music critics and folklorists alike have expressed high praise for her simple and unaffected singing. Composer Roy Harris called her the best folk-singer he had heard. The late Charles Faulkner Bryan, composer and folksong authority, considered her the top singer of genuine American folksongs.

Mrs. Creswell divides her time between her family and her singing. In the past five years she has performed perhaps a hundred recitals in ten or a dozen states, not counting many radio and TV appearances. For some time she had a program on station WSM in Nashville, called "The Hill Girl." Always she is received with growing enthusiasm, and she has done some excellent recordings [29] (see Book Three).

RUFUS CRISP

Down in southeastern Kentucky, Rufus Crisp was one of the favorite musicians at square dances for half a century and more. Born in Allen, Floyd County, Kentucky, on November 17, 1880,[30] he never had any formal schooling, or any special training as a musician. Nor were his parents folk musicians. At the age of fourteen he began learning folksongs and picking the five-string banjo, through his friendship with an old neighbor, Gabe Frazier. From that time until his death, sixty-two years later, Crisp became a devotee of folk music and an expert banjo picker.

The late Mr. Crisp never strayed far from his home town and county, where his occupation was rural mail carrier and where he lived out his days. On February 28, 1905, he was married to Lula Clark. They had one son, Palmer—still living and himself a guitarist —born July 16, 1914. Rufus Crisp came to know a wealth of folk tunes, so many in fact that he often played for square dances all night long and "didn't have to repeat." He was not a collector of folksongs, nor did he do any composing, but he picked up songs as they came along, kept his memory well stored, and played his banjo almost to the day he died—June 9, 1956. He recorded for the Library of Congress Archive in 1946. Pete Seeger, banjo virtuoso and one of his friends, pays high tribute to Rufus Crisp as the one who taught him frailing.*

* A method of plucking all strings on a downward stroke with the back of the fingernails—"good for playing fast, steady rhythms for square dances." See Pete's book, *How to Play the 5-String Banjo*, pp. 18-19.

FOOTNOTES TO CHAPTER 3

[1] See articles in the Montréal *Gazette*, June 21, 1952; *Le Progrès* (Montreal), December, 1952, and March, 1953; *La Semaine à Radio-Canada*, August, 1952, and April, 1953.

[2] Up to the time of his death, at age seventy-six, her father enjoyed singing folksongs. He had a fine baritone voice. Two of her brothers, Jean-Louis and Paul, also know many folksongs. Paul is a choir director in Beauce.

[3] Dr. Barbeau is also a native of Beauce County, P. Q. See Book Two for details on collections of Canadian folksongs.

[4] Many factual details for the above account have been sent to me by Mlle Baillargeon (i.e., Mme Côté). In addition to her folksinging and home activities, she participates in other radio and TV programs: "Match intercités," a sort of "Information, Please" program; "Tour de Chant," on the new TV network; and another TV program called "Point d'Interrogation," in which panel experts "answer questions on various subjects, from sports to the proper way of cooking a sauce béarnaise!" Mlle Baillargeon, a favorite on these programs, is an avid reader with retentive memory and a ready wit.

[5] In the late 1930's, she worked for two years in Quebec City in the law offices of Louis St. Laurent, later to become Canada's popular prime minister.

[6] *Ebony* magazine, March, 1956.

[7] For biographical details I am indebted primarily to Mr. Belafonte. Other sources include *Look* mazagine, August 21, 1956, and *Ebony*, mentioned above.

[8] *Ebony*, March, 1956.

[9] *Time* magazine, April 22, 1957.

[10] *Folksongs on Records* (Boulder, Colorado, 1950), p. 10.

[11] "Sing Me a Homemade Song," by Vincent McHugh, in the January issue of '48, p. 149.

[12] Miss Boette's unpublished master's thesis, at Ohio University Library, is entitled "Selections of Tunes and Variations in the Words of Certain Folk Tunes and Ballads of the Upper Monongahela Valley."

[13] For example, see the issues of December 12, 1953, and February 19, 1955.

[14] *Arkansas Folklore*, IV, 1-15 (January 1, 1954).

[15] I am indebted to the late Mr. Broonzy and to notes from the record, EmArcy MG 26034, for biographical facts.

[16] Louis Nicholas, "In Memoriam: Charles Faulkner Bryan, 1911-1955," *Tennessee Folklore Society Bulletin*, XXI, 79-80 (September, 1955). Mr. Nicholas writes: "He was driving his wife and their two children home from a visit to McMinnville, Tennessee, their home town, when, near Birmingham, he said he did not feel well. He drove the car over to the side of the road and expired almost immediately."

[17] Except when otherwise indicated, biographical facts came to me directly from the late Mr. Bryan. Some facts are drawn from letters and some from an undated brochure he sent me, printed by J. Fischer & Bro., music publishers of New York.

[18] Nan Merriman sang the leading role in a performance at Dumbarton Oaks, Maryland, in 1946.

72   SINGERS OF BALLADS AND FOLKSONGS

[19] In 1954, he wrote: "I used two old folk hymns: Amazing Grace and Goin' Over Jordan."

[20] Another work should be mentioned: a historical drama called *Florida Aflame,* for which he wrote the complete score, based on Indian music. Produced at Lake Wales, Florida, in 1953, it ran for fifty-nine performances.

[21] Four articles had appeared in the *Tennessee Folklore Society Bulletin* (March, June, and September, 1952, and December, 1954). He hoped someday to write a book on the dulcimer and offered tongue-in-cheek apology for rushing into print with inconclusive findings. Now, of course, all students of folksong are grateful for these brief articles. See my discussion on the dulcimer (Interlude I), which owes much to Charlie Bryan.

[22] From Duncan Emrich's notes with the Library of Congress recording, Album XX.

[23] Told to me in an interview at Eureka Springs, October 17, 1953.

[24] *Rayburn's Ozark Guide,* No. 49, Summer issue, July 1956, p. 23.

[25] This beautiful old guitar was a gift from the late Dr. Harold Goddard, professor of English at Swarthmore, and Mrs. Goddard.

[26] Since 1945, many of his arrangements have been published, especially by the following music publishers: Hanson, Inc.; Belwin, Inc.; and Plymouth Music Company, all of New York City; and the Shawnee Press of Delaware Water Gap, Pennsylvania.

[27] "A Happy Man's Sad Music," by Gerald Griffin, Louisville *Courier-Journal,* March 8, 1955.

[28] *Ibid.*

[29] Probably the best of these is an album of four 45's, done by Rebel Records of Nashville.

[30] I am indebted to Palmer Crisp for information about his father, Rufus Crisp.

CHAPTER 4

The Singers, D to G

KATHY DAGEL

For one in her early thirties, Kathy Dagel has lived a full life and a varied one. Born in Oklahoma City on October 14, 1927, she attended grade school, studied ballet, began taking singing and guitar lessons, and was given "everything a child of extra proud and hopeful parents might receive."

In one way or another, her life has been bound up with show business since early childhood. At the age of three she appeared in an Uncle Remus series over station WKY in Oklahoma City. At six she was working at a stable in Oklahoma City, helping to train ponies to jump, and at seven she began trick-riding. (Her great love was, and is, horses.) She spent four years on the road with rodeos throughout the Midwest, performing as a trick-rider and roper. Western ballads and cowboy songs were, of course, a part of this experience.

In her childhood days Kathy was a friend of the aging Pawnee Bill (Major Gordon W. Lillie), Indian interpreter, frontiersman, and originator of Pawnee Bill's Wild West Circus. She often sat before the crackling fireplace in his home on Blue Hawk Peak listening to his wonderful tales, and sometimes he would ask her to sing "The Trail to Mexico" or "Home on the Range." And sometimes she would ride in a parade beside him, an event "to lift one above mortal experience."

From this lively and vigorous childhood she moved on to stunt work in movies, night clubs in Las Vegas, dancing in a burlesque show ("I was a member of the chorus, not a stripper . . . all before I was eighteen"), bit parts in Hollywood radio shows, "and so it goes."

Kathy Dagel has had acquaintance with ballads and folksongs from her earliest remembrance. "In the beginning," she writes, "I learned from Grandpa Baldridge in North Carolina, and from Grandma too," as well as from Negroes who worked on their farm. At the age of three she sang "Go Tell Aunt Rhody" at a church gathering near Grandpa's farm. Soon after her marriage on April 16, 1948, to Verl E. Dagel, at Van Nuys, California, she began to take a more serious and scholarly interest in ballad literature. "These last ten years of my life have been filled with study, reading all the collections . . . from Child to the most recent ones." This has set her to remembering and collecting on her own, primarily in Kansas, Texas, and Oklahoma, in the hope of someday publishing her own personal collection.

Kathy has given perhaps two hundred or more folksong performances, mainly in the Southwest and Northwest, but it is difficult, she says, "to separate the folksongs from other types of appearances, especially with the horses!" She has known the guitar for many years, and her accompaniments are never showy but always skillful and musically right for the song she is presenting. Her appearances at the Ozark Folk Festival in October, 1958, and again in 1959, gave the audience some of the most effective folksinging of that three-day event.

The Dagels live on a farm near Augusta, Kansas. Mr. Dagel works in the electrical department of Boeing Aircraft in Wichita. They have two daughters: Arlana Melissa, born March 30, 1949, and Yolanda Cecile (Loni), born September 22, 1951. They, too, are studying guitar and folksongs and, to quote Kathy again, "I hope to raise my girls in this tradition and thus actively preserve these ballads."

BARBARA DANE

Barbara Spillman ("Dane" is pure fiction—made up by a publicist, Barbara states) was born in Detroit, Michigan, on May 12, 1927. Her formal education was scattered and fragmentary. She attended Cooke Elementary School and began her high-school work in Detroit at Redford High. After a further year at Greenbrier Junior College, Greenbrier, West Virginia, she finally completed her high-school work in Birmingham, Michigan. Then followed one semester at Wayne University in Detroit.

Miss Dane learned folksongs from many sources. Her mother remembered traditional lullabies from an Arkansas childhood. Barbara collected a good deal of miscellaneous material on a trip to Europe in 1947. She has picked up many songs, and done tape-recording, in trips across the country. She has learned from books, records, and other singers. One of her best sources was an elderly neighbor in Berkeley, California, Mrs. Bessie Mercer, from Lincoln and Giles Counties in Tennessee, where traditional music was widely known in an earlier day.

Barbara Dane has been singing folksongs for more than a decade, her first regular performance being given at the Detroit Institute of Art in the fall of 1946. She is married to Byron Menendez, a self-employed maker of contemporary jewelry. They have two children: a son Paul, born June 21, 1952, and a daughter Nina, born December 22, 1955. Barbara has an older son, Nicholas Cahn, by a former marriage. Aside from household activities, Mrs. Menendez assists her husband in the jewelry business, writes folk-music record reviews for *Audience* magazine and, as Barbara Dane, does a good many folk-music programs. For a time she had a folk-music program on FM station KPFA in Berkeley. One of her major activities in 1956 was an extended appearance with Turk Murphy's Band at the Tin Angel, a San Francisco Dixieland club which was pictured in *Life* magazine (August, 1956). At that time she was singing mainly blues and spirituals. In October, 1956, she began a long run at Jack's Waterfront Hangout, singing only folksongs.

PHILIP G. DANUFSKY

Time and again one finds that folksinging is no respecter of professions. People in any and all walks of life sing folksongs. Philip Danufsky makes no pretense of being a professional folksinger, but he likes to sing. Danufsky was born in Newark, New Jersey, on May 2, 1927. He went through high school at Hillside, New Jersey, and from there moved on to the University of Pennsylvania, taking a bachelor's degree in 1946, a master's in 1949, and a Doctor of Medicine in 1951.

Now a physician, Dr. Danufsky's folksong interest is a lively hobby. He is not a collector or a public singer, but sings for his own pleasure and for friends. He has learned folksongs mainly from books and, to a limited extent, from other singers. While in Kansas City in the middle fifties for an internship, he studied classical guitar with Gene Jemison (*q.v.*). Dr. Danufsky likes the folksongs written in the early English modes, and he is particularly interested in Israeli folksongs. "Specific favorites," however, "vary from time to time," he says. People like Danufsky help keep folksongs alive.

ERIK DARLING

When, in the summer of 1958, Pete Seeger found he had too many pots a-cooking on too many fires, he reluctantly resigned from the Weavers, and they had to look elsewhere for a good banjoist. They chose young Erik Darling to make up the foursome.

Erik Darling was born in Baltimore, Maryland, on September 25, 1933. His schooling was somewhat fragmentary, for during his early education he "went to a large number of schools throughout the country." Eventually he finished high school at the Rhodes School in New York. After one year at New York University, he had done with formal schooling and decided "to follow the bumpy road of a folk singer."

Erik learned his "first five guitar chords" from a Miss Marie Allen of Honeoye, New York, and through patience, long hours of practice, and observing others' instrumental styles he has become highly proficient on both the guitar and the five-string banjo. He dates his "activity as a singer of folk songs" from about 1948. Erik collects songs as he travels about, but "as a scholar like Alan Lomax or Cecil Sharp, no." He has traveled and sung in all but half a dozen states, as well as in Canada, England, Germany, France, and Switzerland.

Besides his work with the Weavers, Erik has recorded with groups such as the Tarriers and the Folk Singers, has accompanied Ed McCurdy (q.v.) in a number of albums, and has done an album for Elektra (see Book Three). On September 9, 1957, Erik Darling was married to actress Joan Kugel. They make their home in New York City.

REVEREND GARY DAVIS *

Born on April 30, 1896, in Lawrence County, South Carolina, Gary Davis has been poor most of his life and has had very little schooling. He grew up in a culture that knew blues, work and gospel songs, all of which he learned orally. Some songs, apparently, he has learned from records.

Sometime in his thirties Gary Davis became totally blind. About this time he became a preacher and more and more gave his attention to gospel singing ("he rarely sings secular songs now"). With

* Mr. Barry Kornfeld, "a sort of concert partner" of the Reverend Gary Davis, obtained the information that is the basis for the above sketch. My grateful thanks to Barry Kornfeld and to Mr. Davis. (R.M.L.)

a few weeks' schooling he has learned to read Braille passably well. Singer Barry Kornfeld (*q.v.*), who knows Davis well, considers him "one of the great Negro folk (gospel) singers and instrumentalists still alive today." His main instrument is the guitar but he plays others as well: "I first played banjo when I was 5, played harp [harmonica] at 6 an' started guitar at 7."

According to Kornfeld, Mr. Davis did many 78 rpm records on various "race" and "gospel" labels. In the recent surge of folksong recording, he has also done a number of LP's on the Stinson and Riverside labels (see Book Three). He composes many of the gospel songs he sings, and his method of performing them is unique among folksingers. Gary Davis was married to Ann Hicks in 1940, and makes his home in the Bronx. All his family and friends "are very religious and sing gospel songs."

THE T. M. DAVIS FAMILY

Mr. and Mrs. T. M. Davis are not professional singers, but they have sung folksongs all their lives. Thomas Morris Davis was born August 5, 1882, at Big Rock, Tennessee, and received a grade-school education in southern Indiana. As a small boy he learned folksongs from his older brothers and sisters, from aunts, uncles, and friends. For more than sixty years he has sung folksongs, "mostly for pleasure for myself and my friends," as he puts it.

Lula Smith was born August 11, 1905, in the village of Iconium, Missouri. She completed grade school and had one year of high school at Ozark, Missouri. Her parents and an older sister were singers of folksongs, and Lula has sung folksongs since she was five years old. But, as she points out, never professionally. To quote her: "We sung our folksongs purely because we loved them, and for our friends who also loved to hear them." Though the Davises know many folksongs, they have never collected them "except by memory."

After the death of his first wife, whom he had married in 1908, T. M. Davis married Lula Smith on December 5, 1923. They have five grown children, now all married; their names and years of birth are as follows: Oliva Lenore, 1925; Thomas M., Jr., 1928; George Harold, 1930; Bettye June, 1932; and Mary Jo, 1936. Of the children, the eldest, Oliva, and the youngest, Mary Jo, seem particularly interested in carrying on the family tradition of song. Though both have done radio singing of popular songs, both have done much folksinging.

Mary Jo was born at Springdale, Arkansas, went to the public schools, and graduated from Fayetteville High School in 1954. She first sang in public (aside from singing at school) in 1948 at the

University of Arkansas Field House. She appeared as folksinger at meetings of the Arkansas Folklore Society in June, 1951, and the following three years. She has performed many times at the Ozark Folk Festival held in Eureka Springs, Arkansas, singing unaccompanied in a clear and beautiful voice. Experts in folk music considered her singing the high point in the festival.

Perhaps her most important appearance thus far was in the TV picture filmed and recorded in the Ozarks in 1954 by the Columbia Broadcasting System. This picture, called *The Search*, was a presentation showing how the folksong collector gathers his material. Included in it were many folksingers and folksongs, and the picture has been seen and heard many times over the C.B.S. network. Oliva Lenore has sung at the Arkansas Folklore Society meetings and at the Ozark Festival.

The Davises are fine examples of the folksinging tradition in northeast Arkansas. In recent years they have contributed over seventy-five songs to the Archive of Songs for the Arkansas Folklore Society.[1] Though not highly educated, they are hard-working people, their memories are good, and their singing is authentic. T. M. Davis has been a carpenter and construction worker but is now retired. Mrs. Davis is a machine operator in a garment factory. Mary Jo worked with her mother in the factory until her recent marriage, in the summer of 1955. Among their favorite songs are "Lord Bateman," "Young Johnnie," "Turkish Reveler," "Black Jack Davy," and "Lord Randall." It is hoped they will continue to sing the old songs and help keep alive the ancient art of folksinging.

RICH DEHR

Rich Dehr, a professional songwriter whose songs have been aired and recorded by such singers as Doris Day, Frankie Laine, and Jo Stafford, is one who knows and sings a lot of folk music, too. He was born in Chicago, April 22, 1913. He attended Catholic boarding schools in Chicago, did some study at Notre Dame University, and had two years of further study at the University of Illinois.

Mr. Dehr has known, loved, and sung folksongs as long as he can remember. His mother taught him many early English and Irish folksongs, which she had learned from her Irish parents, Jim and Ann Cleary. One of his aunts used to sing him sad Irish ballads while doing her ironing, and he wept copiously over these sad songs. He learned also from many places in his travels as he was growing up—from people in Missouri, Florida, Louisiana, Indiana, Michigan, Connecticut, and elsewhere.

As for his folksinging career, that began in small cabarets and bars in Chicago. He uses the guitar, but often he sings unaccompanied. He is a collector of ballads in the sense that every good folksinger has his ear alert for one more good ballad. In more than half a dozen states he has given performances, perhaps several hundred altogether. Aside from his popular-song writing, which is usually based on folk melody lines, he has been musical director for some plays, such as *Abe Lincoln in Illinois, Distant Isle, Romance of Scarlet Gulch, Will the Mail Train Run Tonight,* and others, and he has made a good many recordings of folksongs, mainly for Majestic Records. Among these are "John Hardy," "Green Grow the Lilacs," "Bile Dem Cabbage Down," "John Henry," to mention a few.

Rich Dehr was married to Marjorie Helen Higgins in July, 1938. They have three sons: Richard, Dennis, and Jimmy, born in 1941, 1944, and 1949, respectively. These boys, Mr. Dehr reports, know more folksongs than their father: no doubt, Papa Dehr is modest! The Dehrs make their home in California.

ALFRED DELLER

Another Britisher, known to Americans through his concerts in the United States and his recordings, is Alfred Deller, a countertenor * singer of madrigals, folksongs, and other traditional materials. He was born on May 31, 1912, at Margate, Kent, England, and received a grammar-school education there.

Deller is not a traditional singer, that is, he doesn't come from a folksinging milieu, but he has learned folksongs during the past decade and has found them effective in concert work. His first performance was at a school concert in 1927. Of the singers presented in this book, he is one of the few to use the lute. (Wallace House is another.) But in the Alfred Deller Consort, which he directs, he often uses guitar, recorder, viol, or other strings, and sometimes the group sings *a cappella.*

During the past decade and over, Mr. Deller has given some three hundred concerts throughout Europe, North Africa, and North America. Besides the British Isles, he has sung in Germany, France, Switzerland, Holland, Algeria, Tunisia, Morocco. In 1955, 1957, and again in 1959, he has fulfilled coast-to-coast engagements in America.† In recent years he has recorded, on the Vanguard label

* A high voice range between tenor and soprano, sometimes called a male alto. Often it sounds like a man's falsetto. John Jacob Niles (*q.v.*) is a countertenor.

† Under the concert management of Colbert LaBerge, 105 West 55th Street, New York 19, N. Y.

(see Book Three), many madrigals, folksongs, glees, and other early English types of music.

Alfred Deller was married on May 6, 1937, and is the father of three children: Mark, born September 27, 1938; Simon, born October 22, 1942; and Jane, born July 27, 1949. The family home is "Barton Cottage" in Ashford, Kent, England.

DICK DEVALL

Dick Devall (he spells it Devoll), a good example of the old-time cowboy, was born in Texas somewhere around 1890. His schooling was almost negligible, and even in his later years he could barely spell. From the time of his early boyhood he had heard the songs of the cowboys, and he learned well over a hundred of them during his more than forty years on the Texas range.

Devall is married and lives at Reed, a little prairie village in southwestern Oklahoma not far from the Texas border. Over the years he has done considerable recording, some for RCA Victor and Decca, and in 1946, in Dallas, John Lomax recorded a number of Devall's songs which are now in the Library of Congress Archive. His singing, unaccompanied, varies both in text and tune from other versions. As Duncan Emrich points out, "The freedom with which Devall treats music and text is characteristic of many folk singers and accounts, of course, for the wide differences to be found in the many versions of a single song." [2] When speaking of the songs, Dick Devall refers to them as "little ditties." In 1954 at Reed, Oklahoma, Devall was expecting to do some further commercial recording, and he was justly proud of the fact that, as he put it, "they call me a natural balidear." His kind of "natural singing," unfortunately, seems less common than it once was.

MARION DIARD

It may surprise Marion Diard and her family to call her an international folksinger, but she sings folksongs in eleven different languages. She learned many of these during the war years, when she was with the USO and sang and collected songs all around the world. Miss Diard was born December 6, 1920, in a century-old, part-log house at Kimmswick, Missouri, a village on the Mississippi a few miles below St. Louis. After attending elementary school at Kimmswick, she went to Festus (Missouri) High School, graduating in 1938. Her parents and grandparents were singers of folksongs, and Marion learned her first folksongs in the family. Her mother, formerly a grade-school teacher, taught folksongs and games to the children.

And so Marion Diard has been singing ballads and folksongs all her life. In grade schools throughout the Midwest it was a common custom to have a musical program once a week, usually Friday afternoon. In these programs Marion's "career" as a folksinger began. In this early beginning she played the piano as she sang, and this has been her method of presentation ever since. She may possibly be the only traditional folksinger to use only the piano for accompaniment. Like most folksingers, she composes, or makes up, her own accompaniments.

There are other musicians and singers in her family—uncles, aunts, cousins, etc.—but most of them, she reports, went in for classical music and opera. She alone has made folksinging a profession.

Miss Diard has made recordings for radio stations in Bogotá, Colombia, and Caracas, Venezuela. She has occasionally had her own folksong program on radio stations and has made guest appearances on TV. In the fall of 1956, she concluded a series called "Folksongs with Marion Diard" on educational TV station KETC-TV in St. Louis. In January, 1957, she had a similar program on radio station KJCF at Festus, Missouri. Miss Diard has appeared on many folk-festival programs in Missouri, Arkansas, and elsewhere. For instance, in October, 1956, she was a favorite at the three-day Ozark Folk Festival in Eureka Springs, Arkansas. Her singing, unaffected and sincere, shows a genuine appreciation of folk materials.

BOB DUNCAN

Big and affable, easygoing but energetic, Bob Duncan has knocked about the world a good bit as a vagabond, free-lance writer, singer, folklorist, and scholar. He was born September 9, 1927, in Oklahoma City, and went through the conventional public-school training—Whittier Grade School, Taft Junior High, and Classen High School. He attended Oklahoma City University in 1945, did a stretch in the United States Army for eighteen months, and returned to the university in 1947. Transferring to the University of Oklahoma, he took a bachelor's degree in English in 1949, and stayed on for a year's graduate study in Western history.

Bob Duncan's contact with folksongs has been lifelong. His father came from Kentucky and knew folksongs. His mother's early life was spent in a Kansas dugout. She played the piano and she, too, knew folksongs. For his twelfth Christmas, Bob got a guitar and soon began picking up songs, first from his parents, and then in the hobo jungle behind the Tenth Street Brickpit in Oklahoma City. The Brickpit experience led him farther afield: in his teens, particularly in his seventeenth year, he hitchhiked over Oklahoma, picking up tunes from farmers and ranchers. In 1945, he took a walking tour of the eastern United States, collecting some two hundred songs in a three-month trek. And, of course, he picked up many more during his Army service.

Bob has been singing folksongs professionally since 1941, when he was fourteen. He has sung at whisky-filled stag parties, church pie-suppers, to Army groups, women's clubs, and to many college and university audiences. He has given recitals in at least three-fourths of the states of the Union, and his performances run into the hundreds. While in Japan, he managed the Meiji Theatre in Tokyo, emceed many camp shows, and gave folksong programs galore.

In 1948, he was folklore specialist for the Oklahoma University Lecture and Entertainment Bureau. The following year he was curator of local history and folklore at the Oklahoma City Libraries. Both these jobs gave him time and occasion to collect folksongs, local legends, superstitions, and other folklore, and to do ballad singing over an Oklahoma City radio station. When Bob sings and tells stories, he performs in a free-and-easy captivating style that immediately wins an audience.

For a young man, Bob Duncan has done a considerable amount of writing. Stories and sketches have been published in children's magazines and Sunday supplements; popular history features have appeared in *American Heritage*. In 1952, his first book appeared, a piece of social history in a series of sketches about men, women, and black gold, under the title *The Dicky Bird Was Singing*,[3] and in 1959 he published another work in social history, called *Buffalo Country* (E. P. Dutton).

Bob Duncan married Wanda Scott on April 14, 1949. In the fall of 1954, changing their base of activities from Oklahoma to Texas, they became television writers for a Texas series called "Telephone Spotlight on Texas," later adding "Telephone Spotlight on Missouri." This work involved traveling all over the two states, doing stories on every kind of subject imaginable. After some months of this strenuous job, Bob took over the new script department at the Southwest Film Laboratory in Dallas, and Wanda became a script editor. In the fall of 1956, they settled at Eureka Springs, Arkansas, and became the resident directors of the annual Ozark Folk Festival. In September, 1958, the Duncans adopted a daughter, Mary Carole, born February 12, 1958. Early in 1959, the Duncans made a temporary move to California to do script writing for various television studios.

RICHARD DYER-BENNET

The singer of folksongs sometimes develops his talent into a unique art. Richard Dyer-Bennet, singer of folksongs but no ordinary ballad-singer, has often been called the twentieth-century minstrel, for his purpose is to revive the art of medieval song as it was practiced by the minstrels of long ago. As this highly developed art has its basis in genuine folk music, he cannot properly be excluded from an account of folksinging in America.

Richard Dyer-Bennet was born October 6, 1913,[4] of a British father and an American mother. (At twenty-one, he chose to become an American citizen.) After early schooling in Canada, he came to the University of California at Berkeley, where his special interests turned to music and athletics, particularly tennis and soccer. Dyer-Bennet's own words are worth quoting at length, for no one has written a clearer account of his purpose:

I studied English and music at the University of California from 1932 to 1935, and singing with Gertrude Wheeler Beckman from 1934 to 1941. In the summer of 1935 I went to Sweden to meet and hear Sven Scholander, who was then 75 years old. Scholander was not a folk singer, by which I mean that he was not born and brought up in the rural folk singing tradition. He was a trained musician who brought to his work highly developed perceptions of both poetry and music. His repertoire included folk and art songs from all over Europe, and because he had the taste to find a musical approach and a fitting lute accompaniment for each song, he was understood and greatly admired by folk song enthusiasts and chamber music lovers alike. Between 1890 and 1914 he was famous all over Europe, and alone in his time revived to full stature the ancient art of minstrelsy.

I was greatly influenced by Scholander, and tried to develop a comparable approach to the art of song. With him, it was a trinity of poetry, melody, and lute accompaniment. He had no one "style," but seemed to handle each song in a way that befitted. By 1941 I had learned to combine word and melody fairly well, but it was not until 1944 that Rey de la Torre began to show me how to use my fingers on the guitar. Since that time I have been striving towards Scholander's trinity.[5]

Dyer-Bennet's distinctive success over the years has proved how right he has been to follow the great Swedish master in developing his art. Though he was with Scholander only a few days, it is fairly obvious that the mantle of the master fell to Richard Dyer-Bennet. With a hundred songs in German, French, and Swedish, which Scholander gave him, Dyer-Bennet has enlarged his international repertoire to well over seven hundred songs. He has studied the British and American ballads of all types, as well as many Continental songs,[6] and for each song he develops a distinctive guitar accompaniment. For a time Dyer-Bennet used the lute, but soon left it for the more flexible classic Spanish guitar.

On March 4, 1944, Dyer-Bennet gave his first Town Hall recital and, by popular demand, repeated it a month later. This Town Hall recital has become an annual event. Dyer-Bennet reports that he has sung "some 250 concerts, done about 150 weeks of night club work, and recorded 13 albums of song." [7] Records have been made by Harvard University (his first recording and a collector's item), Decca, Mercury, Keynote, Asch, Vox, Disc, Concert Hall Society, and now by his own company. During the war he broadcast some of his own compositions for OWI. In 1946, Leeds Music Corporation published a booklet containing twenty of his songs and ballads, with guitar and piano accompaniments. Four of the songs, both words and music, were composed by Dyer-Bennet; the others are traditional. In the late 1940's, he established a School of Minstrelsy—the first in the United States—at the Aspen, Colorado, summer music camp, but his heavy concert and recording work has forced him to discontinue this project.

Dyer-Bennet's high, clear tenor voice—after long years of study—and his incomparable mastery of the guitar seem peculiarly fitted to the kind of art he has chosen to develop. Here is exemplified a kind of mastery in which the folksong has become an art song. Richard Dyer-Bennet is rightly called the twentieth-century minstrel.

BILL ELLIOTT

When, at sixteen, Bill Elliott was stricken with polio and had to lie in a hospital for thirteen months, he had to give up playing the flute in the school orchestra. Months of illness and depression of spirit, however, could not kill his love of music. No longer able to play the flute, he could pick a guitar and, with the help and encouragement of his folksinging friend Bob Duncan (*q.v.*), he turned to folksongs and found relief and release which nothing else could give.

Bill (William Byron) Elliott was born in Joplin, Missouri, in 1933.

He attended grade school in Joplin and did part of his high school training in New York City, part in Oklahoma City. He attended the University of Oklahoma, taking a degree with a major in geology.

Bill gave his first performance of folksongs in December, 1950, at Tinker Air Force Base, at Oklahoma City. Since then he has performed many times, particularly in and around Oklahoma City and a number of times at the Ozark Folk Festival at Eureka Springs, Arkansas. During his university days and afterward, he worked as disc jockey at radio station KOMA, Oklahoma City, not only playing records but giving the listeners live folksongs with guitar or banjo accompaniment. Bill makes no claim to expertness as a folklorist, but he loves folk music, knows many songs, and performs with skill and sympathetic understanding.

On August 20, 1955, William Byron Elliott was married to Dorothy Dell Skinner.

JACK AND JUNE ELLIOTT

In September, 1955, a couple of happy vagabonds, a few months married, started eastward from California with guitar, banjo, and harmonica to strum and sing their way around the world! Jack Elliott was born August 1, 1931, in New York City, but has spent little time there and doesn't even like to claim it as his home town. For Jack is a born wanderer and, like his friend and mentor Woody Guthrie (q.v.), has knocked about the country by rail and thumb, picking up and making up songs as he goes.[8]

Wanderlust struck Jack in his early teens and, if he's anything like Woody Guthrie, it will never leave him. Naturally, his formal schooling is most meager. Though not born to the tradition of folksinging, he nevertheless has learned his songs in the traditional way—orally. He has picked them up from garage mechanics, hobos, cowboys, other workers and singers, even some from books. By the time he had come of age, he had roamed and sung in more than half the states and in eastern Canada. When he was married on May 15, 1955, the best man played the banjo, and the wedding reception turned into an impromptu folk-music concert, with two banjos, two harmonicas, two guitars, a mandolin, and no end of singing!

Jack recorded some "bad man and hero" ballads for Elektra (EKL-16) in 1955, along with Ed McCurdy (q.v.) and Oscar Brand (q.v.). Jack describes himself as an "intermittent loafer and hobo busher," and it remains to be seen whether marriage will "settle him down." One thing we can count on: in the future, scholarly collectors of folksong are likely to tape a good many numbers from the Jack Elliotts of the world.*

SAM ESKIN

Sam Eskin, who has been working in the field of folksong a long time, was born in Washington, D.C., July 5, 1898. His father was a railroad engineer, the Eskins lived near the tracks, and the turning wheels got in Sam's blood: he's been a restless wanderer since his teens.[9] His formal schooling ended with the eighth grade in Baltimore, Maryland.

In early years Eskin was an avid reader of Jack London, whom he wished to emulate in adventures and in writing. At seventeen, with not much cash in his pockets, he set out for the West, and he soon learned the trick of riding the blinds. He did all kinds of work—on cattle ranches, on the railroads, eventually in the salmon fisheries of Alaska. Later, he went to sea, and his wanderings carried him to ports in the Orient, to Europe, and to Central America.[10]

Sam Eskin wasn't consciously searching for folksongs—at least not at first. But the songs he heard, before he knew they were folksongs, were the songs he liked to sing and remember. Though Sam is not a trained singer, he has a genuine feeling for folksongs and their background. As he himself says: "I never started out to sing folksongs. It just happened. And long before I knew about published collections I became an amateur collector just to find new songs to sing." In time, of course, he studied the collections and enlarged his repertoire.

Over the past thirty-five years Sam has traveled with guitar and recording equipment in forty-eight states and in many foreign countries. He has many discs and tapes—and many memories, too. Not much beyond brief newspaper items has been published about him, for he has had no high-powered press agenting. Though friendly and companionable, he seems paradoxically a lonely figure. A recent writer commented: "The details of his life are scanty, and Eskin does little to lift the veil." [11]

A good deal of Sam's early collecting and singing was done in New York, the Carolinas, Florida, Tennessee, Virginia, Texas, New Mexico, California, Colorado, Kansas, Indiana, and Delaware. Recently he has done much beyond our national boundaries. In the early 1950's he "collected quite a variety of interesting material" in Mexico, also a little in Haiti and Jamaica. In April and May, 1955,

* In April, 1959, *Caravan* (p. 19), edited by Billy Faier, reported that Jack Elliott was singing folksongs at the Club Renaissance in Los Angeles.

he was in Israel, collecting among the Jews and Arabs. From there
he went to Spain for further searching.

With all his collecting, Eskin has done no publishing, except as
his songs are "published" by his singing and his records. In true
scholarly fashion, however, he is careful to give the source of his
songs (person and place, but sometimes *not* the date). In 1954,
he presented a series of folksong programs at the University of
California (Berkeley), bringing to the programs some of the old-
timers who were the sources of his songs. He has made a good
many recordings, a number by Cook Laboratories, Inc.,[12] specialists
in documentary recordings in a series known as "Sounds of Our
Times." And he has recorded sea songs for Folkways.[13]

Sam Eskin was once married and fathered two sons, now grown:
Stanley, born in 1930, and Otho, born in 1935. In recent years
several singers have written their life stories, particularly about
those areas pertaining to folksong.[14] If Sam Eskin ever decides to
turn author and emulate Jack London, he could write a tale interspersed with song that would top them all, when it comes to knocking
about the world looking at the human scene.

BILLY FAIER

Banjo artist, writer, folksong interpreter—Billy Faier is a versatile
and articulate member of the big-city clan of folk musicians. He's
had a long struggle for recognition, but as of this writing he's
definitely on the way up.

William David Faier was born in Brooklyn, New York, on December 21, 1930. He attended public school in Brooklyn and high school
in Kingston, New York. When he was fifteen the family moved to
Woodstock, "an upstate New York artists' colony," where he first
heard recordings of American folk music. This experience impressed
him deeply, and by the time the family moved back to New York
City in 1948, he was ready to devote his life to folk music. One
Sunday afternoon he fell in with the Washington Square Park
musicians—"young people sitting in the Square singing songs and
playing guitars and banjos." To quote him further: "Washington
Square Park has been the traditional gathering place for young
folksingers, mostly amateurs, on Sunday afternoons, for the past
fifteen years."

On finishing high school in 1947, Billy had given up a regular
job to go into folk music, but that road proved rough and full of
disappointment. "Nine years and many, many jobs later," he writes,
"I have been able to maintain myself as a professional musician."

He went to California in 1951. He taught music (especially banjo), worked in night clubs, and gave concerts, performed on radio and TV: "I had a weekly radio program on station KPFA, Berkeley, on which I talked, played records, and sang." In 1952, he spent "a great deal of time" in Modesto, California, collecting songs from some elderly traditional singers.

The stretch of nine lean years, then, was his apprenticeship period, in which he perfected his musical technique, added immensely to his store of folk-music literature, and gained experience in performing, arranging, and writing music until he had developed a style of his own. There is no doubt of a strong Pete Seeger influence in Billy's banjo playing, as Pete has influenced many of the younger folk musicians.

Billy Faier has performed extensively in and around New York, in the Bay area in California, and to a limited extent in New Orleans, Mexico, and Canada. He has made recordings for Elektra, Tradition, and Riverside labels (see Book Three), and in the past few years has written much for the folk-music magazine *Caravan* (see 1958 issues). After some time as one of the assistant editors of that lively little journal, he picked up "the official blue pencil" to become editor in chief. In "spare" moments he will teach banjo, guitar, mandolin, give concerts, do more recordings. Billy Faier has arrived.*

ROBERT E. LEE FLOWERS

"Son of the Old South, Kentuckian by birth, Arkansawyer by adoption, American by the grace of God," Robert Edward Lee Flowers was born March 12, 1865, fifteen miles from Paducah, Kentucky, in a two-story log house. A mile and a half away, the log schoolhouse was the scene of his happy school days.

At twenty-one, Flowers (with others of his family) moved West, eventually settling in the hills near Heber Springs, Arkansas, in a 14' x 16' squatter's cabin with wooden hinges and bunk beds. As Flowers described it, "A commodious fireplace of scrap-rock kept us warm and we heard the wolves howl and the panther scream and saw deer by the half dozen and wild turkeys by the score." In the spring, with the help of neighbors, the Flowers family built a new house, and for a dozen years Robert Flowers was a country-school teacher on a thirty-dollar-a-month salary. Soon he married one of his pupils, Lucy A. Turney.

* Faier is preparing an anthology containing all the folksongs that have been on the hit parade in the 1950's. Tentative title is *Folk Song Hit Parade*, and the publisher is Ballantine Books.

After eight years and five children, Mrs. Flowers died. Robert Flowers married a widow with three children and continued teaching for thirty years more. He was active in Boy Scout work for many years, belongs to the Order of the Arrow, and is probably one of the oldest living scouts.

Flowers learned folksongs in his family and neighborhood as soon as he could talk and sing. His sister Mollie, who took care of him as a child, taught him many songs. For more than eighty years he has known and loved the old songs. When a boy he owned a jew's-harp, an aeolian harp, and, later, a harmonica and a violin. Flowers has made no special point of performing folksongs, but he has sung them on many occasions. He has sung them at home, at school, at picnics, at parties, and in recent years he has performed at the Ozark Folk Festival in Eureka Springs, Arkansas, and the Arkansas Folklore Society has tape-recorded his songs for its archives.

Robert E. Lee Flowers has nine living children, all married and most of them still living in the central part of Arkansas. Now past ninety, he lives with one of his daughters at Quitman, Arkansas.

PAT FOSTER

Born in the early 1920's in the village of Lund, southeastern Idaho, not far from the Bear River, Pat Foster started traveling and singing in his teens and hasn't stopped yet. Calling himself poet, singer, and painter, he traveled with that migrant-minstrel, Woody Guthrie (q.v.), in 1942-43 and before that he worked his way through the Pacific Northwest, California, and the South. His early schooling was in Spokane, Washington, and Oklahoma City. Later, for a short time, he attended the Fruitland Bible School at Wake Forest, North Carolina, but formal schooling has apparently touched him very lightly.

Foster favors the twelve-string guitar. He has performed in night clubs on the West Coast, in forty of the fifty states, in Canada, as well as in Germany, England, France, Italy, and Mexico. He has made recordings for Riverside, Counterpoint, and Elektra (see Book Three). Such magazines as *High Fidelity, Variety, Show Biz,* and *Caravan* have given him favorable reviews.

Pat Foster was once married for a brief time and has a son, Kurt, born August 2, 1953.

JESSE FULLER

Jesse Fuller, folksinger and something of a folk artist-composer, was born in Georgia in 1896.[15] Orphaned early, he had little schooling and soon became a water boy for levee gangs. Thus began his folk education. As a boy he learned the guitar and the harmonica, and frequently he made a little pocket change playing for breakdowns. All his life he has been a day laborer, working with railroad gangs, construction crews, circuses, and traveling about a good deal, playing and singing on the side. About the age of twenty-four he left Georgia and eventually settled in California. He is still a construction worker by day, often handling the rhythmic jackhammer, but at night he becomes a folk artist.[16]

The most remarkable fact about Jesse Fuller is his one-man homemade combo. Besides plucking the guitar, he has a harmonica and a kazoo rigged around his neck, and with his toes (shoes off) he operates the fotdella. Now the fotdella was made and named (he spells it *fotdellar*) by Jesse himself. It is a sawed-off, neckless bass fiddle, set flat and upside down on the floor on short legs and played with five keys which strike the strings. This odd combination, along with Jesse's singing, produces some surprisingly good rhythm and music. Jesse sings many songs remembered from early days, work songs and blues especially, and he composes others. One of his best is "San Francisco Blues." He reminds many listeners of the famous Leadbelly, who for many years was one of his good friends.

As he grows older, Jesse hopes to let up on hard work and turn more and more to music. Singers make easy money, he believes, and he is reported to have said, "I guess I'll just get me some of that e-a-s-y money." After a hard day, he often works on new songs. "I just sit around," he says, "and I kind of get a tune, and if I like it I make up words." [17] Friends have helped him get some records made, and two albums have been released recently.[18]

Jesse Fuller was married in the early forties to Gertrude Johnson. They have three daughters: Jessie Lee, born December 17, 1943; Mae Alice, born July 30, 1945; Janarie, born September 2, 1946.

PATRICK W. GAINER

Among singers and collectors who are trying to preserve the genuine folk culture of the mountain people, none is more active or ardent than Dr. Patrick W. Gainer of West Virginia University. He was born at Parkersburg, West Virginia, on August 25, 1904, and received his elementary schooling at Tanner. He attended high school and took one year of college at Glenville State Normal School, Glenville, West Virginia. From the State Normal he went to West Virginia University at Morgantown, taking a bachelor's degree in

1927 and a master's in 1928. Further interest in study took him to St. Louis University, where he received a Ph.D. in 1933.

Dr. Gainer's familiarity with folksong is lifelong, for his grandfather and all members of the family in that generation were singers of folksongs. Dr. Gainer's activity as a public lecturer–recitalist began in 1928, though he has sung the old songs as long as he can remember. He has collected from singers in all parts of the state and has learned the styles of many singers. Over the years he has presented no fewer than five or six hundred recitals in at least ten different states, and once he performed on the small British island of Ascension off the coast of Brazil. Dr. Gainer sings in a clear tenor voice, often without accompaniment, but generally in recitals he uses what he prefers to call the rebec. This three-string instrument, he says, is "usually mistakenly called a dulcimer." [19]

In 1950, Dr. Gainer organized and directed the West Virginia Folk Festival, held each summer at Glenville. This festival has had wide publicity [20] and, unlike some of the festivals in recent years, is not a mixture of hillbilly singing and the genuine, older folk material. As Dr. Gainer and others have pointed out, hillbilly singing and the hillbilly manner of producing music, as well as the term hillbilly itself (generally a term of contempt), were not known in the hills before the coming of radio. The West Virginia Festival has been concerned, therefore, not with mere popular entertainment, but with preserving the genuine folk arts as developed by the mountain people. The voice of the folksinger, in the traditional manner, has almost been stilled, Dr. Gainer points out. Much has been accomplished through the Folk Festival "to make people aware of their folk heritage so that they would be proud of it and want to preserve it."

As a further means of preserving the traditional songs, and to answer requests from teachers who want the children to hear the songs, Dr. Gainer has initiated the "Folk Heritage Records," the first album appearing in October, 1954. It contains folksongs "collected in the Allegheny Mountains of West Virginia during the last quarter of a century." [21] Others will follow.

Patrick W. Gainer was married to Antoinette Kizinski on June 17, 1926. They have five children, four sons and one daughter, all grown. Dr. Gainer's connection with West Virginia University, where he is a professor of English, goes back to the early 1920's.

BOB GIBSON

Bob Gibson is a newcomer in the field of singing folksongs, having made his first public performance on a television show in Cleveland,

Ohio, in February, 1954. He was born in New York City, November 16, 1931. Early schooling and high school were in and around New York. As for college, he has done some evening courses but taken no degree. His father, for a time a professional singer, eventually became a chemical engineer.

Bob learned his folksongs from other singers, from records, and "from old-timers in small towns." He uses the guitar and five-string banjo and, though he does a little arranging, his purpose is "to keep the song in its traditional form and to sing it in the traditional fashion." He has performed in about a dozen states, at night clubs, folk festivals, and elsewhere, and has had favorable press notices in such papers as the Cleveland *News* and the *Plain Dealer*. He has done recordings for Folkways and Riverside (see Book Three).

On March 29, 1952, Bob Gibson was married to Rose Anna Shean-feld. Singing folksongs began as a hobby, but the hobby began to take so much time, Bob says, "that I had to accept it as my vocation."

SHEP GINANDES

Dr. Shepard C. Ginandes, young Boston psychiatrist, was born in Brooklyn on June 7, 1928. From the Brooklyn public schools he went on to Harvard, taking a Bachelor of Arts degree in 1948 and, at the Harvard Medical School, a Doctor of Medicine in 1951.

Shep Ginandes learned folksongs when he was a teen-ager at summer camps. At sixteen he began singing on his own, giving his first performance in 1944 at a summer camp in New Milford, Connecticut. He has a good ear for languages, particularly French, and from early childhood "listened to foreign programs on radio and mimicked words and accents." He sings not only in French and English but in Welsh, Spanish, German, Yiddish, and Russian.

When Dr. Ginandes received his first degree from Harvard, he went to France and collected a goodly number of folksongs. He plays the guitar by ear, and he plays it with great skill. For French folk dances he plays the vielle.* Apropos his medical studies, Dr. Ginandes writes: "I sang for some of the money it took to get through medical school, and for several years had radio series, weekly, on stations WMEX, WLAW, WBUR-FM, and WXHR-FM—all in Boston."

Besides folksong recitals in several states, in Mexico and France, Dr. Ginandes has made a number of excellent recordings, mainly for Elektra (see Book Three), from 1952 to 1957. These have had

---

* Webster's dictionary defines the vielle as "a large and early form of the medieval viol."

very favorable reviews in journals like *Harper's*, the *Saturday Review*, and the *Journal of American Folklore.**

Shepard C. Ginandes was married to Lois Condon in 1949. They have two sons: David, born January 4, 1952, and Clifford, born November 8, 1956. For a time in the early 1950's Dr. Ginandes was in Europe as a medical officer in the United States Army. The family home is on Trotting Horse Drive in Lexington, Massachusetts, a few miles outside Boston.

JOE GLAZER

Known as the "Political Minstrel" and "Labor's Troubadour," big, burly, and affable Joe Glazer, who is education director for the United Rubber Workers (AFL-CIO), was born in New York City on June 19, 1918, the fifth of seven children. His father, a Jewish immigrant from Poland, was a worker in New York City's garment industry. Joe attended the Manhattan borough public schools and graduated in 1934 from the James Monroe High School. In 1938, he took a Bachelor of Arts degree at Brooklyn College and continued with some graduate studies at New York University. His studies were interrupted by World War II, but beginning again in 1944 and continuing at intervals through 1949, he did graduate work in labor economics at the University of Wisconsin. He acquired no further degrees, however.

Joe Glazer's mother was "a fairly good singer," but his parents were not folk musicians. He learned his folksongs from radio, records, and books, and especially from "traveling around the country working for the labor movement." He has sung folksongs "off and on" since his high-school days (when he got a guitar from Sears, Roebuck for $6.98), and he has been singing them "seriously for the last twelve years." He collects folksongs, too, particularly "labor and protest songs and records."

During his travels and labor activities, Joe Glazer has sung in thirty-five states, in the Canadian provinces of Ontario and New Brunswick, and in both France and England. Naturally, his number of appearances runs into the hundreds, or possibly thousands. Besides strictly labor and political songs, he does a lot of fine old favorites, such as "Roving Gambler," "Buffalo Skinners," "Kevin

---

* Professor Charles Haywood, Queens College, reviewing a batch of Elektra records for the *Journal* (October-December 1954), speaks of Dr. Ginandes' "infectious manner of delivery. . . . [he] possesses a remarkable feeling and understanding of different styles." And concerning *French Traditional Songs* (Elektra 9), Haywood writes: "Ginandes has completely entered and absorbed the spirit of these songs, and he has a good time singing them."

Barry" (a song of revolution from Ireland), "Methodist Pie," and "Go 'Way from My Window." He has made recordings for Folkways Records (see Book Three), Labor Arts, and Sound Studios.[22] Joe is also a composer of many songs in the field of labor and politics. In the strict sense, of course, such songs are topical rather than folk.

The nature of Joe Glazer's singing activities is best summed up in his own words:

> While I do general folksongs, I have specialized in labor, protest and political songs. Have sung at many union conventions, on picket lines, at meetings, union schools, etc. I sang at the AFL-CIO merger convention, and at the merger convention of the Canadian labor movement. I sang in a pageant depicting the history of the CIO presented at the last CIO convention held in New York, in 1955. I sang at the Democratic convention in 1956, appearing on all TV networks. I sang at many rallies where Adlai Stevenson and Estes Kefauver spoke, and my songs were used in many places throughout the campaign.[23]

Joe Glazer was married June 21, 1942, to Mildred Krauss. They are the parents of three children: Danny, born September 8, 1946; Emily, born March 17, 1950; and Patti Lee, born March 7, 1951. The Glazers make their home in Akron, Ohio, headquarters city for the United Rubber, Cork, Linoleum and Plastic Workers of America.*

TOM GLAZER

Among well-established professional ballad singers, few are more widely popular than Tom Glazer, for he has appeared on many radio and television shows, in numerous concerts, and his recordings have had extensive sales. Tom Glazer was born in Philadelphia in 1914. He had the usual public-school education, and he attended City College of New York for three years, but took no degree.

Though Tom Glazer has sung all his life, his first professional appearance occurred at the age of fifteen. Many songs he learned from his mother, who sang a lot of traditional music, and many more he

---

* Joe Glazer is co-editor, with Edith Fulton Fowke, of a new collection of labor songs called *Songs of Work and Freedom*, which is expected off the press in February, 1960. The announcement states: "This book will have 100 union songs, work songs, protest songs and folk songs of social significance." Besides the lyrics, the book will have music "for piano and guitar, and important historical notes." It is sponsored by the Labor Education Division of Roosevelt University.

learned from other folksingers. Ballad singing has been his full-time career since 1943. Also he composes music and lyrics in the popular field. In the past fifteen or twenty years he has done five hundred to six hundred performances at least—he's not sure how many.

Glazer's activities of the past dozen years make a long catalogue—too long for complete listing, but here follow many instances of his folksong activities. He presented "Tom Glazer's Ballad Box" during 1945-47 over the American Broadcasting Company. He was ballad singer, sometimes actor, on "We the People," "Theatre Guild on the Air," "Listening Post," and "True Story." He made his New York Town Hall debut in 1948. He was balladeer-narrator on the RKO short film, *Sweet Land of Liberty*, a featured balladeer on the "Ford Foundation Transcribed Series" on Thomas Jefferson, also on the "Lux-TV Playhouse," and on Columbia "TV Workshop." Finally, he sang sea ballads on the C.B.S. "Radio Theatre" performance of *Moby Dick*, presented November 15, 1955.

Tom Glazer has been a popular ballad singer at colleges and universities, among them Harvard, Princeton, Mount Holyoke, Juilliard, and Antioch. Perhaps no ballad singer has been more popular with children than Tom Glazer. He has been soloist with the Philadelphia Orchestra Children's Concerts, the Worcester Festival Children's Concerts, and he is the storyteller, writer, and balladeer for Young People's Records, Inc. More than two hundred thousand of his children's records sold in 1951, and the number has long since passed the half-million mark. The press has been lavish in praising him,[24] especially for his children's work. In 1947, he received the Annual Record Music Award for his children's recordings. In 1950, the Parents' Institute Certificate was awarded to the Young People's Records, Inc., with the *Parents' Magazine* Seal of Approval. His singing career has indeed been one of continued success.

In 1944, Tom Glazer was married to Miriam Reed Eisenberg, and they are the parents of two children. They live on the Old Revolutionary Road in Scarborough, from where Tom commutes to his work in New York City.

TERRY GOLDEN

Terry Golden is the son of the distinguished Irish patriot-martyr, Peter Golden. On his mother's side he stems from a "solid Republican upstate New York family . . . respectable citizens in the northeast since before the Revolution." Mrs. Peter Golden was an actress with the Ben Greet Players, and Terry was born in Boston, December 4, 1917.[25]

As might be expected, Terry has traveled a good deal and his education, seemingly desultory, was nevertheless thorough. His earliest schooling was at the Horace Mann School in New York City. When Terry was eight, the family moved to California, and he attended public grade school in Pasadena. He had one year at Taos (New Mexico) High School and then completed his high-school work at Fountain Valley, a preparatory school in Colorado Springs. He entered Colorado College in Colorado Springs in 1936, majored in biology, and took a bachelor's degree in 1940. After some years as a border patrolman on the Mexican border during World War II, he did a year of graduate work in English and Spanish at the Texas College of Mines in El Paso, with further graduate work in Spanish at Colorado College.

If a person asks Terry from whom he learned folksongs, he is likely to reply, "Oh, no one in particular, everyone in general." He has, no doubt, learned many songs from other singers, as well as from books and records. But of prime importance are the remembered early years with his distinguished father, Peter Golden. Born in Cork County, Ireland, and migrating to America when he was quite young, Peter Golden was a cousin of Terence MacSwiney, lord mayor of Cork, who led the Brixton Prison hunger strike in World War I days—in the cause of Irish Independence. Golden was a specialist in Irish folksongs and sang them on many occasions.

After a period as assistant stage manager with the Sothern-Marlowe Players and then with the Ben Greet Players, Peter Golden gave up his stage career to devote his life to the Irish Cause. He sang, lectured, wrote prose and verse, and in many ways worked to raise money for Irish Independence. Highly successful in this venture and well known to all people interested in the Cause, he returned to Ireland around 1920 with money and encouragement for the Irish patriots, whom he helped in many ways. After some time in his beloved native land, he returned to America and died in Denver in 1926. Because of his great work for free Ireland, Irish patriots shipped his body back to Ireland for burial in the Martyrs' Plot in the heart of Dublin.[26]

No wonder Terry Golden can sing an Irish folksong and make your heart stand still! All his life he has known the old songs and about "half my life," he reports, he's been singing them for compensation. The "compensation" began at summer tourist camps and when he was a dude wrangler. Terry taught Spanish, history, and biology a couple of years (1945-47) at the Fountain Valley School. Another year he ran a rock crusher in California. (Comment by T. G.: "I can think of better ways to make a living.") Then, after his first formal concert at the Colorado Springs Fine Arts Center, on

January 23, 1948, he took up folksinging and square dancing as a full-time activity.

Terry has been particularly fortunate in his marriage to Sue Ellen (Suzie) Post. They met (blind date) at a square dance in Colorado in 1947. Miss Post had attended the Cheyenne Mountain High School in Colorado Springs and was a member of the famous Lloyd Shaw's Square Dance Team. Later she attended the Katharine Gibbs Secretarial School in Boston, and then worked as secretary to the president of Shepard's Citations, a legal publishing firm. Terry and Suzie were married on December 12, 1949.

Terry has done a lot of folksong recitals—by mid-1956, well over two thousand programs. During the three-year period 1951-54, he worked in the extension departments of the universities of Wisconsin, Kansas, and Minnesota, on their school-assembly circuits, a sort of lyceum business of the universities, providing a variety of entertainment for the schools in smaller towns and rural areas. Terry puts on a program, often with Suzie's help, of folksongs with commentary, and concluding with a square of children for a quick square dance. Sometimes he has done a dozen or more of these programs in one week. Terry said of this activity: "These programs are primarily meant to be entertaining, and if you get in any education, you have to sneak it in edgewise, or the kids aren't going to like it." During the biennium 1954-56, he worked again for the University of Minnesota and for a private agency, the Antrim Bureau of Philadelphia. For the biennium 1956-58, he was with a Western agency, the National School Assemblies of Los Angeles.

In the summer of 1951 and succeeding summers, the Goldens have followed primarily a square-dance circuit, calling dances, singing folksongs, instructing and entertaining at various folk- and square-dance camps about the country. They've covered most of the fifty states. Terry has published several articles on square dancing in *Sets in Order*, a magazine of some 10,000 circulation. They are indeed a pair of busy troupers, who might turn up somewhere east of Cincinnati, or in Alabama, or Tennessee, or Kentucky, or even at their home base at Ranchos de Taos in New Mexico! [27]

CYNTHIA GOODING

Born in Rochester, Minnesota, August 12, 1924, Cynthia Gooding received her early schooling there, and at the Laurel School for Girls in Cleveland, Ohio. After these early years there was further study at Lake Forest, Illinois, and at Branksome Hall in Toronto, Canada. She considered going to college but instead went to live in Mexico for two years.

Miss Gooding does not come from a folksinging family, though her grandmother was a natural musician and taught her a few songs. Her folksong interest developed in Mexico when she was studying the guitar and learning the language, and her first performance was over station XEW in Mexico City in 1945. This appearance was part of a good-will program sponsored by the cultural attaché of the American Embassy. Returning to the States in 1947, she sang for a year at a cabaret called the Soho in Greenwich Village. The effectiveness of her singing is suggested by her offhand concise comment: "It closed when I left to get married."

In the past dozen years Miss Gooding has given several hundred performances, perhaps as many as five hundred. She made a number of appearances in Mexico, but most of her recitals have been in the eastern United States and in the upper Midwest—in such states as New York, New Jersey, Connecticut, Wisconsin, Minnesota, and Illinois. Miss Gooding learned quite a number of songs from a street singer, Marcelo Salazar, in Mexico, but as for serious collecting she says: "I have been a collector in the sense that I spend a great deal of time in the library." The factual details and intelligent comments which she has brought together in notes for her record albums [28] show the thorough and scholarly approach she has developed as a "library collector." With her facility in more than one language (Spanish, Portuguese, Italian, and Turkish as well as English) she is truly developing into an international singer of folksongs. One reviewer speaks of her "magnificent contralto voice" and, in further praise, says: "She is gifted with a wonderful ear for languages, and she exhibits a high competency on the guitar." [29]

Cynthia Gooding was married to Hasan Ziya Ozbekhan, a writer,[30] on July 5, 1948. They are now divorced. They have two children: Ayshe Neriman, born in 1949, and Leyla Faitoute, born in 1954. Miss Gooding now lives in New York City; she says her regular vocation is "singing and mothering!"

DR. AND MRS. I. G. GREER

I. G. Greer was born at Zionville, North Carolina, December 4, 1881. He attended public schools in Watauga County. His higher education was obtained at Appalachian State Teachers College, Boone, North Carolina, and at the University of North Carolina, with further study at Columbia University in New York City.

Dr. Greer has sung ballads all his life, learning them first from his mother as she sang at her loom, and later from friends, neighbors, and students. He became aware of their cultural importance when he was a student under C. Alphonso Smith at the University of North Carolina. Most of his adult life he has collected ballads, and his repertoire totals more than two hundred. Now that he is semi-retired, Dr. Greer hopes to prepare his collection for publication.

Mrs. Greer (nee Willie Spainhour) was born at Boone, North Carolina, July 24, 1888. After completing her studies at Patton's Private School in Morganton, North Carolina, she went on to the Women's College of the University of North Carolina, at Greensboro, graduating in 1907. She has done further study at the Clark School, Northampton, Massachusetts, and at Columbia University in New York City.

Mrs. Greer, whose mother was a music teacher, learned to play the piano as well as the dulcimer. And, like her husband, she learned folksongs from her parents, friends, and students. The Greers have been performing folk music as a team since their marriage in 1916, he as singer and she as accompanist at the piano or on the dulcimer. Their first formal appearance was at the Appalachian State Teachers College in 1917. For their recitals Mrs. Greer writes out the tunes, making up her accompaniments for both piano and dulcimer.

Over the years the Greers have performed in ten different states, giving possibly as many as six hundred recitals. In the summer of 1954, while visiting a son and his family in England, they gave a program at the Cecil Sharp House, near London. The dulcimer Mrs. Greer plays is an antique, made in Watauga County over a hundred years ago. She uses a noter and picks the dulcimer with quills. (See discussion on musical instruments.) In 1929, the Greers made recordings for the Paramount Company of New York. In 1930, and again in 1936, they did recordings for the Library of Congress Archive of American Folk Song.

I. G. Greer, who was given an honorary Doctor of Laws degree by Wake Forest College, was for some years superintendent of the Baptist Orphanage at Thomasville, North Carolina. On January 1, 1928, he resigned that position to become executive vice president of the Business Foundation of North Carolina, Inc., with headquarters at Chapel Hill. The Greers have two sons: I. G. Greer, Jr., and Joseph Philip Greer, both now in their thirties.

FROSIA GREGORY

Frosia Gregory, a Canadian singer of folksongs, mainly on radio and television, was born in Toronto, Canada, May 11, 1922. She received much of her education in that city: first in the public schools, then at the Parkdale Collegiate School, and finally as a senior matriculate at the Royal Conservatory of Music. Later she went to New York for graduate study in music at the Juilliard School.

Miss Gregory is not a traditional singer of folksongs, but became interested in them through the encouragement of Burl Ives (*q.v.*) and Ed McCurdy (*q.v.*). Though she began her singing career at about the age of sixteen, she turned in earnest to folksongs in 1947. She has performed in several Canadian provinces and has beamed short-wave programs to other countries. For accompaniment Miss Gregory uses the autoharp.

In 1940, Frosia Gregory was married to Bob Shuttleworth, but they are now separated. She has two children: Barbara, born in 1945, and Bobby, born in 1947.

ANNE GRIMES

Musician and folksinger, writer and teacher, busy housewife and mother of five, Anne Laylin Grimes was born in Columbus, Ohio, May 17, 1912. Her Ohio ancestors, from the early nineteenth century, were prominent in political and cultural activities of the state. For example, her paternal grandfather, Lewis Cass Laylin, was assistant secretary of the interior under Presidents Taft and Wilson. Anne attended public schools in Columbus, took a Bachelor of Arts degree in 1933 at Ohio Wesleyan University and a Bachelor of Music in 1935 at Ohio State University.

Anne's parents, gifted amateur singers and musicians, were from families of traditional singers. Her father, Clarence Dewey Laylin, a corporation lawyer and former law professor at Ohio State, can play any plucked instrument by ear. In his undergraduate days at Ohio State, he was a playing conductor of the popular Mandolin Club. So Anne Grimes comes by her folk-music interest naturally and has sung folksongs just about all her life. She has learned songs from other relatives and friends, as well as from many informants whose songs and ballads she has collected.

Anne has been giving public recitals of folksongs for more than a dozen years, beginning in the school year 1943-44 with a performance over Ohio State's radio station WOSU. She plays the dulcimer, psaltery, zither, autoharp, and banjo, though generally not using more than two on any one program. She knows the guitar, too, but veers away from it in her public performances because of its all-too-common association with Western and hillbilly music. She does her own arrangements for accompaniment; and like any good folksinger, she often sings unaccompanied. During her collecting she has learned many styles of traditional singing and of playing folk instruments, and these various styles she demonstrates in her programs.

Anne Laylin Grimes has performed hundreds of times—in 1954, she estimated well over five hundred—in areas from Missouri to New York and Tennessee to Michigan. Besides professional appearances before clubs and colleges, always she is a welcome performer at folk festivals and folklore gatherings, not alone because of her authentic singing and excellent musicianship, but also because of her extensive scholarly interest in the field of folklore. (In fact, she is an authority on folk material of Ohio and the Old Northwest Territory.) She has performed for the folklore societies of Tennessee, Ohio, New York, West Virginia, and for the Mountain Festival at Asheville, North Carolina, and the National Folk Festivals in St. Louis—just to mention a few of her many appearances.

Anne Grimes has been collecting folk music off and on for about twenty-five years, more intensively the past dozen years, and she has made a hobby of collecting folk-music instruments. She is particularly well versed in knowledge of the dulcimer. Her rare collection of about a dozen of these instruments was exhibited at the Ohio Folklore Society meetings in April, 1955. (See discussion of folk-music instruments, Interlude I.) Much of her collecting has been done in sections of Ohio, but she has done some taping in Kentucky, West Virginia, and North Carolina. She has a vast amount of material, and of course others are interested in taping *her*, since she, too, is an authentic folksinger. In May, 1953, tapes were made by the St. Louis Department of Audio-Visual Education; some of her material has been used by the American Association of Educational Broadcasters. Other organizations interested in her programs and materials include: The Library of Congress Archive of American Folk Song, Ohio Folklore Archive, Ohioana Library, Ohio Valley Research Project—not to mention a number of schools and libraries.

Anne Grimes has written a good deal on folksong and folklore. Her articles have appeared in *Midwest Folklore, Bulletin of the Ohio Historical Society, Ohio Music Club News,* as well as in various newspapers. Formerly she was a music and dance critic, writing for the Scripps-Howard paper, *The Columbus Citizen.* She has served successively (and successfully!) as secretary-treasurer and vice president of the Ohio Folklore Society, and in 1956 was appointed American folklore chairman of the Ohio Federation of Music Clubs.

Much has been accomplished in the folksong field by Anne Grimes, and her plans call for much more. As if all this weren't enough, she is a busy housewife and mother. On March 16, 1936,

Anne Laylin was married to Dr. James W. Grimes, professor of fine arts, Ohio State University. They are the parents of five children: Steve, born in 1940; Sally, born in 1942; Jennifer, born in 1945; Molly, born in 1947; and Mindy, born in 1950. All this—the children, the collecting and singing, the study and writing—adds up to a busy and fascinating career for one of America's important contemporary folksingers.

DR. GEORGE C. GRISE

George Grise was born September 1, 1918, at Bowling Green, Kentucky. Like Patrick Gainer, Rogie Clark, Brownie McNeil, the late Charlie Bryan, and others, he is a teacher by vocation and a folklorist and singer by avocation. His education through high school was at the Training School of the Western Kentucky State Teachers College at Bowling Green. At the Teachers College he spent his undergraduate days, taking a Bachelor of Arts degree in 1940. For graduate study he went to Peabody College for Teachers, earning a master's degree in 1947 and a Doctor of Philosophy in 1950.

Dr. Grise learned his folksinging under the best environmental conditions—partly from the family, partly from old folks (friends, neighbors, and informants) who sang the old songs, partly from books and records. His father, a nonprofessional singer and fiddler, "grew up amidst much folksinging and playing" and is something of an expert on the harmonica. His mother plays the piano. On the "record" influence, he gives specific credit to John Jacob Niles and Burl Ives.

As for his own singing of folksongs, though he has done some of it all his life, most of his singing up to 1950 was not folk. And after many years of violin playing, he now has developed into an expert country fiddler—no mean accomplishment! In presenting folksongs he frequently uses the autoharp, sometimes the zither "without fretted melody strings," and occasionally the guitar.

Dr. Grise has collected a good deal of folk material ("besides songs, tales and name folklore") in central Tennessee and south-central Kentucky. He has appeared regularly on Nashville's radio station WSM as ballad singer on a program called "Tall Tales," and he has made guest appearances on other programs. He performed a number of times, the first in 1952, at the National Folk Festival in St. Louis. And he sang at the Hillbilly Homecoming at Maryville, Tennessee, in 1953, and again at Knoxville in 1954. He's not sure how many recitals he has given, but "200 won't miss it far," he wrote in 1954. Brief but favorable accounts of his singing have appeared in the St. Louis *Globe-Democrat*, the Nashville *Tennessean*, and the Clarksville *Leaf-Chronicle*.

George Grise did duty as a soldier in World War II and, like any soldier with a voice, he sang a lot. It wasn't folksinging, however, for his serious interest in folksongs did not come to flower before 1950. Dr. Grise is professor of English and chairman of the Division of Languages and Literature at Austin Peay State College, Clarksville, Tennessee. He is married to Marian G. Maxwell, and they live in the country near Clarksville.

WOODY GUTHRIE

Some singers, like Woody Guthrie for instance, defy any easy classification. Testily independent and sharply original, he colors any material he touches. He calls himself "writer, composer, musician" and there are those who will hotly deny or stoutly defend him in all three categories. Folk composer he may well be, and a controversial one for sure.

Woody Guthrie, "ex-GI with an honorable discharge," was born at Okemah, Okfuskee County, Oklahoma, July 14, 1912.[31] To tell it in his own words:

> But will I name the place?
> And month and year and date?
> Bastille's Day, July Fourteen;
> My hour was gettin' late;
> Nineteen & Twelve, Okemah,
> Oklahoma's my blood state.

Okemah is in the east-central Oklahoma Indian Reservation area where a lot of strange names dot the map—Weleetka, Kusa, Hitchita, Wetumka, Vamoosa, Wewoka, Sasakwa. Not that they have any bearing on Guthrie's make-up, but there they are. Woody got some schooling, to about the tenth grade, out in the Texas Panhandle at Pampa, Gray County. After World War II, he had a "few weeks on the GI bill" at Brooklyn College in New York, but—"degrees absent."

Woody started early as a singer, at least "since I was four years old," he reports. He learned many songs from his parents—they weren't professional but "they were very good around home." After them, he says, he learned from just about "everybody I met, seen, and heard." That would include a lot of people, because Woody Guthrie has been a migrant worker all his days: he has wandered all over the United States, much of Canada and Mexico. His remarkable odyssey is told in a salty autobiographical study, *Bound for*

Glory.[32] In this lusty book there is much about migrant workers, riding the rails or crowded freight cars, hobo jungles, guitar picking and singing, fighting and friendship. It's a gay and a sad book of struggling Americans in the Great Depression. As one reviewer said: "He roams from coast to coast, working and playing his guitar and singing for his supper. The songs are made out of what he sees and knows and feels; they are the living folksongs of America." [33]

As a composer of songs and ballads of protest, Woody Guthrie has gained a considerable reputation. Dr. John Greenway in his *American Folksongs of Protest* (see Book Two) gives Guthrie high rating as folk composer. Guthrie analyzes his composing in this manner: "I made up trade union fighting songs and sung on picket lines by taking old songs and putting new words" to them.[34] He can neither "read nor write music notes," but being a natural-born musician (besides the guitar, Guthrie plays the mandolin, fiddle, and harmonica), he can, he reports, "sing down my ballads onto sample records so tunewriters can listen and write all the damned notes they please." [35] Though he has sung many traditional ballads, he makes ballads out of just about everything: "I make up a ballad-song or more every going-coming day," and by now he thinks the number may have run into the thousands. One of his very close friends, Cisco Houston (*q.v.*), said of his composing: "Woody is a man who writes two or three ballads before breakfast every morning."

No doubt, much of his material is spur-of-the-moment oral composing of which there is no record, but many of his songs are on records. By 1953, at least twenty commercial albums had been made, aside from Library of Congress recordings. Among the titles: *Dustbowl Ballads* (2 volumes), *Sodbuster Ballads, Deepsea Shanties,* and *Folksay* (see Book Three for further details). As for their widespread use, Woody writes: "Radio stations bar them and fire discjocks for playing them!"

Woody Guthrie has been married three times, first to Mary Esta Jennings, next to Marjorie Mazia Greenblatt, and now to Anneke Louise VanKirk. He has fathered a brood of six, ranging in ages as follows: Gwendolyn Gail, born in 1933; Carolyn Sue, born in 1935; Bill Rogers, born in 1936; Arlo Davy, born in 1947; Joady Ben, born in 1948; Noralee, born in 1950. To the query whether others in the family sing ballads, he replied: "Not professionally but they are loud around the house."

FOOTNOTES TO CHAPTER 4

[1] *Arkansas Folklore,* IV (January, 1954) and VII (March, 1957).

[2] From the descriptive leaflet accompanying the Library of Congress Record No. AAFS 100. The songs on this record are: "The Dying Cowboy," "Red Whiskey," "Little Dogies," and "My Sweetheart's a Cowboy."

[3] Published by Rinehart & Co., Inc. (New York, 1952), 282 pp. *Buffalo Country* was published by E. P. Dutton & Co., Inc.

[4] *Current Biography,* V, 17-18 (June, 1944).

[5] Quoted, with permission, from the note on the record jacket of Dyer-Bennet's first release under the new company founded by him and Harvey Cort. They plan to release two or three records annually of Dyer-Bennet's singing. See Book Three for further details.

[6] *Current Biography, op cit.,* note 4.

[7] From the record jacket.

[8] I am indebted to Jack and June Elliott for biographical facts. *Cosmopolitan* magazine (April, 1955) carried a brief article about Elliott, with photograph.

[9] From Dr. Desmond Powell's notes to Sam Eskin's first record album, made by Staff Music Corporation (long defunct), Berkeley, California. Used by permission of Dr. Powell.

[10] *Ibid.*

[11] *The Audio Bucket,* II, 3 (January, 1956), published by the Cook Laboratories, Inc., Stamford, Conn.

[12] See Book Three for details.

[13] *Ibid.*

[14] Burl Ives, *Wayfaring Stranger* (1948); Woody Guthrie, *Bound for Glory* (1943); W. Roy MacKenzie, *The Quest of the Ballad* (1919); John A. Lomax, *Adventures of a Ballad Hunter;* Jean Ritchie, *Singing Family of the Cumberlands* (1955). See Book Two for further details on these works.

[15] I am indebted to Jesse Fuller for some facts; also, to his friend and manager, Mr. Norman E. Pierce, owner of Jack's Record Cellar in San Francisco.

[16] In the summer of 1956, Jesse began a long engagement at Ernie and Julie's Cabo-Verdi Cafe, in San Francisco's Latin Quarter.

[17] The Oakland *Tribune,* March 31, 1955.

[18] See Book Three for details.

[19] See my discussion of the dulcimer (Interlude I).

[20] For instance, see *Ford Times,* June, 1954.

[21] This is an excellent recording, with the pressings made by Capitol Records of New York.

[22] In 1953, for Labor Arts, he recorded two LP's now out of print: *Songs of the Wobblies* and *Ballads for Sectarians.* In 1955, he did *Songs of Joe Hill,* an LP for Folkways; and in 1956, Sound Studios of Washington, D.C., recorded *Ballads for Ballots.*

[23] In a letter to me, November 1, 1956.

[24] Various items in the *Library Journal,* the New York *Times, World-Telegram, Look* magazine, *Parents' Magazine, House and Garden, Downbeat,* etc.

[25] I am indebted to Terry Golden's long-time friend, the actor-dancer Jacques Cartier, for many details, as well as to Terry.

26 Two of Peter Golden's sisters (Terry's aunts) were professional musicians, making their life careers in private teaching and with St. Brendan's Church in Brooklyn. Terry's sister, Eithne Golden of New York City, plays the Spanish guitar and sings Spanish and Portuguese folk material. She has been treasurer and a director of the Society for the Classical Guitar (New York City). She has been in the United States Foreign Service, and in New York she has produced radio shows for the Transcaucasian section of the Voice of America. Folksinging has been a hobby with her. In 1956, she was married to a man of Viennese birth, who came to the United States in the 1930's "to get out from under Hitler." He was an orchestra leader in Europe, and now, Terry writes, runs a recording studio in New York City.

27 In 1949, Folkraft of Newark, New Jersey, did a *Terry Golden Album* (F-16) of fourteen songs, and a special single long number (both sides) of "Frankie and Johnny," probably the most complete one on records. (All these are 78 rpm records.)

28 Elektra Records has issued five albums of Cynthia Gooding since 1953 (see Book Three for details). These have been favorably reviewed in such widely diverse publications as the Minneapolis *Tribune*, the Boston *Sunday Post*, the *American Mercury*, *Tennessee Folklore Society Bulletin*, *Harper's Magazine*, *Midwest Folklore*, New York *Times*, St. Louis *Post-Dispatch*, and the *Journal of American Folklore*.

29 Charles Haywood of Queens College, Flushing, New York, reviewing records in the *Journal of American Folklore*, LXVII, 415-20 (October-December, 1954).

30 Mr. Ozbekhan's first novel, *The Isle of Princes*, was published by Simon & Schuster in 1957 and favorably reviewed in the *Saturday Review*, December 14, 1957. Reviewer Ben Ray Redman said of it: "There is not a stock character, a hackneyed situation, nor a commonplace line in *The Isle of Princes*. It opens windows into a world that few Americans can have glimpsed before, and it celebrates the proud past of a proud people."

31 Woody has generously supplied many facts and phrases!

32 Published by E. P. Dutton & Co. (New York, 1943), 428 pp.

33 Louis Adamic in the *Saturday Review*, April 17, 1943.

34 Letter to me, October 5, 1953.

35 *Ibid.*

CHAPTER 5

The Singers,
H to K

KENNETH MARTIN HALL

Kenneth Hall, born in San Jose, California, October 14, 1923, went through eleven grades of schooling at the California School for the Blind, in Berkeley. Folk music runs in the Hall family. His father plays the harmonica, and his paternal grandfather was a Texas fiddler. Kenneth also learned from early recordings and from Blind Sanford of Campbell, California.

At fourteen Kenneth gave his first public performance in Townsend Hall, Richmond, California. He has learned many instruments: the five-string and tenor banjos, mandolin, guitar, fiddle, and harmonica. In 1949, Kenneth Hall, picking his mandolin and singing his way, hitchhiked from the West Coast down through Texas and the Southwest. Now, in spare evenings, he augments his regular income by performing at house parties, square dances, and frequently in bars.

Kenneth is not a collector, except in the way that many singers are collectors: he picks up songs wherever he hears them. Like most singers, he makes up his own arrangements and has his own pickin' style.

In 1950, Kenneth Martin Hall was married to Christine Jarmann. They have two daughters: Kathleen, born March 13, 1952, and Kay, born June 14, 1953. Kenneth's regular occupation is selling brooms for the Blind Home.

FRANK HAMILTON

Born August 3, 1934, in New York City, Frank Hamilton attended Fairfax High School in Los Angeles and studied one semester as a commercial-music major at Los Angeles City College. His mother is a composer, pianist, and teacher of modern dance, and his stepfather knows blues songs.

Frank's folk-music activities began about 1950, with a now-defunct Los Angeles group known as the Sierra Folk Singers. He has met with and learned from "all kinds of singers and players." And he has learned much from books, records, and the Library of Congress Archive. Other singers are particularly enthusiastic about Frank's instrumental techniques and his versatility *—whether on banjo, six- or twelve-string guitar, harmonica, or mandolin. Like many others, he does his own arranging and, in his words, "I have added to, subtracted from, degenerated and maybe regenerated a few songs." His performances run to more than two hundred, mainly in the Southern states and on the East and West Coasts, and he has recorded for Elektra and Riverside labels (see Book Three).

Frank Hamilton was married to Sheila Lofton, a painter, in November, 1957. They have a son, Evan Baird, born October 21, 1958; and Frank has another child by an earlier marriage. Frank is associated with Win Stracke (q.v.) in the Old Town School of Folk Music of Chicago, where Frank is vice president and teacher, and serves also as accompanist and entertainer. (He accompanied Martha Schlamme in her Chicago appearances.) He has done the sound track for two films: A Time Out of War, which received a Venice Festival Award as well as an Academy Award, and The Glidden Tour with Win Stracke, which took a first place at the American Sector of the Brussels World's Fair. Obviously, as an interpreter of folk music, Frank is on the way up.

DONEY HAMMONTREE

Few folksingers can boast of knowing songs for nearly three-quarters of a century, but Doney Hammontree is one of the few. He was born March 13, 1876, at Greenland, near Fayetteville, Arkansas, and has lived in the region all his life. His formal education was obtained in the local public schools, most of the time not over three months during any one year.

Doney's folksong education was relatively ideal and complete—

* See Caravan, October-November 1958 articles by Mark Morris and Erik Darling.

he heard father, mother, brothers, and sisters all sing ballads. Neighbors, too, added to his repertoire. Doney never uses any accompanying instrument and never has collected songs except for his own use. He has composed a few sacred and secular songs, but none for publication.

Doney Hammontree has experienced considerable fame through his knowledge of folksongs. He contributed twenty-three songs to Vance Randolph's *Ozark Folksongs*. An article on Arkansas in *Holiday* magazine (November, 1954) featured a picture of Doney singing a folksong. The Library of Congress Archive of Folk Song has some of his singing on records, and he contributed more than a hundred songs to the University of Arkansas Folklore Archives. Like old Booth Campbell, he was one of the star performers in the C.B.S. television picture called *The Search*, aired in the fall of 1954.

Doney Hammontree was married in 1897 to Mary E. Spadlin. They had six children (Earl, Otto, Oscar, Una May, Cleo, and George), all of them now past fifty. After Mrs. Hammontree's death, he was married, in 1952, to Mrs. Ethel Couch. Mr. Hammontree has had a lifelong interest in Sunday school and church work, having trained classes and led singing for over fifty years. At nearly eighty, he said he was still able to join in singing any part—"soprano, tenor, bass, and a little alto if necessary." This kind of singing was entirely different, he felt, from folksinging. "In all my folksinging," he said, "I have never let it interfere with my church work." For many years Doney Hammontree has been a nurseryman, growing plants and bulbs for sale at Farmington, about six miles from Fayetteville.

ROLAND HAYES

If the reader should inquire why world-famous artists are given a place in a book about folksingers and folksongs in America, the answer is simple: they sometimes sing folksongs, too, or a particular type of folksong. For instance, Carl Sandburg is a great writer, and he sings many lusty ballads of American pioneer life. Peter Hurd is a great painter and an authority on Spanish-New Mexican ranchera songs. Roland Hayes is a world-famous concert tenor and lieder singer, and he sings many Negro spirituals.[*] To quote him: "In order to better understand and perform classic-lieder, one must have gained mastery in what is its basic root—folkslieder."

Roland Hayes, one of seven children, was born on June 3, 1887,

[*] Some other famous Negro artists who include spirituals in their repertoires are: Marian Anderson, Todd Duncan, Inez Matthews, Paul Robeson, William Warfield, Camilla Williams—to name a few.

in Curryville, Georgia. He studied in the public schools there and in Chattanooga, Tennessee, after which he attended Fisk University, taking the regular four-year course and special music courses. He continued his studies for eight years in Boston and, in 1920, made his first triumphal tour of Europe. The rest of his life is well-known musical history—for forty years, Hayes has been a successful concert artist. It is no exaggeration to say that the number of his regular concerts has exceeded two thousand.

Naturally, many honors have come to him, from universities, from governments, from the music critics, and from the great orchestras with which he has made many appearances. Always, in his concerts, he has included Negro spirituals, or, as he prefers to call them, religious folkslieder. Roland Hayes, in fact, is an American institution. He has done much recording and some publishing of his songs (see Books Two and Three for further details). Mr. Hayes makes his home in Brookline, not far from metropolitan Boston.

VALERIE HAYNES

Valerie Haynes, like Bob Gibson, Frosia Gregory, and others, is a newcomer in singing folksongs. She was born in St. Petersburg, Florida, December 16, 1928. Her grade-school training was in the Chicago public schools and at Oberlin, Ohio; her high school, both junior and senior, in North Carolina, Tennessee, and finally in St. Petersburg. In 1953, she took a Bachelor of Science degree at Florida State University, in Tallahassee.

In 1950, after hearing traditional folksinging in the mountains of North Carolina, Miss Haynes bought herself an autoharp, delved into some of the folksong collections, particularly Margaret Boni's *Fireside Book of Folk Songs,* and went to work. Then she listened to other singers and recordings, particularly those of Burl Ives and Susan Reed. On Thanksgiving Day in 1952, she sang a full-hour program of folksongs at the Sportsman's Club, Bainbridge, Georgia. From that time forward, she reports, "I've been at it ever since!"

Miss Haynes has given several score of recitals in North Carolina, Florida, and Georgia and has been a favorite at the Florida Folk Festival. For regular occupation, Miss Haynes works as a secretary. As a special interest she designs puppets for TV shows; and then because she loves to sing, folksongs have become an absorbing hobby.

LEE HAYS

The most popular folksinging foursome in the midcentury is the Weavers, and Lee Hays, singing bass, was one who rode to fame with this group.* Lee was born in Little Rock, Arkansas, in 1914. He attended various grade schools and high schools in Arkansas and Georgia. As for college, Lee reports that he "came along too late and, in depression times, could not afford college." Older brothers and a sister had attended Hendrix College at Conway, Arkansas, and Lee has had "a good deal of informal schooling in night classes" amounting to about three years of credits.

Like some others, Lee Hays had never heard the word folksong until he came to New York in 1936. Soon he began to sing with Woody Guthrie, Leadbelly, Josh White, Burl Ives, Pete Seeger, and others, and first got paid for it with the Almanac Singers in 1940. Lee plays the piano by ear and has always worked with groups, never solo. He helped assemble the "People's Songs Library." To quote him: "I have written several songs, rewritten many, edited a lot, mostly with the Weavers . . . and have had two or three songs sung back to me later as old folk songs!"

Lee likes all kinds of folk music but says he has a strong partiality for gospel songs and blues. The other Weavers once complained, he said, that "no matter what I sing, Hebrew, Spanish, what not, it all comes out like a Methodist hymn!" Besides his working over songs and his singing with the Weavers, Lee does some emceeing, writes short stories, and prepares album notes. For some time the Weavers were recorded by Decca, later by Folkways, and more recently they have gone to the Vanguard label.

FRED HELLERMAN

As a member of the fabulous Weavers and as musical director for Elektra Records, Fred Hellerman has had a hand in much folksong activity for a dozen years past. He was born in New York City on May 13, 1927, and also educated there, from earliest schooling through university. He attended New York University, Columbia University, and in 1949 took a Bachelor of Arts degree at Brooklyn College.

Fred has known folksongs a long time, though his parents were not folk musicians or singers. When he was in the United States Coast Guard (1944-45), he began teaching himself guitar aboard ship. His first professional performance dates from about 1946. Though the guitar is his chief instrument, in the course of much recording activity he has also used the banjo, recorder, drums,

---

* The others are Pete Seeger, Fred Hellerman, and Ronnie Gilbert. Their records have sold in the millions. Because of the pressure of work, Seeger withdrew from the group in 1958, and his place was taken by Erik Darling (q.v.), another fine banjo picker.

celesta, and zither. Since he makes a living as arranger, recording executive, song writer (and rewriter), and guitarist, naturally he has done collecting in various places. "I'm always keeping my ears open," he says. He wrote the song, "Kisses Sweeter Than Wine," has composed music for several plays, and has arranged and composed for Harry Belafonte (*q.v.*), among others.

As a member of the Weavers, Fred has sung in most of the states and in Canada. Though he does not appear often as solo performer, in reality his singing and musical guitar are on hundreds of recordings with others, under the following labels: Folkways, Riverside, Decca, Tradition, Vanguard, Elektra, etc. Fred has much to say about folk music, how one should look upon it and use it, about changing and commercializing it. This sketch may well end with a quote from him on the subject:

> It would seem that the question boils down to looking upon a folksong in either one of two ways: (1) as an inviolate museum piece, which must be kept as antiseptic as possible; or (2) as a *living* expression of a folk culture, susceptible and subject to *all* the forces of the culture. As a living thing, it *must* grow and change.

Obviously, Fred Hellerman has chosen the second way and found it good.

JOE HICKERSON

Joseph Charles Hickerson, a student in the Folklore Department of Indiana University, was born in Highland Park, Illinois, on October 20, 1935. He received his schooling through high school at New Haven, Connecticut, then enrolled at Oberlin College in 1953. After taking a Bachelor of Arts degree in 1957, he went to Indiana for graduate study.

Joe learned folksongs from commercial LP recordings, from friends ("non-traditional singers of folk songs"), and from books. He began singing while a student at Oberlin, appearing before college groups and at children's camps. He uses both the guitar and the five-string banjo, playing them left-handed. He has performed, usually with others, in eight or ten states in some fifty or more recitals. He belonged to a singing group called "The Folksmiths" (see Book Three for recordings) and is now a member of a similar group at Indiana University called "The Settlers," the other members being Bruce Buckley (*q.v.*) and Ellen Stekert (*q.v.*).

Mr. Hickerson approaches folksongs as a serious student, careful in his distinctions of traditional and nontraditional singers and materials. He does not, of course, overlook the genuine entertainment value of the materials he works with. Like some others, he demonstrates that scholarly activities may very often have a popular appeal.

FRED HIGH

Fred High, somewhat of an egocentric and a show-off (he wears funny little hats at folk festivals and, when he writes, he affects outlandish spellings), likes to pose as an uneducated hillman. But he is nonetheless a shrewd and discerning person who knows a considerable body of folksong. He was born at High, Carroll County, Arkansas, January 15, 1878,[1] where he has lived most of his long and useful life. His schooling was meager and intermittent. The country school he attended was overcrowded, the big boys ran over him a good deal, and, besides, the folks needed him at home to pull fodder.

Fred says he has been a jack of all trades, for he has done many things to make a living. For eight years he carried the mail. When High, Arkansas, was made a post office, Fred set up a store that included the post office, and he was postmaster for thirty-five years. He is proud of his "forty-three years for Uncle Sam"—a title he has used for one of his booklets. He once owned a cane mill and made molasses. Later he had an interest in a canning factory, from which he got little profit, and then he farmed a bit, too.

Fred High was married to Janie Hayhurst on June 10, 1900. In 1904, they spent two days at the World's Fair in St. Louis where, Fred reports, "I saw the wonders of my life." The Highs have seven children, all living and all married, and numerous grandchildren.

Like other old-time folksingers, Fred has known folksongs as far back as he can remember. He has sung at the Ozark Folk Festivals in Eureka Springs, Arkansas, along with his sister, Mrs. Briscoe (he calls her Sister Succie), and at the National Folk Festival in St. Louis in 1953 and earlier years. About fifty of his songs have been tape-recorded for the University of Arkansas Folklore Archives. In 1951, he compiled a booklet entitled *Old, Old Folk Songs* containing seventy-three songs (without music)—"One song for each of my years here on earth." His two other booklets, *Forty-Three Years for Uncle Sam* (1949) and *It Happened in the Ozarks* (1954), are compilations of local history and family matters, homely wit and amusing stories. Fred himself advertises and sells these curious little booklets of fact, fancy, and philosophy. Like his sister Succie (Mrs. Mary Briscoe, *q.v.*), he is a living storehouse of old-time songs and other native lore.

MRS. CORA HILLHOUSE

Mrs. Cora Hillhouse, White Springs, Florida, a teacher who uses much folksong material with children, was born in Jasper, Florida, April 24, 1891. She attended rural schools in Florida and the Normal Institute of the Academy of Florida Southern College, at Lakeland. For college study she went to the Georgia State Women's College at Valdosta and later took a bachelor's degree at the University of Florida, in Gainesville.

In her childhood Mrs. Hillhouse learned folksongs in her family, particularly from an aunt, and from many young friends. After a course in folksongs at the University of Florida in 1938, under Dr. Alton Morris, she saw the value of folksongs in teaching, and has been using them ever since. Except for her work in school and her performances at the Florida Folk Festival in White Springs, she has never sung in public. She has collected songs from children in her school work, and in turn she has familiarized many children with the songs.

Mrs. Hillhouse is the widow of J. L. Hillhouse. She has three grown children: two sons, Paul and Clyde; and a married daughter, Grace Hillhouse McClellan. Mrs. Hillhouse does not feel that she has done much in the field of folksinging—it has been a lifelong hobby with her, and she has done a worth-while thing in acquainting many children with the fine old songs.

L. M. HILTON

One of the best singers of Mormon songs, Lavoli M. Hilton was born in Salt Lake City, Utah, February 15, 1896. Latter-day Saints (Mormon) church schools in the Mormon colonies in Old Mexico gave him his early schooling. On the family's return to Utah, he attended Davis County High School in Utah. He had a few courses at Weber College in Ogden and at the University of Utah in Salt Lake City, but took no degree.

L. M. Hilton, though not a professional, has been singing the old songs since he was a small boy. He learned much from his mother, his grandmother, and from many old-timers. For many years he has collected the old songs in Utah, particularly a large number of Latter-day Saints songs of pioneer days. When Utah celebrated her centennial in 1947, Hilton presented 153 recitals of the traditional songs. Since then he averages about fifteen recitals yearly, and on occasion he sings on local Ogden radio stations. He never uses accompaniment. "I just tell the story of the songs and sing them without [instrumental] music," he reports.

Mr. Hilton has made many recordings. In 1946, he made about twenty recordings for the Library of Congress Archive of Folk Song. In 1952, Folkways Records issued an LP album by him containing twelve Mormon folksongs. His only purpose in gathering, singing, and recording the old songs, he reports, "has been, and still is, to keep them alive, preserve them and not let them become forgotten." In this sense, his songs are a part of the social and cultural history of Utah.

L. M. Hilton has been on the police force of Ogden, Utah, for some thirty years. He has been married twice. His first wife was Jennie Goodale, whom he married in 1919. They had five children, now all grown: Janet, Robert ("killed in the Battle of the Bulge in 1945"), Lou Jean, Don Keith, and Jo Anne. The first Mrs. Hilton died in 1940, and he married Mary Hodgson in 1941. They have three children: Clifford, born in 1943; Lawrence, born in 1946; Marney, born in 1950. Officer Hilton modestly disclaims a title which he properly deserves—"Utah's foremost folklore singer."

SAM HINTON

Offhand, biology and balladry don't seem to have much in common. As I have pointed out before, however, a singer of folksongs may turn up just about anywhere. Sam Hinton, biologist and curator, was born in Tulsa, Oklahoma, March 31, 1917. After grade schools in Tulsa and Bartlesville, Oklahoma, he went through high school at Crockett, Texas. Then, after several sessions at Texas A. and M. College, he entered the University of California at Los Angeles, graduating in 1940 with a Bachelor of Arts degree in zoology.

Sam's mother was a piano teacher, and there was much singing in the home, of folksongs and other songs. Though he learned much from his parents, his early knowledge of folksongs came especially from Negro friends in Texas. At five he played the harmonica and at eight the accordion. He has therefore played and sung folk music practically all his life, but his professional singing career really began in 1937 when, with his guitar, he joined a Major Bowes unit as a folksinger. He has performed in almost every state, in Canada and Mexico. Full-length recitals number probably two hundred, and spot entertainments run into the thousands. Naturally, he has been on radio and television many times.

Over the years Sam Hinton has made a sizable collection of folksongs. In the mid-1930's he collected in east Texas and during 1939 in the migrant-worker camps of California. His repertoire has grown to more than four hundred songs from oral sources; some fifty-four of these were contributed to the Library of Congress Archive of

Folk Song. He has done commercial recordings for Columbia and Decca.

Sam Hinton was married to Leslie Forster in 1940. They have two children: Leanne, born in 1942, and Matt, born in 1946. As a serious professional man, biologist Hinton is curator of the aquarium and museum of the Scripps Institution of Oceanography, La Jolla, California. On the side he often writes about folksinging,[2] and he teaches a course in folk music for the University of California Extension. He has had offers to "go on the road" with his guitar, but he is too happy in his work and in his family to make folksinging a full-time profession. Sometimes Sam has qualms about being called a folk-singer, since he hasn't really grown up in the tradition of a folk community. But his wide knowledge of the folksong field and his sympathetic interpretation of the songs save him from any charge of counterfeit. Though not a traditional singer in the strict sense, he is a most effective singer of folksongs and surely one of our best.

LORI HOLLAND

A square-dance crowd at City College in New York gave Lori Holland her first interest in folk music, though her Ukrainian-born grandmother, who sang Russian and Yiddish folksongs, may have planted the seed. Lori was born on March 25, 1932, in New York; got her schooling through high school in the Bronx; and has done some study beyond that in night school. Her father was a piano teacher but with no special interest in folk music. Lori's folksong activity has grown during the past ten years in the square-dance groups of community-church work in New York City, and she has learned much from books, recordings, and friends.

Lori Holland uses the guitar but sometimes sings unaccompanied, and she has made recordings for Folkways and Elektra (see Book Three). She was married on August 23, 1953, to David H. Holland, a statistician for R. H. Macy's in New York. In the spring and summer of 1958, her singing was reviewed in the *New York State Folklore Quarterly* and the *Kentucky Folklore Journal*. Besides her interest in folk music, Mrs. Holland works as a receptionist-secretary at People's Art Center, Museum of Modern Art, in New York City.

WILL HOLT

Will Holt, born in Portland, Maine, April 30, 1929,[3] is not a traditional folksinger; in fact, he is scarcely to be classified as a singer of folksongs, since he does many things with many kinds of music. But because folksongs are important in one way and another in his musical offerings, he belongs in a book of this kind. He attended

Portland public schools and Phillips Exeter Academy, where the guitar and traditional music caught his fancy. He spent a year at Williams College, Williamstown, Massachusettts.

Will Holt's mother is a singer and a piano accompanist. Will's first folksong performance was at the New Hampshire Folk Festival in May, 1947. In the summers of 1948 and 1949, he studied singing under Dyer-Bennet (*q.v.*) at the School of Minstrelsy in Aspen, Colorado, and guitar with Rey de la Torre. In 1950, Will motorcycled through Europe, particularly in Scandinavia, England, France, Austria, Switzerland, and Italy, singing and collecting ("cursorily," he says) many songs. After this venture he spent thirty months in the United States Air Force.

Holt has studied composition, first with Miriam Gideon, later with Irwin Sonenfield, who had been a pupil of the Hungarian composer, Dohnányi. Besides many arrangements, Holt's original compositions include songs, a string quartet, and a trio for violin, 'cello, and guitar. When, therefore, he turns to a folksong for material, the resultant product is likely to be an art song. In this respect he follows his teacher, Dyer-Bennet.

Will Holt appeared on Arthur Godfrey's "Talent Scouts" in November, 1954. By this time his professional career was well under way, and serious magazines were giving him favorable notice (e.g., *Variety*, February, 1954). He has appeared in café society, at such places as the Village Vanguard in New York and the Crystal Palace in St. Louis. He has made recordings for Stinson Records: a first album entitled *A Will Holt Concert* of songs and ballads in 1954, a second entitled *Pills to Purge Melancholy* (from the eighteenth-century English song writer, Thomas D'Urfey) in 1955 (see Book Three).

Holt's full-length concerts have gone beyond fifty, and brief appearances on radio and television have been numerous. He has been featured on Ford Foundation's "Omnibus" and on the Laclede Symphonette television programs. A recent venture will take him on a team-up tour with the "Dance Drama Duo" of Emily Frankel and Mark Ryder, well-known dancer-choreographers. Will Holt is a young man of talents, as singer and guitarist, with considerable accomplishment to his credit and a bright future ahead.

WALLACE HOUSE

Born on the Channel island of Guernsey, Wallace House from his early days has known English folksongs, learned from parents and many friends. "As a boy he sang in the choir of St. Alban's Cathedral and later in oratorios, grand opera choruses and in

operettas, before taking up his main vocation in life—acting." *
When Wallace was nine, the family moved to Toronto, Canada.

After he grew up, Wallace House came to New York, played in
Broadway shows, developed a serious academic interest in ballads
of all countries, "amassed a considerable repertoire of songs which
he performed in clubs, theatre productions and [on] radio." In time
he became a faculty member of two universities, Columbia and
New York University, specializing in folksong courses.

Professor House is looked upon as a distinguished scholar and
performer in the folksong field, appearing on radio and television as
a "ballad-singing actor" and before his university classes. He has
done many recordings, chiefly for Folkways Records (see Book
Three), and, if one may judge by the recordings, his favorite accompanying instrument is the lute.

CISCO HOUSTON

Gil "Cisco" Houston, actor and ballad singer, was born in Wil-
mington, Delaware, August 18, 1918. His father's people came from
the Carolinas, and his mother's from Virginia. One of his grand-
mothers knew and sang many folksongs. Schooling through the
grades and high school was done in Los Angeles, California, but he
did not attend college.

Cisco Houston has knocked about the world a great deal in the
past twenty years and, as he says, he has "swapped songs on cross-
roads, front steps, in general stores, with sailors aboard ships." During the war years he was with the Merchant Marine. His repertoire
is a vast one and his singing experience extensive.

Cisco traveled and sang in many states with his good friend,
Woody Guthric, for whom he has a great admiration. He was also
a personal friend of Huddie (Leadbelly) Ledbetter, "one of the
mightiest singers of our time," says Houston. And he has known and
worked with such other folk artists as Burl Ives and John Jacob Niles.
The number of his concerts, or recitals, in some thirty or forty states
runs into the hundreds—he has no idea how many. Town Hall,
Madison Square Garden and café society in New York, as well as
schools and churches across the land—all have heard and enjoyed his
singing and guitar strumming.

In the dozen years since World War II, Cisco has made folk-

---

* This sketch is drawn almost exclusively from the booklet of Professor
House's Folkways recording of *English Folk Songs* (FP 823), and the details
are used here by express permission of Folkways Records and Service Corporation, 117 West 46th Street, New York 36, N. Y.

song recordings under the Asch, Stinson, Folkways, Disc, and Coral labels. Three of his recent Folkways albums have had highly favor-- able reviews: *900 Miles and Other Railroad Songs* (FP 13), *Cow- boy Ballads* (FP 22), and *Hard Travelin'* (FP 42). Besides strictly folk music, he has done recording for Decca of his own compositions with, as he says, "folk flavor." Among these are "Green Lilac Hill" and "Ramblin' Gamblin' Man." This latter was aired twice on the Sid Caesar "Show of Shows." *

Obviously an artist of Houston's ability would be in demand for radio and television shows. In the latter field, he has appeared on "American Inventory." During the first quarter of 1955, he was heard regularly over the Mutual Broadcasting System "as one of America's most authentic folk artists."

MAX HUNTER

Max Hunter has been singing practically all his life and in recent years has developed a special interest in folksong. Since his work carries him around the country—in an earlier day he would be called a "drummer"—he has gone into collecting, too. Max was born on July 2, 1921, in Springfield, Missouri, where he received his schooling— grade, junior high, and senior high. He has had some college work in night classes but has taken no degrees.

Max has learned folksongs from records, books, and perhaps most of all from people. When he travels, he carries a tape recorder and gets a song wherever and whenever he can. To quote him: "I have not turned down any kind of song. As an example, two songs I got by taking my recorder and guitar into a very dirty beer parlor and buying a very elderly man a half dozen bottles of beer while he sang. Even I was surprised at the songs this old gent knew! I finally had to stop as the beer began to have its effect."

By the end of 1958 Max had collected over three hundred songs, some of which have been placed in the Folklore Archives at the University of Arkansas. Max has sung at the meetings of the Arkansas Folklore Society and at the Ozark Folk Festival in Eureka Springs.

Max Hunter was married to Virginia L. Mercer on December 25, 1939. They have four children: Linda Lou, born in 1942; Dona Sue, born in 1945; David, born in 1948; and Jenny Lynn, born in 1957. Max is vice president and wholesale jobber with the John A. Rhodes Company, a Springfield firm dealing in appliances and industrial supplies. The family home is near Springfield, Missouri. Again, to

* Cisco has also recorded in the popular field with the orchestras of Lynn Murray, Victor Young, Gordon Jenkins, and George Barnes.

use Max's words: "While I am only a beginner in collecting, I have managed to get a fair start. Sometime, if possible, I should like to make collecting and singing a full-time job."

E. G. HUNTINGTON AND EMILY

Once a commercial fisherman and farmer and now a schoolteacher, Gale Huntington is to be numbered among the traditional folksing-ers. Born in New York City on June 4, 1902, he has lived most of his life on Martha's Vineyard. Because his father was a Navy man, Gale was educated—to use his words—"all over the map." He finished eighth grade at Chilmark, Martha's Vineyard, and completed high school in DeLand, Florida. He holds a Bachelor of Arts degree from Stetson University, Long Island, and a master's in history from Boston University.

Gale has known folksongs all his life, having learned them from his parents, who knew many songs but were not professional singers. Later, he married into a "family of folksingers who were mostly whalemen, merchant sailors and fishermen." Gale considers himself only an amateur, performing mostly at home and at parties. He often sings unaccompanied but also uses the guitar, and sometimes he plays the fiddle for square dances. His first professional appearance, if it may be called that, was with Tom Benton at the Museum of Modern Art in New York about 1930.

E. G. Huntington was married to Mildred Tilton in 1933, and they have one daughter, Emily, born January 28, 1936. This fact leads back to Thomas Hart Benton. For many years painter Benton has maintained a summer home on Martha's Vineyard. The Bentons and the Huntingtons were neighbors and the two girls, Emily Hunting-ton and Jessie Benton (q.v.), were playmates. In the mid-1940's, Benton chose Gale Huntington and daughter Emily to pose for what is surely one of Benton's most appealing canvases—"The Music Lesson."

Over the years E. G. Huntington has collected many folksongs, and he has them all written down, both words and tunes. Someday, he says, "I may get them into a book." And if he does, it will be a good book of authentic songs, for—to quote him again—"I sing the songs as nearly as possible as I remember them sung by the singers I got them from." The world beyond the island has already heard some of them on records by Folkways, Elektra, and Riverside (see Book Three).

And by daughter Emily, too, for she—to quote her father—"has turned out to be a full-fledged folksinger." Emily took a Bachelor of Arts degree at Rochester University with a major in music, and is now working on a master's in communications (radio and television) at Boston University. She performs on Tuesday and Thursday evenings at Boston's Café Yana, which features folk music, and she has a half-hour program singing folksongs on Boston University's radio station WBUR-FM. Emily has learned "the music lesson" well from her folksinging father.

PETER HURD

The distinguished artist Peter Hurd * was born in Roswell, Territory of New Mexico, on February 22, 1904. His primary schooling was under Franciscan nuns in Roswell, with some later work in the public schools. He attended the New Mexico Military Institute at Roswell (1917-20), the United States Military Academy at West Point (1921-23), and Haverford College (1923-24) in Pennsylvania.

After these ventures into the academic world, from which he collected no degrees, Peter Hurd turned to the private study of art at the Pennsylvania Academy of Fine Arts and under the tutelage of N. C. Wyeth. Fame and high honors were not long in coming. He has become well known for his frescoes and murals, his portraits and book illustrations, and he is represented in many of the world's galleries, including the Metropolitan Museum in New York.

Peter Hurd owns and operates the Sentinel Ranch in San Patricio, about fifty miles west of Roswell. Here he carries on his painting, plays polo with neighbors, and is rearing his family. Having grown up among Mexican laborers, all his life he has heard and sung their songs. "Some of his songs were learned from an old Mexican woman who was the family cook for many years." † He has learned, too, from wandering singers and has collected songs "throughout New Mexico and on frequent trips to the Republic of Mexico," traveling by "converted station wagon in which he carries his bunk, paints, a supply of food," ‡ and, no doubt, his Spanish guitar.

In 1936, Peter Hurd gave his first folksong performance, singing New Mexican *ranchera* songs at a private viewing of his "first New York one-man show." He's an expert with the six-string Spanish guitar and has performed in eight states, as well as in England and Mexico. Hurd estimates that his recitals run to "possibly as many as a hundred."

---

* This sketch is based mainly on correspondence with Mr. Hurd, but some facts, used by permission of Folkways, are drawn from the booklet of his Folkways record, *Peter Hurd Sings Ranchera Songs* (1957).
† From J. D. Robb's notes with the Folkways record.
‡ *Ibid.*

Peter Hurd was married to Henriette Wyeth, daughter of the artist, N. C. Wyeth, in 1929. They have three children, two sons and a daughter: Peter Wyeth, born March 22, 1930; Carol, born April 9, 1935; and Michael, born February 16, 1946.

DAN ISAACSON

Dan Isaacson, businessman and singer, was born in New York City on November 16, 1931. He attended the Fieldston Ethical Culture School from 1940 to 1949, then entered Cornell University and received a Bachelor of Music Education degree in 1954.

By 1940, Dan was learning folksongs at the Robinson Crusoe boys' camp. He took up study of the guitar and was performing publicly by 1948, first at a settlement camp in New York State. He learned much from records, from friends, and especially through the ballad and folklore courses of Professor Harold Thompson at Cornell University, where he was Professor Thompson's assistant.

Isaacson has performed in about twenty different states, but most of his folksong activity has been in New York State. His appearances number well over two hundred, besides a radio half-hour series each week over stations WVBR and WITJ-FM in Ithaca, New York, for four years. He was also president of the Folk Song Club while at Cornell, and he has been recorded by the Cornell Recording Society (see Book Three).

Dan Isaacson is an industrial and management engineer with L. Isaacson (his father) and Sons, manufacturers of children's knitwear under the Donmoor trade name. He was married to Rhoda Brenner in 1954, and they are the parents of two sons: Gerald Arthur, born November 5, 1956, and Lawrence David, born June 6, 1958. Dan continues his folksong activity by teaching guitar at Lynbrook, Long Island, and by "playing host at the Hewlett Library periodically for folk sings for anyone interested with or without guitar."

BURL IVES

Among living American folksingers, none has more thoroughly captured the popular imagination than Burl Ives. His name is as well known across the land as the name of Harry Truman or Bing Crosby. Mention the word ballad or folksong in any group, young or old, and somebody is bound to think of Burl Ives. He is a tremendous personality, in more ways than one.

Big, burly, 280-pound Burl Icle Ivanhoe Ives was born in Hunt City Township, Jasper County, Illinois, on June 14, 1909. He was one of six children of tenant farmers, Frank and Dellie Ives,[4] whose

English and Irish ancestors had come to America in the seventeenth century. Most of the time their finances were in a precarious state, as they moved from farm to farm, and eventually into town. Burl, youngest of three boys, grew up in a rough-and-tumble way, had to wear hand-me-downs, and often slept in the middle or at the foot of the bed. This and much else is told with understanding and high good humor in his earthy and entertaining *Wayfaring Stranger*, his first book. Burl attended the public schools in Hunt City, a cross-roads village, and graduated from Newton (Illinois) High School in 1927. He was interested in sports and singing but not too much in books. He had two years at the Eastern Illinois State Teachers College at Charleston.

The Iveses were known as a singing family, and his basic training in folksinging came from family members, especially from his grand-mother Kate White. At the age of four he almost became a profes-sional folksinger when, at the annual old soldiers' reunion, he sang fifteen stanzas of "Barbara Allen" for a dollar and loud applause.[5] During his school days, his singing ability and talent for theatricals found him on the amateur stage at every opportunity. For instance, he played the banjo and sang minstrel songs and old ballads between acts in a home-talent show called "Misery Moon the Hoo-dooed Coon." [6]

But college at Eastern Illinois State was too tame for restless Burl Ives. In the summer of 1929, he left to roam over the country on a vagabonding jaunt that lasted about two years. From the folksinging angle, this was Burl's most important education. With banjo, and later guitar,[7] he sang and listened to songs all the way across the land, covering all of the United States, much of Canada and Mexico. With a prodigious and retentive memory, he added immeasurably to his already considerable store. The going was anything but easy. Often he was hungry, sometimes he was suspect and in trouble with the local constables.

It now seems incredible that so beautiful a song as "The Foggy, Foggy Dew" should have once landed him in jail. But Burl tells the story in good faith, and there is no reason to doubt it. It happened in Mona, Utah.[8] He had gone into a restaurant to sing for his supper—a scheme that usually worked—and was promptly thrown out. Next, trying the park, two policemen objected to "The Foggy Dew" as a "dirty song" and to "bums hanging around this town." He was thrown in jail for a day and a night, then driven in a police car out in the desert and ordered to "get the hell out of here." Strange are the ways of fate: when, years later, Fame had touched him with her magic wand, it was "The Foggy, Foggy Dew" that virtually became his trade-mark.

Back home in 1931, Burl thought he might try college again and enrolled in the State Teachers College in Terre Haute, Indiana. But bumming around hadn't settled him down; he soon concluded he couldn't "make with the academic stuff," dropped out, played professional football, sang over a radio station in Terre Haute for a couple of years, and even traveled as a singer with an evangelist.

Eventually he got to New York, played and sang here, there, and everywhere he could to get food and shelter. After many false starts, he got a small singing part in *The Boys from Syracuse*, a part called "tailor's apprentice" written especially for him. Thus began his meteoric rise in the entertainment world. He appeared in *Ah, Wilderness!*, in *I Married an Angel*, and finally in 1940 he made the big-time broadcasting with his ballad program called "The Wayfaring Stranger."

Burl Ives served in the Army for eighteen months (1942-44) and in April, 1942, was a singing star in Irving Berlin's *This Is the Army*.[9] He did much entertaining of servicemen during his Army days and afterward. In 1944, he began a long engagement at Cafe Society Uptown in New York, and in December, 1945, came his formal Town Hall debut. The same year he was a singing cowboy in the film version of Will James's *Smoky*. And the same year he was a featured singer in the Theatre Guild's *Sing Out, Sweet Land*, a great Broadway success. The show moved on to Chicago, where Burl Ives, now famous, had a touching reunion when his whole family came up to see the big show and hear him sing.

This was a moment of triumph for Burl Ives. When he went on stage to sing his first number, "The Foggy, Foggy Dew," the words and story flowed through him in a quiet current of emotion, and he "lifted poetry and music as one would hold up a fine and rare jewel for all to behold." [10] The prodigal son, once more in the bosom of his happy family, his name on the lips of millions, must have let his mind drift back fifteen years when, despised and rejected, he tramped out the lonely night in a Western desert.

The most remarkable thing about Burl Ives is his tremendous zest for life, his variety of interests, his many accomplishments. Besides his top activity as America's best-known folksinger, he is actor, writer, sailor, collector of all sorts of curious things. In folksong concerts he has been heard not only all over America, from the lowliest bar to staid Constitution Hall, but in many other parts of the world —in the Orient, in Russia, England, on the Continent, in Australia and New Zealand. Some think of him as a natural-born singer, even an untutored rustic. Nothing could be further from fact. Natural talent he has, and great sincerity, too, but his seeming simplicity is a seriously studied art, both in singing and in acting, the artlessness of great art.

In 1953, Ives published his first collection of songs,[11] 115 of them from his vast repertoire. The next year appeared his fine collection of tales picked up in his travels throughout the land.[12] In the spring of 1955, Ives began acting a major role, Big Daddy, in Tennessee Williams' Pulitzer Prize play, *Cat on a Hot Tin Roof*. This was his first non-singing role in a major Broadway show.

The popular sale of his many recordings has been nothing less than phenomenal. The big companies like Decca and Columbia have released more than a dozen major LP's in the past dozen years (see Book Three), not to mention the pressings of many lesser companies. The Library of Congress *List of American Folk Songs Currently* [1953] *Available on Records* shows far more entries under Burl Ives than for any other of the three hundred singers listed. His most ambitious single undertaking thus far in recording, however, and the one likely to last the longest, was his educational series for Encyclopaedia Britannica Films. Here, in six albums of thirty 12-inch records (78 rpm unbreakable vinylite), containing 123 songs, he presents "Historical America in Song." [13] In preparation for this series, Ives spent the better part of two years, and the actual recording was done over a period of three months.

In Chicago on December 6, 1945, Burl Icle Ivanhoe Ives married Helen Payne, his former radio script writer. They have an adopted son, Alexander, born February 19, 1949. They bought a primitive old house (no running water, no electricity) on a spit of land out on Long Island,[14] and they maintain a sprawling old-fashioned apartment in New York City, as well as a home in Hollywood.

Burl Ives loves the water. During the early 1940's, when he was singing in night clubs, theaters, and on radio, he lived for four years on an old houseboat, the *Water Gypsy*, anchored off Whitestone Landing in the Long Island Sound. Here he led a quiet but often gay life, and when he went to Hollywood to work in films, he gave a famous party that even Perle Mesta or Elsa Maxwell might have envied. (See *Life* magazine, July 2, 1945.) He loves sailing and he has owned a number of sailing boats. He once told columnist Hal Boyle: "If I didn't have to earn a living I'd spend the rest of my life riding around on a boat." [15]

Nomad that he is, Burl Ives nevertheless likes to collect things. He bought from government surplus a complete set (forty of them) of battleship flags, not to mention a couple of big parade drums he expects to make into lamps. He picked up a Maori war club in New Zealand. In England, he bought two large wooden ship figureheads, one of Pocahontas, one of Vasco de Gama. He bought a new Italian motor scooter and found it "more fun than a Rolls-Royce." He once owned a goat ranch in California. Someday he'd like to play Falstaff, and surely no actor is better fitted for the role, in size, in temperament, in zest for life. But with all this interest in material things, it is well to remember that folksongs are his permanent love, that folksongs catapulted him to fame. Someday, he once told a reporter, he'd like to make a world tour with camerman and soundman and record all kinds of national folk music and dances. No one could do it better, for there is perhaps no other in our time who has the earthy touch common to all kinds of humanity in all parts of the globe.[16]

MERRICK JARRETT

Merrick Jarrett, born in Toronto, Canada, on October 4, 1924, attended private and public schools, leaving high school after three years. He next attended the Radio College of Canada, in Toronto, graduating as a commercial wireless operator. He studied further at the Dominion Business College, also in Toronto.

Merrick's introduction to folksongs stems from his early years, when his mother taught him many children's songs. His interest grew as he listened to numerous recordings, particularly those of Burl Ives, Richard Dyer-Bennet, Josh White, Woody Guthrie, Alan Mills, and Ed McCurdy. Eventually he came to know most of these singers personally. In Gander, Newfoundland, when he was stationed there during World War II as a radio operator, he won an amateur folksong contest and began singing over station VORG. This was in 1943. About this time also he became interested in collecting, and in swapping songs with other singers, eventually building a repertoire of some three hundred songs.

Besides his singing in Newfoundland, Jarrett has performed in the provinces of Quebec and Ontario, as well as in New York and Pennsylvania. He has been heard over the Canadian Broadcasting network on one of the folksong programs of Edith Fowke,* In the main, however, Jarrett prefers not to extend his singing of folksongs into the professional field. Someday he hopes to publish, perhaps privately, his own collection of folksongs.

Merrick Jarrett was married in 1948 and has two children: Linda, born in 1949, and Stephen, born in 1951. Since the war, Mr. Jarrett

* Mrs. Fowke is a folksong record authority and an editor of an excellent collection, *Folk Songs of Canada*. (See Book Two.)

has been in the publishing business, working in the firm of W. J. Gage and Company, Limited, of Toronto. He is in the elementary- and high-school textbook division, as advertising and promotion manager.

GENE JEMISON

Coming a little too late for the sod house or covered wagon, he was nevertheless nurtured on the prairie, the Kansas prairie "that gave him a song and a slogan." Eugene Jemison, artist, teacher, and folksinger, was born on a farm in the Solomon Valley near the village of Alton in north-central Kansas, May 20, 1916. After grade- and high-school days in Osborne County, he attended Washburn Uni- versity, Topeka, taking a Bachelor of Fine Arts degree in 1946.

The next step brought Gene to Kansas City, where he continued his studies and began teaching at the Kansas City Art Institute and School of Design. The institute granted him a Master of Fine Arts degree in 1948 and made him a full member of the faculty. Further interest in study took him to New York, at the Art Students League (1952), Columbia University (1952-53), Hunter College (1953), and the New School for Social Research (1953).

The "song" the Kansas prairie gave him was a folksong. His mother's people were Kentuckians, and his father's family migrated from Pennsylvania to stake out a new home in Kansas. Two uncles and his father were ballad singers, for a time turning professional and touring the Midwest, with fiddle, banjo, and guitar. Gene learned folksongs from his family and neighbors, and he practiced music on the reed organ, a common instrument in the country homes of a generation and more ago. At the age of six Gene made his "debut" in a country school, singing the pathetic and lugubrious ballad, "The Drunkard's Lone Child."

Gene Jemison is a man of many talents, of independent and quiet thoughts. Going away to college and art school didn't dampen his interest in his folksong background. Rather, he sought ways to blend that background with his work in art. Perhaps, too, he was fortunate in that his intellectual life was maturing during the decades that saw the revival of American folksong. He has done painting and many prints based on lines from the old ballads. His belief is that the old songs have a hard core of realism and fundamental honesty, that in them there are strong visual images and powerful ideas use- ful to the painter,[17] that what folk music has to offer is much needed in our society today.

During the past decade Gene Jemison has performed in over a

dozen states, as well as in Mexico and Canada. Aside from spot appearances at folk festivals and elsewhere, he has given well over a hundred recitals. His first folksong album, *Solomon Valley Ballads* (see Book Three), issued in 1954,[18] is a fulfillment of his plan to blend the aural and visual arts. With this LP record of nine songs, Jemison has published a 7" x 9" brochure containing twelve prints interpreting the ballad stories. He has also made a short folk film at Teachers College, Columbia, using similar materials. To quote him on this idea of synthesizing the arts, Jemison has said: "It is my hope to produce a series of films, records, prints, and paintings over the years in which the old idea or custom of illustrating folksongs and ballads may be revived through modern media and techniques, i.e., the motion picture, modern woodblock, and the monotype."

Though Gene's major work is a busy teaching schedule at the Kansas City Art Institute, he finds time for other activities. He has studied folk music with John Jacob Niles, he is a member of the Society for the Classical Guitar, and during the winter he teaches a class in guitar and folk music. He has done some folksong collecting in the Solomon Valley and has taped songs during his stay at International House in New York City, but collecting—except in the music division of many libraries—is not one of his major activities.

Eugene Jemison was married to Louise Burton in September, 1949. They have one daughter, Jeanie, born in 1951, and she, too, is learning folksongs as she grows up.

BUELL H. KAZEE

Buell Hilton Kazee, minister, distinguished Bible teacher, and folksinger, was born August 29, 1900, in a log house on Burton Fork near Falcon, Magoffin County, eastern Kentucky. He grew up in a singing family, where music of the outside world seldom penetrated before 1915, but where the Kazee home was the musical center for ballads, instrumental music, dancing, and religious songs, old and new. He reports that his father led the music, unaccompanied, at church and that his mother "sang Elizabethan ballads over the dish water."

Kazee's early schooling was in a log schoolhouse on Mash Fork in Magoffin County. He graduated from high school in 1920 at Magoffin Institute, a Baptist mission school then at Salyersville, Kentucky, but now at Pleasant Valley in Breathitt County. He took a Bachelor of Arts degree in 1925 at Georgetown College, Georgetown, Kentucky.

Buell Kazee has known folksongs all his life. He began picking the banjo when he was five years old, and one of his early banjos was a homemade instrument.* He had much native ability, developed a fine tenor voice, gave folksong recitals at various times, and as a young man did a great deal of singing and playing in eastern Kentucky and neighboring areas. Meanwhile, he had learned to play the guitar and the piano. Though he has studied harmony and theory, he still plays his instruments largely by ear. Though he had several opportunities to make a career out of folksinging, his first love through the years has been the ministry, which he entered at the age of seventeen.

All his life, however, he has maintained a continuous interest in folk music. His first major performance was at the University of Kentucky in 1925. Kazee reports that, when he first went to college, he was somewhat ashamed of the old songs; but, after a course in Shakespeare, he found himself at home in the Elizabethan world and thereafter began studying and singing the old songs as cultural matter. At one time he worked at collecting ballads and folksongs. On one of his trips, however, he lost a suitcase containing all his collection, and so never tried to make another. During the years 1926 to 1930, Mr. Kazee made no fewer than fifty-two recordings for Brunswick and Vocalion—records no longer on the market except as collectors' items. Among these recordings are such well-known folksongs as "Darling Cora," "East Virginia," "John Hardy," "The Little Mohee," "Rock Island Line," "The Roving Cowboy," "The Butcher's Boy," and "The Hobo's Last Ride." The master discs of these recordings are now owned by Decca.

Kazee has been highly praised for his style of folksinging. For example, Alan Lomax spoke of his singing and playing as some of the most genuine we have on records. He has performed in high schools, colleges, and clubs in several states, and he has done some composing. He wrote the dramatic sequence for *The White Pilgrim,* for which the composer-teacher Lewis Henry Horton made the musical arrangements. This is said to be the first folk cantata in America.[19] He has an unpublished folk operetta awaiting musical arrangement.

---

* Kazee's description of this banjo is worth quoting, since it indicates how folk instruments sometimes came into being: "The neck of the banjo had been whittled out of a piece of walnut, and the hoop or head band was made of a thin split from white oak sapling, bent in the shape of an old-fashioned sieve, with a home-tanned cat hide stretched over it and tacked around the edges with carpet tacks for a 'head.' The holes for the wooden keys were made by a burning iron, and the strings were steel, bought from the country store for five cents. There were, of course, no frets nor brackets on the banjo. This allowed complete freedom for sliding the fretting fingers, and giving the quarter tones so often heard in folk tunes."

Besides his folksinging activities, which have been considerable over the years, Mr. Kazee has been a teacher of voice, a gospel singer, a director of choirs and glee clubs, a writer, and—of first importance to him—a minister of the gospel. For twenty-two years he was pastor of the First Baptist Church in Morehead, Kentucky. Aside from many articles in religious periodicals, he has published a book on religious faith entitled *Faith Is the Victory*.[20] Since 1950 he has been professor of Old Testament at Lexington Baptist College, in Lexington, Kentucky, and he also continues his preaching activities.

Buell H. Kazee was married in June, 1929, to Lucille Jones of Corbin, Kentucky. From this union he has two grown sons: Allan Jones, born March 24, 1930, and Philip Ray, born February 23, 1933. Both young men were in military service in the late 1950's. Philip Ray recently graduated from Georgetown College, his father's alma mater. His first marriage being terminated in 1940, Buell Kazee was married in October, 1950, to Jennie Turnmyre of Wilson, North Carolina.

BRADLEY KINCAID

Radio listeners of the middle 1920's will recall The Prairie Farmer Station, WLS, of Chicago, and a tenor singer who was introduced as the "Original Authentic Folksong Singer." That singer was Bradley Kincaid, "the first to introduce folksongs or mountain ballads to radio," [21] and the person who "sang Barbara Allen on WLS every Saturday night for four years by request."

Bradley Kincaid was born at Point Leavell, Kentucky, July 13, 1895. His parents were Kentucky mountain farmers, and Brad was one of ten children. The family lived in a frame-and-log house of four rooms and a loft. Brad had little schooling until he was nearly grown, attending first to fifth grades three months each year at Stony Point School in Garrard County in central Kentucky. After two years in the lower school at Berea College, he spent two years in the United States Army during World War I, serving one year in France. He returned to Berea College and finished the high-school course in 1922. His next formal schooling was in Chicago, where he attended the YMCA College and George Williams College, graduating from the latter in 1928.

Brad is a traditional folksinger, having heard old songs all his life, learning from his parents and neighbors and later, beginning in 1927, taking "trips through the mountains learning songs from the old settlers." His first guitar was one his father obtained from a Negro friend, in exchange for a foxhound. Brad called this his "houn' dog guitar."

Kincaid's professional career began in August, 1925, when he first sang over radio station WLS. After 1928, for some twenty years he played the vaudeville circuit in theaters throughout the country, usually doing three shows a day. He sang not only the authentic ballads but others that he composed in the folk-ballad style.

In 1922, Bradley Kincaid was married to Irma Forman, a graduate of Oberlin College Conservatory. They have four children, now grown: twin daughters named Barbara and Alene (!) and two sons, Billy and Jimmy. For some time the Kincaids have lived in Springfield, Ohio, where Brad is president and part owner of radio station WWSO.

MARTY KING

Some people have done so much in the folksong field, it becomes a problem to decide what to include in a brief sketch. Martha Bennett King—writer, teacher, folksong enthusiast—is one of these. She was born into the Bennett family October 26, 1902, at Darlington, Wisconsin. Early schooling was at Darlington and at Oak Park, Illinois. She attended the University of Chicago, graduating in 1924 with a Bachelor of Science degree.

Marty King came from a singing family but insists that she is only a singer of folksongs and not a folksinger. Her maternal grandmother, uncles, and her father knew many ballads and folksongs. At one time her father sang with a male quartet that traveled across the country giving concerts: their repertoire included folksongs. From ages fourteen to twenty-one, Marty was trained to be a singer of classical music, but the interest did not last. Her mother had a low opinion of folk music sung by "characters" in the town or by the kitchen help. But Marty hung around anybody who sang anything and "absorbed everything from barroom songs to Negro spirituals and minstrel songs."

Besides family interests, a major activity of Marty King for the past thirty years has been her work in children's literature and the children's theater. Her plays for children, such as *The Snow Queen*, *Peter Peter Pumpkin Eater*, and *Papa Pompino and the Prizefighter*, have been produced all over the country and translated into several foreign languages. They have been published by the Children's Theatre Press, Coach House Press, and Harcourt, Brace and Company. She has become a specialist in children's literature and is a book reviewer for the Chicago *Tribune*'s magazine section. She also directs the *Tribune*'s big annual book fair for children, the Miracle of Books.

Familiar with folksongs all her life, Marty King began singing them professionally in 1947. She gives many programs for women's clubs, teachers' and library groups, and for any group that works with children. Her special interest is "to give a new dimension to American history and American ways of life" through folksong. In the past dozen years she has given programs—hundreds of them—in about half the states of the Union, from Georgia to Minnesota and New York to California. She plays the guitar and sometimes the dulcimer.

One of the fascinating accomplishments of Marty King in recent years is a series of educational recordings entitled "Adventures in Folk Song" (Gloria Chandler Recordings, Inc.). The series portrays the fortunes of the typical American family on their 150-year-long journey through history. Through meticulous research she maintains a high degree of historical accuracy, and through her gift of direct and clear speech she "clothes the dry skeleton of dead events ... with vitality and interest and fun and adventure.... The 95 songs used in the series have been as skillfully woven into scripts as they were woven into the lives of the pioneers." [22]

Marty King has written a great deal about folksongs. A fine example is her long feature article entitled "Folksongs Alive." [23] Here she presents an account of the changing character and the changing uses of folksongs. But she points out how their toughness and genuineness, and "the pure pleasure of singing" them, will keep them alive. She is now assembling a book of folksongs for publication [24] —some she has collected, some drawn from her family background, and many others she has loved and sung. Mrs. King also teaches a class in American folklore and folksong in the downtown college of the University of Chicago.

Martha Bennett was married to William Barrett King in 1925. They have two sons: Thomas Barrett King, born January 13, 1926, and Bennett King, born February 8, 1927. Marty King's lifelong interest in children's education through folksong took a new turn not long ago. She became a proud grandmother: her first grandchild, Sara Church King, was born November 8, 1954.

BARRY KORNFELD

Though he spent a year at Cooper Union studying engineering, Barry Kornfeld, born in New York City on November 17, 1937, soon concluded that engineering was not his field. Earlier schooling was at P.S. 73 in the Bronx and the Bronx High School of Science. He enrolled at Queens College, New York City, spent two years working toward a bio-education major, but found himself entranced by the world of music, particularly folk music. This last has become his prime interest, and he is now working toward a degree in music, class of 1960.

Barry's family were not musicians or folksingers. Singers in the big city have been his mentors, among them the Reverend Gary Davis. He has developed rapidly since 1952, and is looking toward a career in the folk-music field. He has become proficient with the five-string banjo, the guitar, and occasionally uses mandolin, dulcimer, harmonica, and recorder. He plans to become a full-time performer but at present, he writes, "schooling prevents much traveling for this purpose, so I depend on teaching guitar for a living."

Barry has been closely associated with various metropolitan groups of folksong enthusiasts and has published much in the two little magazines in the field, *Sing Out!* and *Caravan*. In fact, he does much editorial work for the latter. In addition to performing, he has been a director of folk music for American Youth Hostels, for the Buck's Rock Work Camp, and has been a faculty member of the Metropolitan Music School and the Scarsdale Adult School. His writing (see articles in *Caravan*, August-September and October-November 1958) displays the easy informality and clarity of a seasoned journalist. The folksong world will hear more of this clearheaded and talented musician, teacher, and writer, Barry Kornfeld.

THE KOSSOY TWINS, ELLEN AND IRENE

Ellen and Irene Kossoy were born in New York City in May, 1938. They attended P.S. 12 together in Queens, after which Irene went to the School of Industrial Art and Ellen to the William Cullen Bryant High School. In the fall of 1956, they entered Blackburn College at Carlinville, Illinois, and remained for two years. In the summer of 1958, Ellen attended the University of Rhode Island and Irene the University of Pennsylvania. In September, Irene returned to Blackburn and Ellen enrolled at Alfred University, Alfred, New York.

The Kossoy twins began singing folksongs in the early 1950's, and they have learned from friends, records, and books. They both play guitar and banjo, occasionally use mandolin and autoharp, and make up their own arrangements. One of their early performances —they sing together as an act—was at the Circle-in-the-Square in New York City on January 27, 1956. They have performed only in New York and Illinois but already have one LP record (see Book Three) to their credit. They intend to continue their folksong activities as a major side line.

MR. AND MRS. ADOLPH KUKLER

The story of the Kuklers is as fascinating and romantic as the Austrian folk music they play and sing. Adolph Hugo Christian Kukler, a descendant of once well-to-do landowners, was born in Vienna, Austria, January 20, 1889.[25] (On a corner shelf in the Kukler living room is a small wooden model of a castle. The original castle was once owned by Mr. Kukler's great-grandfather.) He attended public school in Vienna. When he was twelve, he came with his parents to America, settling in Johnstown, Pennsylvania. He grew up like many an American boy, working at many jobs, from grocery boy to farmer's helper. But there was one difference: Adolph loved music and remembered many old songs, and in Vienna he had learned to play the zither, a skill which he continued to practice in America. (In Vienna, too, he was an altar boy and sang in a church choir.)

Augusta Maria Holzer was born in the historic town of Fuerstenfeld, not far from Vienna. She came to America in her teens with a girl friend and settled in Pittsburgh and, on a visit to Johnstown, she first met Adolph Kukler. But their ways soon parted, for the Holzers moved to New York City, and restless young Kukler moved on to the upper Midwest. Augusta married William Cochran in New York, and they had one daughter, Flora Augusta, born October 7, 1909. William Cochran died April 7, 1911. Some years later, through mutual friends, Adolph and Augusta began a correspondence that eventually led to their marriage. Sixteen years after their first meeting in Johnstown, Augusta boarded a train in New York City for the long journey out to the northern Minnesota village of Blackduck, where they were married on November 24, 1923.

Over the years Adolph Kukler worked at many occupations— farming, mining, logging, and in factories. In the 1940's they were living in Milwaukee, where Mr. Kukler was a crane operator. In 1949, when he retired from this job, they took a vacation to Eureka Springs, Arkansas, where they decided to "settle down for good." In this enchanting setting of the Arkansas Ozarks, these transplanted folksingers pursue their interest in music.

If you should ask the Kuklers from whom they learned folksongs, they would answer, "Oh, in Austria everybody sings them." (It should be noted that they know much other music, too, for the zither is truly a concert instrument.) So the Kuklers have brought another strain of music into the Arkansas hills. Dressed in their native Austrian costumes, they sing at many festivals, blending their voices with the beautiful tones of the zither. They have performed at the Ozark

Folk Festival in Eureka Springs, for the Arkansas Folklore Society in Fayetteville, at the St. Clair (Missouri) Folk Festival, and on many other occasions. By special arrangement, Mr. Kukler "plays the zither for the music of the masses at St. Elizabeth's Catholic Church in Eureka Springs and sings the high mass on Wednesdays." [26] The Kuklers made recordings of zither music and Austrian folksongs in 1951.*

Among their hobbies, the Kuklers enjoy working in a miniature garden which, despite its postage-stamp appearance, yields an abundance of flowers and vegetables. Mr. Kukler is also a skilled cabinetmaker and wood carver, and in his shop makes picture frames, easels, crosses, candlesticks, and some furniture. Still more important is the fine collection of zithers which he has brought together over the years. Oldest of these is an Austrian product made by Anton Kindl in 1810. Several come from the quondam Schwarzer Zither Factory at Washington, Missouri.[27] "Zither music is something of a lost art," Mrs. Kukler says, "and we are trying to bring it before the people by showing our collection of zithers and demonstrating their use." And any visitor dropping in to see the Kuklers and their collection is likely to have a rare treat of zither music. All in all, the Kuklers live a full and happy life in their new-found haven in the Ozarks. (In October, 1959, Mr. Kukler appeared on the television show, "Name That Tune," won some money, and entertained with zither music.)

CHARLENE KUNITZ

California born and educated, with special training in the field of music, Charlene Robbins turned to the singing and teaching of folk music after leaving college. She was born on July 31, 1929, in Los Angeles, where she received her formal education, from elementary school through university. She entered the University of California at Los Angeles in 1948 and was granted a Bachelor of Arts in music in 1952.

Charlene's family were not folk musicians, but her "father had an unusually fine untrained tenor voice." She learned from the usual sources—books and people, singers like Bess Lomax Hawes, Frank Hamilton, Pete Seeger, Vivian Richmond, and others. In 1951, Charlene gave a recital of Spanish folksongs at Royce Hall (U.C. L.A.) and, in 1952, she took up the study of the Spanish guitar.

Charlene Robbins was married to Donald Kunitz on June 27, 1954, and they moved to Kansas City, Missouri, soon afterward. Charlene

* Records are obtainable from Adolph Kukler, 92 South Main Street, Eureka Springs, Arkansas.

has given folksong recitals in half a dozen states, perhaps as many as two hundred performances, besides programs on radio and TV. In the summer of 1958, she did a series of TV films for educational distribution called "Folk Songs for Children" for station KETC in St. Louis. In Kansas City, she has taught guitar at the Conservatory of Music, and in 1958 did a twenty-week series called "This Land of Song" over station WDAF. Her husband, Donald Kunitz, is assistant production manager of a national medical magazine. The Kunitzes have a daughter, Judith Liza, born January 14, 1959.

~~~~~~

FOOTNOTES TO CHAPTER 5

1 Facts gleaned from conversations with Fred High, from letters, and from his booklets.
2 "The Singer of Folk Songs and His Conscience," *Western Folklore,* XIV, 170-73 (July, 1955).
3 I am indebted to Will Holt for biographical facts, with some fill-in of details from Kenneth S. Goldstein's notes on Holt's Stinson album SLP #64.
4 Many sources have contributed to this sketch, the chief ones being Mr. and Mrs. Burl Ives and Burl's fine autobiography, *Wayfaring Stranger* (New York: Whittlesey House, 1948). There are good brief sketches in *Current Biography* (January, 1946) and *The International Who Is Who in Music,* Fifth Edition (Chicago, 1951), as well as accounts in many magazines and newspapers.
5 *Wayfaring Stranger,* pp. 15-20.
6 *Ibid.,* pp. 73-74.
7 *Ibid.,* p. 128. Just outside Kansas City, Burl was knocked off a fast-moving freight by a railroad "bull" who mashed his fingers with a "billy stick." The neck and the head of his banjo were broken beyond repair. Walking back to town, he picked up a pawnshop guitar and hit the road again.
8 *Ibid.* Burl says he was in a little "town called Mona in a Western state." Mention of the desert fixes it as Mona, Utah.
9 *International Who Is Who in Music,* p. 235.
10 *Wayfaring Stranger,* pp. 248-53.
11 *The Burl Ives Song Book* (New York: Ballantine Books, 1953), 304 pp.
12 *Burl Ives' Tales of America* (Cleveland and New York: The World Publishing Company, 1954), 305 pp.
13 Specially produced for schools and released in the early 1950's, the set sold (in 1953) for about $60, but individual albums could be purchased. Titles of the albums: I) *Songs of the Colonies,* II) *Songs of the Revolution,* III) *Songs of North and South,* IV) *Songs of the Sea,* V) *Songs of the Frontier,* VI) *Songs of Expanding America.* The development, as the album titles suggest, is partly chronological, partly regional.
14 G. N. Allen in the Kansas City *Star,* December 4, 1955.
15 Hal Boyle in the Kansas City *Star,* May 13, 1955. Ives has edited a book

of sea shanties, *Sea Songs of Sailing, Whaling, and Fishing* (New York: Ballantine Books, 1956).

16 Hal Boyle again.

17 Winifred Shields, "Art and Artists," Kansas City *Star*, March 19, 1954.

18 Folkways Record, FP 23.

19 Published in 1940 by H. W. Gray Co., New York.

20 Published in 1941 by Wm. B. Eerdmans Co., Grand Rapids, Michigan.

21 So far as I can learn, this claim has not been disputed, though it is a difficult point to check. Kincaid's little booklet, *My Favorite Mountain Ballads and Old-Time Songs*, first published in 1928, is said to be the first folk song-book offered for sale on radio. Now out of print, it went through five or six editions, the last being "upwards of 50,000 copies." I am indebted to Mr. Kincaid for biographical facts and to his introductory sketch in the songbook mentioned.

22 From the review in the *Service Bulletin of the FREC* (Federal Radio Education Committee), February, 1950.

23 *The University of Chicago Magazine*, April, 1955.

24 Illustrated by her brother, Rainey Bennett, and to be published by Doubleday and Co., according to Mrs. King.

25 My good friends, Mr. and Mrs. Kukler, have told me the main biographical details. Some facts are drawn from two brief articles: one by Elizabeth Lewis in the *Northwest Arkansas Times* of Fayetteville, June 22, 1956; the other by Bonnie Lela Crump in the *Arkansas Democrat Sunday Magazine* of Little Rock, April 1, 1951.

26 *Northwest Arkansas Times*, June 22, 1956.

27 See the discussion on musical instruments, Interlude I. The Kuklers appeared on television on the "U. S. Steel Hour," January 16, 1957. They sang Austrian folksongs, played zither music, and exhibited their collection of zithers.

CHAPTER 6

The Singers,
L to M

JOHN LANGSTAFF

Lecturer, teacher, and concert singer, John Langstaff was born in New York City on December 24, 1922. He attended the Choate School in Connecticut, Grace Church Choir School in New York, Curtis Institute of Music in Philadelphia, the Juilliard School of Music in New York, and Columbia University.

John learned folk music from his family—they were amateur musicians—and from traditional singers in the Appalachians and in England. In his singing he sometimes uses the piano or dulcimer, but he likes to sing many folksongs unaccompanied. Though not a field collector, he has published three books (Harcourt, Brace & Co.), all based on folk material: *Frog Went A-Courtin'*, *Over in the Meadow*, and *On Christmas Day in the Morning*.

John Langstaff has performed in well over four hundred concerts, in forty-nine states, in most of the Canadian provinces, and in England, Switzerland, and Holland. His concerts are not exclusively folksongs, of course. He has made a number of LP recordings (see Book Three) and more are in the making.

John Langstaff was married to Nancy Graydon Woodbridge in 1948. They have four children: Carol Diane, John Elliot, Peter Gerry, and Deborah Graydon. Mr. Langstaff is head of the music department of the Potomac School, Washington, D.C., and is an artist-lecturer for the Association of American Colleges. The family home is at Turkey Run Road, McLean, Virginia.

138

LEADBELLY

Any sampling of twentieth-century folksingers would be wholly inadequate without some discussion, however brief, of the famous Huddie Ledbetter, better known as Leadbelly. Much has been written about him and much remains to be written, for his was a strange, enigmatic personality. Perhaps none knew him better than his two friends and benefactors, John and Alan Lomax, who published the first book about him—*Negro Songs As Sung by Lead Belly.**

The exact date of Leadbelly's birth is unknown, but Alan Lomax suggests the year 1888.[1] He grew up on a farm at the eastern edge of Texas, a few miles from Shreveport, Louisiana, of mixed Negro and Cherokee Indian parentage. Very early he showed a keen interest in music and at home he learned lullabies, play songs, and spirituals from his mother. His first musical instrument was a small accordion, then later he acquired a guitar and eventually his famous twelve-string guitar. In his youth he rambled a good deal, but Shreveport was his center of activity, where he seems to have lived a primitive, violent life. Frequently in trouble, he was eventually sentenced to thirty years in the Texas penitentiary. After six years he literally sang his way out of prison with a pardon from obdurate Governor Pat Neff. This was in 1925. In five years he was back in prison, this time at Angola in Louisiana. Again, after four years, he sang his way out with a pardon from Governor Allen. Then came the turning point in his career, for it was about this time, 1934, that he met the Lomaxes.[2]

For the next fifteen years Leadbelly experienced a degree of success, at least musical if not financial, that few would have thought possible. He first traveled with the Lomaxes through the South, ostensibly as a bodyguard, as they collected songs in prisons from Arkansas eastward. Using what now seems like a cumbersome recording machine, they visited state prisons and farms in Arkansas, Alabama, Georgia, South Carolina, and North Carolina. Eventually they reached Washington and Philadelphia, where, under the watchful eye of John Lomax, Leadbelly entertained the scholarly convention of the Modern Language Association. Their destination was New York City, where Leadbelly experienced his years of triumph.

---

* Published by The Macmillan Company in 1936. Part I is a 64-page biography; Part II presents forty-eight songs, together with Leadbelly's incomparable commentary. I am indebted to the Lomax book for some biographical details, as well as to other sources cited. Details used by permission of Alan Lomax.

But he was difficult to hold within respectable bounds—drink and women menaced him. After about a year he broke with John Lomax and went his own way.[3]

Each man, however, had served the other's purpose. Lomax was better able to collect songs in the prisons because of Leadbelly's help; Leadbelly won his freedom and was introduced to the professional world of folksong because of John Lomax's sponsorship. Leadbelly gave many concerts: over the networks, in Town Hall, in Hollywood, to college audiences, and eventually in Paris.[4] He made many recordings (more than one hundred in the Library of Congress Archive), not only for the record companies like Columbia, Musicraft, Victor, Capitol, Asch, Disc, Stinson, and Folkways, but tape recordings for friends and private companies.

Leadbelly died December 6, 1949, at Bellevue Hospital in New York City.[5] The following month, a memorial concert was given by his folksinging friends, Alan Lomax, Josh White, Pete Seeger, and others. How account for the fascination of this restless wandering singer, this "badman minstrel," this "hard-drinking, hell-raising Lead Belly," as *Time* magazine (December 19, 1949) characterized him? His voice was not beautiful. Ramsey and others speak of it as rough and grainy, as having a "nasal twang." But Leadbelly was a personality, a vigorous and compelling personality. Furthermore, he was a superb storyteller. It was his habit to introduce a song with a preliminary spoken story, so that the listener was in the mood when the song came. Thus, as the Lomaxes have pointed out, he was a true folk artist, transmuting the materials he found into something different, often something strange and beautiful, into a new song. Above all, he loved to sing, and he loved his guitar. His friend, Woody Guthrie, said: "The sight and the feel of his music box in his hands lit up those homeless stretches of his spirit." [6]

Alan Lomax's comment on his singing offers a good summing up:

> His steel voice, his steel arm on the twelve strings and his high-voltage personality captured audiences everywhere. More than any other singer, he demonstrated to a streamlined, city-oriented world that America had living folkmusic —swamp primitive, angry, freighted with great sorrow and great joy.[7]

As one reads and ponders Leadbelly's tragic and fascinating story, he is struck by the fact that here was a tortured spirit whose only release was music, sexuality, and strong drink, or to put it more poetically—wine, women, and song!

ARCHIE LEE

Kentucky born, reared, and educated, Archie Lee has spent all his life in his native state, except for a stretch in the Army in World War II. He was born at Albany in south-central Kentucky, July 26, 1920, attended a one-room country school, and at eighteen graduated from Clinton County High School. He studied two years at Western Kentucky State College, before entering the service. In 1940, he again returned to Kentucky State for a semester, transferred to the University of Kentucky, and graduated in 1952 with a Bachelor of Arts degree, majoring in the radio arts.

As Archie Lee's parents, grandparents, and other relatives were (nonprofessional) folksingers, he has known and sung folksongs since childhood. He sang them "publicly" while in elementary school and at ten was learning to use the guitar. Now he uses either the guitar or the dulcimer, making up his own arrangements (not writing them down), but not altering the original tunes. As he said, "I learn and sing most of my songs by ear. If I change them at all, it is usually just the combination of two or more sets of words and an occasional bit of rephrasing."

His *dulcimore* (he prefers that spelling to the more common *dulcimer*) has been in the family for about 140 years. It was handed down to him by his grandmother (nee Alice Guffey) and was made either by or for Sol Guffey (originally McGuffey) in 1817. It is a long oval in shape, has pegholes for four strings, but Archie uses only three strings. Two are tuned in unison and the third is tuned a fifth lower, a common method of tuning for the dulcimer. (See discussion under Musical Instruments.) The tune is developed on one string, either with a noter or one finger, and the other two strings are drones.

Archie Lee is a radio announcer and singer on station WHOP in Hopkinsville, Kentucky, where he has had a featured weekly broadcast of folksongs. In this work he uses both guitar and dulcimore. Preceding his work at WHOP, he broadcast for two years from Lexington, and made occasional guest appearances on radio and TV in Louisville and Cincinnati. Archie has also performed at festivals, such as the Kentucky Folk Festival at Lexington and the National Folk Festival at St. Louis. While in the service, he sang folksongs when he was in Germany.

Aside from his radio work, he has played the guitar in a dance combo. Though he had done no recording of folksongs (up to 1955), he is an effective and authentic folksinger, and has had favorable press notices in the Louisville *Courier-Journal,* the Lexington *Leader,* and the St. Louis *Globe-Democrat.* Archie Lee was married to Annie Ball Davis in 1950.

KATIE LEE

Some singers of folksongs make a specialty of certain types or areas. Such a one is Katie Lee, specializing in folklore of the Southwest and particularly of the great Colorado River country. Katie Lee was born in Tucson, Arizona, October 23, 1919. She attended grade school briefly in Los Angeles, and from the third grade on through high school she was in Tucson. She entered the University of Arizona in 1938 and graduated with a Bachelor of Fine Arts degree in 1942.

Katie's mother was a singer, but her early knowledge of folksongs Katie got from recordings of Burl Ives, from Arizona cowboys on ranches around Tucson, and from Mexicans down along the border in the Nogales area. Folksongs have been a hobby with her since 1940 and a professional interest since 1951. In the latter year, she performed in Hollywood over N.B.C. on the "Great Gildersleeve" show. Since then she has performed on "The Railroad Hour," "The Halls of Ivy," and in several motion pictures. Her regular recitals have been heard in Mexico and about a dozen states—as far east as Connecticut, as far west as California. She sings at colleges and universities, at night clubs and women's clubs, at conventions and on television. The number of her appearances runs into the hundreds.

Recently Katie Lee has developed a special program on the Colorado River. For several summers she has traveled down the Colorado, singing her songs and collecting material from miners, Indians, Mexicans, or other isolated groups. Against a background of color films of the great river, she weaves song and story, with guitar accompaniment, into a superb performance. Her singing has had highest praise from such discerning students of folksong as Burl Ives and Carl Sandburg.

Katie Lee not only sings authentic folksongs, but she makes many adaptations and also composes in the folk idiom. At present she is preparing a book of songs and tales about the Colorado River region, some of it traditional materials, some of it her own compositions. Miss Lee is a member of the ASCAP.

Katie Lee was married in 1942 and divorced in 1945. She has a son, Ronnie Charles Eld, born in Tucson, May 1, 1944.

A. L. LLOYD

Another singer of the British Isles * given place in this account, largely because of his part in recording the Child ballads, is A. L. Lloyd of London. Like Ewan MacColl (*q.v.*), he is a distinguished collector, folklorist, and folksinger.

A. L. Lloyd was born in London on November 29, 1908. His father was an East Anglian fisherman † who sang many sea songs and passed them along to his son. The son went to Australia after his parents died, worked as a sheepherder and shearer, then in the 1930's sailed on Antarctic whaling vessels. These work experiences were the sources of many songs, particularly a large collection of Australian bush songs. Later he collected among coal miners in Great Britain and published *Come All Ye Bold Miners* in 1952. With Alan Lomax, he edited the Bulgarian volume of "The Columbia World Library of Folk and Primitive Music."

A. L. Lloyd has recorded extensively, for Topic and His Master's Voice in London; for Wattle in Sydney, Australia; and for Stinson, Riverside, and Tradition in America (see Book Three for details). Mr. Lloyd prefers to sing unaccompanied, though he has on occasion ("if promoters want me to sing accompanied") used or been accompanied by concertina, guitar, banjo, mandolin, or mouth organ. He has performed before large and small audiences ("whether I got paid or not") some hundreds of times, though he does not think of himself as a "performer." His words are worth quoting here:

> I never get used to the idea and can't take it seriously. At the same time I know lots of songs, enjoyed learning them, and like to give people a chance to learn them too. In the long run, I suppose, my interest nowadays is basically educational, otherwise I would only sing among friends as I was brought up to do. Mostly, I learned the songs first and did the studying afterwards.

Mr. Lloyd's repertoire is a large one—"I imagine it's five to six hundred songs and ballads." To quote him further: "I always mean to keep one of those loose-leaf books that singers have nowadays, containing their songs, but I never find time to compile it!" He is

* See, elsewhere in this book, Ewan MacColl, Isla Cameron, Margaret Barry, Mary O'Hara, and Alfred Deller.

† This account is based on correspondence with Mr. Lloyd, but a few facts are drawn from Riverside Records' announcement of their recordings of *The English and Scottish Popular Ballads,* under the distinguished editorship of Kenneth S. Goldstein.

a member of the editorial board of the English Folk Dance and Song Society and a "Corresponding Member of the International Folk Music Council." In John Huston's production of *Moby Dick,* A. L. Lloyd played the shantyman.

ALAN LOMAX

The student of American folksong would have to search far to find a living person who has done more than Alan Lomax in collecting, recording, and especially popularizing the vast body of our native songs. Son of the distinguished ballad collector and scholar, John A. Lomax, he was introduced early to the songs of the people.

John Lomax's first collection, *Cowboy Songs and Other Frontier Ballads,* had been off the press five years when Alan was born, January 15, 1915, at Austin, Texas. He was the third of four children in the family of John A. and Bess Brown Lomax.[8] The Lomaxes were a singing family, and Alan knew many songs from early childhood. He attended public schools, a preparatory school in Dallas, spent a year at Harvard, and in 1936 took a Bachelor of Arts degree at the University of Texas.

Alan's perennial enthusiasm for the old songs began with a sudden conversion. When, in 1933, John Lomax set out with a crude recording machine to collect songs for the Library of Congress, teen-age Alan was a somewhat reluctant companion, not too much interested in this mission. Soon "they stopped the car in front of a dilapidated cabin," set up their recording instrument, and listened to an old Negro woman as she worked over her washboard. She sang in a clear, rich voice the beautiful spiritual, "God's Goin' to Trouble de Waters," and from that moment "Alan's expression of indifference changed" as he listened "attentively, reverently." [9] He had "seen the light" and thereafter, until John Lomax's death on January 26, 1948, Alan remained his father's constant helper, his strong right arm, his collaborator in many collections. The fruit of that first year of "official" collecting, 1933, was to form the nucleus of what became the Archive of American Folk Song of the Library of Congress, an archive that now contains nearly half a hundred thousand songs.[10] Of this number, the Lomaxes alone, by 1941, through their many collecting ventures, contributed more than ten thousand songs.

Besides the work with his father, Alan Lomax has done much on his own. In 1937, the year of his marriage to Elizabeth Harold, he went to Haiti on a Library of Congress grant to record native songs and dances. During their three-month stay, he and Elizabeth lived in a thatched hut and traveled in a native jalopy.[11] In June, 1937, Alan was made assistant curator of the Archive of American

Folk Song in Washington. (His father had been made honorary curator of the archive in 1934, and so remained until his death.) The year 1939 was a busy one. He supervised recordings of Lead-belly's songs, he made a documentary series of recordings by Ferdinand (Jelly Roll) Morton, he sang folksongs at the White House during the visit of the King and Queen of England, and on Columbia's School of the Air he began a series of broadcasts of the "Wellsprings of America," singing and discussing folksongs and introducing many folksingers to an unseen audience.[12]

In 1943-44, Alan Lomax was with the Office of War Information, and in 1944-45 with the Special Services of the United States Army. In 1946, he joined Decca Records, Inc., as director of folk music. The long list of folk recordings and his informative and enthusiastic notes with the albums show both diligence and scholarship. In 1947, he received a Guggenheim Fellowship to further his researches in folk music. In 1948, he was on the air as "Your Ballad Man Alan Lomax" over the Mutual Broadcasting network.[13]

About 1950, the Columbia Recording Company commissioned Alan Lomax "to assemble for them 30 one-hour LP's entitled *A World Library of Folk and Primitive Music*, edited by the principal folklorists of the world from their collections of records." This task called for a "tremendously complicated world-wide correspondence." [14] By early 1955, fourteen of these albums had appeared and received a long and detailed discussion (ten columns), with quali-fied approval, in the *Saturday Review*.[15] Meanwhile, Lomax was doing a deal of collecting on his own in the British Isles and in Spain, some of which was aired over the B.B.C. during his stay in London in 1953.

The above accomplishments are only a part of Alan Lomax's indefatigable activities. In 1953, a letter from London stated:

> I have four books in the works: 1) *A Summer in Spain*, which will be a journal of the trip with the best of the mate-rial. 2) *Bonny Bunch of Roses*, which will be a book about the British Isles. 3) *The Deep Dark River*, a documentary book about Negro folk singers in the South. 4) A revision of the Leadbelly book.

Now in his middle forties, Alan Lomax is carrying on the great work so effectively begun and developed by his distinguished father.

MRS. MAUD LONG

Maud Gentry, born in Joe, North Carolina, on February 2, 1893, has sung folksongs since early childhood, for her mother, Mrs. Jane

Gentry, was a folksinger. Her early schooling was obtained at Dor-
land Institute, a Presbyterian mission school at Hot Springs, North
Carolina. During 1910 and 1911, she attended the Asheville Normal
Collegiate Institute in preparation for teaching. In 1911, she began
teaching in the North Carolina public schools. During the summers
of 1915 and 1916, she took courses at the University of North Carolina but did not work toward a degree.

Miss Gentry, who used ballads and folksongs in her teaching,
has never commercialized her singing, and she sings without instrumental accompaniment. She was married on June 10, 1922, to Grover
Cleveland Long, an employee of the Southern Railroad. They have
one daughter, Jane Caroline (now married), born May 6, 1929, and
herself the mother of two small daughters. All the family are interested in folksongs and folklore. Mrs. Long, who lists her occupation
as homemaker and teacher, made several recordings for the Library
of Congress Archive of Folk Song in 1946 and 1947.[16]

ROMAINE H. LOUDERMILK

From boyhood on a Kansas farm to ranch life in Arizona—that
phrase spans the career of Romaine Loudermilk, a rancher who
has made cowboy songs his special province. He was born in 1890
on a farm near Chetopa, down in the southeast corner of Kansas,
and he attended public schools in Baldwin. Kansas.

Romaine's father, though not a professional, could play "almost
any musical instrument," and he was well known as a "church and
quartet singer." He knew traditional songs, as well as others, but
wasn't considered a folksinger. Romaine learned folksongs "by ear"
around ranches and cow camps in his early teens. Later, the books
contributed to his repertoire, particularly John A. Lomax's *Cowboy
Songs and Other Frontier Ballads* (1910, 1916). His first public
performance was at a Rotary Club meeting in March, 1918, in
Phoenix, Arizona. By 1922, he was singing cowboy songs over the
radio—one of the first in that numerous tribe!—at station KFAD,
now KTAR, in Phoenix.

Loudermilk has written some Western songs, and over the past
fifty years or so he has done considerable singing at picnics, camps,
folk festivals, on the radio, and in stage shows—generally "along
with other folksingers," he says. He has covered the country from
Wyoming to Arizona and from California to North Carolina. Some
collectors have tape-recorded him, and he has made a few recordings for individuals (none commercially). "I've never cared to make
a business of exploiting my singing," he writes.

About the time of his radio debut, he was married to Jean Fyke. They have one son, Ed, born in 1923. The Loudermilks live at Rancho Manana, not far from Phoenix. Romaine sums up his life and his outlook in these words:

> I was just lucky to be born early enough to get acquainted with some of the cowboys who had worked the ranges through the 70's and 80's, to see occasional actual longhorns on open range. I saw big roundups and drives; saw the old backyard cowboy reunion commercialized into the modern rodeo; saw bands of wild horses on mountain and plain and the gradual change from the genuine Spanish mustang through the bronco era to fine quarter-horses. Have seen altered brands, cow thieves, black-leg, ticks, pink-eye, screw worms, bad men in high places and good men on the dodge, stampedes, range arguments, water troubles, storms, droughts, and lots of bright sunshine and fair weather when

> "Everything's lovely and nothin' is wrong,
> And I'm just lazy-like, lopin' along!"

BASCOM LAMAR LUNSFORD

Few workers in the folk-music field are better known, at least in the eastern half of the United States, than Bascom Lunsford. For well over half a century he's been singing ballads, playing dance tunes on fiddle and banjo, organizing and directing festivals, and in general arousing popular interest in folk culture. Bascom Lamar Lunsford was born March 21, 1882, at Mars Hill, North Carolina.[17] He attended public schools and Camp Academy at Leicester, North Carolina. He spent his college years at Rutherford and Trinity Colleges, then entered law school and was admitted to the bar in 1913.

Bascom's father was a teacher, and his mother, from whom he first learned folksongs, "was a singer of folk ballads." As a boy he sang at school activities, parties, bean stringings, and all kinds of festivities. His first performance, so far as he remembers, was at "some school entertainment in the dim past." Robert W. Gordon, writer and collector of folksongs, interested him in collecting and trying to preserve the songs as he found them. In 1920 and later, he was Gordon's companion on many jaunts through the Southern mountains. In 1935, he recorded 315 songs and ballads for the Columbia University Library. These and over four hundred others were later recorded for the Library of Congress Archive. Over the years Lunsford has gathered about three thousand songs, ballads, fiddle tunes, and dance calls, one of the large private collections in the United States.

Lunsford's best-known work has been his singing and lecturing, his organizing and directing of festivals. In this work his wide knowledge and unbounded enthusiasm have interested both the scholarly world and the general public, especially the mountain people themselves. In 1928, he organized—and still directs—the Mountain Dance and Folk Festival at Asheville, North Carolina. This festival has grown from a few performers with a handful of spectators to several hundred performers with thousands of spectators. In 1946, he organized the Annual Folk Festival at Renfro, Kentucky, which he continues to direct. In 1948, he organized the North Carolina State Fair Folk Festival at Raleigh. In the same year he was invited by the University of North Carolina, Chapel Hill, to help establish and direct the Carolina Folk Festival. His most recent work in this area was his direction of the first East Carolina Folk Festival at Kenansville, North Carolina, in 1952.

Bascom Lunsford has taken part in, or presented himself, well over a thousand concerts in half the states of the Union. He has directed a group of Appalachian folk dancers and singers in programs at Pittsburgh, Dallas, Philadelphia, St. Louis, Chicago, and Washington, D.C. In 1939, he took a group to the White House, where they performed for the King and Queen of England. A climactic point in Lunsford's career was a trip abroad in 1949. He played folk music and sang ballads at Cecil Sharp House in London and also at the First International Folk Music Festival held in Venice, Italy, where he was the United States representative.

Bascom Lamar Lunsford was married to Nellie Triplett in 1906. They have seven children, six daughters and a son. Lamar, Jr., is much interested in his father's folk-music programs and has been an active worker with him. Mr. Lunsford's folk-music work has not been a money-making business. Though he has been paid modestly for some of it, in the main it has been a lifelong labor of love. Consequently, at various times he has been engaged in different projects to support his growing family. Early in his career, he sold shrubs and fruit trees for a nursery. Another time he "robbed" bee trees in the woods and sold the honey. He taught for a while, became an auctioneer, even edited a newspaper.[18] All in all, he's done well enough to buy a farm at South Turkey Creek, Leicester, North Carolina, build a house there, and make it the planning center of his many festival activities.

Bascom Lunsford has had his problems in collecting and promoting folk materials. Early in his career he met with opposition from religious groups to dance music and "sinful" songs. In time this opposition has lessened and has given way to pride in the genuine mountain culture. Another problem has been in the festivals themselves—the problem of presenting genuinely traditional material, and at the same time making it acceptable entertainment. Many are interested merely in entertainment, in the popular sense, and have wanted to bring in current popular music—"country and Western," as hillbilly music is commonly called now. This type of music is not native to the mountains and is scarcely to be considered traditional folk culture. Lunsford, like many other festival directors, has been obliged to make compromises with this "new culture" to the extent that some serious students question "whether his festivals are in the authentic tradition." [19] It is a festival problem the country over: the old culture is crowded by the new, and the old is sometimes crowded out. At any rate, Bascom Lamar Lunsford has been instrumental in bringing to light much good material and, in his long and useful life, has had the satisfaction of seeing the old songs and dances take on a new popularity.

EWAN MacCOLL

Like A. L. Lloyd (*q.v.*), Ewan MacColl * is included in this American collection of singers because of his work in recording the English and Scottish ballads for Riverside Records. He was born on January 25, 1915, in Auchterarder, Perthshire, Scotland, of parents who were folksingers. His Gaelic-speaking mother is still living. He studied in elementary and various other schools in Scotland and England but has not taken any degrees.

From childhood on, Ewan MacColl learned ballads and folksongs from his parents, from his Aunt Margaret Logan, and from other folksingers, among them Jeannie Robertson, Harry Cox, and Charlie Wills. One of his first public performances was a radio program for the B.B.C. in 1934 called "Music of the Streets." Like Lloyd, he prefers to sing unaccompanied; but on occasion he is accompanied by others on the concertina, harmonica, five-string banjo, or guitar. He has given recitals—five or six hundred all told—in the British Isles and all over Europe, including the Scandinavian countries, Poland, Bulgaria, Russia, Italy, Roumania, France, and Germany. His singing has been favorably reviewed time and again.

Mr. MacColl has done a great deal of writing and collecting from

* This brief account is based on correspondence with Mr. MacColl, though a few facts are drawn from the Riverside Records brochure. (See footnote †
on A. L. Lloyd.)

the mid-1930's on, much of it for the B.B.C. He writes "songs and instrumental music using folk idioms." He has published three small collections of folksongs: *Scotland Sings, Personal Choice,* and *Shuttle and Cage.* He has, of course, made many recordings, for Decca, H.M.V., and Topic in Great Britain; for Wattle in Australia; and for Stinson, Tradition, and Riverside in America (see Book Three).

In 1948, Ewan MacColl was married to Jean Mary Newlove. They have one son, Hamish, born July 15, 1950, and he, too, is learning ballads and folksongs.

MAY KENNEDY McCORD

For many years a singer of ballads in the Ozarks and a popularizer of the region's folklore, Mrs. McCord has sometimes been called the "Queen of the Hillbillies." The title is not too apt, however, because after all she is a serious student of folksong and folklore. Somewhat more dignified is her title of Missouri Mother for the year 1950.* May Kennedy was born at the edge of the Ozarks, in Carthage, Missouri, on December 1, 1880.[20] After high school at Galena, Missouri, she spent one year at a private college, Selden's College, at Aurora, Missouri. She did not take a degree.

May Kennedy comes from a musical family. Her mother, a native of Illinois, was a singer, though not particularly of folksongs. A sister became a concert singer. May knew folksongs from her early childhood, not so much from the tradition in her own family, but, as she says, being in the Ozark hills for so many years, she "just absorbed them." In other words, her main source was the "early Ozark pioneers." Not until well into middle life did Mrs. McCord develop a career in folksong activity. In Springfield, Missouri, where she has lived for many years, she has written a column titled "Hill Billy Heartbeats" for the Springfield *Daily News.* And for many years she has popularized the folklore, mainly songs and stories, of the Ozarks over station KWTO. She is excellent with the guitar and knows hundreds of the old songs, her special favorites being the British ballads found in the Ozarks.

Mrs. McCord does not rearrange the folksongs for special effects, and her guitar accompaniments are simple and unobtrusive. "I sing the ballads exactly as I have learned them," she says, "being particular *not* to change them." This fact has made her an authentic source for many songs. She has recorded for the Library of Congress Archive and for a number of universities, including the University of Arkansas at Fayetteville. Vance Randolph's large collection of

* Kansas City *Star,* April 21, 1951.

Ozark Folksongs (*q.v.*) contains seventy-two entries contributed by her. Though she has not herself written a book, much of her material has gone into the making of other books, especially works by O. E. Rayburn and Vance Randolph.

Over the past quarter century her activity as ballad singer and lecturer on folklore has been extensive, ranging all the way "from the English Speaking Union in New York to the Warner Brothers Breakfast Club in Los Angeles." She has been a favorite before music clubs, historical groups, and college audiences; also at various festivals, particularly the National Folk Festival in St. Louis and the Ozark Folk Festival in Eureka Springs, Arkansas. In the latter organization she has been a director and moving spirit during the past decade. Her extensive interests are indicated by membership in many organizations: Missouri State Writers Guild, Ozark Press Association, Springfield Music Club, Ozarks Creative Writers Guild, and by important offices held in these organizations.

On January 3, 1903, May Kennedy was married to Charles Calvin McCord. Their three children are Charles C. McCord, Jr., Mandeva McCord (now Mrs. Herman Henry Janss), and Frank Leslie McCord. Since Mr. McCord's death in 1943, May Kennedy McCord has continued to live in Springfield, carrying on her many activities, especially those relating to the lore and songs of the Ozarks. Asked if her family were particularly interested in folksongs, she replied: "They are mildly interested in ballads but they like to hear me sing them."

ED McCURDY

Elusive and peripatetic Ed McCurdy was born at Willow Hill, Pennsylvania, on January 11, 1919. He attended country school at Middle Spring and finished high school at Shippensburg, Pennsylvania, a few miles away. He picked up one semester of college at the Panhandle A. and M. College at Goodwell, Oklahoma, and did some further study (no degree) at Central State College, Edmond, Oklahoma.

Ed learned a few folksongs from his parents, "some in the field and some by mail," but for the most part he gleaned the libraries for the songs he sings. He plays the guitar and he's been singing all his life, but his activity as a professional singer of folksongs began in May, 1946, over the Canadian Broadcasting network. He has done some collecting in his wanderings, and he composes music, some of it "modern pop, some classical, and some in the traditional folk manner." As writer, actor, and singer he has been in most of the United States and across Canada. His folksinging activity, however, has been mostly on radio and television, though he is also available for concert work.

Recent activities of Ed McCurdy include recordings of folksongs. His first recording was on a Canadian label (Whitehall LP 850) with *Folk Songs of the Canadian Maritimes and Newfoundland.*[21] In 1955, Dr. MacEdward Leach and Harper & Brothers, editor and publishers respectively of *The Ballad Book* (1955), chose Ed McCurdy as an outstanding singer of folksongs to do a musical supplement for the book. The result is an excellent presentation of twenty of the finest ballads on a single LP record. Since then McCurdy has also done many LP albums for Elektra, Riverside, and other recording companies (see Book Three).

In 1945, Ed McCurdy was married to Beryl English in Vancouver, British Columbia. They are the parents of three children: Mary Margaret, born in San Francisco in 1946; and two boys, James Gordon and Dana John, born in Vancouver in 1948 and 1952. Since 1954, the McCurdys have lived in New York City, where Ed is working mainly in radio and television, "particularly on the fine educational series, *Camera Three,* broadcast by C.B.S."

BROWNIE McNEIL

Norman L. (Brownie) McNeil was born in San Antonio, Texas, October 3, 1915. He attended elementary school in San Antonio and graduated from Thomas Jefferson High School in that city. He entered the University of Texas in 1933, graduating four years later with a major in Spanish. He entered the teaching field and began work toward a master's degree in 1939.

Brownie McNeil has known and sung and collected folksongs for many years. His father, who knew a lot of folksongs, was a director of choral singing at county fairs in Rusk County, Texas. A major source and perhaps also a major interest for Brownie, however, was the singing of his great-uncle Frank, an old-time cowboy and trail driver who followed herds up the trail to Abilene, Kansas, in the late 1880's. After listening to Uncle Frank for many years and learning many of his songs, Brownie began collecting seriously about 1932, soon learned to strum the guitar and "began to sing in earnest."

Brownie set out to collect "all that the old cowpokes in South Texas" could give him, and by 1935 he had a "sizable collection of authentic cowboy and trail-driver's songs." When he began graduate study in 1939 (again majoring in Spanish), he undertook a study of the Mexican ballad, mainly because, as he writes. "I had long been interested in the lilting folksongs sung by Mexican cowhands on my father's ranch." In 1941, he was granted the E. D. Farmer International Fellowship by the University of Texas for study in Mexico "on a project whose main purpose was to gather and write a study of Mexican ballads." He completed the master's degree in 1944 and, two years later, published a small group of Mexican border ballads (*corridos*), presenting them in Mexican-Spanish with English translation and giving a history of this particular type, as well as an account of his experiences in collecting.[22]

Brownie's comment about his collecting is interesting and worth quoting:

> By arrangement with the Library of Congress I was sup-plied a recording machine and discs to travel about over the southern portion of Texas and the northern states of Mexico collecting ballads from native folksingers. I was able to record some 60 renditions of ballads, many of them recorded out in the open in remote little Mexican villages.

Copies of these recordings are in the Archive of American Folk Song, Library of Congress, and in the Fine Arts Library, University of Texas. After finishing his degree, Brownie McNeil worked for a time in the Immigration Service along the border, then taught at the University of Houston and, in 1946, was elected president of the Texas Folklore Society.

Brownie McNeil, who sings in a rich, lusty baritone, has built up a considerable repertoire of Southwestern ballads and, with guitar accompaniment, frequently gives folksong programs. His accompani-ments are simple but effective, he is not a composer, and he "sings the ballads and folksongs in their simple native tunes." Consequently, his singing has an authenticity too often lacking in the more sophis-ticated singer. Brownie has given around a hundred regular "paid concerts," and an unknown number of informal amateur programs, in various parts of Texas, Colorado, Louisiana, New York, Con-necticut, and Old Mexico. In 1947, he was invited by the Colorado State Music Teachers Association to conduct a folksinging school on the campus of the University of Denver. In 1950, he was a guest performer on the N.B.C. network TV show, "Broadway Open House," and he has also appeared on C.B.S., as well as on New York City's municipal station, WNYC. In 1949, the Sonic Record Company of Austin, Texas, brought out an album of four 12-inch records of his songs and ballads.

When Brownie McNeil was married to Kathleen Howard in 1941,

they spent their honeymoon on a "second-class train in Mexico collecting ballads." They have two sons: Laird Howard, born in 1942, and John Robert, born in 1945. After a year of teaching at the University of Houston, Mr. McNeil in 1947 went to Trinity University, San Antonio, and then in 1953 joined the English faculty of his alma mater, the University of Texas.

In August, 1956, Mr. McNeil received his Ph.D. degree in American civilization from the University of Texas, his dissertation subject being "The British Ballad West of the Appalachian Mountains." A portion of this work was published in *Mesquite and Willow* in 1957 as one of the publications of the Texas Folklore Society, issued by the University Press in Dallas.

In September, 1956, Dr. McNeil joined the faculty of Texas College of Arts and Industries, Kingsville, Texas, as assistant professor of English and history. "With the matter of the Ph.D. taken care of," he writes, "it's time to get back to singing before the guitar strings get too rusty." Sonic Records issued a new recording of his songs in 1957. Three types of songs are represented in the eleven selections: English ballads, cowboy ballads of the Southwest, and Mexican *ranchero* songs * (see Book Three).

JOSEF MARAIS AND MIRANDA

Among international balladeers none are more popular or more polished than Mr. and Mrs. Josef Marais. These "merry minstrels," as they are aptly called, have performed in many lands the folksongs of many peoples—French and Flemish, Swiss and Swedish, Irish and Scottish, English and American, African Bantu and South African. They are particularly famous for these latter two.

Josef Marais was born on the African veld in Lowry Pass, Union of South Africa, and it was through hearing the natives on the Marais farm (a sheep ranch) in South Africa that he acquired a love of singing by the "folk."[23] Miranda, whose mother was the lieder singer Lily Pardo, was born in Amsterdam, Holland, and received her education at the Barlaeus Gymnasium School in Amsterdam.

Following Josef's first formal schooling in Worcester, South Africa, he was sent to South African College at Cape Town. At that time his special interest was the violin. After beginning his career as violinist with the Cape Town Symphony Orchestra, he went to Europe to continue his studies, first at the Royal Academy of Music in London, then to Professor Otakar Sevcik in Prague, next to Professor Jeno Hubay in Budapest, and finally continuing his studies

* Information on Dr. McNeil's records may be had from him at Texas A. & I. College in Kingsville, Texas.

in Paris. Musical theory and composition, as well as violin, occupied his time.

Josef Marais began working as a professional radio broadcaster in 1938 with the B.B.C. in London. With the outbreak of war in 1939, he joined the Office of War Information and was assigned to the Afrikaans and Dutch division. Here he met Miranda and in time discovered her singing ability. They began working as a team, eventually came to New York, where Marais for several years broadcast the program called "African Trek." Their personal appearances started at the Village Vanguard on October 10, 1945, and, after that, the Ruban Bleu. Soon regular concerts developed from these appearances, with a debut in Town Hall in 1946. They were married in 1947, and from then on they have done coast-to-coast tours, covering the major cities in most of the United States. In 1954, they took what can only be described as the triumphant Continental Grand Tour, singing in England, Holland, France, Belgium, Germany, Denmark, Sweden, and, on their return to North America, across Canada.

Besides being an accomplished violinist, Marais is a fine classical guitarist, and his special arrangements for folksongs are themselves works of art. He is able to weld the song (words) and the tune into a work of art satisfactory to trained and sophisticated music lovers, and yet make a popular appeal to the general public. His own words express it more effectively:

> We believe that our arrangements should be in the spirit of the original, and yet bear the "art" imprint: we consider our function to be that of the minstrel who tries to show the inherent value of a song to the layman, and thus we further the cause of folk-singing, by encouraging the "folk" to sing more songs, and fresh tunes. Our greatest joy is to hear community singing of the songs we originated, or translated, or first planted as seeds in the hearts of amateurs.

For more than a dozen years Marais and Miranda have presented over five hundred regular concerts, not to mention uncounted radio and TV appearances. Obviously, two such popular minstrels have done much recording, mainly for Decca and Columbia (see Book Three), and some of their songs are numbered among the hit-parade and jukebox favorites.[24] Besides his incomparable work in adaptation and arrangements, Josef Marais is a serious composer in folk materials. Such a composition is his folk opera, *Tony Beaver* (libretto by Max Breton), as well as another folk-based work, using African tunes, called *African Heartbeat* (libretto by Charles O'Neal).[25]

Marais and Miranda have taken full and effective advantage of the resurgence of folksong in the past two decades, and their position is a secure one. An item in *Time* (February 2, 1953) suggests that they brought South African "country" music into the popular scene. If the suggestion implies comparison with current American "country-style" (hillbilly) music, it is wide of the mark. It is, of course, true that they do make adaptations of folk tunes, but their work is based on a solid classical musical training. Their songs are never monotonous, never condescending; they are true to the rhythms and spirit of the originals, and even in the simplest songs they show the polish of excellent musicianship. This is not "country" music, as the term is popularly understood. Whether they are presenting a primitive African veld rhythm or a subtle and sophisticated British or Continental ballad, the Marais-Miranda team gives it the imprint of polished artistry that lends dignity and distinction to every song.

THE MARCOTTES, WILL AND JEAN

Wilfred D. Marcotte was born at Willamansett, Massachusetts, on February 11, 1921. He went through the public schools at Belmont, Massachusetts, and attended two sessions at the Wentworth Institute. Jean G. Cleveland was born in Cambridge, Massachusetts, on April 15, 1924. She, too, attended the Belmont schools and met her future husband there.

Neither Will's nor Jean's parents were musicians or folksingers. The Marcottes learned mainly from recordings, from folksinger Bess Hawes and many other friends, as well as from printed sources. Both use the guitar and five-string banjo, and they have been performing since the late 1940's. Their folksong activities have been limited to Rhode Island and Massachusetts. In the main, much of their work has been with groups, as leaders and instructors, and they always perform as a team or with groups.

Will and Jean were married on December 21, 1945. They are the parents of three children: Brooke, born September 9, 1946; Jeremy, born May 17, 1949; and Rachel, born April 3, 1954. They live in Watertown, Massachusetts, where Will's work is structural steel detailing and Jean is housewife and mother. Amateurs like the Marcottes do much to keep folk music alive.

THE MECHAU FAMILY

Paula Mechau and her four children—Vanni, Dorik, Duna, and Michael—have had a unique experience as singers of folksongs in America. They have sung, in unison, over two hundred concerts in a dozen of the Midwest and Rocky Mountain states, beginning in

1943. Their experience is unique not only in the method of presentation but in its beginning and its reason for continuation.

These five are the family of the celebrated Western painter, the late Frank Mechau. Mechau was born in 1904 at Glenwood Springs in western Colorado, where he grew up and came to know intimately the great mountain West. He attended the University of Denver, went on to study at the Chicago Art Institute, then to New York, and eventually to Paris.[26] During lean years in New York he worked at Lord and Taylor's department store, where in 1925 he met Paula Ralska,[27] who was ambitious for a stage career. They were married in the late twenties and in 1929 went to Paris to continue Mechau's art studies. There, in 1932, the first child, Vanni, was born.[28]

And now enters the folksong into their story. Frank Mechau had grown up knowing Western and other traditional songs but apparently gave little thought to them. One evening, when Paula asked him to put the baby to sleep while she did other tasks, she heard him singing a song strange to her ears. He said it was a folksong his mother had often sung. Paula had known Scottish and English ballads as poetry at school and had sung some of them for her own pleasure. So began a new interest for these Americans in Paris, for Frank Mechau was to develop not only a great interest in Western American folklore, much of it reflected in his paintings, but an enthusiasm for ballads and folksongs in particular.[29]

When the Mechaus returned to America, in the depths of the Great Depression, they settled at Redstone, Colorado, a ghost mining town about thirty miles south of Frank's native Glenwood Springs. In 1934, Mechau got a government commission in the PWAP (Public Works of Art Project) to do post-office murals. Thus began his great productive period of a dozen happy years. He made murals for half a dozen post offices: Washington, D.C.; Glenwood Springs and Colorado Springs, Colorado; Fort Worth and Brownfield, Texas; and Ogallala, Nebraska. At Redstone, also, he did paintings for the Denver Fine Arts Library, and other paintings which are now in the galleries of New York, Cincinnati, and Detroit. The children came along at two-year intervals—Dorik in 1934, Duna in 1936, and Michael in 1938—and the growing family continued its interest in singing folksongs. One of the Western songs, "Sierry Peaks," "inspired Frank to paint Saturday P.M., which many consider his greatest work. The galloping horses, the cowboys, and the girl hesitating before the swinging doors of a false-front saloon have the rhythmic quality characteristic of folk songs." [30]

Frank Mechau received a Guggenheim Fellowship in 1934, and the grant was continued for three more years. He taught at the

Colorado Fine Arts Center and "later at Columbia University, where he served as head of the art department from 1939 to 1944." A series of war paintings which he did for *Life* magazine in 1944 was exhibited by the Denver Art Museum in 1945.[31] While the artist was busy with various commissions, Paula and the children were singing folksongs for wounded veterans in Fitzsimons Army Hospital in Denver.

In 1946, Frank Mechau died unexpectedly, and his untimely death left his growing family stunned and stranded. They turned to their best resource: folksongs. Though relatively untrained as singers, they had a family unity, more deeply welded because of their deep loss; and they had sincerity and simplicity, which made their singing unusually appealing. They sang at the Aspen Music Festival in the summer of 1946, as well as at the Western Folklore Conference in Denver. During 1949-50, they spent the winter at Redstone under difficult conditions, cutting their own wood, butchering a buck for meat, and doing other heavy tasks in order to survive the rigors of winter. But most of all that winter they built up a repertoire of several hundred folksongs and were soon ready to expand the radius of their singing. Vanni had learned the guitar and had studied with Richard Dyer-Bennet at Aspen.[32]

So, at the mid-century, a new career developed for the Mechaus. They recorded an album of folksongs in Denver, with notes by singer-composer Earl Robinson.[33] They extended their summer tours beyond Colorado, appearing at many colleges and universities. For instance, in the summer of 1952, their tour of the Midwest and Southwest covered eight thousand miles. For a regular income—the children would soon be ready for college—Paula took up teaching, first at Carbondale and later at Grand Junction, Colorado. Vanni began the study of art at Bennington College in Vermont, and Dorik went to Harvard. Now the children are grown and have gone their several ways. But the singing of folksongs is still a favorite activity with all of them, alone or in the family group, and is likely to remain a part of their heritage.

The words of Paula Mechau, "the mother and the spiritual head of this remarkable singing family," seem particularly appropriate by way of summary:

> We took to singing these folk songs because they express emotions and ideas of great depth and feeling, much deeper and more real than so much of what we hear on the radio, in the movies, and on television. In a way the folk songs help give us a faith to live by.

And the words of Earl Robinson further attest to this faith:

Here we have one of those ever-present contradictions in our history or any people's history, synthesized by the Mechaus; a love for the old, "archaic," the traditional and sanctified, coupled with a quick, living, modern understanding and approach, and directed toward a warm and better future.[34]

ERIK MICKELSEN

A young Western singer with a difference—because he has a serious interest in folk music—is Erik Mickelsen, born on March 26, 1938, in Milwaukee, Wisconsin. Erik's first four years of schooling were in Ridgefield, Connecticut, the next two in a one-room school near the Mickelsen ranch in Montana, two more years at Horace Hurlbut School in Weston, Connecticut, and finally high school at the Fergus County High School, Lewistown, Montana. Erik entered Dartmouth College in the fall of 1956, but had to return home after one quarter because of illness. Later he enrolled at Montana State University at Missoula.

Erik has learned folksongs from neighbors and old-timers in Montana and, like other young singers, from records and books. He uses the guitar, autoharp, sometimes the piano, and on some occasions is accompanied by Robert Beers (q.v.) on the psaltery. Performances thus far have been limited to about fifty or so, in three states mainly—Connecticut, Montana, and Arkansas.* He was first tenor (soloist in ballads and folksongs) with a high-school group called "The Corralaires" who toured Montana, appearing at many towns and colleges, and on TV in Billings. They received first rating in the Missoula, Montana, high-school music festival.

Erik works on his father's cattle ranch near Lewistown, Montana, and expects to finish college and continue his folksong activities.

ALAN MILLS

Since folksinging in itself is not a money-making venture, except in rare instances, it is obvious that singers of folksongs must be ingenious in other ways. Their major careers are surprisingly varied: they may be homemakers, teachers, soldiers, farmers, storekeepers, actors, writers, secretaries, industrial workers, vagabonds, artists— anything and everything. For instance, Canada's most popular singer of folksongs, Alan Mills, hasn't always been a singer of folksongs; in fact, he hasn't always been Alan Mills!

* He was a guest singer at the Ozark Folk Festival in October, 1958.

Al, or Albert, Miller [35] was born September 7, 1913, in Lachine, a suburb of Montreal, P.Q., Canada. At fifteen he left school to become a newspaperman, first with the Montreal *Evening Journal* and later with the Montreal *Herald*. On the side he did some radio work, performed with a group of amateur actors, and sang in a choir.

These several activities gave way to a new interest in 1935. The late John Goss, noted English musicologist and interpreter of folksongs, needed a bass to complete his touring group of singers. Mills (or Al Miller), after some quick training, was able to do the part creditably and for two years traveled over Canada and the United States with the John Goss singers. When this pleasant venture came to an end—victim of the Depression—in New York in 1937, he returned to Montreal to work on the *Herald*, and to part-time radio work. Soon he moved to the *Gazette* and worked on that morning paper for seven years.

But the interest in ballads and folksongs, nurtured under the influence of John Goss, was destined to displace all other activities. The year 1944 was a turning point: he took the name Alan Mills, left the newspaper field, and decided to concentrate on radio work. This decision was a wise one, in part because it brought him into a highly successful financial career, in part because he made Canada aware, through his popular presentation, of her vast wealth of folksong.

From 1947 on, the story of Alan Mills has been one of continued success and popularity. He established the Canadian Broadcasting Corporation program called "Folk Songs for Young Folk" in 1947. Another series, beginning in 1952 with Hélène Baillargcon and the Arthur Morrow Singers and called "Songs of Canada" (later, "Songs *Chez Nous*"), has reached a trans-Canada audience. Further, his songs have been broadcast to Latin America and Europe via the C.B.C. International Service. In February, 1953, in Montreal, he played the leading role in a production of Kurt Weill's folk opera, *Down in the Valley*. In 1953-54, he went on tour, mainly to smaller towns in Canada, giving many folksong concerts.

Mills also gives many free performances in schools, youth organizations, and P.T.A. groups, and assists other groups interested in singing folksongs. For instance, he helped The Laurentian Choral Group (an organization of about forty Montreal housewives and mothers) develop a program of folksongs which, since 1951, has made it possible for them to present an annual festival of International Folk Songs and Dances. As Alan Mills says, "I'm particularly interested in making our Canadian ballads—both 'home-grown' and imported or inherited—known to our own people and to the people of other lands." Hence his enthusiasm and his untiring efforts to cram a "25-hour day into 24 hours."

Alan Mills has done considerable recording of folksongs. One of his early records was an RCA-Victor album (CP-7) called *Let's Sing a Little*. Later recordings have been made by Folkways Records and others (see Book Three). Alan Mills' guitar accompaniments are done by Gilbert Lacombe. This allows him greater freedom for interpretation and acting. For some formal appearances he also uses a harpist. In 1949, *The Alan Mills Book of Folk Songs and Ballads* was published in Montreal (see Book Two).

Alan Mills has often been called the "Canadian Burl Ives." The two men are friends and have much in common. Both had a long struggle before any substantial recognition came. Both have reached the top in popularity in their respective countries. Both have long been interested in acting on the legitimate stage, and to some extent in the movies. There has been one movie "short" featuring Alan Mills, but Ives has done much more in the films. Both have appeared frequently on television. Both are blessed with the "divine gift of friendship" for all kinds of people, and this trait has endeared them to a multitude of admirers across the land.

CAPTAIN MERLIN P. MITCHELL

Merlin Mitchell was born in Gainesville, Texas, on November 14, 1918, in the Red River cattle country where he heard the old songs sung by his family and neighbors. "He listened to the tall talk, absorbed the folk culture, learned to sing and strum the guitar. In the cattle country of Texas, in the pine woods of Florida, in the Rocky Mountains, and in the Ozarks, Mr. Mitchell has met and exchanged talk with the old folks who in their time had to make their own recreation and entertainment." [36]

Merlin's early formal education, through the sixth grade, was in the public schools of Gainesville. When the family moved to Florida, he completed his grade- and high-school studies at Orlando. Before entering military service in 1940, he had two years of college at Rollins College, Winter Park, Florida. After World War II, he enrolled at the University of Texas in 1946 and took a Bachelor of Arts in literature in 1948. He spent the following year at the Univerity of Arkansas, receiving a Master of Arts degree in 1949.

Parents and paternal grandparents were Merlin Mitchell's first folksong teachers, and his folksong activities span some thirty years. At twelve he learned the guitar and began singing Texas ballads to music classes in school. This activity continued with college, and when he went into the Air Force he performed for military and civilian audiences in half a dozen states and in England, North Africa, Germany, Japan, and Korea. His favorite songs are those widely known in Texas and the Southwest, such as "Streets of Laredo," "Old Chisholm Trail," "Bury Me Not on the Lone Prairee," "Trail to Mexico," "Rye Whiskey," "Joe Bowers," "Buffalo Skinners," "Old Paint," and others in a similar vein.

When Mitchell finished his studies at Arkansas in 1949, he was appointed the university's research assistant in folklore. He was among the original organizers of the Ozark Folklore Society (later named the Arkansas Folklore Society). During 1949 and 1950 he tape-recorded over three hundred songs from folksingers in Arkansas for the university's Folklore Archives. Having studied folklore "under the expert direction of such folklorists as J. Frank Dobie of Texas," he was well qualified to work "systematically and discriminatingly." Thus as folklorist and folksinger he "performed for the state an inestimable service in preservation of a great tradition of oral art, which is fast disappearing in our increasingly mechanized civilization." [37]

Merlin Mitchell was married to Barbara Cochran in 1947. They are the parents of four children: David Merlin, born May 23, 1948; Jean Lanius, born January 31, 1950; William Cochran, born February 7, 1952; and James Clifton, born February 3, 1954. Mitchell returned to active duty as a captain in the Air Force and was stationed for some time at Brooks Field, Orlando, Florida. Then he was assigned to duty as military pilot and instructor of Air Force ROTC at Gainesville in north-central Texas, where he lives with his family. His folksinging activities continue nonetheless, and he has performed at many folk festivals, particularly in Texas and Arkansas. His singing is straightforward, ingenuous, and withal sincere and authentic, and particularly effective in the lusty songs of the vast open spaces of the cattle country.

PLEAZ W. MOBLEY

Though he has wandered far from his native Clay County in southeastern Kentucky, Pleaz Mobley has spent most of his life there. He was born in Oneida, January 24, 1913, and his earliest schooling was in a Clay County rural school. After high school he attended a number of colleges in Kentucky, including Berea, Georgetown, and Union, from the last of which he took a Bachelor of Arts degree in the mid-1930's. Later he attended the Jefferson School of Law and received a Bachelor of Laws degree from the University of Louisville.

All his life Pleaz Mobley has been singing folksongs, having learned them early from "parents and neighbors in the hills of Kentucky." Aside from this early absorption, he has collected in Kentucky, Tennessee, and the Carolinas. His first regular performance, with guitar, was given at the Oneida High School in 1926. As a young man he traveled on the old Redpath Chautauqua circuit, singing in practically all the United States and in Canada. Of course, he picked up more songs in these travels. Mobley sings on the Renfro Valley radio programs, and he has his own show "from my log cabin" on the local station in Manchester, Kentucky, where he makes his home. He made recordings for the Library of Congress Archive of Folk Song in 1943 and 1946 (Record Nos. AAFS 56, 58, and 69).

Pleaz William Mobley was married to Jessie L. Johnson in 1937. They have a daughter, Sylvia Phoebe, born in 1939. Mr. Mobley is an attorney-at-law in Manchester and railroad commissioner for the Third District of Kentucky. These sedate and serious activities still leave him considerable time for folksinging.

COLONEL JACOB R. AND WINNIFRED MOON

Jacob Robert Moon was born March 10, 1899, in Goodwater, Alabama, and received his public-school education there. After attending Alabama Polytechnic Institute at Auburn and receiving the Bachelor of Science degree, he entered West Point. In due time he was graduated and given a commission. Following his services in World War II, he retired with the rank of colonel.

Colonel Moon's early interest in and knowledge of folksongs came mostly from the Negroes among whom he grew up. He picked up songs from work gangs on railroads and highways and from backwoods churches. A more extensive interest developed after his marriage, on August 20, 1927, to Winnifred Minter.

Winnifred Minter was born in Monticello, Florida, on July 5, 1898. She attended public school in Columbus, Georgia, and obtained further education at Lorena Hall, a girls' private school, and the Chase Conservatory of Music, both in Columbus. She continued her musical studies at Combs Conservatory, Philadelphia, and at the Alice Parker Studio of Voice, New York City.

Winnifred Minter Moon comes from a family of folksingers and has had a lively interest in folk music all her life. Her father and maternal grandfather were her earliest teachers and informants. She did further collecting from other older members of the family and their friends in Georgia, Florida, Alabama, and the Carolinas. Some of her material also came "from Negroes in small rural churches and communities throughout the South." Mrs. Moon, who uses both the guitar and Irish harp in singing, has made instrumental arrangements of a great many songs in her collection.[38]

Colonel and Winnifred Moon have given many performances, some in the Philippines when stationed there, but particularly throughout the South. "It would be impossible to estimate the number," Mrs. Moon writes, "for we have been singing so long." Some years ago they recorded "a large number of songs to be used on the Voice of America." At another time they made a "transcription of a folksong program with Deems Taylor as master of ceremonies and commentator, entitled *Music from America*. It was aired coast to coast by the Army Recruiting Publicity Bureau on their 'Stars on Parade' series."

The Moons make their home at Ormond Beach, Florida. Since the colonel's retirement from the United States Army, he has been engaged in training and showing hunters and jumpers, and in teaching horseback riding. The Moons have two children, Winnifred Nielsen and Jacob Robert, Jr., now both grown and married.

JIMMY MORRIS

Jimmy Morris, alias Jimmy Driftwood, was born in the heart of the Ozarks at Mountain View, Arkansas, on June 20, 1917. He attended the Richwoods Grammar School, a one-room country school, through the eighth grade, had three years of high school at Mountain View, and finished his high schooling at nearby Marshall. He began country-school teaching immediately and earned college credits between terms. His college work was done at John Brown University, Siloam Springs, Arkansas; Arkansas College, Batesville; and Arkansas State Teachers College, Conway, where he received a Bachelor of Science in education in the early 1940's.

Jimmy learned folksongs mostly in his own family, from his parents, his grandparents, and one of his great-grandmothers. Some folksong knowledge came from friends and neighbors, especially from the older people in his native county. Jimmy can't recall a time when he didn't sing folksongs. As he says, "It was just a part of life back then." He has picked banjo and played fiddle most of his life, too, but his favorite instrument is a homemade guitar— one made by his grandfather Morris "of fence-rail, ox-yoke and bedstead." It is smaller and shallower than the standard-size guitar; the tone is sharper and thinner, but nonetheless melodious.

Jimmy Morris has done some collecting in Arkansas and the South, just as any singer collects as he goes about the country. He sings the old songs exactly as he finds them, and he also composes songs, both words and lyrics, in the folk manner. But Jimmy doesn't make the mistake of calling them folksongs. As he says, "In the strict sense of the word, no one can truthfully say he writes folksongs today. Current compositions called folksongs are misnomers." He is aware that oral circulation, variation of text and tune, and transmission through time are what make a folksong truly authentic. Some of his songs have been published under the name of Jimmy Driftwood.[39]

Jimmy has performed hundreds of times, in twelve or fifteen states, and he is a favorite at parties, picnics, celebrations, and folk festivals. The annual Ozark Folk Festival at Eureka Springs is on his regular beat. Jimmy Morris was married to Cleda Azalee Johnson in 1937. They have two sons: James Risner, born in 1940, and Bing Lee, born in 1943. Asked if others in his family sing ballads, Jimmy replied, somewhat surprised, "Why, naturally." Though Jimmy Morris's regular occupation is schoolteaching, songwriting and singing occupy much of his time.

ABSIE S. MORRISON

Fourth-generation fiddle player Absie S. Morrison was born October 12, 1876, in Searcy County, Arkansas, on the farm where he still lives.* His schooling in the nearby village of Marshall was meager but, as he said, "I learnt my letters." His great-grandfather with three brothers emigrated from Scotland to the Colonies in the mid-eighteenth century, settling first in Virginia. Three of the four fought in the Revolution. Absie's grandfather moved on to Tennessee and eventually to Searcy County, Arkansas, where Absie's father was born in 1842.

All the Morrisons were country fiddlers—great-grandfather, grandfather, father, and finally Absie, who has played the fiddle as long as he can remember. He now owns the fiddle which his great-grandfather played and brought from Scotland nearly two hundred years ago.

For many years Absie Morrison has been farmer, fiddler, and fiddle maker. He has lost count of the exact number he has made and sold, but supposes it might run to seventy-five or more.† Most of his

* These facts are gleaned from an interview with Mr. Morrison on October 20, 1956, in Eureka Springs, Arkansas.

† He had finished making a fiddle in May, 1956, and played it the following October at the Ozark Folk Festival in Eureka Springs. He told me, however, that it was not yet "ripe" because the varnish he used had not set properly, and he intended to refinish it to get a better tone. In fact, when he played it, it sounded "green." Top and back were made from mahogany, and the rest from hard maple.

life, Mr. Morrison has played for country dances or play parties, and in recent years he has been a very active performer at folk festivals, especially in Arkansas, Missouri, and Tennessee. Like many a good fiddler down in the hills, he can play hours by heart without repeating.

Absie Morrison has been twice married, first to Delia Simmons in 1897, who died in 1904, and later to Jennie Cooper, who is still living. From his first marriage there is one son, Hubert Morrison, and from the second marriage, three sons and two daughters. All the children are married and prosperous, Absie reported, and he spoke with pride of his twenty-three grandchildren and four great-grandchildren. Asked if any of his sons were interested in carrying on the family tradition in music, he replied, a little wistfully, "No, they're just interested in raising fine Hereford cattle and making money."

Mr. Morrison has now retired from farm work. Aside from the many activities with his numerous offspring, music is now a major interest with him, and he hopes to devote more time to it and to making fiddles, too. He has traveled some, once as far east as New Jersey, where he made some Victor records in the 1930's—records now out of circulation. But one can hardly say that he has commercialized his talent, and it is hoped that his genuinely fine country talent will not end with him. Perhaps one of his grandsons, or great-grandsons, may be induced to take up the ancient and honorable family tradition of fine fiddle music.

ARTUS MONROE MOSER

A man of many talents and many activities, Artus Monroe Moser has had a lifelong interest in folksongs. He was born September 24, 1894, in Catawba County of west-central North Carolina. His father and mother, of German and Scottish background respectively, moved in 1896 with their growing family to the Swannanoa Valley in the mountainous region of western North Carolina. His elementary schooling was desultory and to some degree fragmentary. When the family moved to the Vanderbilt Estate, he attended the Biltmore High School, graduating in 1917.

Before he had any college training, Artus taught elementary school briefly and was in the Army during 1917-18, serving in France with the 318th Field Artillery of the 81st Division. He then entered the University of North Carolina, took a Bachelor of Arts degree, and, after two more years of teaching, returned to the university for a master's degree. Interest in further studies took him, at various times, to the University of Wisconsin, the Art Institute in Chicago, and the Pennsylvania Academy of Fine Arts in Philadelphia.

Teaching has been a major interest with him. "But at times," he writes, "I am a farmer, a lumberman, an artist, a historian, a lecturer, a college professor, and a sort of Jack-of-all-trades." (He might have added "singer and collector.") He was an instructor in English and speech at the University of Tennessee for three years, 1926-29; professor of English at Lincoln Memorial University, Harrogate, Tennessee, for thirteen years, 1930-43; and professor of psychology and sociology at Asheville-Biltmore College for six years, 1947-53.

As far back as Artus' mother's family can learn, the singing of ballads and folksongs, as well as old-time religious songs, had been a family custom. Though his father occasionally sang and was "a great lover of old-time fiddle-dance tunes," Artus believes that he got most of his taste and ability in singing from his mother's side of the house. He has no memory of a time when he did not sing and collect the old ballads. To quote him again: "My mother sang to us children—there were eight of us—from the very beginning, and I learned from neighbors too." When, in the 1920's, he was a student at the university, he had a renewed interest in singing and collecting because of folklore courses offered there. During his teaching, particularly at Lincoln Memorial and Asheville-Biltmore, he gave many programs to his classes and to other groups. He uses the dulcimer, the guitar, sometimes the banjo, often no accompaniment at all.

Though Mr. Moser has given many programs in the three states of Tennessee, North Carolina, and Kentucky, he considers himself mainly a collector of folksongs and lecturer on folklore. His major collecting activity took place when he was teaching at Lincoln Memorial at Harrogate, in the foothills of the Cumberlands. Often his students furnished him with "sheafs of ballads and many tunes." He recorded on discs and had tunes transcribed. In 1941-42, he submitted some three hundred songs to the Library of Congress, many of them recorded from his own memory—"I can recall literally hundreds of tunes"—from neighbors and others. Mr. Moser sings and records songs exactly as he remembers or finds them, so as "to retain the tunes and spirit of the traditional songs." "I do not think we should change them," he writes, "except unconsciously."

Artus Monroe Moser was married in 1929 to Mabel Eula Young of Salisbury, North Carolina. They are the parents of three children: Dorthea Joan, born December 5, 1935; Artus M., Jr., born December 4, 1937; Janette Irene, born February 28, 1943. The children are musical and all love to sing ballads and folksongs, carrying on the family tradition. Artus, Jr., is "especially versatile on the guitar," and, writes Artus, Sr., "we all have a lot of fun singing the old songs." They have made no commercial recordings, preferring to let their family traditions remain in amateur status.

JEAN MURAI

Brooklyn-born Jean Murai, professional entertainer and singer of folksongs, has used the medium of folksong as an "audience activator," i.e., to bring about mutual understanding among varied cultural groups.[40] Her formal education—elementary, high school, and college—was obtained in New York City. She took a Bachelor of Arts degree in languages and a master's in psychology at Hunter College. In addition to regular academic courses, she studied piano, dancing, and singing.

Jean Murai first learned folksongs in her own family—"Mama sang Yiddish folksongs and still does"—then from many persons and groups in heterogeneous New York City, and finally from the people in whose countries she has visited. She began her professional folksinging career about 1943, as a USO entertainer in World War II. After the war she took up teaching for a time, organizing the first Folksong Workshop at Hunter College, but later returned to the concert stage. Numbered among her concert- and lecture-recitals are those at Town Hall, Boston University, the Brooklyn Museum, the Salon Cultural in Havana, the International Folk Festival, many schools and colleges, and numerous appearances on radio and television.

Miss Murai has traveled widely, having performed in about half the states and in Italy, Spain, Israel, France, Canada, Mexico, Cuba, Puerto Rico, and other West Indian areas. She has made something of a specialty of Latin-American songs and rhythms. Among her many activities, she has become cultural director of the New York Latin-American Folk Group, the aim of which is to bring together the Spanish-speaking groups and to present their authentic folk culture to various audiences.

As a musician, Miss Murai is skillful and versatile. Though she favors the guitar, on occasion she uses the tambourine, concertina, mandolin, chalil (an Israeli recorder), and a number of West Indian instruments such as maracas and Haitian drums. Music critics and audiences alike express enthusiasm over her performances, for she is a performer of great skill. To quote a pair of typical comments: "Her versatility in the field of folksongs is simply phenomenal." "She captivates her audience with enchanting folksongs and a radiant personality." [41]

JIM AND CARMEN MURRAY, JR.

Philip Jesse "Jim" Murray, Jr., was born in Baltimore, Maryland, on December 24, 1925. He went to grade schools in Washington, D.C., and Savannah, Georgia, and to high school in Youngstown, Ohio. What college work he had was spotty and inconclusive. During World War II he had four months of officer training at John Carroll University in Cleveland. He spent the school year 1945-46 at Rockhurst College and 1946-47 at Junior College, both in Kansas City, Missouri. After brief sessions at Kansas City University and Missouri University, he did a two-year study at Huff Business College in Kansas City.

Jim has a natural bent for music, but his interest and activity in folksong are not a family tradition. His father was a jazz musician, used a tenor banjo, and had his own orchestra in the early 1920's. Jim learned folksongs during the war and afterward from "innumerable sources and individuals," among them records, books, periodicals, many folksingers and folk groups. An obvious important influence in his folksong development was the girl he married in 1951, whose "folk" interests are somewhat more extensive than Jim's.

Carmen Harriette Himmaugh was born May 27, 1931, in Memphis, Tennessee. Her father for some years was a union organizer and the family traveled "throughout the South and the Eastern seaboard." Carmen attended grade schools in Memphis, Richmond, and New Orleans and high school in New Orleans. During the summers she and her brother attended the Highlander Folk School at Monteagle in southeastern Tennessee. This region, Carmen reports, is "rich in a folklore of its own, most of it stemming from the descendants of the indentured servants who came over in the early days of our country." Here they learned not only union songs and things written "by the local boys and girls" but also "what outsiders called folk music." Carmen was not aware "that folk music was something different, that is, a category of music in itself," until she was grown. She was aware, however, that it might bring "quizzical if not disapproving looks" (like union music) if sung in school.

Carmen Himmaugh returned to Highlander as a staff member in 1947, and it was then she heard her first "real recording of folk music"—a John Jacob Niles record of "The Seven Joys of Mary." Thereafter, she writes, "I was doomed to sing folk music from that moment on." In 1949, out of admiration for Pete Seeger, she got a five-string banjo. For the most part, however, she sang unaccompanied until after her marriage and "Jim started helping me with my music."

Jim Murray and Carmen Himmaugh were married in 1951. They have two sons: Philip David ("Flip"), born December, 1952, and Richard Nathan ("Ricky"), born September, 1954. The Murrays have sung in a good many different states—Tennessee, Louisiana, Missouri, New Mexico—in Canada, and a number of times at the National Folk Festival in St. Louis. Their repertoire includes more than four hundred songs from many lands, and they have both become proficient on guitar and banjo, Like many singers, they do their own arranging, "mostly by ear," Jim says, and Jim for a number of years has taught classes in "folk guitar."

Besides his United States Army service, Jim Murray has worked at many occupations. For a number of years he was a material control co-ordinator with the Dart Truck Manufacturing Company in Kansas City. Later he worked in the tabulating-machines division of the Remington Rand Corporation. In the fall of 1955, the Murrays moved to Montreal, Canada, where Jim took a job with a quarry and paving outfit. They have found much folksong interest in and around Montreal where, as Jim puts it, "folk activity takes precedence over folk discussion." They have performed on radio and TV, and have also done recitals at McGill University. Earlier, in the States, they had done tape-recordings for the Voice of America. Jim is continuing his folk-guitar teaching in Montreal.*

* Jim and Carmen separated early in 1959. Carmen and the boys are living in New Orleans.

FOOTNOTES TO CHAPTER 6

1 From the Folkways memorial album, *Take This Hammer*, FP 4, released in 1950. *Time* magazine for December 19, 1949, reporting his death, said he was "sixtyish."
2 *Negro Folk Songs As Sung by Lead Belly*, pp. 4-30.
3 *Ibid.*, pp. 38-52.
4 From Alan Lomax's notes on the record, *Take This Hammer*, FP 4. Lomax says he went on "to enchant and terrify a whole generation of college students from the lecture platform."
5 Frederick Ramsey, Jr., "Lead Belly's Legacy," *Saturday Review of Literature*, January 28, 1950.
6 *American Folksong* (New York, 1947), p. 10.
7 Notes on the record, *Take This Hammer*, FP 4.
8 *Current Biography*, September, 1941; *International Who Is Who in Music* (Chicago, 1951), pp. 279, 446; and I am indebted to Alan Lomax for other biographical details.

THE SINGERS, L TO M   171

9 Donald Day, "John Lomax and His Ten Thousand Songs," *Saturday Review of Literature*, September 22, 1945.
10 See Book Two for discussion of collections and archives.
11 Some years later Alan and Elizabeth were divorced. They had one daughter, Ann Littleton, born in 1945. (Letter)
12 *Current Biography*, September, 1941, and *International Who Is Who in Music*.
13 *Ibid.*
14 As Lomax wrote me from London in April, 1953.
15 Frederick Ramsey, Jr., "Girdle Round the Globe," *Saturday Review*, February 12, 1955.
16 Records Nos. AAFS 66, 70, 104, and 105.
17 I am indebted to Mr. Lunsford for many biographical facts. Much has been written about him in local, regional, and national publications. An excellent illustrated article titled "Minstrel Man of the Appalachians," written by Harold H. Martin, appeared in the *Saturday Evening Post*, May 22, 1948. Another good brief sketch appears in *International Who Is Who in Music*, p. 282.
18 *Saturday Evening Post*, May 22, 1948.
19 *Ibid.*
20 *Who's Who in America*, 1950-51. I am indebted to Mrs. McCord for many biographical details.
21 Edith Fowke and Richard Johnson, eds., *Folk Songs of Canada* (Waterloo Music Co., Waterloo, Ont., 1954), p. 194.
22 Mody C. Boatright, ed., *Mexican Border Ballads and Other Lore* (Austin: Publications of the Texas Folklore Society, XXI, 1946) pp. 1-34.
23 I am indebted to Josef and Miranda Marais for many biographical details. Some facts are taken from notes on the sleeve of the Columbia Masterworks Record ML 4894, released in 1954, an unusual recording in which the two voices and guitar are blended with the Pardo Ancient Instrument Ensemble.
24 Among them: "Sugarbush," "Train to Kimberley," and "Ma Says, Pa Says."
25 *Tony Beaver*, published by G. Schirmer, Inc. *African Heartbeat* received its première in August, 1953, in Idyllwild, California, at the Idyllwild School of Music and the Arts, where Marias and Miranda teach each summer.
26 Bulletin of *Frank Mechau Memorial Exhibition*, Denver Art Museum (1946).
27 Paula Ralska was born in Moscow, Russia, January 31, 1907, and when six months old was brought to America. Her family lived on Long Island and in New York, where she graduated from high school.
28 Helen Worden, "The Singingest Family in America," *Collier's*, May 5, 1951.
29 From Paula Mechau's letters.
30 *Collier's*, May 5, 1951.
31 Bulletin of the *Memorial Exhibition*.
32 *Collier's*.
33 This was a private venture, titled the *Mechau Balladeers*, an album of thirteen ballads on three 78-rpm records. Later, Stinson Records, Inc., brought out the same thirteen songs on an LP record (see Book Three).
34 Notes on the Mechau album.
35 Mavis Gallant, "His Songs Tell a Story," *The Standard* (Montreal), February 10, 1951. I am indebted to *The Standard* for the use of Miss Gallant's article. Alan Mills has also sent me many factual details about his career. See also an article by Helen MacNamara, "Alan Mills—Canada's Balladeer," in the magazine *Saturday Night*, December 13, 1952.

[36] Wesley A. Davis, writing in *Ozark Folklore*, I, 12 (January, 1951).

[37] *Ibid.*

[38] For piano as well as for plucked strings. Mrs. Moon writes: "I have many songs which have never been published—some have come down in my family and others, collected from a wide circle of friends and acquaintances in scattered areas, have not been found anywhere else, to my knowledge."

[39] Published in 1953 by Blasco Music Co., Kansas City, Missouri.

[40] I am indebted to Miss Murai for factual data. When asked for her birthdate, Miss Murai wrote: "I'm not old enough to reveal my age!"

[41] Quotes are taken from a publicity dodger.

CHAPTER 7

The Singers, N to R

RUTH NEAL

Born September 11, 1925, into a family of doctors at Indiana in western Pennsylvania, Ruth Neal showed an extremely early interest in music by humming tunes almost before she could talk. This may have been due partly to a doting grandmother who hummed and sang a lot of folk tunes when Ruth was a little girl. At fifteen she was a soloist in her home-town church.

After early schooling in the Training School of Indiana State Teachers College, Ruth Neal went to Harcum Junior College at Bryn Mawr, Pennsylvania. The next move took her to New York's Juilliard School of Music where, among other things, she sang the lead in the American première of Arthur Benjamin's opera, *The Devil Take Her*. Her talents won her a fellowship and eventually she received a Bachelor of Science degree in voice study. She continued her studies at New York University, taking a Master of Arts in personnel administration.

Besides the grandmother's influence, Ruth's father was a versatile singer, and her mother was a conservatory graduate. During her study at Juilliard, on the advice of her singing coach, Sergius Kagen, Miss Neal added folksongs to her repertoire. This proved to be a turning point in her singing career. She gave her first regular folksong recital in 1945 at the famous Cafe Society Downtown in New York's Sheridan Square. She was encouraged by her friend Burl Ives and eventually did a folksong series over New York City radio station WNYC. By now she was ready for a country-wide tour and, under the sponsorship of a New York agency (Roxanna Wells Bureau), she covered some fifteen states, from New England on south and through the Midwest down to Texas and New Mexico. Everywhere she went, press comments showed that "Ruth Neal and her guitar" captivated enthusiastic audiences across the land.

Miss Neal does not devote full time to folksong activity, though it is a major interest. In 1953, she joined the personnel staff at the University of Florida in Gainesville where, incidentally, there is much interest in folklore and folk music. Since May, 1954, Miss Neal has been a favored singer of folksongs at the annual All-Florida Folk Festival, held at White Springs.

CAMILLE L. NICKERSON

Camille Lucie Nickerson, popularly known as the "Louisiana Lady," is an arranger and interpreter of Creole folk music. She was born in New Orleans, where she received her training through high school and normal school. For further education she attended Oberlin College, School of Music, receiving both the bachelor's (in 1916) and master's (in 1932) degrees in music.

Miss Nickerson's father was a musician and teacher, his major instrument being the violin, "but he taught many other instruments." For years he was director of the music department at Southern University in New Orleans. Miss Nickerson learned many folksongs from her father, as well as from many relatives and friends in New Orleans and elsewhere in Louisiana. She began collecting and doing research in folk music about 1931, working first in the Latin Quarter of New Orleans and then in the rural districts of southern Louisiana, especially in the region around Lafayette and St. Martinsville, the region sometimes known as Evangeline country.

As professor of piano and piano pedagogy in the School of Music, Howard University, Washington, D.C., Miss Nickerson naturally gives many recitals. But an important aspect of her public appearance is her work in folk music, for which she uses the guitar as well as the piano. Her programs include "Creole songs, Creole Counjailles (dance tunes), Cries of the Street Vendors, and folksongs of the American Negro, showing the difference between the folk offerings of the American Negro brought up, on the one hand, in Anglo-Saxon environment, and the Creole Negro, influenced by a Latin regime of French and Spanish colonists in Louisiana."

Miss Nickerson has performed on many occasions and in many areas. Her first formal appearance was at the College Alumnae Club in Washington, D.C., about 1940. She has appeared in the major cities across the land—in Times Hall and Riverside Church in New York City, in St. Catherine's College and Kimball Hall in Chicago, in Sharpe Street Church and Dunbar High School in Baltimore, in St. Paul, in Stanford University and Mills College in California, and twice at the National Folk Festival in St. Louis, just to mention a few of her many appearances. Outside the States, she has sung in Canada, Switzerland, and France. Always there have been favorable reviews of her performances in such papers, for instance, as the Washington *Post* (June 7, 1949) and the New York *Times* (March 6, 1944). Miss Nickerson is skilled both as musician and linguist, presenting her materials in a scholarly framework with a popular appeal. A number of her arrangements of Creole folk music have been published, some as solos and some for part singing.

JOHN JACOB NILES

Of the many singers of folksongs in America today, none more richly deserves the title "Dean of American Balladeers" than John Jacob Niles. For more than a generation he has distinguished himself as collector and folklorist, author and teacher, arranger and composer, craftsman and singer.

Niles was born April 28, 1892, in Louisville, Kentucky, and grew up on a farm in Jefferson County,[1] Kentucky, about one hundred miles from the farm in Clark County where he now lives. His background and training for a career in folklore and folk music were unusually fortunate. His maternal great-grandfather, John Frederick Adams, was a maker of pianos.[2] His father *—farmer, carpenter, and humorous philosopher—was a well-known local folksinger and square-dance caller, and his mother was a pianist and church organist. John Jacob had the usual grade- and high-school training, with emphasis on music from both father and mother. He is an excellent pianist, knowing his Bach and Beethoven and other classics, as well as a world of folk music. His later studies in music were done at the Cincinnati Conservatory of Music, the University and Conservatory of Music at Lyons, France, and the Schola Cantorum in Paris.

Niles's folksong collecting goes back nearly half a century when in 1907, at the age of fifteen and still in high school, he began setting down in a five-cent notebook the songs of his native region. That activity was interrupted in 1917 by World War I when he enlisted in the United States Air Corps. Not entirely interrupted, however, for out of that experience came two books: *Singing Soldiers*, a study

* Unschooled in formal education, he learned to write a beautiful hand by attending a night school.

of Negro singing in the Army; and, in collaboration with two friends, the book of Army songs called *Songs My Mother Never Taught Me*.[3] Niles's collecting has been done in many places over the years, but the bulk of it was in the southern Appalachians, mostly in the southeastern counties of Kentucky, with a spill-over into almost every mountain county in North Carolina, Tennessee, Georgia, Alabama, Virginia, and West Virginia. Though some of his material has been published in Schirmer's "American Folk-Song Series," [4] the great body of it—sixty-five classic ballads and over one thousand songs with variants—is still unpublished.[5]

Niles relates with some amusement his experiences in collecting, pointing out that, of course, one cannot expect to find a "folksinger sitting beside every elderberry bush." Folksongs are elusive, he points out, but they can be found. As he says further: "Only twice in thirty-six years of folklore collecting have I resorted to paying money for the privilege of taking down a folk song, though I must admit using chewing tobacco, drinking whisky, bacon, fat-back, lard, string, cotton gloves, cornmeal, wheat-flower, almanacs, corn-cob pipes, aspirin, soda, garden seeds and other blandishments too numerous to mention, as polite bribes." [6]

Niles's singing career is as long and distinguished as his collecting activity. In fact, his first performance was at the age of six in a Presbyterian church in Louisville, when he sang as his mother accompanied him at the piano.* His first "paid" engagement was at the age of fifteen, when he got $1.50 for assisting a group of chautauqua performers in a Saturday-afternoon show. His more serious public performing began about 1910. By 1920 he had given many folksong recitals, and by 1930 he had sung in most areas of America, as well as in England, Germany, Belgium, Holland, France, and Denmark. By another decade he was doing over fifty recitals a year, and before 1950 he had performed in every state of the Union and was known as a folksinger from Finland and Estonia across the world to Vancouver in Canada. Over the years the number of his performances would run into the thousands.

In his recitals Niles uses only materials he has collected and arranged, accompanying himself on one of his homemade dulcimers. These dulcimers are unusual instruments, in fact, unique.[7] In a period of ten years he made twenty-six of them, and on tour he

---

* Mr. Niles mentioned this episode as a memorable occasion. Old-timers still recall, he told me, a very beautiful picture of mother and child, as his mother carried him back on stage for the applause of about five hundred people. Before Niles had reached the age of ten his father had taught him many ballads, including seventeen verses of "Barbary Ellen."

generally carries along three different ones, his choice for a particular song being determined by the nature of the piece and the effect
he wishes to create. His dulcimers are eight-stringed, tuned in octaves
and fifths, and used as a support to the voice but not to carry the
melody. He believes "that the quality of dulcimer tone is improved
by using the fingers to pluck or strum the strings instead of twang-
ing them with the traditional turkey's quill." [8]

A Niles concert strikes the listener as a combination of sophisticated art and homely simplicity. His world-wide travels, extensive
musical training, and vigorous personality make it inevitable that
his genius should modify the simple traditional melody of a song.
Some folklore purists criticize him for this. But whatever modifying
he does only accentuates his genius as arranger and performing
artist. His audiences, at least, find him fascinating and entertaining.
As one reviewer said, "The haunting spell of his voice, pitched in
falsetto range at times, rough hewn and reedy occasionally in the
lower register, grew on the listener." [9] Other reviewers have written
of the "strange haunting beauty" of his singing, of "enraptured
audiences," and of his unique artistry, a troubadour "whom no
imitator has yet successfully imitated."

Besides the "American Folk-Song Series" mentioned previously,
Niles has done a great amount of arranging and composing, much
of which has been published by G. Schirmer, Inc., and Carl Fischer,
Inc. Many of these pieces are for solo voice with piano accompani-
ment, such as "Go 'Way from My Window," "The Rovin' Gambler,"
"I Wonder As I Wander," "Sweet Little Boy Jesus," and others.
Some 150 pieces are arranged for chorus and are widely used, many
of them *a cappella*, in college choruses, or other singing groups.
Among the better known of these are "The Cherry Tree," "Down
in Yon Forest," "Frog Went Courtin'," "I Wonder As I Wander,"
"You Got to Cross That Lonesome Valley," and others.

Among his lengthy compositions is an oratorio entitled *Lamentation*. This was completed in 1950 and first produced in the spring
of 1951 at Terre Haute, Indiana, by the chorus of Indiana State
Teachers College, under the direction of Ruthann Harrison. He
describes this work, in which he uses several folk tunes, as a "prayer
to deliver the world from the curse of Communism." Another long
work is the *Rhapsody for the Merry Month of May* (requiring about
thirty minutes for performance), composed for full chorus and
soprano solo. His most recent work is *Mary the Rose*, a Christmas
cantata, using singers, orchestra, and dancers to interpret the story of
the Nativity. The use of ballet, particularly in a religious production,
shows the impact of television on the modern composer.[10] Some

of Niles's arrangements and compositions have been developed for full orchestra, an example being *Black Is the Color of My True Love's Hair*. This symphonic piece for strings, done in a setting by Patrick McCarthy, was premièred by the Oklahoma City Symphony over WHB on Sunday evening, March 28, 1954.

Many honors have come to John Jacob Niles in the course of his long and busy folksinging career. He has done a good deal of teaching and lecturing, especially in short courses, at such places as Harvard, the Juilliard School, the Curtis Institute, the Eastman School of Music, and at other music schools, colleges, and universities. In 1950, he was granted an honorary Doctor of Music degree by the Cincinnati Conservatory of Music. Early recording of his folksinging was made by RCA Victor; three albums called *American Folk Lore* were issued on Red Seal records over twenty years ago. Recently the Nileses have launched their own recording business under the Boone-Tolliver label and, if one may judge by Mrs. Niles's account of it,[11] the venture has not been too profitable. The opening concert of the 1951-52 season of the Oklahoma City Symphony featured a *John Jacob Niles Suite* composed by Weldon Hart, a symphonic work honoring Niles and using folk tunes made famous by him. More than fifteen years ago, *Life* magazine devoted a feature article to folksinger Niles.[12]

On March 21, 1936, John Jacob Niles was married to Rena Lipetz, a Wellesley College graduate and magazine writer. They have two sons, Thomas Michael Tolliver, born in 1939, and John Edward, born in 1945. Despite his busy career, his many travels and concerts, Niles enjoys a degree of freedom and relaxation with his family on Boot Hill Farm near Lexington, Kentucky. There he makes his dulcimers, plays and works with his boys, and raises hogs that eventually reach the table as fine Kentucky hams and other pork products. There Mrs. Niles acts as his secretary and booking agent and is the general manager of a busy household. Naturally the singing of folksongs is a constant activity in the Niles household. He has taught the boys much of this fine traditional music, and at one time his elder son assisted him in recitals. Such, briefly, is the life story of the dean of American balladeers, John Jacob Niles, one of our most distinguished and most beloved singers and arrangers of ballads, folksongs, and carols.

HERMES NYE

Native Chicagoan, Kansas educated, and Texan by adoption, Hermes Nye was born on February 11, 1908. After early education in a rural school near Topeka, he attended Topeka High School, graduating in 1925. He then entered Washburn College (now University) and remained for two years. After an interval of a year, he entered the University of Kansas at Lawrence, receiving a Bachelor of Arts degree in 1930 and a Bachelor of Laws in 1933.

Nye's Canadian-born father sang a good many lumberjack songs, sea shanties, and other folk ballads learned in Maine and eastern Canada. Beyond that source, Nye has learned songs from other singers, from records and radio programs, and "most of all" from folksong books, of which he has a large collection. He gave his first regular performance, using a Spanish guitar, in August, 1942, in New Orleans. Since that time his performances have numbered several hundred, for the most part in various parts of Texas, Louisiana, and Old Mexico.

Nye went to Texas in his late teens, first to Amarillo but eventually settling in Dallas, where he still lives. He has done ballad singing over Dallas radio stations KSKY and WFAA, and for many years has been an active member of the very active Texas Folklore Society. Nye says he has "a sneaking fondness for the English things from Percy and Child, especially when I can find Texas versions." In 1952, Folkways Records issued the first of Hermes Nye's LP recordings titled *Anglo-American Ballads;* later recordings came out under the titles *Texas Folk Songs* and *Ballads of the Civil War* (see Book Three for details).

Hermes Nye was married to Mary Elizabeth Beasley in 1937. Their son, Eric Beasley, born in 1948, has already learned many of the songs his father sings. Mr. Nye for many years has been associated with the Whittle Music Company of Dallas. Besides his business activities and his singing, Nye does book reviews for the Dallas *Times-Herald,* the *Southwest Review,* and occasionally for the Texas Folklore Society publications.

JOAN O'BRYANT

Singer of folksongs and university teacher, Joan O'Bryant was born in Wichita, Kansas, September 25, 1926. She attended public schools in Wichita and entered the University of Wichita in 1942. During 1945 she studied at the National University in Mexico City and then returned to take a Bachelor of Arts degree in 1946 and a Master of Arts in 1949 at her home university.

When Joan was a child, her maternal grandparents taught her many old songs, and she remembers a great-grandmother, who came from Indiana, as a singer of ballads. But her parents were not singers of folksongs. As a student Joan studied voice and classical music, but folk music has been her major interest, musically, for the past fifteen years. In this field, including playing the guitar, she is largely self-taught.

Joan O'Bryant's public performances began with civic groups in Wichita in the early 1940's. From then on, her singing radius has extended over eight states of the Middle West—north to Wisconsin and Minnesota, south to Arkansas and New Mexico, and west to Colorado. During her stay in Mexico City she was a guest performer over radio station XEW. She has appeared on television, and in 1951 she began a sponsored radio program featuring ballads and folksongs. Her performances are numbered in the hundreds.

Joan has done some collecting of folk material in eastern Kansas and Oklahoma, as well as in the Ozarks, though as yet she has not published. Among her favorite songs are the Child ballads, especially those of the mournful or lonesome kind that have come out of the southern Appalachians. When she appeared at the Ozark Folk Festival in October, 1956, she sang "In Kansas," "Careless Love," "Marble Town," and "Girls, Quit Your Rowdy Ways," and was a favorite among the many singers there. Her guitar accompaniments were particularly effective, and her singing had an authentic, unaffected quality. Though somewhat glamorous herself, she does not believe in glamorizing the folksongs. That kind of treatment, she feels, is a misinterpretation of the songs. Miss O'Bryant has had many favorable press notices on her programs.[13]

Miss Joan O'Bryant is an assistant professor of English at the University of Wichita. Largely through her efforts to preserve the folklore of Kansas, the board of regents of the university has made a grant for establishing an Archive of Midwest Folklore, the first such archive in Kansas. Professor Henry Malone, also of the English staff, is interested in the archive on the linguistic side. Thus far, more than a hundred songs and as many folk tales have been tape-recorded.

MARY O'HARA

Mary O'Hara was born May 12, 1935, in County Sligo, western Ireland. She completed secondary schooling at the Ursuline convent in Sligo town and at Sion Hill, Dominican convent in Blackrock, County Dublin. She next attended the Royal Irish Academy of Music, where she took up study of the ancient Irish harp under M. Ni Sheadha.

Mary learned folksongs at the convent from her singing teacher, Sister Mary Angela, O.P. But many of the traditional Gaelic songs were taught her by such Dublin County singers as Sean Og O

Tuamdha (of Radio Eireann), Mairin Ni Sheadha, and Calum Maclean. She has collected songs in the Hebridean Islands as well as in Connemara, County Galway, Ireland. What may be called Miss O'Hara's official singing debut occurred when she sang over Radio Eireann in May, 1952. Since that date, her singing has been in demand increasingly, she has made three long-playing records * (see Book Three), and the circle of admiring listeners and friends has widened to the Western world. Her recitals, now numbering well over two hundred, have been presented in Ireland, England, Scotland, Wales, Holland, Sweden, Ghana, and, during the winter of 1956-57, in the United States. After appearances on TV in New York, she gave a memorable recital † on February 10, 1957, at the Phillips Gallery in Washington, D.C.

Mary O'Hara met Richard Selig, American poet and scholar, in Dublin in August, 1955. At that time he was a Rhodes Scholar at Magdalen College, Oxford, and he had come from Seattle in the Pacific Northwest. Mary and Richard were married in Oxford, England, on July 23, 1956, and in September they sailed for New York to spend a year in the States.

The unique charm of Mary O'Hara stems from her bell-like high soprano voice, her studied simplicity (a discipline of the highest order) in projecting the songs in both Gaelic and English, and her consummate skill with the ancient Irish harp. According to Liam Clancy (Tradition record TLP-1024), both background and studies have steeped her in traditional Irish music, and she is now considered "one of the most popular singers in Ireland." Her popularity is bound to grow in the New World.

MILT OKUN

Milton T. Okun was born December 23, 1923, in Brooklyn, New York. The New York City public-school system gave him his educa-

---

* Two LP's, released outside the U.S.A. and Canada, were made for the Decca Record Co., Ltd., of England, under the Beltona label (LBE 13 and LBE 20) and appeared in December, 1956, and July, 1958. Reviews of her Tradition record (TLP-1024) have been in superlative terms only. *Songs of Ireland,* wrote Frederic Ramsey, Jr., in the *Saturday Review* (December 27, 1958), "can be counted among the year's finest offerings" in folksongs. In the New York *Times* (January 4, 1959), critic Robert Shelton calls her "a gifted harpist" and "rarely does one hear such splendid rapport between voice and instrument."

† Enthusiastic reviews appeared in Washington, D.C., papers, the *Post-Times Herald* and the *Evening Star* for February 11, 1957. Frank C. Campbell of the *Evening Star* wrote: "Naïveté and worldly wisdom are magically welded [in her singing] into a style that can express all that is human and moving, and totally unaffected by time."

tion, including a Bachelor of Science degree in music education. Later he attended the Oberlin Conservatory of Music of Oberlin College, receiving a Master of Music degree in education.

Milt Okun learned folksongs from hundreds of people and, he reports, "it is impossible to fix the blame." Most responsible, however, is his sister-in-law, Mrs. Beth Griffin Okun, a well-known square-dance caller in the Northeastern states. Okun is a latecomer (beginning about 1950) in singing folksongs, but his enthusiasm and sympathetic interpretation, as he strums guitar or banjo, lend both genuineness and sincerity to his performances.

Okun has taught music at the Joseph Pulitzer Junior High School in Jackson Heights, New York City, and has also conducted a folksong and ballad course in the Extension Division of City College in New York. In the early 1950's, he was director of the Adirondack Folk Song and Dance Festival, held during the summers on the shores of Schroon Lake in upper New York State. Milt Okun has made a number of LP records under the Stinson label (see Book Three). Both his records and live singing have had favorable reviews in many publications.[14]

CHARLES H. OLDFATHER, JR.

Of "singing professors" there are a goodly number in this book, and few of them can give a more satisfying performance than Charles Oldfather, professor of law at the University of Kansas. His guitar accompaniments appear simple—"I'm just a chorder plus," he modestly says—but are in reality complex and carefully controlled, and his relaxed command of a particular folksong is studied artistry of a high order.

Charles Oldfather was born in Crawfordsville, Indiana, on February 10, 1920. He attended public school in Lincoln, Nebraska, and went to the Hotchkiss School at Lakeville, Connecticut, for his high schooling. He entered Harvard College in 1938, transferred to the University of Nebraska in 1940, taking a Bachelor of Arts degree in 1941. After service in World War II, he again entered Harvard, this time the Harvard Law School, in 1945, received the Bachelor of Laws degree in 1948, and came to the University of Kansas in 1950.

Oldfather's parents sang in "church quartets and choirs," and his father played the guitar and knew some folksongs. Beyond this home background he has picked up songs from books and records and "occasionally from other singers." He had some "formal training in voice in prep school and college" and took up the guitar in 1943. Asked how many performances in how many states he had given,

Professor Oldfather replied: "As you know, this is a hobby with me. I have sung, maybe 250 recitals, in four states, and only in the environs of my residences since 1943." He has cut thirteen twenty-five-minute tapes for KFKU, the university FM radio station. His singing has had favorable reviews in Topeka, Lawrence, Salina, and Kansas City papers.

Charles H. Oldfather, Jr., was married to Hortense Casady on May 14, 1942. They are the parents of seven children, whose names and birthdates are as follows: Felicia (May 29, 1943), Timothy (May 31, 1945), Stephen (October 16, 1946), Melanie (January 14, 1950), Christopher (January 13, 1952), Jonathan (June 2, 1955), and William (November 22, 1957). The family home is on a rural route out of Lawrence, Kansas.

HARRY OSTER

Seeing a guitar in a pawnshop turned the trick. While Harry Oster was working on an advanced degree in business administration, his friends had been trying to interest him in folk music. He liked music well enough but hadn't thought much about folk music. He bought the guitar for fourteen dollars and, having bought it, found himself strumming accompaniments to the kind of music his friends got excited about—folk music. The guitar was the start of what has turned out to be a handsome collection of folk-music instruments as well as the spark for a serious interest in America's traditional music.

To begin at the beginning. Harry Oster was born in Cambridge, Massachusetts, April 12, 1923.[15] He went through the public elementary and high schools in Cambridge and, like many a bright boy of eighteen, moved on to Harvard. After a brief interruption by World War II, he returned to Harvard and took a Bachelor of Arts degree in 1946, majoring in English. From Harvard he went to New York for graduate work at Columbia University, intending to work in the field of business administration. In 1948, he took a master's degree in that field, but in the meantime the folk-music interest had taken root.

After a brief interval of teaching at Utica College, a branch of Syracuse University at Utica, New York, he returned to graduate study, this time in the field of English and music at Cornell University. Here, under the leadership of Professor Harold Thompson, he found a lively and active center of folklore. He took both a master's and doctor's degree in English at Cornell, at the same time developing an expert's knowledge and practice in the field of folk-song. In 1953, he joined the faculty of the University of Toledo in

Ohio, and offered the first folksong-folklore course in that institution. In the fall of 1955, he joined the English faculty of Louisiana State University at Baton Rouge. In the spring of 1956, with other interested persons, he helped reorganize and revitalize the moribund Louisiana Folklore Society. With young and active members like Dr. Oster, the society may experience a growth in a region of America where folksong, as well as folklore in general, flourishes abundantly. Dr. Oster collected some folksongs in New York State in 1950, in Ohio in 1953-55, and now is embarking on further collecting in Louisiana.

Though Dr. Oster's parents are not musicians, he reports that "they do sing folksongs occasionally in Yiddish." Oster learned many folksongs from college friends and, of course, from his extensive study of the field. He gave his first folksong performance in June, 1948, at a boys' camp in Maine. During the past decade he has appeared on, or given, many programs, including "Monitor" (N.B.C.), various college programs in Massachusetts, New York, Ohio, Michigan, Maine, and Louisiana. On a 1954 summer European trip, he performed in France and England. For accompaniment he uses various instruments—guitar (twelve-string), dulcimer (one of his own make), five-string banjo, and autoharp. Other instruments in his collection include the lute (purchased in Mexico City), zither, Irish harp-lute, and flute.

As one considers such enthusiastic students and performers of folk music as, for instance, Alan Lomax, Pete Seeger, Carl Sandburg, and Harry Oster, he is tempted to conclude that folksingers are made as well as born!

TOM PALEY

Mathematician and teacher Tom Paley, a handy man with guitar and banjo, was born in New York City on March 19, 1928. He attended public school in New York, went to high school for a time in Hollywood, California, but returned to New York and finished in 1945 at the Bronx High School of Science. He took a Bachelor of Science degree in 1950 at City College of New York, majoring in mathematics. He went to Yale for graduate study, taking a Master of Arts in mathematics in 1952, and continuing toward the doctorate.

Tom Paley's parents were students of classical music, and for a while his mother taught piano, but Tom's interest in folk music does not stem from family tradition. Toward the end of his high-school days he "became actively interested" in folk music and bought a guitar and a five-string banjo. He learned songs from other singers, records, books, and the radio. Folksongs, he believes, have always seemed more natural and enjoyable than the usual run of "popular" music and, despite his serious study and teaching of mathematics, he has found time "to do quite a bit of singing and picking."

Tom Paley has done a good deal of singing of folksongs in the past dozen years, particularly in New York and Connecticut, but also in the other New England states and in Virginia. About his performing Tom says: "I guess most folk singers depend on their voices and merely use a guitar or a banjo to provide a bit of accompaniment, but I have tended to accent my instrumentals more than my singing." * Some of those who have heard him or his recordings believe that his "instrumentals" are far more skillful than his singing. Tom also teaches guitar and banjo, but his major teaching activity has been mathematics at the University of Connecticut and elsewhere.

On June 11, 1959, in Washington, D.C., Tom Paley was married to Claudia Lingafelt. After a gay party that included a host of Washington folk-music enthusiasts, the Paleys left on a concert tour with the "New Lost City Ramblers." †

KENNETH PEACOCK

Having made an LP recording (Folkways) of Newfoundland songs and ballads, Kenneth Peacock is listed here among the singers. The singing of folksongs, however, is a minor activity with him, for he is a distinguished musicologist and collector for the National Museum of Canada.

Kenneth Peacock was born on April 7, 1922, in Toronto, Canada. He was educated in the Toronto public schools, entered the Royal Conservatory of Music, University of Toronto, and was awarded two degrees after studies in music, philosophy, and English. He is a composer of piano, chamber, and orchestral music and has made musical settings of folksongs for concert use.

Mr. Peacock has collected extensively for the National Museum and for a number of years worked with Canada's distinguished folklorist, Marius Barbeau, now retired. In 1951, 1952, and again in 1958, he collected in Newfoundland. Then in western Canada during 1953 and 1954 he collected Indian music of the Canadian Plains. Of his Newfoundland collecting, he wrote this comment: "I'm preparing my Nfd. material for publication in the next year or so. I hope it will be a really definitive cross-section of the island's traditional and local music."

---

* Jacket notes on Elektra record, EKL-12, issued in 1953 (see Book Three).
† Reported in *Caravan*, August-September, 1959.

JOHN B. PENNINGTON

Persons looking for old-time characters down in the Arkansas hills might choose John Pennington of Fayetteville as a good example. He was born in Clay County, Kentucky, on April 14, 1882, the youngest son in a family of ten children. When John was five, his father sold out in Kentucky, loaded the family in a covered wagon, and, after thirty-one days on the road, they finally settled down in Madison County in northwest Arkansas. Here John B. got a meager education in a country school and spent the better part of his life scratching out a living in the niggardly hills.

But life wasn't all hard. "I always delighted in singing from a small boy, and hearing other people sing," he said. He learned many songs and, having a good memory, he collected some three hundred ballads and folksongs, most of these during his early years. Many of his songs have been tape-recorded by the University of Arkansas Folklore Archives. Late in middle life, Mr. Pennington became a salesman and moved to Fayetteville, where he now lives.

DESMOND POWELL

Though he considers himself strictly an amateur in the field, Desmond Powell has been singing folksongs for over forty years, but, he adds, "mostly to myself." In that very thought lies one of the perennially delightful facts about folksongs—the people who sing them, publicly or privately, derive a personal satisfaction that no other kind of singing gives. Desmond Powell was born in Waverly, New York, on July 14, 1899. After a dozen years in the Waverly public schools, he went on to Cornell University, Ithaca, New York, to pick up three academic degrees: an A.B. in 1922, an M.A. in 1924, and a Ph.D. in 1927.

Dr. Powell in his youth learned some folksongs from his mother and an uncle, from an older brother, and "from others in the neighborhood." He plays the guitar and has given a few public performances over the years, but "you can count my public performances on your fingers." He has done some "casual collecting" in southern New York, northern Pennsylvania, and in Arizona, and has recorded for the Arizona Folklore Collection and the Library of Congress.

Dr. Desmond Powell, who is head of the English Department, University of Arizona, Tucson, was married to Janet Gregg MacAdam in 1942. Mrs. Powell, though not a singer, is a student of ballad and folksong literature. Dr. Powell occasionally writes and lectures on the subject of folklore, but modestly insists that he does so "always in the role of amateur."

LE QUATUOR ALOUETTE
de Montréal, P.Q., Canada

Among ensembles devoted to folksinging, none is more popular than Le Quatuor Alouette,[16] authentic interpreters of French-Canadian folksongs. The quartet was founded in 1930 by Roger Filiatrault and André Trottier. The other two members are Émile Lamarre and Jules Jacob.

Soon after 1930 Le Quatuor inherited the repertoire of an earlier singing group called the "Troubadours de By-Town," organized in 1927 by Charles Marchand. The Troubadours sang at the first two festivals of Canadian folksong in Quebec in 1927 and 1928,* but after the unexpected death of Marchand in 1930, their work was disorganized. Oscar O'Brien, an intimate collaborator of Marchand and inheritor of his repertoire, learned of Le Quatuor through Marchand's friend, Trottier, and consented to be director of the group. Their first public appearance under his direction was in 1932.

From that time on, their success was assured, and many popular concerts have established their reputation not only in Canada and the United States but in South America and in Europe. During the past quarter century they have sung on every important occasion and in every important place in Canada. To mention only a few instances. In 1933, they sang at the World Postal Conference in Ottawa, at the Handicraft Guild Exhibition in Toronto, in the Plateau Auditorium in Montreal, and they made twenty-six broadcasts over the Canadian Broadcast Corporation. In 1935, among other appearances, they sang before the Historical Society at Château Ramezay, the Association of Canadian Authors, and gave thirty-seven broadcasts over the C.B.C. In 1936, a notable appearance was made at the anniversary celebration of the founding of Montreal. In 1938, they helped launch "Le Réveil Rural" program for the C.B.C. A crowning achievement came when, in 1939, they were chosen to sing for Their Majesties King George VI and Queen Elizabeth on their visit to Montreal. Recently they have done many C.B.C. television programs.

Their tours of the United States began in 1934 and have continued intermittently ever since. They have sung in such diverse places as the Brooklyn Academy of Arts and Sciences, New Hampshire University, the city of Detroit, the American Legion convention in

* The Quebec festivals sparked a revival of popular interest in Canada's folklore and folksong, but that is another story. Marius Barbeau for many years has been one of the leading spirits in this revival.

Cleveland, and Town Hall in New York. In 1942, they represented Quebec at the National Folk Festival in Washington, D.C. At that time they also sang at the Press Club and at the White House. In 1943, they attended similar festivals in Chicago and Philadelphia.

In 1945, their leader, Oscar O'Brien, entered the Order of the Benedictine Monks at the Abbaye of Saint-Benoît-du-Lac, P.Q., and became a priest in 1952. Direction of Le Quatuor passed to M. Filiatrault, though Dom Oscar O'Brien remains interested in their advancement.

Le Quatuor toured the major cities of Brazil in 1945, and, of course, their trips abroad, particularly in France and Belgium, have been unusually successful. The first of these was in 1934, when the Canadian government made them official delegates to France for the fourth centenary of the discovery of Canada by Jacques Cartier, and they gave many concerts in Paris and other centers. Again in 1937, they toured France and Belgium, giving thirty-five concerts.

From the beginning, Le Quatuor Alouette set out to give artistic interpretation to Canadian folksongs. To understand the quality of their performance and success, one needs to know the background of the singers, or at least of their leader. Roger Filiatrault, one of the original organizers of the group and the present director, was born in Montreal on February 5, 1905. His father was a choir director at a Catholic church. The son was educated in music and the classics at the Séminaire Sainte Thérèse and Collège de Montréal from 1918 to 1923. During these years he studied solfeggio, harmony, voice, and violin. He continued his musical studies in France and Belgium from 1926 to 1930, at the Conservatoire Royal de Musique de Bruxelles and the Conservatoire National de Paris.

In 1930, his formal education completed, Filiatrault returned to Montreal to enter upon a career of teaching music and doing concert work. Though he knew much folk music from his early days, he considers Oscar O'Brien, authority on French-Canadian folk music, his great mentor in that field. Filiatrault has taught in many schools: the School of Music at Université d'Ottawa, École Vincent-d'Indy d'Outrement, École Normale de Musique de l'Institut Péda-gogique, École Supérieure de Musique des Ursulines des Trois Rivières, and École de Musique de l'Institut de Nazareth (for the blind)—to mention a few. Since 1950, he has been assistant director of the Vocal Department of the Conservatoire de Musique et d'Art Dramatique de la Province de Québec.

Roger Filiatrault was married to Isabelle Cardinal September 30, 1950, and they make their home in Montreal.

JARED REED

The son of theater people—"my folks were nomads"—Jared Reed was born April 1, 1924, in Columbia, South Carolina. His father, Daniel Reed, playwright and actor-director,[17] founded the Town Theatre in Columbia; and his mother, Isadora (Bennett) Reed, was a press agent and playwright. The Reed circle of friends included composers and musicians, scholars and folklorists.

Jared's education was unusually good if somewhat scattered. Early schooling was in Rochester, New York, Beaufort, South Carolina, New York City, Palm Beach, Florida, Los Angeles and Hollywood, and Columbia, South Carolina. High-school years were spent at Christ School in Arden, North Carolina, and Riverdale Country School at Riverdale-on-Hudson, New York. After one year (1941) at Wake Forest College, he entered the Marine Corps, won his wings in Naval Aviation, and spent five years in the service.

Jared Reed grew up with folksongs, though the term "traditional singer" does not strictly apply to him. He and sister Susan (*q.v.*) learned songs from parents, from many friends, such as Carl Sandburg, Huddie Ledbetter, and Ralph Cullinan—who came from Ireland via the Abbey Theatre Players. He learned, too, from many traditional singers in the many travels of the Reed family, and from exchanging songs with Aussies and others in the Pacific war area. Collections of ballads and folksongs, as well as recordings, made their contribution also. Jared uses the guitar in his recitals, sometimes the lute or mountain dulcimer, makes his own arrangements, and has done "a little composing both for piano and settings for some of my favorite poems." He's also had occasion to teach guitar and folksinging in the professional training program of the American Theatre Wing.

Jared Reed has had considerable activity in the theater and on television. On Broadway he was featured for a year in the show, *Texas Li'l Darlin'*, and for two years in *Paint Your Wagon*. On radio and television he has performed—among others—on "Kraft Music Hall," "Philco Studio One," and the "Kate Smith Hour." He has given scores of concerts in more than half the states and in Canada.

Jared Reed was married to Janet Cade from 1944 to 1947. They had a daughter, Janet Penelope, born June 8, 1945. Jared was married to Judith Seaton in 1950. As actor and singer, Jared Reed in his middle thirties is apparently well on his way to a long career in entertainment.

SUSAN REED

Susan Reed, sister of Jared, was born in 1927 in Columbia, South Carolina. Like Jared, she traveled about a good deal with the Reed family, and her schooling was done in various places—in South Carolina, California, and private school in New York.

Susan learned her folksongs from many sources—her repertoire is vast—and she has learned them well, presenting her song-stories with the seeming naïveté of an untutored mountain lass. But there is carefully studied art in her simplicity. Sigmund Spaeth characterizes her voice as "the female counterpart of the Burl Ives tenor, and her carefully planned naïveté, including the spoken comments of her concert programs, creates an effect of artless spontaneity that is completely charming." [18]

Very early Susan Reed sang in a church choir in New York City and for the sick and wounded in hospitals in World War II. At seventeen she was singing professionally in Cafe Society Uptown, and her Town Hall debut came in 1946. In the following half-dozen years Miss Reed toured the country extensively, doing club, concert, and college circuits with great success. She owes much to many sources, whether books, records, collectors, actors, traditional singers, or her family. Appearing on Mitch Miller's radio program on October 14, 1956, she mentioned that many Irish folksongs came from her friends among the Abbey Players, especially from Ralph Cullinan and Farrell Pelley. Much earlier, someone had given her an Irish harp, which she uses effectively as accompaniment. The zither and autoharp are among her favorites, too. In fact, for the past dozen years she has been interested in making a collection of stringed folk instruments.[19]

Susan Reed has made records for RCA Victor, Columbia, Elektra, and others (see Book Three). She is married to actor James Karen, and they make their home in New York. A recent report states that they "have just become the parents of a boy, Reed Karen." *

THE SINGING RITCHIES

In America, whole families have grown up in traditions that have set a pattern for a way of life. These traditions may be concerned with religious practices, economic procedures, or social usages of various kinds. Often, traditional folk music has played a major role

* *Caravan* (April-May, 1959), p. 46. The magazine also announces a new Elektra release by Susan Reed called *Songs for Wee Folk,* "a collection of folk songs for children."

in these family usages. One such singing family is that of Balis and Abigail (Hall) Ritchie of Viper, Kentucky.

The Ritchie chronicle has been told with freshness, dignity, and good humor by the youngest of Balis Ritchie's fourteen children, Jean.[20] As early as 1768, the first Ritchies, five brothers, came into the Colonies. Jean's lineal ancestor, James Ritchie, settled in Virginia, moved on to North Carolina, and later pioneered in Kentucky, where six generations of Ritchies have thrived and multiplied during the past two centuries.[21] And these six generations have been singing right down through the centuries to the present day.

Balis Ritchie, now around ninety, not only knew a lot of songs but collected a good many "amongst the people in the county," and at one time hand-printed a little collection called *Lover's Melodies*.[22] Balis made his own musical instruments, such as fiddles and banjos, from gourds, hair from the horse's tail, possum hides, and so on. And, of course, he is a skilled dulcimer player: "Dad would maybe take down the dulcimer off the wall and make the old tunes ring proud in the still, forsaken night." [23]

Balis' cousin, Jason Ritchie—commonly called Uncle Jason—is another who knows a lot of the old songs and the background of the Ritchie family. Born in Perry County, Kentucky, and now around ninety, Uncle Jason has practiced law for some fifty years and, for a number of terms, was county attorney for Knott County.[24] Jason did not sing folksongs in public except at parties and dances, and sometimes for persons collecting. He has a prodigious memory for the songs but hadn't thought much about that until, as he says, "Jean decided to make a collection and I gave her a lot of them." Uncle Jason never uses any accompanying instrument.

All the children * of Balis and Abigail Ritchie know and sing folksongs, though some have done more with them than others. Now that they are all grown and gone from the family circle, their lives have moved in many directions, but the old songs stay with them. Eldest of the children, May Ritchie (Mrs. L. F. Deschamps) reports that she "learned a lot of ballads as a child and had great pleasure in singing them." She was a student at the Pine Mountain Settlement School, Pine Mountain, Kentucky, during the first year (1916-17) that Cecil Sharp came to the mountains to collect ballads. She and others sang for him and did some square dancing at Far House, where Mr. Sharp was a guest.[25]

Una Ritchie (fourth of the fourteen children) with others also sang ballads for Sharp when he visited the Appalachians. She had learned songs from her parents and Uncle Jason and "from old

* Thirteen lived to be grown; one died in infancy.

women ballad singers—notably Aunt Annie Combs."[26] After local
schooling, Una Ritchie went to the Hindman Settlement School,
then attended Science Hill School in Shelbyville, Kentucky, and
later took a degree at Wellesley College. In 1934, she married
Thomas Yahkub. She and her husband led a study group of teachers
and students through India during the summer of 1952 and heard
much Indian folksinging and folk music. Their teen-age daughter
found striking similarities in songs of India and some American
white spirituals.[27]

Always, Una Ritchie has sung folksongs and swapped songs with
singers in India and America, though she has not made singing a
career. One instance of her public performance should be mentioned:
in 1926, on a New York stage (Princess Theatre), she sang ballads
between the acts of Lulu Vollmer's tragic folk play, *Sun-Up*. The
ballads were "Barbara Allen" and "The Brown Girl," and the occasion was a benefit performance given for the Hindman Settlement
School. In 1951, Una Ritchie wrote a pageant, *From Where the
Pattern Grew*, commemorating the fiftieth anniversary of the Hindman School. This work was a "combination of historical matter
interwoven with the singing past of the people in that section,"
an attempt to show our nation's need of rediscovering its past in
the early songs and folkways.

Edna Ritchie (ninth of the fourteen), born in Hindman, Kentucky, in 1910, attended the Pine Mountain Settlement School and
Berea College, Berea, Kentucky, taking a Bachelor of Arts degree
in 1936. Miss Edna has taught in the Hindman School and at Jeff,
Kentucky, not far from Viper. She uses much folksong material in
her teaching, and she is an authority on the play-party games of
the Appalachians. She, too, like her sisters, learned many songs from
her parents, Uncle Jason, other relatives, and many friends. For
accompaniment she uses the dulcimer, autoharp, accordion, or piano.
Not a collector or professional singer, she has sung a great deal for
informal groups, assembly and chapel programs, and at various festivals all the way from North Carolina to Colorado. She once composed and directed an operetta, *Little Black Sambo*, playing her
accompaniments in true folk fashion from memory, and never wrote
them down. "I intended to, but I didn't have time!" she said.

Jewel Ritchie (tenth of the fourteen), born in Viper, Kentucky,
in 1914, received her grade schooling in Viper and at the Pine
Mountain Settlement School, and her high-school training at the
Hindman School. After graduation from high school in 1934, she
attended Berea College for two years, taught school for one year,
then took a four-year course in nurse's training. She became an

Army nurse in 1943, and was stationed in Texas, where she met her future husband, J. B. Robinson, an Army officer. They were married in January, 1944. After their Army service (her husband spent a year overseas), they moved to a farm in southeast Missouri, then later to Indiana, where they now live and are rearing their five children, three girls and two boys.

Besides the Ritchie family interest in singing ballads, Mrs. Robinson reports that her interest in the folksong field was extended by activities at the Pine Mountain and Hindman Schools. She and her sisters attended summer sessions of the John C. Campbell Folk School at Brasstown, North Carolina, where they learned and taught more folk music and dancing, exchanging their songs with others. They also took part in the annual Craftsman's Fair at Asheville, North Carolina. Now, Mrs. Robinson passes along to her children the ballads and the folk games she loved as a girl. "They always like to help do dishes," she writes, "because that is our ballad singing time." Thus the heritage of ballads and folksongs continues, in oral tradition, from one generation to another.

JEAN RITCHIE

Most widely known, most scholarly, and most professional (that is, in the folksong field) of the Ritchie clan is the youngest member in the big family of Balis and Abigail Ritchie. Jean was born December 8, 1922, in Viper, Perry County, Kentucky.[28] Her schooling, through high school, was obtained in Viper, since by the time she came along the village had grown enough to have a high school. She attended Cumberland College, a junior college at Williamsburg, Kentucky, for two years, graduating in 1943 at the head of her class. Then, at the University of Kentucky, she took a Bachelor of Arts degree in social work in 1946, received departmental honors, and was elected to Phi Beta Kappa.

After college, Jean was a teacher and supervisor of elementary education in her native Perry County. From this brief experience she went to work at the Henry Street Settlement (1947-49) in New York City, where she sang folksongs to the accompaniment of her dulcimer.[29] She had not thought there was anything special about these songs, or the way she sang them, until she went to New York. But from that time forward her reputation has grown until she now has become known internationally.

Jean Ritchie was married to George Pickow, a magazine photographer, on September 29, 1950. In the summer of 1951, they went on a picture-taking trip to the North Carolina coast. During this jaunt they tape-recorded several folksingers, and these recordings are now in the Library of Congress. For the year September, 1952, to August, 1953, Jean Ritchie received a Fulbright grant to study folk music in the British Isles. She and her husband traveled extensively in England, Scotland, and Ireland, and by tape recorder they obtained many hundreds of fine old songs. They were able to do this partly because Jean carried along her dulcimer and was always ready to exchange a song with anyone who sang.*

Jean has appeared many times on radio and television, both in the United States and the British Isles. With Oscar Brand (q.v.) she has acted in several film shorts employing folk music, and her photographer husband has done the filming. One such picture is *Courting Songs*, presented in the Paris Theatre of New York. And, of course, recording companies in both London and New York have made Jean's singing widely known throughout the Western world. (See Book Three for details on records.)

In recent years Jean Ritchie has devoted her time to giving folksong recitals and to writing. She has performed in most of the United States, in Mexico, England, and Ireland. While abroad she was the sole representative of the United States at the World Festival of Folk Dance and Song in Biarritz, France, and Pamplona, Spain. She has published three books, two of them brief collections of Ritchie family songs, with story and pictures. The third, published in 1955, is the widely and favorably reviewed biography of her Kentucky family.[30] Another accomplishment: George and Jean Pickow are the parents of two sons, Peter and Johnny, born in 1954 and 1958 respectively.

Jean likes to sing the old songs with dulcimer or sometimes guitar, but mostly, she writes, "I like best to sing the old songs without any accompaniment, the way they used to be sung." Of Jean's singing, no wiser comment than that of Alan Lomax has been given: "Jean's quiet, serene, objective voice, the truth of her pitch, the perfection and restraint of her decorations (the shakes and quavers that fall upon the melody to suit it to the poetry) all denote a superb mountain singer."[31] This, indeed, is genuine folksinging in its truly authentic tradition by one who has become Queen of the Cumberland Mountain Singers.

---

* In December, 1956, Jean and husband George Pickow began issuing a series of records of their tape recordings from abroad. The first of these is a 12-inch LP called *Field Trip* (under the label Collector Limited Editions 1201) containing twenty-one songs. Jean alternates her singing with the field recordings, showing similarities and differences in Old and New World versions. The record is most excellent, both musically and technically.

ROBIN ROBERTS

Robin Roberts, actress and folksinger, was born in Salt Lake City, Utah, on January 12, 1928. Early schooling was in Salt Lake, in Seattle, and high school at Nyack, New York. She entered Sarah Lawrence College in 1945 and took a Bachelor of Arts degree in 1949.

The Roberts family, like many an American family, loved to sing around the piano, and so Robin learned a lot of older music, much of it traditional. But she attributes her serious approach to folksongs to other singers and to many recordings of folksongs, with special credit going to Alan Lomax. Robin got her first job in Paris singing folksongs at the Café L'Abbaye. She uses the guitar, having learned it in her early teens, and occasionally the dulcimer for accompaniment, but keeps her accompaniments simple and effective, "trying very hard to stay as traditional as possible." Miss Roberts has traveled a good deal and has given recitals in half a dozen Eastern states, as well as in France, England, and Ireland. The public press in general has done highly favorable reporting on her appearances.

Though Miss Roberts knows and sings songs of many nationalities, she has a special liking for Irish folk music. She helped Alan Lomax collect in Ireland for Volume I of "The Columbia World Library of Folk and Primitive Music" and has been his assistant in compiling and editing additional volumes in this extensive series.[32] She has herself recorded many songs—"six sides for H.M.V. in London, several for the B.B.C. collection," and a wonderful baker's dozen of *Irish Street Songs* on a Stinson long-play (SLP 63).

Miss Roberts has definite and solid ideas on folk music, and she approaches the whole field with commendable sympathy and understanding. Some of her discerning remarks are worth quoting in rounding out this brief sketch:

> I've always preferred folksongs . . . because they are concerned with the most profound human situations in a very direct, personal and truthful way. . . . From childhood I was attracted to the old ballads because of their wonderful poetry and later discovered the less obvious though real poetry of our American Negro worksongs, chanteys, hymns, etc. . . . The airs are no less beautiful because they spring from a natural need to use certain notes and rhythms corresponding to the words and intention of the songs. . . . The truest way of projecting these qualities is to sing in the style of the people the songs come from. . . .

EARL ROBINSON

"Folk music is the wellspring of my composing work. I owe an incalculable debt to those who made, sang and danced this music, particularly to the Negro people." Thus does Earl Robinson—composer, teacher, conductor, singer, lecturer—modestly characterize the considerable work he has done over the past quarter century.

Robinson was born July 2, 1910, in Seattle, Washington, of parents with strong musical interests. His father picked the mandolin and was a barbershop harmonizer. His mother, a more serious musician, played the piano, violin, harp, and cello. Their son Earl attended Lafayette Grade School and, after graduating from West Seattle High School, entered the University of Washington in 1928. At the university his main interest was music, and he conducted the University Symphony in some of his own compositions. In 1938, he took a Bachelor of Music degree, with a Normal Diploma for teaching.

After college days Robinson took a slow boat to China, working his way by playing the piano. On his return from this Oriental jaunt, he went on a long, roundabout, vagabonding trip through the West and South—a trip that really sealed his interest in folk music and determined the manner of his composing thereafter. Some of the songs he picked up on this leisurely journey were recorded for the Library of Congress Archive of American Folk Song. He learned folksongs, especially early in his career, from itinerant folksingers like Leadbelly, Josh White, Woody Guthrie, Burl Ives, Tony Kraber, and many others.

In New York, in 1935, he joined a little-theater group as musical director, did some acting and sang folksongs, sometimes on the waterfront or in nearby towns, wherever the theater went. His serious activity as a singer of folksongs and as composer in the folk idiom dates from about this time.

Robinson composed "Ballad for Americans" in 1938. The next year it was the featured number in the WPA Federal Theatre production, *Sing for Your Supper*. Late in 1939, when the "Ballad" was aired over C.B.S., the composer woke up to find himself famous. He was granted a Guggenheim Fellowship in 1940. "Ballad for Americans" stimulated the American folksong revival which, by 1940, was in full flower. In June, Earl Robinson and Will Geer presented in New York Town Hall a highly successful *Cavalcade of American Song* featuring a whole gallery of folksingers. The program was presented for the benefit of the New York Committee to Aid Agricultural Workers.

Robinson went to Hollywood in 1943 and for a number of years wrote songs and background scores for films, composing in the folk idiom as well as using genuine folk material. With Lewis Allen he did the songs and background scores for an MGM picture called the *Romance of Rosy Ridge,* the story of a folksinger in Missouri directly after the Civil War. Others include *A Walk in the Sun* (Twentieth-Century Fox), *California* (Paramount), *Man from Texas* (Eagle-Lion), *The Roosevelt Story* (United Artists), and many shorts. And, of course, he had a large share in such productions as *The House I Live In, The Lonesome Train,* and *The Town Crier.*

In the fall of 1951, Robinson went to Brooklyn, where he continues his composing, conducting, singing, and lecturing. He wrote the music for a sound-film entitled *When We Grow Up,* a work on racial understanding and co-operation in a Brooklyn neighborhood. A recent work is the folk opera, *Sandhog,* a study of the early tunnel builders in New York City, written with Waldo Salt and based on a theme from Theodore Dreiser. (Robinson did the score, much of it based on Irish and Negro folk music, and Salt did the libretto.) In early 1956, Robinson completed a score for a General Motors–sponsored picture entitled *Giants in the Land.* It is based on the subject of Diesel power and how machines have made the lot of man better, done entirely in the folk style, containing pioneer ballads, work songs, talking blues, and even a sailor song!

During the past twenty years, along with his many other activities, Robinson has never ceased to be a folksong recitalist. His voice and his guitar have been heard on many a stage, real and improvised, and he has been an inspiration and aid to other singers. The NAACP sponsored an Earl Robinson program in Fort Worth, Texas, in February, 1948. In his travels he has done a lot of collecting and, though he has not published a collection, he has assisted other collectors.[33] He has performed in most of the states, across Canada, "all over" the Hawaiian Islands, in China (Shanghai), and in the Philippines. Like other performers over many years, he has kept no count of his appearances but makes a guess that they might run anywhere from fifteen hundred to two thousand. And, of course, he has done much recording of folk music—Disc, Mercury, Decca, Folkways records, and others.

On February 17, 1937, Earl Robinson was married to Helen Wortis. They have two sons, Perry Morris, born September 17, 1938, and James, born July 23, 1946. The Robinsons make their home in Brooklyn.

FRANK V. ROBINSON

Frank V. Robinson, who has learned his folksongs from records, tape recordings, collections, and other singers, has been singing folksongs for a number of years. He was born December 12, 1925, in San Francisco. His formal schooling was in Berkeley, from grammar school through university. He took a bachelor's degree in psychology in 1950 at the University of California.

Robinson, who uses the five-string banjo, made his first public appearance as a singer of folksongs in October, 1950, at a meeting of the East Bay Folksong Club. In the past half-dozen years he has given approximately 250 performances up and down the West Coast, in Hawaii, and in Mexico. Papers like the Berkeley *Daily Gazette,* the Oakland *Tribune,* and the San Francisco *Chronicle* have given him favorable press notices.

By profession Frank V. Robinson is a photographer. Singing folksongs is his main hobby, sometimes a lucrative one, sometimes not. In July, 1951, he was married to Gene C. Bernardi. They went to Sydney, Australia, in 1956.

BOB ROSS

Born in Newark, New Jersey, Bob Ross was educated in a number of public schools: in Bernardsville, New Jersey; P.S. 51 in Brooklyn; P.S. 36 in St. Albans, New York; and the Jamaica (New York) High School. He did not attend college. He sang spirituals and other songs in church and community functions from the age of six on. It was in the adolescent years that he "discovered folk songs and made them a major part of his repertoire." * He studied Sandburg's *American Songbag,* other books, and other folksingers.

Bob was in the Naval Air Service during World War II. While in the service he entertained many GI's, especially in hospitals. Like many singers, Bob does his own arranging, by ear, and also composes songs in the folk idiom. In the past fifteen or more years he has given hundreds of recitals, mostly in the East and in the service, but once as far west as Kansas and again as far away as Trinidad, British West Indies. Bob Ross was the folksong leader in Kurt Weill's *Down in the Valley* when it was produced at the Actors Playhouse. He does lecture-concerts on folksongs for school children.

Bob Ross was married to Mary Lou Forster in 1943. They have three children: Byron Robert, born July 14, 1946; Gregory Grant,

* From notes with Bob's Folkways record album, FA-2334. (Used by permission of Folkways.)

born March 31, 1950; and Melanie Louise, born June 22, 1955. The Rosses make their home in Merrick, New Jersey.

HERBERT ROTH

Because he preferred singing folksongs to other kinds of music, Herbert Roth, when he graduated from high school, sold his clarinet and bought a guitar.* This was a decade ago, but he had sung traditional music years before that. Herbert Roth was born on November 13, 1930, in Chicago, where he attended elementary school and the Hyde Park High School. His fourth year of high school was in Glendale, California. In 1950, he completed two years at Glendale (junior) College. He spent some time in the Navy and in Japan during the Korean conflict.

In the fall of 1950, Herbert Roth entered Washburn University, Topeka, Kansas, and received a Bachelor of Education degree two years later. Earlier he had been in Red Cross and Boy Scout work, and he had also worked as a professional photographer. With a diploma in his pocket, camera in one hand and guitar in the other, Roth decided to enter the field of teaching. He began at the Quincy Elementary School in Topeka, with additional work at the Children's Service of the Menninger Clinic, where folksongs and the guitar have served him well. Now he is pursuing his studies further at Kansas University, working toward a master's degree in education for emotionally disturbed children.

Roth learned folksongs from friends, from recordings (he has a large collection of folksong records), from whatever source was at hand. Recently he has been delving into the files of the Kansas Historical Society for songs pertaining to the Populist movement. Most of his "recital" singing has been done informally in and around Topeka, or at camps with groups, but he has a genuine scholarly interest in folk music and will do more with it as time permits.

Herbert Roth was married on December 20, 1951, to Muriel Needlman, a student at Washburn University. Asked if Mrs. Roth sings folksongs, Herb replied: "She is occasionally coerced into singing with me!" No doubt, she enjoys folksongs, too.

RUTH RUBIN

An authority on Jewish folksongs, Ruth Rubin (nee Rosenblatt) was born in Montreal, Canada, in 1906. There she received her education in grammar and high school and in the Yiddish Secular School. Later, in New York City, where she worked as a secretary,

* Some details for this sketch come from Margaret M. Hunt's article on Roth in the Topeka *State Journal*, September 27, 1958.

she attended evening courses at Hunter College and at the Jewish Seminary. Though she has taken no degrees, Mrs. Rubin is a distinguished scholar in the folksong field.

Ruth Rubin has always sung folksongs, learning them in her family, particularly from her mother, "a carrier of folksongs," her grandfather, and a great-uncle. Cousins, teachers, and other friends have also contributed to her vast repertoire. In fact, she has learned "from anyone who came along who knew folksongs." As early as the age of seven she sang at the annual Yiddish school concerts where, in true folksong style, she did the songs in her own way.

Mrs. Rubin began presenting recitals—professionally—of Jewish folksongs in the 1940's. From 1945 on, she has done an average of about twenty-five recitals a year. She has performed in many states, from New York to California and Oregon, and frequently in Canada. Often her lecture-recitals are presented in public schools and colleges, as well as in libraries and community centers and before learned bodies. Yiddish love songs and children's songs are among her favorites, but she ranges far in the present and in the past. Very old songs combine with later Yiddish and Israeli materials to make up her programs of love and work songs, cradle and children's songs, humorous and Chassidic songs, holiday and satiric songs. Though Mrs. Rubin has studied piano and has written accompaniments to a few folksongs, she generally sings unaccompanied and does not make special arrangements for the songs.

For many years Mrs. Rubin has been a collector and compiler of Jewish folksongs. Her *Treasury of Jewish Folksong* (see Bibliography, Book Two, for a fuller account), published in 1950, is a standard work in the field. The 110 songs are in the original Yiddish and Hebrew with a free English translation, and are given piano settings by Ruth Post. In addition to the *Treasury*, she has written extensively on her field for the learned journals. Authoritative articles have appeared in the *New York Folklore Quarterly* (1946), the annual *Jewish Music Forum* (Volumes VII and VIII, 1946-47), the *Jewish Book Annual* (1947-48), the Hebrew-English quarterly *Edoth* (1948), the *Journal of American Folklore* (Vol. 65, July-September 1952), the quarterly *Chicago Jewish Forum* (1953-54, Winter), *The Jewish Quarterly* (Autumn 1954), published in London, and in the *Journal of the International Folk Music Council* (1955). Furthermore, she has read papers, "with vocal illustrations," at many meetings of the learned societies—at the Modern Language Association in 1946, the conferences of the American Folklore Society in 1951 and 1954, and at the Seminar on American Culture at Cooperstown, New York, in 1953.

Ruth Rubin has built up from her many informants a recorded library on discs and tapes of over five hundred songs, many of which have already been transcribed. Naturally she has herself done many recordings. Releases of 78's were made by Oriole Records * in 1945 and 1950, and of long-plays in 1954 and 1957, for a total of more than fifty Yiddish and Israeli songs. The latest for Oriole is a recording of *Fourteen Children's Songs*, with guitar and banjo accompaniments done by Pete Seeger. Other companies, like Folkways and Riverside, are issuing Ruth Rubin records (see Book Three).

Despite all her work in the folksong field, Mrs. Rubin lists her regular occupation as housewife and mother. Ruth Rosenblatt was married to Harry Rubin in 1932. They have one son, Michael, born in 1937, now a student at Reed College in Portland, Oregon. Harry Rubin is engaged in the import-export business and is also a member of the board of Westminster Recording Company of New York.

* Address: 8 West 40th Street, New York 18, N. Y.

FOOTNOTES TO CHAPTER 7

[1] Factual details are from interviews with Niles (the first on November 4, 1950), correspondence, and other sources as indicated.

[2] *International Who Is Who in Music* (Chicago, 1951), p. 314.

[3] See Book Two, Bibliography, for further annotations on these volumes. Niles was severely injured in a plane crackup in No Man's Land toward the end of the war in 1918, and it was some years (not until 1927) before he could walk without crutches or other aids.

[4] Of the twenty-seven sets in this series, published between 1920 and 1950, Niles has been responsible for ten. See the Bibliography for further comment.

[5] For some years now he has been working toward a plan for complete publication.

[6] From Niles's *Folk Ballad and Carol,* an eleven-page mimeographed manuscript, p. 4. This manuscript was published as Chapter Six in *The Great Smokies and the Blue Ridge,* The Story of the Southern Appalachians, ed. Roderick Peattie (New York, 1943), pp. 217-38.

[7] See discussion about the dulcimer, Interlude I (Chapter 9).

[8] From the mimeographed manuscript, p. 10, cited above.

[9] C. B. Neibarger in the Kansas City *Times,* November 10, 1950.

[10] This work, scored for woodwinds, horns in F, brasses, celesta, harp, percussion, and strings, had its première on December 16, 1954, at Eastern State Teachers College, Richmond, Kentucky, under the direction of James E. VanPeursem.

[11] "What Are the Wild Waterfowl Saying?" *Saturday Review,* July 25, 1953,

pp. 46-47. Recently RCA Victor has reissued Niles's records on its new Camden label (see Book Three).

[12] By Roger Butterfield, September 6, 1943 (Vol. XV, No. 10).

[13] Wichita *Beacon,* July 10 and October 8, 1953; Wichita *Eagle,* July 29, 1953, and September 26, 1955; Pratt (Kansas) *Tribune,* March 13, 1955; Wellington (Kansas) *Daily News,* April 6, 1955; Pittsburg (Kansas) *Headlight,* June 23, 1956.

[14] For instance: *High Fidelity Magazine,* February, 1955; *Variety,* January 12, 1955; Brooklyn *Daily,* December 17, 1954.

[15] Facts from Dr. Oster and from an article entitled "Professor Even Makes Folk Music Instruments," by Larry Rumley, in the Baton Rouge (Louisiana) *Morning Advocate,* February 19, 1956.

[16] For many details I am indebted to M. Filiatrault, director-administrator of Le Quatuor Alouette.

[17] Daniel Reed appeared at Town Hall, New York, January 15, 1950, in a series of dramatic monologues from E. L. Masters' *The Spoon River Anthology.* (*Saturday Review of Literature,* January 14, 1950.)

[18] "Folk Music to the Fore," *Theatre Arts,* XXXVII (July, 1950), p. 10.

[19] A few details for this sketch are drawn from her program comments, record jackets, and from *International Who Is Who in Music* (Chicago, 1951), p. 343.

[20] Jean Ritchie, *Singing Family of the Cumberlands* (New York: Oxford University Press, 1955).

[21] *Ibid.,* pp. 112 ff.

[22] *Ibid.,* pp. 144-45.

[23] *Ibid.,* p. 276. Also, a letter from Jean Ritchie, May, 1953. Jean's father owns one of the dulcimers made by J. E. (Uncle Eddie) Thomas, famous dulcimer maker of the Cumberlands (see Interlude I).

[24] *Singing Family,* Chapter 8. I am also indebted to Uncle Jason Ritchie for biographical details.

[25] Letter from May Ritchie Deschamps, September 20, 1953.

[26] Letters from Una Ritchie Yahkub, September 30, 1953; February 24 and March 19, 1954; April 24, 1956.

[27] A native of South India and now an American citizen, Professor Yahkub is a teacher of international relations and social studies at Goddard College, Plainfield, Vermont. After studies at Malabar Christian College in India, he came to America and continued his studies at Amherst, Middlebury, and Harvard. He was a Research Fellow on the Rockefeller Foundation. The Yahkubs have one daughter, Molu, born in 1938.

[28] I am indebted to Jean Ritchie Pickow and to other sources as indicated. See also her *Singing Family,* mentioned earlier.

[29] Gladys Burch, "Young Lady with a Dulcimer," *The American Girl,* August, 1951. See also, "Of Ballad Songs and Snatches," in the Dublin (Ireland) *Irish Independent,* November 8, 1952. The dulcimer Jean now uses was made by her husband, George Pickow.

[30] *The Swapping Song Book* (New York: Oxford University Press, 1952), a collection of twenty-one Ritchie family songs for children, illustrated with photographs by George Pickow of members of the Ritchie family in and around the home place in Kentucky; *A Garland of Mountain Song* (New York, 1953), twenty-five songs from the Ritchie family, with piano accompaniments by Hally Wood Gordon; *Singing Family of the Cumberlands,* mentioned earlier. (See Book Two, Bibliography, for further details.)

[31] Foreword, *A Garland of Mountain Song*, p. 11.

[32] The first fourteen volumes rated a discerning ten-column and, on the whole, favorable review by Frederick Ramsey, Jr., in the *Saturday Review*, February 12, 1955.

[33] Among others, B. A. Botkin and Alan Lomax. It should be mentioned, too, that one of Robinson's compositions, "Joe Hill," has almost become a folksong. It has drifted about orally among labor groups and has picked up additional verses. And it appears in a book of folksongs: *The Fireside Book of Folksongs* (New York, 1947) by Margaret Bradford Boni and Norman Lloyd.

CHAPTER 8

The Singers, S to Z

TONY SALETAN

Native New Yorker and Harvard educated, Anthony Saletan was born on June 29, 1931. All his schooling before college, from pre-school through high school (1933-49), was obtained at the Walden School in New York City. During these years he "studied music with a variety of teachers, including Leonard Bernstein." Tony entered Harvard in 1949 and graduated with a Bachelor of Arts degree in 1953. Later he entered the Harvard Graduate School of Education and in 1957 received a "Master of Arts in Teaching in the special field of music."

Though Tony's parents were not professional musicians, they were no strangers to music. His father "played some piano and balalaika." Like other alert city-bred young people, Tony learned folksongs early from many sources—"people, both professional and amateur, in the New York area and many songs from books as well as singers." He began playing the guitar in his early teens and, for some years, he used "songs and instruments mainly to lead groups in singing," especially in recreational work. He sang with a quartet through high school, and during college days "led and performed with an informal four-part singing group." The guitar is his chief instrument, but on occasion he uses the five-string banjo, drum and steel drum, zither, recorder, piano, and even a bagpipe.

Anthony Saletan is putting his musical and folksong knowledge to practical use. As musical consultant for the Newton, Massachusetts, public schools, he has occasion to engage in a variety of activities. "I am currently (1959) performing weekly," he writes, "on an educational TV series which is recorded on video-tape for re-use. It is presented by the Eastern Massachusetts Council for School Television . . . and appears on WGBH-TV, Channel 2, Boston." The series, known as "21-inch Classroom-Music, Grade 2," is used in cities and towns "in the Eastern New England states." To quote him further on the series: "The material for the most part consists of folksongs, folk dances and demonstrations of instruments, and the children in the classrooms sing along with the songs."

For 1959-60, Tony is doing an around-the-world tour that will take about sixteen months. He teaches and leads singing groups and collect songs in a dozen or more countries, especially in the Orient. On his itinerary are "Japan, Taiwan, the Philippines, Indonesia, Borneo, Singapore, Laos, Malaya, and other countries westward." This should be a happy and fruitful experience, for, as Tony says, "I have always believed in and enjoyed getting people to sing *with* me, rather than simply singing *at* them."

CARL SANDBURG

Ordinarily we think of Carl Sandburg as the biographer of Lincoln or poet of bold American idioms. And in these areas he has done a tremendous labor and gained lasting fame. His Lincoln studies and his militant interests in the common workingman have led him also to become a student and performer of American folksong. One critic suggests that "there must have been folk-song singers among his Swedish peasant ancestors." [1] If so, the talent did not appear in his parents. As Sandburg says, "Some peasants sing and some don't. . . . Of the many fine old-time Swedish folk songs, I heard none from the Swedes I grew up with. Nor did I hear of any Swede in Knox County who was supposed to know Swedish folk songs, the sort of a fellow that ballad hunters seek." [2]

Sandburg's folksong interest and education, then, were purely American in development. He does report, however, that his father loved music and that, thrifty and unimaginative as the father was, he once bought a cheap accordion and learned a few tunes, and that on several occasions he delighted to stand at the street corner and listen to a blind Negro sing ballads, particularly the ballad about Jesse James.[3] The many stories Carl Sandburg read about Jesse James (dime novels were popular when Sandburg was a boy) made a profound impression on him.[4]

The main details of Sandburg's biography need not be recounted here, for they appear in many a literary history and reference work.[5]

His interest in folksong, though it may have had some stimulus in early years, is largely a development of his middle years. No doubt, his travels as a hobo,[6] his Army life, his studies of Lincoln, his mixing with common people everywhere, all contributed to his hobby of collecting folksongs which went into *The American Songbag*, published in 1927. And from about that time on, he has added to fame and fortune by reading his poems, lecturing on Lincoln, and—usually for about half of each program—strumming his peculiar bell-shaped guitar and singing folksongs.* Sandburg sings in a rich and sonorous, if somewhat monotonous, baritone, strumming along in a kind of simple chording that is both unobtrusive and effective. He has his own method of timing and emphasis for the songs he sings, and his striking personality always makes him an interesting singer. Several companies have made recordings of his ballad singing (see Book Three).

A. R. SCAMMELL

Though not a professional folksinger, Arthur R. Scammell has nevertheless had considerable folksong activity. He was born November 12, 1913, at Change Islands, Newfoundland. He attended the local schools and then spent one year (1930-31) at Memorial College at St. John's, capital and metropolis of the province. After an interval of eight years' teaching in Newfoundland, he attended McGill University in Montreal, taking a Bachelor of Arts degree in 1942.

Mr. Scammell's mother was a church organist at Change Islands, and singing was a part of the family activity. As a boy he learned and sang Newfoundland ballads, and at the age of fifteen composed a ballad, "Squid Jiggin' Ground," which has since become something of a national song. He has written many other songs, but none has equaled that first youthful success.

As a teacher in Newfoundland, Mr. Scammell sang at school concerts, and he has given many recitals for small groups. His performances have been limited to the eastern provinces of Canada. He has written some articles on Newfoundland folksongs for *Atlantic Guardian*, a local magazine. In 1943, RCA Victor made private recordings for Mr. Scammell of Newfoundland ballads, including his own "Squid Jiggin' Ground."[7] This song, according to Edith Fulton Fowke, distinguished student of Canadian folksongs, "is the most widely known of all Newfoundland songs. Sailors have carried it

---

* He has now laid aside the old bell-shaped guitar in favor of a new expensive modern instrument. Sandburg said, in an interview, that the old one didn't have much tune left in it any more. At eighty, he was still lecturing with wit and brilliance and singing ballads in his rich voice.

"The Music Lesson," from the painting by Thomas Hart Benton. (*Courtesy of the artist and the Associated American Artists*)

Marble plaque commemorating the birth of "Home on the Range." (*Photo by Jim Clark*)

Cabin near Smith Center, Kansas, where "Home on the Range" was written in 1873. (*Photo by Jim Clark*)

"The Jealous Lover of Lone Green Valley," by Thomas Hart Benton. (*Courtesy of the artist and the University of Kansas Museum of Art, Lawrence, Kansas, gift of the Elizabeth M. Watkins Fund of the Endowment Association*)

"The Wreck of the Old 97," by Thomas Hart Benton. (*Courtesy of the artist and Leonard Davidow of Spencer Press, Inc.*)

"Jesse James Train Robbery," from the mural by Thomas Hart Benton in the state capitol at Jefferson City, Missouri. (*Photo by Gerald Massie, Missouri Resources Division*)

"Swing Low Sweet Chariot," by John McCrady. (*Courtesy of the City Art Museum, St. Louis*)

Decorations from the White House piano: "Cowboy Singing" beneath the
prairie stars (*upper left*), "New England Barn Dance" (*upper right*), "Ceremonial Chant of the American Indians" (*lower left*), "Negro Cotton-Picker"
bursting into song (*lower right*). (*Courtesy of Steinway & Sons*)

(*Above*) The White House piano, showing the panel decorations of American folk-music themes. (*Below*) "The Virginia Reel." (*Courtesy of Steinway & Sons*)

"Casey Jones," by Fred Ludekens. (*Courtesy of the artist and* Esquire *magazine*)

inland to the Great Lakes, and it has become a favourite all across Canada." [8] At the ceremony of confederation of Newfoundland and Canada, the song was played on the carillon in the Peace Tower at Ottawa. It was also used by the National Film Board in the film, *Royal Journey,* and was performed by groups of singers at Portugan Cove, Newfoundland, on one occasion when Queen Elizabeth and the Duke of Edinburgh departed from Canada.

A. R. Scammell was married to Isabella Butt in 1938. They live at Town of Mount Royal, Quebec, where Mr. Scammell is a teacher in the high school.

MARTHA SCHLAMME

Among persons singing folksongs today, it is difficult to find anyone as highly praised and universally accepted as Martha Schlamme, beautiful lyric soprano. Though trained as a lieder singer, she has turned to the world of folksong and made it her special province. She was born in Vienna, Austria, in 1930, but in the forties the family fled the wrath of the Nazis, first to France and then to England.

In England she began private training in music—piano and singing —under the prominent lieder singer, Emmy Heith. Martha's parents are very musical people * and from them she learned many folksongs. But like many another singer today, she, too, learned from books and records. Her professional career began in England when, at the age of eighteen, she performed at the Players' Theatre and for the B.B.C. Then, at mid-century, she came to America, where her rise to concert fame as a singer of folksongs is little short of phenomenal.

Why did she change from lieder to folksongs? Her own words tell the story: "Though I was trained as a lieder singer, the appearance [in England] of an Icelandic folksinger, Engel Lund, changed my whole life. She sang songs in about 20 languages—including my own, German and Yiddish—and without her knowing it, inspired me to do the same. She was the most consummate artist I had ever heard. Though I have developed into a different kind of singer, I owe her the inspiration and will never forget her."

Martha Schlamme also sings in many languages and her concert appearances have passed the one-thousand mark. She has given three Town Hall recitals and has appeared "practically all over the country." And, like other good singers, she has recorded extensively, mainly on the Vanguard label in America (see Book Three). Reviews of her concerts and recordings are expressed in only the most compli-

* The Midwesterner is likely to ask, "Who in Vienna isn't?" Look where we will, is there any city on the map that has been a greater source of beautiful music—composers, musicians, singers—than Vienna?

mentary terms.* Like Marais and Miranda, Dyer-Bennet, Theodore
Bikel, William Clauson, Cynthia Gooding, and a few other multilingual singers, she is rightly called an "international balladeer" who
makes folksongs into art songs.

MOLLY SCOTT

Molly Scott was born in Wellsville, New York, on January 11,
1938, where she received her grammar- and high-school education.
From Wellsville she went to Smith College and received a Bachelor
of Arts degree in June, 1959.

Molly first became interested in folk music through her sister
and brother-in-law, members of an outing club in Hanover, New
Hampshire. Then, like others, she learned from books, friends,
recordings, and wherever people sang. In the summer of 1957, she
went out West for her first professional job, singing folksongs at
Timberline Lodge, Mt. Hood, a ski resort in Oregon. She has returned there for Christmas and Easter holiday engagements.

Molly plays the guitar and has performed in ten or a dozen states,
in the East during the winters and in the West during the summers
and other vacation times. In all she has given some 250 to 300 recitals
and has earned a large part of her college expenses. During the
winter of 1958-59, she gave a series of concerts with Bob Coltman
(q.v.). Like other young singers, Molly has appeared on radio
(WAMF at Amherst College) and TV. After graduation from Smith,
she embarked on a full-time career of folksong activity.

TOM SCOTT

Tall, dignified, soft-spoken Thomas Jefferson Scott was born May
28, 1912,[9] in north-central Kentucky at the Campbellsburg tobacco
plantation of his father. Tom's mother was a schoolteacher before
her marriage. After elementary schooling, he attended nearby La
Grange High School, graduating in 1930 and going on to Lexington
to the University of Kentucky. His major interest then, as earlier,
was music. After his college years he continued his musical studies,
both vocal and instrumental, intermittently for the next dozen years,
briefly in Louisville and then in New York. It is reported that a
symphony concert in Louisville opened his ears to the world of
great music.

* See the following for some very glowing accounts: *National Jewish Post*
(October, 1954), Los Angeles *Times* (May 28, 1955), Madison (Wisconsin)
Times (May 20, 1955, and December 12, 1956), *High Fidelity* (October, 1957),
Library Journal (October 1, 1957), *Christian Science Monitor* (April 12,
1958), *The Billboard* (June 24, 1957, and April 21, 1958), Cleveland *Plain
Dealer* (June 5, 1958).

Tom Scott learned to play the harmonica, banjo, and guitar from the Negroes who worked on his father's Kentucky plantation. From them also he learned many spirituals and work songs. In 1936, he left Kentucky to seek a musical career in New York, his chief assets being a solid grounding in musical training, a rich bass-baritone voice, and a wealth of traditional music. He worked as a singing waiter, sang in various musicals and operas, and in 1938 joined the Fred Waring organization. His success was gradual but sure.

For five years Tom Scott was a featured ballad singer with the "Fred Waring Show," and he became one of Waring's major arrangers of program materials. His career with Waring is comparable to that of Stuart Churchill's (q.v.), though Churchill joined the group some years before Scott. Both were very versatile musicians and both were skilled arrangers. Scott, like Churchill, could play six or eight instruments. Waring's music publishing business, known as the Shawnee Press, at Delaware Water Gap, Pennsylvania, published more than a hundred of Scott's choral arrangements of folksongs.

In the early 1940's, Scott struck out with his guitar on a solo folksinging career. In this venture he was eminently successful, whether he appeared on concert stage, at supper clubs, or on radio and TV. In New York, he sang at Town Hall, the Brooklyn Academy of Music, Carnegie Hall, Times Hall, and in such popular supper clubs as Village Vanguard, Cafe Society Uptown, Ruban Bleu, and others. And, of course, his singing was popular in United States Army camps and hospitals across the country and in Europe, during World War II and after, and in many college communities.

Tom Scott is not content to be typed as a singer of folksongs, or even as a good arranger, though he does both supremely well.* For years he has been working as a serious composer, using folksong materials as a basis for symphonic compositions. On March 11, 1954, the Museum of Modern Art presented a whole evening of Tom Scott's orchestral compositions.[10] Among these compositions are the following: *From the Sacred Harp*, a short composition based on white spirituals and premièred in 1946 in Carnegie Chamber Music Hall; *Hornpipe and Chantey*, based on folk themes he heard in Nantucket and premièred in 1946 by the Los Angeles Symphony; a musical portrait of *Johnny Appleseed* (1948) for symphony orchestra; *Fanfare and Cantilena*, premièred by the Louisville Orchestra on November 12, 1952. On February 5, 1956, "Monitor" gave a first radio performance of Tom Scott's *Binorie Variations* (recorded by

---

* I am not alone in feeling that Tom Scott, in his rich bass-baritone and his effective guitar arrangement, does the best performance of "The Foggy, Foggy Dew" of any American singing folksongs today.

the Vienna Symphony Orchestra), an orchestral work based on the old ballad about the two sisters.

On June 11, 1938, Tom Scott married Joy Pride, artist and writer, who has collaborated with him in radio scripts and in writing two books, *Sing of America* and *Folk Songs for Singing*. In 1947, Signature Recording Corporation brought out an album (S-5) of twelve folksongs (78 rpm) with notes by Joy Pride Scott. These were reissued in 1952 as an LP by Coral Records (CRL 56056), a subsidiary of Decca Records, Inc. Among Scott's TV appearances, he has doubled as actor and musical performer on the "Chevrolet Teletheatre," "Lux Video Theatre," the "Robert Montgomery Show," and "The Big Show." [11]

PETE SEEGER

Among students and singers of folksongs today, none holds a more enviable place than Pete Seeger, and few are better known or better informed. Born into a musical family and given unusual educational advantages, he early decided to devote his life to the field of folk music. Pete Seeger was born in New York City on May 3, 1919, third son of Charles L. Seeger and Constance de Clyver Edson Seeger. His father is a distinguished musicologist, conductor, author, editor, and teacher. His mother was a violinist and teacher. At one time both parents were faculty members of the Juilliard School of Music in New York.

Pete's formal education began in the Nyack, New York, public schools. He spent some years in the Spring Hill School at Litchfield, Connecticut, and at Avon Old Farms at Avon, Connecticut, before entering Harvard in 1936. He left Harvard in 1938 without taking a degree. Though his formal education was practically ended, the preparation for his life work was just beginning.

In 1935, when he was sixteen, his father took him to the Folk Festival at Asheville, North Carolina, where he was introduced to a world of music almost entirely unknown to him before: this was the music of the common people, the world of folk music. The experience, for him, was like an old-time religious conversion, for he saw the light that set him on a new way of life. And the musical instrument that captivated him was the five-string banjo. "It was a case of love at first sight," he says. Thereafter his interest in folk music never waned, and his activities in the field have been extensive.

When Pete Seeger left college in the late thirties to look for a job, the Great Depression sent him wandering. Literally and imaginatively he took his banjo on his knee, became a poor wayfaring stranger along the lonesome road, followed the E-ri-ee Canal, and traveled ten thousand miles away from home. This long journey, frequently on the midnight train, took him down in the valley across the wide Missouri. He saw the little old sod shanty in the West, hopped the midnight special train from Sourwood Mountain to the dreary Black Hills, walked out in the streets of Laredo and beyond the Red River Valley. On this long journey he met just about everybody, including the Arkansas Traveler, John Henry, Frankie and Johnny, Casey Jones and Jesse James, Whiskey Johnny and Old Joe Clark, as well as Pretty Polly, Jennie Jenkins, Black-Eyed Susie, the Buffalo Gals, the Danville Girl, and, of course, Darling Cory! No doubt, too, he saw the Grey Goose, Ground Hog, Mister Rabbit, and the Old Gray Mare.

The point is, in the late thirties, he covered the forty-eight states, picked up new ways of playing the five-string banjo, learned hundreds of new songs, and built up a repertoire of ballads, blues, country songs, lullabies, hymns and spirituals, dance tunes and work songs that would take, he says, "from now till breakfast to sing and play 'em all." After this *Wanderjahr*, the United States Army picked him for a three-and-a-half-year stretch, much of it in the Pacific Islands area. During that time he sang to soldiers from the forty-eight states and Canada.

In the past dozen years Pete Seeger's labors in folksong cover a multitude of activities. First of all, his performances for "every imaginable type of audience, from churches to taverns, from street corners to Town Hall and Carnegie Hall, from nursery school children to college audiences"—these have kept him busy and on the road constantly, though now he travels more comfortably and conventionally than by "thumbing rides and grabbing freight trains."

In 1946, Seeger did one of the best of the folk-music shorts, *And Hear My Banjo Play.* He performed in *Dark of the Moon,* a folkplay with a Barbara Allen theme, done by the Los Angeles Repertory Theatre. He campaigned—performing and composing songs—in a cross-country tour with Henry Wallace in 1948. In the same year he published his manual, *How to Play the 5-String Banjo,* which Alan Lomax calls "a most original musicological book . . . a brilliant analysis (and the first one) of our most significant instrumental style." Lomax also credits Seeger with starting a "new national crush for the five-string banjo."

In 1949, Pete Seeger organized with three others a singing group called the "Weavers," and during their three years together their success in theaters, night spots, and on records far surpassed their wildest hopes. Sale of their records has passed the four-million mark. Folkways Music Corporation published their songs in 1951-52 under the titles *The Weavers Sing Folksongs* and *The Caroler's Songbag*. Success of the Weavers "prompted Tin-Pan Alley on a feverish search for folk material from which it has not yet recovered." Pete has, of course, appeared on dozens, yes, hundreds of radio and TV programs in the past fifteen years, and he has recorded over two hundred sides for a dozen different recording companies. (Folkways Records and Service Corporation has been his chief outlet on records. See Book Three.)

In 1954, Pete Seeger published a revised edition of his forty-page, double-column *5-String Banjo* manual. During the winter of 1954-55, he offered a series of six concerts with commentary entitled "American Folk Music and Its World Origins" at the Institute of Arts and Sciences at Columbia University. His appearances at the National Folk Festival in St. Louis in the fifties have been one of the special, anticipated features of that big event. The secret of Pete's success with audiences is not at first evident, but it lies in a number of directions. His tremendous knowledge of folk music, his quiet enthusiasms, his persuasiveness in audience participation, his unfailing, contagious, sharp rhythms with the banjo—all these contribute. Pete Seeger has come a long way since that first visit to a folk festival in 1935, and he has moved consistently in this particular branch of our culture which has so deeply engrossed his talents.

With all his busy activities in writing, recording, performing, Pete Seeger has found time for a family. In 1943, he was married to Toshi Ohta, whom he credits with "patience, perseverance, and perspicacity" in assisting him in many folksong activities. They are the parents of three children. The family home, built by Pete himself, is at Beacon, New York, up the Hudson from New York City on a wooded mountainside.

BROTHER JOHN SELLERS

Singer of gospel songs, blues, and spirituals, Brother John Sellers *
has developed, like Leadbelly and Big Bill Broonzy before him, into something of a fabulous character. (The title "Brother" comes from a religious sect, the Church of God in Christ.) He was born at Clarksdale, Mississippi, on May 24, 1924. His education was brief—only the first four grades at Greenville, Mississippi. When he was about ten, he went to Chicago, where he began to hear singers like Big Bill Broonzy and others.

Brother Sellers began singing publicly about 1939, when he was

* This sketch is based on information received from Mr. Paul Kapp, booking agent for Brother John Sellers. A few facts are drawn from the Vanguard recording, *Blues and Folk Songs* (VRS-9030).

fifteen, at the Chicago Church of God in Christ. His singing activity has grown extensively in the past twenty years. He uses the guitar, but frequently performs with others, such as Blind Sonny Terry (*q.v.*), with harmonica, or with a jazz group. At one time or another in the past dozen years he has performed in most of the states, in Canada, and throughout western Europe along with Broonzy. In religious singing he has been associated with Mahalia Jackson. The number of his performances runs beyond five hundred.

Brother John Sellers has made many recordings, on such labels as RCA Victor, Miracle Records (Chicago), and recently for Vanguard (see Book Three).

JERRY SILVERMAN

With academic musical training and an important book to his credit, Jerry Silverman is evidence of a trend in the folk-music world: combining the scholarly approach with the informal art of folksinging. "I find this," he writes, "a most happy union."

Jerry was born on March 26, 1931, in New York City, began his schooling in the Bronx at P.S. 96, and continued at the Christopher Columbus High School and the Neighborhood Music School, both in the Bronx. He entered City College of New York and took a Bachelor of Science degree in music in 1952. After an interim he began graduate work in musicology at New York University, wrote a thesis on "The Blues Guitar As Illustrated by the Practices of Blind Lemon Jefferson, Huddie Ledbetter and Josh White," and received a Master of Arts degree in 1955. This thesis was the basis for his recently published *Folk Blues,** an impressive collection, with other data, of 110 American songs in this particular genre.

Jerry comes from a musical family. His parents are "non-professional, informal, at-home" singers of many kinds of music. His father plays the mandolin and his mother knows many Yiddish and Russian songs. Jerry learned folksongs in school, at children's camps, from records, and in square-dance groups in the 1940's. At the Neighborhood Music School he studied the guitar with Joe Jaffe. Then, of course, he learned much from well-known singers of folksongs in and around New York, such persons as Woody Guthrie, Josh White, Pete Seeger, Oscar Brand, and many others.

By the mid-1940's Jerry was giving performances, and in 1948 he began appearing on Oscar Brand's "Folksong Festival" over station WNYC. He has sung at Carnegie Hall and at the Tanglewood Festival and, in the course of his travels, has performed in at

---

* *Folk Blues,* by Jerry Silverman (New York: The Macmillan Company, 1958). See Book Two, Bibliography, for further details.

least a third of the states—from California and Idaho to Massachusetts and Vermont—as well as in the provinces of Quebec and Ontario. After this extensive American experience of several hundred performances, Jerry packed his guitar and five-string banjo for a European tour in the spring and summer of 1959. On this sojourn, he "appeared on television from London to Moscow." *

Besides singing folksongs, Jerry is a teacher of guitar. He has begun a series of recordings (see Book Three) of his collection of *Folk Blues,* and for some years he has been music editor of the little magazine, *Sing Out!* In the New York folk-music scene, it would be hard to find a more active devotee of the folk arts than Jerry Silverman.

FRED M. SMITH

Born in northern Wisconsin on July 21, 1888, near Chippewa Falls, where his father ran a logging camp, Fred Smith first learned ballads and other songs from lumberjacks and rivermen. His formal education was limited to a grade school near Chippewa Falls.

Fred's parents knew many songs, too. Because of poor health, the father moved his family to Texas, not far from Corpus Christi, in 1910. Fred married Bessie Gorman in Texas in 1917, and her father was another source for Fred's collection of folksongs. He uses the guitar for accompaniment and recalls that his first performance was in 1914 at Calallen, a small town not far from Corpus Christi. After Fred's father died, the family moved to Arkansas in 1924.

Fred does not sing much in public. As with many traditional singers, he sings for his friends and for his own satisfaction. In recent years he has appeared at the University of Arkansas Folklore Society meetings, Fayetteville, where he tape-recorded a number of songs for the society's archives. He has been on the programs at the Ozark Folk Festival in Eureka Springs.

Bessie Gorman Smith died in 1930. In 1955, Fred Smith married Ruth Keller. By trade Fred is a barber, operating a shop in Bentonville, Arkansas, where he has lived many years. He has had no children by either marriage.

WINIFRED SMITH

Winifred Smith, who has given special attention to songs heard along the Ohio River, was born in Paducah, Kentucky, on April 2, 1930. She attended public schools in Paducah, finishing high school in 1948, after which she went to Nashville, Tennessee, and enrolled at George Peabody College for Teachers. At Peabody she specialized

* *Folk Music, USA,* October, 1959 (Volume I, Number 1).

in music education, graduating in 1952 with a Bachelor of Science degree.

Singing came naturally to Winifred in a family where music was a part of everyday living. Both her mother and sister, who are non-professional singers, taught her many folksongs. Her mother, incidentally, had been a voice student under Mary Wheeler, a collector of many songs along the Ohio River, especially the river-packet songs of the Negro roustabouts. (See Bibliography for annotations on the Wheeler collections, *Roustabout Songs* and *Steamboatin' Days*.) Winifred also learned many songs from an old Negro nurse in her family and later, when she went to Peabody, from the late Charles F. Bryan (*q.v.*), well-known student and singer of folksongs.

Winifred Smith has been doing folksongs publicly for the past ten years and has given over a hundred recitals in half a dozen states. She uses zither accompaniment and sometimes dulcimer. She doesn't compose but, as she says, "I arrange folksong accompaniments in my head but not on paper." After graduation from Peabody, Miss Smith stayed in Nashville, where she works in radio, TV (station WSM), in the schools, and in private teaching of voice and piano. Her programs, of course, are not limited to folksongs, for she is also a soloist at St. George's Episcopal Church.

On May 27, 1954, Miss Smith was married to Mr. John K. Breast, Jr., whose occupation is banking.

MARY AGNES STARR

Mary Agnes Barber was born April 29, 1901, in the French-Canadian settlement of Oconto, on Green Bay, Wisconsin. She attended private schools through high school, graduating in 1919, and carried on further studies by extension, correspondence, and summer courses, mainly at the University of Wisconsin. She taught a country school one year.

Mary Agnes learned folksongs from her mother, an uncle, various cousins and friends, and has been singing them since early childhood. For the past quarter century she has developed a hobby of collecting French-Canadian folksongs and other folklore in her native state, in Michigan, and down the Mississippi Valley into Louisiana. She began presenting programs of French-Canadian folksongs, first appearing in the 1930's on Wisconsin State station WHA. In 1941, she performed for the Waukesha (Wisconsin) Historical Society, and since that time she has performed hundreds of times, in a dozen Midwest states, from Wisconsin to Louisiana, appearing in lecture-recital as "Diseuse and Interpreter" before "almost every type of organization" and in many schools and colleges.

Among Mrs. Starr's many appearances are those at the Wisconsin Historical Society, the Folk Arts Foundation of St. Paul, Minnesota, Southern Illinois University at Carbondale, the University of Wisconsin Laboratory School, the Oconto County Centennial, and for several years at the National Folk Festival in St. Louis and elsewhere. In October, 1955, as artist-representative of the National Federation of Music Clubs, she was a featured performer at the Acadian Bicentennial in Lafayette, Louisiana, and at the Folk Festival held in Evangeline State Park at St. Martinsville, Louisiana.

Mrs. Starr's studies and researches, as well as her singing, have given her prominence in many ways. In 1950, she made recordings at Prairie du Chien, Wisconsin, of old *voyageur* songs as sung by Reuben Valley, who at that time was nearly one hundred years old. These recordings are now in the Library of Congress. Her own singing—and she has specialized in the *voyageur* songs—has been recorded for the Library of Congress and by a Ford Foundation Folk Music Project. She has been very active in the Wisconsin Federation of Music Clubs, as chairman of folk-music research, consulting director for community folk festivals, director of the Little Theatre Folk Festivals at the Wisconsin State Fair, and she is a member of the board of directors as well as vice president of the Badger State Folklore Society. In 1957, she was appointed chairman of folk-music research for the National Federation of Music Clubs.

In 1953, Mrs. Starr prepared, in co-operation with the Bureau of Information and Program Services of the University of Wisconsin Extension Division, *A Bibliography of French-Canadian and French Folk Music,* which is a twelve-page, annotated, mimeographed bulletin of over one hundred items. This very useful bulletin lists books, printed songs and instrumental music, and recordings.*

With all her scholarly and official activities, it must not be forgotten that Mrs. Starr is a "performing folklorist" who helps keep alive our wonderful French-Canadian folk heritage by her very enjoyable programs. She has been praised time and again for her "charming personality and her musical and dramatic ability." This universal praise has extended from the local small-town papers to the metropolitan dailies.

Mary Agnes Barber was married in 1920 to Albert R. Wittock, who died in 1929. They had two children, Joan Ariel (now Dr. Joan A. Diekfuss, D.C., of Pewaukee, Wisconsin), born in 1921, and Sheridan Vincent, born in 1929, who lives in Waukesha, Wisconsin.

* The bulletin may be obtained (15 cents a copy) from the Bureau of Information and Program Services, University of Wisconsin Extension Division, Madison, Wisconsin.

Mary Agnes Wittock married Morton Hull Starr in 1936. Mr. Starr was a fine pianist and organist and frequently assisted Mrs. Starr in preparing and presenting her programs. Since his death in 1955, Mrs. Starr has moved to Pewaukee, not far from Milwaukee, to be near her children. She still carries on her fascinating and useful hobby—the collecting and presenting of our French-Canadian heritage in story and song.

ELLEN STEKERT

Ellen Stekert, a recent graduate (1957) of Cornell University, was born at Great Neck, Long Island, in 1935. Though a relative newcomer in singing folksongs, she "listens to and reads everything pertaining to folk music which she can get her hands on." Consequently, she has learned much from books, records, and other singers, especially at school and in camps.

Miss Stekert plays the guitar, banjo, harmonica, and mandolin. Like others, she makes her own arrangements and, she says, "every time I sing a song the arrangement varies." On a hiking trip through Europe in the early 1950's, she sang frequently ("for meals") in France, Italy, the Scandinavian countries, and the British Isles. She has made recordings for Stinson Records and the Cornell Recording Society (see Book Three). From Cornell, Miss Stekert went to Indiana University to do graduate work in folklore. At Indiana she is a member of The Settlers, a trio (see: Bruce Buckley) that gives folksong recitals in the upper Midwest.

ELEANOR STONE

A goodly number of singers trained in the classical tradition have, in recent years, turned to the singing of folksongs. This is understandable and commendable, since folksongs appeal to both the untutored and the learned in any audience. Another singer in this grouping is Eleanor Stone, born in New York City in 1928 of parents who were highly musical but not singers of folksongs.[12] After elementary school in Brooklyn, Eleanor attended first the High School of Music and Art in Manhattan and then the Manhattan School of Music. She took some work at the New School for Social Research, but her later schooling has been intermittent and she has taken no degrees.

Miss Stone's early interest was in art songs, lieder, and opera, but she has been singing folksongs for the past seven or eight years. These last she has learned from "various national groups in and out of the country" as well as from books and archives of folksong. She uses the guitar, and sometimes the piano, and frequently makes her own arrangements—a common practice with many singers. Miss Stone reports that she has no special interest in the ethnic value of folksongs or in the many variants of a particular song. Since she chooses her songs for their good content and melody, she draws from all sources without regard to race or nation, and her recitals are multilingual.

Relatively new to the folksong field and still quite young, Miss Stone is something of a veteran in folksong recitals. She has performed in most states of the Union, in England, and in Montreal, Quebec, and Toronto in Canada. Though she has kept no accurate account, the number of her performances approaches a thousand. Here, then, is another fine instance of how folksongs are being kept alive in our modern industrialized society.

WIN STRACKE

Win Stracke, a professional singer "whose main objective has been making a living in music" for the past quarter century, has devoted a good share of his time to singing folksongs. He was born February 20, 1908, in the village of Lorraine, out in central Kansas, but the family moved to Chicago while Win was still an infant. The elder Stracke was a minister. After attending Chicago public schools, Win spent about three years at Lake Forest College, a few miles north of Chicago.

Win's parents were German-born immigrants and knew a lot of music of their native land, including folksongs, and, according to Win, "they sang in German exclusively." In high school Win was a member of Noble Cain's *a cappella* choir. For a number of years after his formal schooling he sang "heavy" programs—oratorios, operas, and formal concerts, including appearances with symphonies. For eight years he appeared as soloist with the radio program, "Hymns of All Churches," heard on all networks. In the late thirties and early forties, at the urging of Burl Ives and Carl Sandburg, he began to take folk music seriously. In time it became his chief love.

Stracke's United States Army career of about four years—he was a corporal in antiaircraft—took him to North Africa, Sicily, France, and other European areas. Wherever he went he sang, and wherever he went he picked up more songs. He learned to pick the guitar, too. Though he has not gone out collecting on regular field trips, he is constantly on the lookout for ballads. Like others, he has learned from records, ballad collections, other singers, and "through considerable study at the Newberry Library in Chicago."

In 1948, Win Stracke teamed up with two other singers of folk music, Big Bill Broonzy and Lawrence Lane. With Studs Terkel, folk-music columnist and disc jockey, as the affable narrator, this foursome gave some of the most popular folksong interpretations of recent years. Their program, titled "I Come for to Sing," was first sponsored by the distinguished Renaissance Society of the University of Chicago and suggested a kind of informal history of the country. Lane, a lyric tenor born and reared in the Ozarks, specialized in the early English ballads; Stracke, a big man with a big bass voice, was particularly effective in the songs of loggers and seamen, railroaders and pioneers; and Broonzy (q.v.), as everybody knows, has made history with the folk blues and his marvelous guitar picking. For several years "I Come for to Sing" delighted many audiences throughout the country, especially in the colleges and universities.

During the summer of 1952, Win Stracke appeared on the N.B.C. program called "America's Music." Later in the year this developed into the series known as "The Meaning of America," in which a particular type of folksong was used on each program. For example, the first program was given over to railroad songs. And, of course, since 1950 Stracke has been very busy as an actor-singer on TV, not to mention his regular concert appearances in a program called "A Minstrel's History of the U.S.A." In December, 1957, he established (and directs) the Old Town School of Folk Music,* said to be "America's only school for study of folk-songs." With Win Stracke, as with others, then, we have an example of a well-trained art singer who has made his contribution in interpreting the wealth and variety of American folksong.

Win Stracke was married to Genevieve McMahon in 1942. They have two daughters: Barbara Ellen, born in 1943, and Jane Elizabeth, born in 1947. Mrs. Stracke and the daughters also like to sing ballads and folksongs. It's a fine old American custom that anybody can enjoy!

VIRGIL L. STURGILL

When he appeared at a folk festival held at the University of Virginia, Charlottesville, on May 12, 1950, Virgil L. Sturgill was described as a rawboned mountaineer with an engaging smile and a superb folksinging voice. The description is apt. He was born in the hills of eastern Kentucky in Carter County on April 1, 1897, and got his early education in the one-room log-cabin schoolhouse near his home on Sutton's Branch.

However primitive Sturgill's July-to-Christmas education seems

---

* The Old Town School is self-sustaining, has a weekly attendance of over 150 students (winter of 1958-59), and provides amateurs with training in folksong, instrumental and vocal, and folk dancing.

today, he nevertheless managed to prepare himself for college. He wandered far, however, before getting back to his native state to complete his formal education. First he attended East Central Teachers College at Ada, Oklahoma, then spent some months at the University of Idaho, Southern Branch (now Idaho State College), at Pocatello, and finally did work at the College of Pharmacy in Philadelphia. Then he settled down at the University of Kentucky, where he took a Bachelor of Arts degree in 1926 and some years later (1937) a Master of Arts.

Mr. Sturgill's knowledge and training in folksong have been life-long. As a boy he learned from his mother, grandmother, aunts, uncles, cousins, and neighbors. He remembers also hearing some folksongs on the old-fashioned cylinder records of the Edison Company. And in recent years, with folksinging becoming the fashion, he has learned from other singers. For his first fifty years, however, Mr. Sturgill sang only for personal enjoyment, strictly as an amateur. In August, 1947, he performed at the annual Folk Festival in Asheville, North Carolina, and he gives credit to Bascom Lamar Lunsford (q.v.) for "discovering" him.

In the past decade Mr. Sturgill's folksong recitals have numbered perhaps fourscore or more. He has performed chiefly in Kentucky, Virginia, and North Carolina, but also in Washington, D.C., and Detroit, Michigan. The Library of Congress Archive has recorded eight of his songs, and he has been active in a number of folk festivals in the southern Highlands. Though Mr. Sturgill often sings without accompaniment, he likes to use, especially for small audiences, his three- and four-string "mountain dulcimores." In these smaller gatherings many persons have made private recordings on wire or tape.

In June, 1932, Virgil L. Sturgill was married to Ruth Virginia Norton at Ashland, Kentucky. They have two sons: Jack Norton, born January 23, 1935, and Lee Burris, born August 10, 1939. Mr. Sturgill is eager to have the "priceless heritage of folksong" carried on in his family. He reports with considerable enthusiasm that when the younger son was about fifteen he "suddenly caught fire" and began learning dozens of songs from his father and other folksingers. So the tradition continues.

Virgil L. Sturgill has been vocational adviser, psychologist, and is at present educational therapist at the Veterans Administration Hospital near Asheville, North Carolina.

ANDREW ROWAN SUMMERS

Born December 15, 1912,[13] at Abingdon in southeastern Virginia, Andrew Rowan Summers was educated in the Virginia public schools and by private tutors. He entered the University of Virginia in 1930 with a major interest in music but took up the study of law, receiving his Bachelor of Laws degree in 1935.

Though Summers' parents were not musicians or folksingers, after college he settled in Abingdon and for a decade pursued his interest in folk music. He sought out many old singers in the 1930's, collected a great many songs, and became particularly interested in the dulcimer. He was active in the White Top Folk Festival, which drew singers from the Virginias, Kentucky and Tennessee, and western North Carolina. He heard the dulcimer first at the White Top Festival, and he has since so far perfected his technique on the instrument that he ranks with the best of the traditionalists.

In the 1940's Summers settled in New York, where he has continued his folksong activities. On one occasion he appeared with the N.B.C. Symphony, and he has performed on many radio and TV stations, and has done folksong concerts as far west as San Francisco. His first recording, a Columbia Masterworks in 1941, is titled *Old World Ballads in America*. Since then he has done many other recordings, especially for Folkways Records from 1950 on (see Book Three). In Andrew Rowan Summers, again we have an illustration of the nontraditional singer who has so carefully studied the traditionalists that his singing and dulcimer playing take on a large degree of authenticity.

REBECCA TARWATER

Born in Rockwood in east-central Tennessee, on November 24, 1908, Rebecca Tarwater learned her first folksongs from her grandmother. She attended public schools in Rockwood and later the Smith Studio School in Washington, D.C. Since her parents were not musicians or folksingers, she does not claim to be a traditional singer, though she's been singing folksongs for the past thirty years. "As long as there's the slightest chance that anybody will listen," she said, "I shall keep on singing."

During the 1930's Miss Tarwater did a good deal of singing in and around Washington, D.C. And since her marriage she has sung in New York City and Paris, France. She recorded for the Library of Congress in 1936. Her singing is usually unaccompanied, though she sometimes uses the five-string banjo. She has collected folksongs—

as any interested singer must—though, as she says, "not in any professional or systematic way."

In 1937, Rebecca Tarwater was married to Hugh Mason Hicks, a doctor. They are the parents of three sons: Mason, Jr., born in 1939; Alan Tarwater, born in 1944; and James Byron, born in 1945. They make their home in New York City, and Rebecca Tarwater Hicks lists her "regular occupation" as housewife and mother—a full-time job with three growing boys!

THE CHARLES TATE FAMILY

Way down upon the Suwannee River at White Springs, Florida, many kinds of folk activities have taken place at the Florida Folk Festival, first presented in May, 1953. Aside from Stephen Foster songs, there have been Indian songs and dances; square dancing and other folk dancing; fiddle, harmonica, and dulcimer tunes; *Sacred Harp* songs, lining hymns; Negro spirituals and work songs; singing games, and the songs and games of many nationalities recently come into Florida.

Among the spirituals and work songs, none have been more appealing than those sung by the Charles Tate family. Charles Tate was born at Hawkinsville, Georgia, about 1910.[14] He learned to read and write in the Hawkinsville school, but had little formal education beyond that. In his youth he went to White Springs, married Sippil M. Howard in 1934, and became a farm worker on the Anderson Plantation, working in the turpentine groves. The seven Tate children, born between 1936 and 1945, are named as follows: James, Annie Lee, Sarah Lee, Charles Jr., Minnie Lee, Arthur Lee, and William.

Many Negroes in Florida, as in other states for that matter, still sing as they work. This is particularly true of the Tates as they work in the pine forests gathering sap (oleoresin) to be converted into turpentine and other products. The songs have been handed down orally. The Tates have their own way of singing them, whether spirituals or work songs (sometimes there is little difference), and they scarcely ever sing the same song twice in the same manner. They sing unaccompanied. Here we have an excellent example of the continuity and variation of folksong.

PICK TEMPLE

Another who has had a tremendous commercial success via the folksong route is Lafayette Parker Temple, radio and TV star of Washington, D.C. Professionally known as Pick Temple, he was born January 20, 1911, in a Washington, D.C., hospital, though the family lived in Baltimore. His elementary and teen-age education consisted of eight years at the Boys' Latin School in Baltimore, four years of high school at St. Paul's School, and another year at the naval academy prep school at Severn Park, Maryland. Later he studied "various special courses" in economics and business at the Johns Hopkins University and at George Washington and American Universities in Washington, D.C., but did not take a degree.

Pick Temple has been singing folksongs for a long time. His father played the guitar and his mother the piano. Both parents sang a great deal but were not traditional folksingers. Pick learned many folksongs while at school, but he picked up a great many more in his travels. His particular early interest was railroad ballads, which he picked up "in cabooses, and in the recreation rooms of railroad-men in the various yards across the country." Even with his later success, he remains "very partial to the old railroad ballads." Early in his career, all these were just "songs" that he liked to sing, and he never thought of them as folksongs. In fact, "it wasn't until I was well into my 30's," he writes, "that I even knew what a folksong meant."

In 1948, Pick visited the Folklore Section of the Library of Congress, made some recordings for the library, and began to show a curiosity about collections and other recordings in the library. Up to this time singing folksongs was an amateur side line with him, not a regular occupation. For nineteen years he had been an economist and statistician with the Census Bureau. But with more and more activity on radio and TV, he was able to give up the Census Bureau job and become a professional entertainer. As folklorist Duncan Emrich has pointed out, "From a folksinger, therefore, he evolved— as many others have—into a singer of folk songs, moving easily enough from self-entertainment to the entertainment of others." [15]

Pick Temple sings in a rich and vigorous baritone voice, and he sings easily and naturally. He does his own guitar arrangements, though they are not fixed. Earlier he sang the songs much as he found them, but in recent years, he writes, he has "found it necessary to give more and more attention to 'dressing up' the old songs by arranging them more interestingly, putting more 'expression' into singing them, enunciating more clearly." He alters tunes and phras-ing, tempo and harmony to suit his feeling for a given song. "The arrangements," he says, "are in a state of flux with the passage of time." This fluid quality in "working over" the songs is made easier because everything he does is "strictly by ear." Pick Temple, in other words, is a natural-born artist who insists that he "cannot read or write music at all," even though he wrote an excellent ballad—"The Runaway Logging Train"—in the folksong manner.

All the more remarkable, therefore, is his phenomenal success on radio and TV. Some years ago Temple had a fifteen-minute Sunday folksong radio program in Washington, for which he did careful and extensive study in the Library of Congress, and he made the background information as authentic as possible. It was authentic enough that a Georgetown University professor made it required listening for his students in ballad literature. Temple did not know of the requirement until the series was finished and was "appalled" when he heard about it. Though he modestly makes no pretense of being an authority in the field, his knowledge and practice of folksong are extensive.

In 1950, Pick Temple began a series of TV shows for WTOP-TV (C.B.S.) of Washington, D.C. Beginning as a Sunday show, it soon expanded to three days a week, then daily for three years. The pace has now slackened a bit to six days a week, with a new five-year contract. The number of shows had run to more than twenty-five hundred by late 1959, which Pick thinks "may be a record of some sort." Temple is now a "cowboy" emcee, with "cowboy outfit and all," and with his inseparable dog named Lady. He and Lady are TV heroes to thousands of children in the Washington area.

Besides his radio and TV work, Pick Temple does civic work in the Washington schools—public, private, and parochial—visiting five schools each week for a thirty-minute program of singing and talking to the children. The *Radio-Television Daily* recently (October 24, 1956) carried a brief story about his work, mentioned his sponsor, the Giant Food Stores, and quoted his salary as $1,000 a week.

L. Parker Temple was married in New York City on February 20, 1936, to Jeannette Beatrice Friedman. They have two children: Faye Ilaine, born October 23, 1937, and Lafayette Parker Temple III (they call him Buddy), born September 22, 1948. The children are musical, too: Faye plays the piano as well as the guitar, and Buddy sings folksongs with his father. Before his heavy duties kept him in Washington, Pick Temple had traveled a good deal and had performed in about a dozen states, from Florida and Texas in the South to New York and Pennsylvania in the Northeast. Though his singing has now become completely commercialized, still he is among the many who have shown what possibilities there are in folksong materials. "Purely as a folksinger," he writes, "I had no economic success." When he states that "singing for fun is one thing—doing it for a living is another," he acknowledges the compromise that perhaps many people make with their ideals of art.

SONNY TERRY

Anybody who hasn't heard Blind Sonny Terry * perform with his harmonica, on records or in person, has missed an unusual musical experience in our time. For Sonny Terry, using the humblest of folk instruments, has developed into one of our great folk musicians and might well be compared with many a classical artist. One has only to listen to a few selections to sense the complexity of musical structure and timing of which he is master.

Sonny Terry, born in Durham, North Carolina, in 1911, first performed publicly in churches. Blinded early in life by an accident, he learned to "see" with his harmonica a whole world forbidden to his eyes. By this remarkable sense of "sound-sight" he interprets life and the world about him in some of the most poignant and comical and beautiful performances one can imagine. Whatever the selection—a work song, spiritual, traditional English ballad, or moaning blues—Sonny Terry makes a special work of art out of it. No other performing is like his, none other comparable to it.

In the surge of folk music that developed during the Great Depression and through World War II, Sonny Terry and his fellow artists have fared reasonably well. He has performed throughout the land, as well as abroad, both as soloist and with other artists. One of his favorite accompanists is guitarist Alec Stewart, and he has also been on tour with Pete Seeger. Blind Sonny Terry has been recorded extensively by Stinson, Elektra, Folkways, Judson, Riverside, and on other labels (see Book Three).

PAUL THOMSEN

Featured many weeks on the Lawrence Welk radio and TV show, Paul Thomsen frankly admits that his interest in folksongs is "for the show business angle" and not academic. He is among friends in this book, for a goodly number of the singers discussed here have the same interest.

Paul S. Thomsen was born on February 21, 1935, in Albany, California. He attended grammar school at El Cerrito and high school at Washington Union High School in Centerville, California. Paul's family background was not particularly musical, and he began teaching himself about 1954, using guitar and banjo. His professional singing began in March, 1957, his first engagement being at the Kerosene Club in San Jose, California. He built up his repertoire of songs, particularly in the San Francisco Bay area (one of the very

---

* Some details for this sketch are drawn from Vanguard (VRS-9036) and Elektra (EKL-14) recordings.

active regions of commercialized folk music in the country), and soon "graduated" to the "Lawrence Welk Show," where he has attained a degree of nation-wide popularity.

Before his professional debut, Paul had sung informally "on an amateur basis" all over the European continent and the British Isles. He was married to Joan Perry on August 31, 1958, and went into military service soon thereafter.

RUTH H. TYLER

Writer, student of folklore, and housewife, Ruth H. Tyler was born in 1894 on a farm near Westport Landing, now a part of Kansas City, Missouri. She attended country school for three years and, when the family moved to Bonner Springs, Kansas, completed the grades and high school in that village.

Mrs. Tyler's mother was a self-trained singer and musician who knew many old songs, especially of a religious nature. Much of this knowledge she passed along to her daughter Ruth, who makes no claim, however, to being a singer. She says, "I merely chant the words to old-time tunes—especially play-party games and ballads." She is needlessly modest, for in this art she is unusually skillful.

When Ruth married Ray Earl Tyler in 1919, they moved to Neosho, Missouri, at the edge of the Ozark country. Here they have lived and worked, and here Mrs. Tyler has developed her writing talents and her hobby of collecting Ozark folklore. She has developed an effective written dialect (see, for example, Rayburn's *Ozark Guide* of the past dozen years) and she did radio script used by "Mirandy" on N.B.C.'s old "National Farm and Home Hour" for over five years.

When Neosho held its centennial celebration in 1939, Ruth Tyler began her public activity as a performer of old-time music. Her considerable success stems from her wide knowledge of folklore and from her use of a handmade, primitive Ozark dulcimer—a hammered dulcimer with forty-seven strings.* She plays by heart and performs many a lively tune on this instrument which, though primitive, is skillfully constructed and surprisingly musical in her hands. She has performed many times in the major cities of Missouri and Arkansas, including the National Folk Festival in St. Louis and on most other festival occasions. She is a particular favorite at the annual Ozark Folk Festival held in Eureka Springs, Arkansas, since 1948.

Always there have been favorable press comments on Mrs. Tyler's performances in large and small papers—the Joplin *Globe*, St. Louis *Post-Dispatch*, Kansas City *Star*, *Ozark Guide*, and others.

---

* See further description of the hammered dulcimer, Interlude I.

Ruth Tyler's folk music has been tape-recorded by the University of Arkansas Folklore Archives. Also, recordings were made for N.B.C. by station KVOO of Tulsa, Oklahoma. Mrs. Tyler says she'd like sometime to appear on TV "with this antique instrument" and let the world know what it looks and sounds like. She has appeared on N.B.C.'s "Monitor."

ALEX USHER

Born in St. Louis, Missouri, on January 1, 1929, Alexandra Mac-Nutt was educated at the Community and John Burroughs Schools in nearby Clayton. She spent a year (1947-48) at Wellesley College, where she first became interested in folksongs. Her parents were not singers of folksongs but were artists in allied fields, her mother being a dancer and her father a portrait painter.

After hearing a concert at Wellesley by the famous guitarist, Andrés Segovia, Alex took up the study of the guitar and began a serious study of folk music. She listened to many recordings, especially those of Burl Ives and Richard Dyer-Bennet, studied many folksong collections, and then learned, she reports, "from anyone who knew anything and would be cornered long enough to teach it to me." And she learned well, for in the past decade she has given no fewer than a hundred recitals, besides appearances at various festivals. She performed at the National Folk Festival in St. Louis in 1954 and 1955; at the Mid-America Jubilee in St. Louis on Missouri Day in 1956; at the Hermann *Maifest,* in Hermann, Missouri, in 1957. And she has appeared on the St. Louis educational TV, Channel 9, in two children's plays—*The Finder* in 1954 and *The Happy Page* in 1956.

Alexandra MacNutt was married on June 11, 1949, to Dr. J. Richardson Usher, student and former teacher of history. At present he is a technical writer for the research division of the Central Institute for the Deaf in St. Louis. The Ushers have two sons: David Richardson, born in 1951, and Scott MacNutt, born in 1953. Mrs. Usher has other interests besides folksong activities and being mother to a household. In the spring of 1957, she designed the stage sets for the Midwest Opera Association's performance of *Cavalleria Rusticana* and *I Pagliacci.*

ADELAIDE VAN WEY

Adelaide Van Wey, concert contralto with a special interest in folklore, was born in Rosman, North Carolina, January 24, 1916. Her schooling, from elementary through high school, was obtained at nearby Brevard, the town where she continues to make her home.

She attended Salem College at Winston-Salem, North Carolina, specializing in music and taking a Bachelor of Music degree. Later she studied voice in New York City.

Not a traditional singer in the strict sense, but a classically trained recitalist, Miss Van Wey has known and sung folksongs a good part of her life. She learned them early from mountain neighbors and childhood nurses and gathered them in field trips through the mountains and valleys of her native region and elsewhere in the country. In time her private collection of Creole folksongs, mountain ballads, and Negro spirituals has grown to many hundreds. In 1949, she collaborated in editing a group of *Smoky Mountain Ballads* published by the Omega Music Company, New York.

Miss Van Wey's singing career began professionally in 1940, on radio station WSJS in Winston-Salem, though she had sung in church and elsewhere from the age of five. She has given concerts in a dozen or more states and in Mexico. She knows folksongs from around the world and sings them in many languages. Her recordings are numerous—Cub Records for children; special Creole songs on the earlier Moe Asch Disc Records; and, in 1950, a Folkways record (FP 9) of Louisiana and Smoky Mountain ballads. Both records and recitals have been received with enthusiastic praise.

On February 14, 1941, Adelaide Van Wey was married to Robert Noble Hill. Mr. Hill serves as her accompanist, using piano, zither, or autoharp, and frequently the guitar for recordings. Like any other trained musician, Miss Van Wey cannot avoid stamping her own vigorous personality on the songs she sings, but she is remarkably true to the spirit of the folksongs. Because of her fine work in presenting Creole folksongs—some recordings of these are in the Library of Congress—the city of New Orleans has made her an honorary citizen. The Hills make their home at Silvermont in the town of Brevard, North Carolina, where she grew up and attended school.

JENNY WELLS VINCENT

Learning much from her neighbors in and around San Cristóbal, New Mexico, Jenny Wells Vincent has developed both expertness and authenticity in the singing of Mexican-American and Spanish-American folksongs. Deborah Jeannette Hill was born April 22, 1913, in Northfield, Minnesota. Her education began in the public schools of Winnetka, Illinois, and continued in the North Shore Country Day School. In 1930, she entered Vassar College, majored in music, and received a Bachelor of Arts degree in 1934.

Jenny was reared in a family that "liked music of various sorts," and they saw to it that she had a good musical training both in and outside school. During three years of World War II Jenny Hill entertained in Navy and Army hospitals and at that time, at the suggestion of friends, she added folksongs to her repertoire. This was a turning point in her life, for she has dedicated her talents to the learning, singing, and teaching of folksongs.

Since her first formal recital of folksongs at the Art Gallery in Taos, New Mexico, in 1946, Mrs. Vincent has done much professional singing in the past dozen years. She has performed in some fifteen states in approximately fifty concerts, and has appeared on numerous radio and TV programs. Her singing is known from Boston and New York to Denver and San Francisco. She is particularly liked in schools and colleges because of her wide range of songs and her interest in teaching folksong. Though she has specialized in the Spanish-Mexican-American folksong field, she has developed into an international balladeer, like Marion Diard, Cynthia Gooding, Jean Murai, Pete Seeger, and others. Like them, she sings folksongs of many nations and often in the native languages. For a number of years in the 1940's she had a weekly sustaining program in Santa Fe on station KTRC. And she has been on many festival programs, including the Annual Fiesta in Santa Fe, folklore meetings at Boulder and Denver, Colorado, and the National Folk Festival in St. Louis, and recently (June, 1957) in Oklahoma City.

Jenny Wells Vincent is one of the few professional singers of folksongs to use a small Hohner accordion, and occasionally she uses the guitar. She is a founder and regular staff member of the San Cristóbal Valley School. Mrs. Vincent has made recordings of Spanish-American folksongs, and she sings these songs first in Spanish and then in English. These recordings, done in Taos,[16] are especially good for learning or teaching the songs bilingually.

Jenny Hill's first marriage, to Harry K. Wells, in the late 1930's, ended in divorce in 1947. They have a son, Larry, born in 1942. In 1949, she was married to Craig S. Vincent, builder and farmer, and the Vincents have recently opened the Taos Music Center, specializing in recordings of the Southwest. Though she has traveled widely, Mrs. Vincent has chosen the valley of San Cristóbal, high in the mountains of northern New Mexico, as her home.

FRANK WARNER

For many years an active worker in folklore and collector of folksongs, Frank Warner has traveled along the Eastern Seaboard and in other areas of America with guitar, camera, and recording machine. In exchanging songs with mountain people, fishermen, farmers, miners, lumberjacks, and others, he has built up a remarkable collection of folklore, much of which is now in the Library of Congress.

Frank Warner was born April 5, 1903, in Selma, Alabama. Early schooling was in Selma and, with successive moves of the family, in Jackson, Tennessee, and Durham, North Carolina. He entered Duke University in 1921 and took a Bachelor of Arts degree in 1925. Later formal education included work at the New York School of Social Work, Columbia University, and professional training schools of the YMCA. He began his professional career in 1928 as a YMCA worker in Greensboro, North Carolina, with collecting and singing as a fascinating side line.

Like many others, Frank Warner has learned and sung folksongs as far back as he can remember. As Mrs. Warner has said, he started collecting folksongs before he knew it. He learned them first from growing up among people who sang them and later, "as a vagabond song trader," from many friends and informants. His formal singing career, if it may be called that, began when he was in college. He dates his first performance from 1924, when he sang folksongs "to illustrate a lecture on North Carolina folklore given at the State Fair in Raleigh by Dr. Frank C. Brown of Duke University." (At Duke, Warner was "in turn soloist, manager, president, and student direc- tor" of the College Glee Club.) Since 1924, his singing and collecting have taken him to three-fourths of the states of the Union and into Canada, and his recitals, formal and informal, literally run into the thousands. He has appeared at schools and colleges, before clubs and historical and folklore societies, and in such places as the Philadel- phia Art Alliance, Players Club (New York), New York Public Library, Brooklyn Museum, Town Hall, and Carnegie Hall—to name a few of the many. In his presentations Mr. Warner often uses guitar accompaniment, sometimes no instrument, but he is particularly fond of a homemade wooden banjo presented to him by Nathan Hicks, "a North Carolina mountain man," who made it for him.

Soon after Frank Warner was married to Anne Locker in 1935, they set out on a folklore collecting jaunt which they have repeated in vacation periods as time allowed for more than twenty years. Mrs. Warner's comment here is illuminating:

> Shortly after we were married in 1935, we began (since I shared his enthusiasm) to spend our vacation song hunting in out-of-the-way places, north and south, in a station wagon filled with a guitar, a recording machine, plenty of notebooks and pencils (my particular share of the project), a camera,

and other necessities. These journeys have taken us through the Carolinas from the mountains to the sea, up the coast to the Canadian border, through New Hampshire and Vermont, into the Adirondacks, and down the Hudson. All along the trail we have found people who listened to our songs and swapped with us. As a hobby our song-hunting has been deeply rewarding. It has given us a feel for America that we would not swap for anything.[17]

The Warners have two sons: Jonathan, born in 1943, and Gerret, born in 1946. After his work in Greensboro, Frank Warner went to New York in 1931 and has continued his YMCA work in that area. He has held many important positions in his profession, and in 1952 was appointed general secretary for YMCA work in Nassau and Suffolk Counties. Likewise, in the field of folklore, he has had deserved honors, chief of which is president of the New York Folklore Society.

DICK WEISSMAN

Dick Weissman, whose main interest is the playing and teaching of folk instruments, was born in Philadelphia on January 21, 1935. His schooling began in Brooklyn, but he finished both grade and high school in Philadelphia. He took a Bachelor of Arts degree at Goddard College (Plainfield, Vermont) and is working toward a master's at Columbia.

Dick's interest in folk music started when he was in college, through hearing Burl Ives over the radio. "Then," he writes, "when Disc Records went out of business I bought a lot of Pete Seeger–Woody Guthrie–Leadbelly stuff at a record shop in Philadelphia." Dick specializes in the five-string banjo, the six- and twelve-string guitar, and, to quote him again, "an instrument called the mandocello which I am experimenting with."

Dick has traveled a good deal, performing all over New England, New York and Pennsylvania, Wyoming and New Mexico. His interest in collecting is mild unless, he writes, "I happen to encounter people like Blind Gary Davis, the New York street-singer." Dick has a major interest, too, in composing instrumental and vocal music for both guitar and banjo, some of which has been recorded. He has recorded traditional materials for Riverside, Judson, Counterpoint, and Stinson records (see Book Three), for which he has had favorable press notices. He has teaching studios in Philadelphia and New York.

HARRY AND JEANIE WEST

Among the many husband-and-wife teams * working in the folk-song field are Harry and Jeanie West. The Wests were born in "folkmusic country" and have grown up with a folk-music background. Harry was born in southwestern Virginia in 1926 and Jeanie in western North Carolina in 1933. They first met at the Folk Festival at Asheville, North Carolina, in 1950 and were married a year later.

Though not college trained, they went to the public schools and have learned much on their own in the rough-and-tumble business of growing up. Perhaps what is more important, their musical background extends as far back as they can remember, and they have been singing and playing for many years. As Harry said, "I don't recall the time I could not find some string instrument or another around the house." Harry learned much from his mother, who played the fiddle and picked the mandolin, and Jeanie's mother, too, is a five-string banjo picker. They learned many of their songs from their families and from old people who still remembered the good old songs, or from old-time performers who lived in western North Carolina, east Tennessee, Virginia, and east Kentucky.

Like others in recent years, Harry and Jeanie West have become aware of the meaning of folksong and the many definitions the term has taken on and also of its confusion with other terms. They themselves are broad in their interests and do not confine their singing to any one type, for they sing whatever they like, whether it is folk, or sacred, or country. Harry plays the guitar, mandolin, and five-string banjo, and Jeanie, too, is a guitar and five-string picker. In their singing together they use various combinations of these instruments and their own individual style of picking. They have given many performances in recent years in a number of states, including New York, New Jersey, West Virginia, Virginia, North Carolina, Kentucky, South Carolina, and Florida. Among their particular folksong favorites (in addition to many fine old sacred songs they love to sing—many of these are now known as "spiritual folksongs") are "Black Jack Davy," "East Virginia Blues," "Jimmy Randall" (variant form of Child's "Lord Randall"), "Katy Cline," "Down in the Willow Garden," and "Red Rockin' Chair."

In addition to having learned a wealth of songs from family and friends, the Wests have learned many songs from early records.

* Some others: Robert and Evelyne Beers, Dr. and Mrs. I. G. Greer, Woody and Anneke Guthrie, Josef Marias and Miranda, Colonel J. R. and Winnifred Moon, Jim and Carmen Murray.

For a number of years they have developed a hobby of collecting old folk and country records and, at the present time, they own a valuable collection of over five thousand items. Some of these collectors' items the Wests are reissuing from time to time, when there is sufficient demand. They own and operate a record business and music shop in New York City known as the F-L Music Company. Harry and Jeanie have made a number of excellent LP records (see Book Three), using guitar, banjo, and mandolin accompaniments.

The Wests, like many others in the field, are doing much to keep folksongs and old-time music alive in our day. Though many of the old traditional singers have passed off the scene—in some ways modern industrialism does not seem conducive to the preservation and development of folksong—there are still lovers of good music who are eager and active in preserving our traditional music. Harry and Jeanie West are among the newer generation who are carrying on this fine tradition. And speaking of carrying on a musical tradition from one generation to another, here is one more fact about the Wests: they are the parents of a small son, Everett Glen, born August 3, 1955.

JOSH WHITE

A man of vivid personality and great integrity, Josh White is one of our most distinguished professional folksingers and a top-selling recording artist. He was born February 11, 1915,[18] in Greenville, South Carolina, and named Joshua Daniel after famous Biblical characters much admired by his preacher-father. The religious background has affected him profoundly, for he is a person of great sincerity. Much that he sings is so tinged with the spirit of social protest against injustice that one writer has dubbed him a "preacher in song."

Josh White, whose repertoire seems endless, learned folk music at its source—from a number of itinerant blind minstrels. At the age of seven he left home to lead them on the streets and from one town to another. Successively, over a period of ten years, he was the eyes of blind Joel Taggart, fabulous John Henry Arnold, Willie Johnson, and blind Lemon Jefferson, who was famous all over the South. From them and from others in his wanderings he learned blues, spirituals, work songs, and other folk music. Throughout the South he listened to "railroad workers, turpentine workers, cotton pickers, dock wallopers, and chain-gang prisoners." It was a rough and adventurous life,[19] but he stored his memory with a wealth of song. From his blind mentors, too, he developed his marvelous technique on the guitar.

His learning, however, was not all a matter of memory, for Josh White is also a creative artist in song. His own comment on this point is interesting:

> I was a folk singer long before I knew what it's called. Even when I was a boy I made up and sang songs of ordinary people, trying to convey their joys and sorrows, their grievances and their hopes. In this I was expressing not only my own sentiments but the feelings of humble people generally, whatever their color or their names.[20]

From humble circumstances and through difficult times Josh White has come to fame and success—on the concert stage, on radio and TV, and in recordings. His many appearances over the past twenty years are next to innumerable, but some examples should be mentioned. He sang and played with the Southernaires over N.B.C. On three different occasions he performed at the White House, and he did six concerts at the Library of Congress. In 1941, he went, under government auspices, on a good-will tour to Mexico with the Golden Gate Quartet. During the forties he had long runs at Cafe Society Uptown (three years), the Village Vanguard (twenty-four weeks), Cafe Society Downtown, and many other places in New York. He did weekly broadcasts for the OWI, some of them over the B.B.C. In 1944, he had a fifteen-minute sustaining program over station WNEW, and in 1946-47 he made his first formal concert tour of over thirty Canadian and United States cities. Concert, radio, and TV appearances are still his major activities, along with recordings.

Josh White's recordings are almost as numerous as his live concerts. He is reported to have done his first recording in Chicago, when he was only eleven,[21] but the first of importance was in 1931 (he was then sixteen) when he recorded twenty-eight songs for Columbia Recording Corporation in two days. He made recordings for the Library of Congress Archive of American Folk Song. By 1940, regular commercial recordings were appearing, and since then most of the major companies have pressed his songs—Columbia, Mercury, Decca, London, Period, Folkways, Elektra, Stinson, and others (see Book Three for details).

In his twenties an event occurred which threatened to change Josh White's career. One of his hands was injured in an accident,[22] and he couldn't play the guitar for about five years because of temporary paralysis in the hand. During this time he did some acting on Broadway, performing, among other things, the part of Blind Lemon Jefferson in the play, *John Henry*, in which Paul Robeson did the lead. Though the play had a short run, it brought him some attention and, according to his own account,[23] made him a prey for the Communists. He was used as a front for various organizations, unaware that they were subversive. But Josh White soon cleared himself of any subversion, and anyone would have to go far to find a more patriotic or reliable American. Josh is indeed strongly anti-Communist, but he is likewise, as always, anti-injustice, too.

Josh White was married to Carol Carr in 1935, and they have a number of children, some of whom, like Josh, Jr., follow their father's lead in singing folk music.

MR. AND MRS. ROSS C. WHITMIRE

Away up in the Bighorn National Forest area of Wyoming lives Ross C. Whitmire, onetime cowboy-rancher-farmer and a person who knows many ballads and much folklore. Ross was born on June 24, 1891, on the Huzzah River, Crawford County, in the Missouri Ozarks. What formal education he had was picked up at Cook Station, Missouri, in Whitehall, Montana, and Clearmont, Wyoming.

Ross Whitmire comes from a family of nonprofessional singers and musicians, all of whom knew folk music: "Mother played the organ and uncles played guitar, violin, banjo and zither." Supplementing this family background, Ross learned from old-time fiddlers and singers in both Missouri and Wyoming. From childhood on, he has played the harmonica for his own enjoyment, and as early as 1906 began playing for country dances.

When, in 1918, Ross Whitmire married Alice M. Gideon, musician and teacher in Chicago, his musical activities were not lessened: "My first public performance was at Orchestra Hall, Chicago, on a Folk Series Program given for the schools." Later, he performed at the National Folk Festival in Chicago in 1937, and again in Philadelphia about 1940. Most of his public performing has been at festivals, or before clubs and school groups, but all of it is nonprofessional. He did a little radio work in Chicago, at the time Bradley Kincaid (*q.v.*) was singing Kentucky ballads over station WLS.

Alice Gideon Whitmire, who taught music in the Chicago schools for eight years, has collected and arranged many of the tunes Ross played and sang. Some of these were published about 1935 (Silver, Burdett and Co.) under the title *Highways and Byways* in the "Bronze Book Series." While teaching, Mrs. Whitmire developed a harmonica band of about fifty persons, using the Ross Whitmire versions of folksongs and dance tunes. Obviously the Whitmires have some unusual versions of Western songs.* About 1940, Mrs. Whitmire prepared an article entitled "The Song of the Cowboy" for *Who's Who in Music*.

At the present time Ross Whitmire is the water commissioner for northeast Wyoming, and Mrs. Whitmire is state chairman of Folk Music Research for Wyoming. Their home is at the village of Story, in north-central Wyoming.

DICK WILDER

Dick Wilder, who learned the guitar from an Oklahoma farmer while in the United States Army, was born in New York, September 12, 1923. His education was obtained in the public-school system of New York City, including a Bachelor of Arts degree at Brooklyn College in 1943, when he was only twenty years old. After a year at Princeton, he was in the Army for several years. He then enrolled at Columbia University, received a Master of Arts degree in 1948, and continued his studies during 1950-52.

Though Dick's parents knew and sang Austrian and Slovakian folksongs, he did not show much interest in these matters until, in 1941, he joined the American Square Dance Group under the leadership of Margot Mayo. He speaks of her as the "beloved teacher and friend" who gave him his "first and most permanent inspiration for folk music and early American folk culture." (Miss Mayo at that time was a teacher of education at the Mills School for Nursery, Kindergarten, and Primary Teachers.) After the war he was again with the ASD Group on their tours into various parts of the country visiting folk festivals, fiestas, summer schools and camps. This group collected new songs and other folk materials, most of which was published in their small magazine called *Promenade*. Dick assisted in this collecting and publishing.

Wilder has given a good many performances on his own—well over a hundred by 1955 in about a dozen states, including all of New England, Texas, California, and Colorado. While in the service he performed in France, Belgium, Holland, and Germany. He sings in a rich, deep voice, and though he does particularly well with the lusty sea songs (see Book Three for recordings), he sings all kinds with feeling and understanding.

---

* Mr. Whitmire writes: "We sent Alan Lomax recording and notation of Wyoming versions of Old Paint and Trail to Mexico, which he wanted for his International Collection of Folk Songs. Also, Annabelle Morris Buchanan, Archivist for the Federation of Music Clubs, who is compiling a work on American folk music, has some of our arrangements. Sarah Gertrude Knott, Director of the National Folk Festival, also has a few of them."

Dick Wilder took up the study of medicine in 1954 at the Rochester (New York) Medical School. He was married to Nancy Hay in 1955. Mrs. Wilder also sings folksongs and, though Dr. Wilder will be busy in a growing medical practice, it is not likely that he will ever forego his interest and activity in the wonderful world of folksong.

BETTY VAIDEN WILLIAMS

Born, reared, and schooled in North Carolina, Betty Vaiden has lived most of her life in a region that many think of as "ballad country." Since her family were not folk musicians or singers, however, her interest and activity in the field have been acquired over the past few years.

Betty Vaiden was born at Lincolnton, North Carolina, on January 4, 1913. She attended the public grade schools of Raleigh and received her high-school training at Peace Junior College in Raleigh, North Carolina. In 1930, she enrolled at Converse College, Spartanburg, South Carolina, obtaining a Bachelor of Music degree in 1933. Then followed graduate study at the University of Louisville and, later, further musical studies in Chicago and New York.

Betty has known folksongs from childhood and for half a dozen years has given them intense and serious study. She has collected and recorded materials "from one end of North Carolina to the other" and has picked up songs in Mexico and Europe. Her first full recital was a concert in the Student Union at the University of North Carolina, Chapel Hill, in July, 1954. She uses autoharp, mountain dulcimer, and Spanish guitar accompaniments. Her aim is not to rearrange the songs but to present them "as they were handed down from generation to generation." She has sung in ten different states, mostly in the South, as well as in Mexico, Germany, and Spain. Always there have been favorable press notices, for she is an accomplished coloratura soprano with a wonderful stage presence. She has made recordings, a recent one on the Vanguard label (see Book Three).

Betty Vaiden was married on August 1, 1936, to Dr. Charles Frederick Williams, pediatric consultant for the North Carolina State Board of Health. They have a daughter, Charlotte Bryan, born January 1, 1943. The family home is in Raleigh.

CRATIS WILLIAMS

Another folksinging college professor is Cratis Williams, of Boone, in western North Carolina. He was born at Blaine, Kentucky, April 5, 1911, of mountaineer parents who knew folksongs, and consequently he has known and sung them all his life. He attended a typical one-room country school near Blaine and finished high school at nearby Louisa, Kentucky. He went one year (1928-29) to Cumberland College, Williamsburg, Kentucky, entered the University of Kentucky in 1930, took a Bachelor of Arts degree in 1933, and, mainly through summer schools, a Master of Arts in 1937. He has completed work for the doctorate in English at New York University.

Professor Williams began collecting ballads and folksongs systematically when he was about fifteen. He has collected chiefly in Kentucky, Virginia, and North Carolina, and from his students who come from many parts of the South, but so far he has not published. Though Professor Williams disclaims any knowledge of music, at least through formal training, and generally sings ballads without accompaniment, he can pluck a banjo or other stringed instruments with considerable skill. He is particularly partial to the English and Scottish traditional ballads that have survived in America.

Professor Williams has done many performances over a six-state area, appearing before schools, colleges, conventions, and civic clubs. For instance, in June, 1955, he was the featured entertainer of the North Carolina Rural Carrier Convention. He fills assignments on college lyceum circuits. He has been chairman of the Council for the Daniel Boone Folk Arts Festival. The local press has commented favorably on his ability as a folksinger and student of folk literature.[24] He has made some recordings, once for Disc (*Child Ballads from the Southern Highlands*) and some pressings for private distribution.

In 1937, Cratis Williams was married to Sylvia Graham, who died in 1942. In 1949, he was married to Elizabeth Lingerfelt. They have two children: Sophie, born February 18, 1953, and David, born April 25, 1955. Cratis Williams teaches courses in folksong and American literature at the Appalachian State Teachers College at Boone, where he has been professor of English for a number of years.

STAN WILSON

Stan Wilson is a West Coast singer who has had unusual success with folksongs, calypso, folk blues, and modern songs written in the folk manner. He was born May 2, 1922, in Oakland, California. He attended elementary schools in Oakland and Berkeley and high school in Berkeley. His parents were not singers or musicians, and he is largely self-taught.

Stan recalls that his first performance was in the first grade at school, and he's been singing ever since. Singing of folksongs became a professional interest for him about 1949. He collects songs to add to his repertoire, uses the guitar, and does his own arrangements.

He's published a few songs, including "Rollin' Stone," known as a Western ballad type.

His performances number in the thousands, for singing and playing are his regular occupation as well as his hobby. In the main, he has appeared at the favorite supper clubs in San Francisco, Chicago, Milwaukee, Reno, Las Vegas, and elsewhere. Stan reports as follows on his singing of folksongs: "I sing mostly folksongs because I find I get the greatest feeling from them." He has done several long-play recordings (see Book Three). The San Francisco *Examiner* (September 27, 1953), *Billboard* (November 14, 1953), and other journals have given highest praise to his performances.

Stan Wilson was married to his first wife, Roberta, from 1946 to 1952. They are the parents of three children: Paul, born October 19, 1947; Wayne, born November 30, 1949; and Randy (a girl), born May 7, 1951. He was married to Tamar Hodel in 1953, and they have a daughter, Deborah, born October 24, 1954. The Wilsons make their home in San Francisco.

HALLY WOOD

The composer Sidney Robertson Cowell has pointed out that "good singers of folk song today must not only be born but *made*— as with any of the great and difficult arts." [25] And among the best of the "made" ones is Hally Wood, whose sharp ear and keen mind have given her singing a quality that few not born to the tradition ever attain.

Hally Wood was born in Washington, D.C., September 29, 1922. Early schooling was in Washington, in Oahu, Hawaii, and in a private Episcopal school in San Antonio, Texas. Her father was a nonprofessional musician, playing the organ, piano, and piano-accordion. She attended the University of Texas intermittently, in 1939-40, 1942-43, and 1953-55, doing work toward a bachelor's degree in musical theory.

Though not born to folksinging, Hally Wood has known folksongs many years. Being studious and observant, she has, of course, learned from books and other singers. In 1941 and 1942, she assisted on field trips with John Henry Faulk, who at that time was a Rosenwald Fellow engaged in collecting Negro folk sermons.* Naturally they heard and recorded much Negro folk music. With her training in composition and musical theory, Miss Wood has had occasion to do much transcribing. Aside from work on the Faulk collection, she was a transcriber and music editor for William Doerflinger's

---

* The Faulk collection, as well as much of the Lomax material, is housed in the University of Texas archives.

Shantymen and Shantyboys (1951); she transcribed many tunes for Alan Lomax when he was an editor for Decca Records; she did the piano accompaniments for Jean Ritchie's *A Garland of Mountain Song* (1953); and more recently she has done work on the extensive collection of John and Alan Lomax at the University of Texas.

In recitals Hally Wood sometimes uses the guitar but often no instrument at all. She has given many performances in the past dozen years, from New York to Texas. She has recorded two albums of folksongs (see Book Three), and her singing has had highest praise from both music critics and folksong experts.[26] Miss Wood was once married and has a daughter, Cynthia Tannehill Gordon, born November 28, 1948.

THEODORE WOOD, JR.

Though he makes no claim to the title of folksinger, Theodore Wood, Jr., sometime teacher in the English and History Division of the Massachusetts Institute of Technology, knows a good deal about folksongs. He was born in Medford, Massachusetts, in 1913, received his education in private schools in New York State, took a Bachelor of Science degree in 1935 and Master of Arts in 1940 at Harvard.

Mr. Wood's paternal grandfather was a professional organist though not a singer. His father is an all-round musician and singer, though not of folk music. So Mr. Wood has always been interested in singing, though he has learned folksongs mainly since 1940 from friends, other performers, and recordings. He uses the guitar and works out his arrangements mostly by ear. He has given performances in the New England states, though not many, his main interest being to sing merely for the pleasure of himself and friends. But it should be stressed that his kind of amateur singing helps to keep folksongs alive and interesting.

GLENN YARBROUGH

Born in Milwaukee, Wisconsin, on January 12, 1930, Glenn Yarbrough has developed a considerable folksong repertoire since 1950. He attended Grace Church School in New York City and St. Paul's School in Baltimore. At the age of nine he was a choirboy at Grace Church, and he has had extensive musical training since then.

In 1949, Glenn enrolled in St. John's College, Annapolis. After three years there he had a year of service in Japan and Korea. He had learned many folksongs from student friends and teachers while at St. John's, and his first regular concert was at Christmas time,

1953, in Pusan, Korea. He spent the year 1954-55 at Mexico City College, and in 1956 was at the New School for Social Research in New York City.

Yarbrough's main business is that of musical entertainer, and his folksong concerts have run well over one thousand—this includes night-club spots but not radio and TV appearances. He has performed (he uses the guitar) in a dozen or so of the states, as well as in Japan, Korea, Canada, and Mexico. Both Tradition and Elektra have issued his records (see Book Three), and with his unusual vocal ability and training, he is bound for success in the folksong world.

Glenn Yarbrough was married to Peggy Goodhart on September 21, 1951. They have one child, born in October, 1958.

DAVID ZEITLIN

David Zeitlin, born in Los Angeles in 1932, has learned folksongs from many sources—friends, relatives, and professional singers. He gives special credit to singers Sam Eskin and Carl Sandburg, and to his father, Jacob Zeitlin, who "has sung them for many years." David attended various public schools in Los Angeles and elsewhere, and he had two years of college at Los Angeles City College.

David does his own arranging of folk tunes, using guitar accompaniments or sometimes banjo. Not a professional singer or professional collector, still he has "picked up many songs in many places," and according to his friends is an excellent performer who knows a lot of wonderful folksongs.

Jacob Zeitlin, David's father, is a writer, singer of folksongs, former university professor, and at present a bookseller in Los Angeles. The family, including David, are importers and dealers in rare books and manuscripts, old master drawings and prints. The singing of folksongs in the Zeitlin family is strictly a long-time hobby and, as is often the case, the amateur is often more adept than many a professional.

SUPPLEMENT TO BIOGRAPHICAL SKETCHES

Here follows a list of half a hundred singers and folk musicians for whom, for one reason or another, no biographical data were available. Each has made one or more long-playing folksong records. For some, bits of biographical information are available on the record jackets. Others who are well known—Marian Anderson, Tennessee Ernie Ford, John Greenway, Frank Luther, Paul Robeson, Jo Stafford, William Warfield—have won distinction in various ways and need not be sketched here, but it seemed advisable to include them in this additional listing. Complete identification of their folksong records will be found in Book Three, under the singers' names.

Anderson, Marian

Anderson, Pink

Atcher, Bob

Boguslav, Raphael

Brill, Marty

Britton, George

Brooks, John B.

Campbell, Gerard

Cooper, Clarence

Cuevas, Lolita

DeCormier, Bob & Louise

Donnegan, Lonnie

Dunbar, Max

English, Logan

Ennis, Seumas

Felius, Odetta

Ford, Tennessee Ernie

Galvin, Patrick

Gilkyson, Terry

Gilmer, Julia Ann

Gitter, Dean

Greenway, John

Hall, Dickson

Hemsworth, Wade

Hillel and Aviva

Jacobs, Freddy

Kines, Tom

Labrecque, Jacques

Lee, Charles

Lea, Terrea

Luther, Frank

McFerrin, Robert

McGhee, Brownie

Olsen, Dorothy

Parham, Walter

Pegram, George

Ramsay, Obray

Robertson, Jeannie

Robertson, Walt

Robeson, Paul

Runge, John

Stafford, Jo

Warfield, William

White, Kitty

Williams, Camilla

FOOTNOTES TO CHAPTER 8

[1] Vernon Loggins, *I Hear America ... Literature in the United States Since 1900* (New York, 1937), p. 272.

[2] Sandburg, *Always the Young Strangers* (New York, 1952), p. 84.

[3] *Ibid.*, pp. 84-85.

[4] *Ibid.*, pp. 202-03. Sandburg says that before he was fourteen he had read five paper-covered books on Jesse James. Further, "If England can have her Robin Hood ballads we have a right to our Jesse James song."

[5] A quick summary would include: born of Swedish immigrant parents in Galesburg, Illinois, in 1878; learned to work hard at all kinds of manual labor; spent a year in the Spanish-American War, and returned to graduate from Lombard College; went into newspaper work, first in Milwaukee,

then in Chicago, and thence into the larger writing field; had great success with his Lincoln studies, his poetry readings, and his folksinging;
married Lillian Steichen in 1908, and they reared three daughters; has been
honored by many colleges and universities, and his fame has grown with
the years; his seventy-fifth birthday on January 6, 1953, and his eightieth
in 1958 occasioned nation-wide celebrations. For further details, see such
sources as Loggins, *I Hear America;* L. Untermeyer, *Modern American
Poetry* (New York, 1950); *The Encyclopaedia Britannica* (Chicago, 1947);
Robert E. Spiller *et al., A Literary History of the United States* (New
York, 1948); and, of course, Sandburg's own remarkable and extremely
readable account, *Always the Young Strangers* (New York, 1952).

6 *Always the Young Strangers,* pp. 375-402.

7 Records may be obtained from Mr. Scammell, 1320 Lombard Crescent, Town
of Mount Royal, Quebec, Canada.

8 *Folk Songs of Canada* (Waterloo, Ontario, 1954), p. 53.

9 This sketch of Tom Scott is based on facts gleaned from *Current Biography*
(November, 1946), from his numerous radio and concert appearances
(for instance, many times on the "Fred Waring Show" and on "Monitor,"
February 5, 1956), and from an interview when he appeared in recital at
Junior College of Kansas City.

10 Reported in *Musical Courier,* April 1, 1954.

11 Reported in *Film Music,* XV (Summer 1956), 19-23.

12 Her brother specializes in Israeli folksongs but does not sing professionally.

13 I am indebted to Mr. Summers for biographical facts, with a few details from
notes on his Folkways record jackets.

14 For information on the Tate family I am indebted to Mr. Charles Tate and
to Miss Helen Bixler, secretary and publicity director for the Florida Folk
Festival.

15 Quoted, by permission, from Duncan Emrich's notes on Pick Temple's RCA
record LXA-3022, *Folk Songs of the People.*

16 Amerecord 101, 102, and ALP 102, obtainable from Cantemos Records, P. O.
Box 492, Taos, New Mexico.

17 From jacket notes on Frank Warner's record, *American Folk Songs and Ballads,* Elektra (EKLP-3), 1952.

18 This brief sketch of Josh White is a composite of articles appearing in *Current Biography* (August, 1944), *Negro Digest* (December, 1950), *Ebony*
(March, 1946), *Collier's* (November 16, 1946), of notes on record jackets,
and of firsthand information from hearing Josh sing.

19 *Ebony* (March, 1946) reports that he was beaten by Klansmen in South
Carolina for trespassing on white-owned property.

20 *Negro Digest,* December, 1950, p. 28.

21 *Current Biography,* August, 1944, p. 56.

22 The *Collier's* article reports that his hand was injured when he slipped on icy
pavement as he was carrying a bottle of milk.

23 In a remarkably revealing article titled "I Was a Sucker for the Communists,"
Negro Digest, December, 1950, pp. 26-31.

24 For instance, Charlotte (North Carolina) *Observer,* November 28, 1954;
Shelly (North Carolina) *Star,* April 16, 1955.

25 From notes on the record album, *American Folksongs of Sadness and Melancholy* (EKL-10), sung by Hally Wood.

26 Sidney Cowell emphasizes Hally Wood's ability to develop an individual folk
style after "listening intently" to hundreds of folksingers, and praises her

command of the "impersonal ritualistic style that belongs to the oldest ballads and hymns" (notes on EKL-10). Charles Haywood, reviewing records for the *Journal of American Folklore,* LXVII (October-December, 1954), 415-20, commends her "unfailing sense of pitch and sustained legato" and the "sheer color of her voice," especially in her unaccompanied singing.

INTERLUDE I

CHAPTER 9

Folk-Music
Instruments

I N discussing folk-music instruments, one should keep in mind at the outset some basic general ideas. The first of these is that folksinging does not necessarily require any instrumental accompaniment. Much folksinging, traditional or not, is done "in line of duty"—as one works in the field, around the house, at a shop, or wherever people carry on their everyday activities. In such situations it goes without saying that the singer cannot conveniently carry an instrument over his shoulder, or in his pocket, and make music with it as he works.

In the tens of thousands of recordings made in the field by workers who have recorded for the Library of Congress Archive, or for state and regional archives, much of the singing is done unaccompanied. For instance, a count in the Library of Congress *Check-List of Recorded Songs . . . to July, 1940,* shows that somewhat less than a third of the ten thousand songs used any instrumental accompaniment. Of the 107 records, containing 350 songs, issued for release (up to about 1954), the Library of Congress catalogue indicates that about 200 songs were recorded without any instrument, about 100 had instrumental accompaniment, and about 50 were instrumental only. These figures may not be representative of the many thousands of songs recorded, but they prove the point: folksinging does not require accompaniment. A number of the singers discussed in Book One of this handbook present some songs without instrumental accompaniment (Grace Creswell, Sam Eskin, Dr. I. G. Greer,

Anne Grimes, Jean Ritchie, Hally Wood, etc.), and some others sing entirely unaccompanied (the Davis family, Dick Devall, Doney Hammontree, L. M. Hilton, A. R. Scammell, etc.). Old-time *Sacred Harp* singing of spiritual folksongs is still done without accompaniment also.

A second basic idea is that when instruments are used, they are likely to be small, portable, in the main easily played, relatively inexpensive, and frequently homemade. The folksinger, traditionally, has not been a person of wealth, and hence the more expensive instrument—whether it be harpsichord, piano, Stradivari violin, or a many-stringed harp—has not been within his reach. In any event, the piano, for instance, is too much accompaniment. As Ruth Crawford Seeger has pointed out: "Rich edifices of sound, natural to it, are not natural to folk songs." [1] Ballads and folksongs in many compilations are set to piano music, but the arranger is quick to point out that they were not originally sung in this manner. In an earlier time, too, folk music was even more informal than it is today. The instrumentalist was needed at parties, dances, festivals, or family gatherings and usually carried his instrument along. This is true to some degree today.

A third basic idea is that the folk musician is not likely to be a highly skilled expert, or at least a highly trained one, with his instrument. He may, however, be very clever and capable. Often he plays by ear and may not even read musical notes, but he may be able to do a great deal "on his own" through listening and practice. The current do-it-yourself craze in many of life's activities is nothing new to the folk musician—he has always "done it himself," that is, made his own music. He has not suffered from a lack of self-expression. From the point of view of the sophisticated or the highly trained musician, he may make bad music, but he is personally well-adjusted and in harmony with the universe!

A fourth basic idea is that simplicity of the music does not necessarily mean lack of beauty or importance, or lack of a certain subtlety, one is even tempted to say, complexity. Often the great artist strives for the beauty of simplicity. Often some of the finest folk tunes are the simplest ones. They make a universal appeal to the human heart, and whether expressed simply on a small instrument or in great complexity in a full symphony, the fascination of a recurring melodic line is a perpetual joy.

The broad ideas set forth above no doubt have many exceptions, but perhaps they express some of the larger truths, too. But what instruments do the folk musicians or singers of folksongs use? For the sake of convenience it seems practical to make two obvious groupings: those most commonly used and those less commonly used. In the first group I would place half a dozen instruments: guitar, banjo, fiddle, harmonica, zither (with its modification, the autoharp), and dulcimer.* In the second group the list is almost unending since many ingenious devices are found or fashioned to make music. But important, in varying degrees at any rate, are these: mandolin, accordion, psaltery, recorder, drum (various kinds), lute, harp (small), rattles, and some odd improvised items. It remains now to discuss some of these instruments in detail.

THE GUITAR

"Sometimes I feel like nothin', somethin' th'owed away;
Then I get my guitar and play the blues all day."

FROM AN OLD BLUES SONG

Of all the plucked stringed instruments, it is merely pointing out the obvious to say that the *guitar* † is the most universally popular today. In the Library of Congress *Check-List* mentioned above, the guitar accounted for well over a thousand accompaniments, more than a third of the total. Though not an ancient instrument, it has been used in the Western world since the early Renaissance. The exact place and exact date of its beginnings, like those of most musical instruments, are obscure, though it came West from the Orient and is classed as a member of the lute family.[2] Through the centuries its number of strings, structure, and body form have varied somewhat, but by the early seventeenth century it was approaching its modern simplified form—a mildly curving waist, flat back, long fretted neck, relatively large body, and six single strings.[3] Its portability, its soft tones for vocal accompaniment, its wide range (over three octaves), and its comparative ease in handling and playing have made it the popular instrument among amateurs for well over three centuries. For many generations it has been *the* instrument of the common people, particularly in Italy, Spain, and the Latin countries of the New World,[4] and the Anglo-Saxon world, too, has thoroughly naturalized it.

The folk-music recordings released by the Library of Congress indicate the preponderance of the guitar over other instruments two

* In passing, it is worth notice that the two major mail-order houses in America, Sears Roebuck and Montgomery Ward, have for many years listed in their catalogues the following: guitar, banjo, fiddle (or violin, if expensive enough!), harmonica, accordion, mandolin, zither, and (more recently) autoharp.

† The English word comes directly from the Spanish *guitarra*, which in turn stems from the Greek *kithara*.

to one. Among the two hundred odd singers discussed in the present book, at least two-thirds of them use the guitar (and sometimes other instruments, too). Many of them play the instrument with masterly skill—Bill Broonzy, Richard Dyer-Bennet, Josef Marais, Josh White, and others—though none would claim to be a Segovia!

Folksong collectors and other writers have noted the overwhelming popularity of the guitar. For instance, Eleanor Hague collecting Spanish-American songs before World War I mentions it as "the early instrument throughout Spanish America" and above all others "the most beloved." [5] Alice Corbin, writer of the Southwest, stated that the guitar is the "most inseparable accompaniment of New Mexico folk-songs, and there are few adobes without one." [6] W. A. Owens, collector and authority on Texas folk music, writes that the guitar is especially popular in Texas and many folksingers "have adapted their tunes to simple guitar chords." [7] John W. Work, authority on Negro folk music, comments: "Without question, the most popular instrument among Negro folk instrumentalists is the guitar." [8] Further proof lies in the fact that folksong collections designed for singing almost invariably include chords for the guitar, even when the songs are given piano settings.

THE BANJO

"Now the rain am fallin' in my feather bed I'll snooze
Gonna go to sleep and dream away my Banjo blues."

SPENCER WILLIAMS, "Banjo Blues" [9]

Different in appearance, in sound, in structure from its more elegant cousin, the guitar, the *banjo* also plays a major part in the American folk-music scene. A fleeting glance suggests a long-handled skillet, a closer look says it's a tambourine on a stick, and a more careful examination shows it to be an open shallow drum covered on the top with parchment and having a long fretted neck and four or five strings. As the guitar has come to be thoroughly Latinized or Spanish in character, the banjo by contrast is now thoroughly Americanized. Its strident and insistent plunking, its barbaric yawp, seem peculiarly suited to the restless American character.

Like the guitar, the banjo is somewhat uncertain in place and date of origin. One authority states that it was imported "by slaves from Western Africa," but that it is probably "not an aboriginal instrument." [10] Another states that "the ultimate origin of this instrument is supposed to be Africa, and it was in use amongst the slaves of the Southern U.S.A." [11] Pete Seeger, another authority and a considerable virtuoso on the banjo, agrees that it came from Africa, but "before that the origin is disputed." [12] He states further: "Possibly the Arabs brought it to the African west coast; possibly the Arabs themselves picked it up from civilizations further east." At any rate, it has been popular in these United States for many a decade.

Thomas Jefferson in *Notes on Virginia* mentions the "banjar" as being the chief instrument of American Negroes. A Joe Sweeney of Virginia added the fifth string [13] and gave us the famous five-stringer that for so long dominated the American scene, especially for folk musicians: "It travelled west in the covered wagons, and one could be found hanging on the wall of any farmhouse or mining shack." Historians of the Westward Movement take note of its presence in the camps.[14] It was the favorite instrument of the Negro minstrel shows which dominated the popular entertainment scene from the 1840's on into the twentieth century. One of the earliest collectors of cowboy songs mentions its popularity in the Southwest cattle country.[15]

After the five-stringer was somewhat superseded by the shorter, four-string tenor banjo, it took to the hills and became a back-country instrument, where it is still one of the favorites.[16] With a bit of nostalgia, Seeger writes: "Today, the 5-string banjo is almost forgotten; instrument companies produce very few; a hock shop is the most likely place to find a good one." Even so, it can still be bought by mail order from Sears Roebuck or Montgomery Ward. The upsurge of American folk music, as well as the fine concert work of Pete Seeger himself and the playing of such folk musicians as Banjo Bill Cornett, Bascom Lamar Lunsford, and Frank Warner, may bring it again into popular use.

THE FIDDLE

> "Rabbit in the pea-patch, possum in the pot,
>   Try an' stop my fiddle, now my fiddle's gettin' hot!"
>
>   STEPHEN VINCENT BENÉT,
>   "The Mountain Whippoorwill"

Historically, the word *fiddle* is used to designate a large class of bowed instruments from the Orient and Near East, some of which came into Europe in the Middle Ages,[17] and were perhaps the ancestors of the violin. The violin as we know it today developed in the Renaissance and came to perfection with the Italian makers in the sixteenth and seventeenth centuries, culminating in the supreme work of Stradivari (1644-1737) in the early eighteenth century.[18]

Query: When is a violin a fiddle? As almost any dictionary will show, the word fiddle, in its common American sense, is merely a colloquial term for violin. Sometimes the word is applied humorously or contemptuously. In the folk-music sense, however, it is likely to mean a homemade violin, the manner of playing it, and often the kind of music played. In these senses the instrument has had, and still has, widespread use in America. To give a few examples.

For generations the fiddle has been the main accompaniment at country dances all over New England, and many of the fiddles were homemade, local products and used in families for a long time.[19] Researcher Allen H. Eaton reports finding "more than thirty fiddle, or violin, makers . . ." who had made more than two thousand instruments—some of these makers being native New Englanders, others foreign born.[20] Another writes that "the chief folk instrument in Pennsylvania today is undoubtedly the fiddle—almost indispensable for 'old-time' dancing" or for other instrumental entertainment.[21]

What was true of the fiddle in New England was apparently duplicated in the southern Highlands, as reported by Eaton and others.[22] John Harrington Cox, an early authority on folksongs in the South, tells of meeting in 1918 an old fiddler and maker of musical instruments in West Virginia. Over a period of years this man had made ninety fiddles, as well as guitars and other instruments.[23] In North Carolina, common instruments of the mountain people are the fiddle, guitar, and banjo. Two collectors report that "it would be hard to find anywhere banjo pickers or breakdown fiddlers who can play with a more perfect and contagious rhythm or who have acquired a nimbler technical proficiency than the best of these self-taught musicians." [24]

Similar evidence can be cited as one moves on westward. In a Thomas Hart Benton mural, "History of Indiana," the artist shows, in a background scene, an old-time fiddler and a group of country dancers.[25] Vance Randolph of the Ozarks found the fiddle, as well as the guitar and harmonica, very common throughout the Ozarks.[26] Another writer of the Ozarks, Otto Ernest Rayburn, comments with pride and enthusiasm on the region as peculiarly adapted to the fiddle. He says: "The Ozark region is a geographical center of artful fiddling and expert guitar and banjo picking. These instruments belong to the folk and nowhere in the world are they used to greater advantage. Ozarkers fiddle by the feel of the tune, and notes hung on a staff have little meaning. . . . The James-White River country grows fiddlers as a principal crop and many of them have won state and regional championships with their playing." [27] One might mention here that an old fiddlers' contest is standard entertainment at any festival, state or county fair, cultural or agricultural get-together of whatever nature almost anywhere from the Alleghenies to the Rockies.

Men will have music wherever they go, whatever they do. In the middle 1930's, John Steinbeck's struggling migrant workers in *The Grapes of Wrath*, in spite of all their tragic misery and sadness, still found time for pleasure in tapping feet to the rhythm of harmonica, fiddle, and guitar. Another instance, and a sad one, should be noted here. In October, 1954, when riots rocked the Missouri State Prison in Jefferson City, the governor ordered all radios taken from the cell blocks. The immediate reaction of the inmates was to make their own music, and soon fiddles, guitars, and banjos resounded all over the place.[28]

Back to Thomas Hart Benton. I stated earlier that one distinction between fiddle and violin is the manner of playing. Benton, in many of his paintings, depicts the fiddler playing his fiddle holding it "off the chest," not tucked under the chin. Examples of this method are seen in his "Sourwood Mountain" painting and the murals titled "Arts of the West" and "Arts of the South." [29] Not all the old fiddlers use this method, to be sure, but it is common, as anyone knows who has seen them play. Someone has facetiously pointed out that if a fiddler should dress up in white tie and tails, tuck his instrument up under his chin against a silk kerchief, and start playing—then he becomes a violinist! In this connection Vance Randolph's comment is worth quoting: "Many an Ozark fiddler, even today [1945], does not tuck his instrument under his chin, but nurses it dulcimore-fashion upon his lap. Grasping the bow nearly in the middle, he plays with a short movement very different from that of the conventional violinist." [30]

THE HARMONICA

"During the making of my Missouri mural I traveled all over the state. I met all kinds of people. I played the harmonica and wore a pink shirt to country dances."

THOMAS HART BENTON, *An Artist in America*

Lowliest of folk instruments, easy to play, easy to carry, the *harmonica* has probably given common humanity more musical pleasure than any other instrument. Considering its size, it can deliver a tremendous variety and volume of sound. This very small member of the free-reed family was invented in 1821 by a German, Fredrich Buschmann, and is often known as the mouth organ [31] or, colloquially, French harp. Mouth organs were known in ancient

China, but they were quite different, then and now, from what is the usual meaning of the word in America.[32]

Though the harmonica is fairly easy to play, it is capable of complicated music in the hands of a master. Folk musicians are not exactly Larry Adlers or John Sebastians, but sometimes they can do some pretty tricky stunts. This is attested by Tom Benton's experience when he recorded with a group of highly trained musicians in New York in 1941.[33]

Regarding the instrument's lowly use and surprising virtuosity, we may well conclude this brief comment on the harmonica with a quotation from John Steinbeck:

> A harmonica is easy to carry. Take it out of your hip pocket, knock it against your palm to shake out the dirt and pocket fuzz and bits of tobacco. Now it's ready. You can do anything with a harmonica: thin reedy single tone, or chords, or melody with rhythm chords. You can mold the music with curved hands, making it wail and cry like bagpipes, making it full and round like an organ, making it as sharp and bitter as the reed pipes of the hills. And you can play and put it back in your pocket. It's always with you, always in your pocket. ... And if you lose or break it, why, it's no great loss. You can buy another for a quarter.[34]

THE ZITHER

The common definition of the *zither* is a folk-music instrument having thirty to forty-five strings over a flat horizontal sounding box, and played with a plectrum. Some models show a fretted finger board under several strings on which the melody is played. The word zither comes from the German, which in turn took it from the Latin *cithara* and the Greek *kithara*, the same root word for guitar.

The zither, a member of the psaltery-dulcimer family, had a long and complicated ancestry before coming into Europe and the New World. Something like it was apparently known to the ancient Israelites, the Phoenicians, and the Greeks, as well as to other peoples of the Near and Far East.[35] Today it is a common instrument (but under other names) in Scandinavia, Holland, and particularly in the Austrian, Bavarian, and Swiss Alps, where it is the popular accompanying instrument for folksinging.[36] It does not seem to have been widely used in the United States, and yet there are some rather interesting facts to be noted.*

---

* Available Library of Congress records of folk music do not list any as using the zither for accompaniment.

The year 1864 saw the beginning of a zither factory in the Midwest. German-born Franz Schwarzer, woodcarver by trade and a musician, came to America as a young man and settled on a farm in Warren County, Missouri. There, for his own pleasure, he carved out his first zither. Soon he began making zithers for friends, and thus a business was begun. He moved to Washington, Missouri, and opened a small factory, which eventually employed as many as twenty skilled workers. The factory was a small, red-brick building on a bluff overlooking the Missouri River.

The Franz Schwarzer Zither Company, as it was called, continued in operation for approximately eighty years, and Washington, Missouri, became, not merely the center of the American zither industry, but was known as the Zither Capital of the World. During its eighty years of operation, the factory turned out an annual average of 140 handmade, skillfully constructed zithers of various sizes and quality, ranging in price from $40 to $200. An occasional fine example, with gold and silver decorations and mother-of-pearl inlay, sold for as much as $1,000. The factory had orders from all over the world, and more than eleven thousand fine instruments were sold locally, nationally, and internationally.

The Schwarzer zithers, as the illustrations indicate, were rather elegant instruments. Five melody strings, plucked with a plectrum, were stretched over a fretted finger board, and the remaining strings served as accompaniment. The number of strings varied from thirty-two to forty-five, and the instrument had a range of over six octaves. Carefully air-dried and aged woods—rosewood, tulipwood, mahogany, curly maple, walnut, spruce, burl of many kinds—went into the making of the zithers. These instruments were designed and used for giving formal musical concerts, which obviously included much more than folk music.

After the death of Franz Schwarzer, ownership passed to Herman C. Grohe, who had been associated with the factory for many years. At Grohe's death, in 1925, the factory passed to the last surviving worker, Albert A. Hesse, who died June 28, 1955. Hesse had been taken into the plant in 1891, when he was fourteen, as an apprentice. The factory ceased making new instruments about 1944, but Hesse continued to repair zithers for some years, almost to the time of his death. There is a small collection of the Schwarzer zithers in the State Museum in the Missouri State Capitol Building. Not a vestige of the small, red-brick factory remains on the bluff above the Missouri River, and no sweet strains of zither music float out across the wide Missouri, as some workman turns out another finished product.

In the name of progress, the old factory has been razed to make way for a housing project.[37]

If the zither is no longer much in evidence, except as a museum piece, its simplified modification known as the *autoharp* is sometimes used by singers of folksongs. This instrument is a kind of elementary zither with a series of special buttons or dampers which makes it possible to produce chordal accompaniments almost automatically. If the zither is easy to learn, the autoharp is doubly so. It makes a pleasant and satisfactory accompaniment to the voice when some simple instrumentation is desired.

The autoharp is manufactured today in two or three sizes, a small size with five bars across the strings, and the larger sizes with twelve or fifteen bars. The smaller ones can be played in only two keys, and the larger in five keys. The instrument is frequently used in the schools for simple accompaniment, for pupils in fourth or fifth grade can soon learn it.[38]

Many singers of folksongs have found it a simple and satisfactory addition to the voice. Among singers discussed in Book One of the present work, the following make much use of the autoharp: Bobby Barnes, Mary Ella Boyle, Frosia Gregory, Valerie Haynes—to mention a few.

THE DULCIMER

"The classic beauty of the dulcimer places it at the top of the folk instruments of this country."

CHARLES F. BRYAN, *Tennessee Folklore Society Bulletin*

"Have you ever heard a dulcimer played on a still soft night by a lonesome person?"

JEAN RITCHIE, *Singing Family of the Cumberlands*

The guitar with its soft and mellow tones no doubt holds undisputed first place for all-round use among folk instruments today; the harmonica takes a kind of precedence because of its pocket size and modest cost; the banjo and the fiddle, with sharp and lively, sometimes raucous voices, seem peculiarly fitted to American pioneer exuberance and for a long time have been deservedly popular over the whole country. But surely one of the most fascinating, sweetly musical, and somewhat puzzling (historically) of all plucked stringed instruments is the *dulcimer* (variously called *dulcimore, dulcymore,* or, in Ohio at least, *dulcerine*).

Most histories of musical instruments, and often the general dictionaries, make no mention of the dulcimer as it is commonly known in the eastern United States today, that is, a plucked instrument of three or four strings, and occasionally five, rarely six, strings.[39] The ancient historical dulcimer, to be sure, is quite another instrument. This latter member of the zither family has a trapezoidal shallow sound box over which are stretched many wire strings, usually from thirty to forty, and it is played by striking the strings with two small sticks or wooden hammers. Known as the hammered dulcimer, it is said to be of Persian or Iraquian origin, to have been carried West by the Arabs, then back to China by 1800, where it is still known as the foreign zither, and to many other Oriental countries.[40] It was known in biblical times and is still found among the Israeli and North Africans, as well as in some parts of Europe and America.[41]

We find this hammered dulcimer used occasionally by folk musicians in America. Around 1920, collector Henry W. Shoemaker reported that it was the favorite musical instrument of the Pennsylvania mountain people.[42] Among the available Library of Congress folk-music recordings, however, there is but one record (No. AAFS 41) of hammered-dulcimer pieces, recorded at Ortonville, Iowa, in 1937. In the Ozarks, Ruth H. Tyler owns and plays what is called a primitive Ozark handmade dulcimer which has forty-seven strings. It is built into a box or table with folding legs, so that it is easily portable. Mrs. Tyler thinks the instrument was "made in one of the regional factories circa 1878." She is a skillful artist with the hammers and has given many recitals.[43] The late Charles F. Bryan (see Chapter Three) had two hammered dulcimers in his collection of American folk-music instruments.

But the above examples of the complicated hammered dulcimer are not to be confused with what is sometimes called the American "mountain" dulcimer, the simple, slender instrument of three or four strings. This mountain dulcimer is found, at least in recent years, throughout the Appalachian area as a "native" instrument,* and even north of the Ohio River.

The structural design of this instrument is unique. No matter how many shapes there are within the general pattern, the main features of the design remain relatively constant. This dulcimer is a narrow, elongated fretted instrument, with flat top and bottom. The box is

* A recent (1957) brief account of the structural patterns and present-day use of the dulcimer is to be found in *The Plucked Dulcimer of the Southern Mountains*, by John F. Putnam. This is a sixteen-page mimeographed booklet which may be obtained from the Council of the Southern Mountains, Inc. (College Box 2000, Berea, Kentucky). A note in the booklet states: "A book about the dulcimer is now in process . . . as a joint project of the Council of the Southern Mountains and the Tennessee Folklore Society."

long and shallow, measuring from one and one half inches to possibly three inches in thickness. The usual three or four strings are tightened by pegs placed in the scroll, and there is no movable (or removable) bridge as in the fiddle or other plucked instruments like the guitar, banjo, or mandolin. One feature peculiar to the dulcimer is the long fret piece glued to the flat top and extending the length of the instrument. This fret piece looks like a long "block," about an inch or so wide and deep, but it is hollowed and serves as part of the sound box. (See various illustrations.) Cut in the top of the box on either side of the fret piece and occasionally in the fret piece itself are sound holes—variously shaped in hearts, circles, diamonds, or inverted turns.

Since the instrument was never mass-produced but is handmade and homemade, dulcimer makers have produced many shapes. A common design is the slender-waisted, lengthened hourglass shape—"a little like a long skinny fiddle," to quote Anne Grimes.[44] The larger bulge is at the lower end, the end opposite the scroll. Another shape is a slender oval, or elongated diamond, the greatest width being centered or toward the lower end, i.e., opposite the scroll. (Again, see illustrations.)

Many kinds of wood have been used in making the dulcimer, and a good many persons have made the instrument. One of the early famous makers was James Edward ("Uncle Eddie") Thomas (c. 1850-1933), who generally used walnut, but sometimes maple or birch, and, in a few instances, California redwood.[45] Uncle Eddie Thomas, born in Letcher County in southeastern Kentucky, where he lived out his more than eighty years, was making dulcimers when he was twenty-one and continued to fashion them for over sixty years. How many he made is not known, but conjectures vary from twelve to fifteen hundred.[46] Another famous maker, and a teacher for many years, was Lewis Hinkle, born in the late 1850's, in Upshur County, West Virginia. He, too, used a combination of woods, in one instance "yellow pine, cedar, white oak, poplar, and black walnut." He made several hundred dulcimers during a period of more than fifty years.[47]

Dulcimers are still made and still widely used. Among current makers in the southern Highlands, I should like to mention three. One of these is Jethro Amburgey, who for many years has had charge of woodworking at the Hindman Settlement School. He was born March 11, 1895, at Bath, Kentucky, where Uncle Eddie Thomas lived. He attended the Hindman schools and Berea College and took a Bachelor of Arts degree at Morehead State College in 1937. About 1920, he learned to make dulcimers from Mr. Thomas, and from that time forward he has averaged about one every six weeks. Up to September, 1954, he had made a total of 284 dulcimers. His are numbered, dated, and signed inside one of the heart sound holes.[48] He uses several woods, such as black walnut, cherry, maple and white pine. His chief tools are handsaw, rasp, plane, auger, and pocket knife.*

Another and younger dulcimer maker is Homer Ledford, born September 27, 1927, at Dayton, Tennessee. After schooling in Dayton grade school, Alpine high school, and Livingston Academy, he attended Berea College, Kentucky, for three years, and then finished his college work at Eastern Kentucky State College, Richmond, Kentucky. He spent one year studying crafts and dancing at the John C. Campbell Folk School, Brasstown, North Carolina. Here, in March, 1947, he made his first dulcimer. Since that time he has made and sold some 125 dulcimers, averaging about one a month. His tools are more numerous, possibly more modern, than those of older makers. He uses hand plane, rip saw, electric pointer, band saw, chisels, pocket knife, peghole reamer, special pegmaker (which he developed himself), coping saw, file, pliers, and hammer. He generally uses white pine for the top and back; black walnut for the sides, fret board, and scroll; and maple for the pegs.[49]

Any discussion of dulcimer-making should include a comment on John Jacob Niles, noted balladeer and folksong authority, craftsman, and farmer. (See earlier sketch on him.) Up to the mid-1940's, Mr. Niles had made a total of twenty-six dulcimers over a period of approximately ten years. His instruments are not the conventional type by any means, but rather are broad experiments in the general pattern. They are larger, heavier, and thicker than the "native" variety and usually have eight strings. Their greater size makes them more suitable for concert work in a large hall. For instance, he made one from a cutdown cello—the body flattened and made shallower, the neck or finger board shortened to the scroll. Often he has worked with some local craftsman in developing his instruments, which are capable of rich and deep tones, not common to other types.[50]

The most puzzling problem of all relating to the dulcimer is that of provenience and habitation. What is its origin? How widespread is its use? Such questions are as difficult to answer concerning the dulcimer as they are concerning the old ballads. Is it in truth an original, native American instrument without Old World ancestry, or is its family line merely obscured by time and distance? There

---

* Another maker who uses similar tools and methods is Nathan Hicks of Sugar Grove, Beech Mountain, North Carolina.

are no final answers to these questions, though there are some interesting conjectures.

Maud Karpeles, who helped Cecil Sharp collect folksongs in the southern Highlands in 1916 and the two years following, reports that the dulcimer's introduction into the mountains is obscure, but suggests that it may have stemmed from the early German zither of the Pennsylvania settlers who came into the Southern mountains.[51] Allen H. Eaton, researcher for the Russell Sage Foundation, leans mildly to the same theory, but thinks that possibly it may be an "entirely new instrument." [52] He states categorically that its origin is unknown, as no close prototype "is to be found in the instrument collections of Europe or America." [53]

The late Charles F. Bryan made his own personal search in 1953 in the instrument collections of American museums, and in 1954 in the museums of Europe. He came to practically the same conclusion that Mr. Eaton arrived at some twenty years earlier: we do not know the origin of our plucked dulcimer.[54] He had several hints that similar instruments were to be found in the Scandinavian countries, but his untimely death cut short any further searching.

Recent findings of musicologist Charles Seeger, however, indicate "that the European provenience of the Appalachian dulcimer and of the manner of playing it is clearly marked." Properly speaking, it is, as he states, a fretted zither, of a subclass "well represented in European organography, especially in the northern region, by the Icelandic *langspil,* Norwegian *langeleik,* Swedish *hummel,* Danish *humle,* Lowland *Noordsche balk,* German *Scheidholt,* and French and Belgian *bûche* or *épinette des Vosges.*" But whether its parentage is German, French, or Scandinavian is not clearly established.[55]

Though the exact origin of the plucked dulcimer remains an enigma, we are able, somewhat more clearly, to indicate its habitation. Sharp and Miss Karpeles found the dulcimer only in some of the mountain schools and never in the homes of the people. It should be pointed out, however, that they were searching more for tunes and texts than for musical instruments. Eaton found more dulcimers in Kentucky than in any other state, but noted also that they had been made "for many years" in Virginia, West Virginia, North Carolina, Tennessee, and Georgia.[56] Eaton, Bryan, Niles, and others have considered it indigenous to the southern Highlands. Archie Lee (*q.v.*) of Kentucky plays a dulcimer (he spells it *dulcimore,* for that is "more common among older folk in the Kentucky hills") that, he said, has been in his family at least 140 years. Mrs. I. G. Greer (*q.v.*) plays one that she believes to be over a hundred years old. Her instrument was made in Watauga County, North Carolina. The finding of many instruments in the southern Highlands has led Bryan and others to name the plucked dulcimer the "Appalachian Mountain dulcimer."

But there is evidence that the instrument is not limited to the Southern mountains. Most convincing facts have come from Anne Grimes of Columbus, Ohio, establishing that the dulcimer was known and made in many counties of Ohio, where it is often called a *dulcerine.*[57] One wonders whether further careful research might reveal its presence in early times in southern Indiana or other neighboring regions.

Vance Randolph, whose researches cover most of a lifetime in the Ozarks, said that the old-timers used to talk a great deal about the homemade "dulcimore," but he found it had long since given way to "store-boughten" fiddles and guitars. In all his wanderings in the Ozark region in search of songs and stories, he came across only one dulcimer.[58]

Since the three- to six-stringed plucked or strummed dulcimer is found in areas beyond the southern Highlands, and since it has developed into a truly American folk instrument, perhaps it ought to be renamed. The terms Kentucky dulcimer or mountain dulcimer, or Appalachian Mountain dulcimer, are not broad enough for this instrument which now seems as American as wild turkey or roasting ears. Why should we not call it, simply, the native American dulcimer, even though it isn't altogether "native"?

OTHER FOLK INSTRUMENTS

The half-dozen instruments discussed above—guitar, banjo, fiddle, harmonica, zither, and dulcimer—are by all odds the major folk instruments of America. Others, though important in one way or another, are somewhat minor as *folk* instruments. For instance, the *mandolin,* an eight- or ten-stringed instrument with a pear- or melon-shaped sound box, is an old instrument of the lute family. It was in common use in Italian folk music before it became well known in the rest of Europe, where it was frequently used in art music.[59] Some great composers, including Beethoven, wrote pieces for it, and it is occasionally heard in the modern orchestra. In late-nineteenth-century America, the "mandolin club" was a popular organization in musical centers and sometimes in universities. A few folksingers still use the instrument, as indicated by Library of Congress recordings (Nos. AAFS 8, 43, 75, and 96).

The *accordion* (variant: accordeon; colloquially: windjammer or squeeze box), a member of the free-reed family and first cousin to the harmonica, was first made in Europe in 1822. It was used in

Austrian folk music, later in American jazz, and frequently for dance and popular music.[60] Its use in American folk music is scattered. H. W. Shoemaker reports that there were many accordions in the hunting shacks along the Sinnemahonig and in the lumber camps of Pennsylvania's Black Forest around 1900.[61] It is a common instrument among both the French Creoles and the Cajun-French of Louisiana, as reported by the collector, Irène Thérèse Whitfield.[62] A minor fact worth noting is that Huddie Ledbetter (the fabulous Leadbelly) learned the accordion as a small boy—it was his first musical instrument. His family lived in east Texas, not far from the Louisiana border, where the accordion was well known.[63] Another minor fact is that a similar instrument, the *concertina,* is used by a few singers of folksongs. (See sketches of Jean Murai, Sam Hinton, and Jenny Wells Vincent.)

The *lute,* considered the ancestor of most of our plucked, stringed instruments, has had only sporadic use in the American folk scene. Known to the ancient Chinese and introduced to Europe by the Saracens, it reached its prime in the late Middle Ages, but later gave way to the more popular guitar.[64] It looks somewhat like the modern mandolin, with pear-shaped box, but was usually a larger instrument and was plucked with the fingers, not with a plectrum. It has no bridge, and the head containing the pegbox is bent back at an angle. The lute is shown in many famous paintings of the Renaissance.[65]

Under the late Swedish master, Sven Scholander, the lute experienced a modern revival. His American disciple, Richard Dyer-Bennet (*q.v.*), often used it in his earlier folksong recitals. A Scots woman singer of folksongs, Nemonie Balfour, toured America in the late 1940's and used both the lute and the Irish harp.

Often considered the most ancient of plucked, stringed instruments, the *harp* was known in Babylonia, Egypt, Greece, biblical times, and in Ireland as early as the ninth century A.D. In fact, Ireland is often regarded as its true home—hence the modern name, Irish harp, for the small instrument, though it is said to be Syrian in origin.[66] When Ireland became the Irish Free State in 1922 (later the republic of Eire), she used the small sixteen-stringed Irish harp as a national emblem on her coinage and in other official ways. And, of course, centuries before that the harp was Ireland's heraldic symbol. Extensive emigration from Ireland to America, from the mid-nineteenth century on, brought much Irish folk music and perhaps occasionally an Irish harp, though specific evidence is apparently lacking.

Brief mention should be made here of the *recorder,* a fipple flute (i.e., end-blown) reaching its zenith in the late Middle Ages and passing out of general use in the nineteenth century. But, through the efforts of the Frenchman, Arnold Dolmetsch, his son Carl Frederick, and a few others, it has had a surprising twentieth-century revival.[67] Geiringer reports that "recorders in various sizes—mostly without keys—are now made for revivals of old music, for use in schools of music, and for performances of folk-music." In his fine study, *Handicrafts of New England,* Allen Eaton tells that one of the best musical instrument makers, Mr. William Koch of Haverhill, New Hampshire, spends his full time making recorders of cocobolo wood,[68] for the instrument is in such wide demand by musical amateurs and others the country over. Among singers discussed in this book, the recorder is played by Anne Grimes, Jean Murai, and Pete Seeger.

Musical dictionaries and historians give no space to improvised instruments. This is unfortunate. We should at least give them brief mention in commenting on folk-music instruments, since there is a vestige of the primitive in all of us and probably a hidden sympathy for the Spike Joneses in every community. Kazoos, drums, rattles (of horn, gourd, turtle shell, rattlesnake, etc.), and other percussions were known and in use long before the modern jazz band found them. Besides homemade banjos and fiddles in conventional patterns, researchers have found the common folk using gourd and turtle fiddles or banjos, even cornstalk fiddles, simple flutes, horns, and whistles made from tree bark or cane stalk; not to mention the use of various things of the household such as buckets, washboards, tin cans, muffin tins, water glasses, knitting needles (for fiddle tapping), and what not for percussion or other sound effects.[69] The point is, wherever we find ingenious people, and that is just about everywhere, we will find them making music—of some kind!

An example of this ingenuity is the steel drum, first developed on the island of Trinidad and now spreading northward to the Lesser Antilles and beyond. Pete Seeger, singer and student of folksong, visited Port-of-Spain in the mid-fifties and has written a vivid account of how this "new folk instrument" is made and played. The circular top (or base) of a fifty-five-gallon oil drum is cut off, looking something like a large tambourine or drum. The two-foot disk is then hammered to a concave surface, marked off into small sections which are hammered back into convex areas, and these in turn are tuned to different pitches. A drum head, or pan, may have a range of two octaves, though the lower the pitch the fewer the notes. Rubber-tipped drumsticks are used, and "with a good sense of rhythm, and stamina to stay with it, anyone can join a steel band,"

and so it is a "form of music ideally suited for amateurs." There are limitations, of course, such as "little variety in timbre or tone color" and not much range, but a steel band of twenty to fifty can "overwhelm everything and everybody around it with ringing, melodious, harmonious, jangling, dissonant rhythm." [70]

FOOTNOTES TO CHAPTER 9

[1] *Animal Folk Songs* (New York, 1950), p. 12.

[2] Willi Apel, *Harvard Dictionary of Music* (Cambridge, 1944), p. 313; Karl Geiringer, *Musical Instruments* (New York, 1945), p. 58. See general dictionaries also.

[3] Curt Sachs, *The History of Musical Instruments* (New York, 1940), pp. 374-75; Percy A. Scholes, *The Concise Oxford Dictionary of Music* (London, 1952), p. 251.

[4] *Ibid.* See also, Geiringer, p. 155, and Sachs, p. 374.

[5] *Spanish-American Folk-Songs* (New York, 1917), p. 19.

[6] Foreword to Mary VanStone's *Spanish Folk Songs of New Mexico* (Chicago, 1928).

[7] *Texas Folk Songs* (Dallas, 1950), p. 27.

[8] *American Negro Songs* (New York, 1940), p. 45.

[9] W. C. Handy, *A Treasury of the Blues* (New York, 1949), p. 154.

[10] Apel, *Harvard Dictionary of Music,* p. 72. The word *banjo,* according to several standard dictionaries, is apparently a corruption or variation of the word *bandore,* which in turn goes back to Spanish, Latin, and Greek beginnings.

[11] Scholes, *Concise Oxford Dictionary of Music,* p. 46.

[12] Pete Seeger, *How to Play the 5-String Banjo* (Beacon, New York: Printed by the author, 1954), p. 5. This modest, paperback booklet (quarto size) of forty pages belies the remarkable amount of knowledge that has gone into its making. It is full of humor and history, pictures and personalities, as well as excellent instruction. (Can be obtained from the author at Beacon, New York, for $1.75.) I am indebted to Pete for permission to quote freely—as indeed I have! See the brief biographical sketch of Pete Seeger earlier in this book.

[13] Seeger says this fifth string was added in 1831; Alan Lomax, *Folk Song: U. S. A.* (New York, 1947), p. 78, says it was 1840.

[14] A. B. Hulbert, *Forty-Niners* (Boston, 1931), p. 4.

[15] Jack Thorpe, "Banjo in the Cow Camps," *Atlantic Monthly,* August, 1940.

[16] Again, Seeger. See also, Lomax, cited above.

[17] Sachs, *History of Musical Instruments,* pp. 274 ff. See also, Apel, *Dictionary of Music,* p. 263.

[18] Sachs, pp. 353-59; Apel, pp. 798-802.

[19] Eloise H. Linscott, *Folk Songs of Old New England* (New York, 1939), pp. 57-61; 317-18.

[20] *Handicrafts in New England* (New York, 1949), pp. 374 f.

21 Samuel P. Bayard, *Hill Country Tunes* (Philadelphia, 1944). This view is supported by George G. Korson in *Songs and Ballads of the Anthracite Miner* (New York, 1926) and later works. See Book Two, Bibliography.

22 *Handicrafts of the Southern Highlands* (New York, 1937), pp. 204-06.

23 *Folk-Songs of the South* (Cambridge, Massachusetts, 1925), Introduction.

24 S. Wetmore and M. Bartholomew, *Mountain Songs of North Carolina* (New York, 1926).

25 Pictured in Thomas Craven's *Modern Art: The Men, The Movements, The Meaning* (New York, 1940).

26 See Randolph's *Ozark Mountain Folks* (New York, 1932), pp. 69 ff.; *Ozark Folksongs*, I-IV (Columbia, Missouri, 1946-50), *passim*, and other works.

27 *Ozark Country* (New York, 1941), p. 215.

28 Reported in the Kansas City *Star*, October 24, 1954.

29 Tom Benton's maternal grandfather, Pappy Wise of Kentucky, in his early days had "enough leisure to sit on his store gallery and get expert with the fiddle." Tom, much later, knew him on a cotton plantation in Texas, "an old man with erect gait, long white hair, and a plaintive fiddle."— Benton, *An Artist in America* (New York, 1937, 1951), pp. 66-67.

30 *Ozark Folksongs*, I, 36.

31 Geiringer, p. 247; Sachs, p. 404. The term "French harp" was in everyday use in my boyhood in Oklahoma.

32 Sachs, pp. 182 ff.

33 *An Artist in America*, pp. 285-90. This recording by Decca is called *Tom Benton's Saturday Night*. Incidentally, the harmonica appears often in Benton's paintings.

34 *The Grapes of Wrath*, pp. 447-48.

35 Sachs, pp. 117-18; 137. The psaltery, mentioned in several books of the Bible—Chronicles, Daniel, Psalms—is considered an earlier, simple form of the zither. According to both Sachs and Geiringer it practically ceased to exist beyond the late Middle Ages, and its occasional use now is regarded as a curiosity. (Anne Grimes plays the psaltery on occasion, and Robert Beers makes use of a later, nineteenth-century model.)

36 Geiringer, pp. 130-31; 158.

37 For information on the Schwarzer zither, as well as on the factory, I am indebted first of all to Albert A. Hesse, with whom I had a long interview at his home on Easter Sunday, April 18, 1954. We sat on his front porch and looked across the street at new houses, where once the little factory had stood and where sixty years of his life had gone into the making of beautiful instruments to be used for the delight of mankind throughout the earth. He recalled these years with a sad nostalgia. Some further sources on the zither are the following: a brief account in the St. Louis *Globe-Democrat*, June 27, 1950, written by Edgar C. Scott, Jr.; a six-line note in the *Missouri Historical Review*, XLV, 84 (October, 1950); a notice of Hesse's death in the Kansas City *Star*, June 30, 1955; and some notes from the curator's office of the State Museum at the Capitol Building in Jefferson City. In its later years, the Schwarzer Company also made guitars, mandolins, and "mandolinettes," but the major business was in zithers.

38 Lillian M. Fox, *Autoharp Accompaniments to Old Favorite Songs* (Boston: C. C. Birchard & Co., 1947).

39 It is not mentioned in the *Oxford English Dictionary, Dictionary of American English, Webster's New International Dictionary*, or in *Webster's New World Dictionary*, College Ed. (1952). Neither Karl Geiringer, *Musical*

Instruments (1945), nor Curt Sachs, *The History of Musical Instruments* (1940), makes any mention of it. On the other hand, Percy A. Scholes, *The Concise Oxford Dictionary of Music* (1952), does state: "In Kentucky an instrument called by this name is really a form of psaltery or zither, the strings being plucked." And Willi Apel, *Harvard Dictionary of Music* (1944), states: "In current usage the name dulcimer designates home-made zithers plucked with the fingers." And it is mentioned in *The American College Dictionary* (1947) as "a modern folk instrument related to the guitar and plucked with the fingers."

40 Sachs, pp. 258-59.

41 The late Charles F. Bryan gives an excellent brief account of the hammered dulcimer in the *Tennessee Folklore Society Bulletin*, XVII, No. 2 (June, 1952).

42 *Mountain Minstrelsy of Pennsylvania* (Philadelphia, 1931), p. 200. This work was originally published in 1923 as *North Pennsylvania Minstrelsy*.

43 I have examined this dulcimer and, though it is obviously homemade, it is most skillfully constructed and very effective musically.

44 In her collecting throughout Ohio, Mrs. Grimes has come across many dulcimers. Her findings strongly indicate that the plucked dulcimer is by no means confined to the southern Highlands.

45 Eaton, *Handicrafts of the Southern Highlands*, p. 203.

46 Eaton suggests about fifteen hundred, and J. J. Niles, who knew Mr. Thomas, says the number was well over twelve hundred.

47 Eaton, *Handicrafts of the Southern Highlands*, pp. 203 ff. At the time of his writing, in the 1930's, Eaton contacted about thirty or forty craftsmen in the Highlands making musical instruments, many of them making dulcimers, of course.

48 My information comes directly from Mr. Amburgey, from whom I purchased No. 282 in September, 1954. It is made from white pine and walnut.

49 Information directly from Mr. Ledford.

50 Information in part from Mr. Niles and in part from his discussion of folk music in *The Great Smokies and the Blue Ridge*, ed. Roderick Peattie (New York, 1943), pp. 217 ff.

51 Preface, *English Folksongs from the Southern Appalachians* (London: Oxford University Press, 1932).

52 *Handicrafts of the Southern Highlands*, p. 202. Dr. Patrick Gainer of West Virginia University is convinced that the term "dulcimer" is a misnomer for the ancient rebec.

53 *Ibid.*, pp. 200-01.

54 Bryan, "The Appalachian Mountain Dulcimer Enigma," *Tennessee Folklore Society Bulletin*, XX, 86-90 (December, 1954).

55 Charles Seeger, "The Appalachian Dulcimer," *Journal of American Folklore*, Vol. 71 (January-March, 1958), pp. 40-51. This illuminating and scholarly article, with many illustrations and carefully documented, is the best summary to date on the history of the Appalachian dulcimer.

56 *Handicrafts of the Southern Highlands*, p. 201.

57 I am indebted to Mrs. Grimes for permission to use these findings. She has found the dulcimer in a dozen or more counties, some of her informants giving evidence that it has been known in the area for perhaps a century. Mrs. Grimes has detailed information on many singers and craftsmen, and it is hoped that her findings will soon be published and add further evidence about this remarkable folk instrument.

58 *Ozark Folksongs* (Columbia, Missouri, 1946), I, 36.

59 Geiringer, *Musical Instruments,* pp. 127, 157; Apel, *Harvard Dictionary of Music,* p. 422.

60 Geiringer, pp. 246-47; Sachs, p. 406.

61 *North Pennsylvania Minstrelsy,* pp. 7-8.

62 *Louisiana French Folk Songs* (Baton Rouge, Louisiana, 1939).

63 Reported by the Lomaxes, John and Alan, in *Negro Folk Songs As Sung by Lead Belly* (New York, 1936), p. 5.

64 Sachs, pp. 82, 189-90; Geiringer, pp. 57, 92-93, 155-56.

65 For example: "Concert Champêtre" (Louvre), by Giorgione; "The Jester" (Amsterdam), by Frans Hals; "Merry Lute Player" (Chicago), by Frans Hals; "Venus and the Lute Player" (Metropolitan), by Titian; "Angel with Lute" (St. Peter's, Rome), by Melozzo da Forli.

66 Geiringer, pp. 48-49; Sachs, pp. 80, 92, 135; Apel, p. 326.

67 Apel, p. 631; Geiringer, pp. 62, 212-13; Scholes, pp. 166, 487.

68 Page 45. Webster defines *cocobolo* as a valuable tropical American timber tree.

69 Eaton, *Handicrafts of the Southern Highlands,* p. 198; Bryan, "American Folk Instruments: Improvised Instruments," *Tennessee Folklore Society Bulletin,* XVIII, 65-67 (September, 1952).

70 Peter Seeger, "The Steel Drum: A New Folk Instrument," *Journal of American Folklore,* Vol. 71 (January-March, 1958), pp. 52-57. See also, Putnam Aldrich, "Oil Drums and Steel Bands," *Saturday Review,* September 29, 1956.

BOOK TWO

Collections of ballads
and folksongs

CHAPTER 10

The Collecting
of Ballads and
Folksongs

STUDENTS of English literature are well aware of the importance of early collections of ballad literature and their stimulating influence on English poetry. First of the great collections was that of Thomas Percy (1729-1811), Bishop of Dromore, who published in 1765 *Reliques of Ancient English Poetry*. He had drawn largely on a folio manuscript dated about 1650.[1] Sir Walter Scott (1771-1832) is known to have pored over the *Reliques*, in fact, to have memorized many of the ballads,[2] and to have been stimulated to make his excursions for the collecting of popular poetry, which resulted in his three volumes of *The Minstrelsy of the Scottish Border* (1802-03). *The Minstrelsy* contains about a hundred ballads, historical and romantic, and some imitations—all of them no doubt worked over considerably by Scott.

There was, to be sure, much authentic traditional material in Scott's *Minstrelsy*, for the next great ballad compiler of the nineteenth century included more than half of Scott's pieces.[3] Francis James Child (1825-1896), one of the greatest of ballad scholars,[4] looked toward the modern scientific method of collecting all the variant texts, comparing, sifting, collating, until he had combed all printed and manuscript sources, finally publishing his work in five volumes, or ten large parts, beginning in 1882 and ending in 1898. This work, *The English and Scottish Popular Ballads*, a model for later editors and collectors, contains 305 ballads in over 1,300 variants.[5]

A brief examination of Child's original five volumes, or ten large parts,[6] soon convinces the reader, if physical proof is needed, that here was indeed a tremendous undertaking in scholarship fulfilled beyond fondest hope. The ten parts contain a total of twenty-seven hundred pages. The ballads and their many variants are set forth in the first nine parts, and the tenth part contains additions and corrections. Among other features, a glossary occupies ninety pages, an index of ballad titles fills thirty pages—these are given in thirty-eight languages, including eleven of the Slavic—and finally there is a double-column fine-print bibliography from many languages, using the space of more than sixty pages. The work was issued in a limited edition of one thousand sets and was soon out of print.[7]

But Child had little success, and apparently little interest, in gathering materials from oral, living sources.[8] In fact, it became the general belief, held by some scholars on into the twentieth century,[9] that there was little to be found among the people of an industrialized society. Child's great work did not immediately stimulate a scholarly interest in collecting in America, though his work was carried on by his brilliant pupil and successor, George Lyman Kittredge.

In the main, then, the serious collecting of ballad and folksong materials from oral, living sources is an activity of the present century.[10] True, there had been a few isolated ventures in the field. As early as 1823, according to Phillips Barry, an unknown enthusiast made probably what can be called our first important collection.[11] In 1865, the first serious attempt to garner Canada's French folksongs was made by Ernest Gagnon in his book of over one hundred songs, *Chansons Populaires du Canada*. In 1867, a trio of workers combined their efforts to make the first important collection of Negro spirituals.[12] In 1872, Negro spirituals of the Fisk Jubilee Singers were first put into book form.[13] Some collecting was done under the aegis of the American Folklore Society, founded in 1888. But all these are relatively isolated and, for the most part, small beginnings.

The era of serious, extensive collecting did not get under way until after the turn of the century. A few items, like Jack Thorpe's *Songs of the Cowboys* (1908) and John Lomax's *Cowboy Songs* (1910), appeared early. For the most part, as information on the many collections listed below will indicate, the bulk of the collecting, editing, and publishing of ballads and folksongs in America has been done from World War I to the mid-century. So numerous have been the collections, large and small, that some may believe our best collecting days are behind us. But with new devices, such as the wire and tape recorders, and with a more widespread interest

in folksong as an important phase of our culture, we may be entering upon a new phase of collecting.

In the following chapters the reader will find the collections listed
and grouped according to their nature, with a sufficient annotation
for each collection to indicate both its content and its quality. Within
each chapter (except the first) the works are listed alphabetically
according to titles. There is bound to be some overlapping in this
not-too-rigid grouping, but the grouping, however loose, should aid
in using the book. (A later alphabetized index list of authors, collectors, compilers, and editors will make for easy cross reference.)

Chapter 11 of Book Two lists the works of the ten greatest collectors—or those whom the present writer considers the ten greatest:
Charles Marius Barbeau, Phillips Barry, Frank Clyde Brown, Helen
Creighton, Helen Hartness Flanders, George Pullen Jackson, George
G. Korson, John Avery Lomax, Vance Randolph, and Cecil James
Sharp. Each of these ten, because of unusual skill and singleminded
purpose, has added immeasurably to our store and our knowledge
of ballads and folksongs. (In Chapter 11 only, the titles are alphabetic under each of the ten collectors' names.)

Chapter 12 lists other major collections. These are reasonably
large and well-edited collections, often of a particular state (Ohio,
Indiana, Kentucky) or activity (lumbering, sea life, hoboing, etc.).
So many collections have been compiled for the express purpose of
singing (Sandburg's *American Songbag* or Schirmer's "American
Folk-Song Series") that it seemed advisable to group them together;
hence, Chapter 13. Many good, and not-so-good, small collections
as well as certain items to be classed merely as curiosities make
another group—Chapter 14. Aside from the published collections
of folksongs, there are a number of important archives the reader
should know about, as well as some excellent bibliographical check
lists: these comprise Chapter 15. Supplementary to the five chapters,
a list of useful background books is given which may help the
reader to round out his knowledge in this fascinating field. In this
supplemental list (Chapter 16) are such things as biographies and
autobiographies, critical discussion, some pertinent social-history
studies, and many related works.

FOOTNOTES TO CHAPTER 10

[1] George Sampson, *The Concise Cambridge History of English Literature* (New York, 1941), p. 537. The folio manuscript itself did not get into print until a hundred years after the *Reliques* was published.

[2] George B. Woods, ed., *English Poetry and Prose of the Romantic Movement* (Chicago, 1916), p. 1312.

[3] Evelyn K. Wells, *The Ballad Tree* (New York, 1950), p. 249.

[4] *Ibid.*, p. 251. See also, S. B. Hustvedt, *Ballad Books and Ballad Men* (Cambridge, Massachusetts, 1930), p. 213.

[5] Wells, pp. 253 ff.; Hustvedt, pp. 205 ff.; Sampson, p. 108.

[6] *The English and Scottish Popular Ballads.* Edited by Francis James Child. In Five Volumes (Ten Parts). Boston and New York: Houghton, Mifflin and Company. 1882-1898. Excellent evaluations of Child's accomplishment are to be found in many critical works, two of the best brief ones being Wells and Hustvedt, cited above. Comparable in some ways to Child's work, but depending more on oral sources, is *Last Leaves of Traditional Ballads and Ballad Airs,* collected in Aberdeenshire by Gavin Grieg (1856-1914). Grieg was a village schoolteacher and parish organist in the county of Aberdeen for thirty-five years. He and a friend, the Reverend J. B. Duncan, collected over three thousand texts and tunes. The manuscripts of their collection, now in Aberdeen University, were considered next to Child's in importance by the late Phillips Barry (*British Ballads from Maine*, 1929, p. xii).

[7] The Cambridge Edition, abridged in one volume and edited by Helen Child Sargent and George Lyman Kittredge, with Professor Kittredge's classic introduction, was published in 1904 and remains the standard one-volume text edition. Not until 1956 did any publisher undertake a complete republication of Child. This has now been accomplished by the Folklore Press (509 Fifth Avenue, New York), and the ten original parts are now "completely bound in sturdy cloth covers in three thick books" in a limited printing of five hundred sets.

[8] Hustvedt, pp. 216 ff.

[9] Sampson, p. 108.

[10] By way of comparison, about two-thirds of the collections listed in Margaret Dean-Smith's *A Guide to English Folk Song Collections 1822-1952* (Liverpool, 1954) were done in the present century.

[11] Reported in *The New Green Mountain Songster* (New Haven, 1939).

[12] A collection of 136 *Slave Songs of the U. S.* (New York, 1867).

[13] A collection of sixty-one songs in *The Jubilee Singers and Their Campaign for Twenty Thousand Dollars* (Boston, 1872).

CHAPTER 11

"The Big Ten"
Among Collectors

A. Marius Barbeau

ALOUETTE! (Collection humanitas) *Nouveau recueil de chansons populaires avec mélodies choisies dans le répertoire du Musée National du Canada. Par Marius Barbeau. Montréal: Les Éditions Lumen. 1946. 216 pp.*

This collection of 57 French-Canadian folksongs with simple melodies is another in the series which from time to time have been published by Marius Barbeau. As usual, we have a thoroughly scholarly presentation. The preface points out, among other things, that few of the many popular songs have yet been published: "De notre collection au Musée National, à Ottawa, qui comprend maintenant 9,000 textes et 5,000 mélodies, il n'y en a guère que deux ou trois cents de publiées—et ces publications ne sont guère connues." After the brief preface, each song is presented, first in the melody, then the stanzas, and then a brief comment on the history and development of the song. Some different versions are also mentioned, though not included.

CHANSONS CANADIENNES. (French-Canadian Folk Songs) *Collected by Marius Barbeau. English Words by Paul England. Arranged by Healey Willan. Oakville, Ontario: The Frederick Harris Music Co., Limited. 1929. Vol. I, 37 pp. Vol. II, 39 pp.*

In these two volumes there are 24 songs, for which Willan's

piano settings are sometimes quite elaborate. All are arranged for medium solo voice.

COME A SINGING! CANADIAN FOLK-SONGS. *By Marius Barbeau, Arthur Lismer, and Arthur Bourinot. Ottawa: National Museum of Canada, Bulletin No. 107. 1947. v, 59 pp.*

This booklet, designed for practical everyday use, prints the words and tunes of 30 folksongs. There is no discussion of sources or variants, but a brief headnote documents each song and frequently tells the singer's name. The songs range in subject matter from "Blow the Man Down" and "A Frog a-Wooing" to "Three Lovely Ducks" and "Alouette!" Drawings enliven the text of this handy little volume.

FOLK SONGS OF FRENCH CANADA. *By Marius Barbeau and Edward Sapir. New Haven: Yale University Press. 1925. xxii, 216 pp.*

This very readable collection of 41 folksongs and related material "is an outgrowth of the work of the Canadian National Museum," where the editors were staff members. They have succeeded well in avoiding "the two extremes of technicality and of sentimentalism." A 10-page introduction gives a good background. Few written records precede 1860, the first important collection being Ernest Gagnon's *Chansons populaires du Canada* in 1865, though most of the songs are actually three or four centuries old. By 1925, "over five thousand song records [phonograph], all from oral sources" had been collected for the National Museum, but they found no verification of the Grimm theory of communal origin. Many of the songs were from old France, their sources being obscure. They collected from many singers, two singers giving them over 300 songs each. In this small collection, brief melodies are included (but rather poorly printed), after which the stanzas are printed, first in French, then in English. Each song is preceded by a one- or two-page discussion in English. This is a very satisfactory though small collection, particularly for the English reader whose French is somewhat rusty!

FOLK-SONGS OF OLD QUEBEC. *By Marius Barbeau. Song Translations by Regina Lenore Shoolman. Illustrations by Arthur Lismer. Ottawa: National Museum of Canada. [c. 1935.] Bulletin 75. Anthropological Series No. 16. 72 pp.*

After a 27-page discussion on the origin and varieties of Canadian folksongs and how folksongs have spread from one place to another,

M. Barbeau gives here 15 songs, with simple melodies, and the stanzas in both French and English. In some cases names of singers are given. There is a useful bibliography.

ROMANCERO DU CANADA. *Par Marius Barbeau. Montréal: Éditions Beauchemin. 1937. 254 pp.*
The 50 songs in this book are drawn from the large collection in the Musée National du Canada. Marguerite Béclard d'Harcourt, of Paris, has prepared the tunes for the songs and also written a preface to the volume. Each song is followed by a discussion concerning its origin and backgrounds, a musical analysis, and a listing of variants in both Canada and France. Some song titles: "Voici le printemps," "Renaud, Lisette," "La bergère aux champs," "La plainte du coureur de bois." The book is entirely in French. The music is poorly printed.

B. Phillips Barry

BRITISH BALLADS FROM MAINE. *The Development of Popular Songs with Texts and Airs. By Phillips Barry, Fannie Hardy Eckstrom, and Mary Winslow Smyth. Versions of Ballads included in Professor F. J. Child's Collection. New Haven: Yale University Press. 1929. xlvi, 535 pp.*
The term British here includes not only English and Scottish but Irish as well, and the editors indicate the similarity, often identity, of ballads found in Maine and in the southern Highlands. In this scholarly collection of 56 Child ballads, 8 "secondary" ballads, and fragments (or "jury-texts") of some 30 more, the editors regard each ballad "as an organic whole, text and melody receiving equal attention." The relatively small number of titles scarcely suggests the extent of scholarly research that has gone into this admirable collection: the editors have recorded all versions of both texts and tunes that could be found in the areas of Maine under special study. For example, there were no fewer than fifteen variants of "Lord Randall" and at least seven tunes, seven variants of "The Golden Vanity," five of "Lord Bateman," four of "Barbara Allen," and so on.
The editors pay glowing tribute to the singers (especially by way of dedication to Mrs. Susie Carr Young and Mrs. Annie Viola Marston, both of whom contributed many texts and tunes) whose memories and family histories play such a valuable part in tracing the songs. This book—without doubt a most important study in the field of ballad and folksong literature—concludes with the usual bibliography and special indexes of titles, melodies, and subjects.

FOLK MUSIC IN AMERICA. *By Phillips Barry. Introductory Essay by George Herzog. American Folk-Song Publications, No. 4. New York: National Service Bureau. 1939. A WPA Federal Theatre Project. Mimeographed. xx, 113 pp.*

These fifteen learned, lively, and important essays of Barry are reprinted, in the main, from the *Journal of American Folk-Lore*, the *Southern Folklore Quarterly*, and the *Bulletin of the Folk-Song Society of the Northeast*. They range in time from 1909 to 1937, the year of Barry's death. About 90 folksongs and melodies are included wholly or in part in the book. A Barry bibliography of some 60 items, besides reviews, is included. Barry did not write a book on American folk music, though he might have, had he lived longer. This collection of essays and songs in part fills the gap. Herzog's brief introductory essay tells something of Barry's work in American folksong, which, says Herzog, "may safely be ranked as the most important we have." (p. ix)

MAINE WOODS SONGSTER, THE. *Edited by Phillips Barry. Cambridge, Massachusetts: The Powell Printing Company. 1939. 102 pp.*

Here are 50 of the "vanishing woods songs" that were "sung in camp, and on the drive, when the men were resting and desirous of entertainment." Included also are the melodies, or airs, together with twenty photographs and drawings of Maine woods scenes. "The Notes," says the editor, "in which may be found concise information pertaining to the histories of the songs, have been compiled for all who choose to read them."

C.   Frank Clyde Brown

FRANK C. BROWN COLLECTION OF NORTH CAROLINA FOLKLORE, THE. *The Folklore of North Carolina collected by Dr. Frank C. Brown during the Years 1912 to 1943 in Collaboration with The North Carolina Folklore Society of which he was Secretary-Treasurer 1913-1943. In Seven Volumes. General Editor, Newman Ivey White. Wood Engravings by Clare Leighton. Durham, North Carolina: Duke University Press. 1952, 1957.*

When Dr. Brown died in 1943, the work of organizing and selecting for publication this vast collection was undertaken by Dr. White and a group of ten associate editors. Upon the sudden death of Dr. White in 1948, Dr. Paull F. Baum became the general editor. Up to 1960, the following four volumes of this tremendous collection have been published:

Volume One: GAMES AND RHYMES, BELIEFS AND CUSTOMS, RIDDLES, PROVERBS, SPEECH, TALES AND LEGENDS. (1952) *Edited by Paul G. Brewster, Archer Taylor, Bartlett Jere Whiting, George P. Wilson, Stith Thompson. xiv, 712 pp.*

Volume Two: FOLK BALLADS FROM NORTH CAROLINA. (1952) *Edited by Henry M. Belden and Arthur Palmer Hudson. xxiv, 747 pp.*

Volume Three: FOLK SONGS FROM NORTH CAROLINA. (1952) *Edited by Henry M. Belden and Arthur Palmer Hudson. xxx, 710 pp.*

Volume Four: THE MUSIC OF THE BALLADS. (1957) *Edited by Jan Philip Shinhan. xliv, 420 pp.*

The three remaining volumes (V, VI, and VII) are announced for early publication and will contain The Music of the Folk Songs (V) and Superstitions from North Carolina (VI and VII).

The work of Frank C. Brown, in both quantity and quality, is in the great tradition of Francis James Child. Comparable in scope and quality are the works of Cecil J. Sharp in the southern Appalachians, Marius Barbeau and Helen Creighton in Canada, John and Alan Lomax in the Southwest, Phillips Barry and Helen Hartness Flanders in New England, Vance Randolph in the Ozarks, and the collections of George Pullen Jackson in the field of spiritual folksongs. By way of further comparison one might also mention the scholarly work, by states, of Henry M. Belden (Missouri), George Korson (Pennsylvania), Paul G. Brewster (Indiana), John Harrington Cox (West Virginia), Louise Pound (Nebraska), A. P. Hudson (Mississippi), and Arthur K. Davis (Virginia).

Volumes Two, Three, and Four, with which this present bibliography is concerned, contain respectively 314 ballads and 658 songs, and the music of the ballads. This impressive total of 972 still does not suggest the whole picture, for many of the songs and ballads have many versions. In fact, the grand total of complete and fragmentary variants runs into the thousands. For example, the ballad, "I Wouldn't Marry," has 19 variants; "The Frog's Courtship" has 27; "Lady Alice" has 15; "Lord Thomas and Fair Annet" has 14; "The Jealous Lover" has 23; and so on.

Volume Two, *Folk Ballads*, has three groupings, as follows: I. The Older Ballads—Mostly British; II. Native American Ballads; III. North Carolina Ballads. Volume Three, *Folk Songs*, has many more groupings, thirteen in all, since folksongs are of many kinds. Some of the groupings are as follows: Courting Songs, Drink and Gambling Songs, Play-Party and Dance Songs, Lullabies and Nursery Rhymes, Work Songs, Folk Lyrics, Satirical Songs, and Religious

Songs. This last is the largest single group with 143 songs. Each volume has its special introduction; each song or ballad has its ample scholarly headnotes with comparative folklore, and giving contributor, place, and date of contribution when these last are known. Each volume is fully indexed, and Volume Three lists the names of all contributors.

Volume Four, *The Music of the Ballads* (1957), is an unusually thorough piece of editorial work. In a preface, Professor Shinhan points out the several problems encountered—imperfect wax cylinders, cracks and scratches, confusion in cataloguing—but these difficulties seem nonexistent as the reader runs through the hundreds of tunes for the 314 ballads. A 20-page introduction discussing scales, range, melodic line, meter, over-all rhythm, etc., is somewhat technical for the general reader but perhaps not to the trained musician. Appendix A tabulates the analyses; Appendix B gives the scales (517 in all) of the ballads; and the book closes with three indexes: singers, titles and variant titles, and first lines.

This vast work, a co-operative venture in collecting and editing, stands unchallenged among collections of the present century. It is to be hoped that the three volumes yet to come from the press will continue the scholarly tradition of the present titles. The modern reader may experience one disappointment in this otherwise excellent and vast collection: the tunes for the ballads and songs are printed in separate volumes. If this seems rather awkward, since users of recent collections are in the habit of finding text and tune together, the present method has its rewards: we have a much more careful and complete analysis of the music than in other collections and perhaps than we might have in any other arrangement.

D.   Helen Creighton

SONGS AND BALLADS FROM NOVA SCOTIA. *Collected by Helen Creighton. Toronto and Vancouver: J. M. Dent & Sons, Limited. 1932. xxii, 334 pp.*

This book of 150 songs and a few variants, with both words and simple melodies, represents Miss Creighton's first fruitful venture into the collecting field. The songs were all gathered from "among the fisher-folk in the vicinity of Halifax," where the background is English, Irish, Scottish, and Welsh. A delightful introduction recounts Miss Creighton's experiences in collecting, first using a little melodeon to work out the tunes and later the dictaphone, which proved more satisfactory. Her chief contributor was a Mr. Ben Henneberry, though there were a number of others. One famous song, "Courtship of Willie Riley," done by Mr. Henneberry, runs to 78 stanzas! About 100 of the songs are Canadian variants of traditional English and Scottish songs (many of them Child ballads), and the remainder are native products. As to subject matter, there are songs of love, of the sea, of the broken ring token, of battle, of the nursery, and so on.

There are a few notes of explanation and comparative reference, but little to interfere with the general reader's pleasure. As Professor John D. Robins of Victoria College states in the preface: "There is an academic, clinical approach to folk-songs, and there is a sentimental approach, maudlin or mocking, as the case may be, but the ideal is a combination of the scientific and sympathetic, and that is the one Miss Creighton has shown." Beautifully printed, with highly decorative end papers, this book all in all is a most satisfactory work.

TRADITIONAL SONGS FROM NOVA SCOTIA. *Collected by Helen Creighton and Doreen H. Senior. Toronto: The Ryerson Press. 1950. xvi, 284 pp.*

At first glance this collection of nearly 140 songs, taken down over a period of seventeen years, seems smaller than Miss Creighton's earlier work in the same field (*Songs and Ballads from Nova Scotia,* 1932). Actually, though there are fewer songs (by about 10) and a smaller page, there is more substance, for the print is smaller and the variants are far more numerous. About half of the songs have variants, some as many as half a dozen. The method of collecting and the make-up of the book follow the pattern of the earlier work. A brief introduction tells about the collecting and a tantalizing bit about some of the singers—Dennis Smith, Walter Roast, Mrs. Gallagher, Mrs. Duncan, Enos and Richard Hartlan, and others. Where Miss Creighton formerly collected with melodeon or dictaphone, in the present work she had the skillfully trained musician, Miss Senior, who noted the tunes on the spot.

Miss Creighton has now become the seasoned collector, for by 1950 she has taken down over 900 songs. As John D. Robins states in the preface, she "has consolidated her position as the outstanding collector of folk songs in English-speaking Canada." Though having become more scholarly, she has not lost her "invincible zest" or her "adventurous enthusiasm." This work is not as beautifully printed or as decorative as the earlier work, but still the text and music are entirely satisfying. Unaccompanied tunes are given for all the songs, and the name of each folksinger is given with the song. Brief headnotes add pertinent information, and there is an index of song titles.

E.   Helen Hartness Flanders

BALLADS MIGRANT IN NEW ENGLAND. *By the Collectors Helen Hartness Flanders and Marguerite Olney. With an Introduction by Robert Frost. New York: Farrar, Straus and Young. 1953. xiv, 248 pp.*

More than half of the 97 ballads in this unusually well-edited collection are Child ballads. These are still current in New England, as the editors point out. Mechanical recordings were made during field work in the thirties and forties. Brief headnotes tell who sang each ballad and give the date of recording. In his introductory comment, Robert Frost makes this wise and whimsical observation: "Ballads lead their life in the mouths and ears of men by hear-say like bluebirds and flickers in the nest holes of hollow trees. But that's no reason specimens shouldn't be brought to book now and then for sport and scholarship." (p. xii)

Mrs. Flanders, who began her collecting in 1930, gives much detail about the gathering of these ballads and also a good deal of history of the ballads. The tunes are transcribed by Miss Olney without embellishment in this very interesting and useful book.

GARLAND OF GREEN MOUNTAIN SONG, A. *Edited by Helen Hartness Flanders. Piano settings by Helen Norfleet. Green Mountain Pamphlets, No. 1. Boston: John Worley Company. 1934. 86 pp.*

Here are 24 songs from the Vermont Archive of Folk Songs and Ballads, with moderately easy piano settings. In 1934, the archive was in Springfield, Vermont. (It was then a private collection of Mrs. Flanders.) Headnotes tell briefly of the singers, the time and the place of collecting.

NEW GREEN MOUNTAIN SONGSTER, THE. *Traditional Folk Songs of Vermont. Collected, Transcribed, and Edited by Helen Hartness Flanders, Elizabeth Flanders Ballard, George Brown, and Phillips Barry. New Haven: Yale University Press. 1939. xx, 278 pp.*

Here are 100 songs from the Vermont Archive of Folk Songs, with full texts and tunes (or "whole airs"), together with the extensive scholarly and lively notes of Phillips Barry. Editorial work was completed after Barry died (in 1937) by friends and fellow workers. Many familiar titles are here: "Bold Reynard," "Botany Bay," "The Cowboy's Lament," "The Dreary Black Hills," "The Little Mohea," "The Old Maid's Song," "Springfield Mountain," "The Texas Rangers," "The Two Sisters," etc.—all indicative of how far the folksong travels from one region to another. According to Mrs.

Flanders, the Vermont Archive of Folk Songs contained, in 1939, "472 traditional British songs, 311 early American songs, and 171 versions of different Child ballads" and "there are 421 tunes recorded on dictaphone cylinders." All the songs in the present collection were taken down in the field on dictaphone records. The Vermont Archive was begun only in 1930. In addition to other scholarly data, helpful notes are included on singers and contributors.

VERMONT CHAP BOOK. *Being a Garland of Ten Folk Ballads, together with Notes by Helen Hartness Flanders, Preface by Donald Davidson, Illustrations by Arthur Healy. Hand Set by the Bread Loaf Printers for the Middlebury College Press. Middlebury, Vermont: 1941. viii, 48 pp.*

These 10 ballads are a "delightful and valuable sample" from the Helen Hartness Flanders Collection of Ballads and Folksongs, each preceded by an appropriate block print and a brief note of introduction by Mrs. Flanders. The 10 ballads are: "Song of the Vermonters, 1779," "The Indian Student," "Beckwith Tragedy," "Jonathan's Courtship," "The Segar," "Bill Hopkin's Colt," "Joel Baker," "The Hog-Thorny Bear," "Hard Times," and "The Calais Disaster." Tunes are not included.

VERMONT FOLK-SONGS AND BALLADS. *Edited by Helen Hartness Flanders and George Brown. Brattleboro, Vermont: Stephen Daye Press. 1932. 256 pp.*

The collecting of these 120 songs (including tunes for about half of them) was undertaken by the Committee on Traditions and Ideals of the Vermont Commission on Country Life. Some two dozen of them are Child ballads. Headnotes with each song tell of the singer and the circumstances of collecting. Most of the songs were recorded about 1930. And, according to the editors, "most of the songs or ballads were written down as sung from memory by a person who knew them to have been learned by word of mouth from older generations ... this collection is beholden to oral tradition." (p. 7) There are a few notes on some of the ballads, but no index.

F.   George Pullen Jackson

ANOTHER SHEAF OF WHITE SPIRITUALS. *Collected, Edited, and Illustrated by George Pullen Jackson. Foreword by Charles Seeger. Gainesville, Florida: University of Florida Press. 1952. xviii, 233 pp.*

This latest work of Dr. Jackson rounds out his discussion and his collecting of the spiritual folksongs in America. This fourth volume in his collecting (see also *Spiritual Folk-Songs of Early America,* 1937, and *Down-East Spirituals and Others,* 1942), which contains 363 songs (both texts and tunes), "brings the total number of published American religious folksongs" to over 900—a most impressive accomplishment. Dr. Jackson gathered the songs in this book from the singers themselves, from the various "harp" and "harmony" collections of the nineteenth century, and in some cases from yet unpublished collections. A brief introduction explains some of the background, clarifies his ninefold grouping of the songs, gives "tune-family names," and includes a most helpful map. This map (p. xiii) shows "approximate areas where and times when American Religious Folksongs were and/or are still sung in gatherings." The area began in the Northeast about 1750 and moved west and south, enlarging first and then gradually shrinking, as urban influences became stronger. For this type of singing is essentially *country* singing. There are extensive notes for each song, and the work contains the necessary bibliographies and indexes. Of special interest and value is an unusually fine "Comprehensive Index" of over 18 pages containing titles, first lines, refrains, and choruses of religious folksongs appearing in *all* the collections made by Dr. Jackson. One limitation of the book is the poor and small printing of the musical notes, but it is otherwise an excellent work, both in scholarship and typography.

DOWN-EAST SPIRITUALS AND OTHERS. *Three Hundred Songs Supplementary to the Author's* Spiritual Folk-Songs of Early America. *Collected and Edited by George Pullen Jackson. New York: J. J. Augustin Publisher. 1939. 296 pp. Second Edition 1953.*

This second collection by Dr. Jackson contains 60 "religious ballads," 152 "folk-hymns," and 88 "revival spiritual songs." These songs, he points out, have been gleaned from two areas: "in the *old song books* [and] in rural *group singings.*" But a third area, the homes of *individual singers,* may yield many more songs, he says. The songs included, both text and tune, "are reproduced here exactly as found in the sources." These songs, many of them, were brought to the New World by the Baptists over two hundred years ago, and then later by the Methodists, except for the revival spiritual songs, which are not known before 1800. Extensive notes throughout give added information on individual songs. Simple tunes are given without accompaniment. The book contains an extensive bibliography, index of songs by titles, and an index of first lines; also four full-page illustrations.

From this New England area, the spirituals spread through the South and West, being used by both whites and Negroes.

✻ SPIRITUAL FOLK-SONGS OF EARLY AMERICA. *Two Hundred and Fifty Tunes and Texts with an Introduction and Notes. Collected and Edited by George Pullen Jackson. New York: J. J. Augustin Publisher. 1937. xii, 254 pp.*

After George Pullen Jackson's thorough exploration of "country singings" in his *White Spirituals in the Southern Uplands* (1933), he here makes his first full recognition of spirituals as true folksongs. This came about by his recognition that the tunes, or melodies, came from secular folk tunes, and that the words were somewhat freely composed by persons who were not recognized composers. A learned introduction (of 23 pages) gives us a clear account of all this. In this collection, the first of four, we have 51 religious ballads, 98 folk hymns, and 101 revival spiritual songs—a total of 250 spiritual folksongs, with tunes. The songs were gleaned in the main from the numerous "country singing books" that were popular from 1820 on into the present century. This "country singing" is still very lusty and alive, and is far from dying out. To quote Dr. Jackson: "I demur completely from narrow interpretations of the status, meaning, import, and destiny of folk-lore, folk-songs, *these* folk-songs. I do not participate in the pessimism of the folk-song fatalists." (p. 22)

There are a number of illustrations (some of country singings), many explanatory headnotes with the songs, a bibliography, an index of songs by titles, and an index of first lines. "The Second Edition 1953" is a reprint of the 1937 edition.

STORY OF THE SACRED HARP, 1844-1944, THE. *A Book of Religious Folk Song as an American Institution. By George Pullen Jackson. Nashville: Vanderbilt University Press. 1944. 46 pp.*

The importance of this small volume, part of a centennial celebration, far outweighs its size. The origin, Jackson tells us, of *Sacred Harp* singing is from old Baptist singing—religious, though not denominational, poetry set to remembered folk tunes from early sources. It spread to other denominations, was widely used among country people, apart from more "official" religious songs. Passing along orally for generations, it is true religious folksong. Other works besides the *Sacred Harp* of 1844 were *Christian Harmony* (1805), *Beauties of Harmony* (1813), *Kentucky Harmony* (1815), *Missouri Harmony* (1820), *Union Harmony* (1834), *The Southern Harmony*

(1835), *Southern and Western Pocket Harmonist* (1845), *Hesperian Harp* (1848), *Social Harp* (1855), and the *Colored Sacred Harp* (n.d.).

Sacred Harp singing spread westward as far as Texas and Oklahoma, and northward to Tennessee and southern Missouri. The book of songs, first prepared by B. F. White, was reprinted many times— a fifth edition in 1911 and a new edition as late as 1936. It has outlasted other such harmony books and still is in wide use. It came in time to include fuguing tunes, odes, anthems, and revival songs. *Sacred Harp* singing is four-part singing, in which all four parts have equal prominence. The songs sound "minor" to some listeners because of the "gapped" tunes—they have five-tone or six-tone melodies. Shape notes were used (four at first) and were first published in 1799 by two singing masters. The four notes were eventually increased to seven. This *Sacred Harp* singing is *traditional* singing but not old-fogyish.

A section of the book tells about some of the leading singers, especially the Denson brothers. All in all, it is an interesting and authoritative account of an interesting "American Institution," and Jackson has done a valuable scholarly service in recounting its history.

WHITE AND NEGRO SPIRITUALS, THEIR LIFE SPAN AND KINSHIP. *Tracing 200 years of Untrammeled Song Making and Singing among our Country Folk. With 116 Songs as Sung by Both Races. By George Pullen Jackson. New York: J. J. Augustin Publisher. 1943. xiv, 349 pp.*

This work is not primarily a collection, but rather a discussion and the presentation of evidence in support of Dr. Jackson's views on the relations between white and Negro spirituals. The 116 songs are used for comparative purposes—"melodies of white people paired with the same number of Negro-sung variants."

Part One presents "The Whole Story of American Religious Folk Song as the White People Sang It," in a series of thirteen chapters. Part Two presents "The Whole Story of American Religious Folk Song as the Negroes Sang It," in a series of eleven chapters. Dr. Jackson's conclusion is clear: Most Negro spirituals are derived from white spirituals and are a part of the British-American culture, which has absorbed also other cultural features from other lands. Unbiased, objective observers will find it hard to reject Dr. Jackson's findings.

The book has six appendices, as follows: British and American Books Containing Religious Folk Songs; A List of Abbreviations of

Book and Periodical Titles; A Collection of Wandering Rhyme Pairs (very interesting); A List of Favorite Revival Spiritual Choruses; References to British Isles Sources of Melodies in Tune Comparative List; Index of Titles, First Lines and Refrains of Songs in the Tune Comparative List.

G.   George G. Korson

COAL DUST ON THE FIDDLE. *Songs and Stories of the Bituminous Industry. By George Korson. Philadelphia: University of Pennsylvania Press. 1943. xvi, 460 pp.*

This second volume of Korson's fine work contains story and song material from nine states, collected mostly from the workers but in part from newspapers and journals such as the *United Mine Workers Journal.* Much of the field collecting was done with a recording machine. The three sections of the book are as follows: Minstrelsy in the Coal Camps, Folklore of the Coal Mines, and The Union in Song and Story. Each section contains a wealth of song material, with headnotes indicating source, date, author (if known), and frequently explanatory details. As in other works by Korson, we have here a social history with songs woven into the text. In the preface, Korson states: "A ballad had to pass the test of literary interest and direct relationship to the bituminous coal industry . . . as well as to American folk tradition." A few musical transcriptions (about a dozen) are done by Ruth Crawford Seeger. The volume contains about 140 songs and ballads, a really significant collection. An appendix gives brief biographies of nine "bards and minstrels" and mentions dozens of others.

MINSTRELS OF THE MINE PATCH. *Songs and Stories of the Anthracite Industry. By George Korson. Philadelphia: University of Pennsylvania Press. 1938. xii, 332 pp.*

Here we have a good regional (Pennsylvania) collection of stories, ballads, and songs, and biographical sketches of singers. There are texts of 85 ballads and songs, with simple melodies included for about a dozen of them. The stories and legends told often suggest the source of the songs. An appendix gives brief biographical sketches of fourteen minstrels, and mention is made of many more. Most of the bards were Irish, some of them wandering minstrels who sang their songs unaccompanied, though a few used the fiddle. In this very useful collection there is a glossary of anthracite words and phrases, a brief bibliography, and an index.

PENNSYLVANIA SONGS AND LEGENDS. *By George Korson, Editor. Philadelphia: University of Pennsylvania Press. 1949. 474 pp.*

This important collection contains 116 ballads and songs, about one-third of them in Pennsylvania German (followed by English translations) and most of them with simple musical notation. The legends bulk larger, in amount, than the songs and ballads. Fourteen scholars have combined their talents to discuss such topics as the British folk tradition, Amish hymns as folk music, Conestoga wagoners, railroaders, lumberjacks and raftsmen, coal miners, canallers, and so on. Much scholarly research has gone into this study.

SONGS AND BALLADS OF THE ANTHRACITE MINER. *A Seam of Folklore Which Once Ran Through Life in the Hard Coal Fields of Pennsylvania. Gathered and Edited by George G. Korson. New York: Frederick H. Hitchcock, The Grafton Press. 1926 and 1927. xxviii, 196 pp.*

A note on the obverse of the title page states: "This work first appeared in the United Mine Workers Journal." The more than 50 songs and ballads (some are fragments and variants) are each preceded by an introductory discussion or setting, giving the narrative an organic continuity. This interspersed narrative makes the book unique among collections because it tells more than usual about the singer. "These homespun songs and ballads," writes Korson, "provided an escape from his troubles and served as a medium of expressing his sorrows."

The general introduction discusses background. The best minstrel period flourished, he says, from the Civil War to the end of the century. The early miners were mainly British, to be succeeded later by Slavic people. The author makes a sevenfold division of the songs and ballads, as follows: Life in the Mine Patch, When the Heart Was Light, On Being a Miner, The Collier Boys, Four Mine Accidents, One Strike, and The Mollie Maguires (i.e., terrorists). These songs are not traditional, in the usual sense of the word, but the material presented here shows how songs and ballads came into being during the latter part of the nineteenth century in America.

The author, George Korson, a newspaper reporter many years, made his researches mainly in 1924 and 1925. He names about fifty people who sang for him or sent him songs, not to mention "probably several hundred" who gave aid in one way or another. By 1925, the scene had changed markedly. "Romance no longer colors the anthracite coal industry. And in its flight it has taken balladry and minstrelsy with it," writes Korson. Unfortunately there is no index in this otherwise excellent study.

H.   John Avery Lomax

ᐟAMERICAN BALLADS AND FOLK SONGS. *Collected and Compiled by John A. Lomax and Alan Lomax. With a Foreword by George Lyman Kittredge. New York: The Macmillan Company. 1934. xxxix, 625 pp.*

In this big book, as Kittredge points out, "There is something for every mood and for every intelligent taste." This work and its sequel, *Our Singing Country* (New York, 1941), represent one of the great collecting and compiling tasks in several decades and, with other works (*q.v.*) by the Lomaxes, make them easily among the dozen most important collectors of our century.

The present work includes about 275 songs, drawn from many areas and representing every phase of American life. Most of the songs were collected by the Lomaxes, but many others have contributed to this omnibus volume. The Lomaxes group their songs into twenty-five sections, beginning with railroad songs and ending with the spirituals. In between there are songs of the levee, the chain gangs, bad men, the mountains, whiskey, party and childhood, the cowboy, the miner, the sailor, the logger, war, and pioneers. Nothing is lacking here to show the vigor, the variety, and the vastness of a great and growing country. In his brilliant introduction, John Lomax says the purpose is "to present the best examples of the most noteworthy types, words and tunes. We offer," he continues, "a composite photograph of what we and others, in field and forest, on mountain and plain, by the roadside and in the cabin, on big cane or cotton plantations and in prison camp, have set down of the songs of the people. . . ."

For most of the songs there are unaccompanied tunes, and headnotes or footnotes give some account of each song or its source. An extensive bibliography, some items having brief annotations, was compiled by Harold W. Thompson, and there is an index of song titles.

COWBOY SONGS AND OTHER FRONTIER BALLADS. *Collected by John A. Lomax. With an Introduction by Barrett Wendell. New York: Sturgis & Walton Company. 1910. xxvi, 326 pp.*

This collection of 112 songs (18 of them with tunes) is a pioneer work in American balladry. It is the first of several works in the field by one of our most important collectors. The songs are not grouped by subject or theme, but "have been arranged in some such haphazard way as they were collected—jotted down on the table in the rear of saloons, scrawled on an envelope while squatting about a campfire, caught behind the scenes of a bronco-busting outfit," says Lomax in an introductory Collector's Note. Here are printed, in many cases for the first time, many of the now well-known songs, such as "The Cowboy's Lament," "The Dying Cowboy," "Jack o' Diamonds," "Jesse James," "A Home on the Range," etc. Lomax points out that in the main the songs are anonymous, but that all were popular with the "range riders," some of them "current all the way from Texas to Montana." He admits "softening" some of the songs, for "polite society is not quite willing" to hear them in their original directness. Lomax was to spend another quarter century or more making further collections.

In 1916, the Macmillan Company took over the plates of the book, reprinting the earlier work, adding 41 songs and 88 more pages, making a total of 153 songs in 414 pages. There was a reissue in 1927. Then, in 1938, there was a "revised and enlarged edition" as follows:

COWBOY SONGS AND OTHER FRONTIER BALLADS. *Revised and Enlarged. Collected by John and Alan Lomax. Edward N. Water, Music Editor. New York: The Macmillan Company. 1938. xxxviii, 431 pp.*

This completely revised, reset, and enlarged edition now contains 207 songs besides some variants. More than a hundred of the songs have unaccompanied melodies. There are a few explanatory headnotes and footnotes and, unlike earlier editions, this one is indexed. The present edition groups the songs under seven headings, as follows: I. Up the Trail; II. The Round Up; III. Dodge City, the End of the Trail; IV. Campfire and Bunkhouse; V. Off Guard; VI. Son of a Gun; VII. Way Out West. This grouping gives a consistent, satisfying arrangement, making the present volume all in all the best cowboy song collection now extant. This 1938 edition has had many reprints and, in 1948, was reissued without further change except in price. Perhaps this will be the final edition of that now famous little book of the year 1910.

FOLK SONG: U.S.A. *The 111 Best American Ballads. Collected, adapted, and arranged by John A. Lomax and Alan Lomax. Alan Lomax, Editor. Charles Seeger and Ruth Crawford Seeger, Music Editors. New York: Duell, Sloan and Pearce, Inc. 1947. xvi, 407 pp.*

This sixth and last collection made by the Lomaxes, while John

Lomax was still living, exhibits some striking differences from their previous volumes. First of all, most of the songs have appeared in their earlier works. Then, this is a book to place on the piano and to sing from, as all the songs have piano arrangements by the distinguished Seegers. Further, some of the songs are composites. As Alan Lomax writes in the preface: "In this volume we have created our own versions of the songs, combining all the best stanzas we could find." Perhaps most important of all are certain editorial paraphernalia. For example, the songs are grouped into eleven sections, each section having a long introduction of six to sixteen double-column pages, in which a history and a setting are given for each song: these are very useful introductions, particularly for those who want to brush up on backgrounds. Finally, there are three important appendices: I. Sources and References; II. Selected List of 126 books and other sources, with a good deal of useful annotation; III. Selected List of Records, with valuable information about the singers and the recordings. Two indexes, one of explanatory material and the other of song titles and first lines, round out this excellent and usable volume. Though "the selections will certainly be caviled at," as the Lomaxes are the first to point out, it would be difficult to find a better cross-country selection of American folksongs.

NEGRO FOLK SONGS AS SUNG BY LEAD BELLY. *"King of the Twelve-String Guitar Players of the World," Long-Time Convict in the Penitentiaries of Texas and Louisiana. Transcribed, Selected and Edited by John A. Lomax and Alan Lomax. New York: The Macmillan Company. 1936. xiv, 242 pp.*

This fascinating work might well be called "The Saga of Lead Belly," for this notorious but gifted Negro recounts his life story in talk, chant, and song. The 64 pages of Part I present the biography proper, as told by the Lomaxes (but much of it in Lead Belly's dialect), a harrowing and sometimes tragi-comical story of the dangerous existence of a powerful and gifted Negro in and out of jails and penitentiaries. The most remarkable fact of all is that on two occasions his gifted singing influenced two governors to grant him a pardon. Part II gives the songs—"sinful songs" they are called, to distinguish them from spirituals. There are 48 of these, chosen from over a hundred that the Lomaxes considered genuine folksongs, from a repertoire of many hundreds that Lead Belly sang. The songs are interspersed with Lead Belly's commentary, a kind of primitive philosophical interpretation. There is little doubt that he frequently altered the songs as he went along—in a way, personalized them, for he was a genuine folk artist. There are reels, work songs, hollers, blues, regular ballads, and others, each with simple musical notation.

OUR SINGING COUNTRY. *A Second Volume of American Ballads and Folk Songs. Collected and Compiled by John A. Lomax and Alan Lomax. Ruth Crawford Seeger, Music Editor. New York: The Macmillan Company. 1941. xxxiv, 416 pp.*

A spill-over volume organized on much the same plan as the Lomaxes' 1934 collection, here are over 200 songs and ballads grouped under six major headings, as follows: Religious Songs, Social Songs, Men at Work, Outlaws, Hollers and Blues, and Negro Gang Songs. These groupings are further subdivided. In this volume are some groups not found in the earlier collection: Bahaman, courting, Louisiana French, and Southern farmer songs.

Archibald MacLeish, at that time chief librarian of the Library of Congress, contributes a significant short introduction, naming the Lomaxes as "the two men who created, under the brilliant direction of Herbert Putnam, the Archive of Folk Song in the Library of Congress." He also indicates that by 1940 the library began to make these songs available by recordings to the general public. The preface, by the Lomaxes, tells about many of the singers, and further indicates that these songs come mainly from their own collecting; the 1934 volume had drawn on others to some extent. Composer Ruth Crawford Seeger did the transcribing and in the music preface discusses the process of transcribing, offering suggestions for singing. As usual, there are clarifying headnotes. Again, Harold W. Thompson is the bibliographer, and there is an index of songs and an index of first lines.

SONGS OF THE CATTLE TRAIL AND COW CAMP. *Collected by John A. Lomax. Foreword by William Lyon Phelps. New York: The Macmillan Company. 1919. xviii, 189 pp.*

Here is a three-part collection of 74 songs, some of them anonymous, but a goodly number of them by known authors, such as Arthur Chapman, H. H. Knibbs, Badger Clark, Frank Desprez, James Barton Adams, R. V. Carr, C. F. Lummis, and others. The three parts are: Cowboy Yarns, The Cowboy off Guard, and Cowboy Types. Only by the broadest stretch of definition could these be called folksongs or poetry, though some of them have become well known, for instance, Chapman's "Out Where the West Begins" and Lomax's "The Old Mackenzie Trail." But they have had little *oral* circulation; no tunes are included, since most of these have not been set to music.

Continued popularity is indicated by a reissue in 1927. Then, in 1950, another firm (Duell, Sloan and Pearce) brought out a new edition containing dozens of attractive drawings by many prominent artists. An interesting volume, but not to be confused with the collections of more genuine folk materials by the Lomaxes.

I. Vance Randolph

OZARK FOLKSONGS. *Collected and Edited by Vance Randolph. Edited for the State Historical Society of Missouri, by Floyd C. Shoemaker, Secretary, and Frances G. Emberson, Research Associate. Columbia, Missouri: The State Historical Society of Missouri. 1946-50. In Four Volumes. Total pages, 1,729.*

Anyone who examines, even superficially, this vast collection recognizes at once that here is one of the great folksong collections of this century. Vance Randolph, long-time resident of the Ozarks, has been "more or less identified with the region" for half a century and has been collecting songs and stories most of that time. As he points out (I, 31), "Nearly all of the songs in this collection derive, directly or indirectly, from the singing of the 'old residenters.'" The songs are of all kinds and are not selected for either musical or literary excellence; but in true scholarly fashion, Randolph has set them down exactly as they were sung. As he says, "All temptations to 'improve' either the texts or the melodies have been virtuously resisted." (I, 34)

Randolph includes simple melodies with the songs, though his chief interest, since he makes no pretense to being a musician, is "in the words of the old songs rather than in the tunes." (I, 35) He first worked with assistants who "set down the tune directly from the singer's lips" but after 1938 he used a portable machine with acetate discs.

Randolph did not find much instrumental music along with the songs. Many songs were done without accompaniment, though some singers preferred to use the guitar or banjo. He heard much talk about the homemade "dulcimore," but saw only one in many years of travel in the Ozarks. Important instrumental music, he concluded, was that played at backwoods dances—fiddle music. He has recorded some 130 of these fiddle tunes, many of them for the Library of Congress in 1941-42.

These four volumes contain a total of 883 songs with tunes and, counting variant forms, the separate texts run to nearly 1,700 items. To mention the volumes in detail, Volume I, appearing in 1946, contains 130 British ballads and songs. Of these, 41 are Child numbers and the others are later importations. Volume II, appearing in 1948, contains 211 songs of the South and West. These include songs about murderers and outlaws; Western, Civil War, Negro, and temperance songs. Volume III, appearing in 1949, contains 253 humorous and play-party songs. Volume IV, appearing in 1950, contains 289 religious songs and other items. Here is the old-time "brush-arbor" music, and here also are about 200 miscellaneous items not classifiable under any one type.

Volume I has an extensive bibliography of over 400 items prepared, in part at least, by the staff of the State Historical Society of Missouri. Headnotes, besides containing bibliographical data, give the provenience, singer, and date of each song. Each volume is enlivened with eight to ten halftone photographs (done by Randolph) of the singers. The volumes are not separately indexed, but Volume IV has indexes for all volumes: titles, first lines, and contributors and towns. Finally, this magnificent collection is rounded out by colored end papers picturing an Ozark river scene done by Missouri-born artist Thomas Hart Benton.

J. Cecil James Sharp

ENGLISH FOLK-CHANTEYS. *With Pianoforte Accompaniment, Introduction and Notes. Collected by Cecil J. Sharp. London: Simpkin, Marshall, Hamilton, Kent & Co., Ltd. 1914. xvi, 75 pp.*

This collection of 60 songs contains 26 capstan chanteys and 34 pulling chanteys, set to simple piano accompaniments, and all of them taken down by Sharp from old retired sailors. Sharp defines the chantey "as a song used by sailors during their work and devised, not only to keep them amused, but also, by assuring unanimity of action, to aid them in the efficient execution of their collective task." (p. xi) Capstan chanteys are used in work of a "regular rhythmic character," while pulling chanteys are used in work that is "irregular and spasmodic."

Though these 60 songs were collected from *English* sailors, many of them were, of course, known to American sailors, since sea songs tend to become international. Well-known ones in the American tradition are: "Drunken Sailor," "Rio Grand," "Sally Brown," "Shanadar" (Shenandoah), and others.

ENGLISH FOLK SONGS FROM THE SOUTHERN APPALACHIANS. *Comprising 122 Songs and Ballads, and 323 Tunes. Collected by Olive Dame Campbell and Cecil J. Sharp. With an Intro-*

duction and Notes. New York and London: G. P. Putnam's Sons. 1917. xxviii, 341 pp.

Here we have, in this 1917 edition, the first book publication of Sharp's collecting activities in America. This is the result of his first nine weeks of work in the southern Appalachians. Miss Maud Karpeles took down the words in shorthand, while Sharp noted the tunes. A 20-page introduction discusses his methods of collecting, the kind of people who inhabited the region, their habits and culture, and the nature of the songs and ballads, about 37 of which are found in Child or other collections. Though Sharp was an outside observer, he was in no sense an unsympathetic or condescending one, but entered wholeheartedly into the life of the people, as in fact he had done in some fifteen years of previous collecting in England. Sharp gives the simple, unaccompanied tunes with each ballad and song, his belief being that words and tune should not be separated; and with each he also gives singer, place, and date.

There are brief notes at the end of the book. For this volume the collecting was done from 1907 to 1916, the earlier part of the collecting (1907-10) being done by Mrs. Campbell, since Sharp did not come to America until 1916. The work set a high standard for many later collectors.

ENGLISH FOLK SONGS FROM THE SOUTHERN APPALA-CHIANS. *Collected by Cecil J. Sharp. Comprising two hundred and seventy-three Songs and Ballads with nine hundred and sixty-eight Tunes. Including thirty-nine Tunes contributed by Olive Dame Campbell. Edited by Maud Karpeles. Vols. I and II. London: Oxford University Press. 1932. xxxvii, 436 pp.; xi, 411 pp.*

This greatly enlarged second edition of the Sharp collection, published eight years after his death, more than doubles the number of songs and ballads and triples the number of tunes recorded in the 1917 edition. The original Sharp introduction (the 1917 one) is reprinted here, and Miss Karpeles adds an illuminating 9-page preface. The general make-up of the work is the same as the 1917 edition, the ballads in Volume I and the songs in Volume II, many variants recorded, and name of singer, place, and date given, along with simple tunes. Miss Karpeles includes many more extensive notes and bibliography than were given in the 1917 edition.

Miss Karpeles writes that Sharp spent a total of forty-six weeks in the mountains—nine weeks in 1916, nineteen in 1917, and eighteen in 1918. She accompanied him on all these searchings, she taking down the words and he the tunes. "In this way," she writes, "we noted songs from 281 different singers, obtaining a total of 1,612 tunes, representing about 500 different songs." (p. xii)

In each volume there is a full index of titles for *both* volumes. In 1952, the Oxford Press brought out a second impression, and a recent scholarly review points out the genuine worth and permanence of this great collection: "Indeed, it becomes increasingly clear that this probably is not only the best *regional* collection we shall ever get, but the most representative of the whole British tradition in the United States." *

* Bertrand H. Bronson in *Journal of American Folklore*, LXVII, 95 (January-March, 1954).

CHAPTER 12

Other Major
Collections

AMERICAN BALLADS AND SONGS. *Collected and Edited by Louise Pound. The Modern Student's Library. New York: Charles Scribner's Sons. 1922. xxxvi, 266 pp.*

This collection of the twenties, with its scholarly 25-page introduction and brief clarifying notes on each ballad, remains one of the best of the early, representative across-America collections. Miss Pound states that the aim of the collection is "to display the typical songs and ballads liked by the people and lingering among them." Here are brought together 120 ballads and songs (142, counting variants) grouped under seven headings: I. English and Scottish Ballads in America; II. Other Imported Ballads and Songs; III. Native Ballads and Songs; IV. Ballads of Criminals and Outlaws; V. Western Ballads and Songs; VI. Miscellaneous Ballads and Songs; VII. Dialogue, Nursery and Game Songs.

The notes give the provenience and often a bit of history of each ballad. The introduction is one of the best, if brief, statements of the true meaning of folksongs, of their growth in America, and suggestions about their continuance. Miss Pound was, of course, one of the most reliable scholars in the folksong field.* This small collection has none of the tunes, which all collectors now consider of equal importance with the texts. Though Miss Pound recognizes that "the

---

* See also her *Poetic Origins and the Ballad* (New York, 1921) and her "Oral Literature" (Chapter XXVII), *The Cambridge History of American Literature,* IV (New York, 1921).

song is the life of the words," she contends that the words have more stability than the tunes and more significance for social history.

AMERICAN FOLKSONGS OF PROTEST. *By John Greenway. Philadelphia: University of Pennsylvania Press. 1953. x, 348 pp.*

This informative volume is a combination of song, folksong, history, and biography. Approximately 225 songs and ballads (out of an original collection of some 2,000, according to Greenway) are included in the running text. The book is a pioneer work in a neglected field: the relation of song (and folksong) to social unrest. The author calls his work "an introduction rather than a scientific analysis, an impressionistic panorama rather than a blueprint."

After a survey of the background, he discusses, and includes, protest songs of the Negroes, the textile workers, the miners, migratory workers, the farmers, and a number of other groups such as seamen, steel and automobile workers, and even lumberjacks. Excellent biographical accounts (some of the best so far in print) are given of Ella May Wiggins, Aunt Molly Jackson, Woody Guthrie, and Joe Glazer—representative figures among current composers of the protest song. These persons were, of course, singers and adapters of traditional folksongs as well as makers of new songs. Devotees of the conventional and traditionally established concept of what constitutes folksong will object to Dr. Greenway's broadened definition of the term.[*] After examining various earlier definitions, he comes to this conclusion: "A folksong, therefore, is a song concerned with the interests of the folk, and in the complete possession of the folk." Such a definition ignores the ideas of persistency and transmissional changes; Dr. Greenway feels, however, that we should not overlook (and eventually lose) an important body of song for want of a definition.

Simple tunes are included for about 30 of the songs. An appendix lists about 300 songs of protest on phonograph records, and there are indexes and a bibliography. This is indeed an excellent study, but the title might better be *American SONGS of Protest.*

AMERICAN NEGRO FOLK-SONGS. *By Newman I. White. Cambridge Mass.: Harvard University Press. 1928. xi, 501 pp.*

This collection of over 700 songs and fragments (without music) was made over a period of a dozen years—from 1915 to 1927. The songs were taken down from oral or manuscript sources, none of them from printed sources. Much annotation and discussion are given

[*] See, for example, W. Edson Richmond's review of Dr. Greenway's book in *Journal of American Folklore*, LXVII (January-March, 1954), 96.

with the songs, providing a kind of history of origin and development. Informants and dates are carefully noted. There are 14 chapters in the work, beginning with The Negro Song in General and continuing with various groups, such as Religious Songs, Social Songs, Work Songs, and others.

Five appendices give additional matter, such as a few specimens of tunes, minstrel items, Negro "ballets," etc. There is an excellent bibliography of well over 200 items, many with brief annotations; and there are indexes of titles and first lines. All in all, this is one of the liveliest and most scholarly collections of Negro folksongs. In the light of recent methods, the chief drawback is the lack of tunes.

AMERICAN PLAY-PARTY SONG, WITH A COLLECTION OF OKLAHOMA TEXTS AND TUNES, THE. *By B. A. Botkin. The University Studies of the University of Nebraska, Vol. XXXVII. Lincoln: Published by the University. 1937. 400 pp.*

When Botkin made a survey among teachers and students at Oklahoma University in 1926-27 and in the high schools throughout the state, he uncovered 128 play-party songs in over 1,000 variants. Some six hundred students and many teachers helped in the collecting (their names and addresses are given), and most of the state's counties (63 out of 77) were represented. Oklahoma, being a kind of "last frontier" from 1889 on, had settlers from many areas, including a dozen states; hence, the great variety and numbers of songs collected.

Part One, a third of the volume, discusses the American play-party song in a series of chapters as follows: Origins and Backgrounds, The Play-Party and the Game, Play-Party and the Dance, Play-Party and the Song, Language and Style. Part Two gives the Oklahoma Texts and Tunes. The book is a learned study, with all the scholarly paraphernalia, completed at the University of Nebraska under Dr. Louise Pound, noted ballad scholar. An appendix prints a series of interviews on the social status of the play-party, and there is an extensive bibliography.

ANTHOLOGY OF JEWISH MUSIC. *Sacred Chant and Religious Folk Song of the Eastern European Jews. Compiled and Edited by Chemjo Vinaver. With original notations and commentary in English and Hebrew. Frontispiece Drawing by Marc Chagall. New York: Edward B. Marks Music Corporation. 1955. 292 pp. [At the back, introductory matter (xii pages) is given in Hebrew.]*

This first volume in a projected series contains "to a great extent, music hitherto unpublished and unrecorded," music that was a "once-living folk tradition." The editor obtained transcriptions of folk tunes by a "number of people selected from many Jewish immigrants," older persons who remembered chants and melodies "from their childhood or early youth in the old country."

The anthology contains 103 songs, about half of them sacred chant and the others religious folksong. Complete musical notation is given for each song, and the words are in both English and Hebrew. Careful study of this work throws light on much American-Yiddish and Israeli folksong of today.

BALLAD BOOK, THE. *Edited by MacEdward Leach. New York: Harper & Brothers. 1955. xiv, 842 pp.*

It was perhaps inevitable that the long-time secretary-treasurer of the American Folklore Society, Dr. MacEdward Leach, should do a book of ballads. The present well-edited, comprehensive volume is a representative anthology of 370 British and American ballads, with variants and Scandinavian analogues. Dr. Leach's 44-page introduction attests to his wide scholarly interest and ability in the folklore field.

The ballads are presented in two large groups without further division: I. Ballads of England and Scotland with American and Danish Variants; and II. American Ballads by Origin or Adoption. Brief but adequate headnotes for each ballad give its history and source of the text. The latter pages of the book include a selected bibliography, a selected list of ballad recordings (many of them especially recommended for their authenticity), an index of titles, and a long glossary (nearly 1,000 items) of unusual forms and meanings. This last feature, a great aid in reading the ballads, includes terms from Middle English to modern industrialism.

Some readers will regret that Dr. Leach does not include any tunes. His main reason is that no system of musical notation is really adequate for the ballads, since folksinging "shows subtle variations in pitch, rhythm, phrasing, accentuation [from stanza to stanza and singer to singer] that cannot be captured by conventional notation." (p. xiii) Since there are many satisfactory recordings available in our time, anyone wishing to use this anthology for teaching purposes will have ample means of demonstration.

BALLADS AND SEA SONGS FROM NOVA SCOTIA. *Collected by W. Roy Mackenzie. Cambridge, Massachusetts: Harvard University Press. 1928. xxvi, 421 pp.*

This excellently edited volume contains 162 songs and ballads

(16 of them Child numbers), 39 variants, and, in a separate section of the book, 42 folk tunes. Besides a very lively introduction, there are scholarly headnotes preceding each song and ballad, as well as a note telling where the collecting was done and who the singer was. A surprisingly large number, over 140, of the songs were collected from singers in Pictou County, many of them at the seaport towns of River John and Pictou on the north shore of Nova Scotia. Naturally, in such a collection as this, there are many fine old ballads, such as "Bonny Barbara Allan," "The Turkish Lady," "The Lass of Mohee," "Young Charlotte," "Santy Anna," "Reuben Ranzo," "Blow the Man Down," "The Dying Cowboy," "Rolling River," etc.

There are indexes of titles and first lines.

BALLADS AND SEA SONGS OF NEWFOUNDLAND. *Collected and edited by Elizabeth Bristol Greenleaf. Music Recorded in the Field by Grace Yarrow Mansfield and the Editor. Cambridge, Massachusetts: Harvard University Press. 1933. xliv, 395 pp.*

This work contains 185 songs, with over 100 tunes, and, in addition, 14 dance tunes. Nineteen items are identified as Child ballads. In the early twenties, Mrs. Greenleaf (then Miss Bristol) was a summer volunteer teacher in Dr. Wilfred Grenfell's mission in northern Newfoundland; at that time she first heard the folksongs of genuine oral tradition. Later she helped organize the Vassar College Folklore Expedition (of two persons!) in the summer of 1929, and so developed this fine collection of ballads and sea songs. All songs were recited or sung by native Newfoundlanders (dozens contributed), whose names and addresses are given with each ballad or song. Tunes were written down by Mrs. Mansfield, since the expedition did not carry a recording machine. Bibliographical and other explanatory notes follow each ballad and song. A most interesting 20-page introductory essay by Mrs. Greenleaf tells a great deal, not only about her methods and experiences in collecting, but much about the life of the hardy Newfoundlanders. "Folk-song in Newfoundland," says Mrs. Greenleaf, "owes a great debt to the people of Irish descent," because of their "genius for music." An excellent collection, with eight pages of illustrations.

BALLADS AND SONGS. *Collected by the Missouri Folk-Lore Society. Edited by H. M. Belden. The University of Missouri Studies: A Quarterly of Research. Volume IV, Number 1, January 1, 1940. Published at the University of Missouri, Columbia. xviii, 530 pp.*

In this big book, one of the best edited of the state collections, Belden has brought together well over 400 songs and ballads, counting variants and fragments. (For instance, about 15 of "Barbara Allen.") The work of collecting was done mainly by members of the Missouri Folk-Lore Society (founded in 1906) from 1903 on, in which over a hundred people collected and contributed. About 30 of the Child ballads are included and numbered. No special groupings are made, but in the preface Belden indicates that about all the usual subject types are found in the state—songs on the returned-lover theme, the rejected lover, humorous and comic pieces, satire, Irish songs, religious and play-party songs, etc. The editor emphasizes that all parts of the state, not merely the Ozarks, are given to folksinging, and that all classes and ages of people sing: "It does not appear that ballads in Missouri belong to any particular age, sex, or class of society."

Explanatory headnotes, which include mention of the songs in other collections, give useful information on provenience. Some 60 tunes are included, as well as a full index and bibliographical data.

BALLADS AND SONGS FROM OHIO. *Collected and arranged by Mary O. Eddy. Introduction by James Holly Hanford. New York: J. J. Augustin Publisher. 1939. xxvii, 330 pp.*

Twenty-five of the 153 separate ballads and songs (besides many variants) in this collection are listed as Child ballads. The collector found many of her songs in or near Perryville, her native town in Ashland County, Ohio. The collection represents "a very intensive research in a comparatively small area." Mary O. Eddy knew her sources intimately, for her great-grandfather had founded Perryville in 1810, and many of her sources were relatives or old friends. An index names over one hundred persons from whom she gathered her materials, and pictures are included of several of them. In accordance with recent practice, simple tunes are included for most of the songs. There is a minimum of useful information on the ballads throughout this well-edited regional collection, for which Hanford has written a scholarly introduction.

BALLADS AND SONGS OF INDIANA. *Collected and edited by Paul G. Brewster. (Indiana University Publications, Folklore Series, No. 1). Bloomington: Indiana University. 1940. 376 pp.*

This collection of 100 ballads and songs, many of them having two or more variants, comes mainly from eighteen counties in the southern part of Indiana. The editor has not "improved" the texts but has kept to "the original copy furnished by the contributor." Twenty-seven of the 100 are Child ballads, and simple tunes are given for about 30 of the songs; but, the editor reports, "ballad-singing, as an active tradition, is practically non-existent in Indiana." Headnotes name the contributors, give reference to other texts or discussions, and set forth other pertinent facts. There are indexes of titles, first lines, and tunes in this useful and scholarly work.

BALLADS AND SONGS OF SOUTHERN MICHIGAN. *Collected and edited by Emelyn Elizabeth Gardner and Geraldine Jencks Chickering. Ann Arbor: University of Michigan Press. 1939. London: H. Milford, Oxford University Press. 1939. xviii, 501 pp.*

Here is a collection of 200 ballads and songs (from a manuscript collection of over 900) grouped under nine appropriate headings: I. Unhappy Love; II. Happy Love; III. War; IV. Occupations; V. Disasters; VI. Crimes; VII. Religion; VIII. Humor; IX. Nursery. Twenty-nine are Child ballads and are numbered accordingly. Head-notes give valuable data on sources, references to other texts, and the name of each contributor who recited or sang the ballad. A later section gives brief biographical accounts of the informants. Musical notations are given with many of the ballads and songs. A lengthy introduction (26 pages) tells of the development of the collection, and discusses also "Some Factors in the Study of Folk Song." Many of the songs were taken directly from persons who had been in lumber camps or had learned them from lumberjacks. The golden age of the lumber camps (1870-1900) did great service, the editors report, in preserving and distributing folksongs. All in all, this is a very useful and scholarly work.

BALLADS AND SONGS OF THE SHANTY-BOY. *Collected and Edited by Franz Rickaby. Cambridge: Harvard University Press. 1926. xli, 244 pp.*

This book of 84 songs and ballads (including variants), with simple tunes for more than half of them, is a very scholarly work with full introduction, notes, glossary, and indexes of titles and first lines. The songs, collected immediately after World War I, "from men who worked in the woods of Michigan, Wisconsin, and Minnesota," come from the "Golden Age of American Lumbering (1870-1900)." After that period, as the editor points out, the machine more and more dominates, and the songs become less significant. Many of the songs have an Irish background, or an Irish singer, though Scotch and French-Canadian are also significant. Brief headnotes tell the sources (which may have further discussion in the notes). As to content, the songs concern many things in life besides lumbering. The glossary is most helpful, for many of the terms (birl, deacon seat, peavy, scaler, switch-hog, wanigan, etc.) are too technical for the general reader.

BALLADS OF THE KENTUCKY HIGHLANDS. *By Harvey H. Fuson. London: The Mitre Press. 1931. 219 pp.*

In addition to a useful introduction of 35 pages, this small volume contains, without tunes or any musical notation, 103 songs and some 20 quatrains, either jigs or stanzas on the war "from the memory of the Author." The introduction discusses the background of the people as a mixture of English and Scotch-Irish of the finest stock. Fuson is native to the region and is critical of Cecil Sharp, an outsider, who spoke ill of their education though well of their manners and culture. The great contribution, says Fuson, of the mountain people is their ballad literature: "Through this literature, handed down from generation to generation by way of oral transmission, and added to from time to time, they have kept up a culture and a refinement that is nothing short of marvellous." (p. 26)

Fuson does not distinguish between ballads and folksongs. He makes a ninefold division, under such headings as Old Ballads and Songs, Other Ballads and Songs, Play Songs, Nursery Rimes, War Songs, Old Religious Songs, etc. With each title he includes the name of the person who sang or gave him the song. All told, there were about two dozen singers, including Fuson himself.

CHANSONS FOLKLORIQUES FRANÇAISES AU CANADA, *Leur Langue Musicale. Par Marguerite et Raoul d'Harcourt. Québec: Presses Universitaires Laval. Paris: Les Presses Universitaires de France. 1956. xii, 449 pp.*

The 240 songs in this book, as Marius Barbeau tells in the preface, are drawn from songs in the National Museum at Ottawa, Canada. They were originally collected by MM. Barbeau and E.-Z. Massicote, on phonograph records, during the years 1916-18. The editors' introduction gives the background of the songs, pointing out that French folk music stems from both peasant and scholar over the past three centuries, that many of the great Canadian singers have now passed out of the picture, that most previous works have emphasized the words and have neglected the music. The present book has been written for those who love music.

The work has three main divisions. Part One is a brief discussion of the singers, of whom there were about forty that contributed in 1916-18. The chief singer was François Saint-Laurent, from whom about 200 songs were recorded. Most of the singers were of humble origin, without formal education, and they sang for the love of singing.

Part Two, in several chapters, discusses the musical language of the songs, i.e., the scales, modes, styles, rhythms, movements, and forms. These somewhat complicated matters, as the editors point out, have had a long and slow development through the centuries. The troubadours (eleventh to thirteenth centuries) and later the trouvères had much influence on folk music, as earlier they had been influenced by Gregorian church music. So, as the music comes down into the eighteenth and nineteenth centuries, and then is finally recorded in the twentieth, it is the product of many complicated forces.

The d'Harcourts study these various features in detail with each of the 240 songs, as they are presented in Part Three, which constitutes the bulk of the work. Simple tunes are given for each of the songs, and comments clarify their "musical language." The songs are grouped under twelve subject headings, such as History and Legend, Religion, Love, Marriage, Soldier Life, Drinking and Feasting, Travels, etc.

This well-printed and very scholarly study is presented entirely in French. At the end of the book there is a bibliography of works cited, as well as a detailed table of contents.

CHANSONS POPULAIRES DU CANADA. *Recueillies et publiées avec annotations, etc. Par Ernest Gagnon. Huitième édition (conforme à l'édition de 1880). Montréal: Librairie Beauchemin Limitée. 1908. xvii, 350 pp.*

This book, entirely in French, of about 110 songs including variants was the first serious attempt to collect the folksongs of French Canada. Some of the songs are mere fragments, but many others run from a dozen to two dozen stanzas. The work, first published in 1865, is a landmark by a distinguished composer and musician, and, of course, represented only a beginning in a vast field. As the editor says: "Le nombre de nos chansons populaires est incalculable." Since 1865, more than 10,000 have been collected. Here one finds many that have practically become world-wide in their appeal. Naturally, "À la Claire Fontaine" leads the field. ("Depuis le petit enfant de sept ans jusqu'au vieillard aux cheveux blancs, tout le monde, au Canada, sait et chante la *Claire Fontaine*.") Each song is prefaced by a brief comment, after which the simple melody is set down, and then the several stanzas. The book concludes with some thirty pages of Remarques Générales, in which Gagnon discusses the musical character of the songs, and points out that they must be judged according to their time and background and not according to modern musical standards. This very important early collection deserves a better printing than it has in the present edition.

FOLK-SONGS DU MIDI DES ÉTATS-UNIS. *Par Josiah H. Combs. Paris: Les Presses Universitaires de France. 1925. 230 pp.*

This work in two parts—one part discussion and the other a collection of 61 folksongs—was a doctoral dissertation made by Professor Combs at the University of Paris. A prefatory note states: "Les chansons ajoutées à cet ouvrage ont été choisies parmi une liste d'environ deux cents, que j'ai rassemblées au cours des quinze dernières années. Dans la plupart des cas, elles ont été recueillies auprès des chanteurs populaires mêmes." The songs were gathered from Kentucky, Virginia, West Virginia, Tennessee, Arkansas, Oklahoma, and Texas. Part One of the study discusses such matters as the region from which the songs came, questions of origin and authorship, how the songs were found and collected, classification of the songs (some English, some American), and the disappearance of folksong in the modern world. Usual footnotes and bibliographical references accompany the study, and headnotes mention singers or contributors and their addresses. (The author's mother was an important contributor.) The discussion (i.e., Part One) is in French, and the songs are in English. No tunes or melodies included.

FOLK-SONGS FROM THE SOUTHERN HIGHLANDS. *Collected and Edited by Mellinger Edward Henry. New York: J. J. Augustin Publisher. 1938. xiii, 460 pp.*

These 180 ballads and songs (with over 140 variants, making a total of well over 300) were recorded from the years 1928 to 1931, taken down by the Henrys from persons in the Highlands who sang or recited them. A few variants come from other sections of the United States. Pictures are included of some ballad singers and scenes, and a very few simple tunes are given. Twenty-nine of the total are indicated as Child ballads. Headnotes give locations of some of the songs and ballads in other collections, as well as names and addresses of persons who contributed.

A most interesting introduction (27 pages) by M. E. Henry tells much about the geography, economics, and culture of the southern Highlands—which he began visiting in 1917, though he had known the Blue Ridge of the Virginias as a boy. He tells of his travels and especially of experiences in collecting the songs. His serious collecting activity began in 1923 (or was it 1928?). This is indeed one of the fine collections of songs and ballads of the southern Highland region. There are indexes of titles and first lines.

FOLKSONGS OF ALABAMA. *Collected by Byron Arnold. University: University of Alabama Press. 1950. xiv, 193 pp.*
Here are 153 folksongs arranged, not according to subject groups, but according to the more than forty singers who gave Mr. Arnold the songs on his six-week collecting tour of Alabama in the summer of 1945. "I was so much interested in the singers themselves as personalities," writes Mr. Arnold, "and in the wide range of material in their singing, that in organizing this book I have grouped each singer's songs and included a biography with the songs." Headnotes for the songs usually tell how or where each singer learned the songs. Pictures are also included of most of the singers. The songs fall under four general headings, and could be so grouped: (1) ballads of British origin, of which there are 11; (2) ballads and songs of American and Alabama origin (more than 100); (3) Negro spirituals and work songs, of which there are 34; and (4) 10 play-party songs. No variants are given of the songs, though the author notes that there were some, and he indicates where many of the folksongs are to be found in other collections—such as those by White, Belden, Hudson, Brewster, Cox, Lomax, and others. In accordance with recent practice, Arnold has collected "the tunes of all the songs for inclusion in the present volume." This is indeed a fine regional collection; though not as scholarly or as large as some of the recent collections, it is perhaps more popular and usable for the general reader.

FOLK-SONGS OF AMERICA. *By Robert Winslow Gordon, Formerly in Charge of the Archive of American Folk Song of the Library of Congress. Sponsored by Joint Committee on Folk Arts, W.P.A. Issued by Folk-Song and Folklore Department, Herbert Halpert, Supervisor. New York: National Service Bureau, Publication No. 73-S. December, 1938. iv, 110 mimeo. pp.*
This interesting volume is a series of fifteen essays on American folksong, with many illustrative examples; in fact, about 100 songs in whole or in part are given in the text. The essays appeared originally at irregular intervals in the New York *Times Sunday Magazine*, from January 2, 1927, to January 22, 1928. The first essay tells the scope of Gordon's study and lays the plans for extensive travels to do collecting. The following essays tell of his experiences in collecting in North Carolina, Georgia (especially of Negro materials), in jails and lumber camps, and of his looking for outlaw ballads.

(Gordon considers "Frankie and Johnny" "by all odds the most popular of the American underworld songs."—p. 45) Lumberjack songs, he points out, came mainly from 1870 to 1900, and not many since then. Fiddle tunes and banjo tunes are included; the songs, that is, and not the music, for no musical notation is presented here. Besides the types mentioned above, there are nursery songs, songs of the pioneers, and cowboy songs.

FOLKSONGS OF FLORIDA. *Collected and Edited by Alton C. Morris. Musical Transcriptions by Leonhard Deutsch. Gainesville, Florida: University of Florida Press. 1950. xiv, 464 pp.*

This excellent collection, one of the finest of state collections, of over 300 folksongs of Florida of the white population, grew out of a doctoral study at the University of North Carolina. Some one hundred native singers helped the collector, Dr. Morris, and he is careful to give credit with each song. (In one remarkable instance, about 80 songs came from one woman, a Mrs. G. A. Griffin, in her late seventies.) Simple tunes are included for more than half the songs. The great variety of Florida's population, the somewhat cosmopolitan character of the state, the long coastline, the Southern character of north Florida and the Northern character of south Florida—all these and other factors make for great variety in the folksongs. Dr. Morris has two major divisions—Songs of the New World and Songs of the Old World—which are further subdivided. In the first there are songs of war and historical events, songs of the West, of the sea, badmen, disasters, love and domestic affairs, religion, work, nursery, and play-party songs. The second section contains mainly English and Scottish songs (Child ballads to the number of 34), but also some Bahaman and Irish or Anglo-Irish songs. A unique find was Child ballad No. 208, "Lord Derwentwater"—its first appearance in America. An introductory essay, headnotes, and other notes by Dr. Morris are most illuminating, as they give considerable social history and "living background" of the region. As in other good studies, there are helpful indexes and a lengthy bibliography.

FOLKSONGS OF MISSISSIPPI AND THEIR BACKGROUND. *By Arthur Palmer Hudson. Chapel Hill: The University of North Carolina Press. 1936. xii, 321 pp.*

The nearly 200 songs in this collection were gathered from white people in Mississippi, most of them of British or Irish ancestry. The songs include those which Hudson had printed previously in the *Journal of American Folklore* in 1927 and in *Specimens of*

Mississippi Folk-Lore in 1928. The songs were collected from all over the state and represent a cross-section of folksongs then current. About 40 of them are Child ballads. Others are varied in subject matter—Western, outlaw and criminal, war, nursery, and others. The author, a leading scholar in the folklore field, has four excellent background chapters besides ample headnotes and footnotes, a fine bibliography, and indexes of titles and first lines. No melodies or tunes are given (the work was published during Depression years), but otherwise this is an excellent state collection.

FOLK SONGS OF OLD NEW ENGLAND. *Collected and Edited by Eloise Hubbard Linscott. With an Introduction by James M. Carpenter. New York: The Macmillan Company. 1939. xxi, 337 pp.*
This collection contains 28 singing games "with diagrams and directions," 35 country dances "with directions, charts, calls, and fiddle tunes," 17 sea chanteys and fo'castle songs, and 77 folksongs and ballads—in all a total of 157 songs. Old singers were the source of many of these songs, many of them (both songs and singers!) in the family background of the editor. Not particularly intended as a scholarly collection, but rather as a *usable* one for home or group activity, this is nevertheless a sound collection.
The editor precedes each group with a brief discussion, and the headnotes for each song give the singer or informant and other pertinent details. Music is included for all the songs and dances. One point is particularly significant in the comments of the editor: These songs and dances were the heritage of educated and important people in the community, not merely of the so-called common folk. It is often thought that ballads and folksongs come only from the unlettered. Though much of the flavor and background of old New England is in this fine book, any student of folksong is also aware that much of the material is widely known and sung in other sections of the country.
Toward the end of the volume there are brief accounts of about forty singers, fiddlers, and prompters—the chief sources of the collector. A condensed reference list shows where each song appears in other collections, but there is no index.

FOLK-SONGS OF THE ROANOKE AND THE ALBEMARLE. *By Louis W. Chappell. Morgantown, West Virginia: The Ballad Press. 1939. 203 pp.*
These 120 folksongs (tunes included for 65 of them) are divided into six categories of 20 songs each: British Ballad Survivals; Sea Ballads and Songs; Other Ballads and Songs; Nell Cropsey Songs

and Others; Religious Songs; Other Songs. The Nell Cropsey songs might seem most puzzling to the uninitiated: they are concerned with the disappearance and death in 1901 "of a popular young woman of Elizabeth City, North Carolina" (p. 108) and, according to Chappell, these songs had wide currency.

The songs in this collection were gathered from twenty-eight singers (with names and addresses listed) at various times from 1924 to 1938. There is an index of titles.

FOLK-SONGS OF THE SOUTH. *Collected under the Auspices of the West Virginia Folk-Lore Society and Edited by John Harrington Cox. Cambridge: Harvard University Press. 1925. xxxi, 545 pp.*

From the scholar's viewpoint, this is one of the most satisfactory regional collections of American ballads ever made. In an introduction, Dr. Cox tells of the organizing of the West Virginia Folk-Lore Society, of his activities in collecting ballads and of the many who helped him and the society, and a good deal about his meetings with ballad singers. The work contains 185 ballads and songs collected in West Virginia and nearby areas. Many of these are given in many variants; for example, nearly a dozen versions of "Barbara Allen" and at least nine of "John Hardy." Some 33 of the ballads are numbered as being in the Child collection. Each ballad is preceded by headnotes indicating where else it may be found in print, and telling also when and from whom it was collected for the society. The work includes half a dozen photographs of ballad singers whom Dr. Cox knew or knew about. In the latter part of the volume there are 29 "folk tunes," simple melodies without accompaniment, edited by Miss Lydia I. Hinkel, of West Virginia University. Further, there is an index of titles and first lines, and finally a folded-in map of West Virginia. All in all, a most valuable book for the student of folksong.

GAMES AND SONGS OF AMERICAN CHILDREN. *Collected and Compared by William Wells Newell. New and Enlarged Edition. New York and London: Harper & Brothers, Publishers. 1883, 1903. xv, 282 pp.*

Anybody who remembers his childhood cannot but delight in this fine early collection of 190 pieces, drawn from all parts of the country and organized into sixteen categories, such as the following: Love-Games, Playing at Work, Humor and Satire, Bird and Beast, Guessing-Games, Games of Chase, Counting Out Rhymes, and others. Many of the games are explained in prose, others are presented in rhyme, and about forty of them have accompanying tunes. Some well-known numbers: "Virginia Reel"; "Oats, Pease, Beans, and Barley Grows"; "Happy Is the Miller"; "There Was a Tree Stood in the Ground"; "Ring Around the Rosie"; "Pease Porridge Hot"; "Blind-Man's Buff"; "Hop-Scotch"; "The Needle's Eye"; "Pussy Wants a Corner"—to mention but a few.

This very scholarly edition has long been considered a standard work. The editor gives the source of each game and song collected. A long introductory section tells of the diffusion of the games and songs, their background, their relation to ballad literature, and their origins. An appendix lists many collections of children's games and sets forth comparisons and references.

HAITI SINGING. *By Harold Courlander. Chapel Hill: The University of North Carolina Press. 1939. xii, 273 pp.*

This scholarly and useful work is both a history and a collection, the author having spent parts of five years (1932-37) in Haiti, making his study and collection with the help of many people. He tells much of the complicated African background, much of the social and economic life of the people, and, of course, concentrates on the importance and meaning of their music. The middle third of the book is given over to the songs, usually with English translations, and the latter part gives the music or tunes for the songs, some 126 of them. There are photographs, notes, glossary, references, and an index in this excellent volume.

HILL COUNTRY TUNES. *Instrumental Folk Music of Southwestern Pennsylvania. Collected and Edited by Samuel Preston Bayard. Philadelphia: American Folklore Society. 1944(5). xxvii, 130 [unnumbered] pp.*

This small book contains about 100 tunes collected from nine different fiddle and fife players. The tunes are hornpipes, reels, quadrilles, schottisches, waltzes, and other dance tunes. A 19-page introduction presents detailed information on fiddling techniques. There are brief notes on the nine players, chief of whom was Mrs. Sarah Gray Armstrong of (near) Derry, Pennsylvania, who gave the editor more than a third of the tunes. Some of the fiddlers were good singers of folksongs, too. After the tunes, the editor gives comments on origins, variants, diffusion, and in some cases printed sources for the tunes. This kind of music is blood brother to folksong music, and as yet has had all too little investigation in the United States. As Bayard points out, "We know little about instrumental folk music in the United States . . . we possess as yet no large quantity of musical material gathered from many different parts of the

country—nothing comparable with the mass of our recorded traditional song melodies."

LORE OF THE LUMBER CAMPS. *By Earl Clifton Beck. Ann
Arbor, Michigan: University of Michigan Press. 1948. xii, 348 pp.*

This revised and enlarged edition of Beck's earlier work, *Songs
of the Michigan Lumberjacks* (1941), contains 118 songs. There is
little change from the plan and content of the earlier work (*q.v.*),
except the added 14 songs. The editor gives much pertinent discussion in the headnotes for each song.

LOUISIANA FRENCH FOLK SONGS. *By Irène Thérèse Whitfield.
University, Louisiana: Louisiana State University Press. 1939. xiv,
159 pp.*

This is a carefully prepared collection of 103 folksongs transcribed,
as Miss Whitfield heard them sung, "with special care as to phonetic
and musical rendition." The songs are presented in three classifica-
tions: I. Louisiana-French Folk Songs; II. Cajun Folk Songs—the
largest group (48)*; and III. Creole Folk Songs. These groupings
are further classified as to subject matter, with such headings as
Lullabies, Songs of Love and Marriage, Drinking Songs, Comic
Songs, Songs of Animals, of Satire, of War, of Food, and so on.
Phonetic transcriptions of all the songs, translations (from Creole
to French), footnotes, indexes, and a bibliography—all attest to the
scholarly work done for this collection.

MINSTRELSY OF MAINE. *Folk-Songs and Ballads of the Woods
and the Coast. Collected by Fannie Hardy Eckstrom and Mary
Winslow Smyth. Boston: Houghton Mifflin Company. 1927. xvi,
390 pp.*

This collection of 119 songs and ballads (with the source included
for each one) is interspersed with valuable editorial comment, including some interesting essays, such as The Pursuit of a Ballad
Myth (about "The Jam on Gerry's Rocks"), How the Folk Rewrite
a Song, The Function of the Singer, and Of Ballads and Ballad-
Making. The book has a twofold division, as suggested in the title.
The Woods songs are divided chronologically, the first from 1825
to 1875, the middle group near the end of the century, and the
later ones since the turn of the century. Among the Coast songs
there are deep-sea songs, chanteys, pirate songs, mournful songs,

---

* In 1955, this "largest group" was republished by the Louisiana State University Press under the title *Acadian Folk Songs* "in commemoration of the
Acadian Bicentennial Celebration." The earlier work (1939) is now out of
print.

coastwise songs, and then, for good measure, a few songs of the pioneers. There is a wealth of information and entertainment in this book, though unfortunately no tunes are included for any of the songs. Indexes of first lines and titles are given.

MOUNTAIN MINSTRELSY OF PENNSYLVANIA. *Being a Third Edition of* North Pennsylvania Minstrelsy, *Revised and Enlarged. Compiled by Henry W. Shoemaker. Philadelphia: Newman F. McGirr. 1931. 319 pp.*

The revised and enlarged edition contains the same introductory material as the 1923 edition, and also a short 1931 introduction. Again, there are about 140 songs, but the "enlarged" part consists of about 80 additional fragments. As in the earlier editions, the melodies are not included. This edition is without illustrations, but the printing is better than in the earlier editions. (See annotation on *North Pennsylvania Minstrelsy*.)

NEGRO AND HIS SONGS, THE. *A Study of Typical Negro Songs in the South. By Howard W. Odum and Guy B. Johnson. Chapel Hill: The University of North Carolina Press. 1925. vii, 306 pp.*

The 209 songs in this collection, presented primarily as a sociological study, were collected from northern Mississippi and northern Georgia. The three main groups are Religious Songs, Social Songs, and Work Songs. The editors present a good deal of discussion along with the songs, interpreting the life of the Negro through his music. As industrialization advances, these songs tend to disappear, or change completely. Some of them are crude, some beautiful.

Melodies are not included. There is a brief bibliography and an index of songs.

NEGRO FOLK RHYMES, *Wise and Otherwise. With a Study by Thomas W. Talley of Fisk University. New York: The Macmillan Company. 1922. xii, 347 pp.*

This volume contains about 350 folk rhymes, characterized in the introduction as "genuine folk-songs—lyrics, ballads, rhymes—in which are crystallized the thought and feeling, the universally shared lore of the folk." The items range from very short simple rhymes to songs of many stanzas. For instance, "Frog Went A-Courting" has 25 stanzas. The "Study" takes up about the last third of the volume. A very few melodies are given, though most of the pieces are meant to be sung or chanted or used as play tunes. There are love songs, dance songs, nursery and animal rhymes, and many play songs. This is an excellent collection and study of a special type.

NEGRO WORKADAY SONGS. *By Howard W. Odum and Guy B. Johnson. Chapel Hill: The University of North Carolina Press. 1926. xvi, 278 pp.*

Primarily a sociological study, in "The University of North Carolina Social Study Series," this is nevertheless a very important collection. There are some 250 songs here, illustrating many types of subject matter: blues and lonesome songs, badman ballads, jail and chain-gang songs, work, love, and religious songs. In general, melodies are not given, except for about fifteen type examples. This collection is unique in one respect: the songs were collected directly from Negro workers and singers in the years 1924-25 in the Carolinas, Tennessee, and Georgia. Other collections in other years have yielded different songs, or some of the same songs in variant forms, since this material is extremely fluid. The editors do not claim folksong status for all items in the volume, but many, perhaps most of them, are folk creations. There is an excellent chapter on the John Henry legend, with about fifteen different versions of the famous song. There is a selected bibliography and an index to songs.

NORTH PENNSYLVANIA MINSTRELSY. *As Sung in the Backwoods Settlements, Hunting Cabins and Lumber Camps in the "Black Forest" of Pennsylvania, 1840-1923. Collected by Henry W. Shoemaker, in Collaboration with John C. French and John H. Chatham. Second Edition. Altoona, Pennsylvania: Published by the Times Tribune Company. 1923. 233 pp.*

This somewhat quaint, poorly printed and bound collection contains a surprising amount of interesting material. The "Black Forest," a squarish area about eighty miles each way, produced most of the nearly 140 songs here included. The people are of a mixed ancestry of English, Scotch-Irish, Huguenot, Dutch and German, and American Indian. Hence the great mixture and variety of their songs in this unusual background.

The songs are preceded by a number of essays (43 pages), two of them by Shoemaker, who makes a strong plea for the integrity of the mountain people and their culture as opposed to modernization—the mountain people whom he considers "a reserve fund against luxury and decadence." (p. 12) By 1920, he had written and collected some "forty books and pamphlets" on Pennsylvania folklore. The present collection, he states, "is in no way complete," for "there are hundreds of old songs yet to be had." (p. 18) A few notes tell the sources of the songs, which seem to be of every variety and have no special groupings here, and the text is interspersed with pictures of about a dozen old folksingers. Except for two brief samples, no melodies are given.

ON THE TRAIL OF NEGRO FOLK-SONGS. *By Dorothy Scarborough, Assisted by Ola Lee Gulledge. Cambridge: Harvard University Press. 1925. 289 pp.*

Chiefly a group of essays, with songs interspersed, this is the first of several authoritative works by Miss Scarborough on Negro folksongs. There are something over 100 songs with tunes, and over 200 more additional texts and fragments. The ten chapter-essays tell of Miss Scarborough's labors in running down the texts, and the even more elusive tunes, as she worked all through the South from Texas on eastward in her tireless search for folksong materials. Some may not agree with her comment that the Negro has "produced the largest and most significant body of folk-song created in America" (p. 283), but few will question the value of her great contribution in bringing to light many songs and tunes. In the various essays she includes many kinds of Negro folksongs—traditional songs and ballads as preserved by the Negro, indigenous Negro ballads, dance songs or reels, game songs, lullabies, songs about animals, work songs, railroad songs, and blues. No spirituals are included in this volume. The author's reminiscent accounts are sprightly and entertaining. This is an important work, but unfortunately without an index.

A PIONEER SONGSTER: *Texts from the Stevens-Douglass Manuscript of Western New York, 1841-1856. Edited by Harold W. Thompson, Assisted by Edith E. Cutting. Ithaca, New York: Cornell University Press. 1958. xxii, 203 pp.*

This collection of 89 song texts, as the subtitle indicates, is a ballad-collector's hoarding of the mid-nineteenth century. Miss Cutting had edited the songs in 1945 as a master's dissertation under Professor Thompson's guidance, and a few songs from the manuscript had been published here and there. But not until 1958 was the whole manuscript adequately presented in print. Professor Thompson's introduction gives a brief background of the times which produced the songs, comments on the character and condition of the manuscript, and discusses the classification of the songs.

The songs are presented in three groups: I. Songs and Ballads from the British Isles; II. American Songs and Ballads; III. Minor Groups—English and American. In group I are 9 Child ballads and 27 on love, historical, and Irish themes. In group II are seven divisions of 38 songs ranging from love themes to white spirituals.

In group III are 15 songs on Indian, moral, tearful, and satirical themes.

Professor Thompson has prepared brief introductions for the divisions within the three groups, and Miss Cutting has written headnotes for each song. Since no tunes were in the original manuscript, none are given in the present text. The ballad student is not surprised to find in the text such titles as "Barbara Allen," "The 'Prentice Boy," "Skewball," "The Hunters of Kentucky," "The Dying Californian," "Old Dog Tray," and "The Roving Bachelor"; and to find also that these versions may be different from any he has come across before. This well-edited and beautifully printed text concludes with a general bibliography and an index of songs.

ROLL AND GO. *Songs of American Sailormen. Compiled by Joanna C. Colcord. With an Introduction by Lincoln Colcord. Indianapolis: The Bobbs-Merrill Company. 1924. xxiv, 118 pp.*

This well-edited book of 86 sea songs is the first collection of any size and importance on the American side, though a good number of British collections had previously appeared. After the introduction and foreword, the compiler gives the shanties in a running text discussion, together with the tunes. Nine full-page pictures of the old sailing vessels add to the text. The later Colcord edition (1938) gives a few more songs and further details of the era in which they developed. (For fuller discussion, see the entry on *Songs of American Sailormen.*)

SHANTYMEN AND SHANTYBOYS. *Songs of the Sailor and Lumberman. Collected and Compiled by William Main Doerflinger. New York: The Macmillan Company. 1951. xxiii, 374 pp.*

Other collections will be made, but in some ways this remarkable gathering of sailor and logger songs can be called a definitive edition, so thorough is the job and so competent is the editing. Here are 167 songs and 50 variants, making a total of 217 in all.

The songs originated, for the most part, from 1820 to 1860—the great years of shantying, after a decline in the seventeenth and eighteenth centuries. Though by now most of the old-time shellbacks and lumbermen have gone, the collecting was done in the early thirties and forties, when enough old singers were still around to share their songs and experiences. Most of the versions here are given as sung directly into the recording machine, over a period of about twenty-five years in which the collecting was done.

Doerflinger is not the first to suggest the similarity of sailor and logger songs,* or to point out that sailors and loggers both were a rugged lot of rovers. Their lives intermingled up and down the eastern coast of North America, and sometimes a man was a sailor in the summer and a logger in the winter. But Doerflinger is perhaps the first to bring their songs together in a single, integrated collection.

Concerning the arrangement or "stowage plan" of the book, Doerflinger has three groups of shanties (short-haul, halyard, and others), a group of deep-water songs, two groups of fishing-bank and forecastle songs, two groups of logger songs, and three groups (bold adventure, murder, and romantic) common to both logger and sailor. Each group is skillfully set into a running text of interesting commentary, and there is an excellent chapter on The Rise of Shantying. Simple, unembellished tunes are included. An unusual feature of the book is the series of short biographical sketches of about twenty fine singers. Then, very useful for the scholar, a long section of notes (pp. 324-59) gives detailed information on each song—who the singer was, history of the song if known, versions in other collections, and so on. There is an excellent bibliography of nearly 200 items and an index of song titles. All in all, this is one of the finest collections of recent years.

SLAVE SONGS OF THE GEORGIA SEA ISLANDS. *By Lydia Parrish. Music Transcribed by Creighton Churchill and Robert MacGimsey. Introduction by Olin Downes. New York: Creative Age Press, Inc. 1942. xxxii, 256 pp.*

This very interesting collection, quarto size, contains about 100 songs or musical pieces, divided into five main groups, as follows: Afro-American Shout Songs; African Survivals on the Coast of Georgia; Ring-Play, Dance, and Fiddle Songs; Religious Songs; and Work Songs. The last two groups comprise about two-thirds of the whole.

Mrs. Parrish spent about twenty-five years in the collecting and study of these primitive songs, some of them extremely complicated in rhythm and notation. She points out the difficulty in transcribing them in ordinary Western musical notation. Though she does not mention Dr. George Pullen Jackson by name, her explanations suggest sharp disagreement with him on the origins of Negro spirituals. She felt that experience with the native singers was the best authority—as opposed to the books in libraries.

Each group of songs is preceded by a scholarly discussion. The songs are presented with unaccompanied melodies. The book is

* See Joanna Colcord, *Roll and Go* (Indianapolis, 1924), Foreword.

enhanced by the inclusion of 25 full pages of photographs. There is a selected bibliography but no index in this important volume of music from the Georgia Sea Islands.

SLAVE SONGS OF THE UNITED STATES. *Edited by William Francis Allen, Charles Pickard Ware, and Lucy McKim Garrison. New York: Peter Smith. 1929. Copyright 1867. Reprinted 1929. xliv, 115 pp.*

This collection of 136 songs, all with unaccompanied simple tunes, taken directly from Negroes, is of prime importance because it represents, in all probability, the first serious attempt at a general collection of Negro songs throughout the South. Most of the songs, however, are from South Carolina and Virginia, with the greatest number from Port Royal Islands off South Carolina. The editors expressed their purpose when they stated "that these relics of a state of society which has passed away should be preserved while it is still possible." (p. iii) But they recognize that they "have only gleaned upon the surface, and in a very narrow field." (p. x) Most of the songs are "sperichils" or of some religious nature. Fewer than a dozen are secular. A 38-page introduction by Allen tells of their collaboration during most of a year in collecting the songs, and also gives a good deal of detail on how the songs were sung (and danced) in Negro meetings. Most of the songs seem to have come from group meetings. Much is told of dialect(s), especially of the Port Royal Islands, and of the very extensive simplification of language. The editors had received much help from Colonel T. W. Higginson, whose "own valuable collection had appeared in the *Atlantic Monthly*" (p. xxxvii) early in 1867. From the titles (though words may vary in modern versions) one recognizes such well-known songs as "Roll, Jordan, Roll," "The Lonesome Valley," "Nobody Knows the Trouble I've Had," "I'm Going Home," and others. Because of its primacy, this collection, though small, will retain its position of major importance among all collections of Negro folksongs in the United States.

SONG CATCHER IN THE SOUTHERN MOUNTAINS, A. *American Folk Songs of British Ancestry. By Dorothy Scarborough. New York: Columbia University Press. 1937. xviii, 476 pp.*

This second important collection by Miss Scarborough came from her "questing for folk songs" in Virginia and North Carolina in the summer of 1930, with a specially made hand dictaphone. Out of an original collection of some 600 items, this book contains well over 200 songs. The tunes are given in a special section (pp. 385-457), separate from the songs and ballads. Part One (80 pp.) is a lively account of the indefatigable searchings of the author. Part Two gives the ballads, many of them with many variants (e.g., 9 for "Barbara Allen," 6 for "Pretty Polly," 6 for "The House Carpenter," 7 for "The Gypsy Davy," and so on). Part Three gives the songs, also with variants. Three indexes are included: Index of First Lines, Index to Music, and General Index. All in all, this is a rich and rewarding study, not only for the content, but for the lively style of the author. Miss Scarborough died in 1935, and the book was seen through the press by her friends at Columbia University.

SONGS ALONG THE MAHANTONGO. *Pennsylvania Dutch Folksongs, gathered and edited by Walter E. Boyer, Albert F. Buffington, [and] Don Yoder. Lancaster: The Pennsylvania Dutch Folklore Center. 1951. 231 pp.*

This fine collection presented in a lively style shows how interesting research can be! The three scholarly editors, native to this region of Pennsylvania Dutch heritage, have brought together over 60 songs, giving them in both Pennsylvania Dutch dialect and in English translation, including the unaccompanied tunes also.

The Mahantongo valley is a somewhat isolated area of east-central Pennsylvania, inhabited by descendants of Germans and Swiss who came about the time of the Revolution. Though most of them now know English, 95 per cent of them speak the Pennsylvania Dutch dialect, too. The songs come mostly from German, Swiss, and Alsatian backgrounds—and the editors have collated the songs in collections of Germanic folksongs published in Europe.

Here are songs of childhood, courtship and marriage, farm life, play-party (or "snitzing" party), tavern, and religious songs. Many have never before been published. Many are gay, with an earthy humor. Tunes were taken down by wire recorder from about forty singers, whose brief biographies are included. It is interesting to note that dances of the region do not seem to be Germanic in origin, but English and Irish, according to the editors. There are ample explanations with the songs, a pronunciation key, a bibliography, an index of songs, and some gay illustrations. This is indeed a well-done, important small collection.

SONGS OF AMERICAN SAILORMEN. *By Joanna C. Colcord. With an Introduction by Lincoln Colcord. New York: W. W. Norton & Company, Inc. 1938. vii, 212 pp.*

On the obverse of the title page appears this statement: "A former edition of this work entitled *Roll and Go, Songs of American Sailor-*

men, was published in 1924 under the copyright issued to the Bobbs-Merrill Company, Indianapolis, Ind."

These 108 songs stem from the great days of the clipper ships, roughly from 1812 to 1860. They are grouped as follows: Short-Drag Shanties, Halliard (or Halyard) Shanties, Windlass or Capstan Shanties, and Forecastle Songs. An explanatory introduction tells of the clipper-ship era and gives information on the editor, who was specially qualified to make such a collection as this: "Born at sea among the islands of the South Pacific in the cabin of a sailing ship, the daughter of a ship master, she is descended from five generations of deep-water seamen on the New England coast, masters and builders of square-rigged vessels. Up to the age of eighteen she spent most of her girlhood at sea on board her father's command, sailing on China voyages; and from this experience she acquired, as if by nature, the essential feeling of ships and the sea." (Introduction, p. 20) (Her father went to sea about 1874.)

Miss Colcord says that, in the main, shanties "consisted of short solo passages, each followed by a chorus." (p. 25) She also points out that the origin of shantying is lost in the unrecorded past. (p. 27) The same can be said for many kinds of folksinging. Explanatory headnotes are given with each song, and a brief discussion precedes each of the four groups. Simple, unaccompanied tunes are set down, and a few variants are included. A chapter by Miss Colcord on The Singing Sailor illuminates the song texts which follow.

Here are a few titles of famous songs: "A-Roving," "Blow the Man Down," "Captain Kidd," "Derby Ram," "Drunken Sailor," "Haul Away Joe," "The Lass of the Mohea," "Shenandoah," "Stormalong," "Whiskey Johnny." The book is illustrated with drawings by Gordon Grant and with pictures of some famous clipper ships. All in all, this is one of the fine collections of American sea songs.

SONGS OF THE MICHIGAN LUMBERJACKS. *By Earl Clifton Beck. Ann Arbor: University of Michigan Press. 1941. xi, 296 pp.*

This volume contains 104 songs, collected by Beck and a legion of "student helpers and other friends." All kinds of songs sung by the lumberjacks are here—songs of the shantyman's life, men at work and play, stories of love and death, moniker songs, French-Canadian songs, bunkhouse ballads, and others. A few of the songs have simple tunes. There are illustrations, especially of Paul Bunyan episodes and of log brands (not unlike cattle brands). An appendix (12 pp.) includes "Tall Tales" (in prose), and there is a brief bibliography, an index of songs, and an index of tunes.

SONGS SUNG IN THE SOUTHERN APPALACHIANS. *Many of Them Illustrating Ballads in the Making. Collected by Mellinger Edward Henry. London: The Mitre Press. n. d. xxiii, 253 pp.*

The 19-page introduction is dated December, 1933, and headnotes indicate that most of the songs were recorded from August, 1929, to December, 1933. A few are earlier and some not dated. Though no publication date is given, 1934 is generally accepted.

These songs, approximately 150 and many fragments, are more "contemporary" and less "traditional" than the songs in Henry's other large collection, *Folk-Songs from the Southern Highlands* (*q.v.*), and apparently belong to the same collecting period; but the text is less carefully edited and the notes are less complete. Headnotes usually give dates of collecting, as well as the informant and the place. As in the other collection, the introduction is personal and informative, telling much about the region and the inhabitants. Curiously, neither introduction makes reference to the other collection. There are no tunes, but there is an index of titles, alphabetical, in lieu of a table of contents.

"SOUND OFF!" SOLDIER SONGS FROM YANKEE DOODLE TO PARLEY VOO. *By Edward Arthur Dolph. Music Arranged by Philip Egner. Ilustrated by Lawrence Schick. Foreword by Peter B. Kyne. New York: Cosmopolitan Book Corporation. 1929. xv, 621 pp.*

"SOUND OFF!" SOLDIER SONGS FROM THE REVOLUTION TO WORLD WAR II. *Compiled by Edward Arthur Dolph (1896-   ). Music Arranged by Philip Egner. Illustrated by Lawrence Schick. New York: Farrar and Rinehart, Inc. 1942. xxvii, 621 pp.*

This big collection of old and recent songs, as the editor points out, contains not only the true folksongs of the Army but other songs adopted by the Army—probably the "most comprehensive collection of American soldier songs" ever made. Kyne says Dolph has "saved from oblivion ballads that were born of historic events and reared in hardship, danger, and blood." Here are over 300 songs, with piano accompaniments, going back to Revolutionary times and coming down to include (in the 1929 edition) World War I. Headnotes by Dolph give a brief and very useful history of each song. Numerous small drawings by Schick add touches of humor. There is a bibliography and an index of first lines.

The 1942 edition is a reprint and not a new edition. The introductory matter merely adds 12 pages of World War II material—otherwise there is no change from the 1929 edition.

SPANISH FOLK-POETRY IN NEW MEXICO. *By Arthur Leon Campa. Albuquerque: The University of New Mexico Press. 1946. [x], 224 pp.*

This scholarly study and collection of nearly 200 New Mexican folksongs is done by one of our leading authorities on Mexican-Spanish culture. Campa divides his songs into *romances, corridos, decimas,* and *canciones,* with the comment that *canciones* has come to be a sort of generic name for the entire field of New Mexican folksong. Discussions of the songs, or groups of songs, are in English, but the songs themselves are all in Spanish (with no translations). The learned introduction gives considerable historical background and tells much about the art and practice of folksinging in New Mexico. The ballad in this area dates back to the end of the sixteenth century, having come with the Spanish conquerors. (p. 17) The singers are troubadours, skilled with the guitar, and there are many of them today in New Mexico. (p. 25) This is an excellent collection, with many notes, footnotes, and a bibliography, but unfortunately no index.

TEXAS FOLK SONGS. *Collected by Willam A. Owens. Musical Arrangements by Willa Mae Kelly Koehn. Publications of the Texas Folklore Society, Number XXIII. Dallas: University Press in Dallas. 1950. 302 pp.*

This collection of 118 folksongs, with tunes in a piano setting, represents the work of one collector, apparently over about a dozen years with a recording machine, mainly in east Texas. "Collector's Notes" and headnotes give information, much of it autobiographical, about the background in which the collector worked, himself one of the folk in east Texas. Many of the songs he knew from early childhood. He attended East Texas State Teachers College, later Southern Methodist University, and finally the University of Iowa. Owens makes several divisions of his songs—British and American Ballads, Sad and Comic Songs, Children's Songs, and War Songs. Both his texts and tunes show variation from collections made, for instance, by the Lomaxes and, of course, variations from other collections made in other parts of the country. This collection is made interesting and somewhat different from many others because of the personal, less objective, approach to the materials.

TRADITIONAL BALLADS OF VIRGINIA. *Collected under the Auspices of the Virginia Folk-Lore Society. Edited by Arthur Kyle*

Davis, Jr. Cambridge: Harvard University Press. 1929. xviii, 634 pp.
with nine pages of illustrations and a [folding] map of Virginia.

Davis brings together here 51 traditional ballads (i.e., Child ballads) in a great number of variants. Each variant has a scholarly headnote, and the variants are exceedingly numerous. In fact, counting them all, there are some 650 items, though only 440 are printed in this volume. Some ballads have many variants, such as "The Three Ravens" (20), "Lady Isabel and the Elf-Knight" (28), "Lord Thomas and Fair Annet" (36), "Fair Margaret and Sweet William" (29), "Lord Lovell" (37), "The Lass of Roch Royal" (52), and, largest number of all, "Bonny Barbara Allen" (92). In each case the collector and the singer of each variant is given in the headnotes, as well as the time and place of collection. The latter part of the book includes 148 tunes.

There is a long introduction (56 pages) in which Davis gives definitions and a good deal about balladry in America, and in particular a very illuminating history of the ballad movement in Virginia.

The Virginia Folk-Lore Society was founded in 1913 by Professor C. Alphonso Smith, who was its first president and later the permanent archivist.

This is one of the best edited of the state collections of ballad literature. More recent editors might deplore separation of the ballad tunes from the words, but this is really a minor defect in a brilliant and scholarly edition.

TRADITIONAL MUSIC OF AMERICA. *By Ira W. Ford. New York: E. P. Dutton and Co., Inc. 1940. 480 pp.*

This anthology of traditional American music (melodies without accompaniment) is a collection of many kinds: the first major portion (more than a third of the book) includes over 300 fiddle tunes, especially for square and round dances; the "squares" including quadrilles, clogs, reels, jigs, hornpipes, etc., and the "rounds" including waltzes, schottisches, galops, polkas, mazurkas, etc. A second part presents many traditional dance calls. A third part presents old-time play-party songs and dancing games. Still another portion, containing over 150 songs, presents ballads and songs of entertainment. This is a very useful book of old-time music, dancing, and song.

TRADITIONAL TUNES OF THE CHILD BALLADS, THE. *With Their Texts, according to the Extant Records of Great Britain and America. By Bertrand Harris Bronson. Volume I, Ballads 1 to 53.*

Princeton, New Jersey: Princeton University Press. 1959. xxxvii, 465 pp.
This handsome quarto is obviously the beginning of a significant and definitive work by a distinguished scholar. A brochure about the book states: "Here is the musical counterpart to the famous Francis James Child collection of English and Scottish ballads from the 13th to 19th centuries. Professor Child's canon established the texts; Professor Bronson's present work provides both tunes and texts, systematically ordered and grouped in accordance with the intrinsic character of the tunes themselves."

In this first monumental volume (others are to follow), Professor Bronson has brought together from manuscripts, printed sources, and phonographic records most of the folk tunes (approximately a thousand) of these 53 ballads (of the 305 in the Child canon). The book is printed in two columns, the tunes and their sources preceding the ballad stanzas.

A scholarly introduction discusses the primary importance of the tunes, the Child canon, the aims and editorial procedure of the work. Each ballad is preceded by its special introduction and a listing of the variants. Then all variants, both words and tunes, are presented. To get an idea of the immensity of Dr. Bronson's task, and his accomplishment, the reader notes that "Lady Isabel and the Elf-Knight" (Child No. 4) has 141 variants that, all told, occupy sixty-two pages of double-column print. Obviously, here is one of the great studies in ballad literature of the present century.*

Reviews in superlative terms come from sources as diverse in purpose and method as the sedate and scholarly (London) *Times Literary Supplement* (July 10, 1959) and the popular magazine of folk music, *Caravan* (June-July, 1959).

. TREASURY OF JEWISH FOLKSONG, A. *Selected and Edited by Ruth Rubin. Piano settings by Ruth Post. Drawings by T. Herzl Rome. New York: Schocken Books, Inc. 1950. 224 pp.*
Here is a varied collection of 110 songs, coming apparently from all over Europe and western Asia, presented in the main in Yiddish dialect, with English translations. The translations, says the editor, are "free renditions from the Yiddish or the Hebrew" and are not meant to be sung. (The English words do not fit the musical notation.) Many kinds of songs are here included: cradle songs, children's songs, love songs; holiday, partisan, and work songs; and new songs from the new Israel. These songs, of course, are not yet American;

* When Professor Bronson's work is completed, my discussion of it will be placed, obviously, in Chapter 11, among collectors of the very first order.

that is, they are not in the American idiom. Yet, to quote the editor, "The mass migration to America of the Jews of Eastern Europe, in the eighties and nineties of the last century, brought the Yiddish folk song to the New World; and that song became the basis for the new tunes created on American soil." (p. 12) In other words, these songs are entering the broad stream of American folksong.

VIKING BOOK OF FOLK BALLADS OF THE ENGLISH-SPEAKING WORLD, THE. *Edited by Albert B. Friedman. New York: The Viking Press. 1956. xxxv, 473 pp.*

This anthology of folk ballads, with its illuminating 27-page introduction, its clear and concise headnotes, and its excellent variety of ballads, is obviously designed as a practical classroom text. And a good one it is. Here are 144 ballads arranged in fifteen subject-matter groups, from Supernatural to Humor and including such categories as Romantic Tragedies, Tabloid Crime, Ballads of the Scottish Border, Accidents and Disasters, Cowboy and Frontier Ballads, and others.

Besides the 144 ballads, the editor offers a good many variants and fragments, so that the total number actually reaches 208. Friedman's groupings show that subject types persist from early times on down; for example, in his largest group (XII), designated Outlaws, Pirates, Badmen, and Heroes, he begins with Robin Hood and concludes with John Hardy and Dupree. In addition to some 30 tunes throughout the text, Friedman includes a brief bibliography (not annotated), a discography (of accessible LP records), and an index to titles and first lines. This no doubt will prove to be a popular text.

CHAPTER 13

Compilations
Designed for
Singing

ALAN MILLS BOOK OF FOLK SONGS AND BALLADS, THE.
*Musical Arrangements by Arthur Morrow. Illustrations by Ted
Graham. Montreal: Whitcombe & Gilmour Limited. 1949. 93 pp.*
     This small quarto of 55 songs, drawn from Mills' weekly broad-
casts over C.B.C., is designed for ready use at the piano or with
guitar. The black-and-white illustrations are created, and the songs
mainly chosen, for children, though the young of all ages may enjoy
them. These are traditional songs from the Scotch, Irish, English,
Canadian (French and English), and American. A good representative collection, this book is another one in the growing list of the
singer's choice.

AMERICA SINGS. *Stories and Songs of Our Country's Growing.
Collected and Told by Carl Carmer. New York: Alfred A. Knopf.
1942. 243 pp.*
     This is a four-part book of East, Midwest, South, and Far West,
a collection of twenty-nine stories, together with a folksong for each
story, done in simple language and musical setting for boys and girls.
Easy musical arrangements have been done by Edwin John String-
ham, and dozens of color illustrations by Elizabeth Black Carmer.
Here are "Stormalong," "Old Dan Tucker," "The Boatman Dance,"
"Old Smokie," "The Boll Weevil," "John Henry," "Good-By Old
Paint," and others. A delightful and fascinating book for juveniles.

AMERICAN ANTHOLOGY OF OLD-WORLD BALLADS. *Compiled and Edited by Reed Smith. Settings by Hilton Rufty. New York: J. Fischer & Bro. 1937. xxxii, 72 pp.*

Here is a quarto volume of 25 Child ballads with piano settings of the ballad airs. From over 800 of the known ballad airs, Reed Smith has chosen these 25 as "the most attractive that have been recovered and recorded in America." A lengthy, scholarly introduction (12 columns) entitled "The Ballad Field" discusses such matters as age and number, ballads as songs, the tunes, singing the ballads, and the general importance of music in ballad study. Rufty contributes a Musical Introduction, and there are detailed notes, both interesting and scholarly, on the history of each of the 25 ballads. A selected bibliography includes some brief annotations which indicate the number of "traditional ballad airs" in each work. This book, designed for practical use at the piano, is surely one of the very choice volumes for the singer.

AMERICAN FOLK MUSIC FOR HIGH SCHOOL AND OTHER CHORAL GROUPS. *Collected and Edited by George Pullen Jackson. Arranged by Charles Faulkner Bryan. Boston: C. C. Birchard and Company. 1947. 80 [unnumbered] pp.*

The title clarifies the purpose of this group of 25 songs, some, but not all, with harmonization and simple accompaniment.

AMERICAN FOLK SONGS FOR CHILDREN. *Traditional American Songs. By Ruth Crawford Seeger. Illustrated by Barbara Cooney. Garden City, New York: Doubleday & Company, Inc. 1950. 80 pp.*

Here are 43 folksongs chosen especially for small children, placed in a simple musical setting for easy singing, and decorated with pictures to delight anyone young in heart. The dozens of gay and whimsical black-and-white illustrations by Barbara Cooney add humor and brightness to the bright and humorous songs. Surely this is a choice book for any family with growing youngsters.

AMERICAN FOLK SONGS FOR CHILDREN IN HOME, SCHOOL AND NURSERY SCHOOL. *A Book for Children, Parents and Teachers. By Ruth Crawford Seeger. Illustrated by Barbara Cooney. Garden City, New York: Doubleday and Company, Inc. 1948. 190 pp.*

Here is an interesting, usable book of about 100 genuine folksongs for home and school use, prepared by a distinguished musician, teacher, and mother of four. The songs are set in simple piano arrangements, and they all come from standard collections or recordings. One very interesting feature of the book is the series of helpful introductory essays (48 pages) telling how the book grew, what value there is in using folksongs in home and school, and suggesting how the songs may be sung and enjoyed. There is an eightfold grouping that would particularly appeal to children, such as Action Songs, Outdoor Activities, Singing Games, Home Activities, and the like. The pages are brightened with Barbara Cooney's gay and whimsical drawings. Both content and make-up of the volume amply justify the title-page description.

AMERICAN FOLK SONGS FOR CHRISTMAS. *By Ruth Crawford Seeger. Illustrated by Barbara Cooney. Garden City, New York: Doubleday & Company, Inc. 1953. 80 pp.*

A companion book (the same in size and format) to the editor's *American Folk Songs for Children* (1950), this collection contains "fifty-five songs and one fiddle tune." Again, as in the earlier volume, the dozens of drawings give a charm to the book which only the singing of the songs can equal.

AMERICAN MOUNTAIN SONGS. *Compiled by Ethel Park Richardson. Edited and Arranged by Sigmund Spaeth. New York: Greenberg, Publisher, Inc. 1927. 120 pp.*

These 61 songs are arranged for singing to simple piano accompaniment. The compiler has grouped them as follows: Ballads—Americanized and American, Lonesome and Love Tunes, Spirituals, and Nonsense Songs. These mountain songs, writes Spaeth, "deal with the universal realities, which are fundamentally the same, whether in the environment of the cities or the wild places of nature." Mrs. Richardson, a native of the mountain region, gathered the songs in the mountain districts of Tennessee, the Carolinas, North Georgia, Kentucky, Virginia, and Missouri. Her 10-page introduction is a good explanation and defense of the speech and way of life of the hill people. Her reason for the collection is a desire to preserve the fine old songs in the face of a growing industrialism. Since much collecting has been done in the past quarter century, singers will recognize many of the fine old songs, such as "Careless Love," "Soldier, Won't You Marry Me," "Frankie Baker" (variant of "Frankie and Johnnie"), "Shortenin' Bread," "Sourwood Mountain," and others. At the end of the volume, 15 pages of notes add useful bits of information on the songs.

In the spring of 1956, Mrs. Richardson, seventy-two, won $100,000 on the TV show, "The Big Surprise," for her knowledge of folk music, and the publisher brought out a new printing (not a new edition) of *American Mountain Songs*.

AMERICAN NEGRO SONGS. *A Comprehensive Collection of 230 Folk Songs, Religious and Secular, with a Foreword by John W. Work. New York: Howell, Soskin & Co. 1940. x, 259 pp.*

This excellent collection includes discussion on (a) Origins, (b) The Spiritual, (c) The Blues, (d) Work Songs, and (e) Social and Miscellaneous. The editor takes note of the controversy over the origin of Negro songs, especially spirituals. He recognizes influences from white sources, but considers the songs more than imitative, pointing out certain features, such as the "call and response" chant, as peculiarly African in origin. The songs, most of which are religious (about 200), have a four-part vocal arrangement without instrumental accompaniment. Here are included many of the songs used by the Jubilee Singers, from 1871 down to the present day. The editor notes that the spirituals were called Jubilee songs until rather recently. He points out (p. 28) that the spirituals are choral and communal, the blues are solo and individual—"the one intensely religious," the other "intensely worldly." Some universal favorites such as "Go Down Moses," "I Couldn't Hear Nobody Pray," "Little David," "Roll Jordan Roll," "Steal Away to Jesus," "Swing Low," "Going to Shout All Over God's Heav'n"—all these and many more are included. An adequate bibliography and an index of song titles make this a useful collection.

AMERICAN SONGBAG, THE. *By Carl Sandburg. New York: Harcourt, Brace and Company. 1927. xxiii, 495 pp.*

Sandburg calls this collection a "ragbag of strips, stripes, and streaks of color from nearly all ends of the earth." (Introduction) The collection contains "280 songs, ballads, ditties, brought together from all regions of America"—from pioneers, workers, hoboes, river gangs, Mexicans, sailors, lumberjacks, and from singers of spirituals. Sandburg says that about 100 of the 280 have not before been published—"they have been gathered by the compiler and his friends from coast to coast and from the Gulf to Canada." Further characterizing the composite nature of the work, Sandburg points out that "pioneers, pick and shovel men, teamsters, mountaineers, and people often called ignorant have their hands and voices in this book, along with minstrels, sophisticates, and trained musicians." The subject matter, as one may see at a glance, concerns the "rich and poor; robbers, murderers, hangmen; fathers and wild boys; mothers with soft words for their babies; workmen on railroads, steamboats, ships;

wanderers and lovers of homes." The songs, all of which include the musical scores and harmonizations, are grouped into twenty-four not-too-logical divisions, with such group titles as Dramas and Portraits, Pioneer Memories, Prison and Jail Songs, Southern Mountains, Railroad and Work Gangs, and so on.

One of the most interesting features of the whole work, after the songs themselves, of course, is Sandburg's series of explanatory headnotes appearing with each song. These are sometimes amusing commentary, sometimes important history—always in the vivid, racy style of the compiler. The book contains occasional illustrations, frequently amusing, which Sandburg says come "chiefly from songsters and broadsides of 1840 and 1850."

AMERICAN-ENGLISH FOLK-SONGS. *Collected in the Southern Appalachians and Arranged with Pianoforte Accompaniment. By Cecil J. Sharp. New York: G. Schirmer, Inc. (and G. P. Putnam's Sons). 1918. vii, 57 pp.*

A collection of 12 songs, designed for singing, with brief notes indicating minor changes in wording. The tunes are unchanged, says Sharp, and "are presented precisely as they were noted down, without any alteration whatsoever." These songs are drawn from the first edition (1917) of Sharp's famous collection in the southern Appalachians.

AMERICANS AND THEIR SONGS. *By Frank Luther. New York: Harper and Brothers Publishers. 1942. xiv, 323 pp.*

This collection of 117 songs, most of them with piano accompaniment, attempts a sort of three-hundred-year "history of America set to music." Luther begins with songs sung by the Pilgrims and moves on down through three centuries and twenty-eight chapters, weaving a story, or informal history, of America along with the songs. Many of them are traditional folksongs, but Luther makes no separation of traditional and popular works: his purpose is rather to portray the social history, no matter what the song. One finds many old favorites of the genuine folksongs in the collection, from "Barbara Allen" to "The Old Chisholm Trail." Perhaps a third of the songs would fall under the classification of true folksong. In any case, the book is good reading and good singing.

ANIMAL FOLK SONGS FOR CHILDREN. *Traditional American Songs. By Ruth Crawford Seeger. Illustrated by Barbara Cooney. Garden City, New York: Doubleday & Company, Inc. 1950. 80 pp.*

Most of the 43 songs in this book come from traditional singing (taken from the Archive of American Folk Song in the Library of Congress), and the others are reprinted from folklore books. The author's introduction tells how they were chosen (from many hundreds, of course) and suggests ways of singing and enjoying them. These suggestions grow out of the experience of the Seeger family, where four children were growing up.

There are four groups of the songs, as follows: I. Woods and Field (e.g., "Mister Rabbit," "Peter Squirrel," and "Old Ground Hog"); II. Dogs and Hunting (e.g., "Oh, Blue," "The Deer Song," and "Old Fox"); III. Farm and Ranch—20 songs here—(e.g., "The Gray Goose," "Little Pig," "The Old Cow Died," and "The Kicking Mule"); IV. And Others (e.g., "Crocodile Song," "Daddy Shot a Bear," "Wolves A-Howling"). The tunes are set in easy piano accompaniments (guitar or banjo may be used) and, as in other books in this series, the numerous black-and-white drawings (about 75) of Barbara Cooney are intensely human and humorous and a constant delight to the eye. Following the table of contents, there is an alphabetical list of song titles.

BEFO' DE WAR SPIRITUALS. *Words and Melodies collected by E. A. McIlhenny. Boston: The Christopher Publishing House. 1933. 255 pp.*

This collection of 120 songs was made by the editor from his own memories and from Negroes who lived and grew up on the family sugar plantation in southern Louisiana. A long introduction (23 pages) gives details of the life and singing of the Negroes on Avery Island. The music is four-part harmony. McIlhenny deplores the later changes in the spirituals, though he points out that they were almost never sung twice in the same manner. All in all, this is an interesting and useful collection.

BLUES, AN ANTHOLOGY. *Edited by W. C. Handy. With an Introduction by Abbe Niles. Illustrations by Miguel Covarrubias. New York: Albert & Charles Boni. 1926. 180 pp.*

Here are 50 of the more famous blues songs, both instrumental and vocal, from "Careless Love" (Arr. W. C. Handy) to Gershwin's "Rhapsody in Blue." Forty pages of introduction and notes by Niles and eight full-page drawings by Covarrubias add clarification to this particular type of music, always close to folksong. (See annotations on the 1949 edition later in this chapter.)

BOOK OF AMERICAN NEGRO SPIRITUALS, THE. *Edited with an Introduction by James Weldon Johnson. Musical arrangements by*

J. Rosamond Johnson. Additional numbers by Lawrence Brown. New York: Viking Press. 1925. 187 pp.

This fine collection of 61 spirituals, all with piano settings, is the first of several works by the distinguished Johnson brothers. A long introduction or preface (some 40 pages) discusses backgrounds and origins. The controversial question of origin is discussed at length, with J. W. Johnson's belief very positively set forth: "The Spirituals are purely and solely the creation of the American Negro; that is, as much so as any music can be the pure and sole creation of any particular group." (p. 17) The later findings of George Pullen Jackson (*q.v.*) do not accord with this theory; however, regardless of origin, authorship, or backgrounds, we have here some of the finest spirituals in a wholly sympathetic musical setting: "Swing Low, Sweet Chariot," "Somebody's Knockin' at Yo' Do'," "Deep River," "I'm Troubled in My Mind," "Nobody Knows de Trouble I See"— to name a few perennial favorites.

BURL IVES IRISH SONGS. *Edited with New Piano Accompaniments by Michael Bowles. New York: Duell, Sloan and Pearce. 1958. x, 126 pp.*

The result of visits to Ireland in 1952 and 1953, this quarto volume of 50 songs reflects another facet of the versatile and musical Burl Ives, whose background is heavily Irish. As Ives wisely says in "A Personal Note," "Fifty songs can barely skim the wealth of Irish songs," but here are enough to give the American public an excellent sampling "in simple modern form with adequate accompaniment." The two categories present, in Part I, thirty songs of "Love, Laughter, and Daily Events" and, in Part II, twenty songs of "Wit, Courage, and a Fighting Nation." Each song is followed by a brief paragraph of background information, or folklore and legend, just enough to give the singer or listener a useful bit of orientation. The book is beautifully printed and rests comfortably open at the piano. A short, favorable review by Walter Raim appeared (Winter 1959) in the folksong magazine, *Sing Out!*

BURL IVES SONG BOOK, THE. *American Song in Historical Perspective. Song Versions by Burl Ives. Text by Burl Ives. Arranged for the Piano by Albert Hague. Illustrations by Lamartine Le Goullon and Robert J. Lee. New York: Ballantine Books. 1953. xiv, 304 pp.*

This personal collection of 129 songs represents a historical development in song, from Colonial times on down. Most of them are folksongs, of course, but Ives wisely does not use the term in his title. Though Ives does not claim to be an "authority on folk songs in the academic sense," he is nonetheless well informed and, as everybody knows, a master showman in folksinging and one with a seemingly endless repertoire.

The songs are grouped into five chapters, as follows: Colonial America, 1620-1775; Revolutionary America, 1775-1790; The Growing Country: On the Sea, 1790-1850; Religious, Professional, and Folk Singing, 1800-1850; The Frontiers of America, 1800-1850. Ives writes a brief and very readable introduction for each chapter, and there are brief notes on some of the songs. Otherwise there are no footnotes, variants, cross references, or other scholarly trappings. The latter pages contain a title index, an index of first lines, a very useful listing of Burl Ives recordings (for Decca, Columbia, and the Encyclopaedia Britannica), a key to the guitar chords, and a biographical sketch of Ives. The book is a beautifully printed quarto and rests easily on the piano. There are many color illustrations, some full page, in this excellent volume, which surely will make a popular appeal.

CANADIAN FOLK SONGS (Old and New). *Selected and Translated by J. Murray Gibbon. Harmonizations by Geoffrey O'Hara and Oscar O'Brien. Decorations by Frank H. Johnston. New York: E. P. Dutton & Co. 1927. xxii, 105 pp.*

The purpose of this minor collection of 30 songs is to present bilingually a group of the better-known French-Canadian songs, apparently for group singing. The translator suggests that mixed groups of French and English might sing in the two languages at once! Two-thirds of the songs (both melody and words) are drawn from the famous *Chansons populaires du Canada* of Ernest Gagnon. Except for the harmonizations and translations, the book has little originality.

CANADIAN SONG BOOK, A. *Edited by Ernest Macmillan. London and Toronto: J. M. Dent & Sons, Ltd. 1929. xii, 180 pp. Published under the Auspices of the National Council of Education.*

Over half of the 109 songs in this work are folksongs or traditional melodies. They come from many nations, though they are mainly British, American, Canadian and French. "The present book is designed," the editor says, "to serve the Canadian home, club, school and college." The songs are given piano settings, the book is well printed and easy to read, and sources and notes are given for many of the songs.

CARL SANDBURG'S NEW AMERICAN SONGBAG. *New York: Broadcast Music, Inc. 1950. 107 pp.*

A collection of 59 songs taken in part (40 per cent, Sandburg says) from *The American Songbag*, in part from other collections, and in part directly from singers. This small book is an extension of *The American Songbag*, which appeared in 1927. Many kinds of songs—religious, "period pieces," mountain, Negro, Western, comic—are grouped in nine typical, colorful Sandburg sections. There are interesting headnotes and other colorful comments, for Sandburg is no pedestrian editor: his original genius permeates even the slightest discussion. The book is illustrated with drawings and old prints.

CENTURY OF PROGRESS IN AMERICAN SONG, A. *By Marx and Anne Oberndorfer. Honorary editor: Dr. Frederick A. Stock. Associate editors: Arthur Olaf Anderson, Noble Cain, Dr. J. Lewis Browne, and others. Chicago: Hall & McCreary Company. 1933. 160 pp.*

The 190 songs in this book, most of them arranged for four-part singing, are in the main folksongs, drawn from many lands. The book was prepared for the 1933 world's fair in Chicago and is representative of many types in our nation's song: Indian, Negro, pioneer, patriotic, sailor, mountaineer, sentimental, college, religious songs, and others—all are here. An essay entitled "America's Heritage of Song" precedes the songs. Names of poets and composers, when these are known, are given with the songs. There are no footnotes, headnotes, or other scholarly paraphernalia in this collection, obviously designed for popular use.

FIRESIDE BOOK OF FOLK SONGS. *Selected and edited by Margaret Bradford Boni. Arranged for the piano by Norman Lloyd. Illustrated by Alice and Martin Provensen. New York: Simon and Schuster, Inc. 1947. 323 pp.*

In this delightful and colorful book designed and produced by the Sandpiper Press and Artists and Writers Guild, Incorporated, we have what will likely become more common as interest in ballad and folksong develops further: an attempt—and a fine accomplishment this one is—to make our folksong materials more appealing to a wider public. The makers of this book, all of them accomplished and practicing artists, have brought together 147 folksongs, from many nationalities, but practically all of them well known in America. The songs are grouped under five major heads, as follows: Ballads and Old Favorites (56); Work Songs, English and American (23); Marching Songs and Songs of Valor (22); Christmas Carols

(20); Old Hymns and Spirituals (26). Brief discussion precedes each major section, then follow the songs with their excellent piano settings. If one is a bit surprised to find in a folksong collection such numbers as "The Star-Spangled Banner," the Russian "Meadow-lands," "God Save the King," "La Marseillaise," and such old-timers in religion as "My Faith Looks Up to Thee," "Stand Up, Stand Up, for Jesus," and "Rock of Ages"—the answer is that they have truly become songs of the people, though they can scarcely be said to follow the oral tradition of the true folksong. Scarcely a page of this book escapes the lively and humorous brushes of the Provensens, who have helped the editor and arranger make the songs come alive in literally hundreds of gay pictures, emphasizing many phases of the infinite variety of folksong. The end papers, even, contribute to the gaiety of scene and color. There are useful indexes of first lines and titles. This is a must book for any fireside or, for that matter, any lover of good singing.

FOLK BLUES.* *Compiled, Edited and Arranged for Voice, Piano and Guitar. By Jerry Silverman. New York: The Macmillan Company. 1958. 308 pp.*
Called a "superb collection" of 110 American folk blues, many appearing in print for the first time, this work stems from Mr. Silverman's graduate studies at New York University. There are biographical sketches of famous practitioners of the blues songs, such as Blind Lemon Jefferson, Leadbelly, Josh White, and others. Besides "musicological consideration of the art form," the book contains a full bibliography and discography. Indexed.

FOLK HYMNS OF AMERICA. *Collected and Arranged by Annabel Morris Buchanan. New York: J. Fischer & Bro. 1938. xl, 94 pp.*
Except for one instance, these 50 hymns are arranged for four-part *a cappella* singing. An introduction gives a good brief history of the hymns, and tells also of the shape-note hymn books. Many of the hymns were traditional in the editor's family background. The hymns are grouped as follows: general, camp meeting, secular songs in sacred form, and traditional carols. The editor gives a tabulated classification of the 50 hymns, showing source, composer (if known), tonic, mode (Aeolian, Ionian, or Dorian). Full discussion (some 22 pages of notes) is presented preceding the hymns; there is also an excellent bibliography of some 150 items. This is an excellent collection for study and for enjoyable singing.

* I have not seen a copy of Mr. Silverman's book. (R. M. L.)

FOLK SONGS FROM NEWFOUNDLAND. *Collected and Edited by Maud Karpeles. With Pianoforte Accompaniments by R. Vaughan Williams, Clive Carey, Hubert J. Foss, and Michael Mullinar. Volumes I and II. London: Oxford University Press. 1934. v, 144 pp.*

These two quarto volumes, designed for use at the piano, contain 15 ballads and 16 songs set to music by the above composers (15 by Vaughan Williams, 7 by Carey, 4 by Foss, and 5 by Mullinar). The arrangements on the whole are simple, in keeping with the materials. There is a brief introduction (repeated in Volume II) and, at the end, some explanatory notes.

Maud Karpeles, who had accompanied Cecil Sharp in his collecting in the Appalachians, had hoped to accompany him to Newfoundland, but Sharp died in 1924. Miss Karpeles made two trips of six weeks each (in 1929 and 1930) to Newfoundland, collecting some 200 songs, including variants, from which the present texts are printed. Most were collected from fishermen and their families—people of British descent from Ireland and west England. The notes give names and addresses of singers, also other printings of the ballads, for many of the old ones are here, such as "Earl Brand," "Gypsy Laddie," "Sweet William," "Hind Horn," "The Cuckoo," and others.

FOLK SONGS OF CANADA. *Edith Fulton Fowke, Literary Editor. Richard Johnston, Music Editor. Illustrations by Elizabeth Wilkes Hoey. Waterloo, Ontario: Waterloo Music Company Limited. 1954. 198 pp.*

This excellent collection of 77 songs, designed to reach a large audience, may well become one of the most popular books of Canadian folksongs yet published. For the songs range from the eastern reaches of Newfoundland to the western provinces, the musical (piano) settings are very simple, and the editorial paraphernalia are neither intrusive nor voluminous. The collection is not a large one (at least three Canadian regional collections each has more than twice as many songs), but it is representative of the many phases and vast stretches of Canadian life, as indicated by the tenfold grouping: Out of the Past, Men of the Sea, Up the River, In the Woods, Out West, Let Joy Be Unconfined, The Christmas Story, Songs of Love, Of Men and Maids, and A Little Laughter.

The editors are themselves not collectors but enthusiastic compilers who have drawn freely on the scholarly collections of Marius Barbeau done for the National Museum of Canada, and the works of Helen Creighton, Elizabeth Greenleaf, W. Roy Mackenzie, and others. A brief introduction by Mrs. Fowke (who incidentally has one of the largest folksong record collections in Canada) gives an excellent account of the main sources of Canadian folksongs and some details on the collectors: numerous songs came from the pioneer settlers of New France, others from the sea folk of Newfoundland, English-Canadian songs from the Nova Scotians, and other sources are suggested.

This is avowedly a popular collection designed chiefly for group singing, and the editors frankly admit to "a certain amount of adapting and editing." Scholars may frown on this practice, but the singing layman will not. Mrs. Fowke gives English translations (where needed) along with the French songs and also contributes explanatory notes on each song. The book has helpful "Notes on the Music" by Dr. Johnston, a composer, conductor, and professor of music at the University of Toronto. A brief bibliography, some information on Canadian folksongs on records, an index of titles and first lines, and Mrs. Hoey's lively black-and-white drawings round out the materials in this readable and singable work of representative Canadian folksongs.*

FOLK SONGS OF MANY NATIONS. *Collected and Edited with Preface and Annotations. By Louis C. Elson. Philadelphia: The John Church Company. 1905. 171 pp.*

Here are 87 songs from 19 countries—9 from America; 31 from England, Ireland, and Scotland; 9 from Germany; and the others from here and there. Each song has a simple piano setting. Elson says his purpose is to set these songs "in contrast with each other." In an introductory essay, The Influence of Folk-Song upon Classical Music, he states further: "Mr. G. W. Chadwick has effectively developed some distinctly American themes in two of his symphonies, being the first eminent composer to elevate our folk-song into the symphonic domain."

FOLK SONGS OF OLD VINCENNES. *French Texts collected by Anna C. O'Flynn and Joseph Médard Carrière, English Versions by Frederic Burget and Libushka Bartusek, Introduction and Notes by Joseph Médard Carrière, Melodies Collected and Harmonized by Cecilia Ray Berry. Chicago: H. T. Fitz-Simons Company. 1946. 95 pp.*

These 38 songs, prepared for voice and piano, in both French and English, are relics of an early French civilization in the Middle

---

* In 1957, Mrs. Fowke and Dr. Johnston published *Folk Songs of Quebec,* an anthology of French-Canadian songs.

West. "The purpose of publishing these songs," writes Burget in the preface, "is to perpetuate in some manner the folk lore of the oldest French territory now part of our country." Explanatory notes are given along with each of the songs in this carefully edited, scholarly collection.

Carrière gives a brief history of the town of Vincennes. The French were dominant as late as 1855, but by 1900 they were a small minority, and by 1930 they had practically disappeared.

Most of the songs can be traced to French-Canadian sources though some may have come upriver from New Orleans. Many of them came from one French woman folksinger in her seventies, Joséphine Thériac-Caney. The collection shows the usual variety of "love and work songs, carols, lullabies, play-party songs, complaintes, pastourelles, religious ditties, and humorous verse." This is an important though small collection.

FOLK-SONGS OF THE FOUR SEASONS. *Thirty-Three Traditional Melodies Associated with Festivals and Folkways. The Text and Translations by Susanna Myers. The Harmonization by Harvey Officer. New York: G. Schirmer, Inc. 1929. 79 pp.*

In this large quarto the songs, drawn from twenty-two national groups around the world, are grouped under the four seasons, the largest number (13) belonging to winter. Some two dozen background stories, from authentic folklore (though sources are not named), precede the various songs. The piano settings are very simple. This is a useful and carefully prepared text for home and school singing.

FOLK-SONGS OF THE KENTUCKY MOUNTAINS. *Twenty Traditional Ballads and Other English Folk-Songs. Notated from the singing of the Kentucky Mountain People and arranged with piano accompaniment. By Josephine McGill. Introductory note by H. E. Krehbiel. New York: Boosey & Co. 1917. 106 pp.*

The descriptive title page gives the main details of this excellent small collection. Miss McGill's collecting, done in the autumn of 1914 in two Kentucky counties, preceded the work of Cecil J. Sharp. Her informants were a dozen mountain singers, including several of the Ritchie family and children at the Hindman Settlement School. Thirteen of the 20 songs are numbered Child ballads. Though most of these songs were not generally known when Miss McGill made her collection, such songs as "Barbara Allen," "The Cherry Tree," "The Gypsie Laddie," and others have now reached a high degree of popularity.

Krehbiel points out the growing interest in both the collecting and singing of folksongs, and suggests that a reawakening of general interest seems evident. The piano accompaniments are easy and satisfactory. There is no discussion of the songs or of the collecting methods.

FOLK-SONGS OF THE WEST AND SOUTH. *Negro, Cowboy, and Spanish-Californian. Harmonized by Arthur Farwell. New Center, Massachusetts: The Wa-Wan Press. 1905.*

This Volume IV, Number 27 of the "Wa-Wan Series of American Compositions," contains 6 songs in elaborate piano settings: 2 Negro spirituals ("De Rocks A-Renderin'" and "Moanin' Dove"), 1 cowboy song ("The Lone Prairee"), and 3 Spanish-American folksongs ("The Black Face," "The Hours of Grief," and "Bird Dance Song"). Words are given in both Spanish and English for two of the songs.

GARLAND OF MOUNTAIN SONG, A. *Songs from the Repertoire of the Ritchie Family of Viper, Kentucky. Edited with Notes by Jean Ritchie. With Piano Accompaniment by Hally Wood Gordon. Drawings by Alberta Sordoni. Foreword by Alan Lomax. Produced under the Supervision of Milton Rettenberg. New York: Broadcast Music, Inc. 1953. 69 pp.*

This excellent thin volume, in large quarto (9" x 12"), is a musical prelude to Jean Ritchie's family history, *Singing Family of the Cumberlands,* published in 1955. The 24 songs are given a handsome setting, with delightful drawings in black on backgrounds of yellow, green, or brick red. Jean provides a running commentary of personal history for each of the songs. The book concludes with an excellent full-page photograph of Carl Sandburg and Jean Ritchie singing folksongs. This is certainly one of the most delightful of the small personal collections.

HISPANIC FOLK SONGS OF NEW MEXICO. *With Selected Songs Collected, Transcribed, and Arranged for Voice and Piano. By John Donald Robb. University of New Mexico Publications in the Fine Arts, Number One. Albuquerque: The University of New Mexico Press. 1954. viii, 83 pp.*

This excellently printed large paperback quarto contains 15 songs in Spanish, with English translations. Current in New Mexico but not necessarily originating there, they come from Dean Robb's large collection of about 1,300 songs recorded (by disc, wire, and tape) in New Mexico. A fourth of the booklet is given over to discussion of the Hispanic songs in New Mexico and of these 15 songs in particular. Obviously more publication is likely to come out of this New Mexican–Spanish treasure, found and recorded by John D. Robb, dean of fine arts at the university.

LIFT EVERY VOICE! *The Second People's Song Book. Edited by Irwin Silber. With an Introduction by Paul Robeson. Illustrated by Jim Lee. New York: People's Artists Inc. 1953. 96 pp.*

This group of 76 songs, most of them folksongs, drawn from many countries, is dedicated to the cause of peace. "Here are union songs, love songs, lullabies and play songs, songs of historic struggles for democracy and freedom ... songs ... from plain people the world around." There are five groups, with these descriptive titles: "Study War No More" (Songs of Peace); "Commonwealth of Toil" (Songs of Labor); "Wasn't That a Time" (Songs of Historic Struggles); "A Man's a Man for All That" (Songs of Real People); "One Great Vision Unites Us" (Songs of Freedom). The songs are well printed in piano settings, with guitar chords indicated. This is an international collection, small though it is, with songs from the French, Spanish, Yiddish, Hebrew, German, and others, but English translations are given for all of them.

LONESOME TUNES: FOLK SONGS FROM THE KENTUCKY MOUNTAINS. *The Words Collected and Edited by Loraine Wyman. The Pianoforte Accompaniment by Howard Brockway. New York: The H. W. Gray Company. 1916. [viii], 102 pp.*

Words, melodies, and piano accompaniments of 25 songs found in Kentucky are here presented "as nearly as possible as we heard them sung by the people." Fifteen native singers are mentioned (as sources) in the introductory comment, though specific credit is not given with each song. The collection begins with "Barbara Allen" and includes such favorites as "Billy Boy," "Frog Went A-Courting," "The Little Mohee," "Sourwood Mountain," etc.

L'ORDRE DE BON-TEMPS. *(The Order of Good Cheer) Ballad Opera based on French Canadian Folk Songs. Libretto by Louvigny de Montigny. English Translations by J. Murray Gibbon. Music Arranged by Healey Willan. Oakville, Ontario: The Frederick Harris Co. 1928. 36 pp.*

This "ballad opera" in piano setting, from materials collected by Marius Barbeau, consists of 12 songs with three Indian dances as a conclusion. The songs, given in both French and English, are arranged in a sort of climactic sequence, for three different soloists and choruses. There are no stage directions or indications for acting, nor is there much plot. The work is more like an operetta than an opera. The title page carries this explanation: "*L'Ordre de Bon-Temps*, the name of the society of good cheer founded by Champlain at Port Royal in 1606, tells the story of the life at the garrison during those bitter winters when the Order stood for the best in good living and Poutrincourt's table groaned beneath the luxuries of the winter forest: flesh of moose, caribou and deer, beaver, otter, hare; with ducks, geese, grouse and plover; sturgeon, too, and trout and other fish speared through the ice in the neighbouring bay. These repasts were always attended by ceremonial followed by song and the guests were frequently Indian chiefs."

MELLOWS. *A Chronicle of Unknown Singers. By R. Emmet Kennedy. Decorations by Simmons Persons. New York: Albert and Charles Boni, Inc. 1925. [viii], 183 pp.*

A brief foreword states that "mellow is the Negro word for melody, and by this term their devotional songs are called in southern Louisiana." A longish introduction (32 pages) gives some of the background of life in New Orleans and environs, where these 27 songs, mostly spirituals (besides over 20 fragments) in elaborate piano settings, were gathered by Kennedy. Each song is preceded by a brief account of the circumstances of its recording, with a narrative of the singer (or singers) who performed it, many of whom were intimate, long-time friends of the author. All the singers were Negroes or Creole Negroes. More than twenty-five "unknown" singers are named and presented in the brief accounts. This book is both entertaining and informative in its account of folk music on Louisiana plantations in post-bellum days about the turn of the century. It presents an excellent record by one who is native to the region, whose common people he knows intimately. Included among the songs are: "Dry Bones," "Poor Little Jesus," "Lonesome Valley," "I Got Two Wings," "Heaven," "Little David, Play on Your Harp."

MORE MELLOWS. *By R. Emmet Kennedy. New York: Dodd, Mead and Company. 1931 [xii], 178 pp.*

This continuation of the earlier work, *Mellows* (1925), is developed in much the same pattern and includes 12 "harmonized spirituals," 7 unharmonized, 2 harmonized folksongs, and 16 "ballets without the music." In addition, there is (as in *Mellows*) extensive introductory discussion on how the songs were collected, both from congregation singing and from individual singers. The ballet-making of several Negro folk-artists is given in some detail. More than half the book is given over to discussion.

NURSERY SONGS FROM THE APPALACHIAN MOUNTAINS. *Arranged with Pianoforte Accompaniment by Cecil J. Sharp. Illustrated in Silhouette by Esther B. Mackinnon. London: Novello and Company, Ltd.*

First Series, 1921. 36 [unnumbered] pp.

Second Series, 1923. 40 [unnumbered] pp.

These thin quartos are lively and gay in both song and picture. Surely they fulfill Sharp's idea of reviving folksong for everyday use. The two series contain 35 songs, that is, the poems with simple musical accompaniments. Here are many old favorites of the nursery, which many persons had perhaps not thought of as folksongs: "Early Sunday Morning," "Billy Boy," "The Frog and the Mouse," "The Old Grey Goose," etc.

OLD SONGS HYMNAL. *Words and Melodies from the State of Georgia. Collected by Dorothy G. Bolton. Music Arranged by Harry T. Burleigh. New York: The Century Company. 1929. Approx. 200 [unnumbered] pp.*

This is a collection of 187 Negro spirituals, taken down by the collector as they were sung in the churches throughout Georgia. The melodies are arranged for simple, four-part singing. The purpose is to preserve these fine old spirituals, which had been sung only from memory (both words and tunes are here presented anonymously), as the minister or "some older brother or sister" would "line" them for the congregation. The songs are grouped in eight divisions, not too sharply classified, as follows: Folk Songs in the Making; Narrative Songs; Songs of Admonition; Songs of Striving, Weariness and Aspiration; Songs of Conversion; Songs of Devil and Hell; Songs of Death; and Songs of Judgment, Resurrection and Reward. Here one finds many of the well-known favorites: "Didn't It Rain," "He Never Said a Mumbling Word," "I Couldn't Hear Nobody Pray," "Little David, Play on Your Harp," "Shoes," "Swing Low, Sweet Chariot," "The Gospel Train," etc. The book is offered "with the hope that in these songs the human heart will continue to find expression for its deepest emotions of joy, of sorrow, of inspiration and that exaltation of the soul which gave them the name—spirituals." The work has a brief foreword and alphabetical index, and it is, all in all, an excellent collection.

ONE HUNDRED FOLKSONGS OF ALL NATIONS. *Edited by Granville Bantock for Medium Voice. The Musicians Library. Boston: Oliver Ditson Company. 1911. xxxvii, 175 pp.*

This large quarto includes songs from about fifty nationalities

(1 to 11 from each nation), ranging in time and place from China to the American Indian. The songs are all in piano settings, and all the non-English ones are given in translation along with the original version. Brief notes for each song and an extensive bibliography occupy 30 pages in the front of the volume. Here is a practical book for use at the piano, though the United States songs ("Old Folks at Home," "Tenting on the Old Camp Ground," and "Dixie") are perhaps not too aptly chosen. Such an over-all collection, however, tends to illustrate the striking similarities of folksongs in all nations.

RAILROAD SONGS OF YESTERDAY. *By Sterling Sherwin and Harry K. McClintock. Foreword by William M. Jeffers. Illustrated. New York: Shapiro, Bernstein & Co., Inc. 1943. 48 pp.*

This paper-bound thin quarto of 20 old railroad songs, with piano and guitar accompaniments, and embellished with twenty-five photographs from the files of about a dozen railroads, will strike a nostalgic note in any person who has lived near a railroad; or who, from his youth up, has heard "Casey Jones," "I've Been Working on the Railroad," or " De Gospel Train." Most, though not all, numbers in the collection are traditional and are therefore properly classified as folksongs.

RELIGIOUS FOLK-SONGS OF THE NEGRO AS SUNG AT HAMPTON INSTITUTE. *Edited by R. Nathaniel Dett. Hampton, Virginia: Hampton Institute Press. 1927. xxvii, 236 pp.*

This book of 165 songs stems from a collection first brought together in 1874, used by the Hampton singers to raise money for the school. It was revised and added to from time to time, and its continued use, even to the present day, attests its great popularity. There are three prefaces from earlier editions and a foreword by Dett. In 1874, Thomas P. Fenner wrote in the first preface: "One reason for publishing this slave music is that it is rapidly passing away." He mentioned also that the words of the hymns were "common property throughout the South."

Dett in his foreword gives considerable discussion to the matter of origins: he contends that the music of these folksongs "is original to the Negro, in so far as any folk music is original"—a view sharply at variance with the findings (somewhat later than 1927) of George Pullen Jackson.

The songs are grouped in a sort of chronological life-sequence, under twenty-six headings, with such group titles as Hymns of Admonition, Consolation, Deliverance, Praise, Tribulation, etc. The musical arrangement is for four-part choral singing without instrumental accompaniment. The 1874 edition is only two years later than the earliest collection of Jubilee songs from Fisk University, also used to raise money for the school. There are full indexes of subjects, titles, and first lines.

RICHARD DYER-BENNET, THE 20TH CENTURY MINSTREL. A COLLECTION OF 20 SONGS AND BALLADS. *With Guitar and Piano Accompaniments. Piano Settings by John Ward. Radio City, New York: Leeds Music Corporation. 1946. 48 pp.*

Four of these are composed, both words and music, by Dyer-Bennet. The others are traditional. This is a good personal collection of one famous singer whose reputation is international.

ROLLING ALONG IN SONG. *A Chronological Survey of American Negro Music. With Eighty-Seven Arrangements of Negro Songs, including Ring Shouts, Spirituals, Work Songs, Plantation Ballads, Chain-Gang, Jail House and Minstrel Songs, Street Cries, and Blues. Edited and Arranged by J. Rosamond Johnson. New York: The Viking Press. 1937. 224 pp.*

This potpourri, not all folksongs, is well characterized by the descriptive title page. The editor has drawn a bit on Stephen Foster, Paul Laurence Dunbar, and Benjamin Hanby (author of "Darling Nelly Gray"). Above all this is a "singing" book. Perhaps the most unusual section is that called "De Chain Gang"—an Original Musical Episode Based on [Eight] Traditional Negro Idioms, a sort of choral medley. The editor's introduction is a hurried sketch of "random notes," to use his words, on the growth of Negro music in America.

ROUSTABOUT SONGS. *A Collection of Ohio River Valley Songs. Words and Melodies Collected by Mary Wheeler. Arranged by William J. Reddick. With an Introduction by Irwin S. Cobb. New York: Remick Music Corporation. 1939. 48 pp.*

This quarto collection of 10 songs, arranged for the piano, represents an original collecting and arranging task of songs taken down from the singing of Negro workmen on the wharves and on the river packets. The work is illustrated with seven pages of photographs—by James A. Wallen of Huntington, West Virginia—of many of the steamboats, some of the Negro singers, and various river scenes. Mary Wheeler continued her collecting from this romantic and bygone era in her more ambitious work, *Steamboatin' Days* (*q.v.*), published in 1944.

SAINT HELENA ISLAND SPIRITUALS. *Recorded and Transcribed at Penn Normal, Industrial and Agricultural School. By Nicholas George Julius Ballanta-(Taylor) of Freetown, Sierra Leone, West Africa. New York: G. Schirmer, Inc. 1925. xviii, 93 pp.*

A lengthy foreword by Mr. Ballanta explains many technicalities of the spirituals which he collected from this particular island area, just off the coast of South Carolina. His original collection was about 100 songs, and about a dozen are added from other sources. All are arranged for four-part singing. The spelling varies considerably from that in other collections of spirituals. Here are some characteristic titles: "At De Jedgment Bar," "Cyan' Hide Sinner Cyan' Hide," "Ebery Time I Feels de Spirit," "Give Me Jedus," "I Ain't Gwine Grief Muh Lawd No Mo'," "Roll, Jerdon Roll," "When I Git in Heben in Muh Elbow Chair."

SCHIRMER'S AMERICAN FOLK-SONG SERIES. *New York: G. Schirmer, Inc. [27 sets in the Series, Collected, Edited, and Arranged by various persons, as indicated below:]*

Set Number

1. FOLK-SONGS FROM THE KENTUCKY HIGHLANDS. *Collected by Josiah Combs, with Piano Accompaniments by Keith Mixson. 1939. 40 pp.*

    Here are 16 songs, 2 with variants, drawn from Josiah Combs' "private collection of several hundred songs." These come largely from Knott County, in what Combs calls the "pure feud belt." Some, like "Giles Collins" or "Slago Town," are American adaptations of British ballads; others, like "The Government Claim," are purely American. There are brief headnotes.

2. BAYOU BALLADS. *Twelve Folk-Songs from Louisiana. Texts and Music Collected by Mina Monroe. Edited with the Collaboration of Kurt Schindler. 1921. vii, 55 pp.*

    These are songs of the Negroes on the Labrauche Plantation of St. Charles Parish, a plantation once owned by the grandmother of the collector. The songs were sung in French Creole dialect, and Miss Monroe gives them also in English and standard French. Notes precede the songs, which are arranged in simple piano settings.

3. MOUNTAIN SONGS OF NORTH CAROLINA. *Collected by Susannah Wetmore and Marshall Bartholomew. Arranged with*

Set Number

Pianoforte Accompaniment by Marshall Bartholomew. 1926. iv, 43 pp.

These 14 songs were collected from 1917 to 1924 from "among the mountain people of western North Carolina." There is a brief background introduction, and there are notes for each song, giving the place and date of collecting, and the singer.

4, 5, 6, 7. NEGRO FOLK-SONGS. *Recorded by Natalie Curtis-Burlin. Hampton Series, in Four Books.*

Book I. 1918. 42 pp.
Book II. 1918. 44 pp.
Book III. 1918. 40 pp.
Book IV. 1919. 50 pp.

Each of these four books contains songs (19 in all) arranged for male quartet, and all were recorded at Hampton Institute. Each book has an extensive foreword (2 to 8 pages), and each song is preceded by an elaborate introduction. Half of the songs are spirituals, half are work and play songs.

8. SEVEN KENTUCKY MOUNTAIN SONGS. *As sung by Marion Kerby and John J. Niles. Collected and Arranged by John J. Niles. Cover Design by C. M. Sutherland. 1929. 13 pp.*

This is the first of several Niles books in the Schirmer series, and some of these songs come from his earliest collecting—around 1908. Among the 7 songs are "The Cherry Tree," "If I Had a Ribbon Bow," and "The Legend of Fair Eleanor and the Brown Girl." There is a brief preface, and Niles's notes give time and place of collecting, as well as the singers.

9. SEVEN NEGRO EXALTATIONS. *As Sung by Marion Kerby and John J. Niles. Collected and Arranged by John J. Niles. 1929. [iv], 15 pp.*

Niles's preface praises the durability of Negro music, and notes on each song give the place and occasion of singing, as well as other illuminating comment. Many of the songs, in both sets 8 and 9, are "jump-up" songs—meaning a song that "does not tell a connected story, each verse standing by itself."

10. SONGS FROM THE HILLS OF VERMONT. *Sung by James and Mary Atwood and Aunt Jenny Knapp. Text Collected and*

Set Number

Edited by Edith B. Sturgis. Tunes Collected and Piano Accompaniments Arranged with Historical Notes by Robert Hughes. 1919. ix, 57 pp.

A quarto of 13 old songs with somewhat elaborate piano settings, and the songs considerably "improved" in arrangement and content. As the editor states: "We thought it best to make some slight alterations to render the text suitable for present-day publication." Among the old songs are "Botany Bay," "Soldier's Return," "Spinster's Lament," and "Birds' Courting Song."

11. SPANISH SONGS OF OLD CALIFORNIA. *Collected and Translated by Charles F. Lummis. Pianoforte Accompaniments by Arthur Farwell. 1923. 31 pp.*

The 14 songs in this booklet are chosen from a large collection of over 450 Spanish folksongs which Lummis gathered in the Southwest over a thirty-eight-year period. He began his collecting in the 1880's and none too soon, for he felt that the time to collect from the people directly was rapidly passing. The piano settings are simple and effective.

12. THIRTY-SIX SOUTH CAROLINA SPIRITUALS. *Collected and Harmonized by Carl Diton. For Church, Concert and General Use. 1928. 54 pp.*

These songs in four-part harmonizations were collected in 1913 at an island settlement off the coast of South Carolina where, according to the collector, there was very little white influence.

13. AMERICAN COUNTRY DANCES, *Vol I. Twenty-Eight Contra-Dances. Largely from the New England States. Edited by Elizabeth Burchenal. Piano Arrangements by Emma Howells Burchenal. 1918, 1945. xvi, 62 pp.*

In 1916, Elizabeth Burchenal founded the American Folk-Dance Society and was its first president. In the preface to this collection she reported that the society is "assembling an Archive of American Folk-Dance." Many of these dance tunes are popular "old Irish and Scottish jigs" now thoroughly Americanized. The full notes for each dance are designed to make the book very practical. Most of the 28 are "longways" dances,

Set Number

among them such titles as these: Virginia Reel, Old Zip Coon, Pop Goes the Weasel, Boston Fancy, Speed the Plough, Arkansas Traveler. Though piano arrangements are given, formerly the music was by a single fiddler, who also "called."

14. SONGS OF THE HILL-FOLK. *Twelve Ballads from Kentucky, Virginia, and North Carolina. Collected and Simply Arranged for the Piano, by John Jacob Niles. 1934. 25 pp.*

For these 12 ballads Niles gives town and county of origin, but does not include informant or the specific date.

15. BEECH MOUNTAIN FOLK-SONGS AND BALLADS. *Collected, arranged, and provided with piano accompaniments by Maurice Matteson. Texts edited and foreword written by Mellinger Edward Henry. 1936. vii, 59 pp.*

Here are 29 songs, all recorded in the summer of 1933 in the Beech Mountain district of North Carolina, "one of the shorter cross-ranges lying between the Blue Ridge and Allegheny Mountains," as Henry points out in the foreword. M. E. Henry stresses the need to obtain the melodies, or airs, along with the text, else the collector has "but half a ballad." A footnote to each song gives source of text, name of singer, with date and place of recording the air. Here are many songs which, since 1936, have become more famous through use by professional singers: "Barbara Allen," "Careless Love," "Old Smoky," etc.

16. TEN CHRISTMAS CAROLS FROM THE SOUTHERN APPALACHIAN MOUNTAINS. *Collected and simply arranged with accompaniment for piano by John Jacob Niles. 1935. 22 pp.*

A selection of songs recorded from 1912 to 1934, from four states. Sometimes specific source (person, place, and date) is given, sometimes not. Among the carols are the very beautiful "Seven Joys of Mary," "The Cherry Tree," and "On the First Day of Christmas" (or, "The Twelve Days of Christmas"). This last one is given with melody only.

17. MORE SONGS OF THE HILL-FOLK. *Ten Ballads and Tragic Legends from Kentucky, Virginia, Tennessee, North Carolina, and Georgia. Collected and Simply Arranged with accompaniment for piano by John Jacob Niles. 1936. 21 pp.*

Town, county, and state are given to show sources of the songs, and in some cases dates and informants.

Set Number

18. BALLADS, CAROLS, AND TRAGIC LEGENDS FROM THE
SOUTHERN APPALACHIAN MOUNTAINS. *Collected and
Simply Arranged with piano accompaniment. By John Jacob
Niles. 1937. 22 pp.*
There are 10 songs here, with place of collection noted and
a few other explanatory notes. Most of the songs were collected
in North Carolina and Kentucky.

19. COUNTRY SONGS OF VERMONT. *Collected by Helen H.
Flanders, with Piano Accompaniment by Helen Norfleet. 1937.
50 pp.*
These 24 songs were collected and recorded, "usually by
dictaphone," in the early 1930's in Vermont. There is no duplication of the same editor's *Garland of Green Mountain Song*
(1934) except for "The Bailiff's Daughter," but this is a variant
recording from another singer. Some of these are Child ballads.
Mrs. Flanders has added informative headnotes.

20. BALLADS, LOVE-SONGS, AND TRAGIC LEGENDS FROM
THE SOUTHERN APPALACHIAN MOUNTAINS. *Collected
and Simply Arranged with piano accompaniment by John Jacob
Niles. 1938. 21 pp.*
Five of these 10 songs are Child ballads. A note on one of the
songs, "Jack o' Diamonds," states that the verses were "collected
from workmen engaged by my father between the years of 1910
and 1917."

21. AMERICAN-ENGLISH FOLK-SONGS FROM THE SOUTH-
ERN APPALACHIAN MOUNTAINS. *Collected and Arranged
with piano accompaniment by Cecil J. Sharp. 1918. [iv], 27 pp.*
These 6 songs are chosen from the first edition of Sharp's
larger work, published by Putnam in 1917. They are "representative examples of the traditional song bequeathed to the mountain singers by their immigrant British forefathers." Brief notes
indicate singer and place of collection.

22. AMERICAN-ENGLISH FOLK-BALLADS FROM THE
SOUTHERN APPALACHIAN MOUNTAINS. *Collected and
Arranged with piano accompaniment by Cecil J. Sharp. 1918.
[iv], 31 pp.*
Again, 6 numbers as in Set 21, with the same introductory
comment and similar notes on the ballads.

Set Number

23. FIFTEEN SHAKER SONGS. *Selected and Arranged by Conrad Held. With a Preface by Edward D. Andrews. 1944. 31 pp.*

The 15 spiritual folksongs chosen for this collection come from many composed in the late eighteenth- and early nineteenth-century activities of this peculiar sect. Andrews gives a brief history of their migration to America in 1774, their growth in New York and New England (with a colony in Ohio), and their gradual disappearance in modern times. They worked in a communal, relatively celibate, peaceful, and industrious organization. The Shakers were an offshoot of the Quaker and Camisard faiths.

24. THE ANGLO-AMERICAN BALLAD STUDY BOOK. *Containing Eight Ballads in Current Tradition in the United States of America. Collected and Arranged by John Jacob Niles. 1945. 38 pp.*

These 8 ballads are presented in simple piano settings, together with Mr. Niles's interesting and scholarly notes. The time and place of collection are noted, and also in what other American collections each ballad appears. Most famous in this group are "Bonny Barbara Allan" (Barbary Ellen) and "The Farmer's Curst Wife."

25. AMERICAN FOLK-SONGS FOR YOUNG SINGERS. *Collected and Arranged for Chorus by Maurice Matteson. 1947. 102 pp.*

The 49 songs in this collection—half for singing in unison, the others for two- and three-part singing—are drawn from half the states across the land, from Far West to Northeast. There are five groups: Folk-Songs of Home Life, the Farm, the Family, the Children, the Holidays; Folk-Songs of the Dance, Party Games, the Banjo and Fiddle; Folk-Songs Inspired by the Music of Other Lands or Peoples—The American Indian, England, Sweden; Folk-Songs of Travel, Places, Nature; Folk-Songs of Animals and Birds.

This book attempts no complete picture of the American scene through folksong, but rather aims to include "*Singable songs* for children." Matteson's brief and illuminating notes for each song tell just enough to interest and orient the modern singer. There are a few illustrations in this usable book.

Set Number

26. THE ANGLO-AMERICAN CAROL STUDY BOOK. *Containing English Carols in Their Early Traditional Form and Surviving Versions Traditional in the United States. Collected and Arranged by John Jacob Niles. 1948. 44 pp.*

Eight carols in 17 versions (English and American) in easy piano settings are given here. Niles's careful and useful notes accompany each of the carols. The American "surviving versions" are from Niles's extensive collecting, done over many years.

27. THE SHAPE-NOTE STUDY BOOK. *Selected from "The Sacred Harp" (1844) and "The Southern Harmony" (1835). Piano Settings and Annotations by John Jacob Niles. 1950. 20 pp.*

Eight songs in conventional piano settings comprise this small collection. A brief preface discusses the background and explains the use of the shape notes in these words: "It is now an accepted fact that the shapes, as they now stand, were adopted to give the beginner additional help in locating the pitch of the notes and to speed his understanding of *a cappella* singing." (p. 2) Notes accompany each song, and Niles pays high tribute to George Pullen Jackson, our leading authority on spiritual folksongs in America. Best known of the songs in this small group is "Wayfaring Stranger."

SEA SONGS OF SAILING, WHALING, AND FISHING. *Song Versions by Burl Ives. Text by Burl Ives. Music Transcribed by Albert Hague. New York: Ballantine Books. 1956. [x], 134 pp.*

This paperback singable collection of 68 sea songs, with Burl Ives' introduction and brief notes, contains songs of whaling, piracy, work songs, sailor songs about women and home, and other nostalgic pieces. Many favorites, like "The Golden Vanity," "Blow the Man Down," "Haul Away, Joe," "Maid of Amsterdam," "Shenandoah," are included. Tunes are given, together with guitar chords. There is a title index and a listing of Burl Ives Decca recordings.

John Huston, director of the *Moby Dick* film, writes a foreword for the book, saying, among other things, that some of these songs "just sang themselves into our picture." The songs, however, are not in Melville's classic of the great whaling days, though he mentions the sailors' singing.

SECOND BOOK OF NEGRO SPIRITUALS. *Edited with an Intro duction by James Weldon Johnson. Musical arrangements by J. Rosamond Johnson. New York: The Viking Press. 1926. 189 pp.*

This collection of 61 spirituals is a continuation of the (first) *Book of American Negro Spirituals* by the same competent editors. The two volumes of six-score songs are but a small part of the "five or six hundred known" to exist, and the editors believe many have been lost. Well edited and printed, these volumes are likely to remain standard collections for some time.

SEVENTY NEGRO SPIRITUALS. *Edited by William Arms Fisher, for High Voice. Boston: Oliver Ditson Company. 1926. xxxvi, 212 pp.*

This large quarto is one of the volumes in "The Musicians Library," of which over a hundred volumes have been issued. There is a preliminary essay on Negro spirituals and brief biographical sketches, with photographs, of ten interpreters of spirituals (such as Avery Robinson, H. T. Burleigh, J. Rosamond Johnson). The songs are given rather elaborate settings for concert singing. Many notes and a bibliography complete this fine collection.

SING OF AMERICA. *Folk Tunes Collected and Arranged by Tom Scott. Text by Joy Scott. Wood Engravings by Bernard Brussel-Smith. [New York]: Thomas Y. Crowell. 1947. xii, 84 pp.*

Tom Scott's collection of 35 songs in this small quarto, the thirty-one woodcuts and thirteen decorated initials by Brussel-Smith, and the illuminating folk-tale commentary by Joy Scott—all this makes a most authentic record and interpretation of American folksong. Here are work songs and sailor songs, courting songs and spirituals, trail-driving songs and settlers' tunes, sad songs and gay. Included are these favorites: "Hammer Song," "Billy Boy," "Little Mohee," "Barb'ra Allen," "Sweet Betsy from Pike"—to mention a few. All but three in the collection are traditional tunes and tales, for which Tom Scott has made excellent piano settings, and additional guitar chords. The three exceptions are Joy Scott's lyrics on "Paul Bunyan," "Johnny Appleseed," and "Pecos Bill"—all set to music by Tom Scott. Any lover of story, song, or picture will find this a satisfying little book.

SINGING COWBOY. *A Book of Western Songs. Collected and Edited by Margaret Larkin. Arranged for the Piano by Helen Black. New York: Alfred A. Knopf, Inc. 1931. xvii, 196 pp.*

Margaret Larkin has made an interesting book out of these 42 Western songs in piano settings, each song preceded by an explanatory headnote. As she states in the introduction: "I gathered them with my voice and my guitar, and the basis of choice was that they be worth singing over and over." Most of them came directly from people in the cattle trade, in roundups or in rodeos. Sandburg contributed a few of them. The book is enlivened with seventeen full-page old prints, most of them drawn from Joseph G. McCoy's *Historic Sketches of the Cattle Trade in the West and Southwest.* McCoy, a pioneer Western cattle shipper, published this book in 1874. A 15-page glossary, explaining about fifty terms used in the cattle business, is included for the uninitiated, and there is an index of first lines.

SINGING HOLIDAYS: THE CALENDAR IN FOLK SONG. *By Oscar Brand. Musical Arrangements by Douglas Townsend. Illustrated by Roberta Moynihan. New York: Alfred A. Knopf, Inc. 1957. xiv, 258 pp.*

In this beautifully designed and printed quarto, Oscar Brand, long-time director of folk music for New York City's municipal radio station, has chosen thirty special dates "in the busy American year" and illustrated them "with some ninety appropriate folk songs," all of them more or less in the category of "game" songs. Some particularly happy choices are: "I Will Give My Love an Apple" (Saint Valentine's Day), "The Bold Volunteer" (Washington's Birthday), "The Cuckoo" (Spring), "Alouette" (Pan-American Day), "The Tree in the Wood" (Arbor Day), "Green Grow the Lilacs" (Flag Day), "When Johnny Comes Marching Home" (Veterans Day).

Townsend's piano arrangements are "simple and direct." This book, like all good books designed for children, is for the young in heart. (Cf. the Ruth Crawford Seeger folksong collections for children, illustrated by Barbara Cooney.) Gay end papers and about seventy-five black-and-white (and sometimes red) drawings liven up further the lively songs.

The indexes (songs and first lines) are separately paged (i to v), a common practice in Knopf books.

SONG FEST. *Edited by Dick and Beth Best. Illustrated by David Hunt. New York: Crown Publishers, Inc. 1955. 160 pp.*

Here is the song collection used by the Intercollegiate Outing Club Association (with about forty member colleges) founded in 1932, mainly of clubs in the eastern United States and Canada. The most surprising fact about this rather small book is that it contains well over 300 songs, with words and tunes given for all of them.

"In recognition of the present trend toward folk songs and ballads," the preface states, "many of these have been added." Easily more than half of the collection are folksongs. The editors make seventeen not-too-strict groupings under such titles as Folk Songs and Ballads, College Songs, Songs of National Origin, Drinking Songs, Chanties, Fiddle Tunes, Spirituals, etc. And a further surprising fact is that no composers, authors, arrangers, or others are given credit anywhere in the volume, the assumption being that all these songs are in the public domain. Indexes of songs and of first lines are included, but no explanatory notes. An earlier edition was published in 1948.

SONGS MY MOTHER NEVER TAUGHT ME, THE. *According to John J. "Jack" Niles, Douglas S. "Doug" Moore, and cartoons by A. A. "Wally" Wallgren. New York: The Macaulay Company. 1929. 227 pp.*

The 56 songs (with piano settings) in this gay collection are for the most part Army adaptations of many old songs. Among them are "Mad'moiselle from Armentieres," "Santy Anna," "Limey Sailor Song," "Sally Brown," "Frankie and Johnny." Headnotes and brief discussions tell the occasion of many of the songs and also indicate that the printed versions have been pretty carefully expurgated. Wally's drawings add to the gaiety of the texts.

SONGS OF AMERICAN FOLKS. *By Satis N. Coleman and Adolph Bregman. Illustrated by Alanson Hewes. New York: The John Day Company. 1942. 128 pp.*

This collection of 47 songs, in easy piano settings, is "meant to be a sampling, a representative choosing, of authentic American songs that represent the 'folk' element, and that are *good to sing*." (p. 7) They are especially suited to junior and senior high-school singing. The editors make nine groupings, not too rigid in classification. Many favorites are here: "Springfield Mountain," "Sweet Betsy from Pike," "Cindy," "The Blue-Tail Fly," "Dese Bones Gwine Rise Again," "'Tain't Gwine Rain No Mo'," and others. There are hoedowns, spirituals, westerns, mountain, pioneer, occupation, and badman songs here. All in all, a good collection, especially arranged for good singing.

SONGS OF EARLY AMERICA, 1620-1830. *Compiled and Arranged by Elie Siegmeister. Radio City, New York: Edward B. Marks Music Corporation. 1944. 56 pp.*

Most of the 16 songs in this quarto booklet are folksongs arranged for four-part singing, with piano and guitar accompaniment. A brief introduction comments on the revival of old songs in America. These songs were performed in the early 1940's all over America by Siegmeister and his American Ballad Singers, and all are recorded on Bost Records. Siegmeister gives brief notes on each of the songs in this excellent small collection.

SONGS OF THE OPEN RANGE. *Compiled and Edited by Ina Sires. With Piano Accompaniments by Charles Repper. Boston: C. C. Birchard & Co. 1928. [vi], 60 pp.*

Each of these 29 songs is preceded by a brief headnote, and about three dozen words (*cayuse, dogies, locoed, sour-dough,* etc.) are explained in a glossary. In a preliminary Collector's Note, Miss Sires acknowledges a debt to Howard Thorpe and John A. Lomax, whose early collections preceded hers. She secured the melodies, however, "directly from the cowboys, by visiting ranches, attending dances, and riding on roundups in the western states where people still dance all night to the tune of the fiddle." Her early life was spent on a ranch. She has included many of the songs that have now become familiar throughout the land.

SONGS OF THE RIVERS OF AMERICA. *Edited by Carl Carmer. Music Arranged by Dr. Albert Sirmay. New York: Farrar and Rinehart, Inc. 1942. xi, 196 pp.*

This fascinating quarto of about 100 titles is only partly in the folksong field. Carmer, in the table of contents, divides the songs as to East, South, and West. But the general categories are four in number: songs of nostalgic yearning; songs of historical content; traditional folksongs of the rivers; and minstrel show songs. All are arranged for piano and for popular singing. With each title the river is named, if the title does not provide it. Dates of composition are given also with many of the songs. Small block-print pictures adorn many pages, pictures that appeared originally in the "Rivers of America" series. There are indexes of titles and first lines. A useful and beautiful text.

SONGS OF YESTERDAY. *A Song Anthology of American Life. By Philip D. Jordan and Lillian Kessler. Garden City, New York: Doubleday, Doran & Co., Inc. 1941. 392 pp.*

Here is a fine collection of nearly 100 old-time popular, sentimental, and melodramatic songs both lively and lugubrious, mainly of eighteenth- and early nineteenth-century vintage. The editors include both the original words and complete musical settings of the songs, as well as appropriate historical introductions to the nineteen groupings. These songs differ for the most part from the true ballads or folksongs. Though popular, they have not lasted as well through oral transmission as the true folksongs. For most of them both author and composer are known, thus setting them apart further from most traditional folksong literature. In general, too, they were composed for group singing. Except for a few names like Stephen Foster, the authors of the stanzas are minor figures. All in all, a useful and usable book of our older popular music, in what might be called a handsome setting, illustrated with a goodly number of contemporary prints. In the words of Jordan and Kessler, "These are the songs of our people. They are homely songs, easy to sing and to enjoy." And this book is a fine chapter in our social history.

SPANISH FOLK SONGS OF NEW MEXICO. *Collected and Transcribed by Mary R. VanStone. With a Foreword by Alice Corbin. Chicago: Ralph Fletcher Seymour. 1928. 41 pp.*

This slim quarto of 23 songs given in simple musical setting has both Spanish and English words. These are some of the folksongs sung by the native Spanish-speaking people of New Mexico, writes Alice Corbin in the foreword. She further mentions that the guitar is "the most inseparable accompaniment of New Mexico folk-songs, and there are few adobes without one."

SWAPPING SONG BOOK, THE. *By Jean Ritchie, Photographs by George Pickow. Piano Arrangements by A. K. Fossner and Edward Tripp. New York: Oxford University Press. 1952. 91 pp.*

This little book of 21 southern Appalachian songs done for children is a delight in picture, song, and story. Jean Ritchie tells a story for each song, which in turn is clarified by the full-page photographs of local mountain scenes, done by her husband, George Pickow. This little gem is one in the series of Oxford books for boys and girls.

30 AND 1 FOLK SONGS FROM THE SOUTHERN MOUNTAINS. *Compiled and Arranged by Bascom Lamar Lunsford and Lamar Stringfield. New York: Carl Fischer, Inc. 1929. iv, 56 pp.*

Only a brief selection from the many hundreds of songs Mr. Lunsford knows, this small booklet was designed to make more popular a number of the best mountain songs. Here are such favorites as "Black Jack Davie," "Little Turtle Dove," "Jinnie Jinkins," "Sourwood Mountain," "John Henry," "Careless Love," "Old Smoky." Simple piano settings are done by Lamar Stringfield.

TREASURY OF AMERICAN SONG, A. *By Olin Downes and Elie Siegmeister. New York: Howell, Soskin & Co. 1940. 351 pp.*

Most of the 142 songs in this large quarto are folksongs, ranging from early American ones like "Bunker Hill," "Springfield Mountain," and "Erie Canal" to "Hinky Dinky" ("Mademoiselle from Armentieres") and "Tom Joad." They come from all periods of our history and from all walks of life—political activities, whaling and sailing, cowboy and frontier life, the city and the mining camp. They do not pretend to be *belles lettres*, but they tell much about our way of life and are therefore among our most revealing records.

Downes writes an interesting introductory essay on our popular music, suggesting (as he has done on other occasions) its use to our serious composers; and Siegmeister discusses the piano settings he has given the songs, reminding us that folksongs have no fixed or final versions. The editors group the songs into sixteen subject and time categories, with brief introductions for each category and also for each song. There is an index of song titles in this excellent and usable collection. A second, revised and enlarged edition (408 pages) was published by Knopf in 1943.

TREASURY OF NEGRO SPIRITUALS, THE. *Edited by H. A. Chambers. London: Blandford Press. 1953. 125 pp.*

Here are 35 traditional spirituals and 7 modern compositions, most of them in easy piano settings by H. A. Chambers. Marian Anderson writes a brief foreword for the collection.

TREASURY OF THE BLUES, A. *Complete Words and Music of 67 Great Songs From Memphis Blues to the Present Day. Edited by W. C. Handy. With a Historical and Critical Text by Abbe Niles. With Pictures by Miguel Covarrubias. New York: Published by Charles Boni. Distributed by Simon and Schuster, Inc. 1926, 1949. 258 pp.*

The descriptive title page effectively suggests the content of this enlarged, standard work. The songs are grouped under three heads: The Background, The Blues, and Blues-Songs. In addition, under Larger Forms, three piano excerpts are given, one from John Alden (*Krazy Kat Ballet*) and two from Gershwin (*Rhapsody in Blue* and *Concerto in F*). The songs are all in piano settings, about half of them done by Handy. Abbe Niles' long introduction, titled "The Story of the Blues" (they began in 1912), and, in the latter pages, the same writer's "Notes to the Collection" give an authoritative history of the genre. (These two sections run to 41 double-column pages.)

The full-page drawings, nine in all (three portraits—Handy, Gershwin, and Berlin—and six interpretations), by Covarrubias add immensely to this handsome quarto designed for use at the piano.

TREASURY OF THE WORLD'S FINEST FOLK SONG, A. *Collected and Arranged by Leonhard Deutsch. With Explanatory Text by Claude Simpson. Lyrics versified by Willard Trask. Illustrations by Emery I. Gondor. New York: Howell, Soskin, Publisher, Inc. 1942. 430 pp.*

This collection of 171 songs from thirty-four countries or nationalities includes 17 from the English, Scottish, Irish, and American. The largest groups are Slovakian (19) and Hungarian (16). Except for the few American pieces, these songs are all European, and all are presented in English. They are given musical settings for the piano, and each national group is prefaced by a brief introduction. This large quarto is beautifully and practically made for use at the piano. There are some appropriate illustrations and a brief general introduction.

TWELVE NEGRO SPIRITUALS. *Arranged for Solo Voice by William Grant Still. "Literary Treatments" by Ruby Berkley Goodwin. Illustrations by Albert Barbelle. Edited by Wellington Adams. Vols. I and II. New York: Handy Brothers Music Co., Inc. 1937. Approx. 120 pp.**

These two slim quartos present 12 songs in a story setting and piano arrangements. There are appropriate drawings, photographs of Still and Goodwin, and a brief biographical sketch of Still by Verna Arvey. Perhaps the best known of the songs in the collection is "All God's Chillun Got Shoes." As always, the brilliant work of W. G. Still sets these songs apart as permanent contributions to our musical literature.

TWENTY KENTUCKY MOUNTAIN SONGS. *The Words Collected by Loraine Wyman. The Melodies Collected and Piano Accompaniments Added by Howard Brockway. Boston: Oliver Ditson Company. 1920. 115 pp.*

Except for a brief prefatory statement by Miss Wyman, this handsome quarto of 20 songs, obviously designed for use at the piano, is without notes or other explanatory data. Eight singers are mentioned by name as contributors of the songs, and beneath each title is given the county where the song was collected. "Barbara Allen," strangely enough, did not get in this collection ("she" is in most of them), but here are "The Swapping Song," "The Old Maid," "Pretty Polly," etc.

---

* I have examined only Volume I of this small collection.

VINGT-ET-UNE CHANSONS CANADIENNES. *Arrangées par Achille Fortier, Alfred La Liberté, Oscar O'Brien, Leo Smith et Ernest MacMillan. Avec des Traductions en Anglais et Introduction par J. Murray Gibbon. Editées par Ernest MacMillan. Oakville, Ontario: The Frederick Harris Music Co., Limited. 1928. 53 pp.*

The title page is also given in English. A brief preface and an introduction are in French. Most of these songs, in rather elaborate piano settings for solo and chorus, from the collections of Ernest Gagnon and Marius Barbeau, are well known in French Canada, particularly such titles as "C'est la belle Françoise," "Je n'ai pas d'amant," "La Plainte du Coureur des Bois," "Les jeunes filles à marier," "Les trois dames de Paris," "Lisette," etc.

'WAY UP ON OLD SMOKY. *Songs of Mountain Folk, Cowboy Music, Play Party Tunes, Work Songs, Spirituals, Blues, Campus Melodies, Love Songs, Ballads. Chosen and Arranged for Girls' and Women's Voices. By Elie Siegmeister and Rufus A. Wheeler. Boston: Ginn and Company. 1950. 106 pp.*

Most of the 39 songs in this collection are folksongs done in easily singable piano settings, for this small quarto is made for use at the piano. Included are such popular numbers as "The Blue-Tail Fly," "Cindy," "I've Been Working on the Railroad," "Lolly-Too-Dum," "Sourwood Mountain," "The Streets of Laredo." There are no explanatory notes—none are needed for this sort of book—but there is an index of titles and sources.

WORK AND SING. *A Collection of the Songs That Built America. Selected and Arranged by Elie Siegmeister. With a Commentary, Annotations and a Critical Bibliography. Illustrated by Julian Brazelton. New York: William R. Scott, Inc., Publisher of Young Scott Books. 1944. 96 pp.*

This squarish volume of 31 songs (most of them folksongs), designed primarily for the schoolroom, is adequately described by the following comment on the title page: "A treasury of American Work Songs of yesterday and today, including Songs of the Sea, capstan and short-drag chanteys; Songs of the West, ballads of the shanty-boys, cowboys' herding songs, Conestoga wagon songs; Songs of the Railroads and River Boats, from track gangs and blasting crews, from the Ohio River and the Erie Canal; Songs of the Country, of farmers, cotton-pickers, share-croppers; Songs of the City, street cries, modern factory and union songs."

Bold and humorous drawings by Brazelton add to the vigor of the texts.

CHAPTER 14

Minor Compilations and Curiosities

AFRO-AMERICAN FOLKSONGS. *A Study in Racial and National Music. Third Edition. By Henry Edward Krehbiel. New York: G. Schirmer. 1914. xii, 176 pp.*

This small book, by a former distinguished music critic of the New York *Tribune*, is a pioneer work in approaching scientifically the study of Afro-American folk music. The author here attempts "by comparative analysis to discover the distinctive idioms of that music, trace their origins and discuss their correspondences with characteristic elements of other folk-melodies, and also their differences." In a series of eleven chapters he elaborates his views, concluding that these are genuine native folksongs, African in basic origin but original American products nonetheless; and, further, that they may well be the inspirational background for a new American music. Two chapters are devoted to Creole music. He includes about 50 songs (with piano accompaniments) for illustrative purposes. He cites the work of Anton Dvořák as proof of what can be done with Afro-American musical materials.

ALLAN'S LONE STAR BALLADS. *A Collection of Southern Patriotic Songs, made during Confederate Times. Compiled and Revised by Francis D. Allan. Galveston, Texas: J. D. Sawyer, Publisher. 1874. 200 pp. + 24 pp. of Advertisements.*

This small volume, brought together by Allan, a publisher's agent, contains 177 "songs" or poems (without music) which, according to the compiler, were sung around the campfires during the war. According to his account, these are original songs of the people, presumably in oral circulation for the most part, and not from the books but from the singing soldiers. If this were the case, then many of them might be considered true folksongs. Yet most of them are too complex and sophisticated to be considered traditional folksongs. Some have known authors, others are anonymous, in this interesting and curious collection.

AMERICAN FOLK TALES AND SONGS. *And Other Examples of English-American Tradition as Preserved in the Appalachian Mountains and Elsewhere in the United States. Compiled with Introduction and Notes by Richard Chase. Drawings by Joshua Tolford. Music Edited with the Assistance of Raymond Kane McLain, Annabel Morris Buchanan, and John Powell. A Signet Key Book. New York: The New American Library of World Literature, Inc. 1956. 240 pp.*

The title-page description of this pocket paperback suggests the content. The first half of the book consists of 29 tales, classified as Ancient, Jack, Fool Irishman, and Tall. The second half gives 49 ballads, songs, hymns, games and country dances and fiddle tunes, besides a few odds and ends, and music for the second part uses the shape notes. Other items are a title index, a brief bibliography of suggested further reading, a few pages called an "Amateur Collector's Guide," and, perhaps best of all, a most excellent brief introduction. As collector and compiler, Richard Chase has long been interested in promoting our folk culture, and this little book, like many others by him, is packed with genuine material.

AMERICAN FOLKSONG. *By Woody Guthrie. Illustrations by York Cunningham, Jr., and Woody Guthrie. New York: Disc Company of America. 1947. 48 pp.*

A lithographed booklet containing an autobiographical sketch, an account of Leadbelly and his New York home, and 30 of Guthrie's songs, without tunes. Best known of these songs are "Tom Joad," "Jack Hammer John," "Pretty Boy Floyd," "Billy the Kid," and "Sharecropper Song." Many of the songs are propaganda for union organization. Guthrie is an important figure in John Greenway's *American Folksongs of Protest* (*q.v.*).

AMERICAN SEA SONGS AND CHANTEYS FROM THE DAYS OF IRON MEN AND WOODEN SHIPS. *By Frank Shay. Illustrated by Edward A. Wilson. Musical Arrangements by Christopher*

Thomas. New York: W. W. Norton and Company, Inc. 1948. 217 pp.
"An earlier version of this work entitled Iron Men and Wooden
Ships *was published in 1924." (See below)*

Frank Shay's collection of 78 sea songs is grouped into four divisions as follows: Chanteys, Forecastle Songs, Wardroom Ballads,
and Miscellaneous. Shay, once a sailor, got many of the songs directly
from sailors, a few from other collections, and some from the Archive
of American Folk Song. Most of the old favorites are here: "Sally
Brown," "Haul Away, Joe," "Shenandoah" ("loveliest melody of all
sailor songs," says Shay), "High Barbaree," "Blow the Man Down."
Edward Wilson's decorative end-papers and dozens of lively illustrations, sixteen full-page and in color, add zest to the book.
Simple tunes are included for most of the songs. There is a brief
introduction and an index of song titles. Though a good collection,
it does not compare with the more authoritative work of Joanna
Colcord.

BARBER SHOP BALLADS. *A Book of Close Harmony Edited by
Sigmund Spaeth. Illustrated by Ellison Hoover. Foreword by Ring
Lardner. New York: Simon & Schuster. 1925. 61 pp.*

About half of this curious little square volume (7½" x 7½") is given
over to discussion of the type, methods of singing, and dedication.
Then the dozen selections are presented, together with further comments. There are plenty of amusing decorations. Obviously here
are such old standbys as "Sweet Adeline," "In the Evening by the
Moonlight," and "Goodnight Ladies"; and there is one genuine
folksong: "I've been Workin' on the Railroad." Later, Spaeth revised
the books, as follows:

BARBER SHOP BALLADS AND HOW TO SING THEM. *By
Sigmund Spaeth. New York: Prentice-Hall, Inc. 1940. xvi, 125 pp.*

This much enlarged and more serious treatment of the type contains about 40 selections. Again, there is much discussion of method,
as well as a comment on barbershop singing contests and a comedy
sketch entitled "Barber Shop Harmony." More genuine folksongs
are included, too, such as "Red River Valley," "Ezekiel Saw the
Wheel," and "Polly Wolly Doodle." The book has no index.

BLACK CAMEOS. *By R. Emmet Kennedy. Decorations by Edward
Laroque Tinker. New York: Albert & Charles Boni. 1924. xv, 210 pp.*

This book is a series of 28 "verbal transcriptions of Negro life in
southern Louisiana," interspersed with a number of spirituals.
Simple melodies are given with the 17 spirituals included here. The

dialect shows a strong Creole influence. In the main, the book is a
series of episodes, sad and gay, in the Negroes' lives, with frequent
discussion of those who sang. Black-and-white drawings add to the
text. No index.

BLOW HIGH, BLOW LOW. *Illustrated by Edward A. Wilson.
New York: Published by the American Artists Group, Inc. 1941.
32 pp.*

The 7 sailor ballads in this gay little gift volume, with Wilson's
fourteen salty drawings, are interesting merely as a curiosity. "Blow
the Man Down," "Whiskey for My Johnny," "The Maid of Amsterdam," "High Barbaree," and "Boston" are the traditional pieces; the
other two are modern additions. There are no notes or comments—
perhaps none are needed.

BOOK OF SHANTIES, A. *By C. Fox Smith. Boston and New York:
Houghton Mifflin Company. 1927. 93 pp.*

These 31 shanties, or working songs, mainly capstan and halliard
(a few bunt and pumping), are taken in part from other collections
and in part from old sailors. (Smith is not always clear, in the
prefatory note to each song, what his source is.) Melodies are given
with the shanties. Shantying was at its best, says Smith, from 1850
to 1875. The somewhat nostalgic introduction discusses the term
"shanty" as to spelling, meaning, and source, with no very clear conclusion. Smith considers the tunes far superior to the words, these
latter often making little sense. In this collection are the universal
favorites: "Rio Grande," "Sally Brown," "Blow the Man Down,"
"Amsterdam," "The Wide Missouri," and "Rolling Home"—to mention a few.

CAPSTAN BARS. *By David W. Bone. With eight woodcuts by
Freda Bone. New York: Harcourt, Brace and Company. 1932. 160 pp.*

Here we have a valuable though small collection (only 23 songs in
all) of chanties by an experienced seaman who sang these work
songs of the sailor and who gives us the proper setting for the songs.
It was Captain Bone's purpose to preserve these songs, as far as possible, as they were in the old days, because, he writes, "in the process
of adapting them to the requirements of professional singers they
are in danger of becoming polished and shiny." Both the "musical
airs" and the time for the songs were worked out by expert musicians
as Bone sang them the songs, and these simple tunes are noted in the
text. Bone admits to some editing of the sailor text in order to "tone
down the frank prolations of lusty fellows" on shipboard. Otherwise

both words and tunes may be considered highly authentic. The author classifies the chanties as short haul, halyard, debt and credit, capstan, out of the blue, and windlass and pump. Here we have such old favorites as "Early in th' Morning," "Blow th' Man Down," "The Rio Grande," "Shenandoah (frequently heard as "Across the Wide Missouri")—this last one being, says Bone, "the most beautiful of them all." These chanties, unlike many folksongs, were sung with solo part and chorus. (In Bone's text chorus is indicated by italics.) "Chanties were not sung on board ship to any instrumental accompaniment," since they were used for work rhythms and not for casual entertainment. Captain Bone's reputation as both sailor and writer gives interest and value to this small but valuable collection.

CAROLINA LOW-COUNTRY, THE. *By Augustine T. Smythe, Herbert Ravenal Sass, Alfred Huger, Beatrice Ravenal, Thomas R. Waring, Archibald Rutledge, Josephine Pinckney, Caroline Pinckney Rutledge, DuBose Heyward, Katherine C. Hutson, [and] Robert W. Gordon. New York: The Macmillan Company. 1931. xi, 327 pp.*

This book is a composite study and collection by a group in the early 1920's in Charleston, South Carolina, known as The Society for the Preservation of Spirituals. The society sang not only for their own pleasure in their various homes, but branched out, giving concerts in many cities, including New York. There are background chapters or discussions by each of the persons named on the title page. The latter third of the book is given over to 49 Negro songs or spirituals. The melody is given for each song, and place of collection is noted. The dialect of this region is interesting and somewhat different from that in other areas of the South.

This collection is important in the light of what went into the making of *Porgy and Bess*, on which DuBose Heyward collaborated. There are a number of illustrations from paintings by Alice R. Huger Smith, from etchings by Elizabeth O'Neill Verner, and from pen-and-ink drawings by Albert Simons. There is no index to this otherwise excellent volume.

COOPERATIVE RECREATION SERVICE, DELAWARE, OHIO, publishes a series of inexpensive booklets (20 to 25 cents each), about 4″ x 7″, of AUTHENTIC FOLK SONGS AND RECREATION MATERIALS. Here follow some examples of their pocket booklets, in some of which the material has been edited and "improved":

1. AMIGOS CANTANDO. *Edited by Phyllis and Olcutt Sanders. 1948. 32 pp. Thirty-three songs in both Spanish and English.*

2. HANDY PLAY PARTY BOOK. *Copyright 1940 by Lynn Rohrbaugh. 135 pp. Contains 108 songs and singing games from South, West, and abroad.*

3. LITTLE BOOK OF CAROLS. *48 pp. Forty carols from ten different nations.*

4. LOOK AWAY. *Fifty Negro Folk Songs. Edited by Walter F. Anderson. 48 pp.*

5. SONGS OF ALL TIME. *1946. 64 pp. Contains 72 songs published for the Council of Southern Mountain Workers.*

6. SWEET FREEDOM'S SONG. *"A little book of well loved All-American Songs for celebrating Ohio's 150 years." 100 pp. About 120 songs, some not folksongs.*

7. WORK AND SING, AN INTERNATIONAL SONGBOOK. *100 pp. About 120 songs from many languages, with English translations.*

COWBOY JAMBOREE: WESTERN SONGS & LORE. *Collected and Told by Harold W. Felton. Musical Arrangements by Edward S. Breck. Illustrations by Aldren A. Watson. Foreword by Carl Carmer. New York: Alfred A. Knopf. 1951. [xii], 110 pp.*
This is another in the Felton series of folksong and folklore books for young people published by Knopf. (The list also includes *Legends of Paul Bunyan; Pecos Bill: Texas Cowboy; John Henry and His Hammer.*) Each of the 20 songs is preceded by a story setting, and each is humorously and delightfully illustrated. Here are the best of the famous Western songs, from "The Chisholm Trail" and "The Lone Prairie" to "Home on the Range" and "Good-By, Old Paint." The popular juvenile conception of the cowboy as brave, heroic, lonely, and humorous is well presented.

COWBOY LORE. *By Jules Verne Allen, "The Singing Cowboy." Illustrations by Ralph J. Pereida. San Antonio, Texas: Naylor Printing Company. 1933. xv, 165 pp. [with an additional eight pages advertising other books]*
A lively, nostalgic discussion on "Life of the Cowboy" (42 pages), a chapter on "Cattle Brands" with about a hundred brands illustrated, a "Cowboy Dictionary" of about 150 terms and sayings, and then about 100 pages of "Songs of the Range," with music in piano arrangements. There are 36 songs "taken down" from Allen's singing and "set to music" by Mrs. G. Embry Eitt of San Antonio, Texas. Many old favorites are here: "Jesse James," "Jack o' Diamonds," "Git Along, Little Dogies," "The Old Chisholm Trail," "Buffalo

Skinners," "The Zebra Dun," and even "Barbara Allen," which turns
up in every section of the country and in almost every collection
of traditional songs and ballads. Concerning the source of his songs,
Allen says that the "trail driving period lasted from 1867 to 1895,"
and that 90 per cent of the early trail-drivers were Confederate
veterans—which accounts, he thinks, for the Southern flavor of many
of their songs.

CREOLE SONGS OF NEW ORLEANS. *Compiled by Clara G.
Peterson. Philadelphia: L. Grunewald Co., Ltd. 1902. 18 pp.*

The 12 songs in this collection, in Creole-Negro dialect, are
presented in simple piano settings. Mrs. Peterson was a sister of
Louis Moreau Gottschalk (1829-1869), a brilliant pianist, and a
composer of many piano pieces. Many of his compositions—"La
Savane" (Op. 3), "Bananier," "Bamboula" (Op. 2), and "Banjo"
(Op. 15)—were based on Creole melodies, and Gottschalk earned
a great popular reputation with them. English translations are given
for the 12 songs. According to John Tasker Howard, *Our American
Music* (New York, 1939, p. 209), Gottschalk's mother was a Creole.

DARLING CORIE. *Opera in One Act. Music by Elie Siegmeister.
Libretto by Lewis Allan. New York: Chappell & Co., Inc. 1953-54.
64 pp. quarto*

For six principals, a chorus, and an orchestra of twenty-five pieces,
this brief opera, based on the famous ballad, consists of a prologue,
ten scenes, and an epilogue. Scenes are titled: I. The Boy and Girl;
II. The Stranger; III. Sunday; IV. Fire and Brimstone; V. Conscience; VI. Fear; VII. Farewell; VIII. The Wedding Party; IX. The
Wedding Party Square Dance; X. Return.

DEVIL'S DITTIES. *Being Stories of the Kentucky Mountain People.
Told by Jean Thomas, With the Songs They Sing. Cyril Mullen
Drew the Illustrations. Chicago: W. Wilbur Hatfield. 1931. viii, 180
pp.*

After several chapters or stories (64 pages) on the life of the
mountain people, Jean Thomas, herself a mountaineer, gives the
texts and tunes (with simple harmonizations) of 55 ballads and
songs. The discussions include accounts of weddings (the infare),
funerals (funeralizin'), courtings, baptizings, play parties, county
fairs, etc.—all told somewhat sentimentally and with their musical
or ballad accompaniment. No attempt is made to point out printing
of the texts in other collections. One interesting feature of the book
is the presentation of a locally famous singing fiddler—Jilson Setters,

The Singin' Fiddler of Lost Hope Hollow. Other singers are discussed. Though an interesting presentation, the book has small importance as a collection of songs and ballads.

EAST TENNESSEE AND WESTERN VIRGINIA MOUNTAIN BALLADS. (*The Last Stand of American Pioneer Civilization.*) *By Celestin Pierre Cambiaire. London: The Mitre Press. [c. 1934]. xli, 179 pp.*

After a long introduction explaining the Anglo-Norman background of the region and especially the French element, Cambiaire includes 72 songs and ballads, a dozen songs for parties and games, and then a collection of 25 of his own verses. Tunes are not included for any of the songs and ballads. A footnote (p. 124) states: "In some ballads and songs ... the writer had to supply verses and even stanzas, as the mountaineers remember, at times, only parts of the old poems." Such practice, of course, gives doubtful value to the work as a scholarly collection, but the 40-page introduction is an interesting essay on the background.

FAMOUS SONGS AND THEIR STORIES. *By James A. Geller. New York: The Macaulay Co. 1931. viii, 248 pp.*

Except for a few songs like "Casey Jones," these 55 pieces and their stories are not folksongs, but popular and vaudeville numbers. Some titles: "Sweet Genevieve," "Little Annie Rooney," "After the Ball," "The Bowery," "Oh Promise Me," "Down Went McGinty," "Sweet Adelaine," etc.

FISHERMEN'S BALLADS AND SONGS OF THE SEA. *Compiled by Procter Brothers, and Respectfully Dedicated to the Hardy Fishermen of Cape Ann. Gloucester, Massachusetts: Procter Brothers, Publishers. 1874. 204 pp.*

To the modern student of folksong, the title of this quaint little book is somewhat misleading. Of the 120 pieces in the collection, few could properly be called folksongs or folk ballads. For most of them are by known authors, some of whom are Bret Harte, Celia Thaxter, H. W. Longfellow, O. W. Holmes, William Cowper, J. G. Whittier, and Thomas Hood. A few anonymous pieces might be called folksong, such as "A Wet Sheet and A Flowing Sea," "Hull's Victory," "Poor Bessie Was a Sailor's Wife," and "Tom Turner." But none of the commonly known sea songs of recent collections are to be found in this early book. There is, of course, a good deal of interesting poetry of the sea here, especially of a popular kind, brought together primarily for sailors and fishermen. The text is adorned with about one hundred small woodcuts, and the last twenty pages of the volume are devoted to advertising—everything from harness to tinware!

FLYING CLOUD. *And One Hundred and Fifty other Old Time Songs and Ballads of Outdoor Men, Sailors, Lumber Jacks, Soldiers, Men of the Great Lakes, Railroadmen, Miners, etc. Compiled by M. C. Dean. Virginia, Minnesota: The Quickprint. n.d. 134 pp.*

This curious little paper-bound volume is a combination of popular poetry, Irish songs, barbershop numbers, and some traditional ballads. It includes such poems as "Ben Bolt," My Old Kentucky Home," "Listen to the Mocking Bird," "In the Evening by the Moonlight," "Where the River Shannon Flows," "Home Sweet Home," "Old Folks at Home," etc. Among the well-known Irish popular melodies (which comprise over half the book) are: "Ireland Must Be Heaven for My Mother Came from There," "Colleen Bawn," "Rose O'Grady," "Come Back to Erin," "I Was Born in Killarney," "Wearing of the Green," etc.

But interspersed among the popular and sentimental pieces are a number of genuine ballads: "The Arkansaw Navvy" (about working on the railroad in Arkansas), "The Lass of Mohe(e)," "Young Monroe," "Caroline of Edinburg Town," "Young Charlotte," "Joe Bowers," and "The Klondike Miner." "Flying Cloud," the opening poem of sixteen stanzas, is a ballad of an African slaver turned pirate and of the fate that befell her crew.

The book contains no table of contents, no index, no headnotes nor other discussion, no melodies, and there is no logical organization. The poems are poorly printed on very cheap paper.

This small work is included in many bibliographies as *The Flying Cloud*, but the title page does not carry the word *The*. Furthermore, the copy I examined shows no evidence of any date, though 1922 is given by some who list the book.

FOLK DANCES OF TENNESSEE. *Old Play Party Games of the Caney Fork Valley. By Lucien L. McDowell and Flora Lassiter McDowell. Ann Arbor, Michigan: Edwards Brothers, Inc. 1938. 79 pp.*

The Caney Fork Valley in the Cumberland foothills lies between the Cumberland and Tennessee Rivers and was somewhat isolated from the usual westward movement. This rich, hidden valley, settled by English and Scotch-Irish beginning about 1800, developed its own culture, until recent times. Mr. and Mrs. McDowell, born there in the 1880's, have brought together in this mimeographed booklet, with the help of a dozen or so friends, folk material (songs and dances) of the play-party games. The play-party game was a substitute entertainment for dancing, which was prohibited on religious grounds. As the McDowells say, "It seems to have grown out of unending conflict between the natural desire to dance and to be merry and the stern religious prohibition of all worldly pleasure." (p. 4) Tunes, figures, and verses are given for 25 of the play-party games, and an addition of 6 old square-dance tunes. Among the 25 are many old favorites: "The Miller," "Old Dan Tucker," "Coffee Grows on White Oak Trees," "Jenny, Put the Kettle On," "Skip to My Lou," "The Needle's Eye," etc.

FOLKLORE FROM IOWA. *Collected and Edited by Earl J. Stout. Published by The American Folk-lore Society. New York: G. E. Steckert and Co., Agents. 1936. x, 228 pp.*

Part I of this publication (to p. 141), titled "Ballads and Folk-Songs from Iowa," prints 112 songs and ballads, with many variants. Headnotes indicate contributors and singers. Except for eight examples, melodies are not given.

Part II is given over to "Current Beliefs from Iowa" and includes 1,351 items.

FOLK SONG CHAPBOOK, A. *Collected by Marion Kingston. The Beloit Poetry Journal, Vol. 6, No. 2, Chapbook No. 4. Cover Design and Illustrations by Franklin Boggs. Beloit, Wisconsin: Beloit College. 1955. 38 pp.*

An interesting collection of 40 folksongs (without tunes), all gathered from oral tradition and not before printed, at least in these versions. The songs come from many sections of the country. Some are counting-out rhymes, some humorous game songs, some nonsense, and some are recent parodies. Examples: "Tyin' Knots in the Devil's Tail," "Mouse Went A-Courtin'," "The Trooper and the Maid."

FOLK-SONGS MAINLY FROM WEST VIRGINIA. *By John Harrington Cox. Introductory Essay and supplementary references by Herbert Halpert. American Folk-Song Publications #5. WPA Federal Theatre Project, Publication No. 81-S. New York: National Service Bureau. June, 1939. xxiii, 88 pp.*

This well-edited mimeographed volume contains 55 songs, including the variants, and 46 melodies. This is the second group of songs from Professor Cox's large collection, the first group being *Traditional Ballads* (American Folk-Song Publications #3). Each song has a headnote showing when, where, and from whom the song was gathered. Most of the songs were collected in the 1920's. At the volume's end are several pages of explanatory notes, five pages of bibliography, and a page of errata with corrections that pertain to the melodies.

FOLK TUNES FROM MISSISSIPPI. *Collected by Arthur Palmer Hudson and Edited by George Herzog. Music Research Department. New York: National Play Bureau (Publication No. 25), Federal Theatre Project, WPA. July, 1937. xxii, 54 pp., mimeographed.*

Simple melodies are given with each of the 45 songs, stanzas not being given separately from melodies (but as in a hymnal). Headnotes name the singers and the "notators" (who took them down). At the end there are notes to the songs, a melodic index, and some explanatory comments on the melodic index.

Hudson states that the tunes were "collected from white people in Mississippi between the years 1923 and 1930." His preliminary comment tells briefly about some of the singers. This pamphlet is a supplement to his work of the previous year, *Folksongs of Mississippi and Their Background* (1936).

FRANKIE AND JOHNNY. *By John Huston. Illustrated by Covarrubias. New York: Albert & Charles Boni. 1930. 161 pp.*

This dramatic stage version of the famous bawdy ballad, a triangle of love and death, is done as a prologue, three scenes, and an epilogue. Huston based his adaptation on many oral versions "which he had discovered throughout the country." Thirteen of these versions are printed in the latter third of the volume. "The Story of the St. Louis Version" is a 9-page discussion of the ballad's origin. Police and hospital records in St. Louis indicate that Frankie Baker shot Allen Britt because of jealousy on October 15, 1899. Early versions of the ballad are titled "Frankie and Albert." But similar ballads are known to have existed much earlier, even before the Civil War, as collectors have pointed out. (See especially, Vance Randolph, *Ozark Folksongs*, II, 125 ff.) Its origin, therefore, is still uncertain, and it has been collected all over America. Randolph found six versions in the Ozarks. Covarrubias' illustrations add gaiety and glamor to Huston's drama.

FRONTIER BALLADS. *Heard and Gathered by Charles J. Finger. Woodcuts by Paul Honoré. Garden City, New York: Doubleday, Page & Company. 1927. 181 pp.*

This book of hard cases and rough life on the frontier contains about 65 songs (some are fragments) from lawless lands, presented in a running and vigorous narrative. Finger reports that many are here printed for the first time. He further reports that here is "a true account of the manner of their singing by gold hunters in the Andes, men on shipboard, hard-cases who were beach combers, fellows in the calaboose, South Sea smugglers, sealers, bartenders, and some who have since achieved fame." Simple tunes (poorly printed) are included for about half of the ballads, and Honoré's woodcuts lend color and vigor to the text. Among the old favorites in this collection are "The Dying Hobo," "The Jealous Lover," "The Amsterdam Maid," "Jesse James," "The Cowboy's Dream," "Blow the Man Down," "Sam Bass," "Bluetail Fly," "John Hardy," "Young Charlotte." There is an index to first lines.

"GENTLEMEN, BE SEATED!" *A Parade of the Old-Time Minstrels. By Dailey Paskman and Sigmund Spaeth. With a Foreword by Daniel Frohman. Profusely illustrated from old prints and photographs and with complete music for voice and piano. Garden City, New York: Doubleday, Doran & Company, Inc. 1928. xvii, 247 pp.*

This sumptuous volume is an informal history of the old-time minstrel show and of the people who were important in that kind of entertainment. It includes over 40 songs with words and music, and discusses many others. Perhaps half of the songs were (or are now considered) folksongs, such as "De Blue Tail Fly," "Arkansas Traveller," "Jim Crow," "Oh Susanna," "Old Dan Tucker," "Wake Nicodemus," etc. Aside from the songs, the book is fascinating reading—an excellent piece of social history.

GIFT TO BE SIMPLE, THE. *Songs, Dances and Rituals of the American Shakers. By Edward D. Andrews. New York: J. J. Augustin, Publisher. 1940. xi, 170 pp.*

Section I is a collection of over 40 songs and rituals, with texts illustrating various types of Shaker songs, including a good deal of background discussion. Section II is Tunes and Music, a collection of tunes with texts, about 90 in all. Section III discusses the dances. One surprising fact to the outsider is the variety of songs and dances among the Shakers: hymns and anthems, ritualistic songs, Indian and Negro songs, songs in unknown tongues, vision songs, etc.

An introduction gives a brief history of the Shaker movement. This strange, monastic-like sect began in England about 1750 and a group came to America in 1774. By the Civil War the group numbered about six thousand members, in eighteen different societies, but declined thereafter, until today only a few hundred members remain. Their doctrine was a kind of primitive Christianity, based on celibacy and community of goods—a sort of pure communism. This book, therefore, portrays a curious piece of folk culture in our varied social history.

GOLD RUSH SONG BOOK, THE. *Comprising a group of twenty-five authentic ballads as they were sung by the men who dug for gold in California during the period of the great gold rush in 1849. Compiled by Eleanora Black and Sidney Robertson. With music. San Francisco: The Colt Press. 1940. ix, 55 pp.*

The lengthy title pretty well characterizes this little volume of songs which "describe the trip to California and daily life in the mines." Many are from songsters that appeared before 1860, especially from the compilations of composer, arranger, and collector John A. Stone, who published *Put's Original California Songster* in 1854 and *Put's Golden Songster* in 1858. In all probability, few of these songs are now in oral circulation—with the exception of "Sweet Betsy from Pike," which has had a happy revival among current folksingers.

HAMPTON AND ITS STUDENTS. *By Two of Its Teachers, Mrs. M. F. Armstrong and Helen W. Ludlow. With Fifty Cabin and Plantation Songs. Arranged by Thomas P. Fenner, In Charge of Musical Department at Hampton. New York: G. P. Putnam's Sons. 1874. 256 pp.*

Two-thirds of the book is a historical account of Hampton Institute. The 50 songs are arranged for piano. Many old favorites are here: "Peter, Go Ring Dem Bells," "Swing Low, Sweet Chariot," "Nobody Knows de Trouble I've Seen," "In Dat Great Gittin'-up Mornin'," "De Old Ark a-Moverin' Along," "My Lord, What a Mornin'."

HISTORY SINGS. *Backgrounds of American Music. By Hazel Gertrude Kinscella. Lincoln, Nebraska: The University Publishing Company. 1948. 560 pp.*

In the seven sections of this book, which is somewhat chronological and somewhat sectional, Miss Kinscella has brought together a sort of history-anthology of many writers of both prose and poetry. The work is designed as a background text to supplement the study of American history, literature, art, and music. The many short items are not satisfactorily welded into a unified story, but there is much good reading and a deal of useful fact. Much ballad and folksong material is printed here and there, but it is poorly documented.

HOBO'S HORNBOOK, THE. *A Repertory for a Gutter Jongleur. Collected and Annotated by George Milburn. Decorations by William Siegel. New York: Ives Washburn. 1930. 295 pp.*
This volume of 86 pieces, grouped into eight categories, is an excellent collection of hobo and tramp songs, done by a collector who did some hoboing himself and who saw and heard this material as something that was fast disappearing in a highly mechanized society. Though the collection is in no sense complete or scientific, it presents the materials in an interesting manner. Each song is preceded by a headnote of explanation or origin. Many of the songs are satiric, none romantic in the usual sense, many of them are parodies, many humorous; and since the hobo often rode the rails, many of them are railroad songs. The groupings are as follows: Monika Songs, The Lehigh Valley Sequence, Parody and Burlesque, Wobbly Songs, Homeguard Versions, Hobo Classics, "Packing the Banner," and The Road.
A brief introduction on "Poesy in the Jungles," a glossary of about 150 hobo terms—very useful for the uninitiated—about a dozen and a half tunes, and an index of titles complete this interesting volume. Some of these ballads, such as "The Big Rock Candy Mountains," "The Son of a Gambolier," "The Wabash Cannonball," have been made known generally in recent years by folk or popular singers.

IRISH STREET BALLADS. *Collected and Annotated by Colm O. Lochlainn, and Adorned with Woodcuts from the Original Broadsheets. Dublin: Printed and Published at the Sign of the Three Candles in Fleet Street. London: Constable & Co., Ltd. 1939. xvi, 235 pp.*
These 102 ballads, all with unaccompanied airs, represent a sampling of the popular songs of over two hundred years, which have gone into oral circulation in Ireland and elsewhere in the world. They are taken from Lochlainn's accumulation of twenty-five years. In a commentary toward the end of the volume, Lochlainn tells when and where he heard each ballad. The eighty-one small, quaint woodcuts are a delightful adornment to the text, and there is an index of first lines. A goodly number of these ballads, or variants of them, are well known in America, such as "The Dark-Eyed Sailor," "The Girl I Left Behind Me," "If I Was a Blackbird," "Lillibulero," "The Real Old Mountain Dew," "The Women Are Worse Than the Men" (or, "The Farmer's Curst Wife"), etc.

IRON MEN AND WOODEN SHIPS. *Deep Sea Chanties, edited by Frank Shay. Decorations and Woodcuts by Edw. A. Wilson.*

Introduction by William McFee. Garden City, New York: Double-day, Page & Company. 1924. xx, 154 pp.

One is tempted to say that this quarto collection was brought together for the sake of the decorations, many of them in full-page color and all of them extremely lively. The "songs of work and songs of leisure" stem mainly from the mid-nineteenth century. Here are 47 songs in all; no music is included, nor are sources given, except a few in some brief notes. William McFee, sailor and novelist of the sea, gives an 8-page introduction in which he evokes the mood of the chantey era, by telling an episode of singing, and discusses the passing of this type of singing with the passing of the sailing vessels. "A true chantey," says McFee, "is as authentic as a saga, and like a saga it is composed independent of the written word; it is handed on from one votary to another like a prophecy, a legend, or a tradition." (p. xv)

JUBILEE SINGERS AND THEIR CAMPAIGN FOR TWENTY THOUSAND DOLLARS, THE. *By Gustavus D. Pike. With Photographs by Black. Boston: Lee and Shepherd Publishers. 1872. 219 pp.*

Nine chapters (160 pages) give the history and purpose of missionary work among the freedmen, a brief account of Fisk University, a personal account of the original nine singers (all born in slavery), and then an account of their first trip throughout the North and their earning of $20,000 for Fisk. An appendix gives the original 61 songs used by the singers. In most cases they are given in a four-part arrangement, but for some there is only the simple melody. Here follow some of the more familiar titles: "Nobody Knows the Trouble I See, Lord," "Swing Low, Sweet Chariot," "Roll, Jordan, Roll," "Didn't My Lord Deliver Daniel," "Go Down, Moses," "Steal Away," "Ride On, King Jesus," "Mary and Martha," "I'm Troubled in My Mind." This small collection is, of course, a very important early work.

JUBILEE SONGS: COMPLETE. *As Sung by the Jubilee Singers, of Fisk University, Under the Auspices of the American Missionary Association. Price 25 cents. New York: Biglow and Main. [1872.] 64 pp.*

Apparently a first printing, this pamphlet contains 61 songs. Of the total, 21 are given with simple melody, and the remaining 40 are harmonized for four-part singing. Four-line stanzas usually range from three to six for each song, but "Go Down, Moses" has twenty-four stanzas. This is a rare early printing.

KING'S BOOK OF CHANTIES. *By Stanton H. King. Official Government Chanty-Man. Boston: Oliver Ditson Company. 1918. vi, 26 pp.*

This little pocket booklet of 28 chanties, with tunes, is presented by an authentic chantyman. King states in the preface: "The chanties in this book are as I heard them sung, and have often sung them myself when a sailor on our deep water American sailing ships." Here are many of the fine old standard numbers: "Blow the Man Down," "Hanging Johnnie," "The Wide Missouri," "Rolling Home," etc.

MADEMOISELLE FROM ARMENTIERES. *Illustrated by Herb Roth. With a discussion of the song and its origin, by John T. Winterich. Mount Vernon, New York: The Peter Pauper Press. 1953. 60 pp.*

The publisher's note states: "Of the hundreds of verses of *Mademoiselle from Armentieres* that have been recorded in print, we have selected the funniest and the liveliest [101 in all], but have eliminated the bawdiest." And, as every veteran of World War I knows, there are hundreds of verses—even thousands—never recorded in print. As Winterich points out, "It is, of course, not a song, but a whole anthology.... It is everywhere outrageously critical and utterly defamatory." (p. 51) Winterich's discussion of the origin shows that it goes a long way back, perhaps with its roots among the early Greeks. Herb Roth's thirteen drawings are outrageously funny. By all odds it was the most popular song (or anthology) of the whole A.E.F.

MORE PIOUS FRIENDS AND DRUNKEN COMPANIONS. *Songs and Ballads of Conviviality, Collected by Frank Shay. Magnificently Illuminated by John Held, Jr. Musical Arrangement for any degree of Inebriety by Helen Ramsey. New York: The Macmillan Company. 1928. 190 pp.*

A continuation of *My Pious Friends* of the previous year, but with more tunes included. This second collection has 63 songs and ballads, all in the ribald and humorous vein of the previous volume.

MY FAVORITE MOUNTAIN BALLADS AND OLD-TIME SONGS. *By Bradley Kincaid. As Sung over WLS, The Prairie Farmer [radio] Station. Chicago. 1928. 47 pp.*

This thin little pamphlet in gray paper covers (about 7 inches square) prints 33 of the old ballads (with simple tunes) as sung by Kincaid over the radio. It is probably the first folksong collection offered for sale by a radio station. Now out of print, the booklet went through five or six editions, the last being over 50,000 copies.

MY PIOUS FRIENDS AND DRUNKEN COMPANIONS. *Songs and Ballads of Conviviality, Collected by Frank Shay. Magnificently Illuminated by John Held, Jr. New York: The Macmillan Company. 1927. 192 pp.*

This ribald and humorous, delightful and defiant collection of 67 songs of the Prohibition era is Shay's attempt to bring together "the songs professional drinkers sing when in a convivial mood." Most of them are traditional songs. He says further, "They are presented in all their tawdry garments, unprettified save that in some cases their faces and hands have been washed so they may properly appear in company." (p. 13) The songs come from many drinking haunts and from many people. Credit is given for particular songs. A few tunes are given, though not many, and the three dozen wood engravings of John Held, Jr., are "magnificent."

MY SPIRITUALS. *By Eva A. Jessye. Illustrated by Millar of the Roland Company. Edited by Gordon Whyte and Hugo Frey. New York: Robbins-Engel, Inc. 1927. [vi], 82 pp.*

These 16 songs, in an attractive quarto, arranged and presented by the distinguished singer and choir director, come from her background in Coffeyville, Kansas, where she was born and reared. No scholarly impedimenta intrude to mar the beauty of the songs. "It is simply a recording of some songs I grew up with," Eva Jessye writes. And yet the factual narrative setting—actual experiences out of her childhood and youth told with a disarming simplicity and beauty—makes this one of the most satisfying of small collections we yet have of spirituals. "Collecting these songs has not been a difficult task," she says. "I was not obliged to delve in remote corners of the South or coax them from reluctant elders. They are the songs of my childhood and of my own people. I have sung them all my life." Each song is preceded by a brief account which sets the mood, and the musical accompaniment is for piano.

NEGRO SINGS A NEW HEAVEN, THE. *By Mary Allen Grissom. Chapel Hill: The University of North Carolina Press. 1930. [viii], 101 pp.*

These 45 Negro spirituals, with simple unaccompanied melodies, are presented in six groups: Songs of Death, Songs of Heaven and Resurrection, Bible Stories in Song, Songs of Exhortation, Songs of Service and Personal Experience, and Shouting Songs and Songs of Triumph. The compiler's foreword states that "most of the songs included in this volume have been taken directly from the Negroes in their present-day worship, and have been selected from those sung in the neighborhood of Louisville, Kentucky, and certain rural sections in Adair County." The book is without notes or an index but is handsomely printed.

"NEGRO SPIRITUALS" [an article and a collection] *By T. W. Higginson. Atlantic Monthly, June, 1867, pp. 685-94.*
  Higginson was with a Negro regiment in the Civil War and made his collection and observations at that time. Included here are 37 songs. He writes that "almost all the songs were thoroughly religious in their tone, however quaint their expression, and were in a minor key, both as to words and music." (p. 687) He points out that they learned the songs by ear and consequently often strayed away from the original words, making entirely new songs. These songs, he said, were "more than a source of relaxation; they were a stimulus to courage and a tie to heaven." (p. 693)

NORWEGIAN EMIGRANT SONGS AND BALLADS. *Edited and Translated by Theodore C. Blegen and Martin B. Ruud. Songs Harmonized by Gunnar J. Malmin. Minneapolis: The University of Minnesota Press. 1936. [x], 350 pp.*
  These 60 or so songs and ballads in Norwegian, with English translations, are taken mainly from newspapers of the middle years of the nineteenth century and are set in historical sketches by the editors. Many of the songs are controversial in nature, some favoring and some opposing emigration. They are a part of the folk movement to a new country, people wanting new adventure and new economic advantage. The translations are done in prose and are therefore somewhat difficult to relate to conventional folksong patterns. Piano settings have been included for eleven of the Norwegian airs, familiar folk tunes from the "old country." For the American reader this book is perhaps more valuable as social history than as song. Not indexed.

OLD, OLD FOLK SONGS. *Compiled by Fred High. Berryville, Arkansas: Braswell Printing Company. [1951] 53 pp.*
  To quote Fred: "I, Fred High, of High, Arkansas, have compiled 73 Old, Old Time Songs of several kinds to suit young and old. . . . I am now 73 years of age past, and this book contains one song for each of my years here on earth." (Fred High was born in 1878.)

Here is a hodgepodge of garbled folksongs, together with some rural verses. Fred's eccentric spelling adds to the humor. He gives credit to different ones who have contributed songs. No tunes are included. Fred High has hawked this booklet at many folk festivals.

OLD SONGS AND SINGING GAMES. *Collected and Edited by Richard Chase. Chapel Hill, North Carolina: The University of North Carolina Press. 1938. xii, 52 pp.*

This small volume contains 21 songs, ballads, and singing games, together with some explanatory notes and figures for use in teaching. There is a brief bibliography.

PEOPLE'S SONG BOOK, THE. *Edited by Waldemar Hille and others. Foreword by Alan Lomax. Preface by B. A. Botkin. New York: Boni and Gaer, Inc. 1948. 128 pp.*

Here we have a collection of 100 crusading songs—"old and new songs of faith in freedom and protest against oppression," says Botkin in the preface. Some are folksongs, some are not. The editors make a four-part division, as follows: Songs That Helped Build America, World Freedom Songs, Union Songs, and Topical-Political Songs.

PIONEER SONGS. *Compiled by Daughters of Utah Pioneers. Arranged by Alfred M. Durham. Collection of Songs used by the Pioneers enroute to and in the early settlement of the west. Also songs inspired and composed by the Pioneers in memory of their experiences. Copyrighted by Daughters of Utah Pioneers, 1932, Publishers. iv, 278 pp.*

No place of publication is given for this collection, but presumably it is Salt Lake City; however, the book was printed in Cincinnati by the Otto Zimmermann & Son Co., Inc., Music Printers.

Many of the more than 200 songs in this collection are, of course, not folksongs. There are included such songs as "America," "Annie Laurie," "Count Your Blessings," "Home Sweet Home," "Lead Kindly Light," and so on. But there are genuine folksongs, too, such as "Billy Boy," "The Lass of Mohee," "Old Dan Tucker," and others. Possibly a third or so of the songs could be classed as folksongs. There are also four traditional dance tunes.

The Daughters of Utah Pioneers was organized in 1901, with the purpose of preserving the culture and traditions of the past. This collection of songs shows what the Mormons, in their westward movement, sang along the way and afterward. Most of the songs are arranged for four-part singing, with piano accompaniment.

PLAY-PARTY IN INDIANA, THE. *A Collection of Folk-Songs and Games with Descriptive Introduction, and Correlating Notes. By Leah Jackson Wolford. Indiana Historical Collections, Vol IV. Indianapolis: Indiana Historical Commission. 1916. 120 pp.*

Part I, a brief introduction, gives an account of the play-party in Indiana in the latter nineteenth century and in the early years of the present century. Part II gives the games—58 in all—including verses, music, and explanatory notes. Part III classifies the games and offers a selected bibliography of books and periodicals.

PRAIRIE SINGS, THE. NORTHWEST KANSAS FOLKSONGS. *By Mildred Miranda McMullen. Lawrence, Kansas: University of Kansas. Typewritten Master's Thesis. January, 1946. [iii], 203 pp.*

The 133 songs in this collection were taken down from the "old settlers." The author gives a running narrative which serves as a connecting link "between the social history of the early days and the songs with which the settlers lived." (p. 2) Many of the songs were obtained from the author's mother and a friend, both of whom had come as "babes" to the prairie country, back in the seventies and eighties. There are seven chapters in Part One, each with a group of songs; and then Part Two is called "Songs of the Pioneers" and not divided into chapters. The author reports that the fiddle, the banjo, and the guitar were common in the early days in northwest Kansas. (p. 130) Tunes are included for all the songs, and footnotes give additional information.

Many of the songs found in oral tradition in northwest Kansas are well known elsewhere (as one might expect) and appear in many other collections: "Buffalo Gals," "Casey Jones," "The Dying Cowboy," "Fair Charlotte," "The Gypsy Davy," "Home on the Range" (Kansas' own native folksong), "Jesse James," "Little Mohee," "Red River Valley," "Skip to My Lou," etc. There is an index of song titles and a brief bibliography. This study is an excellent collection and discussion and should have wider currency than a typed thesis can give.

PUT'S GOLDEN SONGSTER. *Containing the Largest and Most Popular Collection of California Songs Ever Published. By the Author of* Put's Original California Songster. *San Francisco: D. E. Appleton & Co. Copyright 1858 by John A. Stone. 64 pp.*

This is a small (4″ x 6″) paperback pamphlet containing 31 "songs" without music. Except for a few items like "Sweet Betsy from Pike," these are not folksongs, but popular pieces supposed to be sung to popular tunes. Certain airs are suggested, such as "Blue-tail Fly," "Wait for the Wagon," "Lily Bell," "Comin' through the Rye," "Rosin the Bow," "Ben Bolt," "Old Dog Tray," etc., but the verses are apparently Stone's compositions. The last two pages name one hundred "Mining Localities Peculiar to California." Some color-ful names of these mining localities: Hell's Delight, Last Chance, Gouge Eye, Puke Ravine, Skunk Gulch, Dead Mule Cañon, Shin-bone Peak, Gospel Gulch, Lousy Ravine, Poverty Hill, Rough and Ready, Rat Trap Slide, Poker Flat, Coyote Hill, Git-up-and-git, Gopher Flat, Gold Hill, Stud-Horse Cañon, Centipede Hollow, Push-Coach Hill, etc.

Put's Original California Songster was published in 1854 and contained 37 songs.

READ 'EM AND WEEP. *A Treasury of American Songs—the Songs You Forgot to Remember—Some Sad, More Merry, Some Sentimental; With a Wealth of Amiable Anecdote, Comment and Fascinating Folklore—A Flavorful Feast of Melodious Music. By Sigmund Spaeth. With an Album of Elegant Art. Foreword by Richard Rodgers. New York: Arco Publishing Company. 1926. New and Revised Edition, 1945. 248 pp. + 14 pp. of the Album.*

In this discussion-collection there are about 200 songs presented in whole or in part, most of them with some musical notation. They are mainly music-hall and minstrel songs, but a few are (or have become) folksongs, such as "Casey Jones," "Erie Canal," "Frankie and Johnnie," and "Zip Coon." Most of them are popular songs which have not lasted beyond a few seasons.

ROUND THE LEVEE. *Edited by Stith Thompson. Publications of the Texas Folklore Society, Number I. 1916. Reprint edition, 1935. 111 pp.*

This copy prints, without music, 46 Texas play-party songs and games, which had been collected by R. E. Dudley and L. W. Payne, Jr. They suggest procedures for further collection of play-party materials.

This small volume also has a brief history of the Texas Folklore Society up to 1935.

SAN FRANCISCO SONGSTER, 1849-1939, A. *Cornel Lengyel, Editor. Volume Two: History of Music in San Francisco Series. San Francisco: Works Progress Administration, Northern California. 1939. 208 [mimeographed] pp.*

A note on the title page calls this "an anthology of songs and ballads sung in San Francisco from the gold rush era to the present, illustrative of the city's metamorphoses from camp to metropolis, and serving as lyric footnotes to its dramatic history."

Part I contains 52 ballads of the Forty-Niners, about one-third of them with tunes. Among these are "Crossing the Plains," "Sweet Betsy from Pike," "Jo Bowers," "Hog-Eye Man," "The Days of Forty-Nine." Part II (From Camp to City) contains 19 songs, most of them minstrel or broadside numbers. Part III (Metropolitan Song) contains 46 songs, mainly topical songs but also some urban folk ballads of protest. Within the three parts there are four, five, and six groups respectively, each group having a name (such as Cross Country and Round the Horn) and a brief introduction. "Most of the included ballads," the editor writes, "will serve as anonymous footnotes to the rich history of a region."

A number of appendices give sources of texts and tunes, music publishers in San Francisco, composers and representative early songsters, lists of the contents of some of these songsters, names of old mining camps near San Francisco, a general bibliography on balladry, and a title index. All in all, this is a well-edited and useful regional collection.

SEA SONGS AND SHANTIES. *Collected by W. B. Whall, Master Mariner. The Songs Harmonized by R. H. Whall and Ernest Reeves. Sixth Edition, Enlarged. Glasgow, Scotland: Brown, Son & Ferguson, Ltd., Publishers. 1927. Reprinted 1948. xx, 154 pp.*

Sea songs being international, such a collection as Whall's must be included in any American bibliography, since some of the songs are peculiarly American ("The Plains of Mexico," "The Hog-Eye Man," "Shenandoah," etc.) and no doubt all were sung by American sailors.

A first edition appeared in 1910, a second in 1912 containing about 50 songs, a fourth in 1920 with 63 songs, and a sixth with no further additions.

Included, besides many line drawings, are twenty-three plates of famous ships and some description of each. Captain Whall mentions "Dixie" as a favorite shanty with the sailors. Other well-known favorites: "Sally Brown," "Across the Western Ocean," "Bound for the Rio Grande," "A-Roving," "Blow the Man Down," "High Barbaree," "Haul Away Jo," "Rolling Home." Headnotes give historical background of the songs and other interesting commentary. An appendix has notes on some of the illustrations.

These songs were taken down by Captain Whall, as they were actually sung by the seamen, during his eleven years at sea, from

1861 to 1872. A nostalgic introduction gives a good deal of background for the songs in this authentic and fascinating collection.

SERIES OF OLD AMERICAN SONGS. *Reproduced in Facsimile from Original or Early Editions in the Harris Collection of American Poetry and Plays [of] Brown University. With Brief Annotations by S. Foster Damon, Curator. Providence, Rhode Island: Brown University Library. 1936. Approximately 200 [unnumbered] pp.*

These 50 songs, in facsimile reproduction with typed explanatory notes, come mainly from the music-hall or minstrel stage. They date from 1759 to the Civil War, roughly a hundred-year period. Some of them have come into the realm of traditional folksong, such as "The Hunters of Kentucky," "The Pesky Sarpent" (or, "On Springfield Mountain"), "Johnny Sands," "Old Rosin the Beau"; but most of them would be classified rather as popular stage songs and not, strictly speaking, as folksongs. The illustrated title pages have a quaint flavor.

SHANTY BOOK, THE. PART I. SAILOR SHANTIES. *Collected and Edited with Pianoforte Accompaniment, by Richard Runciman Terry, with a Foreword by Sir Walter Runciman, Bart. London: J. Curwen & Sons, Ltd. 1921. xvii, 59 pp.*

Sir Walter, an old sailor, states in the foreword: "Whatever landsmen may think about shanty words—with their cheerful inconsequence, or light-hearted coarseness—there can be no two opinions about the tunes, which, as folk-music, are a national asset." Part I contains 30 shanties, mainly windlass, capstan, and halyard. The editor's introduction shows a careful handling of the materials and gives information on musical forms, origins, and notes on each shanty. Terry gives high praise to W. B. Whall's collection, first published in 1910, but this, too, is a good brief collection.

SHANTY BOOK, THE. PART II, SAILOR SHANTIES. *Collected and Edited with Pianoforte Accompaniment, by Sir Richard Runciman Terry, with a Foreword by Sir Walter Runciman, Bart. London: J. Curwen & Sons, Ltd. 1926. xi, 69 pp.*

Again, with high praise to Whall above all others for his work in shanties, Terry prints 35 shanties in Part II. The two parts constitute an important collection of the twenties. Terry reports that an old sailor once told him that anything could be made into a shanty, and so their songs were picked up from every source and from every kind of subject matter. It is interesting to see included as shanties such songs as "Billy Boy, Can't You Dance the Polka?," "John

Brown's Body," "Paddy Works on the Railroad," and "The Banks of Sacramento."

SINGING SOLDIERS. *By John J. Niles. Illustrated by Margaret Thorniley Williamson. New York: Charles Scribner's Sons. 1927. xii, 171 pp.*

When he was a first lieutenant pilot in the United States Air Force (World War I), John J. Niles decided to make a collection of songs sung in the Army. His early observation was that the white soldiers, for the most part, sang conventional songs and that, if he were to find anything particularly original, it would be among the Negro troops. Among these "natural-born" singers he came upon something original—"a kind of folk music, brought up to date and adapted to the war situations"—music with the "haunting melodic value" he had found in Negro music when he was a boy in Kentucky.

The volume is an account of that collecting which extended over a number of years. In the account, Niles gives the texts and tunes of about 30 songs. Though some of the titles—like "Ole Ark," "Going Home Song," "Jail House," "Long Gone," and "Roll, Jordan, Roll"— suggest the usual Negro spiritual or blues song, the words are adapted to the war situation and reflect the feelings of loneliness, hunger, grief, humor, and homesickness.

SONGS AND BALLADS OF THE AMERICAN REVOLUTION. *With Notes and Illustrations by Frank Moore. New York: D. Appleton & Company. 1855. xii, 394 pp.*

Some of the 92 pieces, according to Moore, are "taken from the newspapers and periodical issues of the time; others from original ballad sheets and broadsides"; and still others from old soldiers who remembered them. There are parodies and satires and patriotic pieces. Some are by known authors, like "Liberty Tree" of Thomas Paine, but the majority are anonymous. Perhaps none have survived in oral tradition, since their substance is topical rather than universal. Music is not included for any of them, though some of them must have been sung.

SONGS AND BALLADS OF THE MAINE LUMBERJACKS. *With Other Songs from Maine. Collected and Edited by Roland Palmer Gray. Cambridge: Harvard University Press. 1924. xxi, 191 pp.*

There are 51 songs and ballads in this small collection, made by Professor Gray when he taught at State University. Three old woodsmen (Mr. Shedd, Mr. Fowler, and Mr. Chadbourne), all over seventy, sang and recited many ballads for him, as he took them down. One lumberjack told him how the songs were made—something happens, and then they put it in song, many contributing. Of the subject matter, Gray states: "Elemental emotions and simple interests, brave deeds, adventure, work, joy, sorrow, love, life's romance, life's tragedy—these are the burden of their songs. They are typical and descriptive of the lumberjack, the seaman, the warrior, and common folk. Thoroughly human, they touch all hearts." About one-third of the number are strictly lumberjack songs; others are old ballads or historical songs; also included are half a dozen "Maine broadsides." The book has a brief introduction, good headnotes, but no music. Nor is there any bibliography (except in headnotes) or index.

SONGS FROM THE OLD CAMP GROUND. *By L. L. McDowell. Genuine Religious Folk Songs of the Tennessee Hill Country. Ann Arbor, Michigan: Edwards Brothers, Inc. 1937. 85 pp.*

This lithoprinted volume contains 45 songs with tunes. They all come from oral sources, from the memory of Mr. McDowell, his family and friends, in a limited, once-isolated area of the Tennessee hills. Writes Mr. McDowell: "Every part of every melody is written, to the best of my ability, from my memory of the old songs as I heard them in my childhood around the Old Camp Ground." The text is very carefully prepared and documented, with introductory remarks and explanatory comments. There are three groups: I. Traditional Rote Songs (e.g., "Over on the Golden Shore," "Going Over Jordan"); II. Traditional Song Refrains (e.g., "I Will Arise and Go to Jesus," "I Am Bound for the Promised Land"); III. Old Hymns (e.g., "Amazing Grace," "Glorious Things of Thee Are Spoken"). Mention should be made of one other song in the collection: "One More River to Cross," a folksong title that, apparently, gave the novelist John Galsworthy a title for one of his stories. This small book is indeed a very satisfying, authentic group of religious folksongs.

SONGS LINCOLN LOVED. *By John Lair. With an Introduction by William H. Townsend. New York: Duell, Sloan and Pearce. Boston: Little, Brown and Company. 1954. ix, 85 pp.*

This interesting volume presents and discusses 47 songs considered among the favorites of Abraham Lincoln. Some are sentimental songs of the time, a few are folk hymns, many are minstrel tunes, and a goodly number are old folksongs. Among the minstrels are "Jim Crow," "Jim Crack Corn," and "Zip Coon." Among the folksongs are "Barbara Allen," "Old Dan Tucker," "Skip-to-My-Lou," and "Who

Laid de Rail?" This small book, a handsome piece of publishing, is sumptuously illustrated with old prints of songs, performers, many cartoons, etc.

SONGS OF HAWAII. *Arranged by A. R. Cunha. Assisted by W. H. Coney and Solomon Hiram. Drawings and Translations by Allan Dunn. Honolulu, Hawaiian Islands: Bergstrom Music Co. 1902. 47 pp.*

These 21 songs, most of them folksongs, "respectfully dedicated to the Princess Kawananakoa of Honolulu, T.H.," are given in the original Hawaiian language, and seven of them have English translations. All have piano accompaniments. An introductory note mentions that the musical instruments of old Hawaii (drums and reeds mainly) have given way to guitar, banjo, mandolin, ukulele, and flute. The ukulele, according to the dictionary, is a small four-string guitar of Portuguese origin which became popular in Hawaii about 1877.

SONGS OF THE COWBOYS. *Compiled by N. Howard ("Jack") Thorpe. With an Introduction by Alice Corbin Henderson. Boston: Houghton, Mifflin Company. 1921. Enlarged Edition of one first published in 1908. xxii, 184 pp.*

Unscholarly but early, this collection of 101 songs (about one-fourth of them composed by Thorpe) gives many that have since become famous: "The Cowboy's Lament," "The Dying Cowboy" ("Oh bury me not on the prairie . . ."), "Git Along Little Dogies," "The Old Chisholm Trail," "Old Paint," "The Zebra Dun," etc. Much of Thorpe's collecting preceded the elder Lomax's. Brief headnotes tell where, from whom, and (sometimes) when Thorpe gathered the songs. Many were by known authors but had wide oral circulation in the cow country. Mrs. Henderson gives a brief sketch of Thorpe, an old-time cattleman and cowpuncher, a colorful character and something of a folk poet. There is a glossary of ranching terms, an index of first lines, but no tunes.

The 1908 edition of 2,000 copies, said to be the first book of cowboy songs ever published, was printed in Estancia, New Mexico, and sold at 50 cents a copy. The printing cost Thorpe 6 cents apiece. Jack Thorpe, who died in 1940, was one of the old-time cowboys. For some fifty years in Texas, New Mexico, Arizona, and other areas, he drifted all over the cow country, carrying his banjo, punching cattle, singing and hunting songs.[*]

[*] *Atlantic Monthly*, CLXVI, 192-203 (August, 1940).

SONGS OF THE GOLD MINERS. *A Golden Collection of Songs As Sung By and About the Forty-Niners. By Sterling Sherwin and Louis Katzman, and an Introduction by Beth Moore. With Chord Accompaniments for Ukulele, Tenor Banjo and Guitar.* New York: Carl Fischer, Inc. 1932. 44 pp.

This pamphlet contains 20 songs, among them "Crossing the Plains," "Clementine," "The Days of Forty-Nine," and "Sweet Betsy from Pike." Sherwin collected them in the "gold country" direct from old miners or their descendants. This is a good if small collection.

SONGS OF THE SEA AND SAILORS' CHANTEYS: AN ANTHOLOGY. *Selected and Arranged by Robert Frothingham.* The Riverside Press, Cambridge, Massachusetts: Houghton Mifflin Company. 1924. xxii, 288 pp.

This rollicking collection, from Shakespeare to Masefield, of over 150 sea songs contains about 30 traditional chanteys, variously indicated as "long drag," "short drag," "capstan," "pumping," and just "old sea songs." The chanteys have simple, unaccompanied tunes.

SOUTH CAROLINA BALLADS. *With a Study of the Traditional Ballad Today. Collected and Edited by Reed Smith.* Cambridge: Harvard University Press. 1928. xi, 174 pp.

More than half of this small but important book is given over to discussion of problems relating to the ballads—defining ballad and folksong (Smith considers the former a narrative, the latter a lyric), the pros and cons of communal authorship and transmission, changes or "degeneration" in transmission, and other problems. Variant forms of 14 ballads and 2 songs are recorded as found in South Carolina. Simple tunes are included with some of them. Headnotes give detailed information on the finding of the ballads and tell of their appearance in other collections and in other sections of the country.

SOUTHERN HARMONY, AND MUSICAL COMPANION, THE. *By William Walker.* Philadelphia: E. W. Miller. 1835 [*First Edition*], 1847, 1854. *Reproduced in Facsimile as* The Southern Harmony Songbook, *American Guide Series, by The Federal Writers' Project of Kentucky, WPA. Sponsored by The Young Men's Progress Club of Benton, Kentucky.* New York: Hastings House, Publishers. 1939. xxxii, 336 pp.

Here is an example of the famous "harmony" books of religious folksongs, set forth in shape notes, that were so very popular in rural areas throughout the nineteenth century. This collection contains 335 songs and was widely used throughout the South. Over 600,000 copies were sold in the quarter century before the Civil War. George Pullen Jackson, chief authority on religious folksongs, writes an introductory essay on Walker and *Southern Harmony*. There are also pictures of many of the old-timers and information on Benton's Big Singing, begun in 1884 and continued annually to this day.

SPANISH-AMERICAN FOLK-SONGS. *As sung and played by Mrs. Francisca de la Guerra Dibblee [and 15 other singers]. Collected by Eleanor Hague. Lancaster, Pennsylvania, and New York: The American Folk-Lore Society. 1917. Memoirs of the American Folk-Lore Society, Vol. X. 115 pp.*

The 95 songs in this collection are gathered from Chile, Argentina, and all the way up to California and Arizona. As Miss Hague comments in her introduction: "This little volume stirs but the uppermost surface of the vast sea of charming music lying to the south of us." (p. 24)

The songs are all recorded from native singers, taken down by phonograph record or dictation. An English translation accompanies the Spanish texts, which include the tunes without any accompaniment. A 15-page introduction discusses backgrounds, and there is a brief bibliography at the end. Miss Hague includes source and singer with each song. Many of the songs, of course, are known in our own Spanish Southwest.

STEAMBOATIN' DAYS. *Folk Songs of the River Packet Era. By Mary Wheeler. Baton Rouge, Louisiana: Louisiana State University Press. 1944. xiv, 121 pp.*

This book of 66 songs, with eleven full-page illustrations, contains the words and melodies of the songs "taken down from the singing of old Negroes who in their youth worked on the boats." These are tales of the river life of the Ohio, Mississippi, and Tennessee rivers. These are called "rouster songs," because they were sung by the roustabouts, the Negro workers on the docks and the river packets. Besides the songs, the book contains a good deal of background material pertaining to the river-boat activities, by way of introductory and concluding matter. There are eight sections of songs, as follows: Work Songs, Songs of Boats, Soundings, Spirituals, Songs of Meditation, Love Songs, Dance Songs, and Songs of Lawlessness. The introduction states that the first steamboat on the Ohio was the *New Orleans,* built in Pittsburgh in 1811, and that "the most romantic period of the packet boat was just prior to and following the War Between the States." A sampling of titles includes "Careless Love," "I Am Waitin' on the Levee," "Red Sea," and others less well known.

STORY OF "HOME ON THE RANGE," THE. *By Kirke Mechem. A Reprint from* The Kansas Historical Quarterly, *pp. 313-339, Vol. XVII, Number 4. November, 1949. Topeka, Kansas: The Kansas State Historical Society. 33 pp.*

This interesting research essay establishes several things: the dates and the names of the author and the composer of "Home on the Range," and the methods whereby the peregrinations of an ordinary, simple art-song caused it to become a folksong. The song first appeared in print in 1873 in a newspaper called the *Smith County Pioneer.* The author was Dr. Brewster Higley, a practicing physician in pioneer Smith County, Kansas; the man who "made up" the music but never wrote it down was another pioneer and businessman, Daniel E. Kelley. The song came to light in this century, when John A. Lomax found it on the Texas ranges among the cowboys and published it in 1910 as a folksong. It has enjoyed folksong status ever since, being sung all over America and in Europe, Asia, Antarctica (by Richard E. Byrd), and wherever Americans have ranged over the modern world. No one was much concerned about the author or composer until in 1934, when suit was brought for infringement of copyright by someone who claimed authorship. Then researches began which, in 1935, led to establishment of the author and the composer.

STORY OF THE JUBILEE SINGERS, WITH THEIR SONGS, THE. *By J. B. T. Marsh. Revised Edition. Sixty-Fifth Thousand. Boston: Houghton, Mifflin and Company. 1881. viii, 243 pp.*

The first half of this book (eleven chapters and 120 pages) gives the story of the struggle to establish Fisk University and the part the Jubilee Singers played in that story. Chapter XI is particularly interesting because of the factual data, "Personal History of the Singers." "At different times twenty-four persons in all have belonged to the company," twenty of whom had been slaves, the account says. Rather full biographical sketches are given of ten of the singers.

The second half of the book gives the songs, 112 in all, most of them harmonized for four-part singing. Many of the great and popular favorites are here: "Deep River," "Inching Along," "John Brown's Body," "Mary and Martha," "Steal Away," "Swing Low, Sweet Chariot," and many others.

SWING AND TURN: TEXAS PLAY-PARTY GAMES. *By William A. Owens. Dallas, Texas: Tardy Publishing Co. 1936. xxxiii, 117 pp.*

This collection of 64 singing games is divided into three groups: Children's Games (6), Longways Dances (7), and Ring Games (51).

Simple melodies and explanation of movements are given for each of them. The collector's introduction gives a full and clear account of the play-party and the reasons for its development: a desire to relieve the tedium of lonely frontier or country life, and a means of light and rhythmic entertainment in place of dancing. This last was tabooed by the Protestant churches and was considered, like card playing, as an instrument of the devil.

Many or perhaps most of the singing games in this collection are known in other parts of America. Who, for instance, hasn't heard of or swung to "Itiskit Itaskit," "Weevily Wheat," "The Girl I Left Behind Me," "Old Dan Tucker," "Pig in the Parlor," "Old Joe Clark," "Skip to My Lou," or "She'll Be Comin' Round the Mountain"? The play-party singing stanza is usually four lines, with much repetition.

The collector has included explanations of a list of terms used in the play-party games (needed for the uninitiated, no doubt), a brief bibliography, and an index of first lines. This is a valuable collection, of more than Texas-wide interest.

TALES AND SONGS OF SOUTHERN ILLINOIS. *Collected by Charles Neely. Edited with a Foreword by John Webster Spargo. Menasha, Wisconsin: The Collegiate Press, George Banta Publishing Co. 1938. xix, 270 pp. and a double-spread map.*

Part II of this book, slightly more than half of it, is devoted to 83 ballads and songs. Neely divides them into ten chapters, the usual groupings being suggested, such as British Ballads, Other Imported Ballads, American Ballads, Western Songs, Nursery and Game Songs, etc. Some variants are given, headnotes add explanatory comments, and footnotes (at the chapter ends) give sources, including singers and their addresses. There is an index, but except for a few samples, melodies are not included.

Neely, who died prematurely on March 11, 1937, was a teacher of English at Southern Illinois Teachers College, Carbondale, and had collected these tales and songs during the previous twelve years.

TEXAS AND SOUTHWESTERN LORE. *Edited by J. Frank Dobie. Publications of the Texas Folk-Lore Society, Number VI. Austin, Texas: Published by the Texas Folk-Lore Society. 1927. 260 pp.*

About half of this volume (pp. 121-237) is devoted to discussion and printing of ballads and songs, the largest group (63 pages) called "Ballads and Songs of the Frontier Folk" edited by Dobie and containing over 30 songs. As always, Dobie's discussions are lively and informative. The whole volume contains 80 songs and ballads, and a considerable variety—songs of the cowboy, the tramp, battle and war songs, badman ballads, Mexican songs, love songs, etc.

THEY KNEW PAUL BUNYAN. *By E. C. Beck. Illustrated by Anita Eneroth. Ann Arbor: University of Michigan Press. 1956. [x], 255 pp.*

Many of the 67 songs and poems in this third collection by Beck had appeared already in his *Lore of the Lumber Camps* (1948), which was an enlarged edition of his *Songs of the Michigan Lumberjacks* (1941). Thus, except for the slight variants and for a further swatch of "Tall Tales from the Thick Timber," this volume adds little to the earlier volumes. Sixteen tunes are included, the drawings by Eneroth are lively, and there is an index of songs and poems. Such well-known numbers as "The Curst Wife," "Drill Ye, Tarriers," "The Jam on Gerry's Rocks," and "Little Brown Bulls" are included.

TRADITIONAL BALLADS, MAINLY FROM WEST VIRGINIA. *By John Harrington Cox. Introductory Essay and Supplementary References by Herbert Halpert. American Folk-Song Publications, No. 3. Edited by Dr. George Herzog and Herbert Halpert. New York City: National Service Bureau, WPA. March, 1939. Mimeographed. xiv, 109 pp.*

In this collection done under the auspices of the West Virginia Folk-Lore Society there are 37 melodies and 49 texts, including fragments and variants. More than half of them are from West Virginia, and others were recorded in Kentucky, California, Indiana, and elsewhere. Halpert's introduction discusses "truth in folksongs" and some attitudes of the singers. The book is rounded out with 15 pages of scholarly notes and references on the ballads, and 5 pages of bibliography, listing approximately eighty items without annotations. Headnotes give the names of singers or other sources, as well as time and place of collecting.

TREASURY OF AMERICAN BALLADS: GAY, NAUGHTY, AND CLASSIC, A. *Edited with an Introduction and Notes by Charles O'Brien Kennedy. Illustrated by Barye Phillips. Special Vista House Edition. New York: The McBride Company. 1954. xvii, 398 pp.*

Of the 232 ballads in this collection, 77 are listed as anonymous. In other words, most of the items are literary ballads, though some with known authors have had wide oral circulation. Among these are "Oh! Susanna" (Foster), "Old Dan Tucker" (Emmet), "When

Johnny Comes Marching Home" (Gilmore), "John Brown's Body" (Bishop), etc. The work contains no tunes, few notes, and no references, though it has an index of first lines. It is a collection designed merely for popular reading.

A similar volume was done by Kennedy in 1952 for Fawcett Publications, Inc., and reprinted as a Premier paperback in 1956.

TREASURY OF FOLK SONGS, A. *Edited and Compiled by Sylvia and John Kolb. New York: Bantam Books. 1948. Revised 1955. xvi, 240 pp.*

This popular international collection of 90 folksongs, with tunes, contains most of the famous ones, from old Scottish ballads to compositions by Woody Guthrie. The editors have made a dozen groupings, with brief introductions. Headnotes offer interesting comments, not for the scholar but for the uninformed layman—the person who sings many of these songs before he ever sees them in a book. There's a brief preface, an index of titles and first lines, a list of one hundred helpful books (and a good list it is), and a guide to recordings of most of the songs in the book. Here indeed is a pocketful of folksongs for 35 cents, and its many printings attest its genuine popularity.

UNSUNG AMERICANS SUNG. *Edited by W. C. Handy. New York: Handy Brothers Music Company. 1944. 236 pp.*

This is an interesting book of songs, poems, brief biographies, and drawings (by Beauford De Laney) of famous American Negroes, past and present. There are 39 musical compositions, most of which are not folksongs. Exceptions might be "The Memphis Blues" and "John Brown's Body."

VOICE OF HAITI, THE. *By LeRoy Antoine. New York: Clarence Williams Music Pub. Co., Inc. 1938. 41 pp.*

In this large quarto volume are 32 native Haitian ceremonial folksongs, with tunes, given in the native Creole-French patois, and all with English translations. Antoine states that the songs had not been printed before. An introduction tells of the social and religious background, especially voodooism, which produced the songs. The compiler, LeRoy Antoine, a native of Haiti, writes: "All of the songs in this book are authentic, having been procured through first-hand information and personal associations with the natives, while on a six months' visit to the interior of Haiti." The latter pages contain seven scores for the three drums commonly used for voodoo rhythm.

WEEP SOME MORE, MY LADY. *By Sigmund Spaeth. Garden City, New York: Doubleday, Page & Company, 1927. xv, 268 pp.*

This book, containing well over 150 songs with tunes, is another in the Spaeth series of old-time songs that were once popular. The editor includes them as "typical examples of the sentiment of a past generation" and gives ample discussion along with the songs. Some titles of the ten chapters are: The School of Self-Pity, The Eternal Story, Ballads and Near-Ballads, Mottoes and Moralizing.

The connection of this kind of song with folksong is that some of these popular songs get into oral circulation and virtually become ballads or folksongs; or, some of them are drawn from authentic folksong material. Examples of these are: "Blue-Eyed Ellen" ("The Jealous Lover of Lone Green Valley"), "Buffalo Gals," "Young Charlotte," "The Dying Hobo," and "Stackalee." Aside from the songs themselves, the book is highly diverting, informative reading matter.

CHAPTER 15

Archives and Bibliographical Items

A. *Archives*

Though it might be desirable, a complete listing and description of folklore archives is not attempted here, for that problem lies outside the scope of this work. Furthermore, this task has been undertaken by a committee of the American Folklore Society under the guidance of Thelma G. James of Wayne State University, Detroit. In April, 1956, Miss James reported, among other things, that "there are vast quantities of all kinds of folklore materials already collected in this country," that these materials are "almost entirely unarchived" and are "virtually inaccessible to either archivists or scholars." [1] This AFS committee on archiving hopes in time to prepare an "accurate list of the archives of American Folklore" and to develop a "workable classification system for these archives."

Indiana University has undertaken, through its Divisions of the Research Center in Anthropology, Folklore and Linguistics, to set forth and clarify some of the problems in archiving by establishing a quarterly magazine or bulletin titled *The Folklore and Folk Music Archivist*. The bulletin, edited by George List, supervisor of the Indiana University Archives of Folk and Primitive Music, is described in its first issue (March, 1958) as "a publication devoted to the collection, documentation, indexing and cataloguing of folklore and folk music." In "A Very Preliminary Statement" in this first issue, William Hugh Jansen, archivist at the University of Kentucky,

393

pointed out that "no greater chaos can be imagined than that which prevails among various set-ups which are, or might be, termed folk archives in the United States."

The present chapter, therefore, can undertake only a brief comment on one area of some folklore archives known to the writer, namely, the area of folksong. To begin with, a few observations are in order. A goodly number of singers discussed in Book One have their own private archives from which, frequently, they build a program or publish songs. In particular I would mention Horton Barker, George W. Boswell, Edgar Rogie Clark, Paul Clayton, Richard Dyer-Bennet, Sam Eskin, Dr. I. G. Greer, Anne Grimes, L. M. Hilton, Marty King, Bascom Lamar Lunsford, Brownie McNeil, Josef Marais, Winnifred Moon, Artus Moser, John Jacob Niles, Jean Ritchie, Ruth Rubin, Frank Warner, and Josh White. Many of those named, as well as others, at one time or another, have given materials to various state or national archives. On the other hand, in order to build up an extensive repertoire, some singers have gone to the archives, as well as to the book collections of ballads and folksongs. And, of course, there's no objection to picking up a few songs by listening to other singers' commercial recordings. Among those who have extended their repertoires by one or more of these methods, one might mention Harry Belafonte, Oscar Brand, William Clauson, Bob Duncan, Cynthia Gooding, Ed McCurdy, Alan Mills, Jean Murai, Pete Seeger, Hally Wood. One more point, perhaps too obvious to need statement, is that any number of the published collections discussed in Book Two are the products of some archive. To be mentioned here are the *Frank C. Brown Collection of North Carolina Folklore* (four volumes published and three more projected), collections published by Marius Barbeau and others from the Canadian archives in the National Museum at Ottawa, the several B. A. Botkin *Treasury* folklore books, which draw heavily on the Library of Congress holdings, Helen Hartness Flanders volumes from the Flanders Ballad Collection in Vermont, and several booklets in "Schirmer's American Folk Song Series" from the John Jacob Niles collection.

But to mention briefly some of the archives in more specific detail. The Archive of American Folk Song of the Library of Congress, Music Division, is the chief archive in the United States. A part of the introductory note of the combined catalogue of phonograph recordings states:

> The Archive of American Folk Song, now a part of the Folklore Section of the Library of Congress, was established

in 1928 when Robert W. Gordon was appointed the first curator. Subsequent curators of the collections were John A. Lomax, his son, Alan Lomax, and B. A. Botkin. Through their efforts and those of the present staff the collections have grown to be world famous and include over 10,000 acetate recordings with over 40,000 different songs and ballads, fiddle tunes, harmonica and banjo pieces, and other indigenous American folk music. In addition to material from the United States, the Archive houses also folk music from many Latin American countries, from Europe and the rest of the world as well. . . . Almost every region of the United States is represented in the Library's collection of field recordings and encouragement is now being given to the establishment of archives in each state, in order that scholars may have locally available the materials of their own region. These regional archives are normally housed in the library collection of a state university.[2]

Early in 1953, the library began to issue some of its folksong materials on long-playing microgroove records.[3] (See Book Three for further details.)

In 1949, the Arkansas Folklore Society began collecting songs, by tape recorder, for the University of Arkansas Folklore Archives. By early 1957, a total of 855 songs, in 962 texts, had been collected successively by Merlin Mitchell, Irene Carlisle, and Mary Celestia Parler. Miss Parler is archivist for this collection.[4]

A Northern California Archive is being developed at Chico State College under the direction of Hector Lee.[5]

Florida Folklore Archives are being built up at Florida State University at Tallahassee under the direction of Professor J. Russell Reaver.[6]

In the very active Folklore Center at Indiana University, Bloomington, there are recordings of some 20,000 items, "with representation of a large portion of the cultural areas of the world." This is designated the Archives of Folk and Primitive Music, originally founded by George Herzog at Columbia University and brought by him to Indiana University at the time he was appointed professor of anthropology (1948). The archives also "maintains a collection of folk, primitive and Oriental musical instruments."[7]

In Kansas, the Board of Regents of the University of Wichita has made a grant for establishing an archive of folklore, the first in the state. Miss Joan O'Bryant, teacher of English, collector and singer of folksongs, has been active in tape-recording several hundred songs and folk tales.[8]

In Kentucky, Professor William Jansen is organizing and directing the Kentucky Folklore Archives at the University in Lexington.[9] A Western Kentucky Folklore Archive was established in 1953 by D. K. Wilgus at Western Kentucky State College, Bowling Green. Of the 11,000 items, some 3,500 are songs. "An adjunct to the archive is a collection of approximately 2,000 commercial recordings, largely hillbilly." [10]

Cecil Sharp's original manuscript collection, out of which came *English Folk Songs from the Southern Appalachians* (Oxford, 1932), "is in the Clare College Library at Cambridge [England], and there are also complete copies in the Harvard College Library, Cambridge, Massachusetts, and in the New York Public Library." [11] The Harvard College Library has, of course, many manuscript collections, including those of Francis J. Child, George L. Kittredge, Phillips Barry, and others.

In the New England area off the Harvard campus, the most important archive is the Helen Hartness Flanders Collection at Middlebury College, Middlebury, Vermont. Established in 1941 by Mrs. Helen Hartness Flanders of Springfield, Vermont, with her private collection as a nucleus, the archive began with 1,500 items of Vermont and New Hampshire tradition. Among the items were fiddle tunes, ballads and folksongs of American and British origin, hymnals, and singing games. Since 1941, the collection has grown to nearly 10,000 items, collected from all the New England states. Included, besides American and British materials, are ballads and folksongs of French-Canadian, Finnish, German, Polish, Russian, Spanish, and Swedish origin—all these gathered in New England. The materials are on cylinder, disc, and tape. In addition to the recorded materials, the college and friends in 1943 started a library which now contains over 1,500 volumes, as well as other materials such as songsters, articles, and folksong albums, "selected to contribute to the comparative study of the ballads and folksongs recovered in New England." [12]

Much Pennsylvania folksong, as well as other folklore, has been collected under the direction of Henry W. Shoemaker and George G. Korson, both of whom have been important figures in the Pennsylvania Folklore Society. These materials are placed in the archives of the State Museum Building at Harrisburg.[13]

In 1947, Richard M. Dorson began the collecting of folklore, with the help of his students, at Michigan State University, East Lansing, Michigan. A vast amount of materials was brought together, "distributed in seven file boxes," one of which was American folksongs, fiddle tunes, and folk dance.[14] When Professor Dorson, in 1957, was appointed professor of history and folklore at Indiana University, the Michigan State archive was transferred to Indiana.[15]

Wayne State University in Detroit, Michigan, began a folklore archive in 1939, under the direction of Miss Emelyn E. Gardner and continued under Professor Thelma James. "It has become the task of the Wayne University Folklore Archives to deal with the traditional materials of the ethnic groups in the [metropolitan Detroit] area." Professor James mentions "tales and songs" as being among the larger groups in the archives.[16]

In New Mexico, the Folklore Archive of Hispanic Folk Music has been developed under the leadership of Dr. John Donald Robb, dean of the College of Fine Arts at the University of New Mexico, Albuquerque. During a number of years Dean Robb has collected something over "1300 popular and folk tunes of the Southwest" on discs, wire, and tape recordings. These he has transcribed to phonographic records, in duplicate, one for the university library and one for his personal use.[17]

The Archive of Ohio Folklore and Music was established at the Miami University Library, Oxford, Ohio, in 1948 and became the official archive of the Ohio Folklore Society in 1951.[18] "The general collection includes standard books and periodicals, and some 2,000 commercial recordings, relating to the whole range of world folklore. The special collections are an Ohio collection, which includes the Bruce Buckley Scioto County Collection (tape and manuscript); the Bascom Lamar Lunsford Collection of North Carolina folklore (tape and manuscript); and an Afro-American collection (primarily commercial recordings, books, and tape)." [19]

An extensive job of collecting folksongs in Oklahoma has been carried on by Ethel and Chauncey Moore. Beginning in 1925 and continuing for twenty-five years, they have collected over 400 titles in 1,400 different texts and 1,100 different tunes, all from oral sources, by "direct transcription at first and later, by tape recording." [20]

Collecting and archiving have been done in Texas for a long time, with much material housed at the University of Texas in Austin. The work of the Lomaxes is discussed elsewhere in this book, but it should be mentioned that the great body of their folksong material is housed at the university. In 1941-42, Mr. John Faulk, working on a Rosenwald Fellowship, made a collection of Negro folk sermons and folk music, which he later gave to the university. He was assisted by Hally Wood Gordon, who later transcribed much of the Faulk music as well as many songs in the Lomax collection.[21]

In the Old Dominion State of Virginia, long considered a sort of folksong paradise, collecting and archiving have been extensive in the past generation, particularly under the leadership of Dr. Arthur Kyle Davis, Jr., archivist of the Virginia Folklore Society. (A later item in the present chapter describes Dr. Davis' *Folk-Songs of Virginia, A Descriptive Index.*) Besides the Folklore Society Archives, there is the Winston Wilkinson collection of folk music in the Alderman Library, University of Virginia, Charlottesville. It is a two-volume work called "The University of Virginia Collection of Folk Music," totaling 657 pages in typescript and containing 321 items, e.g., hymns, ballads, carols, etc.[22]

In West Virginia, Dr. Ruth Ann Musick, secretary-archivist of the state's Folklore Society since 1950, has accumulated a large body of ballads and folksongs—"disc records in a large file cabinet and a bookcase shelf of tapes"—some of it ready for publication.[23] Before the recent revival of the WVFS, much work in collecting had been done before 1925 under the leadership of John Harrington Cox of West Virginia University, and further materials have been added by Dr. Patrick W. Gainer (*q.v.*), collector and folksinger, and a member of the English faculty, West Virginia University, Morgantown.

Concerning the archives in Canada, I shall make only brief mention. By all odds the most significant work in folklore has been done by the distinguished French-Canadian Dr. Marius Barbeau. For nearly forty years he was anthropologist and folklorist for the National Museum of Canada at Ottawa, during which time, beginning about 1915, he collected more than 10,000 songs and ballads and 6,000 melodies. Many of these are still in manuscript or on phonograph discs, though some books based on them have been published.[24] (See the entries under Barbeau at the beginning of Book Two.) Additions by others have brought the total to more than "7,000 melodies and 13,000 texts."[25]

Recently the collectors Carmen Roy (for the Gaspé Peninsula), Helen Creighton (for Nova Scotia), Margaret Sargent McTaggart and Kenneth Peacock (for Newfoundland) have added still more songs to Canada's store. To the above figures should be added over 3,000 recordings of Indian songs, "the most important individual collection of native music on the continent."[26] And mention should be made of the extensive French-Canadian Archives of Folklore, which includes thousands of songs, housed at the Université Laval in Quebec, under the direction of Professor Luc Lacourcière.

An interesting semiprivate collection in Canada is housed at Newcastle, New Brunswick, in the Old Manse Library, under the care of Miss Louise Manny. There are, in fact, "three folksong collections," one sponsored by Lord Beaverbrook (about 50 songs on discs and tapes), another collected by Miss Manny and a friend (some 50 songs on discs and tapes), and a third group made for a local radio station, CKMR. These collections are constantly being augmented, and the Beaverbrook Collection was apparently done for the University of New Brunswick at Fredericton.[27]

The preceding paragraphs on various archives, though somewhat sketchy and admittedly incomplete (see, again, the opening paragraph), will give the reader some idea of the vastness of materials yet unpublished. Perhaps, too, these paragraphs hint at the possibilities of further collecting that may be done and further archiving that must be done.

B. *Bibliographical Items*

AMERICAN BALLADRY FROM BRITISH BROADSIDES. *A Guide for Students and Collectors of Traditional Song. By G. Malcolm Laws, Jr. Publications of the American Folklore Society: Bibliographical and Special Series, General Editor, MacEdward Leach, Volume VIII. Philadelphia: The American Folklore Society. 1957. xiii, 315 pp.*

In organization, this work follows Laws' earlier study, *Native American Balladry* (1950), the first half being a series of four chapter discussions: I. The Types of British Broadside Ballads Traditional in America; II. The Origin and Distribution of the Broadside Ballads; III. Broadside Balladry as Traditional Song; and IV. Broadside Ballad Forms and Variants.

The second half is a series of three appendices, the first being the longest (169 pages) and offering a bibliographical syllabus of 290 British broadside ballads current in American tradition. The ballads are grouped into eight categories (war, sailors and the sea, crime and criminals, family opposition to lovers, lovers' disguises, faithful lovers, unfaithful lovers, humorous and miscellaneous), and a summary of each ballad in a few sentences, with a single stanza, gives the gist of the story. Then references locate the ballad in collections. Appendix II lists 85 British and 26 American ballad printers of the nineteenth century. Appendix III lists some American recordings of British broadside ballads (95 titles are given), these drawn from Lumpkin's *Folksongs on Records* (*q.v.*) and a *Check-List of Recorded Songs* (*q.v.*) published by the Library of Congress. This most useful book for student and collector concludes with an excellent selected bibliography (nearly 200 items) and an index of the ballad titles.

AMERICAN FOLK MUSIC. *Compiled by Annabel Morris Buchanan. Native Folk Music Found in America, Including Anglo-American (English, Scotch, Irish), Indian, Negro, Creole, Canadian, Mexican and Spanish-American, and a small amount from German, Norwegian, Hungarian and Portuguese sources. Sacred and Secular Forms, Presented in Songs, Tunes, Bibliography, Collections, Choral and Instrumental Settings, American Compositions Based on Native Traditional Material with Old-World Forms for Comparison. [Compiled] For National Federation of Music Clubs. New York: National Federation of Music Clubs. 1939. 57 pp. [mimeographed]*

The above long title page satisfactorily describes the contents of this compact bibliography. The material is organized into twelve parts, the first seven being the major groupings and the remaining "a small amount from the German . . ." etc. Within each part there are listings of collections, history, and criticism; songs, instrumental works, operas, chamber music, band, and orchestra. There are brief annotations, and though in many cases the bibliographical information is far from complete, this is a useful and in many ways satisfactory bibliography.

AMERICAN FOLK SONG AND FOLK LORE. *A Regional Bibliography. By Alan Lomax and Sidney Robertson Cowell. New York: Hinds, Hayden & Eldredge, Inc. 1942. 59 pp.*

This little booklet, one of the Service Center Pamphlets of the American Education Fellowship, is a useful, popular bibliography which lists over 400 items with very brief annotations. The items are classified into thirteen sections, partly regional (The North, The Negro South, The West, etc.) and partly as to subject matter (Occupational Ballads, White Spirituals, Dances and Games, etc.).

AN ANALYTICAL INDEX TO THE JOURNAL OF AMERICAN FOLKLORE, VOLS. 1-67, 68, 69, 70. *By Tristram P. Coffin. Publications of the American Folklore Society: Bibliographical and Special Series, General Editor, MacEdward Leach, Volume VII. Philadelphia: The American Folklore Society. 1958. xvi, 384 pp.*

Long needed, even in the tentative state Coffin describes in his delightful introductory essay, "Troubles of a Harmless Drudge," this *Analytical Index* is most welcome and will indeed be useful to all students of folklore. Its double-column 384 pages of fine print are organized into eight parts as follows: (1) Titles of Articles, Notes, etc.; (2) Authors of Articles, Notes, Reviews, etc.; (3) Book Reviews, by Author of Book Reviewed; (4) News and Notices; (5) Subjects and Areas in Folklore; (6) Nationalities and Ethnic Groups;

(7) Songs and Rimes: Titles and First Significant Lines; (8) Tales: Types, Incidents, Characters, Objects, etc. Coffin calls on "scholar slavery" to proofread the present paperback index, in anticipation of a definitive index of the journal's first seventy-five years to be published about 1964.

A BIBLIOGRAPHY FOR THE STUDY OF AMERICAN FOLK-SONGS WITH MANY TITLES OF FOLK-SONGS (AND TITLES THAT HAVE TO DO WITH FOLK-SONGS) FROM OTHER LANDS. *By Mellinger Edward Henry. London: The Mitre Press. n. d. 142 pp. "This edition is limited to 750 copies."*

For a straight, uncritical, alphabetical author-listing of materials on folksong, these 142 pages can be useful. But many items are incomplete and no annotations are given. The book is not dated, though no entries appear after 1936. A quick calculation indicates that there are about 2,800 entries. The Prefatory Note states, in part: "This is not a scientific bibliography. No effort has been made to list separately authors or editors and subject matter. . . . Nor have all titles listed herein been examined. . . . If full information concerning an item is sometimes lacking, it has not been possible, under the circumstances, to supply it."

A BIBLIOGRAPHY OF NORTH AMERICAN FOLKLORE AND FOLKSONG. *By Charles Haywood. New York: Greenberg. 1951. xxx, 1,292 pp.*

Only such adjectives as prodigious and magnificent begin to characterize adequately this most scholarly, most usable, and most nearly complete bibliography in the field of folklore and folksong. Here we have in nearly 1,300 pages of double-column print a systematic presentation of the materials for research in the field, the like of which had never before been attempted. To say that workers in folksong and folklore are eternally indebted to Dr. Haywood is to say the obvious.

For so large a work, the compiler has a relatively simple plan of organization. The whole work is laid out in two books. Book One covers "The American People North of Mexico" and Book Two covers "The American Indians North of Mexico." Part One of Book One is a General Bibliography on Folklore and Folksong. Part Two is Regional Bibliography, including these six regions (besides Canada and Alaska): the Northeast, the South and southern Highlands, the Midwest, the Southwest, the West, and the Northeast. Then each of the six regions has its separate folklore and folksong entries; after this, the entries for each state of the region are given in the same manner. Part Three is Ethnic Bibliography, including the Negro and the non–English speaking groups. Part Four is Occupational Bibliography, and Part Five is Miscellaneous.

Many of the bibliographical entries carry useful annotations. An extensive index (pp. 1161 to 1292) makes it possible to find any entry quickly.

THE BRITISH TRADITIONAL BALLAD IN NORTH AMERICA. *By Tristram P. Coffin. Publications of the American Folklore Society: Bibliographical Series, Volume II, 1950. Philadelphia: The American Folklore Society. 1950. xvi, 188 pp.*

"The purpose of this book," Coffin states in the introduction, "as it covers the field to May 1950, is to offer the ballad scholar and particularly the student of ballad variation, a key to the published material on the Child ballad in America." Following a 20-page essay entitled "A Description of Variation in the Traditional Ballad of America," the author devotes the bulk of his work (132 pages) to "A Critical, Bibliographical Study of the Traditional Ballad of America." This long section studies in detail the text of some 140 Child ballads, giving story types, location of printed texts, and further comment on discussions about each ballad. A most useful and scholarly work in the study of variations. There are nine pages listing hundreds of items in a "general bibliography" used in preparing the work.

CHECK-LIST OF RECORDED SONGS IN THE ENGLISH LANGUAGE IN THE ARCHIVE OF AMERICAN FOLK SONG TO JULY, 1940. *Alphabetic List with Geographical Index. A-K to p. 216 and L-Z, pp. 217-456. Geographical Index, pp. 1-138. [total mimeographed pages: 594] Washington, D. C.: The Library of Congress, Music Division. 1942.*

Begun in 1933 with the extensive collecting of John and Alan Lomax, the archive has grown to contain upward of 40,000 "different songs and ballads, fiddle tunes, harmonica and banjo pieces, and other indigenous American folk music." The present *Check-List* of about 10,000 recordings represents the work done by the Lomaxes between 1933 and 1940. The actual number of different songs, however, is approximately 6,000, since many have been recorded more than once in a state or section. To note a few instances: "The Arkansas Traveler" is recorded 26 times, "Amazing Grace" 16 times, "Barbara Allen" 64 times, "Black-Eyed Susan" 10 times, "Jesse James" 11 times, "The House Carpenter" 42 times, and any number of other songs two or three times each.

Each entry includes song title, name of performer(s) with address(es), musical instrument(s) used if any, name of collector(s), and call number of the disc. The Geographical Index is a cross-indexing by states and by counties within states. Though not all the states are represented in this listing up to 1940, songs are recorded from thirty-six states, the District of Columbia, and the Bahamas. Those predominating in number of recordings are Alabama, California, Florida, Kentucky (largest number), Louisiana, Michigan, Mississippi, North Carolina, South Carolina, Tennessee, Texas, and Virginia. Numbers from counties in the other two dozen states are scattered.

The recordings, done "in the field" on aluminum or acetate discs, have great authenticity if far less polish than studio performances. In 1940, the Carnegie Foundation granted funds for a Recording Laboratory in the library's Music Division for duplication of the records. (The introduction states that duplicates of the disc of any song may be had by writing the archive.) Hundreds of the songs are now available on nonbreakable 78's, and several dozen long-playing albums have been issued. (These are obtainable only from the Recording Laboratory, Music Division, Library of Congress, and not from commercial houses.)

FOLK MUSIC OF THE UNITED STATES AND LATIN AMERICA. *Combined Catalog of Phonograph Records. Washington, D. C.: The Library of Congress, Division of Music. 1942. Reprinted 1953. 47 pp.*

The catalogue contains a statement about the Archive of American Folk Song by Duncan Emrich; an introductory note, then the descriptive contents of the albums now issued for sale, an alphabetical list of album titles, and an alphabetical list of song titles. There are 107 records (78 rpm) containing 341 songs now available for purchase. Some have recently been issued on long-playing records. (See Book Three.)

FOLK-SONG OF NEBRASKA AND THE CENTRAL WEST, A SYLLABUS. *By Louise Pound. Nebraska Ethnology and Folk Lore Series. Addison E. Sheldon, Editor. [Lincoln, Nebraska] Nebraska Academy of Sciences Publications, Vol. IX, No. 3. 1915. 89 pp.*

This useful small book is an annotated syllabus of approximately 325 folksongs found in Nebraska and the Central West. The editor, the late Dr. Pound, distinguished folklorist and authority on ballad literature, groups the songs into 32 categories, beginning with English and Scottish popular ballads, continuing with such groupings as pioneer and Western songs, elegies and complaints, songs of the lost at sea, religious pieces, temperance songs, railroad songs, humorous songs, songs dealing with Indian material, and finally ending with skipping-rope songs or rhymes.

The editor has attempted to include in the *Syllabus* "what the people have cared to preserve, regardless of question of origin, or quality, or technique." (p. 4) In the songs for each group except one, Dr. Pound gives a brief sentence-summary of each folksong with an opening stanza. This makes for easy identification. In one group, pioneer and Western songs, she has printed the full texts of the 16 songs in that group. Other items in the *Syllabus* are a brief introduction, a few old Western pictures ("The Little Old Sod Shanty," etc.), an index, but no tunes.

FOLK-SONGS OF VIRGINIA. *A Descriptive Index and Classification of Material Collected under the Auspices of the Virginia Folklore Society. By Arthur Kyle Davis, Jr. Durham, North Carolina: Duke University Press. 1949. lxiii, 389 pp.*

The subtitle indicates the purpose of this excellent bibliographical study. Davis states that the number of folksongs collected by the Virginia Folklore Society "is now well over three thousand." (p. ix)

This work does not contain the folksongs but lists them by title, when and where and by whom collected, and lists *all* the collecting that has been done of any one song. Some songs have been collected dozens of times in as many different places. For instance, 36 different "collectings" were made of "The Frog's Wooing," 22 of "Sweet William," 18 of "The Derby Ram," 26 of "Barbara Allen," etc. All told, the book lists 2,454 versions or variants of 974 songs, including 263 versions of 61 Child ballads.

The introduction gives a brief history of the Virginia Folklore Society and its work. All its collected materials (manuscripts, recordings, etc.) are now housed in the basement of the Graduate House at the University of Virginia.

FOLKSONGS ON RECORDS. *Compiled and Edited by Ben Gray Lumpkin, with Norman L. ("Brownie") McNeil and forty other collectors. Issue Three, Cumulative, including essential material in issues one and two. Published by Folksongs on Records, Boulder, Colorado, and Alan Swallow, Publisher, Denver. 1950. [viii], 98 pp.*

This paper-bound issue lists nearly 4,000 folksongs on records. Lumpkin's purpose is a laudable one and clearly stated: it is to "help to distinguish genuine folksong records from imitations." Many of the records listed are out of print or circulation, but many can be obtained by record-finder companies. Lumpkin's comments on the quality and character of the recordings are useful to the student and collector alike. After the main section, there are a bibliography of recent books and articles, a list of collectors and contributors, and various indexes to recordings.

A GUIDE TO AMERICAN FOLKLORE. *By Levette J. Davidson. Denver: The University of Denver Press. 1951. xii, 132 pp.*

This elementary handbook is compact, useful, and well organized. There are fifteen chapters, each with a brief explanatory discussion, followed by a bibliographical listing of basic readings and general references, and this in turn is followed by ten or a dozen suggestions for further study and for collecting. Sample chapter titles: What Is Folklore?; Folk Heroes; Songs, Ballads, and Rhymes; Folk Wisdom; Folk Music, Dances, and Games; How and What to Collect. Several appendices offer information on folklore scholarship in America; folklore specialists; and archives, museums, and libraries.

A GUIDE TO ENGLISH FOLK SONG COLLECTIONS, 1822-1952. *With an Index to their Contents, Historical Annotations and an Introduction. By Margaret Dean-Smith. Foreword by Gerald Abraham. Liverpool, England: The University Press of Liverpool in association with The English Folk Dance & Song Society. 1954. 120 pp.*

Strictly speaking, this book lies outside the present study, but I include it for two reasons: first, to show how the author handles a complicated bibliographical problem; second, because it has much detail on Cecil Sharp, who added to his already considerable fame by his great collection of songs of the Appalachians.

After the long introduction, Miss Dean-Smith lists about 85 English collections from 1822 to 1952, each carrying an annotation of some length, sometimes more than half a page of fine print. The alphabetical index of the individual songs occupies over half of the whole volume. There is much more in these 120 pages than might at first be supposed: the book is a small quarto, the print is small and, in the index, the text is printed in double columns.

GUIDE TO LIFE AND LITERATURE OF THE SOUTHWEST. *Revised and Enlarged in both Knowledge and Wisdom. By J. Frank Dobie. Dallas: Southern Methodist University Press. 1952. viii, 222 pp.*

A reader might not expect a guidebook to be delightful reading.

Dobie's *Guide* is just that, as well as being very useful. The "delight" begins on the copyright page in these words:

"Not copyright in 1942
Again not copyright in 1952
Anybody is welcome to help himself to it in any way."

This *Guide* "grew up" with Dobie's quarter century of teaching at the University of Texas. There are thirty-five chapters and "A Preface with Some Revised Ideas." Though there are hundreds of titles cited, the work is largely discussion and not intended as a formal, scholarly bibliography. There is, however, plenty of learning here, but the author wears it lightly. To get an idea of content, the reader notes such chapter headings as these: General Helps, Indian Culture, Backwoods Life and Humor, Fighting Texians, Pioneer Doctors, Circuit Riders and Missionaries, Cowboy Songs and Other Ballads, Mining and Oil, Negro Folk Songs and Tales, and even a chapter on Subjects for Themes.

Some twenty illustrations by Tom Lea, Charles M. Russell, and others are included. A most excellent and extensive index (25 pages) makes the volume doubly useful. (All honor to whoever invented the book index!)

INTERNATIONAL CATALOGUE OF RECORDED FOLK MUSIC. *Edited by Norman Fraser. With a Preface by R. Vaughan Williams and Introduction by Maud Karpeles. Prepared and published for UNESCO by The International Folk Music Council in association with Oxford University Press. 1954. Printed in Great Britain. xii, 201 pp.*

This is a bilingual catalogue, the title page and all other preliminary material being given in both English and French, as is the descriptive information throughout. The information is presented according to continents, beginning with Africa and ending with Oceania (Australia included). Within continents, the order is by nations, with record-company headings also. Surprisingly enough, Africa occupies more than a third of the space in the catalogue. Information is incomplete and fragmentary in many areas, particularly Asia, but the present work is of great value, since nothing like it has appeared before.

Maud Karpeles, in the introduction, states that "we have refrained from including any entry [as folk music] that has not been guaranteed by an expert."

A LIST OF AMERICAN FOLKSONGS CURRENTLY AVAIL-
ABLE ON RECORDS. *Compiled by the Archive of American Folk
Song of the Library of Congress. Washington, D. C.: Library of
Congress. 1953. 176 pp.*

The archive has co-operated with the Record Industry Association
of America to produce this catalogue of commercial records. The
opening note states: "No critical evaluation has been made, nor is
any distinction here noted between recordings made in the field of
untrained singers and those made under studio conditions by professional artists."

Listed here are more than 1,500 folksongs by twenty-four of the
leading record manufacturers. The listing is alphabetical by song
title, beginning with an abolitionist hymn and ending with a Zuñi
"Komache" song. The song title is followed by the performer's name,
then by the album title, and finally by the publisher or publishers,
i.e., the record makers. There is an index of album titles and performers' names. Besides groups, some 300 singers and other performers are named.

Though not complete or free of errors, this is a useful catalogue,
obtainable for 60 cents from the Superintendent of Documents,
Government Printing Office, Washington 25, D. C.

NATIVE AMERICAN BALLADRY. A DESCRIPTIVE STUDY
AND A BIBLIOGRAPHICAL SYLLABUS. *By G. Malcolm Laws, Jr.
Publications of the American Folklore Society: Bibliographical Series,
Volume I. Philadelphia: The American Folklore Society. 1950. xii,
276 pp.*

The first half of this very useful volume, the "Descriptive Study"
part, is a series of eight chapters in which the author attempts to
systematize the vast amount of fact in the American ballad field.
Chapter titles suggest the content of the author's discussions: A
Definition of Native American Balladry, American Ballad Types,
American Ballads as Dramatic Narratives, The Origin and Distribu-
tion of American Ballads, The American Ballad as a Record of Fact,
American Ballad Forms and Variants, The Negro's Contribution to
American Balladry, and The British Ballad Tradition in America.

The second half is a series of appendices. Longest and most valuable of these is Appendix I, a bibliographical syllabus of the 185
native ballads in oral tradition. The ballads are grouped into nine
subject categories (war, cowboy and pioneer, lumberjack, sailor,
criminal and outlaw, and so on), and a summary of each ballad in a
sentence or two, with a sample stanza, gives the gist of the story.

Additional brief appendices mention native ballads of doubtful currency in tradition, ballad-like pieces, and imported ballads and folksongs. The study concludes with a bibliography and an index of the songs and ballads, discussed or mentioned in the study.

PHONOLOG. THE ALL-IN-ONE RECORD CATALOG. *Published and Printed in the U. S. A. by Phonolog Publishing Company, Los Angeles, since 1948.*

This loose-leaf compendium, called the encyclopedia of the record industry, is described as a "catalog of all known records currently available, carefully indexed and classified for ready reference ... and kept up to date with weekly corrections and additions." There are some 600 company labels, or recording companies (some of them inactive), and the chief value of *Phonolog* is in the "currently available." Large record stores which subscribe to *Phonolog* (the cost runs to $8 a month after an initial fee) discard sheets as the material becomes noncurrent and new sheets are added. The work is useful in checking the availability and content of many long-playing records.

RESEARCH IN PRIMITIVE AND FOLK MUSIC IN THE UNITED STATES. *A Survey by George Herzog. Washington, D. C.: American Council of Learned Societies, Bulletin No. 24. April 1936. iv, 97 pp.*

The first half of this useful work is devoted to primitive, or Indian, music; the second, to folk music. Each half is primarily an essay devoted to the history of what has been done, up to 1936, and what problems lay ahead. Much of what Herzog suggested needed doing, has been accomplished in the past two decades. There are extensive lists and bibliographies, with especially valuable listing of archives and unpublished collections, some of which have been published in recent years.

FOOTNOTES TO CHAPTER 15

[1] *Journal of American Folklore Supplement,* p. 9. Miss James gives further consideration to problems of archiving in the June, 1958, *Folklore and Folk Music Archivist.*
[2] Written in 1948, reprinted in 1953, in *Folk Music of the United States and Latin America* (Washington, D.C.: The Library of Congress, Division of Music), by Duncan Emrich, Chief, Folklore Section.

3 The *JAF Supplement* (April, 1955) reported that the Library of Congress, Archive of American Folk Song, received a grant of $25,000 from the Carnegie Corporation for the purpose of issuing additional long-playing records.
4 *Arkansas Folklore,* A Publication of the Arkansas Folklore Society, IV, 1-15 (January, 1954) and VII, 1-10 (March, 1957).
5 *JAF Supplement* (April, 1955).
6 *Ibid.* (April, 1956).
7 *The Folklore and Folk Music Archivist,* I (March, 1958).
8 Details from Miss Joan O'Bryant.
9 *JAF Supplement* (April, 1956).
10 *The Folklore and Folk Music Archivist,* I (December, 1958).
11 *English Folk Songs from the Southern Appalachians,* I, Preface, xii (Oxford, Second Impression, 1952).
12 For details on the Flanders Ballad Collection I am indebted to the curator, Miss Marguerite Olney.
13 *JAF Supplement* (April, 1955).
14 *Midwest Folklore,* V, 51-59 (Spring, 1955).
15 *The Folklore and Folk Music Archivist,* I (March, 1958). In 1954, Indiana University began its annual, summer-long Folklore Institute of America. Courses under distinguished scholars and visiting folklorists are given in all areas of folk literature. In 1958, the institute was under the direction of Dr. Richard M. Dorson.
16 *Midwest Folklore,* V, 62-64 (Spring, 1955).
17 From the preface, *Hispanic Folk Songs of New Mexico,* by John Donald Robb (Albuquerque, 1954).
18 *Midwest Folklore,* III, 45-46 (Spring, 1953).
19 *The Folklore and Folk Music Archivist,* I (September, 1958).
20 For details I am indebted to Mr. and Mrs. Chauncey Moore and to Mr. Vance Randolph. The University of Oklahoma Press is considering publication of a part of the Moore collection.
21 For details I am indebted to Hally Wood Gordon.
22 For details on the Wilkinson manuscript I am indebted to Mr. James A. Bear, Jr., Division of Rare Books and Manuscripts, Alderman Library, University of Virginia.
23 Details from Dr. Ruth Ann Musick.
24 An excellent summary of the life and work of Dr. Barbeau, who retired at mid-century, can be found in *Les Archives de Folklore,* Vol. II: *Hommage à Marius Barbeau* (Publication de l'Université Laval, Montréal: Les Éditions Fides, 1947).
25 *Journal of American Folklore,* Vol. 67, p. 100 (April-June, 1954).
26 *Ibid.*
27 For details I am indebted to the librarian, Miss Louise Manny, of Newcastle, New Brunswick, Canada.

CHAPTER 16

Supplemental Section of Background Books

ADVENTURES OF A BALLAD HUNTER. *By John A. Lomax.*
Sketches by Ken Chamberlain. New York: The Macmillan Company.
1947. xiv, 302 pp.

Here is one of the best of the autobiographies of ballad men.
Lomax tells of his early days in Texas, life at college, interest in
cowboy songs, an interim outside ballad hunting, then of the later
years of his life in which he collected extensively over the country,
particularly in the penal institutions of the South. A fascinating and
chatty account of the many people he knew and of his many interesting activities. Not indexed.

ANGLO-AMERICAN FOLKSONG SCHOLARSHIP SINCE 1898.
By D. K. Wilgus. New Brunswick, New Jersey: Rutgers University
Press. 1959. xx, 466 pp.

In this attractive study of four chapters and two appendices, **Dr.**
Wilgus presents a careful and learned account of folksong scholarship during the past sixty years. The two opening chapters, "The
Ballad War" (I and II), tell of the many problems concerning origins, authorship, texts, music, early collecting, etc. Chapter Three,
"Folksong Collections in Great Britain and North America," is a long
critical history (over 100 pages) about collecting in the twentieth
century. Chapter Four, "The Study of Anglo-American Folksong,"
gives much needed organization and discussion to the scholarly
studies about ballads.

Appendix One, "The Negro-White Spirituals," is concerned with the long dispute over origins. Appendix Two, "A Selective Discography of Folk Music Performances on Long-Playing Records," lists about 150 records and gives brief annotations, but song titles are not included.

Extensive footnotes, an excellent selected bibliography, a useful glossary of 160 terms relating to folksong study, and a full index round out this useful study.

ARTIST IN AMERICA, AN. *By Thomas Hart Benton. New and Revised Edition with 79 Illustrations. New York: University of Kansas City Press—Twayne Publishers. 1937, 1951. 324 pp.*

The "New and Revised" part of this book consists of Clarence Decker's foreword titled "Tom Benton—The Kansas City Years" and a final chapter by Benton titled "After," added to the original eight chapters. This vigorous and lively account of Tom Benton's rediscovery of the American scene, and of one artist's part in it, is good background reading no matter what the field. And it is particularly good for the student of folksong because of Tom's interest in the common man and because of his use of ballad and folksong materials in his paintings. Though it is a personal history against the background of art during the first third of this century, there is no denying its great value as social history.

BACKWOODS AMERICA. *By Charles Morrow Wilson. With Illustrations by Bayard Wootten. Chapel Hill: The University of North Carolina Press. 1935. 209 pp.*

Here are seventeen chapters of colorful journalistic writing about the "American Peasants" of the "backhill Ozarks of Arkansas and Missouri," as observed by Wilson (native of the region) during the early years of this century. Illustrated by 32 full-page photographs. The book gives, in general, high praise to the backwoods as compared to city life, for there is more leisure and independence in spite of fewer gadgets and conveniences. One chapter, "Mountain Ballads," quotes nine ballads without music. The backwoods has changed much since Wilson wrote these delightful essays. Not indexed.

BALLAD BOOKS AND BALLAD MEN. *Raids and Rescues in Britain, America, and the Scandinavian North since 1800. By Sigurd Bernhard Hustvedt. Cambridge, Massachusetts: Harvard University Press. 1930. ix, 376 pp.*

This work, a sequel to Hustvedt's *Ballad Criticism in Scandinavia and Great Britain during the Eighteenth Century* (1916), tells a great deal about collectors and published collections of ballads. After a chapter on "Definitions and Distinctions," he discusses Sir Walter Scott's work and that of his followers, then moves "South of the Border" to England, then to Scandinavia and especially the work of Svend Grundtvig in Denmark, and finally to Francis James Child and others in America. Two long appendices—one giving the Grundtvig-Child correspondence (first printed here) and the other giving the Grundtvig-Child index of English and Scottish ballads—round out the study. This scholarly study is a necessary background for anyone interested in balladry. There are an extensive bibliography and an index.

BALLAD MAKIN' IN THE MOUNTAINS OF KENTUCKY. *By Jean Thomas. With Music Arranged by Walter Kob. New York: Henry Holt and Company. 1939. xviii, 270 pp.*

Jean Thomas, a court reporter and native of the hill country, gives an account of mountain life in several south Kentucky counties. She tells of feuds, war, stillin' and drinkin', hymn makin', killin', etc., and her account is interspersed with ballads, about 120 in all. Music is given for 23 of them. The interesting thesis which she develops is that ballad composing still goes on, that people use current events set to the old tunes.

BALLAD OF TRADITION, THE. *By Gordon Hall Gerould. A Galaxy Book. New York: Oxford University Press. 1957. First published in 1932. viii, 311 pp.*

This soft-cover reprint should give greater currency to the late Professor Gerould's excellent background study. His prefatory remark that "we can no longer ignore the part that music has played in the history of balladry, and less than ever can we look at ballads as verses printed in books" at once shows his intent to treat ballads as living literature.

In ten chapters he discusses such problems as the relation of British and Continental ballads, tunes and characteristics of ballads, their importance as social history, the nature of ballad variation, and their relation to broadsides. Chapter Ten examines the "rich store of melodies and texts found in America" in the generation since the last volume of Child's great work came off the press in 1898. An appendix gives the texts of a dozen ballads of American origin.

There is a selected bibliography of nearly 200 items, and an index of ballad titles as well as a general index. Here indeed is a basic book for ballad and folksong study, a book at once lively and scholarly for both scholar and layman.

BALLAD TREE, THE. *A Study of British and American Ballads, Their Folklore, Verse, Music. Together with Sixty Traditional Ballads and Their Tunes. By Evelyn Kendrick Wells. New York: The Ronald Press. 1950. ix, 370 pp.*

Though this work is not presented as a collection, the author's "Sixty Traditional Ballads and Their Tunes" were, for the most part, collected from 1916 on from singers who lived, some in Maine, some in the Appalachians. *The Ballad Tree* is a solid scholarly study in the history, dispersion, and mutation of ballads as they have been kept alive in oral tradition from medieval days down to the present.

The work begins with the Robin Hood ballads, discusses various related topics, such as the supernatural, the Christian elements, origins, eighteenth- and nineteenth-century revivals, the work of Francis James Child, Cecil J. Sharp, and some later collectors. There are many helpful illustrations from photographs and old prints, an extensive bibliography (not annotated), and several indexes. This book can be used effectively in courses in ballad and folksong, especially if used with one of the standard collections supplemented by a generous supply of folksong records.

BEST OF THE AMERICAN COWBOY, THE. *Compiled and edited by Ramon F. Adams. With [13] drawings by Nick Eggenhofer. Norman: University of Oklahoma Press. 1957. xiv, 289 pp.*

Dividing the material into three parts (The Cowboy, The Range, and The Trail), Adams reprints twenty-seven firsthand accounts of cowboy life, giving the reader interesting and authentic material on our "most popular American folk-hero." Adams's headnotes describing some of the cowboy literature help the reader interpret the selections and add useful bibliographical details. Not indexed.

BODY, BOOTS & BRITCHES. *By Harold W. Thompson. Philadelphia: J. B. Lippincott Company. 1940. 530 pp.*

This rollicking book of New York folklore is not, the author points out, "a book of ballads." Nonetheless, woven into this wild and rambunctious narrative of fascinating anecdotes, told in the speech of the folk, he has included about 130 songs and ballads in whole or in part, and sometimes with a number of variants. Certainly this is one of the most fascinating books of upcountry folklore to be published in recent years, for upstate New York, like the big city itself, is a mixture of many peoples and ideas and beliefs.

BOUND FOR GLORY. *By Woody Guthrie. Illustrated with Sketches by the Author. New York: E. P. Dutton & Co., Inc. 1943. 428 pp.*

This is Woody Guthrie's lusty account, in the unliterary vernacular, of his hoboing days from one part of the country to another. The account begins with a gang of bums rolling along in a boxcar, Woody with his guitar, singing his way and "bound for glory." The book has many bits of his song creations—he is called by many a true folk artist of the working people. The story ends with him still riding the rails. The book has a genuine fascination, and is surely a lively and realistic account of the hobo's life.

CABINS IN THE LAUREL. *By Muriel Earley Sheppard. With Illustrations by Bayard Wootten. Chapel Hill: The University of North Carolina Press. 1935. ix, 313 pp.*

An account of the life of mountain people in the Toe River Valley area of western North Carolina, near the Tennessee border. Profusely illustrated with full-page photographs. Not indexed.

CECIL SHARP. *By A. H. Fox Strangways and Maud Karpeles. London: Oxford University Press. First published 1933, Second Edition 1955. xvi, 225 pp. + 16 plates at end.*

The standard biography of Sharp done by two of his friends and coworkers, the revised edition by Miss Karpeles alone, as Mr. Fox Strangways died in 1944. The work tells of Sharp's musical education, his interest in the revival and collecting of folksongs in Great Britain, his teaching career, and his important collecting in America. At the end, a listing of Sharp's publications, sixteen photographic plates, and an adequate index.

CHISHOLM TRAIL, THE. *By Wayne Gard. With Drawings by Nick Eggenhofer. Norman: University of Oklahoma Press. 1954. xi, 296 pp.*

This is a standard history of one of the most colorful and fascinating of all the cattle trails coming up from Texas. Besides the drawings, the book is illustrated with photographs and old prints. There is an excellent bibliography and an index.

CHISHOLM TRAIL, THE. *A History of the World's Greatest Cattle Trail. Together with a Description of the Persons, a Narrative of the Events, and Reminiscences Associated with the Same. By Sam P. Ridings. Illustrated. Guthrie, Oklahoma: Co-Operative Publishing Company. 1936. [x], 591 pp.*

This somewhat ponderous volume, overlaid with much legal phrasing (Sam Ridings was a small-town lawyer), contains much firsthand information about the old trail. Sam Ridings, born soon after the Civil War, was close to many persons who had traveled the Chisholm Trail, and he has done a useful piece of work in setting down a vast amount of detail. Many stirring episodes with Indians and outlaws are set forth. In spite of stylistic difficulties, it is fascinating reading. The book is well printed, except for the fifty or so illustrations. Snatches of many cowboy songs are given, such as "Sam Bass," "Dying Cowboy," but, curiously enough, not "The Old Chisholm Trail." There are interesting discussions on such problems as relations with the Indians, days on the long trail, shifting of the trail, freighting activities, and information about the cowboy capitals —Abilene, Ellsworth, Newton, Dodge City, and Caldwell. The index is all too brief.

COWBOY DANCES. *A Collection of Western Square Dances. By Lloyd Shaw. With a Foreword by Sherwood Anderson, Appendix: Cowboy Dance Tunes arranged by Frederick Knorr. Revised Edition. Caldwell, Idaho: The Caxton Printers, Ltd. 1952. 417 pp.*

This big collection of some 75 Western dances, first published in 1939, is a standard authority in its field. Part I discusses the dances in considerable detail with illustrations and diagrams, and Part II does the same for many of the calls. Scores of drawings and about 150 pictures from photographs add much to the explanations. The latter portion of the book contains a glossary of about 100 technical terms, 33 typical dance tunes in piano settings, a long listing of phonograph recordings, and an index. The book has had thirteen printings in as many years.

DOWN IN THE HOLLER. A GALLERY OF OZARK FOLK SPEECH. *By Vance Randolph and George P. Wilson. Norman: University of Oklahoma Press. 1953. x, 320 pp.*

In this learned work, portions of which appeared as articles in *Dialect Notes* and *American Speech,* the author's purpose is to set down what they have heard "the Ozark hillman say, how he said it, and what he meant by it." The result is a fascinating linguistic study of a particular area. Chapters deal with pronunciation, grammar, survival of early forms, euphemisms and taboos, and many kinds of sayings. The work is both instructive and entertaining. The last chapter (a fourth of the book), "An Ozark Word List," is a useful dialect dictionary. Annotated bibliography and index.

ENGLISH FOLK SONG: SOME CONCLUSIONS. *By Cecil J. Sharp. Revised by Maud Karpeles, with an Appreciation by Ralph Vaughan Williams. London: Methuen & Co., Ltd. 1907. Second Edition 1936. Third Edition 1954. xxi, 143 pp.*

These twelve chapters say some of the best and wisest things that have ever been written about folksongs. Though Sharp was to do much collecting after 1907, both in England and America, his conclusions for the most part have been verified by time. Hence this work should be known to the student of folksong of whatever country. And any comment by Ralph Vaughan Williams (who died in 1958 at the age of eighty-five) is worth a second reading.

FOLK-SAY, *A Regional Miscellany. Edited by B. A. Botkin. Norman: The Oklahoma Folk-Lore Society. 1929. 151 pp. Not indexed.*

FOLK-SAY, *A Regional Miscellany. Edited by B. A. Botkin. Norman: University of Oklahoma Press. 1930. 473 pp.*

FOLK-SAY, *A Regional Miscellany. Edited by B. A. Botkin. Norman: University of Oklahoma Press. 1931. 354 pp.*

FOLK-SAY IV: THE LAND IS OURS. *Edited by B. A. Botkin. Norman: University of Oklahoma Press. 1932. 297 pp.*

These four volumes, collected and published under the leadership of B. A. Botkin for the Oklahoma Folk-Lore Society, contain a wealth of stories, songs, sayings, reminiscences, and other material of early days in Oklahoma. The three later volumes are fully indexed.

FOLK SONG OF THE AMERICAN NEGRO. *By John Wesley Work. Nashville, Tennessee: Press of Fisk University. 1915. 131 pp.*

The ten chapters of this book aim to chart the history and scope of American Negro folksong. John W. Work, a professor in Fisk University, was a long-time student of Negro music. He classifies the songs as songs of joy, sorrow, faith, hope, love, determination, adoration, patience, courage, and humility. He discusses the origin of the songs, their preservation and development, and gives an account of the singing of the Jubilee Singers. Some songs and fragments are included by way of illustration, but this book is not intended as a collection. No index.

FORTY-NINERS. *The Chronicle of the California Trail. By Archer Butler Hulbert. Fully Illustrated. Boston: Little, Brown and Company. 1931. xvii, 340 pp.*

This authentic and rollicking account is a composite from "every available diary or journal . . . on pioneer experience in the region." In this manner the author works out "a story of actual experience covering 2200 miles of plain, desert, butte, mountain, river, and ravine"—a story as it was lived between the years 1848 and 1853. (Preface) The work contains a few of the Westward Movement songs which reveal "the raw incident and local color of the trail."

Hundreds of rare illustrations reproduced from materials in the Huntington Library add humor, color, and authenticity to the lively text.

FROM AN OZARK HOLLER. STORIES OF OZARK MOUNTAIN FOLK. *By Vance Randolph. Illustrated by Richard A. Laederer. New York: The Vanguard Press. 1933. 252 pp.*

Good in folklore and dialect, this early work of twenty-two stories is entirely fictional. Some stories had appeared earlier in magazines. Each story has a woodblock print at the heading. One story is titled "A Good Song Well Sang."

FUNK & WAGNALLS STANDARD DICTIONARY OF FOLK-LORE, MYTHOLOGY, AND LEGEND. *Volume I: A-I; Volume II: J-Z. Maria Leach, Editor. New York: Funk & Wagnalls Company. 1949, 1950. xii, 1,196 pp.*

This scholarly dictionary, twelve years in the making, is the work of some thirty-three folklore specialists. It contains just about everything one could want by way of definition, explanation, or discussion in the broad field of folklore—meaning of particular terms, discussion of individual folksongs, etc.

GREAT SMOKIES AND THE BLUE RIDGE, THE. *The Story of the Southern Appalachians. Edited by Roderick Peattie. New York: The Vanguard Press. 1943.*

The contributors to this excellent survey are Edward S. Drake, Ralph Erskine, Alberta Pierson Hannum, John Jacob Niles, Donald Culross Peattie, Henry S. Sharp, and Arthur Stupka. Topics covered in the ten chapters include early settlers and explorers, the mountain people, trees and wild flowers, crafts and folk music, climate and seasons, and the geological characteristics. Niles writes an informative chapter on "Folk Ballad and Carol."

HANDICRAFTS OF THE SOUTHERN HIGHLANDS. *With an Account of the Rural Handicraft Movement in the United States and Suggestions for the Wider Use of Handicrafts in Adult Education and in Recreation. By Allen H. Eaton. Containing Fifty-eight Illustrations from Photographs Taken for the Work by Doris Ulmann. New York: Russell Sage Foundation. 1937. 370 pp.*

This three-part study, by one of the Russell Sage Foundation's researchers, discusses (1) Mountain Handicrafts of Pioneer Days, (2) Revival of the Handicrafts in This Century, and (3) the Rural Handicraft Movement and its uses today. There are chapters on spinning, weaving, furniture, woodwork, pottery, mountain music, and handmade instruments. An excellent, authoritative work with a selected bibliography and a full index.

Mr. Eaton has written a companion volume entitled *Handicrafts in New England* (New York: Russell Sage Foundation, 1949).

HOLY OLD MACKINAW: A NATURAL HISTORY OF THE AMERICAN LUMBERJACK. *By Stewart H. Holbrook. New York: The Macmillan Company. 1938. viii, 278 pp.*

This lively and somewhat informal history, in which the author has "tried to set down an honest picture of the American lumberjack, at work and at play, as he has performed for the past three centuries," is presented in twenty brief chapters and includes a "Logger's Dictionary" and an excellent index. Chapter 11, "Ballads of the Woods," gives parts of a dozen songs, without music.

IRISH FOLK MUSIC. *A Fascinating Hobby. With Some Account of Allied Subjects including O'Farrell's Treatise on the Irish or Union Pipes and Touhey's Hints to Amateur Pipers. By Capt. Francis O'Neill. Illustrated. Chicago: The Regan Printing House. 1910. 359 pp.*

This book is a series of essays which first appeared in magazines while Captain O'Neill, general superintendent of the Chicago police force, was pursuing his "fascinating hobby" of collecting Irish folk music. There are eighteen chapters or essays on various phases of Irish music, such as the stories of tunes, the origins of tunes, accounts of early collections, information on Irish dances, the Irish pipes and pipers, and other matters. There is obviously much useful information here, and much entertainment, too. The book is well indexed.

Advertisements at the end of the volume tell of O'Neill's three collections of the music: one book of 250 selections of airs, jigs, reels, hornpipes, etc., for piano or violin; another book of about 1,000 gems of *The Dance Music of Ireland;* and a third book of some 400 pages, called *The Music of Ireland,* containing 1,850 airs in all (not harmonized). Much of this Irish music has, of course, come into our American heritage.

IRISH FOLK MUSIC AND SONG. *By Donal O'Sullivan. With Illustrations by Muriel Brandt. Dublin: At the Sign of the Three Candles. Published for the Cultural Relations Committee of Ireland by Colm O. Lochlainn. 1952. 62 pp.*

As everyone knows, Ireland's folk music has had wide influence on American folk music and dance, and so this booklet is worth including in a work on American folksong. Third in a series of booklets on Ireland's culture, this brief discussion of Irish folk music tells about seven early collectors, about the Irish harpers and their music, later Irish folk melodies, Anglo-Irish songs, folk dances and fiddlers of Ireland, and concludes with the idea that Ireland has too long neglected giving serious study to this area of her culture. Author O'Sullivan is director of folk-music studies at Dublin University and a member of the International Folk Music Council.

JOHN HENRY. *Play by Roark Bradford. Music by Jacques Wolfe. Sets by Albert Johnson. New York: Harper & Brothers. 1939. 91 pp.*

This is a dramatization of the prose work published in 1931. This musical play of three acts is filled with much singing of songs close to folksongs, and some are folksongs. The first production starred the singer-actor Paul Robeson as John Henry. The story has practically the same characters and development as the prose work. In both prose story and drama John Henry is portrayed as a cotton-rolling man (one who piled bales of cotton on steamboats), but the well-known folksong today portrays him as a "steel-driving man" working on the railroad.

JOHN HENRY: A FOLK-LORE STUDY.* *By Louis W. Chappell. Jena, Germany: Walter Biedermann. 1933. 144 pp.*

An exhaustive, critical study of the ballad and its backgrounds, with an appendix of some fifty versions of "John Henry" and "John Hardy." The book does not include music but lists early recordings.

JOHN HENRY: TRACKING DOWN A NEGRO LEGEND. *By Guy B. Johnson. Chapel Hill: The University of North Carolina Press. 1929. [xiv], 155 pp.*

Johnson here studies the John Henry tradition, concluding that there probably was an actual person so named, but that the legend itself is more significant and more alive than the person. He concludes also that John Henry and John Hardy are two different persons and that we do have documentary evidence about Hardy. The latter half of the book deals with the John Henry songs—hammer songs and the ballads—of which there are several dozen versions. In the conception of the Negro workman, John Henry is the great and good hero, in contrast to John Hardy, a criminal.

LAND OF SADDLE BAGS: A STUDY OF THE MOUNTAIN PEOPLE OF APPALACHIA, THE. *By James Watt Raine. New York: Council of Women for Home Missions and Missionary Educa-*

* I have not seen this book. (R. M. L.)

tion Movement of the United States and Canada. 1924. x, 260 pp.

A former head of the English Department at Berea College tells of life in the Appalachians, under such chapter titles as the following: The Spell of the Wilderness, Elizabethan Virtues, Mountain Speech and Song, Moonshine and Feuds, The Mountains Go to School, Religion of a Stalwart People. The time of which he wrote was somewhat before industrialism reached the area. He gives details on the speech of the people and some examples of ballads. There are about a dozen illustrations from photographs. Not indexed.

LAY MY BURDEN DOWN: A FOLK HISTORY OF SLAVERY. *Edited by B. A. Botkin. Chicago: University of Chicago Press. 1945. xxi, 286 pp.*

"These narratives . . . are from the large-scale collection of life-history and interview material gathered by the Federal Writers' Project. A now imperishable part of our American heritage of history and folklore, the collection includes interviews with more than two thousand former slaves." (Jacket note)

The narratives are grouped in five parts under the titles: Mother Wit, Long Remembrance, From Can to Can't, A War Among the White Folks, and All I Know about Freedom. Several hundred episodes are given, most of them vividly moving. There are some illustrations from photographs of elderly Negroes, and at the end is a list of informants and interviewers. Not indexed.

MULES AND MEN. *By Zora Neale Hurston. With an Introduction by Franz Boas. Ten Illustrations by Miguel Covarrubias. Philadelphia: J. B. Lippincott Company. 1935. 343 pp.*

An interesting book of Negro folklore, with tales and sayings, a few songs with music, and valuable comment on voodoo practices. Miss Hurston, a graduate in anthropology (Barnard College), presents "the Negro's reaction to everyday events, to his emotional life, his humor and passions." (Boas) Part I consists of 70 folk tales, and Part II of about 30 "hoodoo" rituals. The book is not indexed, but has an appendix of 9 songs, a glossary, hoodoo formulae, etc. Alan Lomax calls this one of the finest books in American folklore.

MUSIC IN THE SOUTHWEST, 1825-1950. *By Howard Swan. San Marino, California: The Huntington Library. 1952. x, 316 pp.*

The first half, or seven chapters, of this book is particularly applicable to the study of folk-music backgrounds. The author discusses the various phases of music among the Mormons, in the mining camps, missions, on the ranches, and in the cow counties. The remaining chapters, however, are devoted to genres of music other than folksong.

NEGRO SLAVE SONGS IN THE UNITED STATES. *By Miles Mark Fisher. With a Foreword by Ray Allen Billington. Published for The American Historical Association. Ithaca, New York: Cornell University Press. 1953. xvi, 223 pp.*

This work (not a collection), the outgrowth of a doctoral dissertation at the University of Chicago, is a study of Negro thought through the study of Negro spirituals. Dr. Fisher's contention is that the spirituals were not merely religious folksongs, but a record of the hidden thoughts of the Negro people in bondage. In other words, the songs are highly symbolic, with many inner and hidden meanings. This is a very interesting and important analysis, and Dr. Fisher's ingenious and thoughtful interpretation makes a convincing case for the identification of the desire for heavenly reward with the desire for freedom from slavery.*

OZARK COUNTRY. *By Otto Ernest Rayburn. American Folkways. New York: Duell, Sloan and Pearce. 1941. ix, 352 pp.*

This fourth volume in the "American Folkways" series presents a regional study in sixteen chapters, in which the author discusses sociological backgrounds, the scenery, customs and traditions, superstitions and legends, crafts and skills, music and other arts of the hill people. Presented in a readable style, with a highly favorable viewpoint, it is recommended as an excellent introduction to the region, especially for folk backgrounds.

The "American Folkways" series has now run to more than two dozen volumes. Here follow the additional titles,† with publication dates:

Edwin Corle, DESERT COUNTRY (1941)
Haniel Long, PIÑON COUNTRY (1941)
Stanley Vestal, SHORT GRASS COUNTRY (1941)
Stetson Kennedy, PALMETTO COUNTRY (1942)
Wallace Stegner, MORMON COUNTRY (1942)
Eric Thane, HIGH BORDER COUNTRY (1942)
Jean Thomas, BLUE RIDGE COUNTRY (1942)
Harnett T. Kane, DEEP DELTA COUNTRY (1944)

---

* A detailed and illuminating review of Dr. Fisher's study was written by Arthur Palmer Hudson for *American Literature*, XXVI, 453-56(November, 1954).
† I have not examined all of these volumes. In the main, those that I have seen show the same high quality of content and style found in *Ozark Country.*

Thames Williamson, FAR NORTH COUNTRY (1944)
Gertrude Atherton, GOLDEN GATE COUNTRY (1945)
Meridel LeSueur, NORTH STAR COUNTRY (1945)
Clarence M. Webster, TOWN MEETING COUNTRY (1945)
Carey McWilliams, SOUTHERN CALIFORNIA COUNTRY (1946)
H. C. Nixon, LOWER PIEDMONT COUNTRY (1946)
Homer Croy, CORN COUNTRY (1947)
Donald Day, BIG COUNTRY: TEXAS (1947)
Lloyd Graham, NIAGARA COUNTRY (1949)
Alfred Powers, REDWOOD COUNTRY (1949)
William B. Bracke, WHEAT COUNTRY (1950)
Albert N. Williams, ROCKY MOUNTAIN COUNTRY (1950)
Hodding Carter and Anthony Ragusin, GULF COAST COUNTRY
    (1951)
George Swetnam, PITTSYLVANIA COUNTRY (1951)
North Callahan, SMOKY MOUNTAIN COUNTRY (1952)
William C. White, ADIRONDACK COUNTRY (1954)
Oscar Lewis, HIGH SIERRA COUNTRY (1955)
Clark McMeekin, OLD KENTUCKY COUNTRY (1957)
Baker Brownell, THE OTHER ILLINOIS (1958)

OZARK MOUNTAIN FOLKS. *By Vance Randolph. New York:
The Vanguard Press, Inc. 1932. xvi, 279 pp.*
    In Chapter IX of this study, Randolph tells, under the title of
"The Sport of Ballad-Hunting," of his early activities of ballad
collecting. At the suggestion of an Eastern professor (unnamed),
he made a collection of a number of the traditional British ballads
in the Ozarks region. Thirteen ballads are recorded in this volume,
together with a simple musical notation of the melodies. He found
some variation of words and stanzas in the same community, each
ballad singer insisting that his particular version was the true one.
This work, the second book of a serious nature on the region by
Randolph, throws much light on his early writing.

OZARK SUPERSTITIONS. *By Vance Randolph. New York: Columbia University Press. 1947. viii, 367 pp.*
    This entertaining and scholarly volume discusses all sorts of super-
stitions of the region—matters of the weather, water witching, domestic affairs, birth and death, medicines, ghost stories, and so on. A
10-page annotated bibliography of over sixty items mentions most
of the literature on the subject (to publication date), and there is
an extensive index.

OZARKS: AN AMERICAN SURVIVAL OF PRIMITIVE SOCIETY, THE. By Vance Randolph. New York: The Vanguard Press. 1931. 310 pp.

Of the twelve chapters in this social history, the first of his many important books, Vance Randolph devotes one chapter to the passing of the play-party and another to Ozark folksongs. About a dozen play-party songs are given, with tunes. The longish chapter (pp. 166-222) on folksongs is a prelude to Randolph's later great work in the field. Musical accompaniments by fiddle, guitar, and harmonica were very common, he reports, but many singers used no accompaniment. (p. 176)

PANORAMA OF AMERICAN POPULAR MUSIC. The Story of Our National Ballads and Folk Songs—The Songs of Tin Pan Alley, Broadway and Hollywood—New Orleans Jazz, Swing and Symphonic Jazz. By David Ewen. Englewood Cliffs, New Jersey: Prentice-Hall, Inc. 1957. x, 365 pp.

The early chapters, particularly Chapter 2 ("The People Sing: Our Folk Music") and Chapter 3 ("Gonna Sing All Over God's Heaven: The Songs of the Negro") are most pertinent to the special student of folksong. The whole book, of course, like many of Ewen's studies, is packed with a vast body of readable facts. It is well indexed also.

POETIC ORIGINS AND THE BALLAD. By Louise Pound. New York: The Macmillan Company. 1921. 247 pp.

This now-famous series of discussions sets forth Miss Pound's arguments against many of the romantic ideas on the origins and history of balladry. She condemns the communal theory, the idea that the ballad is early and primitive, that it originated in the dance, that it belongs wholly to the illiterate, and that ballad-making is a closed account. In fact, she cites much evidence against these once-popular, romantic ideas. In general, time has sustained her views, as many research developments of the past thirty-five years have shown.

QUEST OF THE BALLAD, THE. By W. Roy MacKenzie. Princeton, New Jersey: Princeton University Press. 1919. xiii, 247 pp.

This book is an account of MacKenzie's collecting activities in Nova Scotia, and of his belief that the ballad is going out of fashion. He gives accounts of many of the old singers of the regions, sometimes including their pictures, and he laments that the younger people have little or no interest in the art of native song: ". . . the persons who appear and reappear in the following pages are, with the fewest exceptions, men and women of three-score years and upwards." With the advance of civilization, he concludes, ballad singing declines. An interesting book of experiences and conclusions, in many respects an autobiography in a very lively style. Some ballads are included here and there.

RAINBOW ROUND MY SHOULDER. *The Blue Trail of Black Ulysses. By Howard W. Odum. Decorations by Harry Knight. Indianapolis: The Bobbs-Merrill Company, Publishers. 1928. 322 pp.*

These twenty-two chapters give an account of the black workman-singer in the South trying to adjust himself to the new industrial era and trying also to retain a measure of freedom. He is a wanderer, a lonely creature, taking life and love wherever he can find them, and singing as he goes, sometimes happy but more often sad and blue, for his life is hard and precarious. The author gives snatches of hundreds of songs, some of them recognized folksongs, others composed by Black Ulysses in his strange odyssey. This book is an interesting sociological account and is a valid background of much recent Negro music, especially in the blues manner.

SAINTS OF SAGE AND SADDLE. *Folklore Among the Mormons. By Austin and Alta Fife. Bloomington, Indiana: Indiana University Press. 1956. xiv, 367 pp.*

This carefully developed study of Mormon lore and history is presented in a prologue, seventeen chapters, and an epilogue. The main body of the text has a four-part arrangement: I. Mantle of the Prophets; II. Saga of the Saints; III. Faith of the Fathers; IV. Saddles among the Sage. The basis for the whole study is best expressed in the authors' words in a bibliographical note: "The most significant sources of information for the preparation of this work consist of the lived experience of the authors as Mormons in Mormon communities, and of the interviews which they have conducted with hundreds of Mormons throughout the length and breadth of Mormondom over a period of more than fifteen years." There is evidence, too, of the use of archived materials and many published sources.

The epilogue consists of seventeen Mormon folksongs, "at best a random sampling from the hundreds of Mormon songs" in the Fife Mormon Collections. More songs, or parts of them, are scattered throughout the chapters.

Both Gentile and Mormon are likely to find this learned study surprisingly colorful and entertaining. Bibliography, illustrations from photographs, footnotes, index, and end papers (map of Utah) satisfactorily round out the work.

SIDEWALKS OF AMERICA. *Folklore, Legends, Sagas, Traditions, Customs, Songs, Stories and Sayings of City Folk. Edited by B. A. Botkin, Indianapolis: The Bobbs-Merrill Company, Inc. 1954. xxii, 603 pp.*

Like Botkin's other "Treasury" books, this one is packed with good reading on the lore of city life and ways.

SINGING FAMILY OF THE CUMBERLANDS. *By Jean Ritchie. Illustrated by Maurice Sendak. New York: Oxford University Press. 1955. vi, 282 pp.*

Jean Ritchie's family story in the once-isolated Cumberlands of Kentucky is an important piece of social history, told with sharp vision and keen sympathy. Love of singing the old songs kept the large family unified. (Words and music of 42 songs are woven into the text.) Life was hard and sometimes painful, but it also had richness and gaiety and freedom. It is told in a vigorous style with plenty of down-to-earth colloquialism.

SOD-HOUSE FRONTIER, 1854-1890, THE. *A Social History of the Northern Plains from the Creation of Kansas and Nebraska to the Admission of the Dakotas. By Everett Dick. Illustrated. Lincoln, Nebraska: Johnson Publishing Company. 1954. xviii, 550 pp.*

From the preface we learn that "the present volume is an attempt to depict the life of the common man on the cutting edge of the frontier immediately following the date when it leaped across the Missouri River into Kansas and Nebraska and across the Red River into the vast domain now known as North and South Dakota." Here is a scholarly and extremely readable account, in thirty-five chapters, under such titles as Log-Cabin Days, Road Ranches, The Sod House, Hunting and Trapping, Fuel and Water, Coming of the Iron Horse, The Prairie Town, The Pioneer Doctor, etc.

First published in 1937, this is a reprint on the one hundredth anniversary of the Kansas-Nebraska Act of 1854. The work is profusely illustrated with thirty-two old prints and photographs, and it has an extensive bibliography and an excellent index. Some attention is given to music and entertainment on the frontier of the Midwest, such as Dick's comment (pp. 367-70) on the great importance of the fiddler at frontier dances in the seventies and eighties.

SONGS OF AMERICA. *A Cavalcade of Popular Songs. Edited with Commentaries by David Ewen. Arrangements by Mischa and Wesley Portnoff. Chicago: Ziff-Davis Publishing Company. 1947. 246 pp.*

The 58 songs in this volume are given mainly to illustrate the discussion, which is in reality a history—and a good brief one—of the development of popular song in America. Ewen begins with the early broadsides of Colonial days, goes on to native folksongs, Negro songs and minstrels, and patriotic songs; thence to the expansion movement which brought work songs of all kinds—cowboy, miner, railroad; then follows a discussion and sampling of variety music-hall songs and sentimental ballads. The final discussion (without samples) recounts a brief history of Tin Pan Alley, the development of ragtime, the blues, jazz, and so-called swing music, closing with some account of melody snatching from the classics.

Perhaps a good half of the songs included are now considered folksongs, though the line between folksong and popular song is not always a sharp one.

SOUTHERN HIGHLANDER AND HIS HOMELAND, THE. *By John C. Campbell. New York: Russell Sage Foundation. 1921. xxii, 405 pp.*

Campbell, a teacher in the region for twenty-five years, and later a worker for Russell Sage, presents here a readable account of the southern Highlands, in effect a sociological study that is warmly human and personal. The time is about the turn of the century. He discusses many phases of the region and its people: topography, population, home life, religious denominations, education, resources, and ways to improve the economic, social and cultural life. Chapter IV, "The Rural Highlander at Home," tells much about recreation, customs, ballads, funerals, rural arts of weaving, etc. He mentions the fiddle, banjo, and dulcimer as common musical instruments. There are many statistical details, tables, and an extensive bibliography and index. A must book for any student of the southern Highlands. The book contains about one hundred excellent illustrations from photographs.

STORY OF AMERICAN FOLK SONG, THE. *By Russell Ames. With a Foreword by Helen L. Kaufmann. New York: Grosset & Dunlap, Publishers. 1955. xii, 276 pp.*

This compact book in "The Little Music Library" series is an informal but scholarly history of American folksong. Ten chapters, interspersed with numerous samples from hundreds of songs, tell the story. Ames discusses the background, Colonial and Revolutionary days, the frontier, slavery, war, the trades, itinerant life—all in the pattern of folk music. No tunes and no index.

SUN SHINES BRIGHT, THE. *By Kentucky's "Traipsin' Woman" Jean Thomas. New York: Prentice-Hall, Inc. 1940. xiv, 275 pp.*
  This reminiscent account, a sort of autobiography, is concerned with Jean Thomas' life among the hill people, but perhaps is presented mainly to tell about her avocation of "ballad huntin'" and her establishing the Singin' Gathering each June at her cabin on Mayo Trail, and to present a true picture of the Kentucky mountaineers. It is a highly sentimental approach, but does give interesting reminiscences.

TREASURY OF AMERICAN FOLKLORE, A. *Stories, Ballads, and Traditions of the People. Edited by B. A. Botkin. Foreword by Carl Sandburg. New York: Crown Publishers. 1944. xxviii, 932 pp.*
  A six-part "Paul Bunyan of a book" which "breathes of the human diversity of these United States." And as Sandburg further says, "There have been small fry collections of folklore . . . but this one is a big shot." The first five parts (about five-sixths of the book) contain prose tales (occasionally some verses) classified under these titles: Heroes and Boasters, Boosters and Knockers, Jesters, Liars, Folk Tales and Legends. Part Six, entitled "Songs and Rhymes," contains (besides play rhymes, catch colloquies, singing and play-party games) a section of ballads and songs, most of them with simple musical notations. There are some 65 representative ballads and songs of sailormen, rivermen, lumberjacks, cowboys, miners, farmers, jailbirds and hoboes, mountaineers, and Negroes.

TREASURY OF NEW ENGLAND FOLKLORE, A. *Stories, Ballads, and Traditions of the Yankee People. Edited by B. A. Botkin. New York: Crown Publishers. 1947. xxvi, 934 pp.*
  Part Five of this fattest of Botkin's "Treasuries" is titled "Songs and Rhymes" and includes 47 folksongs and ballads with melodies, besides a batch of rhymes and jingles without melodies. Grouped into several categories such as Songs of Old and New England, Hymns of Faith and Freedom, Sea Songs and Chanteys, Lumberjack Songs and Ballads, Nursery and Humorous Songs, Game and Dance Songs—the collection presents many familiar pieces. To mention a few: "The Pesky Sarpent," "Canada I O," "The Little Pig," "Johnny Sands," and "Derby Ram." Ample footnotes of sources and other information are given and, from the reader's viewpoint, the

wonder is that so bulky a book can present so much material in such readable fashion.

TREASURY OF RAILROAD FOLKLORE, A. *The Stories, Tall Tales, Traditions, Ballads and Songs of the American Railroad Man. Edited by B. A. Botkin and Alvin F. Harlow. New York: Crown Publishers, Inc. 1953. xiv, 530 pp.*

Part Five, or 30 pages, of this colorful collection of railroad folklore is devoted to ballads and songs, some 18 in all, including "Casey Jones" and others. The whole work is good background study for folksong and folk history.

TREASURY OF SOUTHERN FOLKLORE, A. *Stories, Ballads, Traditions, and Folkways of the People of the South. Edited with an Introduction by B. A. Botkin. With a Foreword by Douglas Southall Freeman. New York: Crown Publishers. 1949. xxiv, 776 pp.*

Part Five, about 65 pages of this big book, is titled "The Singing South" and includes 53 songs of various kinds: lullabies; dances; British songs and ballads; work, mountain, religious, and topical songs. Melodies are included, as well as footnotes showing sources and other facts.

TREASURY OF WESTERN FOLKLORE, A. *Edited by B. A. Botkin. Foreword by Bernard DeVoto. New York: Crown Publishers, Inc. 1951. xxvi, 806 pp.*

Part Six, less than a tenth of this omnibus of Western lore, is titled "Western Songs and Ballads," of which there is a total of 53 about miners, Indians and pioneers, Mormons, cowboys, loggers and others. Melodies are included, as well as a good many footnotes giving sources and other details. Much of this well-edited material is drawn from the Archive of American Folk Song, Library of Congress.

WAYFARING STRANGER. *By Burl Ives. New York: Whittlesey House. 1948. 253 pp.*

A frank, sometimes amusing, sometimes sad or sentimental, account of Burl Ives' struggle from his birth in 1909 to his success on the stage. He gives much family background, as the family moves from one farm to another; he tells where he learned many songs in his vast repertoire and of the many people who contributed. The book shows Ives to be full of life and energy, a down-to-earth character in his outlook and his interests. The style is easy, informal, and entertaining. Naturally there are snatches and samples of folk-songs. Not indexed.

WE ALWAYS LIE TO STRANGERS. TALL TALES FROM THE OZARKS. *By Vance Randolph. Illustrated by Glen Rounds. New York: Columbia University Press. 1951. x, 309 pp.*

This book is the first in what purports to be a long series out of the store of Randolph's collecting over the years. The collection is presented in ten groups according to subject matter: Steep Hills and Razorbacks, Fabulous Monsters, Rich Soil and Big Vegetables, Hunting Yarns, Snakes and Other Varmints, Backwoods Supermen, High Wind and Funny Weather, Fish Stories, and Miscellaneous Tales. An annotated bibliography and an index complete the volume.

Other titles in the series so far published, all by Columbia University Press—each (except the last) with notes by Herbert Halpert showing sources and relations to European folk tales, illustrations by Glen Rounds, and bibliography of works cited—are the following:

WHO BLOWED UP THE CHURCH HOUSE? AND OTHER OZARK FOLK TALES, *100 stories (1952) xix, 232 pp.*

THE DEVIL'S PRETTY DAUGHTER AND OTHER OZARK FOLK TALES, *91 stories (1955) xvi, 239 pp.*

THE TALKING TURTLE AND OTHER OZARK FOLK TALES, *100 stories (1957) xviii, 226 pp.*

STICKS IN THE KNAPSACK AND OTHER OZARK FOLK TALES, *97 stories (1958) xvii, 171 pp. With Notes by Ernest W. Baughman.*

WHITE SPIRITUALS IN THE SOUTHERN UPLANDS. *The Story of the Fasola Folk, Their Songs, Singings, and "Buckwheat Notes." By George Pullen Jackson. Chapel Hill: The University of North Carolina Press. 1933. xv, 444 pp.*

In the thirty-four chapters of this scholarly study, Dr. Jackson tells the story of the shape-note singers and their songs—and their attempts at survival in the face of urbanization of American life and importations from abroad. His study covers the subject of spiritual folksongs from New England on down through the South and westward. To quote from his foreword: "How and where I found them ["the aged handbooks of spiritual folksong"], what strange sorts of songs they contained, whence the unique notation in which the songs are recorded, who made, collected, and sang them, how, when, and where they came into being, and how and where their singing persists at present—these are a few of the problems which . . . have provided matter for discussion in *White Spirituals*."

The book contains many illustrations, particularly of the leaders among the rural singers. There is a brief bibliography, a list of abbreviated titles, and an index.

As evidence of his findings in *White Spirituals*, Dr. Jackson, in the twenty years after 1933, presented his four volumes of approximately 900 spirituals (see titles elsewhere in this study), establishing his position as the major collector and authority in this particular folk genre.

YANKEE WHALER, THE. *By Clifford W. Ashley. With an Introduction by Robert Cushman Murphy and a Preface to the pictures by Zephaniah W. Pease. Garden City, New York: Halcyon House. 1942. xxviii, 156 pp. + 112 plates.*

A fascinating book on whaling out of the New England ports during the nineteenth century, this bit of social history is recounted in a series of twelve chapters, telling of whaling life and methods, and is interspersed with many illustrations, some in color, from paintings and photographs. There is an extensive glossary of whaling terms. Indexed. Earlier editions were published in 1926 and 1938.

"Cowboy Singing," by Thomas Eakins. (*Courtesy of the Metropolitan Museum of Art*)

Steuben glass: The "Stephen Foster Bowl," designed by Sidney Waugh (*upper left*), "Prairie Smoke," designed by Sidney Waugh (*upper right*), "The Western Group," designed by Bruce Moore (*below*). (*Courtesy of Steuben Glass*)

Steuben glass: "The American Ballad Series," designed by Sidney Waugh. (*Courtesy of Steuben Glass*)

"Sourwood Mountain," by Thomas Hart Benton. (*Courtesy of the artist and Hyman Cohen*)

Anne Grimes with part of her collection of folk-music instruments.

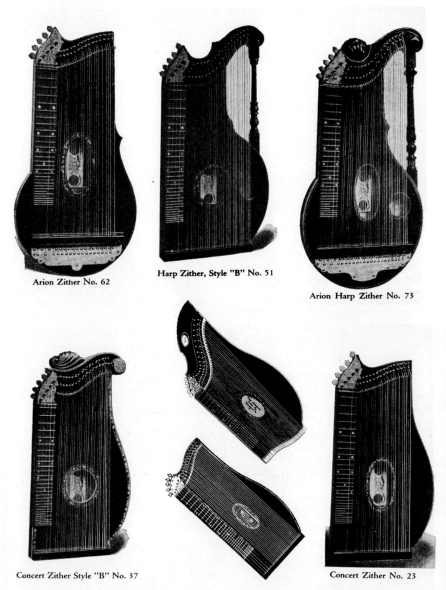

Arion Zither No. 62

Harp Zither, Style "B" No. 51

Arion Harp Zither No. 73

Concert Zither Style "B" No. 37

Concert Zither No. 23

A group of handmade zithers from the Franz Schwarzer Zither Company of Washington, Missouri.

Jethro Amburgey of Hindman, Kentucky, making a dulcimer (*left*), and Homer Ledford of Louisville, Kentucky, playing a dulcimer (*right*).

The late Lon Jordan of Farmington, Arkansas, demonstrates the old fiddler's method of bowing. (*Photo by Vance Randolph, reprinted by courtesy of the State Historical Society of Missouri, publisher*)

Nemonie Balfour, a Scottish singer who toured America in the 1940's, playing the medieval lute. In the background, an ancient Irish harp.

Ruth H. Tyler playing a primitive Ozark hammered dulcimer.

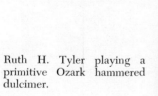

INTERLUDE II

CHAPTER 17

Folklore Societies
and Folk Festivals

A. Folklore Societies and Journals [1]

Anyone interested in the wonderful world of folksong soon learns that a vast amount of research goes on in the field of folklore. Activities of many folklore societies, including their publications, give ample evidence of this research which, on the whole, is the work of specialists. A good share of it, unfortunately, is pretty much unknown to the general public. More's the pity, for often, tucked away in these journals of very modest circulation,* there is much lively and entertaining information.

The chief organization among folklorists is the AMERICAN FOLK-LORE SOCIETY, founded in 1888 and now in its seventy-second year. In the same year, the society began publication of the *Journal of American Folklore,* a quarterly that now runs to a hundred pages or more in each issue. Besides the regular issues of the *Journal,* the society from time to time publishes "Memoirs" (about fifty volumes have appeared to date) and various "Bibliographical and Special Series" (nine volumes to date), the last being V. Propp's *Morphology of the Folktale* (1958). Sometimes a regular issue of the *Journal* is devoted to a special problem or field, as for instance

---

* For instance, as of January 15, 1958, the *Journal of American Folklore* had 1,150 subscribers. Of this number, 510 are institutions (learned organizations; college, university, and public libraries, etc.), only 10 persons are life members, and 10 are honorary members.

a "Canadian Number" (April-June, 1950, and again, April-June, 1954),[2] or "Slavic Folklore: A Symposium" (July-September, 1956), or "Traditional India: Structure and Change" (July-September, 1958)—this last one a volume of over three hundred pages. Furthermore, the society sponsors or encourages regional, state, and local societies. These may have a very tenuous connection with the parent national body, which in no way exercises control over the smaller groups. These smaller groups may or may not be affiliated with the American Folklore Society.

Here follows an alphabetical listing of various state [3] and regional societies, with details (incomplete) about their beginnings and their publications. In 1906, Arizona organized what proved to be a short-lived branch of the American Folklore Society. Presumably now the Arizona activities are merged with the Western folklore group.[4]

The ARKANSAS FOLKLORE SOCIETY, first called the OZARK FOLKLORE SOCIETY, was organized on April 30, 1949, "in the study of Vance Randolph in Eureka Springs." The first president was the distinguished writer, John Gould Fletcher (1886-1950), who is credited with "conceiving the idea of a folklore society which would arouse interest in, collect, and preserve the rich traditional culture of Arkansas and the contiguous Ozark regions." [5] The name Ozark Folklore, first used for both the society and its small publication, was changed after two years to Arkansas Folklore. The society has been vigorously active in the past decade in collecting folk material (songs, ballads, tales, and sayings particularly) for the University of Arkansas Folklore Archives, Fayetteville, and in sponsoring folk festivals (though not the annual Ozark Folk Festival held at Eureka Springs). The society organ is Arkansas Folklore, a mimeographed bulletin published intermittently, the most important numbers being "A Check List of Arkansas Songs" (January 1, 1954, and March, 1957).

The CALIFORNIA FOLKLORE SOCIETY, with headquarters at the University of California, Berkeley, came into being at the home of Archer Taylor in March, 1941. The society began the publication of the California Folklore Quarterly in January, 1942. When the Quarterly was expanded to include more of the Western states, the name was changed, in January, 1947, to Western Folklore. Its pages (often more than one hundred in each issue) contain a wealth of folk material of the West, including tales and songs, customs and superstitions, proverbs, place names, etc., and it remains one of the major regional quarterlies. Like the Journal of American Folklore, it occasionally issues special numbers, such as the April, 1956 issue, edited by T. M. Pearce, devoted to the New Mexico

Folklore Society. In scholarship and readability, in format and make-up, it is a quarterly of the highest standards.

The COLORADO FOLKLORE SOCIETY was organized in Denver at the Western Folklore Conference in 1947. Its activities are closely associated with those of the Western group.

The *Journal of American Folklore* (January-March, 1958) lists John A. Munroe as president, Harold W. T. Purnell as vice president, and Charles W. Dickens as secretary of the DELAWARE FOLKLORE SOCIETY.

Florida folklore activities are part of the SOUTHEASTERN FOLKLORE SOCIETY, which was founded in 1934 at the University of South Carolina (see below, South Carolina Folklore Society). The *Southern Folklore Quarterly*, at present edited by Alton C. Morris, first appeared in March, 1937, and was published at the University of Florida in co-operation with the Southeastern Folklore Society. A most distinguished feature of this quarterly is its annual "Folklore Bibliography," by Professor Ralph S. Boggs. From a modest beginning of half a dozen pages in the issue of March, 1938, this annotated bibliography has grown to more than eighty pages in recent issues, filling a whole number of the *Quarterly*.

A short-lived ILLINOIS FOLKLORE SOCIETY, branch of the AFS, was organized in 1911. Later, in 1936, the society was reconstituted and is now an active organization, with headquarters at Southern Illinois University, Carbondale. The *JAF* (January-March, 1958) lists Edith S. Krappe as president, Harold Briggs as vice president, William E. Simeone as secretary-treasurer, and Jesse W. Harris as editor of the *Bulletin*, as well as Illinois regional editor of *Midwest Folklore*. (A CHICAGO FOLK-LORE SOCIETY existed from 1891 to 1904.)

Folklore activities in Indiana are carried on by the HOOSIER FOLKLORE SOCIETY, one of the most active in the upper Midwest, founded at Indiana University, Bloomington, in 1937. The society began issuing the *Hoosier Folklore Bulletin* (mimeographed) in 1942. This was changed to *Hoosier Folklore* (printed) in 1946. Activities of the society are now reported in *Midwest Folklore*, published at Bloomington.

The KANSAS FOLKLORE SOCIETY was organized at Fort Hays Kansas State College in February, 1957, under the leadership of Dr. Samuel J. Sackett. The society began with approximately one hundred members, has held several state meetings and folk festivals, and promises to become active in collecting songs, tales, and other folklore.

The KENTUCKY FOLKLORE SOCIETY was organized in 1912. A *Folk Song and Poetry Magazine* was begun in 1926 and continued for a dozen years. After a period of comparative inactivity, the society is again among the more active ones, and its official publication is the *Kentucky Folklore Record.*

Among the early state societies was the LOUISIANA FOLKLORE SO-CIETY, founded in 1892 by Professor Alcée Fortier of Tulane University. Fortier and others kept the society going for a few years, but it died out before the turn of the century. In the spring of 1956, the society was again organized and gives promise of renewed activity under the lead of such folklore students as Dr. Corinne Sourcier of Natchitoches, Dr. and Mrs. Calvin Claudel of Chalmette, and Drs. N. M. Caffee, Harry Oster, and Fred Kniffen, all of Baton Rouge.

Sometime before the turn of the century, Maryland formed a branch of the American Folklore Society, but it seems not to have survived into the present.

Folklore activities in Massachusetts were a part of the FOLK-SONG SOCIETY OF THE NORTHEAST, which was founded in March, 1930, by Phillips Barry, Mary Winslow Smith, and Fanny Hardy Eckstrom. This society did much collecting in the years 1930-37 and issued twelve *Bulletins.* When Barry and Miss Smith died, both in 1937, the society became inactive. Manuscript collections were left to the Widener Library of Harvard. In a real sense, the Flanders Ballad Collection at Middlebury College, Vermont, is the spiritual successor of the Folk-Song Society of the Northeast.

The first meeting of the MICHIGAN FOLKLORE SOCIETY was held in March, 1940, though the society had its inception the previous year under the sponsorship of Wayne University, Detroit. It has been an active society for the past twenty years, with a regional editor reporting for *Midwest Folklore.*

Midwest Folklore is the quarterly regional journal established at mid-century and published by Indiana University. The region includes the eight upper Midwest states of Illinois, Indiana, Kentucky, Michigan, Minnesota, Ohio, and Wisconsin—each with its regional editor.

Folklore activities in Minnesota find publication through the Minneapolis journal called *North Star Folk News,* with Mrs. Lewis R. Jones as editor. Mrs. Jones is also Minnesota regional editor for *Midwest Folklore.*

The MISSISSIPPI FOLKLORE SOCIETY was organized in the spring of 1927, with Dr. A. P. Hudson of the University of Mississippi as the chief guiding spirit. Under his leadership much collecting was done, but the society became relatively inactive when he went to the University of North Carolina in 1930. The introduction to Dr. Hudson's *Folksongs of Mississippi and Their Background* (Chapel Hill, North

Carolina, 1936) gives an account of the organizing and purpose of the society.

The MISSOURI FOLK-LORE SOCIETY was organized at the University of Missouri in the fall of 1906, under the leadership of Dr. H. M. Belden (1866-1954), who had come to the university in 1896. Under his guiding hand the society entered into considerable collecting activity up to about 1925. Several pamphlets were published between 1909 and 1916, but the major publication, *Ballads and Songs Collected by the Missouri Folk-Lore Society* (Columbia, 1940), did not get into print until long after the society lapsed into inactivity. Dr. Belden's edition of the *Ballads and Songs* is a work of major importance (see Book Two, Bibliography), but after he ceased to be active, leadership in the Ozarks area passed to the Arkansas Folklore Society.

There is much recent and scattered folklore activity in the Idaho-Montana area, but apparently no regional or state organization to give it direction.

Before World War I, the NEBRASKA FOLKLORE AND ETHNOLOGY GROUP was active in collecting and publishing a series of pamphlets. The ballad and folksong work was for many years carried forward under the leadership of the distinguished folklorist, the late Dr. Louise Pound (1872-1958). Her *Syllabus* and *American Ballads and Songs* (see Book Two, Bibliography, for discussion of both) are important contributions.

Folklore activities of New Hampshire are merged with the FOLK-SONG SOCIETY OF THE NORTHEAST and later with the Flanders Ballad Collection.

The NEW MEXICO FOLKLORE SOCIETY was organized in 1930 and developed much activity, centered at the university, Albuquerque. After 1935, its work was merged with the HISPANIC INSTITUTE OF NEW YORK and, with the founding of the MEXICAN FOLKLORE SOCIETY in 1938, the New Mexican Society went into a decline. Under the stimulus of Dr. John R. Robb, dean of fine arts at the university, it was reconstituted in 1946 and is experiencing a new life. Its chief organ is the *New Mexico Folklore Record*, which has been published at the university since 1946.

Among the very active state societies is the NEW YORK FOLKLORE SOCIETY, organized in 1944 and affiliated with the New York State Historical Association. The following year, a lively magazine was established, the *New York Folklore Quarterly*, under the sponsorship of the Farmers' Museum, Cooperstown. A typical issue (Winter 1952) runs to eighty pages. Such important folklorists as Frank Warner,

Harold W. Thompson, B. A. Botkin, Carl Carmer, Moritz Jagendorf, and others have long been identified with the society and its quarterly. Extensive archives of folklore are housed at Albany, Cooperstown, and at Cornell University in Ithaca.

The first meeting of the NORTH CAROLINA FOLK LORE SOCIETY, active for many years, was held at Raleigh in 1913. Frank C. Brown was the chief organizer. *North Carolina Folklore*, journal of the society, has been published intermittently. The society's activities are centered at the university, Chapel Hill. According to *The University of North Carolina Record* of May 25, 1954, the university organized the Folklore Council in 1935 to promote an interest in all aspects of folk life and to collect, study, and interpret all phases of folklore. The Institute of Folk Music, organized in 1931, is now a division of the Folklore Council.

Many interests of the OHIO FOLKLORE SOCIETY, active for many years, are merged with the regional group in *Midwest Folklore*, with Tristram P. Coffin the regional editor.

The OKLAHOMA FOLKLORE SOCIETY was organized in 1915 at the University of Oklahoma. Interrupted for a time by World War I, it became active soon afterward and, in 1929, published *Folk-Say, A Regional Miscellany* under Ben Botkin's editorship. The society has functioned sporadically since 1940.

The PENNSYLVANIA FOLKLORE SOCIETY was organized at Harrisburg in 1927, and in the same year the society undertook a series of *Publications* which continued for four years. Much collected material is in the Division of Archives, Department of Public Instruction, at the state capital. Work has been carried on in conjunction with the Pennsylvania Federation of Historical Societies. The society has sponsored festivals, state and local, from 1936 on. In recent years, publication has centered in the *Keystone Folklore Quarterly*, and two of the leading spirits in the society are George Korson and the late Henry W. Shoemaker.

Another active organization in the state is the PENNSYLVANIA GERMAN FOLKLORE SOCIETY, begun at Allentown in 1935, incorporated in 1941. A Pennsylvania Dutch Folk Festival at Kutztown (*see below, Folk Festivals*), begun in 1950, has attracted wide interest. Muhlenberg College at Allentown, Franklin and Marshall College at Lancaster, and State Teachers College at Kutztown—all in eastern Pennsylvania, not far distant from one another or from the state capital —have been active in folklore matters. Extent of the society's activities is evident in *Publications of the Pennsylvania German Folklore Society*, for more than a decade under the able editorial guidance of Preston A. Barba of Emmaus.

The SOUTH CAROLINA FOLKLORE SOCIETY was organized at the University of South Carolina, Columbia, in 1913 and, over a period of years, much material was collected and placed in the university library. After 1934, when the SOUTHEASTERN FOLKLORE SOCIETY was organized, the South Carolina Society's affairs have merged with that organization.

South Carolina is the only state boasting an all-Negro folklore organization. The society has flourished for the past fifteen years as the SOUTH CAROLINA NEGRO FOLKLORE GUILD, under the able leadership of Cora V. Green (president) of Orangeburg County, J. P. Burgess (vice president-treasurer) of State College at Orangeburg, and J. Mason Brewer (director-secretary) of Samuel Huston College at Austin, Texas.

The TENNESSEE FOLKLORE SOCIETY was organized at Cookeville in 1934. The following year appeared the first issue of a mimeographed quarterly publication, the *Tennessee Folklore Society Bulletin*. The *Bulletin* has appeared without interruption, and 1959 marked the twenty-fifth anniversary of a continuously active and lively state folklore society.

The TEXAS FOLKLORE SOCIETY was founded in 1909 by John A. Lomax, L. W. Payne, and others at the University of Texas. The annual *Texas Folk-Lore Society Publications* appeared in 1916 and has continued ever since. After World War I, the society underwent some reorganization about 1922, and it has remained the most active and important folklore society of the Southwest. J. Frank Dobie, writer and sometime professor at the University of Texas, was for many years the vigorous editor and guiding spirit of the society.

Activities of the VERMONT FOLKLORE SOCIETY have not been differentiated from the Helen Hartness Flanders ballad work, now centered at Middlebury College.

The VIRGINIA FOLKLORE SOCIETY, founded at Richmond in 1913, began with ninety-one charter members under the direction of C. Alphonso Smith, its first president and permanent archivist. An annual *Bulletin* was issued for a dozen years. After Dr. Smith's death in 1924, Arthur Kyle Davis, Jr., took over as editor and archivist. Much collecting has been done in all counties of Virginia, and for many years the Virginia Folklore Society was among the most active, though it is less so now.

The state of WASHINGTON organized a FOLKLORE SOCIETY at Seattle in 1957-58. This group gives promise of doing much-needed collecting in the Pacific Northwest.

The WEST VIRGINIA FOLKLORE SOCIETY was organized in 1915 at Morgantown, with Professor John Harrington Cox of the University of West Virginia as first president, archivist, and general editor. Professor Cox was the chief officer and collector for many years. Several volumes were published under the auspices of the society, which became inactive soon after World War I. In the summer of 1950, the society was revived and reorganized and has continued active. A mimeographed bulletin was issued in the spring of 1951, and soon thereafter it became a quarterly bulletin called *West Virginia Folklore*. The society meets annually in conjunction with the West Virginia Education Association, and usually holds a summer meeting at Fairmont State College. Dr. Ruth Ann Musick of Fairmont has been secretary-archivist since the society's revival in 1950. The society sponsors a folk festival every summer, and there is much unpublished material in its archives.[6]

Much individual collecting has been done in Wisconsin from 1910 on, though a folklore group was not organized until 1938. It was incorporated in 1947 as the BADGER STATE FOLKLORE SOCIETY. A journal, *Badger Folklore*, has been published irregularly, and some Wisconsin activities are merged with the *Midwest Folklore* regional group centered at Indiana University.

A few observations may be drawn from the preceding facts and remarks on folklore societies. (1) About two-thirds of the states maintain active organized folklore groups which hold meetings, stimulate collecting, sometimes sponsor folk festivals, and frequently publish some sort of journal or bulletin. (2) Regional activities are strong in several sections, as shown by the publications *Western Folklore, Southern Folklore Quarterly, Midwest Folklore, Publications of the Texas Folklore Society,* and the *New York Folklore Quarterly*. (3) With the concentration of folklore scholars, archived material, courses and institutes of folklore, there is strong evidence that the nation's major center of scholarly folklore activity today is located at the University of Indiana, Bloomington. (4) With the recent organizing of new folklore societies and the reconstituting of some older ones, with increased publications, archiving and recording of materials, there is much more folklore business in the whole country than ever before. This last point suggests the need to give brief discussion to another matter—the folk-festival movement in America today.

B. *Folk Festivals*

Questions discussed earlier in this book as to what is meant by a folksong and a folksinger suggest that we should also attempt some definition of the folk festival. Obviously it is a time of joy and gaiety, a coming together for mutual entertainment, in which the "folk" or common people are the participants, usually in various kinds of traditional music and dance. Recent writers on all sorts of American festivals [7] have suggested that we Americans never miss a chance to launch a festival, no matter what the occasion: it may be roses, rodeos, square dances, maple syrup, wild flowers, cotton, tulips, music, logging, Indian powwows, holidays, pioneer and patriotic celebrations—anything for a get-together! But our concern here is with one kind of festival only—the folk festival that gives emphasis to the presentation of traditional music and dance.

Writing in the first issue of the *Southern Folklore Quarterly* (March, 1937), Annabel Morris Buchanan, an authority on our folk music, sets forth some functions of the folk festival and offers a few guiding principles. Her main contention is that a folk festival "should encourage only the highest type of native material, traditionally learned and traditionally presented." Participation should be spontaneous and not too much planned or rehearsed. Activities should be strictly noncommercial, with no thought of exploiting the folk musician. The aim should be to preserve, to exhibit, and to continue the customs and culture of the common people. [8]

It would be excellent if the above principles could be strictly adhered to. But, as anyone knows who has attended folk festivals, there is often a compromise, or shall we call it a blending, of the purely traditional "traditionally presented" with the more recent popular entertainment arts, in order to gain public attention or to advertise local interests. This is not all bad, however, much as it may be deplored by the purist. Often such a blending is the only link between the antiquarian interests of the scholarly few and the general public. But "the genuine folk festival," as Stith Thompson has pointed out, "should have a great deal to do with educating the public" to what is genuine and what is counterfeit. [9] Our purpose in Interlude II, however, is not to theorize but rather to present a few facts about folk festivals, naming and describing some of the more prominent ones.

Though folk festivals in America had pretty generally died out before the twentieth century began, mention should be made of one particular annual festival of early date: since 1884 the "Big Singin'" of spiritual folksongs at Benton, Kentucky, has survived, and to this day is still vigorously carried on. The basic book for this festival is *The Southern Harmony* (1835), the shape-note hymn book of William (Singin' Billy) Walker. [10]

National folk festivals in England have been held since 1911 and in Russia since 1933. The National Folk Festival Association of

America, founded in 1934, grew out of a number of other folk projects, notably the California Folk Dance Federation, the Folk Arts Center of New York, the Catskill Annual Folk Festival, and the Annual Mountain Dance Folk Festival. The International Folk Festival was first held in London in 1935 and, except for the war years, it has flourished ever since, with meetings in various European countries.[11]

Folk festivals have flourished widely, if somewhat sporadically, in the United States since the early 1930's. If any one person can be called the fairy godmother of the folk-festival movement in America, that person is Sarah Gertrude Knott. Working with a National Advisory Committee of prominent folklorists,[12] she planned and directed the first National Folk Festival held in St. Louis in 1934, and she has continued as organizer and director for the past quarter century. Not only that, "since then [1934], in each state," she writes, "where the National has been held, and in a number of others, we have encouraged and actually directed folk activities on a community, state, and regional basis." The "we" of the quotation is none other than Sarah Gertrude Knott, for she writes all too modestly about her ceaseless and effective activities in folk festivals.[13]

Over the past quarter century the folk-festival movement, as pointed out by Miss Knott, has gone through three stages, with a five-to-ten-year range for each stage. The first stage held rather strictly to "native material traditionally learned and traditionally presented," to repeat Mrs. Buchanan's phrase. Participants were from rural areas and were "almost all natural born singers and dancers."

In time, as the festival developed wider interest and importance, there evolved a second stage in which the "basic cultural offerings of newer citizens from Scandinavia, Poland, Lithuania, Czechoslovakia, Italy, Israel, Greece, and other countries" began to be included. This was an inevitable and valid development as our need to understand other cultures in order to understand ourselves was increasingly brought to public attention.

The third stage showed a further moving away from the native traditional, both as to material and the participants. People from rural areas became less active in the festivals, and city folks, many of them with a new interest in folklore, more and more took over though they were often not traditional singers or dancers. This has meant a change in emphasis, a change which many serious folklorists deplore. Even so, state and regional festivals seem to flourish with unremitting vigor, some of them relatively "pure" and some with much mixture of "new" performers.[14]

It might be useful, at this point, to summarize briefly the National Folk Festival and then go on to some of the state and regional festivals. In 1935, the festival was held in Chattanooga; in 1936, in Dallas; in 1937, in Chicago; and in 1938 to 1942 inclusive, in Washington, D.C. For four years the National Festival went to Philadelphia, then once in Cleveland, and finally "back home" in St. Louis [15] until 1957, when Oklahoma City held the festival in conjunction with the semi-centennial celebration of statehood.

In St. Louis, where the National Folk Festival has held forth in Kiel Auditorium during half its years, the *Globe-Democrat* has been its major sponsor. A typical three-to-four-day program includes Indian songs and dances; fiddle, harmonica, banjo, and dulcimer tunes; songs of the cowboys, lumberjacks, French voyageurs, Spanish-Americans, Pennsylvania Dutch; folksongs and ballads of Tennessee, Ohio, New England, the Ozarks, and other regions; national folk dances of Ireland, England, Mexico, Cuba, Poland, Germany, Lithuania, and American square dances; Negro spirituals and work songs. The festival uses some one thousand or more performers, from half or more of the states and from twenty to thirty different nationalities. During the festival perhaps twenty to thirty thousand spectators are entertained and enlightened.[16]

To look briefly now at some of the state and regional festivals. An early festival—and one that has successfully managed over the years to hold on to the traditional Anglo-Saxon materials, resisting hillbilly influences—is the White Top Folk Festival, first held in 1931. The scene is White Top Mountain near Marion in southwestern Virginia, and the director for many years has been Annabel Morris Buchanan.[17] There have been participants from five to ten nearby states, and on some occasions over ten thousand visitors have come for the three-day events. A typical festival was that held in mid-August of 1934 in which more than two hundred persons took part, among them twenty-two old ballad singers, twenty competitors in fiddling, and about twenty groups of mountain bands (three to five persons playing fiddle, banjo, and guitar).[18]

One of the oldest state festivals still continuing annually is the Mountain Dance and Folk Festival at Asheville, North Carolina, which Bascom Lamar Lunsford organized in 1928. Under his direction (in recent years his son Lamar, Jr., has assisted) the Asheville festival has grown from a few performers and a handful of spectators to hundreds of performers and thousands of spectators from across the nation. In 1946, Lunsford organized the Annual Folk Festival at Renfro, Kentucky; and in 1948, both the Carolina State Fair Folk Festival at Raleigh and the Carolina Folk Festival for the University at Chapel Hill. Though he is getting along in years (he was born in 1882), he has continued to guide these and other festivals.[19]

In Denver, the Western Folklore Festival, in conjunction with the regional Western Folklore Conference, has been held annually in the summers since 1941. The late Levette J. Davidson, of the University of Denver, was the guiding spirit of this conference and festival. Here we have had a well-balanced blend of scholarly discussions, excellent traditional singing of ballads and folksongs by qualified singers (not always traditional), and a variety of folk and square dancing to top off the more serious discussions.

A similarly balanced blending of scholarship and entertainment has been accomplished, since 1947, by the Arkansas Folklore Society in its Annual Meeting and Folk Festival each summer at the university in Fayetteville. Aside from the usual scholarly papers and reports, there has been excellent singing of ballads by traditional singers, old and young, as well as banjo, fiddle, and zither music. Most of the performers have been recorded or taped for the University of Arkansas Archives.

A somewhat different kind of folk festival, one having a far greater popular appeal, is the Ozark Folk Festival established at Eureka Springs, Arkansas, in 1948 by Otto Rayburn and other business leaders of the resort town. As a sort of showpiece, a parade contrasting old and new opens the three-day festival. Impromptu shows and street dances are held in the afternoons, but the main performances are the three nights of entertainment in the town auditorium. Here there is ballad singing, fiddling and banjo picking, an old fiddlers' contest, novelty acts, barbershop-quartet singing, and square dancing.[20] Rayburn directed the festival for six years, and recent directors have been Bob and Wanda Duncan. The directors have tried to maintain a balance between the genuinely traditional folk arts and the later popular arts. The task has proved to be a tightwire act for a seasoned diplomat.

Pennsylvania has had, and still has, a number of folk festivals, one as early as 1934 at Allentown. A recent one to attract wide attention is the Pennsylvania Dutch Folk Festival at Kutztown, begun in 1950 and held in conjunction with seminars on folk culture sponsored by the Pennsylvania Dutch Folklore Center of Franklin and Marshall College, Lancaster, Pennsylvania. The seminars and festival are described as "four days of study, fun, and above all else, fellowship with those sharing kindred interests in the wide field of Americana." The Americana includes the "largest exhibition of regional cookery ever held in America," colorful Dutch handicrafts by leading craftsmen, a display of heirlooms and antiques, and decorative and home arts of the Pennsylvania Dutch. Then, of course, as in any good folk festival, a generous offering of traditional dancing and singing—hoedown and jigging dances, square dancing, ballads and folksongs. To sum up, "There is something for every taste, no matter the age." [21]

The All-Florida Folk Festival, first presented in May, 1953, at the Stephen Foster Memorial, White Springs, Florida, on the banks of the Suwannee River, got under way with immediate success as one of the larger state festivals. Its full-blown character can be attributed to the organizing and directing genius of indefatigable Sarah Gertrude Knott. The three-day program was almost as extensive and varied as those of the National Folk Festivals and followed a similar pattern. Opening with Indian songs and dances, the program moved on to American square dances, British ballads and folksongs; Negro games, spirituals, and other songs and tales; fiddle, harmonica, guitar, and banjo tunes. Then groups of various nationalities in Florida—and what a melting-pot state it is!—presented their songs and dances: Spanish, Irish, Czechoslovakian, Mexican, Scandinavian, Israeli, Greek, and others. This all-Florida festival is sponsored by the Stephen Foster Memorial Commission and the Florida Federation of Music Clubs. As one writer put it, "Sarah Knott has introduced Floridians to themselves and to their visitors as they had never been known before." [22]

The several folk festivals discussed above—in such varied areas as Arkansas, Colorado, Florida, Missouri, North Carolina, Pennsylvania, Virginia—suggest to the reader how extensive our folklore is today. These festivals serve to call attention to our native culture and to popularize it. Festivals have brought to light many singers of folksongs, as well as many old songs, and these enrich our culture. Many songs have been taped and recorded at festivals and thus have enriched the archives, local and national. But the festivals discussed are only a few of the many in the past quarter century. Some others should be mentioned,[23] if only to suggest further the number and variety:

The American Folk Song Society, founded in 1930 at Ashland, Kentucky, by Jean Thomas.

The Mountain Folk Festival of Berea, Kentucky, under the auspices of Berea College, begun in 1935.

The Adirondack Folk Song and Dance Festival, directed by Milt Okun, held during summers as Schroon Crest on Schroon Lake, New York.

The annual New England Folk Festival, organized in 1944 and held in different cities.

The Minnesota Folk Festival of Nations, begun in 1928 in St. Paul and continued intermittently.

Folk and Square Dance Festivals, held in Lincoln, Nebraska, occasionally from 1941 on.

Steamboat Springs, Colorado, host to a Square Dance Tournament for the past dozen years.

The Folk Dance Festival of Oakland and the Country Dancers Festival of Healdsburg, California, active since the mid-1940's.

Any number of Indian dance festivals and other fiestas in New Mexico and Arizona.

More than twenty-five years ago an annual Old Fiddlers' Contest, organized at Athens, Texas; dozens of fiddlers competing (prize money is negligible), and unflagging interest among the thousands of spectators.

Several cities, such as Duluth, Cleveland, Kansas City, not to mention New York City (mecca of all wandering singers of folksongs!), staging their own folk festivals from time to time.

So the folk-festival movement continues and is likely to grow in the years to come, particularly as we become more conscious of our folk backgrounds, collect more of the folk materials, establish more folk museums, and record more and more of the folk music, vocal and instrumental. With that comment, it is appropriate that we should look next, in Book Three, to the impressive number of recordings of ballads and folksongs done in the past ten years.

FOOTNOTES TO CHAPTER 17

[1] Though some of my information on folklore societies is firsthand knowledge, I am much indebted to listings in Professor Charles Haywood's *Bibliography*, to the listing in *JAF* of "National, State, and Regional Folklore Societies," but above all I have freely used, with his kind permission, the articles of Wayland D. Hand: "North American Folklore Societies" (*JAF* 56: 161 ff., July-September, 1943) and "North American Folklore Societies: A Supplement" (*JAF* 59: 477 ff., October-December, 1946).

[2] A Canadian branch of the American Folklore Society was organized in 1916, and there are various societies in the provinces. Typical of these is the Alberta Folklore and Local History Project, which was established in 1943 and which published the *Alberta Folklore Quarterly*.

[3] I have not been able to uncover any organized state-wide folklore activity in the following states: Alabama, Alaska, Connecticut, Georgia, Idaho, Iowa, Maine, Montana, Nevada, New Jersey, North Dakota, Oregon, Rhode Island, South Dakota, Utah, and Wyoming.

4 The Western folklore group publishes the journal *Western Folklore* (see California Folklore Society).

5 *Ozark Folklore*, I, 4, (May 30, 1951).

6 I am indebted to Dr. Ruth Ann Musick for details about the revival of the West Virginia Folklore Society.

7 Two recent studies are the following: Helen R. Coates, *The American Festival Guide*, A Handbook of More Than 200 . . . Festivals and Celebrations in the United States and Canada (New York: Exposition Press, 1956), 299 pp.; Robert Meyer, Jr., *Festivals U. S. A.* (New York: Ives Washburn, Inc., 1950), 438 pp.

8 Summarized from Mrs. Buchanan's article, "The Function of a Folk Festival," *SFQ*, I, 29-34 (March, 1937).

9 In *Western Folklore*, IV, 11 (Spring 1954).

10 Meyer, *Festivals, U. S. A.*, p. 147.

11 Summarized from *The American Peoples Encyclopedia*, VIII, 751, Franklin J. Meine, Editor-in-chief (Chicago: The Spencer Press, Inc., 1952).

12 Among them, George Pullen Jackson, Constance Rourke, Mary Austin, Ben A. Botkin, Arthur L. Campa, May Kennedy McCord, Frances Densmore, and Bascom Lamar Lunsford. The first three named are no longer living.

13 Her article, "The Folk Festival Movement in America," appearing in *Southern Folklore Quarterly*, XVII, 143-55 (June, 1953), gives an excellent brief summary. I am indebted to Miss Knott and to *SFQ* for permission to use details from the article.

14 Knott, "Folk Festival Movement," *SFQ*, cited above.

15 *Ibid.* The 1942 Washington, D.C., festival was repeated in Madison Square Garden, New York City.

16 Summarized from programs and from articles in the St. Louis *Globe-Democrat*, April 9-11, 1954.

17 Other distinguished folklorists and musicians associated with this annual festival are R. W. Gordon, Richard Chase, Mr. and Mrs. Mellinger Henry, Alton Morris, Maurice Matteson, A. P. Hudson, and John Powell.

18 As discussed in *Musical America*, LIV, 8 (September, 1934), by George Pullen Jackson. See also, Allen H. Eaton, *Handicrafts of the Southern Highlands* (New York, 1937), 199.

19 Information comes direct from Bascom L. Lunsford.

20 See my article, "Ozark Folk Festival," *Ford Times*, L, 24-27 (October, 1958); also, *Caravan*, Issue 14, p. 13 (December-January, copyright 1958).

21 Details come direct from the Pennsylvania Dutch Folklore Center, Franklin and Marshall College, Lancaster, Pennsylvania.

22 Helen B. Bixler, Live Oak, Florida, to whom I am greatly indebted for details on the Florida festival. Miss Bixler is secretary of the All-Florida Folk Festival Commission.

23 The various ones listed are mentioned here and there in either Coates, *American Festival Guide*, or Meyer, *Festivals U. S. A.*, both cited earlier. My listing, intended to be representative, makes no pretense to completeness, as information is scattered and incomplete or lacking.

BOOK THREE

Folksong titles
and discography

CHAPTER 18

A Check List of
Folksong Titles

THE numbered, alphabetized list of 844 titles, given below, of best and/or best-known folksongs is drawn from about forty collections. The list is based in part on a song's appearance in some of the collections, in part on its being recorded on long-playing records, and in part on personal choice of the writer. The number 844 is accidental, not arbitrary. Another writer, drawing on the same collections and recordings (and possibly more than are included here), as well as on his personal preferences, no doubt would come up with a different list, but the differences should not be many.

The following folksong collections were used, and they are listed here in the alphabetic order of the key letters at the left of each title. Full descriptions of these and hundreds of other items appear in Book Two, Bibliography.

AAFS	*Check-List of Recorded Songs in the English Language in the Archive of American Folk Song to July, 1940* (1942)
ACM	A. C. Morris, *Folksongs of Florida* (1950)
AKD	A. K. Davis, Jr., *Folk-Songs of Virginia, A Descriptive Index and Classification* (1949)
APH	A. P. Hudson, *Folksongs of Mississippi* (1936)
Ark.	*A Check List of Arkansas Songs in the University of Arkansas Folklore Archives* (1954), with *Supplement I* (1957)

CJSi ii	C. J. Sharp, *English Folk-Songs from the Southern Appalachians*, 2 vols. (1932)
CS	Carl Sandburg, *The American Songbag* (1927)
EBG	Elizabeth B. Greenleaf, *Ballads and Sea Songs of Newfoundland* (1933)
G+C	E. E. Gardner and G. C. Chickering, *Ballads and Songs of Southern Michigan* (1939)
GPJ-A	George P. Jackson, *Another Sheaf of White Spirituals* (1952)
GPJ-D	———, *Down-East Spirituals* (1939, 1953)
GPJ-S	———, *Spiritual Folk Songs of Early America* (1937)
GPJ-U	———, *White Spirituals in the Southern Uplands* (1933)
GPJ-W	———, *White and Negro Spirituals* (1943)
HC-*SB*	Helen Creighton, *Songs and Ballads of Nova Scotia* (1932)
HC-*TS*	———, *Traditional Songs from Nova Scotia* (1950)
HHF+	Helen H. Flanders, *et al., The New Green Mountain Songster* (1939)
HHF+MO	Helen H. Flanders and Marguerite Olney, *Ballads Migrant in New England* (1953)
HMB	H. M. Belden, *Ballads and Songs* [Missouri] (1940)
J+Ji	J. W. and J. R. Johnson, *The Book of American Negro Spirituals* (1925)
J+Jii	———, *A Second Book of American Negro Spirituals* (1926)
JCC	Joanna C. Colcord, *Roll and Go: Songs of American Sailormen* (1924, 1938)
JHC	J. H. Cox, *Folk-Songs of the South* (1925)
JWW	J. W. Work, *American Negro Songs* (1940)
Li	John A. and Alan Lomax, *American Ballads and Folk Songs* (1934)
Lii	———, *Our Singing Country* (1941)
Liii	———, *Folk Song: U. S. A.* (1947)
LP	Louise Pound, *American Ballads and Songs* (1922)
MB+ES	Marius Barbeau and Edwin Sapir, *Folk-Songs of French Canada* (1925)
NCFii	*North Carolina Folklore, Vol. II: Folk Ballads* (1952)
NCFiii	*North Carolina Folklore, Vol. III: Folk Songs* (1952)
NIW	N. I. White, *American Negro Folk Songs* (1928)

PGB   P. G. Brewster, *Ballads and Songs of Indiana* (1940)
VRi, ii, iii, iv   Vance Randolph, *Ozark Folksongs* (1946-50)
WAO   W. A. Owens, *Texas Folk Songs* (1950)
WCH   W. C. Handy, *A Treasury of the Blues* (1926, 1949)
WMD   W. M. Doerflinger, *Shantymen and Shantyboys* (1951)
WRM   W. R. Mackenzie, *Ballads and Sea-Songs from Nova Scotia* (1928)

A word of explanation is needed about the method of listing the songs titles that follow. They are set down in alphabetic sequence, the words *a, an,* and *the* being disregarded in the sequence and placed at the end of the title. *De* for *the* is disregarded also, but *dese* and *dem* (*these* and *them*) are entered under *d* and not under *t*. All *I* entries precede *I*-plus-verb contractions; for instance, *I will* precedes *I'm,* just as *I have a* precedes *I'm a,* etc. A hyphenated word is treated as one word. In other words, strict alphabetic order (except for *a, an,* and *the*) is followed regardless of contractions, hyphens, or dialect spellings.

If a song is one of the numbered Francis James Child ballads, the title is followed by C and the appropriate number; example: "James Harris, or The Daemon Lover" (C 243). Next, various collections where the song may be found are given according to the key letters above, and with each set of key letters, in parentheses, the number of times or variants in a particular collection; * example: HMB(9) means that the song shows nine variants or versions in H. M. Belden's *Ballads and Songs.* Following the key letters, several of the more common variant titles are set down. Some (though not necessarily all) of these variant titles may be entered and numbered elsewhere in their alphabetic sequence, but data are given only under the title considered the standard or common one. Example: "The Cruelty of Barbara Allen" is entered and numbered under C with the following notation, (*See:* Bonny Barbara Allen). If the reader is still in doubt as to method, a glance at the entries "Bonny Barbara Allen" and "James Harris" will show how the tabulation works.†

* Page numbers are not included, since the songs are readily found by indexes in the collections. A more complete and specific listing of sources for individual ballads is used in Coffin's *The British Traditional Ballad in North America* (1950) and in Laws's *Native American Balladry* (1950) and *American Balladry from British Broadsides* (1957), but the purpose in the present study is to suggest a few sources that may be available to the interested student.

† When the listed title is better known as an instrumental or dance tune than as one to be sung, that fact is noted by the abbreviation: *instr.*

In Chapters 19 and 20, where long-playing records are listed with song titles, the song-title number in the present chapter is set down in front of the song title of the recording. (See Chapter 19 for further explanation.)

1. Ain't Gonna Be Treated This-a Way
   (*See:* Going Down the Road Feeling Bad)
2. Alabama Bound (instr.) AAFS(5), Li
3. All Around the Maypole AAFS(5)
4. All God's Chillun Got Wings AKD, Ark., J+Ji, JWW, NCFiii(4), NIW
   All God's Chillun
   Going to Shout All Over God's Heaven
   I Got Shoes
5. All My Sins Are Taken Away AAFS(4), NCFiii, NIW
   All of My Sins Been Taken Away
6. Alouette!
7. Alphabet Song   AAFS(2), AKD, HC-*SB*, VRiv(6)
8. Amazing Grace   AAFS(16), Ark., Li, Liii
9. Amsterdam Maid, The AAFS(2), JCC, WMD(2)
   A-Roving
   I'll Go No More A-Roving
10. Another Man Done Gone AAFS, Liii
11. Apprentice Boy, The
    (*See:* Sheffield Apprentice, The)
12. Arkansas Boys, The Ark.(3), VRiii(3)
    Missouri Boys
    Ways of Arkansas, The
13. Arkansas Traveler (instr.) AAFS(26), Ark.(3), AKD, HMB(2), JHC(4), Li, NCFiii, PGB(2), VRiii
14. A-Roving
    (*See:* Amsterdam Maid, The)
15. As I Walked Out
    (*See:* Rolly Trudum)
16. As I Walked Out in the Streets of Laredo
    (*See:* Cowboy's Lament, The)

17. As I Was Going to Nottingham Fair
    (*See:* Earl Brand)
18. As I Went Walking One Morning in May
    (*See:* One Morning in May)
19. Aunt Rhody
    (*See:* Go Tell Aunt Rhody)
20. Babes in the Woods, The AAFS(5), ACM(2), APH, Ark.(3), AKD(2), CJSi, G+C, HMB(2), NCFii, LP, PGB, VRi(5)
    Little Babes in the Woods, The
    Poor Babes in the Woods, The
    Two Babes in the Woods
21. Babylon; or, The Bonnie Banks o' Fordie (C 14) AKD, NCFii
    Baby Lon
22. Bachelor's Hall   AAFS, ACM, Ark., G+C, VRiii
23. Backwoodsman, The
    (*See:* Green Mountain Boys, The)
24. Bailiff's Daughter of Islington, The (C 105) ACM, AKD, APH, CJSi(2), EBG, HC-*TS*(3), HHF+, HMB
    Bailiff's Daughter, The
    Comely Youth, The
    There Was a Youth
25. Ballad of Davy Crockett, The
    (*See:* Davy Crockett)
26. Ballad of the Good Old Rebel, The
    (*See:* Good Old Rebel, The)
27. Ballit of de Boll Weevil, The
    (*See:* Boll Weevil)
28. Bamboo Briars, The
    (*See:* Sheffield Apprentice, The)
29. Bangum and the Boar
    (*See:* Sir Lionel)
30. Banks of the Brandywine, The G+C(2), WRM

31. Banks of Claudie, The   AAFS,
    AKD, APH, HMB, JHC, G+C,
    WAO, WRM
    Banks of the Claudy (Cloddy,
    Cloddie), The
32. Banks of Sacramento
    (*See:* Sacramento)
33. Banks of the Nile, The
    (*See:* Sailor's Sweetheart)
34. Banks of the River Dee, The
    G+C(5), LP(2)
    Banks of the Obadee
    On the Banks of the Old Pedee
    On the Banks of the Old T. B.
    On the Banks of the Old Knee
35. Banks of the Sweet Dundee, The
    AAFS(4), AKD, CJSi(3),
    G+C(3), HC-*TS*, HMB(2),
    JHC(2), VRi(2), WRM
    Banks of Sweet Dundee, The
    On the Banks of the Sweet
    Dundee
    Farmer's Daughter, The
36. Barbara Allen
    (*See:* Bonny Barbara Allen)
37. Bay of Mexico, The
    (*See:* Santy Anna)
38. Bear Went Over the Mountain,
    The   AKD(3)
39. Beaulampkins
    (*See:* Lamkin)
40. Beefsteak When I'm Hungry
    (*See:* Cindy)
41. Big Rock Candy Mountain, The
    Liii
42. Bile Dem Cabbage Down
    AAFS(5), NCFiii, NIW
    Boil Them Cabbage Down
43. Billikins and His Dinah
    (*See:* Villikins and His Dinah)
44. Billy Boy   AAFS(21), ACM,
    AKD(20), APH(4), Ark.(3),
    CJSii(3), HC-*TS*(4), HMB(2),
    JHC(4), Li, LP, NCFiii,
    VRi(7)
    Charming Billy
    Oh, Where Have You Been, Billy
    Boy
    My Boy Billy
45. Billy Grimes   AAFS, ACM(2),
    AKD(6), CJSii, HMB, NCFii
    Billy Grimes, the Drover
    Sweet Sixteen

46. Billy the Kid   AAFS, Li(2)
47. Birmingham Jail, The
    (*See:* Down in the Valley)
48. Black, Black
    (*See:* Black Is the Color)
49. Black-Eyed Davy
    (*See:* Gypsy Laddie, The)
50. Black Gal   AAFS(8), CJSii, Li
    That Black Gal
    That Old Black Gal
51. Black Is the Colo(u)r   CJSii,
    Liii
    Black, Black
52. Black Jack Davy
    (*See:* Gypsy Laddie, The)
53. Black-Eyed Susie   AAFS(10),
    HC-*TS*(2), Li, Liii,
    NCFiii(2), VRiii(2)
    Black-Eyed Susan
54. Blessings of Mary, The
    (*See:* Joys of Mary, The)
55. Blind Child, The   AAFS(6),
    HMB(5)
    Blind Girl, The
56. Blow, Boys, Blow   AAFS(2),
    ACM, JCC, WRM
    Blow, Bullies, Blow
    Blow Boys, Bully Boys, Blow
57. Blow the Man Down   AAFS(2),
    AKD, CS, JCC(3), Li,
    WMD(5), WRM(2)
58. Blue-Tailed Fly, The   AAFS(2),
    ACM, AKD(5), NCFiii(5),
    WAO
    Jenny Crack Corn
    Jim Crack Corn
    Jinny Crack Corn
59. Bol' Lampkin
    (*See:* Lamkin)
60. Bold Jack Donahue
    (*See:* Jack Donahue)
61. Bold Kidd, the Pirate
    (*See:* Captain Kidd)
62. Bold Pedlar and Robin Hood,
    The   (C 132) HC-*SB*,
    HC-*TS*, HHF+MO
    Bold Robin Hood and the Pedlar
63. Bold Reynard
    (*See:* Fox Chase, The)
64. Bold Robin Hood and the Pedlar
    (*See:* Bold Pedlar . . .)

65. Boll Weevil   AAFS(18), ACM,
Ark., AHP, CS(2), Li, Liii,
NCFiii(2)
Boll Weevil Been Here
Ballit of de Boll Weevil
Boll Weevil Rag
Boll Weevil Blues
Mister Boll Weevil
66. Bolts and Locks
(See: Locks and Bolts)
67. Bonaparte's Retreat (instr.)
AAFS(12), CJSii, JCC, Li,
NCFii(4), WMD(2)
Boney's Defeat
Isle of St. Helena, The
Bonyparte
Boney (John Franswor)
68. Bonny Barbara Allen (C 84)
AAFS(64), ACM(4),
AKD(26), APH(16),
Ark.(10), CJSi(16), CS,
EBG, G+C(3), HC-TS(7),
HMB(16), JHC(12), LP(2),
NCFii, VRi, WAO, WRM(3)
Barbara Allen
Cruelty of Barbara Allen
Barbry Ellen
Sweet William
Love of Barbara Ellen, The
Barbree Ellen
Unworthy Barbara Allen
Barbery Allen
69. Bonny Black Bess AAFS(2),
Ark., LP, NCFii, VRii(3),
WRM
My Bonnie Black Bess
My Poor Black Bess
70. Bonny Bunch of Roses AAFS,
EBG, HC-SB, WRM(2)
71. Bonny Wee Window, The   VRi
72. Boots and Leggins
(See: Old Shoes and Leggins)
73. Boston Burglar, The
AAFS(12), ACM, AKD(14),
Ark., G+C(3), HC-SB, JHC,
LP(2), NCFii, PGB(5), WAO
Charlestown
Boston Murderer, The
Frank James, the Roving Gambler
Charleston Jail
Jail at Morgantown, The
74. Botany Bay   G+C, HHF+, VRi

75. Bought Me a Cat AAFS(2),
Ark.
I Bought Me a Cat
I Had Me a Cat
76. Bound for the Promised Land
AAFS(2), GPJ-S, Liii
77. Boys, Keep Away from the Girls,
I Say   AAFS(2), Ark.
Boys, Stay . . .
78. Bramble Briar,The
(See: Sheffield Apprentice,
The)
79. Brennan on the Moor   AAFS(3),
HC-TS, CJSii, HMB(2), Lii,
VRii, WRM
Young Brinnon on the Moor
80. Bright Sherman Valley
(See: Red River Valley)
81. Broken Heart, The   HMB(3),
VRiv(9)
Broken Vow, The
False-Hearted Lover, The
Railroad Flagman, The
Brown-Eyed Girl, The
Peggy Walker
False Lover, The
82. Broken-Hearted Lover, The
(See: Unquiet Grave, The)
83. Broken Token, The
(See: Pretty Fair Maid in Her
Garden)
84. Brown Girl, The (C 295)
(Cf. C 73) ACM, AKD,
APH(2), CJSi(11), CS,
HC-TS(2)
Rich Lady from London
Rose of Ardeen
Pretty Sally
85. Brown Jug, The
(See: Little Brown Jug)
86. Buck Creek Girls
(See: Cripple Creek)
87. Buffalo Gals (instr.) AAFS(13),
AKD (2), Liii, NCFiii(2),
VRiii(4)
Round Town Girls
Won't You Walk Out Tonight?
Buffalo Girls
88. Buffalo Skinners, The
AAFS(4), Ark., CS, Li, Liii,
LP
Craigle's Buffalo Hunt
Range of the Buffalo, The

89. Bully of the Town (instr.)
    AAFS
90. Bury Me Beneath the Willow
    (*See:* Weeping Willow, The)
91. Bury Me Not on the Lone Prairie
    AAFS(4), AKD, APH, Ark.,
    CS, Liii, LP, VRii(2)
    Lone Prairie, The
    Oh, Bury Me Not on the Lone
    Prairie
    Bury Me Out on the Lone Prairie
    Oh, Bury Me Not
92. Butcher Boy, The   AAFS(12),
    ACM(2), AKD(26), APH,
    Ark.(2), G+C(7), HC-*SB*,
    HMB(8), JHC(3), LP(2),
    NCFii(14), PGB(9), VRi(8),
    WAO, WRM
    Butcher's Boy, The
    Forsaken Lovers, The
    Railroad Boy, A
    Farmer's Boy, The
    In London City
    There Is a Tavern in the Town
    In Boston Town
    In Johnson City
93. Bye-O-Baby Bunting
    AAFS(10), AKD(2)
    Bye You Baby Bunting
    Baby Bunting
    Rockabye Baby
    Rockababy Bunting
94. Cackling Hen
    (*See:* Old Hen Cackled)
95. Calomel Song, The   AAFS,
    APH, HMB, LP, NCFiii,
    PGB(2)
    Calomel
96. Cambric Shirt, The
    (*See:* Elfin Knight, The)
97. Canaday-I-O
    (*See:* Michigan-I-O)
98. Captain, Captain, Tell Me True
    (*See:* Sailor Boy, The)
99. Captain Kidd   ACM, G+C,
    HHF+MO, JCC, LP, NCFii,
    WRM
    Bold Kidd, the Pirate
100. Captain Wedderburn's Court-
    ship   (C 46)
    AAFS(2), CJSii(3), HC-*TS*(2),
    NCFii
    I'll Give My Love an Apple

I Gave My Love a Cherry
Riddle Song, The
101. Careless Love   AAFS(18),
    Ark., CS, Li, Liii, VRiv(3),
    WCH
    Dink's Song
    When My Apron It Hung Low
    When I Wore My Apron Low
102. Caroline of Edinborough Town
    AAFS, AKD, APH, Ark.(2),
    CJSi, G+C, HHF+, JHC(2),
    VRi, NCFii, WRM
    Edinboro' Town
    Young Caroline
    Edinburgh Town
    Caroline of Eddingburg Town
103. Casey Jones   AAFS(14), ACM,
    APH, CS(2), Li, Liii(2), LP,
    NCFii(2)
    Mama Have You Heard the
    News?
104. Charles Guiteau   AAFS(4),
    ACM, AKD(5), APH, Ark.,
    HMB, LP, NCFii(12),
    VRii(5), WAO
    Charlie Guiteau
    James A. Garfield
    Charles Getaw
    Death of Bendall, The
105. Charleston Jail
    (*See:* Boston Burglar, The)
106. Charming Beauty Bride, The
    AAFS(2), ACM(2), AKD(11),
    HMB, JHC, NCFii(4), PGB,
    VRi, WAO
    Once I Courted a Charming
    Beauty Bride
    First Girl I Courted, The
    I Courted for Love
    Irish Molly-O
    Fair Beauty Bride
    Widow's Daughter, The
    Seven Year Song
107. Charming Billy
    (*See:* Billy Boy)
108. Cherry Tree Carol, The (C 54)
    AAFS(2), ACM, AKD, CJSi(6),
    GPJ-D, HC-*TS*(2), LP,
    NCFii(2), VRi
    Sweet Mary and Sweet Joseph
109. Chickamy, Chickamy, Crany,
    Crow   AAFS, AKD, VRii(3)
    Chick-A-Ma-Craney-Ma-Crow

Chickee Chickee Ma Craney Crow

110. Chicken Reel (instr.) AAFS(4), CS
111. Chickens A-Crowin' (*See:* Sourwood Mountain)
112. Chilly Winds AAFS(2), Lii
113. Chisholm Trail (*See:* Old Chisholm Trail, The)
114. Christ Was Born in Bethlehem (*See:* Jesus Was Born . . .)
115. Cindy (instr.) AAFS(18), AKD(4), Liii, NCFiii(6), VRiii(2)
    Get Along Home, Cindy
    Beefsteak When I'm Hungry
    Run Along Home, Cindy
    Sindy—A Jig
116. Clinch Mountain (*See:* Rye Whisky)
117. Coffee Grows on White Oak Trees AAFS(8), ACM, APH, Ark.(2), Liii, NCFiii(9)
    Green Coffee Grows on a White Oak Stump
118. Colony Times (*See:* In Good Old Colony Times)
119. Colorado Trail, The CS
120. Come All Ye Fair and Tender Ladies AAFS(12), ACM(2), AKD(3), CJSii(18), Liii, NCFiii(6), VRi(3), WAO
    Come All You Young and Tender Ladies
    Come All You Pretty Fair Maids
    Fair and Tender Ladies
    I Wish I Were a Little Sparrow
121. Come All You Jolly Cowboys AAFS(2), VRii(2)
    Come All You Roving Cowboys
    Come All Ye Lonesome Cowboys
122. Come In, Come In, My Own True Love (*See:* One Morning in May)
123. Come Men and Maids (*See:* Silver Dagger, The)
124. Come Sit by My Side, Little Darlin' (*See:* Red River Valley)

125. Comely Youth, The (*See:* Bailiff's Daughter of Islington, The)
126. Comin' Round the Mountain (*See:* She'll Be Comin' Round the Mountain)
127. Common Bill AAFS, ACM, AKD(6), APH, Ark.(2), CS, G+C, NCFii(5), VRi(2)
    Silly Bill
    Green Bill
    I'll Tell You of a Fellow
128. Corn Shucking Song (*See:* Possum Up a 'Simmon Stump)
129. Cotton-Eyed Joe AAFS(5), Ark., Li, Lii, NIW
130. Couldn't Hear Nobody Pray (*See:* I Couldn't Hear Nobody Pray)
131. Courting Song, The (*See:* Quaker's Courtship, The)
132. Courting Too Slow (*See:* On Top of Old Smoky)
133. Cowboy Waltz (instr.) AAFS
134. Cowboy's Dream AAFS, Li, Liii, VRii(2)
    One Night as I Lay on the Prairie
135. Cowboy's Lament, The AAFS(18), ACM, AKD(12), Ark.(5), CS, G+C(2), HHF+, HMB(9), JHC(6), Liii, LP, NCFii(12), VRii(5), WRM
    Streets of Laredo, The
    Unfortunate Rake, The
    Dying Cowgirl
    As I Walked Out in the Streets of Laredo
    Dying Cowboy, The
    Dying Cowboy's Prayer
    Wild Cowboy, The
136. Craigle's Buffalo Hunt (*See:* Buffalo Skinners, The)
137. Crawdad AAFS(6), Ark., Liii
    Crawdad Song
    Sweet Thing
    Sugar Babe
138. Creation (*See:* Dese Bones Gwine Rise Again)

139. Cripple Creek (instr.)
　　AAFS(28), AKD(6), CJSii(2),
　　NCFiii(2)
　　Buck Creek Girls
　　Buck Creek Gals
140. Cruel Brother, The (C 11)
　　AAFS, CJSi(2), LP, NCFii(2)
　　Two Cruel Brothers, The
　　Oh Lily O
141. Cruel Mother, The (C 20)
　　AAFS(2),　AKD,　CJSi(13),
　　JHC, VRi
　　Down by the Greenwood Side
　　Greenwood Siding, The
142. Cruel Ship's Carpenter, The
　　(See: Ship Carpenter, The)
143. Cruelty of Barbara Allen, The
　　(See: Bonny Barbara Allen)
144. Cuckoo Is a Pretty Bird, The
　　AAFS(5),　ACM,　AKD(9),
　　CJSii(13), HC-TS(3), VRi(4)
　　Cukoo Song, The
　　Sorry True Lover, A
　　False-Hearted Lover, A
　　Cuckoo, The
145. Cumberland Gap (instr.)
　　AAFS(14), AKD(4), Li,
　　NCFiii, VRiii
146. Daemon Lover, The
　　(See: James Harris)
147. Daniel in de Lions' Den
　　AAFS(2),　AKD(2),　CJSii,
　　GPJ-A, NCFiii
148. Dark-Eyed Sailor　AAFS(2),
　　EBG,　G+C(4),　HC-SB,
　　HC-TS(2), HHF+, NCFii(2),
　　WMD, WRM
149. Darling　Cory　AAFS(7), Lii,
　　Liii
　　Darlin' Corey
　　Darling Cora
150. Davy Crockett　AAFS(4), AKD,
　　HMB, JHC(2), Li, VRiii(2)
　　Ballad of Davy Crockett, The
151. Days of '49　AAFS(4), Liii,
　　VRii, VRiv(2)
　　In Eighteen-Forty-Nine
　　Days of Forty-Nine, The
152. Death of Queen Jane, The (C
　　170)　AAFS, AKD, CJSi(2)
153. Death of a Romish Lady, The
　　(See: Romish Lady, The)

154. Death of Young Monroe
　　(See: Jam on Gerry's Rocks,
　　The)
155. Deep River　J+Ji, Li, WCH
　　Deep River Blues
156. Derby　Ram,　The　AAFS(8),
　　AKD(18), APH, Ark., CJSii(3),
　　G+C(4),　HC-TS(2),　HMB,
　　JCC, Lii, NCFii(2), PGB(2),
　　VRi(3)
　　Darby Ram, The
　　Ram of Derby, The
　　There Was a Sheep of Darby
　　Derby Sheep, The
　　Great Sheep, The
　　Old Tup, The
　　Sheep of Darby
　　Ram in Darby, The
157. Dere's No Hidin' Place Down
　　Dere
　　(See: No Hiding Place)
158. Dese Bones Gwine Rise Again
　　AAFS(10), AKD, CS, Li, Lii,
　　NCFiii(2)
　　Dem Bones
　　Creation
　　Dry Bones
159. Devil and the Farmer, The
　　(See:　Farmer's　Curst　Wife,
　　The)
160. Devilish Mary　AAFS(5), ACM,
　　AKD(2), Ark., CJSii(2), Lii,
　　VRiii(4)
161. Devil's Nine Questions, The
　　(See:　Riddles　Wisely　Ex-
　　pounded)
162. Diamond Joe　AAFS(4), Lii
163. Didn't My Lord Deliver Daniel?
　　AAFS, Ark., J+Ji
164. Didn't They Crucify My Lord?
　　(See: Were You There When
　　They Crucified My Lord?)
165. Dinah and Villikins
　　(See: Villikins and His Dinah)
166. Dink's Song
　　(See: Careless Love)
167. Dog and Gun, The (or My)
　　(See: Golden Glove, The)
168. Down by the Greenwood Side
　　(See: Cruel Mother, The)
169. Down by Yon Weeping Willow
　　(See: Weeping Willow, The)

170. Down in That Lonesome Valley
(*See:* That Lonesome Valley)
171. Down in the Low (Lone) Green
Valley
(*See:* Jealous Lover, The)
172. Down in the Valley   AAFS(5),
ACM(2), Ark., CS, HMB, Li,
Liii, NCFiii(2), VRiv, WAO
173. Down the Banks of the Ohio
(*See:* On the Banks of the
Ohio)
174. Dreary Black Hills, The
AAFS(4), CS, Li, LP, HHF+,
HMB(2)
175. Drill, Ye Tarriers, Drill   AAFS,
ACM
176. Drowsy Sleeper, The   AAFS(6),
ACM, AKD(25), Ark.(2), EBG,
G+C(6),   HMB(8),   JHC(2),
LP(2),   NCFii(5),   PGB(6),
VRi(6), WMD
Bedroom Window
Wake   Up,   Wake   Up,   You
Drowsy Sleeper
Little Sparrow, The
Untrue Lover, The
Who Is at My Bedroom Win-
dow?
Death of William and Nancy
Green Willow Tree, The
177. Drunkard's Dream, The
AAFS(8), EBG, HMB, JHC(2)
178. Drunken Sailor, The
(*See:* What Shall We Do with
a Drunken Sailor?)
179. Dry Bones
(*See:* Dese Bones Gwine Rise
Again)
180. Ducks in the Mill Pond
(*See:* Jim Along Josie)
181. Dupree   AAFS, ACM(2), AKD,
Lii, NCFii
Frank Depre
Frankie Dupree
182. Dying Californian, The
AAFS(7), AKD(4), APH,
GPJ-S,D, HMB, JHC, VRii,
LP
183. Dying Cowboy, The
(*See:* Cowboy's Lament, The)
184. Earl Brand (C 7)   AAFS(2),
ACM, AKD(7), APH, Ark.,

CJSi(12),   EBG,   JHC,
NCFii(7), WRM
Seven Brothers or Lord William
Sweet William and Fair Ellen
As I Was Going to Nottingham
Fair
Seven Horsemen
Lord Robert
Earl Bran
Fair Ellender
Seven Brothers
Seven Sleepers, The
185. Early, Early in the Spring
(*See:* Girl I Left Behind Me,
The)
186. East Virginia   AAFS, Lii
187. Edinburgh Town
(*See:* Caroline of Edinborough
Town)
188. Edward (C 13)   AAFS(4), ACM,
AKD(3),   APH(2),   CJSi(10),
HHF+MO,   LP,   NCFii(3),
VRi(4), WAO
What Blood on the Point of Your
Knife?
How Come That Blood on Your
Shirt Sleeve?
Brother's Blood
What's on Your Sword?
Dear Son
189. Egyptian Davio
(*See:* Gypsy Laddie, The)
190. Eighth of January (instr.)
AAFS(10)
Eighth Day of January, The
191. Elfin Knight, The (C 2)
AAFS(6), ACM, AKD(5), Ark.
CJSi(2),   G+C,   HHF+,
HMB(3),   NCFii(3),   PGB(5),
VRi(2)
192. En Roulant Ma Boule   MB+ES
193. Erie Canal, The   CS(3), Li, Liii
Raging Canawl, The
E-r-i-e, The
Erie Was Rising, The
194. Erin's Green Shore   AKD, Ark.,
EBG, JHC(4), VRi
Irishman's Dream Song, The
Irish Dream, The
195. Every Night When the Sun Goes
In   CJSii, Li
196. Every Time I Feel the Spirit
AAFS, Ark., J+Ji

197. Ezekiel Saw the Wheel AAFS,
     J+Jii, JWW
     'Zekiel Saw the Wheel
     Ezek'el Saw the Wheel
198. Fair and Tender Ladies
     (*See:* Come All Ye Fair and
     Tender Ladies)
199. Fair Annie of Lochyran
     (*See:* Lass of Roch Royal, The)
200. Fair Beauty Bride
     (*See:* Charming Beauty Bride)
201. Fair Charlotte
     (*See:* Young Charlotte)
202. Fair Ellen(der)
     (*See:* Earl Brand)
203. Fair Ellender and the Brown
     Girl
     (*See:* Lord Thomas and Fair
     Annet)
204. Fair Margaret and Sweet Wil-
     liam (C 74) AAFS(27),
     AKD(8), APH(2), CJSi(17),
     G+C, HHF+MO, HMB(4),
     JHC(7), Lii, LP, NCFii(7),
     PGB(5), VRi(4), WAO, WRM
     Lady Margaret and Sweet Wil-
     liam
     Prince William and Lady Mar-
     garet
     Lady Margaret's Ghost
     Sweet William and Fair Ellender
     Lady Marg'ret
     Sweet William
     Sweet William and Lady Mar-
     garet
205. Fair Young Maid, A
     (*See:* Pretty Fair Maid in the
     Garden)
206. False Knight Upon the Road,
     The (C 3) AKD, CJSi(2),
     HC-SB, HC-TS(2),
     HHF+MO, HMB, LP, PGB
     Boy and the Devil, The
     Fause Knight Upon the Road,
     The
     False Knight, The
207. False Lamkin
     (*See:* Lamkin)
208. False Lover, The
     (*See:* Broken Heart, The)
209. False-Hearted Lover, The
     (*See:* Cuckoo Is a Pretty Bird,
     The)

210. False Young Man, The
     (*See:* One Morning in May)
211. Fare You Well, My Own True
     Love AAFS(4), Liii,
     NCFiii(3)
     I'll Hang My Harp on a Willow
     Tree
     Fare Thee Well
212. Farmer's Boy, The
     (*See:* Butcher's Boy, The)
213. Farmer's Curst Wife, The (C
     278) AAFS(6), ACM,
     AKD(8), APH(2), Ark.,
     CJSi(7), G+C(5), HC-SB,
     HC-TS(5), JHC, HHF+MO,
     HMB(2), NCFii, PGB, VRi(2),
     WRM
     Old Woman and the Devil, The
     Devil and the Farmer, The
     Woman and the Devil, A
     Old Man Under the Hill, The
     Ten Little Devils
     Farmer's Wife, The
     Kellyburnbraes
     Scolding Wife, The
214. Farmer's Daughter, The
     (*See:* Banks of the Sweet
     Dundee)
215. Fatal Wedding, The AAFS(2),
     APH, AKD(6), Ark.(3), EBG,
     HMB(3), LP, NCFii, PGB(4),
     VRiv
216. Father Grumble AAFS(2),
     AKD(18), APH, Ark.(2),
     HMB, JHC(7), LP, NCFii(4),
     PGB, VRi(3), WAO
     Old Man Who Lived in the
     Wood, The
     Old Father Grumble
     Old Grumbler
     Old Crumbly Crust
     Grumbler's Song, The
     Darby and Joan
217. Fight at Bunker Hill, The
     (*See:* Last Fierce Charge, The)
218. Fire Down Below AAFS, JCC
219. First Girl I Courted, The
     (*See:* Charming Beauty Bride,
     The)
220. Flat River Girl, The
     (*See:* Jack Haggerty)

221. Flop-Eared Mule (instr.)
     AAFS(6)
     Lop-Eared Mule
     White Cockade
222. Flo(r)ella
     (See: Jealous Lover, The)
223. Flying Cloud, The AAFS(3),
     EBG, HC-SB, HC-TS(2),
     HMB, JCC, Li, WMD(2),
     WRM
     Edward Hollander
224. Foggy Dew, The CJSii, CS,
     VRi
     Weaver, The
     Foggy, Foggy Dew, The
225. Forsaken Lover
     (See: Unconstant Lover, The)
226. Fox and the Goose, The
     (See: Gray Goose, The)
227. Fox Chase, The AAFS(6),
     AKD(3), NCFii(5)
     Fox and the Hounds, The
     Come All Ye Jolly Sportsmen
     We Hunted and We Hollered
     Fox Hunt
     Bold Reynard
     Three Jolly Welshmen
228. Fox Stepped Out One Moon-
     shiny Night, The
     (See: Gray Goose, The)
229. Frank James, the Roving Gam-
     bler
     (See: Boston Burglar, The)
230. Frankie and Johnny AAFS(14),
     ACM, AKD(5), APH, Ark.(2),
     CS(5), HMB, Li(2), Liii,
     NCFii(10), NIW, VRii(6)
     Frances She Shot Albert
     Frankie Baker
     He Done Her Wrong
     Frankie Silver(s)
     Aggie and Alfred
     Frankie and Albert
     Josie
     Sadie
231. Frankie Dupree
     (See: Dupree)
232. Frog and the Mouse, The
     (See: Frog Went A-Courting)
233. Frog Went A-Courting
     AAFS(34), ACM(7), AKD(36),
     APH, Ark.(11), CJSii(11), CS,
     G+C(8), HC-TS(7),

HHF+MO, HMB(7), JHC(7),
Li, NCFiii(27), PGB(10),
NIW, VRi(10), WAO, WRM
Frog and the Mouse
Marriage of the Frog and the
     Mouse, The
Froggy Vould A-Vooing Go
Uncle Rat's Courtship
Master Frog Went A-Courting
Miss Mousie
Mr. Frog
234. Frozen Girl, The
     (See: Young Charlotte)
235. Fuller and Warren AAFS(4),
     APH, HHF+MO, HMB(4),
     PGB(7), VRii(3)
     Warren and Fuller
     Sons of Columbia
236. Gallant Ship, The
     (See: Mermaid, The)
237. Gallows Tree
     (See: Maid Freed from the
     Gallows, The)
238. Gamb(o)ling Man, The
     (See: Roving Gambler, The)
239. Geordie (C 209) AAFS, AKD,
     Ark.(2), CJSi(6), EBG, G+C,
     HC-TS(3), HMB(3), JHC,
     NCFii, VRi(4)
     Life of Georgia, The
     Lovely Georgie
     Georgie
     George E. Wedlock
     Georgia
240. George Collins
     (See: Lady Alice)
241. Gerry's Rocks
     (See: Jam on Gerry's Rocks,
     The)
242. Get Along Home, Cindy
     (See: Cindy)
243. Get Up and Bar the Door (C
     275) AAFS, ACM, AKD,
     EBG, HC-TS, JHC, NCFii(2),
     VRi(2)
     Joan and John Blount
244. Giles Collins
     (See: Lady Alice)
245. Girl I Left Behind Me, The
     AAFS(7), AKD(5), APH,
     Ark.(3), G+C(2), Li, NCFii(7),
     VRi(4), VRiii(3), WMD
     Maid I Left Behind Me, The

Early, Early in the Spring
Gal I Left in Arkansas, The
Maggie Walker

246. Git Along, Little Dogies
AAFS(4), ACM, CS, Li, Lii,
Liii, LP
Whoopee Ti Yi Yo, Git Along
Little Dogies
Little Dogies

247. Git Along Liza Jane
(*See:* Liza Jane)

248. Git On Board   AAFS(2), J+Ji

249. Give Me That Old Time Religion
(*See:* That Old Time Religion)

250. Go Down Moses   J+Ji, JWW,
Liii, NCFiii

251. Go Down, Old Hannah
AAFS(10), Lii

252. Go Tell Aunt Rhody   AAFS(7),
Ark., Liii, VRii(4)
Aunt Rhody
Go Tell Aunt Dinah (or, Patsy,
Tabby, Tildy, Phoebe, Nancy)

253. Go 'Way from My Window
AAFS, CS, Li, NCFiii
Go 'Way f'om Mah Window

254. Going Down the Road Feeling
Bad AAFS(10), AKD, Liii,
NCFiii
Blowing Down the Road Feelin'
Bad
Ain't Gonna Be Treated This-a
Way

255. Goin' to Boston (instr.)
AAFS(2), CJSii, Li, VRiii(2)
We'll All Go to Boston

256. Goin' t' Lay Down My Sword
and Shield
(*See:* Study War No More)

257. Going to Shout All Over God's
Heaven
(*See:* All God's Chillun Got
Wings)

258. Golden Glove, The   AAFS,
AKD(7), HMB(5)
Dog and Gun, The
Wealthy Young Farmer, A
Nobleman's Daughter, The
Hunting with a Dog and Gun
I'll Tell You of a Squire
Squire, The

259. Golden Slippers   AAFS(2),
NCFiii

260. Golden Vanity, The
(*See:* Sweet Trinity, The)

261. Golden Willow Tree, The
(*See:* Sweet Trinity, The)

262. Good Old Mountain Dew
(*See:* Mountain Dew)

263. Good Old Rebel, The   AAFS,
AKD(4), APH, JHC, Li(2),
NCFiii(4), VRii(3)
I'm a Good Old Rebel
Ballad of the Good Old Rebel

264. Goodbye, My Lover, Goodbye
AAFS, NCFiii(2)
See the Train Go Round the
Bend

265. Goodbye, Old Paint   AAFS(3),
Ark., CS, Li, Liii(2)
I Ride an Old Paint
Leadin' Old Paint
Ridin' Old Paint
Old Paint

266. Gospel Train, The (De)
AAFS(5), AKD(2), NCFiii(3),
NIW
That Gospel Train Is Coming

267. Gosport Tragedy, The
(*See:* Pretty Polly)

268. Gray Goose, The   AAFS(9),
AKD(7), Ark., G+C, JHC,
HC-*TS*(3), NCFiii(5), PGB,
VRi(4)
Fox Stepped Out One Moon-
shiny Night, The
Fox and the Goose, The
Old Mother Flip-Flop
Fox Is on the Town, The
The Fox
Old Fox Walked Out
Fox Started Out, The

269. Great Grandad   AAFS, NCFii,
VRiii

270. Great Titanic, The
(*See:* Sinking of the Titanic,
The)

271. Green Bed, The   AAFS(2),
AKD(9), CJSi(4), HMB(3),
NCFii(5), WRM
Young Johnny
Daughter Polly
Bring Down Your Daughter
Polly
Liverpool Lady, The
What Luck, Young Johnny?

272. Green Coffee Grows on a White
    Oak Stump
    (*See:* Coffee Grows on White
    Oak Trees)
273. Green Corn   AAFS(4), VRii(2),
    WAO
    I'll Meet You in the Evening
274. Green Grass Growing All
    Around   AAFS(4), Ark.,
    VRiii
275. Green Grow the Laurels
    AAFS(2), AKD(3), Ark.,
    CJSii, G+C(2), HMB, JHC(2)
    Green Grow the Lilacs
    Red, White, and Blue, The
    Green Grows the Wild Isle
    I Once Had a Sweetheart
    Green Laurels
    Green Grow the Rashes
276. Green Grow the Lilacs
    (*See:* Green Grow the Laurels)
277. Green Mossy Banks of the Lea,
    The   G+C, HC-*SB*, WRM
278. Green Mountain Boys, The
    AAFS(2), G+C, Lii
    Backwoodsman, The
    I Came to This Country in 1865
279. Green Willow Tree, The
    (*See:* Drowsy Sleeper, The)
280. Greenland Whale Fishery, The
    AAFS, HMB, JCC, Lii
    Whale Song, The
    Greenland Fishery
281. Greensleeves
282. Greenwood Siding, The
    (*See:* Cruel Mother, The)
283. Ground Hog   AAFS(14),
    AKD(3), CJSii, JHC, Li,
    Liii, NCFiii(3), VRiii(2)
    Old Ground Hog
    Groun' Hog
    Ground Hog Song, The
284. Grumbler's Song, The
    (*See:* Father Grumble)
285. Gypsy Davy, The
    (*See:* Gypsy Laddie, The)
286. Gypsy Laddie, The (C 200)
    AAFS(15), ACM(2), AKD(8),
    Ark.(3), CS, CJSi(10), APH(2),
    EBG(2), HC-*TS*, HMB(3),
    JHC(4), Lii, NCFii(7), VRi(8),
    WAO
    Gypsen Davy

Black Jack Davy
Black-Eyed Davy
Heartless Lady, The
Egyptian Davio
It Was Late in the Night When
    Johnny Came Home
Gyps of Davy, The
Dark-Clothed Gypsy, The
287. Gypsy's Warning, The
    AAFS(3), PGB(2), VRiv
288. Hand Me Down My Walking
    Cane   AAFS(2), AKD, Ark.,
    NCFiii
    Walking Cane
289. Hanger, O Hanger, Go Slacken
    the Line
    (*See:* Maid Freed from the
    Gallows, The)
290. Hanging Johnny   AAFS(2),
    JCC, WMD
291. Hangman, Hangman
    (*See:* Maid Freed from the
    Gallows, The)
292. Hard Times   AAFS(7), AKD(3),
    APH, G+C, JHC, Li,
    NCFiii(5)
293. Haul Away, Joe   AAFS(4),
    AKD, JCC, Lii, WMD(2)
    Haul Away, My Rosy
    Haul Away, My Johnny-O
294. He Done Her Wrong
    (*See:* Frankie and Johnny)
295. He Never Said a Mumblin' Word
    AAFS(6), JWW, NCFiii
    Never Said a Mumblin' Word
    Never Spoke a Mumble
296. Hebrew Children   AAFS,
    AKD(4), GPJ-U,S
    Way Over in the (de) Promised
    Land
297. He's Gone Away
    (*See:* Ten Thousand Miles)
298. High Barbaree   AAFS, JCC,
    ACM(2), Lii, NCFii
    Hi Barbaree
    High Barbary
299. Hog Drovers   AAFS(10), APH,
    Ark., VRiii
    Hog Rovers
300. Hog-Eyed Man, The   AAFS(6),
    CS, CJSii, JCC
    Hog Eye

301. Hold On
    (*See:* Keep Your Hand on the Plow)
302. Home on the Range   AAFS(4), Liii, VRii(2)
    Western Home, The
303. Horse Named Bill, The   CS
304. House Carpenter, The
    (*See:* James Harris)
305. How Come That Blood on Your Shirt Sleeve?
    (*See:* Edward)
306. Hunters of Kentucky, The   CS, HMB, VRiv
    Packenham
    Packing Ham
    Old Packingham
307. Huron Carol, The
308. Hush, Little Baby   AAFS(2), Lii
309. I Asked My Love to Take a Walk
    (*See:* On the Banks of the Ohio)
310. I Bought Me a Cat
    (*See:* Bought Me a Cat)
311. I Can't Set Down
    (*See:* Set Down, Servant)
312. I Couldn't Hear Nobody Pray   AAFS(3), J+Ji, JWW
    Couldn't Hear Nobody Pray
313. I Gave My Love a Cherry
    (*See:* Captain Wedderburn's Courtship)
314. I Got a Girl at the Head of the Holler
    (*See:* Sourwood Mountain)
315. I Got Shoes
    (*See:* All God's Chillun Got Wings)
316. I Met Her in the Garden Where the Praties Grow   CS
317. I Must Walk That Lonesome Valley
    (*See:* That Lonesome Valley)
318. I Once Had a Sweetheart
    (*See:* Green Grow the Laurels)
319. I Ride an Old Paint
    (*See:* Goodbye, Old Paint)
320. I Was Born About Ten Thousand Years Ago   AAFS(3), CS, Liii, NCFiii(5), VRiii(3)
    I Went to See My Susan

321. I Wish I Was a Mole in the Ground   AAFS(2), Li, NCFiii
    Mole in the Ground
322. I Wish I was a Single Girl   AAFS(3), ACM, AKD(7), NCFiii(3), WAO
    Single Girl, The
    Drunkard's Wife, The
    When You Was a Single Girl
323. I Wish I Was Single Again   AAFS(13), AKD(17), CS, HMB(4), Li, Liii, LP, NCFiii(10), VRiii(4), WAO, WRM
    When I Was Single
    I Wish to My Lord I Was Single
324. I Wish I Were a Little Sparrow
    (*See:* Come All Ye Fair and Tender Ladies)
325. I Wonder As I Wander   NCFiii
326. Ida Red   AAFS(10), Ark., Li, VRiii
327. If He'd Be a Buckaroo   AAFS, Li
328. I'll Give You a Paper of Pins
    (*See:* Paper of Pins)
329. I'll Go No More A-Roving
    (*See:* Amsterdam Maid, The)
330. I'll Hang My Harp on a Willow Tree
    (*See:* Fare You Well, My Own True Love)
331. I'll Not Marry at All   ACM, Ark., LP
    I'm an Old Livelong Maid
332. I'm a Good Old Rebel
    (*See:* Good Old Rebel, The)
333. I'm Bound for the Promised Land   AAFS, NCFiii, VRiv
334. I'm Going to Georgy (instr.)   AAFS(4), CJSii
335. I'm Sad and I'm Lonely
    (*See:* Troubled in Mind)
336. I'm Troubled in Mind
    (*See:* Troubled in Mind)
337. In Boston Town
    (*See:* Butcher Boy, The)
338. In Eighteen-Forty-Nine
    (*See:* Days of '49, The)
339. In Good Old Colony Times, or The Three Sons   AKD(6), LP, NCFii(4), VRi
    Three Sons, or Noble King, The

Noble King, The
Colony Times
Three Rogues, The
340. In London City
    (*See:* Butcher Boy, The)
341. Indian Lass, The
    (*See:* Little Mohea, The)
342. Irene   AAFS
    Goodnight Irene
343. Irish Lady, The
    (*See:* Rich Irish Lady, The)
344. Irish Washerwoman   AAFS(9),
    HMB(3), VRiii(4)
    Down, Down, Down Derry
    Down
    Benton County, Arkansas
    Irish Wash-Woman
345. Irishman's Dream Song, The
    (*See:* Erin's Green Shore)
346. Isle of St. Helena, The
    (*See:* Bonaparte's Retreat)
347. It's Me, Oh Lord   AAFS(3),
    Ark., J+Ji, JWW, NCFiii(3),
    Standin' in the Need of Prayer
348. I've Been Workin' on the Rail-
    road   AAFS(2), NCFiii(3)
    Working on the Railroad
349. Jack Donahue   AAFS(3), APH,
    LP, WRM
    Bold Jack Donahue
    Jack Donahoo
350. Jack Haggerty   AAFS, G+C(6),
    NCFii, WMD
    Jack Haggerty's Lament
    Flat River Girl, The
351. Jack Monroe   AAFS, HMB(5),
    NCFii(4)
    Poor Jack Is Gone A-Sailing
    Young Jack the Farmer
    Jack the Sailor
    Wealthy Merchant, The
352. Jack O' Diamonds   AAFS(4),
    APH, Lii, NCFiii(4)
    Lillie, O Lillie
353. Jack Was Every Inch a Sailor
    EBG
354. Jail at Morgantown, The
    (*See:* Boston Burglar, The)
355. Jam on Gerry's Rocks, The
    AAFS(6), ACM, CS, G+C(6),
    HC-*TS*, HHF+, JHC(4), Li,

Liii,   NCFii(3),   WMD(2),
WRM(2)
In the Jam at Gerry's Rocks
Gerry's Rocks
Jack Monroe
Young Monroe
Death of Young Monroe
356. James A. Garfield
    (*See:* Charles Guiteau)
357. James Harris (The Daemon
    Lover)   (C 243) AAFS(42),
    ACM(2), AKD(25), APH(2),
    Ark.(4), CJSi(22), CS, G+C(3),
    HHF+, HMB(9), JHC(21),
    LP, NCFii(14), PGB(9),
    VRi(16), WAO
    House Carpenter, The
    Demon Lover, The
    I Have Forty Ships
    House Carpenter's Wife, The
    Salt, Salt Sea, The
    Salt Water Sea
    Sweet Wildee
    Sea-Faring Man, The
358. James Whalen
    (*See:* Lost Jimmie Whalen)
359. Jealous Lover, The   AAFS(6),
    ACM(3), AKD(19), APH(2),
    Ark.(6),   EBG,   G+C(3),
    GPJ-D, HHF+, HMB(18),
    JHC(8), LP(2), NCFii(23),
    PGB(13), VRii(10), WAO,
    WMD
    Down in the Low (Lone) Green
    Valley
    Flo(r)ella
    Lorilla
    Flo Ella
    Lone, Lone Valley, The
    Pearl Bryan(t)
    Blue-Eyed Ella
    Under the Weeping Willow
    Jealous Lover of Lone Green
    Valley, The
    Look Across the Low Green
    Valley
360. Jenny Jenkins   AAFS(3), Ark.(2),
    Lii, Liii, NCFiii(4), WAO
    Jinny Jinkins
    Julie Jenkins
    Tooley Wooley Iser
361. Jesse James   AAFS(11), ACM,
    AKD(4), APH(3), Ark.(4), CS,

G+C(2), HMB, JHC, Li(2), Liii, LP, NCFii(9), VRii(7), WAO
I Went Down to the Depot

362. Jesus Born in Bethlea   AAFS, AKD, CJSii, GPJ-D, NCFiii
Christ Was Born in Bethlehem

363. Jim Along Josie (instr.)   AAFS, VRiii(2)
Ducks in the Mill Pond

364. Jim Fiske   AAFS(2), HMB

365. Jimmy Randolph
(See: Lord Randal)

366. Jinny (Jimmy) Crack Corn
(See: Blue Tail Fly, The)

367. Joe Bowers   AAFS(6), AKD(4), APH, Ark.(3), HMB(4), Li, LP(2), NCFii, JHC, VRii(4), WAO

368. John Hardy   AAFS(19), ACM, AKD(9), CJSii, JHC(9), Li, Liii, NCFii(3), VRii(3)

369. John Henry   AAFS(53), ACM, AKD(6), Ark.(2), CS, JWW(2), Li(2), Lii, Liii(2), NCFii(9), NIM(2), WCH
Steel Drivin' Man, The
I Been a Miner
Swannanoa Tunnel
John Henry Blues

370. John Riley   AAFS(6), HC-TS(4), Lii, VRi(2)
Johnny Riley
Young Riley
George Riley

371. John Rogers, the Miller
(See: Young Johnny, the Miller)

372. Johnny Booker   AAFS, AKD(3), JCC, WMD
Going to Mill
Johnny Boker

373. Johnny Doyle   AAFS(5), ACM(2), AKD(2), APH, CJSii(2), JCC, NCFii, VRi(3), WRM
Samuel Moore and Johnny Doyle
Paddy Doyle
Johnny Dyles
Johnny Dyers

374. Johnny Randal, My Son
(See: Lord Randal)

375. Johnny Sands   AAFS, ACM(2), AKD(4), APH, HMB(5), NCFii(4), PGB(3), VRiv(2)
Johnny Vands
Johnny Sams

376. Johnny's Gone to Hilo   AAFS, ACM, AKD, JCC(2), Li, WMD
Tom's Gone to Hilo
O Johnny Come to Hilo
Johnny Walk Along to Hilo
Tommy's Gone to Hilo

377. Johnson's Ale
(See: When Johnson's Ale Was New)

378. Jolly Is the Miller   AAFS(3), ACM, AKD, APH, HMB
There Was a Jolly Miller Boy
Jolly Miller, The

379. Joshua Fit de Battle ob Jerico   GPJ-A, J+Ji, Liii
Jeric(h)o

380. Joys of Mary, The   AAFS(3), AKD, Ark., GPJ-A,D, HC-TS(2), HHF+MO, JHC, HHF+, NCFii
Blessing of Mary, The
Mary's Twelve Blessings
Seven Great Joys
Wessel Cup, The
Ten Blessings of Mary, The
Seven Joys of Mary, The
Mary's Blessings (Joys)
Twelve Miracles, The

381. Jump Jim Crow   AAFS, Ark., VRii

382. Just A-Goin' Over Jordan
(See: Roll, Jordan, Roll)

383. Kansas Boys   CS

384. Katharine Jaffray (C 221)   HC-SB, HC-TS(3), HHF+, NCFii

385. Keep Your Hand on That Plow, Hold On   AAFS, CJSii, GPJ-A, Lii, Liii
Hold On

386. Kemo Kimo   AAFS, AKD(9), NCFiii(2), NIW, PGB(3), VRii(4)
Kim-bo, Kime-bo
Cremo, Crimo, Kady
Kimo, Kimo

Kitchie Ki-me-O
Had an Old Hat
387. Kevin Barry   AAFS, CS
388. Keys of Heaven, The
(*See:* Paper of Pins)
389. Killiecrankie (instr.)   AAFS,
APH
390. Kim-bo, Kime-bo
(*See:* Kemo Kimo)
391. Kind Wife
(*See:* Our Goodman)
392. Kitchie Ki-me-o
(*See:* Kemo Kimo)
393. Kitty Wells   AAFS(4), ACM(2),
AKD(6), Ark.(3), JHC,
NCFiii(13), PGB(3), WAO
Katy Wells
Katie Wells
394. Knoxville Girl, The
(*See:* Wexford Girl, The)
395. La Claire Fontaine, À   MB+ES
396. Lady Alice (C 85)   AAFS(13),
ACM(3), APH(4), JHC(5),
NCFii(15), VRi(2)
George Collins
Giles Collins
Dame Alice Was Sitting on
Widow's Walk
Young Collins
George Coleman
John Collins
George Carey
397. Lady Isabel and the Elf Knight
(C 4)   AAFS(7), ACM(2),
AKD(12), APH(4), CJSi(9),
EBG(3), G+C(3), HC-*TS*(7),
HMB(9), JHC(9), NCFii(7),
PGB(3), VRi(5), WRM(3)
Seven King's Daughters, The
Salt Water Sea, The
Seven Sisters, The
King's Seven Daughters, The
Pretty Golden Queen, The
Six King's Daughters
Six Fair Maids, The
Polly and William
398. Lady Margaret and Sweet
William
(*See:* Fair Margaret and Sweet
William)
399. Lady Who Loved a Swine, The
Lii, NCFiii
Old Woman and Her Pig

400. Lake of Ponchartrain, The
AAFS(3),   Ark.(3),   HC-*SB*,
HHF+, VRiv
Lake of Passing Train
On the Lakes of Ponchartrain
Ponsaw Train, The
Creole Girl
401. Lamkin (C 93)   AKD, Ark.,
CJSi(5), G+C(3), PGB,
NCFii(2), VRi
Lord Arnold's Castle
Beaulampkins
False Lamkin
Bol' Lampkin
402. Lane County Bachelor, The
(*See:* Starving to Death on a
Government Claim)
403. Lass of Mohea, The
(*See:* Little Mohea, The)
404. Lass of Roch Royal, The (C 76)
AAFS(5),   ACM,   AKD(14),
APH(2), Ark., CS(3), CJSii(9),
NCFii(2), NCFiii(5), JHC(3),
PGB(10), VRi(8), WAO
Who Will Shoe Your Pretty Little
Foot?
True Lover's Farewell, The
Fair Annie of Lochyran
Oh, Who Will Shoe My Foot?
Who's A-Gonna Shoe . . . ?
405. Last Fierce Charge, The
AAFS(4), HMB(3)
Fight at Bunker Hill
Soldier Boys, The
406. Last Night I Dreamed of My
True Love
(*See:* Locks and Bolts)
407. Lazy Man, The
(*See:* Young Man Who
Wouldn't Hoe Corn)
408. Lead Me to the Rock   AAFS,
GPJ-D, JWW
409. Leather Breeches (instr.)
AAFS(17), AKD(2), NCFiii
Leather Britches
410. Lexington Murder, The
(*See:* Wexford Girl, The)
411. Life of Georgia (Georgie), The
(*See:* Geordie)
412. Lily of the West, The   AAFS,
Ark.(2), CJSii, HC-*SB*,
HMB(2), NCFii, VRii(3)

413. Lining Track   AAFS, Liii
Track Lining Song
Line 'Em
Can'cha Line 'Em
414. Lis'en to de Lam's   J+Ji, JWW
415. Listen to the Mocking Bird
AAFS(5), CJSii(2)
Mocking Bird, The
416. Little Babes in the Woods
(See: Babes in the Woods)
417. Little Birdie in the Tree
AAFS(6), Ark., NCFiii, VRii(2)
Sweet Little Bird
418. Little Black Moustache, The
AAFS, ACM, AKD(3), Ark.(2),
NCFii(6), VRiii(3)
That Little Black Moustache
Black Mustache, The
419. Little Black Train, The   Lii,
NCFiii, NIW
420. Little Brown Bulls   AAFS(9),
G+C, Lii
421. Little Brown Jug   AAFS(8),
AKD(5), Ark.(2), HMB(2),
Li, NCFiii(7), VRiii(4)
422. Little David, Play on Your Harp
AAFS(5), J+Ji, JWW,
NCFiii(2), NIW
423. Little Joe, the Wrangler
AAFS(2), Ark., VRii
424. Little Mathy Grove
(See: Little Musgrave and
Lady Barnard)
425. Little Mohea, The   AAFS(25),
ACM, AKD(16), APH(2),
Ark.(7), HHF+, HMB(7),
JHC(3), Li, LP, NCFii(12),
PGB(7), VRi, WAO, WRM(2)
Lass of Mohea
Pretty Mohea, The
My Little Mohee
Maumee
Little Maumee
Indian Lass, The
Sad Mohea, The
426. Little Musgrave and Lady Bar-
nard (C 81)   AAFS(8),
AKD(5), CJSi(17), G+C,
HC-SB, HC-TS(2), HMB(2),
JHC, LP, NCFii(5), VRi(3),
WRM(5)
Little Mathy Grove
Mathy Grove

Lord Daniel's Wife
Lord Musgrave
Lord Barney
Young Little Mathy Groves
Lord Danaver and Little Mus-
grave
Little Moth Grove
427. Little Old Log Cabin in the
Lane, The
(See: Little Old Sod Shanty
on the Claim)
428. Little Old Sod Shanty on the
Claim   AAFS(4), AKD, CS,
LP, VRii(2)
Little Old Log Cabin in the
Lane, The
429. Little Omie Wise   AAFS(16),
ACM(2), AKD(7), APH,
Ark.(2), CJSii(7), HMB(2),
LP, NCFii(8), VRii(8)
Little Ona
Poor Oma Wise
Poor Annie
Little Omie
Pretty Oma
Little Oni
Naomi Wise
Omie Wise
430. Little Rosewood Casket, The
AAFS(6), AKD(10), Ark.(2),
HMB, NCFii(24), VRiv(3),
WAO
Rosewood Casket, The
Little Rosebud Casket
Package of Old Letters, A
431. Little Saro
(See: Pretty Saro)
432. Little Sparrow, The
(See: Drowsy Sleeper, The)
433. Little Willie
(See: Twa Brothers, The)
434. Liza Jane   AAFS(16), AKD(2),
CJSii(3), CS, Li, NCFiii(3),
NIW(3), VRiii(3)
Eliza Jane
Goodbye, Suzan Jane
My Liza Jane
Po' Liza Jane
Git Along Liza Jane
435. Locks and Bolts   AAFS(5),
AKD(8), Ark., CJSii(5),
HMB, NCFii, PGB
Bolts and Locks

My Lonely Darling
Last Night I Dreamed of My
True Love
I Dreamed Last Night of My
True Love

436. Lolly-Too-Dum
(*See:* Rolly Trudum)

437. London Bridge Is Falling Down
AAFS(10), VRiii
London Bridge
London Bridge Is Burning
Down

438. Lone Prairie, The
(*See:* Bury Me Not on the
Lone Prairie)

439. Lonesome Cowboy AAFS(2),
Ark., CS, Li, VRii(3)
Wandering Cowboy, The
Poor Lonesome Cowboy
He Was Just a Lonely Cowboy
·Roving Cowboy, The

440. Lonesome Dove AAFS(4),
NCFiii, VRiv

441. Lonesome Grove, The AKD(4),
CJSii(4), GPJ-S

442. Lonesome Road AAFS(7), CS,
Lii(2), NCFiii(2), WCH
Long Lonesome Road
Goin' Down That Long Lone-
some Road
Look Down That Long Lone-
some Road
Look Up, Look Down That
Lonesome Road
Down the Lonesome Road
Lonesome Road Blues

443. Long Lonesome Road
(*See:* Lonesome Road)

444. Long Time Ago AAFS(4), JCC,
Li, WMD(6)

445. Look Down That Long Lonesome Road
(*See:* Lonesome Road)

446. Lord Arnold's Castle
(*See:* Lamkin)

447. Lord Bateman
(*See:* Young Beichan)

448. Lord Danaver and Little Mus-
grave
(*See:* Little Musgrave and
Lady Barnard)

449. Lord Daniel's Wife
(*See:* Little Musgrave and
Lady Barnard)

450. Lord Lovel (C 75) AAFS(9),
ACM(3), AKD(6), APH,
CJSi(5), CS, G+C(3),
HC-*TS*(2), HMB(8), JHC(5),
LP(2), NCFii(7), PGB(7),
VRi(2)
Lord Lover
Lord Lovinder
Lord Leven
Lord Lovel and Lady Nancy
Lord Lowell

451. Lord Randal (C 12) AAFS(11),
ACM, AKD(6), APH(2), Ark.,
CJSi(13), G+C, HC-*TS*(3),
HHF+MO, HMB(8), JHC(12),
LP(2), NCFii(4), PGB, VRi(4)
Jimmy Randall
My Rambling Young Son
Mama, Make My Bed Soon
Johnny Randall
Willie Ransome
Cup of Cold Poison, The
Johnny Randal, My Son

452. Lord Thomas and Fair Annet
(C 73) AAFS(21), ACM(3),
AKD(13), APH(5), Ark.(5),
CJSi(31), EBG, G+C(2),
HC-*SB*, HMB(12), HC-*TS*,
JHC(11), LP, NCFii(14),
PGB(8), VRi(10), WRM
Lord Thomas and Fair Ellener
Brown Girl, The
Three True Lovers
Fair Ellender
Fair Ellender and the Brown
Girl
Lloyd Thomas

453. Lost Jimmie Whalen, The
AAFS(2), HC-*TS*, CS, Li
James Whalen
James Whaland

454. Love of Barbara Allen, The
(*See:* Bonny Barbara Allen)

455. Lowlands Low, The
(*See:* Sweet Trinity, The)

456. Lumberjack's Alphabet, The
AAFS(3), G+C(7), HHF+,
HHF+MO, WMD
Lumbermen's Alphabet

457. Madam, I Have Come
     A-Courting
     (*See:* Quaker's Courtship, The)
458. Maid Freed from the Gallows,
     The (C 95)   AAFS(7),
     ACM(4), AKD(4), APH(6),
     Ark.(3), CJSi(11), CS(2),
     G+C, HC-*TS*(4), HHF+,
     HMB, LP, NCFii(13), PGB,
     JHC(7), VRi(6), WAO
     Gallows Tree
     Hanger, O Hanger, Go Slacken
     the Line
     Hold Your Hands, Old Man
     By a Lover Saved
     Hangman, Hangman
     Hangman's Tree
     Hangman's Song, The
     Sycamore Tree, The
459. Maid I Left Behind Me, The
     (*See:* Girl I Left Behind Me,
     The)
460. Maiden in the Garden, The
     (*See:* Pretty Fair Maid in the
     Garden)
461. Man Who Wouldn't Hoe Corn
     (*See:* Young Man Who
     Wouldn't Hoe Corn)
462. Marching Down to Old Quebec
     (*See:* My Pretty Little Pink)
463. Marriage of the Frog and the
     Mouse, The
     (*See:* Frog Went A-Courting)
464. Martha and Mary
     (*See:* Mary and Martha)
465. Mary   and   Martha   AAFS(2),
     AKD, J+Jii
     Martha and Mary
     Mary and Martha Jes' Gone
     'Long
466. Mary of the Wild Moor
     AAFS(3), ACM, AKD(7), Ark.,
     HMB(6), JHC(4), NCFii, PGB,
     WRM
     Wind That Blew Over the Wild
     Moor, The
     On a Cold Winter's Night
     Wild Moor, The
467. Mary's Blessings
     (*See:* Joys of Mary, The)

468. Mary's Twelve Blessings
     (*See:* Joys of Mary, The)
469. Massa Had a Yaller Gal
     (*See:* Yaller Gal)
470. Meet Me in the Moonlight
     (*See:* Prisoner's Song, The)
471. Mermaid, The (C 289)
     AAFS(9), ACM, AKD(3),
     APH, CJSi(4), EBG, HC-*TS*,
     HMB, JHC, Lii, NCFii(2),
     WRM
     Gallant Ship, The
     Sinking Ship, The
     Pretty Fair Maid with a Tail,
     The
472. Methodist Pie   VRii(2)
473. Michigan-I-O   AAFS, G+C(3)
     Canaday-I-O
474. Midnight Special   AAFS(7),
     Liii, VRii
475. Milkmaid, The   AAFS(2),
     AKD(4)
     Milking Maid, The
     Oh, Where Are You Going My
     Pretty Little Maid?
     Where   Are   You   Going,   My
     Pretty Maid?
476. Miller Boy, The
     (*See:* Young Johnny, the
     Miller)
477. Miller's Daughters, The
     (*See:* Twa Sisters, The)
478. Mister Boll Weevil
     (*See:* Boll Weevil)
479. Mocking Bird, The
     (*See:* Listen to the Mocking
     Bird)
480. Mole in the Ground
     (*See:* I Wish I Was a Mole in
     the Ground)
481. Molly Bawn   ACM(3), APH(2),
     Ark., G+C, JHC(3), NCFii(2),
     VRi(6)
     Polly Band
     Song Ballet of Mollie Bonder,
     The
     Johnnie Randle   (Cf. Lord Ran-
     dal C 12)
     Molly Vander
     Shooting of His Dear
482. Molly Malone   AKD
     Cockles and Mussels

483. Monkey's Wedding, The
   AKD(3), CS, G+C, NCFiii(3)
   Monkey Married the Baboon's
   Sister
484. Moonshiner, The   AAFS, AKD,
   CS, NCFiii
   Roving Moonshiner, A
   Moonshiner's Dream
   Kentucky Moonshiner
485. Mountain Dew   AAFS(3), Ark.,
   Li
   Good Old Mountain Dew
486. Mustang Gray   AAFS, Li
487. My Bonnie Black Bess
   (See: Bonny Black Bess)
488. My Father's Gray Mare
   (See: Young Johnny, the
   Miller)
489. My Home Is Over Jordan
   (See: Roll, Jordan, Roll)
490. My Horses Ain't Hungry
   (See: On Top of Old Smoky)
491. My Lord, What a Mornin'
   AAFS(3), J+Ji, JWW
   My Lord What a Mourning
492. My Mother and Father Were
   Irish
   (See: Pig in the Parlor)
493. My Pretty Little Pink   AAFS(4),
   AKD, CS, WAO
   Pretty Little Pink
   To Mexico
   Marching Down to Old Quebec
   Valuable Soldier, A
   Play Song, A
494. My Sweet Sailor Boy
   (See: Sailor's Sweetheart)
495. My Yellow Gal
   (See: Yaller Gal)
496. Naomi Wise
   (See: Little Omie Wise)
497. Needle's Eye   AAFS(5),
   APH(2), Ark., NCFiii, VRiii(2)
   Threading the Needle
498. New Buryin' Ground   AAFS(5),
   NCFiii
499. New River Train   AAFS(4),
   AKD(2), Ark.(2)
500. Nightingale, The
   (See: One Morning in May)
501. No Hiding Place   J+Ji, JWW
   Dere's No Hidin' Place Down
   Dere

502. No, Sir, No   AAFS(4), ACM,
   Ark.(2), NCFiii(4), VRiii
   O, No, John
   No Sir! No Sir!
   Spanish Merchant
503. Noble Sku-ball, The
   (See: Stewball)
504. Nobody Knows the Trouble I've
   Seen   AAFS, J+Ji, NCFiii
   Nobody Knows
505. Nottingham Fair   CJSii(2),
   VRiii
   Nottamun Town
506. Now, Now, Now
   (See: Risselty, Rosselty)
507. O Mary, O Mary
   (See: Rye Whisky)
508. O, No, John!
   (See: No, Sir, No)
509. Ocean Burial, The   AAFS,
   JHC, WMD
   Oh Bury Me Not in the Deep,
   Deep Sea
510. Oh, Bury Me Not in the Deep,
   Deep Sea
   (See: Ocean Burial, The)
511. Oh, Bury Me Not on the Lone
   Prairie
   (See: Bury Me Not on the
   Lone Prairie)
512. Oh Mary, Don't You Weep
   AAFS(2), JWW, NIW
513. Oh Susannah   AAFS(5),
   NCFiii(9), NIW
   Suzanna, Don't You Cry
   Suzanna Gal
   Suzanna
514. Oh, Who Will Shoe My Foot?
   (See: Lass of Roch Royal,
   The)
515. Ol' Ark's A-Moverin' an' I'm
   Goin' Home, De   J+Jii, JWW
516. Old Bangum
   (See: Sir Lionel)
517. Old Blue   AAFS(3), APH, Ark.,
   Lii, Liii, NCFiii, VRii(2)
518. Old Chisholm Trail, The
   AAFS(8), ACM, Ark.(2), Li,
   Liii(2), LP, NCFiii, VRii
   Chisholm Trail
   Chizzum Trail, The

519. Old Christmas Ballad
(*See:* Twelve Days of Christmas, The)

520. Old Dan Tucker AAFS(9),
AKD(9), Ark.(4), Li, Liii,
NCFiii(6), PGB(2), VRii(5)
Dan Tucker

521. Old Father Grumble
(*See:* Father Grumble)

522. Old Gray Goose Is Dead, The
AAFS, CJSii, HC-*TS*, Li, Liii,
WAO

523. Old Gray Mare AAFS(4),
AKD(3), CJSii(3), CS, NCFiii
Old Gray Horse, The

524. Old Groun(d) Hog
(*See:* Ground Hog)

525. Old Hen Cackled, The (instr.)
AAFS(22)
Cackling Hen
Old Hen Cackled and the
Rooster Laid an Egg
Old Hen, She Cackled, The

526. Old Joe Clark (instr.)
AAFS(37), AKD(12), Ark.,
CJSii, Li, Liii, NCFiii,
VRiii(12)

527. Old Man in the North Countree,
The
(*See:* Twa Sisters, The)

528. Old Man Who Lived in the
Woods, The
(*See:* Father Grumble)

529. Old Man's Courtship, The
(*See:* Old Shoes and Leggins)

530. Old Ninety-Seven
(*See:* Wreck of the Old 97,
The)

531. Old Paint
(*See:* Goodbye, Old Paint)

532. Old Quaker, The
(*See:* Quaker's Courtship, The)

533. Ol' Rattler
(*See:* Rattlesnake)

534. Old Rosin the Bow
(*See:* Rosin the Bow)

535. Old Sally Goodin
(*See:* Sally Goodin)

536. Old Ship of Zion AAFS(9),
GPJ-U,S,W, NIW

537. Old Shoes and Leggins
AAFS(3), Lii, NCFiii(5),
PGB(2), WAO
Old Man's Courtship, The
Old Shoe Boots and Leggins
Boots and Leggins
Old Boots

538. Old Smok(e)y
(*See:* On Top of Old Smoky)

539. Old Time Religion
(*See:* That Old Time Religion)

540. Old Tom Bolen
(*See:* Tom Bolyn)

541. Old Woman All Skin and Bones
AAFS(4), AKD(11), HMB(3),
JHC(2), NCFiii(9), PGB,
VRi(2)
There Was an Old Woman All
Skin and Bones
Old Skin and Bones
Skin and Bones Woman, The
Skin and Bones

542. Old Woman and Her Pig
(*See:* Lady Who Loved a
Swine, The)

543. Old Woman and the Devil, The
(*See:* Farmer's Curst Wife,
The)

544. Old Zip Coon
(*See:* Zip Coon)

545. Omie Wise
(*See:* Little Omie Wise)

546. On Springfield Mountain
(*See:* Springfield Mountain)

547. On the Banks of the Ohio
AAFS(2), AKD(2), NCFii(8),
NCFiii, VRii(3)
I Asked My Love to Take a Walk
Down the Banks of the Ohio
I'll Never Be Yours
Banks of the Bedea

548. On the Banks of the Old Pedee
(*See:* Banks of the River Dee,
The)

549. On the Banks of (the) Sweet
Dundee
(*See:* Banks of the Sweet Dun-
dee, The)

550. On the Lakes of Ponchartrain
(*See:* Lake of Ponchartrain,
The)

551. On Top of Old Smoky
AAFS(8), ACM, HMB, Liii,
NCFiii(7), WAO
Courting Too Slow
Old Smok(e)y
My Horses Ain't Hungry

552. Once I Courted a Charming
Beauty Bride
(See: Charming Beauty Bride,
The)

553. One More River to Cross
AAFS, GPJ-D,S NCFiii,
VRii(2)
One More River

554. One Morning in May   AAFS(9),
ACM(2), AKD(3), HMB(6),
PGB
False Young Man, The
Come In, Come In, My Own
True Love
As I Went Walking One Morn-
ing in May
Nightingale, The

555. One Night As I Lay on the
Prairie
(See: Cowboy's Dream)

556. Orphan Girl, The   AAFS(6),
HMB(2), PGB(5)

557. Other Side of Jordan, The
(See: Roll, Jordan, Roll)

558. Our Goodman (C 274)
AAFS(7), ACM, AKD(7),
Ark.(2), APH, CJSi(5),
HC-TS, HMB(2), JHC(3),
NCFii(4), PGB, WRM
Arrow Goodman
Kind Wife
Three Nights' Experience

559. Over the River to Feed My
Sheep
(See: Weevily Wheat)

560. Ox-Driving Song   AAFS(2), Lii

561. Oxford Girl, The
(See: Wexford Girl, The)

562. Paper of Pins   AAFS(17), ACM,
AKD(20), APH, Ark.(3),
G+C(2), HMB(3), Li, LP,
NCFiii(13), VRiii(3)
I'll Give You a Paper of Pins
Way Love Begins, The
Keys of Heaven, The
Nothing But Gold

563. Pearl Bryan(t)
(See: Jealous Lover, The)

564. Pick a Bale o' Cotton   AAFS(6),
Li, Liii

565. Pig in the Parlor   AAFS(2),
NCFiii(3), VRiii
We Have a New Pig in the
Parlor
My Father and Mother Were
Irish

566. Pizen Serpent Song, The
(See: Springfield Mountain)

567. Plains of Mexico
(See: Santy Anna)

568. Plenty Good Room   AAFS,
JWW

569. Po' Boy   AAFS(4), CS, Li,
WAO
Po' Boy, Long Ways from Home

570. Po' Laz'us   AAFS(17), JWW,
Lii, Liii
Po' Ol' Laz'rus

571. Po' Liza Jane
(See: Liza Jane)

572. Polly Oliver
(See: Pretty Polly)

573. Polly Wolly Doodle All Day
AAFS, NCFiii
Sing Polly Wolly Doodle

574. Poor Babes in the Woods
(See: Babes in the Woods)

575. Poor Jack Is Gone A-Sailing
(See: Jack Monroe)

576. Poor Lonesome Cowboy
(See: Lonesome Cowboy)

577. Poor Oma Wise
(See: Little Omie Wise)

578. Poor Pilgrim, The   AKD,
GPJ-D, VRiv(2)
Tossed and Driven

579. Poor Wayfaring Stranger
(See: Wayfaring Stranger)

580. Pop Goes the Weasel   AAFS(3),
AKD(4), NCFiii, VRiii(2)

581. Possum Up a 'Simmon Stump
AAFS(2), NCFiii(7), VRii
Corn Shucking Song
Possum Up a Gum Stump
Old Bob Ridley
Possum Sits on a 'Simmon Tree,
De

582. Preacher Went A-Huntin'
     AAFS, AKD, Ark., NCFiii(2)
     Preacher and the Bear, The
583. Prentice Boy, The
     (See: Sheffield Apprentice,
     The)
584. Pretty Fair Maid with a Tail,
     The
     (See: Mermaid, The)
585. Pretty Fair Miss in the Garden
     AAFS(8), ACM(2), AKD(30),
     APH, Ark.(5), CS, JHC(6),
     NCFii, VRi(5), WAO
     Maiden in the Garden, The
     Pretty Fair Damsel
     Pretty Little Girl in Her Garden
     Fair Young Maid, A
     Broken Token, The
     Fair Damsel, The
586. Pretty Little Pink
     (See: My Pretty Little Pink)
587. Pretty Mohee, The
     (See: Little Mohea, The)
588. Pretty Polly   AAFS(32),
     AKD(4), Ark., CJSi(3), CS,
     EBG(2), G+C(3), HC-SB,
     HC-TS(3), HMB(2), JHC(3),
     Lii, Liii, NCFii(5), NCFiii,
     PGB(2), VRi(2), WAO, WRM
     Polly Oliver
     Ship's Carpenter, The
     Come, Pretty Polly
     Young William
     Gosport Tragedy, The
     Polly and Willie
     Young Beeham
589. Pretty Sally
     (See: Brown Girl, The)
590. Pretty Saro (instr.) AAFS(9),
     AKD(10), APH, Ark., CJSii(4),
     NCFiii(2), PGB, VRiv(2)
     Little Saro
     My True Love
     Pretty Sairey
     Miss Saro
     Way Down in Lone Valley
591. Prince William and Lady Mar-
     garet
     (See: Fair Margaret and Sweet
     William)
592. Prisoner's Song, The   AAFS,
     AKD(3), CS, HC-SB, WRM
     Prisoner Walls

Sweet Lulur
Meet Me in the Moonlight
I Have a Ship on the Ocean
593. Quaker's Courtship, The
     AAFS(2), ACM, AKD(7), CS,
     HC-SB, HC-TS, HMB,
     G+C(3), LP, NCFiii, VRiii(4),
     WRM
     Old Quaker, The
     Quaker's Wooing
     Honest Quaker
     Madam, I Have Come A-Court-
     ing
     Courting Song, The
     Uh Huh, Boo Hoo
594. Raging Canawl
     (See: Erie Canal, The)
595. Railroad Bill   AAFS(5), CS,
     JWW, Li
596. Railroad Flagman, The
     (See: Broken Heart, The)
597. Raise a Ruckus (Tonight) (instr.)
     AAFS(5), Li, Liii, NCFiii
598. Ram of Derby, The
     (See: Derby Ram, The)
599. Rambling Boy, The   AAFS(8),
     AKD(4), Ark., HMB, NCFii,
     VRii(2)
     Wretched Rambling Boy, The
     Waynes County Girl, The
600. Range of the Buffalo, The
     (See: Buffalo Skinners, The)
601. Ranzo
     (See: Reuben Ranzo)
602. Rattlesnake   AAFS(7), Li
     Ol' Rattler
     Rattlesnake Song
603. Red Light Saloon, The   WMD
604. Red River Valley AAFS(3),
     CS, Liii, NCFiii(6), VRiv(4)
     Bright Sherman Valley
     Come Sit By My Side, Little
     Darlin'
     Little Lonely Valley
     Red River Blues
605. Reuben Ranzo AAFS, JCC,
     WMD(2), WRM
     Ranzo
606. Rich Irish Lady, The   AAFS,
     HMB(5)
     Irish Lady, The
     Brave Irish Lady, A
     Sally Sailsworth

607. Rich Lady from London
  (*See:* Brown Girl, The)
608. Riddle Song, The
  (*See:* Captain Wedderburn's Courtship)
609. Riddles Wisely Expounded (C 1) AKD(3)
  Devil's Nine Questions, The
  Devil and the Nine Questions, The
610. Ride On, King Jesus   AAFS(3), JWW
  Ride On, Jesus
611. Rio Grande   AAFS(3), AKD, JCC, Li, WMD(2), WRM(3)
  We're Bound for the Rio Grande
612. Risselty, Rosselty   AAFS(2), Ark., VRiii(2), WAO
  Now, Now, Now
  Ti Risslety Rosslety
613. Rockabye Baby, the Cradle Is Green
  (*See:* Bye-O-Baby Bunting)
614. Roger(s) the Miller
  (*See:* Young Johnny, the Miller)
615. Roll, Jordan, Roll   AAFS(3), Ark., GPJ-S,D,U,W J+Ji, JWW, Lii, NCFiii(3), NIW, VRii(2)
  Other Side of Jordan, The
  Just A-Goin' Over Jordan
  My Home Is Over Jordan
  Over Jordan
616. Roll on the Ground   AAFS(2), AKD(3)
  Saroah
  Roll on the Ground, Boys
617. Roll the Old Chariot Along   CS, G+C, NCFiii
  We'll Roll the Old Chariot Along
618. Rolling Home   AAFS(2), WMD(2)
619. Rolly Trudum   AAFS(6), APH, Ark.(3), Lii, Liii, VRiii(3), WAO
  Raleigh Truedom
  As I Walked Out
  Lolly-Too-Dum
  Rally Trudam
  I Must and Will Get Married
620. Romish Lady, The   AAFS(10), ACM, AKD(4), APH, Ark.,

GPJ-S, HMB(5), Lii, NCFii, PGB(2), VRiv, WAO
  Death of a Romish Lady, The
  Roman Lady, The
621. Root, Hog, or Die   AAFS(4), Ark.(2), HMB, NCFiii, VRiii(5)
622. Rose of Ardeen
  (*See:* Brown Girl, The)
623. Rosewood Casket, The
  (*See:* Little Rosewood Casket, The)
624. Rosie (instr.)   AAFS(12), Li
625. Rosin the Bow (instr.)   AAFS(5) AKD(2), APH, Ark., HMB, LP, NCFiii, VRiv
  Old Rosin the Beau (Bow)
  Rossen le Beau
626. Roving Cowboy, The
  (*See:* Lonesome Cowboy)
627. Roving Gambler, The   AAFS(6), AKD(6), Ark., CS(3), CJSii(2), G+C, Li, LP, VRiv(3), WAO
  Gambling Man, The
  Gambler, The
  Yonder Comes My Pretty Little Girl
  Roaming Gambler, The
  Guerrilla Man, The
628. Roving Moonshiner, The
  (*See:* Moonshiner, The)
629. Run Along Home, Cindy
  (*See:* Cindy)
630. Rye Whisky   AAFS(12), Ark.(3), Li, Liii, VRiii(6), WAO
  Clinch Mountain
  O Mary, O Mary
  Irish Rye Whisky
631. Sacramento   CS, JCC, Liii, WMD(3)
  Banks of Sacramento
632. Sailor Boy, The   AAFS(3), Ark., G+C, HMB(7), JHC(2), NCFii(12), VRi(5), WAO, WMD
  True Sailor Boy
  Sailor's Trade
  Oh Father, Go Build Me a Boat
  Susie's Search for Her Lover
  Sailor Boy and His Bride, The
  Captain, Captain, Tell Me True

633. Sailor Cut Down in His Prime,
The
(*See:* St. James Infirmary
[Hospital])
634. Sailor's Sweetheart AAFS,
VRi(6), VRiv(2)
Banks of the Nile, The
My Sweet Sailor Boy
635. Sailor's Trade, The
(*See:* Sailor Boy, The)
636. St. James Infirmary (Hospital)
AAFS(9), CJSii(2)
Sailor Cut Down in His Prime,
The
637. Sally Brown AAFS(4), JCC,
WMD(2), WRM(2)
638. Sally Goodin (instr.)   AAFS(23),
AKD, Ark.(2), NCFiii(5),
VRiii(2)
Old Sally Goodin
Hunks of Pudding and Pieces of
Pie
The Jaybird and the Sparrow
639. Salt (Salt) Sea, The
(*See:* James Harris)
640. Salt-Water Sea, The
(*See:* Lady Isabel and the Elf
Knight)
641. Sam Bass AAFS(6), AKD(2),
Ark.(3), CS, HMB(3), Li, Liii,
LP, VRii(2), WAO
Young Sam Bass
642. Santy Anna AAFS(10), AKD,
CS, HMB, JCC, Lii(2), Liii,
VRii(2), WMD, WRM
Plains of Mexico
Bay of Mexico, The
On My Way to Mexico
Trail to Mexico, The
Had a Little Fight in Mexico
Hills of Mexico
643. See the Train Go Round the
Bend
(*See:* Goodbye, My Lover,
Goodbye)
644. Set Down, Servant AAFS(6),
JWW, Li, Liii
I Can't Set Down
Can't Set Down
645. Seven Brothers, or Lord William
(*See:* Earl Brand)
646. Seven Joys of Mary, The
(*See:* Joys of Mary, The)

647. Seven King's Daughters, The
(*See:* Lady Isabel and the Elf
Knight)
648. Seven Year Song
(*See:* Charming Beauty Bride,
The)
649. Shady Grove AAFS(4),
NCFiii(2)
650. Shantyman's Life AAFS(2),
CS, G+C(2), HC-*TS*,
WMD(2)
651. Shearfield Apprentice Boy, The
(*See:* Sheffield Apprentice,
The)
652. Sheep of Darby, The
(*See:* Derby Ram, The)
653. Sheffield Apprentice, The
AAFS(4), AKD(2), CJSii(5),
EBG(2), G+C, HC-*SB*,
HC-*TS*(3), HMB(3), JHC(3),
LP(2), NCFii(3), PGB(3), VRi,
WRM
Prentice Boy, The
Bomberry Brier, The
Bramble Briar, The
Apprentice Boy, The
Bamboo Briars, The
Shearfield Apprentice Boy, The
654. She'll Be Comin' Round the
Mountain AAFS(2), CS(2),
NCFiii, PGB
Comin' Round the Mountain
655. Shenandoah AAFS, CS, JCC,
Li(2), Liii, WMD
Wide Missouri, The
Wild Miz-zou-rye, The
Wide Mizzoura, The
656. Ship Carpenter, The AAFS(5),
ACM, HC-*TS*(4), HHF+,
CJSi(21)
Cruel Ship's Carpenter, The
657. Ship That Never Returned, The
AAFS(3),   AKD(5),   Ark.(2),
CS, NCFii(11), VRiv(2)
658. Shoo-Fly AAFS(4), AKD(4),
VRii
Shoo-Fly, Don't Bother Me
659. Shoot the Buffalo AAFS(7),
APH, Ark.(2), CJSii, Li, Liii,
NCFiii, VRiii
Chase the Buffalo
660. Shooting of His Dear
(*See:* Molly Bawn)

661. Short(e)nin' Bread AAFS(11),
     AKD, Ark., Li, NCFiii(9),
     NIW, VRii(2)
662. Shorty George AAFS(4), Li,
     Liii
663. Shule Aroon   AAFS, APH, Ark.,
     HMB, NCFii, VRi(3)
     Shule Agrah
     Shule, Shule
664. Silk Merchant's Daughter, The
     AAFS(2), ACM, AKD, APH,
     EBG, CJSi(4), G+C, JHC,
     NCFii(2), PGB, VRi, WMD(2)
665. Silver Dagger, The AAFS(6),
     ACM, AKD(18), Ark.(5),
     CJSii(2), G+C, HMB(8),
     JHC(3), LP(2), NCFii(3),
     PGB(4), VRii(6)
     Young William
     Wounded Affections
     Come Men and Maids
     Broken Hearts
     Warning, The
     Lover's Farewell, The
     Young Men and Maids
666. Sing Polly Wolly Doodle
     (See: Polly Wolly Doodle)
667. Single Girl, The
     (See: I Wish I Was a Single
     Girl)
668. Sinking of the Titanic, The
     AAFS(11), Ark.(8), CS, NIW,
     VRiv(2)
     Great Titanic, The
     Wreck of the Titanic, The
     Titanic Sinking
     Destruction of the Titanic
669. Sioux Indians, The AAFS(3),
     VRii
     Indian Fighters, The
670. Sir Lionel (C 18) AAFS(2),
     AKD(5), CJSi(4), HHF+MO,
     HMB(4), Lii, VRi
     Bangum and the Boar
     Old Bangum
     Wild Hog, or Ole Bangum
     Old Bangham
     Wild Hog
671. Skewball
     (See: Stewball)
672. Skin and Bones
     (See: Old Woman All Skin
     and Bones)

673. Skip to My Lou AAFS(2),
     ACM, AKD(2), APH, Ark.(2),
     Li, Liii, VRiii(7)
     Skip-Ta-Ma-Lou, My Darling
674. Soldier, Soldier, Won't You
     Marry Me? AAFS(13),
     AKD(5), CJSii(3), HC-TS(2),
     JHC, NCFiii(6), PGB, VRi(2),
     WAO
     Soldier and the Lady
     Soldier and the Maid
675. Soldier's Joy (instr.) AAFS(22),
     AKD
676. Soldier's Song, The
     (See: Sweetheart in the Army,
     A)
677. Sometimes I Feel Like a Moth-
     erless Child AAFS(2), J+Jii,
     JWW, Liii
678. Sometimes It Causes Me to
     Tremble
     (See: Were You There When
     They Crucified My Lord?)
679. Song Ballet of Mollie Bonder
     (See: Molly Bawn)
680. Sourwood Mountain (instr.)
     AAFS(29), ACM, AKD(5),
     CJSii(3), CS, Li, Liii,
     NCFiii(11), VRiii(5)
     I Got a Girl at the Head of the
     Holler
     Chickens A-Crowin'
681. Springfield Mountain AAFS(7),
     ACM(2), AKD(17), APH,
     Ark.(3), CJSii(2), G+C(2),
     HHF+, HMB(3), JHC, Liii,
     NCFii(7), PGB, LP(4),
     VRiii(4), WAO
     On Springfield Mountain
     O Johnny Dear, Why Did You
     Go?
     On Fieldmount Spring
     Greenfield Mountain
     Pizen Serpent Song, The
     Rattlesnake Song, The
     Shrattledum Snake, The
     Down to Mow That Hay
682. Stagolee AAFS(16), Li(2)
     Stackerlee
683. Standin' in the Need of Prayer
     (See: It's Me, Oh Lord)

684. Starving to Death on a Government Claim CS, Liii, LP, VRii
Lane County Bachelor, The
685. State of Arkansas, The AAFS(6), AKD(2), Ark.(6), Liii, VRiii(6)
Arkansas in '82
Six Weeks in Arkansas
Sanford Barnes
686. Steal Away AAFS(2), Ark., J+Ji, JWW
Steal Away to Jesus
687. Steel Drivin' Man, The
(*See:* John Henry)
688. Stewball AAFS(14), AKD(6), Ark.(3), HHF+, Li, NCFii(2)
Skewball
Noble Sku-ball, The
Cue Ball
Squeeball
Skewbald
689. Stormalong AAFS(2), JCC, WMD
Old Stormy
690. Strawberry Roan ACM, Li(2), VRii
691. Streets of Laredo, The
(*See:* Cowboy's Lament, The)
692. Study War No More AAFS, JWW
Goin' t' Lay Down My Sword and Shield
693. Susie's Search for Her Lover
(*See:* Sailor Boy, The)
694. Suzanna, Don't You Cry
(*See:* Oh Susannah)
695. Swapping Song, The AAFS, NCFii(6)
I Swapped My Horse and Got a Mare
When I Was a Little Boy
Sister, Sister, Have You Heard?
696. Sweet Betsy from Pike AAFS(3), CS, HMB, Li, Liii, VRii(2)
Betsy from Pike
697. Sweet Mary and Sweet Joseph
(*See:* Cherry Tree Carol, The)
698. Sweet Trinity, The (The Golden Vanity) (C 286) AAFS(23), ACM(3), AKD(4), APH, Ark., CJSi(12), EBG(2), HC-*SB*,

HC-*TS*(6), HHF+MO, HMB(3), JCC(2), JHC(4), LP, Liii, NCFii(5), PGB(2), VRi(5), WRM
Lowlands Low, The
Golden Vanity, The
Green Willow Tree, The
Young Edwin (Edmund) in the Lowlands Low
Merry Golden Tree, The
Turkish Revelee, The
Golden Willow Tree, The
699. Sweet William (I)
(*See:* Bonny Barbara Allen)
700. Sweet William (II)
(*See:* Fair Margaret and Sweet William)
701. Sweet William and Fair Ellen (der)
(*See:* Earl Brand)
702. Sweet William and Lady Margaret
(*See:* Fair Margaret and Sweet William)
703. Sweet William's Ghost (C 77) AKD(2), EBG, NCFii
Lady Margaret
Sweet Willy
704. Sweetheart in the Army, A HMB(5), PGB
Soldier's Song , The
Sailor's Return, The
705. Swing Low, Sweet Chariot AAFS(2), Ark., J+Ji, JWW, Li
706. Take This Hammer AAFS(5), AKD, Lii, Liii, NIW
Ten Pound Hammer
Nine-Pound Hammer Killed John Henry
This Old Hammer
Dis Old Hammer
707. Ten Blessings of Mary
(*See:* Joys of Mary, The)
708. Ten Pound Hammer
(*See:* Take This Hammer)
709. Ten Thousand Miles AAFS(6), AKD, Ark., CS(3), JCC, Li, VRiv(2)
He's Gone Away
710. Tennessee Wagoner, The
(*See:* Wagoner, The)

711. Texan Boys   HMB, Liii
     When You Go A-Courtin'
     Texian Boys, The
712. Texas Rangers, The   AAFS(17),
     ACM(2),   AKD(3),   Ark.(4),
     HHF+, HMB(8), Lii, LP,
     NCFii(4), PGB, VRii(5)
     Texican Ranger
     Texas Cowboy, The
713. That Black Gal
     (See: Black Gal)
714. That Little Black Moustache
     (See: Little Black Moustache,
     The)
715. That Lonesome Valley
     AAFS(2), GPJ-S, JWW, Liii
     I Must Walk That Lonesome
     Valley
     Down in That Lonesome Valley
716. That Old Time Religion
     AAFS(8), GPJ-S, J+Ji, JWW,
     NIW, VRiv
     Old Time Religion
     'Tis the Old Time Religion
     Give Me That Old Time Re-
     ligion
     This Old-Time Religion
717. Them Golden Slippers   AAFS,
     Ark.
     Golden Slippers
718. There Is a Tavern in the Town
     (See: Butcher Boy, The)
719. There Was a Tree
     (See: Tree in the Wood)
720. There Was a Youth
     (See: Bailiff's Daughter of Is-
     lington)
721. There Was an Old Woman All
     Skin and Bones
     (See: Old Woman All Skin
     and Bones)
722. This Old Hammer
     (See: Take This Hammer)
723. Threading the Needle
     (See: Needle's Eye)
724. Three Black Crows, The
     (See: Three Ravens, The)
725. Three Jolly Welshmen
     (See: Fox Chase, The)
726. Three Little Babes, The
     (See: Wife of Usher's Well,
     The)

727. Three Ravens, The (C 26)
     AAFS(2), ACM, AKD(2),
     APH, Ark., CJSi(3), HC-TS,
     HMB(2), JHC(2), NCFii,
     PGB, VRi(2), WAO
     Three Black Crows
     Twa Corbies, The
     Three Crows
728. Three Sons, or Noble King, The
     (See: In Good Old Colony
     Times)
729. Tobacco Is a Noxious Weed
     AAFS(2), Ark.
     Tobacco Song
730. Tom Bolyn   AAFS,   CJSii(2),
     HMB, Lii, VRiii
     Old Tom Bolen
     Tom Bo-lin
731. Tom Dooley   AAFS(4),   AKD,
     Liii, NCFii(3)
732. Tom(my)'s Gone to Hilo
     (See: Johnny's Gone to Hilo)
733. Tossed and Driven
     (See: Poor Pilgrim, The)
734. Track Lining Song
     (See: Lining Track)
735. Trail to Mexico
     (See: Santy Anna)
736. Tree in the Wood   AAFS,
     ACM, AKD(6), CJSii(3),
     G+C, HC-TS(2)
     There Was a Tree
     Curious Tree, A
     Oakum in the Woods
737. Troubled in Mind   AAFS(6),
     CS, J+Ji, NCFiii(2)
     I'm Troubled in Mind
     I'm Sad and I'm Lonely
738. True Lover's Farewell, The
     (See: Lass of Roch Royal,
     The)
739. True Sailor Boy
     (See: Sailor Boy, The)
740. Turkey in the Straw (instr.)
     AAFS(12), Ark., CS(2),
     NCFiii, VRii(3)
741. Turkish Lady, The
     (See: Young Beichan)
742. Turkish Revelee, The
     (See: Sweet Trinity, The)
743. Turnip Greens (instr.)
     AAFS(5), APH, VRii
     Greasy Greens

744. Twa Brothers, The (C 49)
    AAFS(4), ACM, AKD(7),
    APH(2), Ark.(2), CJSi(13),
    HC-*TS*, HMB, JHC(2),
    NCFii, PGB(2), VRi(4)
    Two Little Boys, The
    Cruel Brother, The
    Two School Boys, The
    Little Willie
    Two Brothers, The
745. Twa Corbies, The
    (*See:* Three Ravens, The)
746. Twa Sisters, The (C 10)
    AAFS(12), ACM, AKD(11),
    APH, Ark., CJSi(13), EBG,
    G+C(2), HHF+, HHF+MO,
    HMB(6), JHC(2), NCFii(5),
    PGB(5), VRi(8)
    Old Man in the North Countree,
    The
    Miller's Daughters, The
    Two Young Daughters, The
    Two Sisters, The
    Down by the Waters Rolling
    Two Little Sisters
747. Twelve Days of Christmas, The
    AAFS, ACM, HHF+MO,
    HMB, NCFii, PGB(2)
    Old Christmas Ballad
748. Twelve Miracles, The
    (*See:* Joys of Mary, The)
749. Two Cruel Brothers, The
    (*See:* Cruel Brother, The)
750. Two (or Ten) Little Devils
    (*See:* Farmer's Curst Wife,
    The)
751. Two School Boys, The
    (*See:* Twa Brothers, The)
752. Uncle Ned NCFiii(3), NIW,
    VRii
753. Unconstant Lover, The AAFS,
    HMB(3), NCFiii(6), PGB
    Forsaken Lover
    Young Girls, Take Warning
    Cuckoo Is a Pretty Bird
    Inconstant Lover, The
    Little Sparrow
    On Constant Loveyer, The
754. Under the Weeping Willow
    (*See:* Jealous Lover, The)
755. Unquiet Grave, The (C 78)
    AKD, EBG(2), NCFii(2)
    Broken-Hearted Lover, The

Auld Song from Cow Head, The
    Restless Grave, The
756. Unworthy Barbara Allen
    (*See:* Bonny Barbara Allen)
757. Van Dieman's Land HC-*SB*,
    WRM
758. Villikins and His Dinah
    AAFS(2), ACM, AKD(16),
    APH, G+C(3), HC-*SB*, HMB,
    JHC, NCFii(5), VRi(2)
    Wilkens and Dinah
    Billikins and His Dinah
    Young Diana
    London Merchant, A
    Dinah and Villikins
    Merchant's Daughter, The
759. Virginia Reel AAFS
760. Wabash Cannonball, The (instr.)
    AAFS(4), Ark., VRiv
761. Wagoner, The (instr.)
    AAFS(10), Ark., HMB
    Tennessee Wagoner, The
762. Wagoner Boy, The AAFS(8),
    AKD(19), CJSii(6), NCFiii(8)
    Gypsy Song, The
    Wagoner's Lad, The
    Sweet Mary
    Kitty Wagner
    Farewell, Sweet Mary
763. Waillie, Waillie! CS
    Waly, Waly
764. Wait for the Wagon APH,
    VRiii
765. Wake Nicodemus NIW
766. Wake Up, Wake Up, You
    Drowsy Sleeper
    (*See:* Drowsy Sleeper, The)
767. Walking Cane
    (*See:* Hand Me Down My
    Walking Cane)
768. Wanderin' CS
769. Wandering Cowboy, The
    (*See:* Lonesome Cowboy)
770. Warren and Fuller
    (*See:* Fuller and Warren)
771. Way Love Begins, The
    (*See:* Paper of Pins)
772. Way Over in the Promised Land
    (*See:* Hebrew Children)
773. Wayfaring Stranger AAFS(7),
    AKD, GPJ-S, Liii
    I'm a Poor Wayfaring Stranger
    Poor Wayfaring Stranger

774. Ways of Arkansas, The
(*See:* Arkansas Boys, The)
775. We Have a New Pig in the
Parlor
(*See:* Pig in the Parlor)
776. We Hunted and We Hollered
(*See:* Fox Chase, The)
777. Wealthy Young Farmer, A
(*See:* Golden Glove, The)
778. Weaver, The
(*See:* Foggy Dew, The)
779. Weeping Willow, The
AAFS(6), AKD(2), CS,
NCFiii(11), VRiv
Down by Yon Weeping Willow
Under the Weeping Willow Tree
Bury Me Beneath the Willow
O Bury Me Beneath . . .
780. Weevily Wheat (instr.)
AAFS(19), AKD(5), Ark.(3),
CS, Li, NCFiii(2), VRiii(7)
Over the River to Feed My
Sheep
Presbyterian Waltzing
781. We'll All Go to Boston
(*See:* Goin' to Boston)
782. We'll Roll the Old Chariot Along
(*See:* Roll the Old Chariot
Along)
783. We're Bound for the Rio Grande
(*See:* Rio Grande)
784. Were You There When They
Crucified My Lord?
AAFS(3), Ark., J+Jii, JWW
Didn't They Crucify My Lord?
Sometimes It Causes Me to
Tremble
785. Western Home, The (or My)
(*See:* Home on the Range)
786. Wexford Girl, The   AAFS(18),
ACM(2), AKD(9), APH,
Ark.(5), CJSi(5), EBG(2),
G+C(2), HMB(2), JHC(2),
NCFii(13), PGB, VRii(12),
WAO, WMD(2), WRM
Knoxville Girl, The
Oxford Girl, The
Miller's Apprentice
Lexington Murder, The
Rexford Girl, The
Wedding Day, The
Cruel Miller, The
Murdering Miller, The

787. Whale Song, The
(*See:* Greenland Whale Fish-
ery, The)
788. What Blood on the Point of Your
Knife?
(*See:* Edward)
789. What Shall We Do with a
Drunken Sailor?   AAFS,
HC-*TS*, WMD(2)
Drunken Sailor, The
Early in the Morning
790. What Was Your Name in the
States?   CS
791. What'll We Do with the
Baby-O?   AAFS(6), CJSii
What You Goin' to Do with the
Baby?
792. When I Was Single
(*See:* I Wish I Was Single
Again)
793. When I Wore My Apron Low
(*See:* Careless Love)
794. When Johnson's Ale Was New
AAFS(2), WMD
Johnson's Ale
When Jones's Ale Was New
795. When the Saints Come Marchin'
Home   AAFS(3), Ark.(3)
796. When the Work's All Done Next
Fall   AAFS(3), AKD(5),
Ark.(2), CS, NCFii
Lonely Cowboy
Cowboy's Song, A
797. When You Was a Single Girl
(*See:* I Wish I Was a Single
Girl)
798. Where Are You Going, My Pretty
Maid?
(*See:* Milkmaid, The)
799. Whisky Johnny   AAFS(2),
AKD, CS, JCC, Li, WMD(3),
WRM(2)
800. Whistle, Daughter, Whistle
AAFS(2), ACM, AKD(2), Ark.,
CJSii, NCFii(3), VRi(3)
801. White Pilgrim, The   AAFS(2),
APH, Ark., GPJ-A, HHF+,
PGB, VRiv(4)
802. Who Is Tapping at My Bed-
room Window?
(*See:* Drowsy Sleeper, The)

803. Who Killed Cock Robin?
     AAFS(4), ACM
804. Who Will Shoe Your Pretty
     Little Foot?
     (See: Lass of Roch Royal,
     The)
805. Whoopee Ti Yi Yo, Git Along
     Little Dogies
     (See: Git Along Little Dogies)
806. Wicked Polly AAFS(2), ACM,
     AKD(4), GPJ-S, HHF+MO,
     JHC, Li, LP(2), NCFiii(4),
     PGB, VRiv(5)
     Dying Girl, The
     Poor Polly
     Young People Hark
807. Wide Missouri, The
     (See: Shenandoah)
808. Wife of Usher's Well, The (C 79)
     AAFS(20), ACM(3), AKD(10),
     APH(2), Ark., CJSi(18),
     HHF+MO, HMB(2), JHC(7),
     PGB, VRi(2), WAO
     Three Little Babes, The
     Woman Lived in a Far Coun-
     try, A
     Lady from the West Counteree,
     The
     Lady and a Lady Gay, A
     Lone Widow, The
     Three Babes, The
     Moravian Song, A
809. Wife Wrapped in Wether's Skin,
     The (C 277) AAFS(5), ACM,
     AKD(7), APH, CJSi(5),
     HC-TS, HHF+MO, HMB(2),
     JHC(5), LP(2), NCFii(4),
     PGB(3), VRi
     Dan-doo
     Old Man That Lived in the
     West, The
     Kitty Lorn
     Gentle Virginia
810. Wild and Reckless Hobo
     AAFS(3), AKD, Ark., VRiv
811. Wild Bill Jones AAFS(10),
     AKD(2), CJSii, VRii
812. Wild Colonial Boy, The AAFS,
     G+C(2), Lii, WRM
     Wild Colloina Boy
813. Wild Cowboy, The
     (See: Cowboy's Lament, The)

814. Wild Hog, or Old Bangum
     (See: Sir Lionel)
815. Wild Miz-zou-rye, The
     (See: Shenandoah)
816. Wild Moor, The
     (See: Mary of the Wild Moor)
817. Wild Mustard River, The
     AAFS, G+C, Lii
818. William Hall AAFS(5),
     CJSii(6), HMB(3)
819. Willie and Mary HMB, PGB,
     VRi
     Mary and Willie
820. Willy Reilly AAFS(2), HMB,
     PGB
821. Wind That Blew Over the Wild
     Moor, The
     (See: Mary of the Wild Moor)
822. Won't You Walk Out Tonight?
     (See: Buffalo Gals)
823. Working on the Railroad
     (See: I've Been Working on
     the Railroad)
824. Wreck of the C. & O., The
     AAFS, JHC, Li
825. Wreck of the Old 97, The
     AAFS(4), AKD, Ark.(2),
     NCFii(7), VRiv
     Old Ninety-Seven
826. Wreck of the Titanic, The
     (See: Sinking of the Titanic,
     The)
827. Wretched Rambling Boy, The
     (See: Rambling Boy, The)
828. Yaller Gal AAFS(16), Li,
     NCFiii(6)
     Yaller Gal and Brown-Skinned
     Woman
     I Got a Long Tall Yaller Gal
     My Yellow Gal
     Massa Had a Yaller Gal
829. Year of Jubilee AAFS(2), Ark.,
     JWW, NIW, VRii
     Jubilee
     Year of Jubelo, The
830. Yonder Comes My Pretty Little
     Girl
     (See: Gamb(o)ling Man, The)
831. You Got to Cross That Lone-
     some Valley AAFS(3), CS,
     GPJ-S
     You Got to Cross It foh Yohself

832. Young Beichan (C 53)
     AAFS(14), ACM, AKD(4),
     APH, Ark.(3), CJSi(12),
     EBG, G+C, HC-*TS*(6),
     HHF+MO, JHC(4), NCFii,
     VRi(5), WRM(3)
     Lord Bateman
     Lord Bakeman
     Turkish Lady, The
833. Young Brinnon on the Moor
     (*See:* Brennan on the Moor)
834. Young Charlotte   AAFS(16),
     ACM, AKD(2), APH, Ark.,
     CS, EBG, G+C(3), HC-*SB*,
     HHF+, JHC(7), HMB(17),
     LP, PGB(5), VRiv(8),
     NCFii(3), WAO, WRM
     Frozen Girl, The
     Song Ballet of Young Shollity,
     The
     Fair Charlotte
     Charlotte
835. Young Edward in the Lowland
     Low   AAFS(5), Ark.(2),
     NCFii(2), PGB, VRi, VRii(3)
     Young Edwin
     Young Edmond Dell
     Driver Boy, The
836. Young Girls, Take Warning
     (*See:* Unconstant Lover, The)

837. Young Johnny
     (*See:* Green Bed(s), The)
838. Young Johnny, the Miller
     AAFS(7), EBG, G+C,
     HMB(2), LP, PGB
     Rogers the Miller
     John Rogers the Miller
     Miller Boy, The
     My Father's Gray Mare
     Johnny O'Rogers
839. Young Man Who Wouldn't Hoe
     Corn   AAFS(2), AKD(7),
     APH, Ark., HMB, JHC, Liii,
     LP, PGB, NCFiii, WAO
     Man Who Wouldn't Hoe Corn
     Lazy Man, The
840. Young Monroe
     (*See:* Jam on Gerry's Rocks,
     The)
841. Young People Who Delight in
     Sin   AAFS(3), AKD, Ark.
842. Zebra Dun   AAFS(2), VRii
843. 'Zekiel
     (*See:* Ezekiel Saw the Wheel)
844. Zip Coon   AKD, Ark.(2), HMB,
     NCFiii(2), VRii
     Old Zip Coon
     Old Zippy Coon

CHAPTER 19

Long-Playing
Records of
Individual Singers

OME seven hundred long-playing records (33⅓ rpm) are listed
in the present chapter and in the one following. The listing
approximates completeness for the decade 1948 to 1958, that
is, from the beginning of the long-play to the beginning of stereo. No
attempt is made here to include the 78 rpm recordings, since earlier
publications * have made listings of these.

* See, for instance, the following works, all of which are discussed in Book
Two, Bibliography, Chapter 15, of the present study:
  *Check-List of Recorded Songs in the English Language in the Archive of
American Song to July, 1940* (Library of Congress, Music Division, 1942); *Folk
Music of the United States and Latin America, Combined Catalog of Phono-
graph Records* (Library of Congress, Music Division, 1948); *Folksongs on
Records*, Compiled and Edited by Ben Gray Lumpkin, *Issue Three* (Boulder
and Denver, Colorado, 1950); *International Catalogue of Recorded Folk Music*,
edited by Norman Fraser, prepared and published for UNESCO (Oxford Uni-
versity Press, 1954); *A List of American Folksongs Currently Available on
Records*, compiled by the Archive of American Folk Song (Library of Congress,
1953). No one of the above pretends to a complete listing, though Lumpkin's
Folksongs on Records is about as accurate and complete (to 1950) as the reader
is likely to find.
   Another work, which I have not seen or included in the Bibliography, is *The
World's Encyclopaedia of Recorded Music*, by Francis F. Clough and G. J.
Cuming (London: Sidgwick and Jackson, Ltd., in assoc. with The London
Gramophone Corporation, 1952). According to an advertisement in the Schwann
Catalogue (July, 1952), this cloth-bound, royal-octavo volume of 880 pages
(priced at $17.50) is "the *only* Encyclopaedia that includes *all* electrically-
recorded music of worthwhile interest from *every* record producing country in

Much has happened in the recording industry since 1948 and, in addition to the company catalogues, much has appeared in print. In October, 1949, W. Schwann, Inc., issued its first catalogue of long-playing records, a thin booklet of about two dozen pages (large print), including eleven record labels and a total of 674 listings. Five years later (September, 1954), the Schwann catalogue had expanded to 160 pages (fine print), listing long-playing records of 233 labels. Schwann published its one hundredth issue in April, 1958, a catalogue of 204 pages (still finer print!) listing some 20,000 long-playing records on 312 different labels. *

High Fidelity, "The Magazine for Music Listeners," began publication in 1951, and by late 1952 hi-fi recordings were becoming common in the catalogues. Early in 1950, catalogues listed both 10-inch and 12-inch records; early in 1957, many record companies began to withdraw the 10-inch record; by the end of 1958, the 10-inch record had all but disappeared. Along came stereophonic recordings in early 1958, and Schwann made its first listings of stereo in the June, 1958, catalogue. The 33⅓ long-play has crowded out the 78's. Now, it remains to be seen whether or how soon the stereos will displace the monaural long-plays.

Reviews of long-playing folksong recordings have been spotty and scattered until the early 1950's. *The American Record Guide*, established in 1933, contains monthly reviews in all categories—classical, popular, folk, and jazz. The literary magazines such as *Harper's, Atlantic Monthly, Saturday Review* give serious consideration to folk-music recordings as well as to other categories. *The Journal of American Folklore* as early as 1901 took notice of folksong recordings and has reviewed a limited number of long-plays since 1948. Over one hundred of the records listed here have been reviewed in *The Journal.*

The problem in these two chapters, however, is not the quality of records or the number of folksong-record reviews. It is, rather, the listing of the long-plays as accurately and completely as possible, within the decade 1948-58. Both completeness and accuracy are to be taken in the relative and not the absolute sense. The problem in some ways is not unlike a detective story, moving from one

---

the world, *both available and deleted* . . . in classified lists for easy reference . . . brought up to May/June 1951." [Italics in the original]

* There are, of course, other good catalogues besides Schwann's. *The Long Player,* comparable to the Schwann, began publication in early 1952. Both catalogues began early to categorize their listings, with *The Long Player* predating Schwann with a separate folksong listing.

shadowy clue to another. Ideally the way to make a satisfactory discography is to see every record in order to list the pertinent facts, but this has not been possible.*

Aside from seeing the records, then, the compiler is forced to seek other sources of information. A major source is the catalogues from the various recording companies. Sometimes these catalogues do not give full information, especially of song titles, but company officials have been generous in answering inquiries and in supplying additional details. Besides the Schwann and *Long Player* catalogues mentioned earlier, two other sources have proved invaluable: (1) the *One-Spot Record Finder*,† published in monthly and trimonthly sections for record dealers, which lists all records by labels as well as by artists and song titles; (2) the *Phonolog: The All-in-One Record Catalog*, a loose-leaf continuous compendium, published since 1948 and described in Book Two of this study. Not infrequently also an appeal to singers for information on their recordings brought excellent results.

Something should be said here about the song titles listed on the records. The terms *folksong* and *folksinger* are very often interpreted liberally by recording company and singer alike. It is obvious that they do not hold to a strict definition, and the reader (listener) will be obliged to exercise his own critical judgment as to what he thinks is or is not a folksong. The same problem confronts the compiler, whether to admit this or that record to the listing, and I have preferred to err on the side of inclusiveness. Included here the reader (listener) will find not only the well-established, traditional ballads and folksongs but also carols and hymns, spirituals, all kinds of work songs, and what are known as folk blues and folk jazz. Often there are popular, non-folk numbers along with genuine folksongs. It seemed best to list whatever was on the record, since it was next to impossible to hear every recording and try to determine the folk or non-folk character of a song.

Finally, a word of explanation is due the reader on the *method* of listing. In the present chapter, the records are listed in alphabetic order according to the singer's last name. (In the chapter following, they are listed alphabetically according to the over-all record title.) The singer's name is followed by the record title, and then, in parentheses, is given the number of songs and the accompanying

---

* I have examined somewhat fewer than half of the seven hundred records listed in these two chapters.

† Published for the record trade by Tunnis "One-Spot" Publishers (Oak Park, Illinois) since the mid-1950's.

instrument, if any. The next line contains the record maker's name (often shortened, e.g., RCA Victor or Folkways), the identifying letters and numbers (EKL-131 or RLP 12-631), the record size (10″ or 12″), and the date of release if known. The song titles are listed next. If the reader notices variation in wording or spelling, as indeed he will notice in the titles which appear and reappear, this variation is not to be interpreted as an excess of typographical errors. Rather, this is in the nature of folksong: words and spellings vary just as the content and tunes of the songs vary.*

A number at the left of a song title refers to a title in Chapter 18, where a selected listing of folksong titles is given for further reference. This numbering will sometimes aid the reader in checking the song for variants in the standard collections of ballads and folksongs.

Allison, John: HEROES, HEROINES & MISHAPS (*Vol. I, American Folk Song Series*) (*12—guitar*)   Ficker   C-10001   12″   (1957)

285	Gypsy Davy	824	Wreck on the C & O Road
	The Riverman's Daughter		The Wild Goose Grasses
826	The Titanic		The Bowery Grenadiers
	Peggy	696	Betsy from Pike
260	The Golden Vanity		The Cow Chase
	Slow Mule	763	Waily, Waily

Anderson, Marian: SINGS ELEVEN GREAT SPIRITUALS (*Franz Rupp at the piano*)   RCA Victor   LRM-7006   10″

155	Deep River	677	Sometimes I Feel Like a Mother-
	He's Got the Whole World in		less Child
	His Hands		Let Us Break Bread Together
615	Roll, Jerd'n Roll	568	Plenty Good Room
250	Go Down, Moses	196	Everytime I Feel de Spirit
	Crucifixion		If He Change My Name
			O What a Beautiful City!

Anderson, Marian: SINGS SPIRITUALS (*10—piano*)   RCA Victor   LM 110   10″

504	Nobody Knows the Trouble I See		Sinner, Please
	Hear De Lam's A-Cryin'		Honor, Honor
491	My Lord, What a Morning		On Ma Journey
784	Were You There?	266	De Gospel Train
	Soon-A Will Be Done	610	Ride On, King Jesus

---

* Furthermore, song titles taken from catalogues cannot be relied upon for accuracy in wording or spelling.

Recently, the quarterly folksong magazine *Sing Out!* began a department called "Folk Music on Records." The four 1959 issues of the magazine list 146 new releases, from approximately twenty different labels. Listings include folksongs of all nations, but song titles are not given.

Anderson, Marian: SINGS SPIRITUALS (*11—piano*)   *RCA Victor*
LM-2032   12"

504 Nobody Knows the Trouble I
See
155 Deep River
He's Got the Whole World in
His Hands
615 Roll, Jord'n, Roll!
250 Go Down Moses

677 Sometimes I Feel Like a Motherless Child
Let Us Break Bread Together
568 Plenty Good Room
196 Every Time I Feel de Spirit
If He Change My Name
O What a Beautiful City

Anderson, Pink: CAROLINA STREET BALLADS and Davis, Rev. Gary:
HARLEM STREET SPIRITUALS (*15*)   *Riverside   RLP 12-611   12"*

Anderson:

369 John Henry
Every Day in the Week
270 The Ship Titanic
Greasy Greens
825 Wreck of the Old '97
I've Got Mine
He's in the Jailhouse, Now

Davis:

Blow Gabriel
Twelve Gates to the City
Samson and Delilah
Keep Your Lamp Trimmed and
Burning
There Was a Time That I Was
Blind
Oh, Lord, Search My Heart
Get Right Church
You Got to Go Down

Archer, Frances and Beverly Gile: COMMUNITY CONCERT (*16—guitar*)
Disneyland   WDL-3023   12"

I Know My Love
172 Down in the Valley
Soontag
Le Coeur de Ma Mie
How Should I Your True Love
Know
It Was a Lover and His Lass
Ritka Arpa, Ritka Buza
Imi Au Ia Oe
He Ono

51 Black Is the Color of My True
Love's Hair
Scetate
Pajarillo Barranqueno
301 Hold On
53 Black-Eyed Susie
773 Wayfarin' Stranger
Nine Hundred Miles
Do Lord

Archer, Frances and Beverly Gile: FOLK SONGS FROM FAR CORNERS
(*12—guitar*)   *Disneyland   WDL-3006*

Fast Freight
655 Shenandoah
Maybe Tomorrow
253 Go 'Way from My Window
Uncle Reuben
Windmill

302 Home on the Range
Towdy Owdy (Bird Song)
My Lagan Love
Red Rosy Bush
705 Swing Low, Sweet Chariot
Sinful People

Arkin, Alan: FOLKSONGS (and 2½ that aren't) ONCE OVER LIGHTLY
(*12—guitar*)   *Elektra   EKL-21   10"*

A Knave Is a Knave
Kisses Sweeter Than Wine

137 Crawdad Song
Tom With-A-Grin

119 Colorado Trail
     The Mad Count
     So Early in the Morning
     Tobacco Union

I'm Gonna Marry in the Fall
269 Great Grandad
     Lavender Cowboy
     Ann Boleyn

Arnold, Eddy: WANDERIN' (14–guitar)   RCA Victor   LPM-1111   12"

768 Wanderin
627 The Rovin' Gambler
442 The Lonesome Road
172 Down in the Valley
36   Barbara Allen
551 On Top of Old Smoky
313 I Gave My Love a Cherry

677 Sometimes I Feel Like a Mother-
     less Child
773 The Wayfaring Stranger
807 Across the Wide Missouri
101 Careless Love
604 Red River Valley
696 Sweet Betsy from Pike
302 Home on the Range

Atcher, Bob: EARLY AMERICAN FOLK SONGS (7–guitar)   Columbia
     HL 9006   10"   (1949)

36   Barbary Allen
     De Ladies Man
472 Methodist Pie
160 Devilish Mary

614 Young Rogers the Miller
538 Old Smoky
306 The Hunters of Kentucky

Atcher, Bob: SONGS OF THE SADDLE (Traditional Cowboy Songs)
     (8–guitar)   Columbia   HL 9013   10"

302 Home on the Range
604 Red River Valley
690 The Strawberry Roan
423 Little Joe the Wrangler

91   Bury Me Not on the Lone Prairie
134 The Cowboy's Dream
     I've No Use for the Woman
518 The Old Chisholm Trail

Baillargeon, Hélène (with children's chorus): CHANTS DE NOËL
     (CHRISTMAS SONGS) OF FRENCH CANADA (16)
          Folkways   FC 7229 (FW829)   10"

Venez
Divin Messie
Les Anges
Il Est Né
Entre le Boeuf et l'Âne Gris
Nouvelle Agréable
Les Choeurs Angéliques
Dans Cette Étable

Ça, Bergers, Assemblons-Nous
Nous Étions Trois Bergerettes
D'où Viens-Tu Bergère?
Le Petit Noël
Vive le Vent
Les Beaux Santons
Ballade de Noël
La Guignolée

Baillargeon, Hélène and Alan Mills: DUET SONGS OF FRENCH CANADA
     Folkways   (16–guitar)   FW 6918 (FP918)   10"   (1955)

J'entends le Moulin
Fringue! Fringue!
J'ai Tant Dansé
Auprès de Ma Blonde
La Plume Qui S'envole au Vent
Mon Père Avait 500 Moutons
Là-Bas, sur Ces Montagnes
Le P'tit Avocat

C'est le Bon Vin Qui Danse
Marie-Madeleine
Le Retour du Marin
Pambelibelo
Voilà La Récompense
C'est à Boire
Le Petit Mousse
I Went to the Market

Baillargeon, Hélène and Alan Mills: SONGS OF ACADIA (*French and English texts incl.*) (*16*)   Folkways   FW 6923   10"

Où Vas-Tu Mon P'tit Garçon?	6	Au Chant de l'Alouette
395 À la Claire Fontaine		La Belle
Ma Virginie		Si J'avais Su
Derrière Chez Nous		Dans les Prisons de Nantes
Patrons! La Mer Est Belle!		Angélique
Sur la Montagne du Loup		Wing-Tra-La
J'ai une Brune		Dessus la Fougère
Ave Maria Stella		
Joséphine		

Barry, Margaret: SONGS OF AN IRISH TINKER LADY (*12*)   Riverside
RLP 12-602   12"

She Moves through the Fair	The Cottage with the Horseshoe
The Cycling Champion of Ulster	O'er the Door
The Factory Girl	My Lagan Love
The Hills of Donegal	The Galway Shawl
The Turfman of Ardee	The Bold Fenian Men
Moses Ritoorel-i-ay	The Flower of Sweet Strabane
	Belfast Hornpipe

Belafonte, Harry: CALYPSO (*11–guitar, orch., chorus*)   RCA Victor
LPM-1248   12"

Day O	Star O
I Do Adore Her	The Jack-Ass Song
Jamaica Farewell	Hosanna
Will His Love Be Like His Rum?	Come Back Liza
	Brown Skin Girl
Dolly Dawn	Man Smart

Belafonte, Harry: "MARK TWAIN" AND OTHER FOLK FAVORITES
(*12–guitar, orch., chorus*)   RCA Victor   LPM 1022   12"   (*1954*)

Mark Twain	226	The Fox
Man Piaba	674	Soldier, Soldier
369 John Henry		The Next Big River
Tol' My Captain		Delia
Kalenda Rock		Mo Mary
The Drummer and the Cook	451	Lord Randall

Belafonte, Harry: SINGS HIS FAVORITES (*11–guitar, orch., chorus*)
RCA Victor   LPM-1150   12"

Waterboy	In That Great Gettin' Up
Troubles	Mornin'
Suzanne (Every Night When the Sun Goes Down)	Noah
	Unchained Melody
Matilda	Jump Down, Spin Around
Take My Mother Home	Sylvie
Scarlet Ribbons for Her Hair	

Belafonte, Harry: * SINGS OF THE CARIBBEAN (*11—guitars, chorus*)
RCA Victor   LPM-1505   12"

Scratch, Scratch
Lucy's Door
Cordelia Brown
Don't Ever Love Me
Love, Love Alone
Cocoanut Woman

Haiti Cherie
Judy Drownded
Island in the Sun
Angelique-O
Lead Man Holler

Bender, Bill: FRONTIER BALLADS AND COWBOY SONGS (*6—guitar*)
Stinson   SLP #18   10"

696 Sweet Betsy from Pike
88   Buffalo Skinners
     Sam Hall

352 Jack o' Diamonds
486 Mustang Grey
361 Jesse James

Bennett, Marjorie (Marty King): SING A SONG OF CHILDHOOD (*28—
autoharp, mountain dulcimer, guitar, Irish harp*)   Judson Records   J-3028   12"

     A Little Song A-Singing in My
     Heart
     The Rummy-Dummy Line
     I Saw a Ship A-Sailing
     Jolly Old Roger
803 Who Killed Cock Robin?
     Where Is Thumbkin?
252 Go Tell Aunt Rhody
156 The Derby Ram
     Bingo
     All the Pretty Little Horses
791 What'll We Do with the
     Baby-O?
     One Elephant Went Out to Play
     Oats and Beans and Barley Grow

38   The Bear Went Over the Moun-
     tain
     The Carrion Crow
     Michael Finnegan
308 Hush, Little Baby
     Bobby Shaftoe
     The Animal Fair
     Mr. Rabbit
     Ten Little Indians
     I Know an Old Lady
     This Old Man
232 The Frog and the Mouse
     I Had a Rooster
     The Lady & the Crocodile
     The Muffin Man
     ABC Song

Bikel, Theodore: AN ACTOR'S HOLIDAY (*Folksongs of Many Lands*) (*22*)
Elektra   EKL-105   12"

Khag Laro'e
Rue
Ay Te Tsi Nye Te
Vi Zenen Mayne Yinge Yoren
Mangwani Mpulele
Wheel of Fortune
Le Mineur

Be'er Bassadeh
Los Cuatro Muleros
Vira
Na Konye Voronom
395 A la Claire Fontaine
Welcum to Scotland
Ma Guitare et Moi

* Additional Belafonte records issued by RCA Victor in late 1958 or early
1959 include the following:
AN EVENING WITH BELAFONTE   LPM 1402   12"
BLUES   LOP 1006   12"
LOVE IS A GENTLE THING   LPM 1927   12"
BELAFONTE SINGS THE BLUES   LPM 1972   12"
PRESENTING THE BELAFONTE SINGERS   LPM 1760   12"
HARRY BELAFONTE AT CARNEGIE HALL   LOC 6006   2-12"

Scalinatella
Blow the Candles Out
Kto Yevo Znayet
Snyezhnaya Kolibellnaya

Perrine Etait Servante
Khof Shakett
Stenka Razin
Folklore Limited [?]

Bikel, Theodore: FOLKSONGS OF ISRAEL (*13—guitar*)   *Elektra*
EKL-32   10"

Dodi Li
Mi Barechev
Hechalil
Ptsach Bazemer
Karev Yom
Shech Abrek
Sissoo Vessimchoo

El Ginat Egoz
Shomer Mah Milel
Hana'ava Babanot
Ana Pana' Dodech
Shim'oo Shim'oo
Lyla Lyla

Bikel, Theodore: FOLKSONGS OF ISRAEL (*18—guitar, with clay drum by Michael Kagan*)   *Elektra*   EKL-132   12"

Arava, Arava
Oozy Vezimbrat Yah
Orcha Bamidbar
Sookah Bakerem
Dodi Li
Mi Barechev
Ada
Hechalil
Ptsach Bazemer

Karev Yom
Shech Abrek
Sissoo Vessimchoo
El Ginat Egoz
Shomer Mah Mile.
Hana'ava Babanot
Ana Pana' Dodech
Shim'oo Shim'oo
Lyla, Lyla

Bikel, Theodore: * JEWISH FOLK SONGS (*16—guitar, orch.*)   *Elektra*
EKL-141   12"   (1958)

Der Rebe Elimelech
Di Yontevdike Teyg
Sha Shtil
Di Ban
Kum Aher Du Filozof
Di Mezinke
A Sudenyu
Achtsik Er Un Zibetsik Zi

Di Mame Iz Gegangen
Margaritkelech
Mu Asapru
Lomir Zich Iberbeten
Homentashn
A Chazn Oyf Shabes
Reyzl
Tumbalalayka

Boguslav, Raphael: SONGS FROM A VILLAGE GARRET (*14*)   *Riverside*
RLP   12-638   12"

	MacPherson's Lament	780	Weevily Wheat
	Bowling Green		High Germany
729	Tobacco's but an Indian Weed	440	Turtle Dove
	Moneymusk	829	Year of Jubilo
	Crows in the Garden		The State of Elanoy
	The Flying Dutchman	88	Buffalo Skinners
599	Rambling Boy	762	Wagoner's Lad

* In 1959, Elektra issued a Bikel record (EKL-175) titled BRAVO BIKEL.

Bonyun, Bill: WHO BUILT AMERICA? (*16—guitar*)   *Folkways*
FC 7402   (*LP-2*)   10"

763	Waly, Waly	278	Green Mountain Boys
	Praetes	193	Erie Canal
642	Santy Ano	684	Government Claim
65	Boll Weevil	175	Drill Ye Tarriers
	Happiness Song	361	Jesse James
113	Chisholm Trail	659	Shoot the Buffalo
	Mi Chacra		So Long
	Salangadou		Shluf Kind, Kleine Jonges

Bonyun, Bill and Gene: YANKEE LEGEND (*19—guitar*)   *Heirloom Records*
HL-500   12"   (*1957*)

	Yankee Doodle	528	The Old Man Who Lived in the
763	Waly Waly		Wood
	Psalm III		Johnny Has Gone for a Soldier
839	The Young Man Who Couldn't	360	Jenny Jenkins
	Hoe Corn	260	The Golden Vanity
	Song of the Fishes (Boston	233	The Frog in the Spring
	Come All Ye)		Katie Cruel
456	Lumberman's Alphabet		Doodle Dandy
	Three Jolly Rogues of Lynn		Riflemen of Bennington
	The Connecticut Peddler	57	Blow the Man Down
	Father Abby's Will		The Herring

Brand, Oscar: ABSOLUTE NONSENSE (*18*)   *Riverside   RLP 12-825   12"*

303	A Horse Named Bill		The Frozen Logger
	Fooba-Wooba John		Talking Blues
	Midnight on the Ocean		The Bold Fisherman
156	The Derby Ram		In the Vinter
	Good Peanuts		Kafoozalum
	Anne Boleyn		Bunch of Roses
87	Buffalo Gals		Ain't Gonna Rain No More
	The Old Woman and the Pedlar	542	The Old Lady Who Loved a Pig
659	Shoot the Buffalo		
	Alaska		

Brand, Oscar: AMERICAN DRINKING SONGS (*Acc. Erik Darling*) (*17*)
Riverside   RLP 12-630   12"

421	Little Brown Jug	630	Rye Whiskey
	Vive l'Amour		Drunk Last Night
	Quartermaster Corps	262	Good Old Mountain Dew
	Three Jolly Coachmen		Old King Cole
603	Red Light Saloon	377	Johnson's Ale
	Mother Rackett's		Copper Kettle
	No More Booze	193	The E-RI-E Was Rising
	I've Been a Moonshiner		Bootlegger's Song
		799	Whiskey Johnny

Brand, Oscar: BACKROOM BALLADS (8–*guitar*)   *Chesterfield*
CMS-101   10"

	Maid of Amsterdam	603	Red Light Saloon

Maid of Amsterdam   603   Red Light Saloon
730   Tom Bolynn   Sunday School
Early One Morn   Old King Cole
The Fireship
Ramblin' Wretch

Brand, Oscar: BAWDY SONGS AND BACKROOM BALLADS   *Audio*
Fidelity   *ADFL 906*   10"
(song titles not available)

Brand, Oscar: BAWDY SONGS AND BACKROOM BALLADS (*Vol. 1*)
(*15–guitar*)   *Audio Fidelity*   *AFLP 1906*   12"

Roll Your Leg Over   Her Name Was Lil
No Hips at All   Bell Bottom Trousers
One-Eyed Reilly   The Sergeant
Blow the Candle Out   526   Old Joe Clark
Sam Hall   558   Our Good Man
Limericks   The Fireship
The Chandler's Wife   Rollin' Down the Mountain
Around Her Neck She Wore a
    Yellow Ribbon

Brand, Oscar: BAWDY SONGS AND BACKROOM BALLADS (*Vol. 2*)
(*14–guitar*)   *Audio Fidelity*   *AFLP 1806*   12"

Zulaika   The Same the 'Ole World Over
Winnipeg Whore   The Hermit
Chris Colombo   A Gob Is a Slob
Ball o' Yarn   224   Foggy Dew
Squire of Great Renown   156   Darby Ram
Limericks   53   Black-Eyed Susie
193   Erie Canal
Crusher Bailey

Brand, Oscar: BAWDY SONGS AND BACKROOM BALLADS (*Vol. 3*)
(*14–guitar*)   *Audio Fidelity*   *AFLP 1824*   12"

Seven Old Ladies Locked in a   Roll Your Leg Over (cont'd)
    Lavatory   Three Prominent Bastards
We Go to College   Red Wing
The Jolly Tinker   Ball of Ballynoor
Bella   She'll Do It Again
Cats on the Rooftops   Kafoozalem
Humoresque   The Bastard King of England
Ring Dang Doo

Brand, Oscar: BAWDY SONGS AND BACKROOM BALLADS (*Vol. 4*)
(*14–guitar, banjo*)   *Audio Fidelity*   *AFLP 1847*   12"

115   Cindy   Basket of Oysters
730   Tom Bolynn   Green Grow the Rashes
Plymouth Town   Cuckoo's Nest
Two Maidens   Sweet Violets

The Money Rolls In
Chicago
The Old Sea Chest

Wayward Boy
Don't Call Me
Roll Me Over

Brand, Oscar: BAWDY SEA SHANTIES (*Vol. 5*) (*14—guitar, with Dave Sear on banjo*)   *Audio Fidelity*   AFLP 1884   12"   (*1959 ?*)

You're a Liar   376 Johnny Come Down to Hilo
Good Ship Venus   Turalai
We Set Sail   Backside Rules the Navy
Can't Ya Dance the Polka   57 Blow the Man Down
Bell Bottom Trousers   Jinny Wren Bride
A Clean Song   Keyhole in the Door
                                                  There's Nothing Else to Do
                                                  Lulu

Brand, Oscar: G. I. AMERICAN ARMY SONGS (*Assisted by Fred Hellerman*) (*17*)   *Riverside*   RLP 12-639   12"

I Don't Want No More of Army   Old Soldiers Never Die
    Life   The G.I. Blues
The Freaking Fusileers   The Sergeant
I'll Tell You Where They Were   Roll Me Over
The Raw Recruit   He Ain't Gonna Jump No More
Beneath a Bridge in Italy   Home, Boys, Home
Mademoiselle from Armentieres   Around Her Neck
807 The Wide Missouri   The Regular Army O
The Soldier's Life   Follow Washington

Brand, Oscar: PIE IN THE SKY (*Satire in Folksong*) (*16—guitar, with Dave Sear on banjo*)   *Tradition*   TLP 1022   12"

Pie in the Sky   The Clerks of Parch's Grove
Talking Atom   Give My Regards
Ninety Cents Butter   The Tenderfoot
The Dodger Song   The Mormon Engineer
Arkansas   734 Track Lining Chant
Tammany   The Battle of the Kegs
The Downtrodden Landlord   Rum a Dum Dum
Down, Down, Down   A Dollar Ain't a Dollar Anymore

Brand, Oscar and Fred Hellerman: LAUGHING AMERICA (*12—guitar, banjo*)   *Tradition*   TLP 1014   12"

Robin A-Thrush   Kafoosalem
Talking Guitar Blues   Donderbeck
292 Hard Times   129 Cotton-Eye Joe
730 Tom Bolynn   65 Lookin' for a Home
320 I Was Born About 10,000 Years   The Smeller Song
    Ago   The Old Soldiers of the King
                                            A Hole in the Bucket

Brill, Marty: THE ROVING BALLADEER (*Folk Songs*) (*12—guitar*)   *Mercury*   MG20178   12"

Diggin' for Old Black Coal   14 A-Rovin'
Mon Piaba   Black Lace
                                      The Ash Grove

369	John Henry	588	Pretty Polly
	Timber		Poor Miss Bailey
281	Green Sleeves	51	Black Is the Color
	Pauvre Petite Lolotte		

Britton, George: PENNSYLVANIA DUTCH FOLK SONGS (14–guitar)
Folkways   FA 2215 (FP615)   10″   (1955)

Lei Lie, Lei Lo	Siss Net Alli Daag Luschdich
Lauterbach	Leewe
Alle Yahr en Kindlein	Reidi, Reidi, Geili
Wie Kumm Ich an des Gross-	Des Bucklich Mennli
wadder's Haus?	Eiei, Rete, Ridddieoo
Unser Saiwi	In Einem Kiehlen Grunde
Schloof Bobbeli Schloof	Schpinn, Schpinn
Joe Raetel	Meedli, Widdu Heiere

Brooks, John Benson: FOLK JAZZ, U.S.A. (12)   Vik (of RCA)   LX-1083   12″

	The New Saints	655	Shenandoah
	Venezuela		Joe's Old Folks
51	Black Is the Color		Saro Jane
	Betsy	68	Scarlet Town
451	Randall My Son	773	Wayfarin' Stranger
440	Turtle Dove	149	Darling Corey

Broonzy, Big Bill: BIG BILL'S BLUES (10–guitar)   Columbia   WL 111
12″   (1958)

	Bossie Woman		When I've Been Drinking
	Texas Tornado Blues		Martha Blues
	Tell Me What Kind of Man	705	Swing Low, Sweet Chariot
	Jesus Is		Key to the Highway
737	Trouble in Mind		Goodbye Baby Blues
	See See Rider		

Broonzy, Big Bill: BLUES (12–guitar)   EmArcy   Em. 36137   12″   (1958)

442	Walkin' the Lonesome Road	I Know She Will
	Mopper's Blues	Hollerin' Blues
	Get Back	Leavin' Day
	Hey, Hey	Southbound Train
	Willie Mae	You Changed
	Stump Blues	Tomorrow

Broonzy, Big Bill: BLUES CONCERT   Dial Records   Dial-306   10″   (1952)
(song titles not available)

Broonzy, Big Bill: COUNTRY BLUES (12–guitar)   Folkways   FA 2326   12″

	In the Evening	230	Frankie and Johnny
	When Things Go Wrong		South Bound Train
	Diggin' My Potatoes		Joe Turner No. 2
	Poor Bill Blues		Hey Hey Baby
737	Trouble in Mind		Saturday Evening Blues
	I Wonder When I'll Be Called		
	a Man?		
	Louise		

Broonzy, Big Bill: FOLK BLUES (*8—guitar*)   *EmArcy*   *MG-26034*   *10"*

369	John Henry	58	Blue Tail Fly
137	Crawdad		Bessie Smith
	Bill Bailey		Leroy Carr
	Make My Get-Away		Richard Jones

Broonzy, Big Bill: HIS STORY (*Interview with Studs Terkel*) (*8*)
  Folkways   *FG 3586*   *12"*

Plow-Hand Blues (Early Days)   Mule Ridin'-Talking Blues
C. C. Rider   Key to the Highway (Traveling)
Willie Mae Blues   Black, Brown, and White
This Train (Experiences)   Joe Turner Blues No. 1

Broonzy, Big Bill: SINGS   *Period   Per. 1114   10"*
    (song titles not available)

Broonzy, Big Bill: SINGS AND JOSH WHITE COMES A-VISITING
    Period   SLP 1209   12"   (1958)
    (song titles not available)

Broonzy, Big Bill: SINGS (BLUES)   *Period   SPL 1194   10"   (1956)*
    (song titles not available)

Buckley, Bruce: OHIO VALLEY BALLADS (*9—guitar, dulcimer*)   *Folkways*
    FA 2025 (FP23/2)   10"

	Molly Bonder	563	Pearl Bryan
	Sidney Allen		Lola Williams' Fate
	Rowan County Crew	641	Sam Bass
	Lola Viers	369	John Henry
	Rarden Wreck		

Cameron, Isla: THROUGH BUSHES AND BRIARS (*19*)   *Tradition*
    TLP 1001   12"

	Keel Row	Sandgate Nursing Song
	Through Bushes and Briars	Scots Curse
	The Seeds of Thyme	Sweet Scented Lavender
	To the Begging I Will Go	Johnny Todd
451	Lord Randal	Died for Love
	The Water Is Wide	Frog and the Crow
674	Soldier, Soldier	Baloo Baleary
	Christ Child Lullabye	Lowlands of Holland
108	The Cherry Tree Carol	Croodin Doo
	Lark in the Morning	

Campbell, Gerard: THE WANDERING MINSTREL (*17—guitar*)   *London*
    LL 1714   12"

421	Little Brown Jug	71	Bonnie Wee Window
	Three Lovely Lassies from		Darlin' Girl from Clare
	Bannion		Dumb-Dumb-Dumb
	Dacent Irish Boy		Trottin' to the Fair
	Master McGrath		Killeter Fair

484 Moonshiner
     Outlandish Knight
436 Lolly-too-dum-day
     Maid of Sweet Brown Knowe

362 Real Ol' Mountain Dew
     Larry's Goat
     Kitty of Coleraine
     Killyburn Brae

Cansler, Loman: MISSOURI FOLK SONGS (*14—guitar*)   *Folkways*
     FH 5324 12" (1959)

 Sally
 Arthur Clyde
 When I Went for to Take My
  Leave
 Judgment Day
 Lovers' Quarrel
746 The Two Sisters
 Kickin' Mule

106 Charles Guiteau
     I Told 'em Not to Grieve After
      Me
367 Joe Bowers
     Housekeeper's Complaint
     What Is a Home without Love?
     The Blue and the Gray
     Far Away

Charles, Lee: SWING LOW, SWEET CHARIOT (*Negro Spirituals and*
   Jubilees) (17) *Riverside RLP 12-651 12"*

196 Every Time I Feel the Spirit
677 Motherless Child
 Good News
 Round About the Mountain
 Oh, Freedom
147 Daniel
504 Nobody Knows
 Ride Up in the Chariot
 Let Us Break Bread Together

 In That Morning
 Poor Pilgrim
379 Joshua
 Honor, Honor
705 Swing Low, Sweet Chariot
 I Got a Home in That Rock
 No More Auction Block
 Little Boy

Child, Marilyn and Glenn Yarbrough: ENGLISH AND AMERICAN FOLK-
SONGS (*17—guitar acc. Fred Hellerman*) *Elektra EKL-143 12" (1958)*

 We Come for to Sing
 Wee Cooper O' Fife
 Lilli-I-O
76 Bound for the Promised Land
 Weel May the Keel Row
773 Wayfaring Stranger
506 Nickety Nack
 Three Jolly Sailor Boys
 Gentle Johnny, My Jingalo

 Everywhere I Look This Morn-
  ing
 Mary Had a Baby
 New York Girls
604 Red River Valley
 An Irish Fragment
 Buffalo Boy
803 Who Killed Cock Robin
 Now Let Me Fly

Clark, Keith: BALLADS OF LaSALLE COUNTY, ILLINOIS (*Composed and*
  sung by K. Clark) (*11—guitar*) *Folkways FA 2080 10"*

 Father Marquette & the Jesuit-
  Indian
 The Ballad of Starved Rock
 The Sloopers from Stavanger
 Elsie Strawn Armstrong
 Pioneer
 The Lincoln & Douglas Debate

 The Rules of the Board of
  Trustees
 The Diary of Willy Price
 The Magnetic Doctress
 Wild Bill Hickok
 The Cherry Mine Disaster

Clark, Rogie: LEGEND OF JOHN HENRY *Allegro AL-8 10" (1950)*
      (song titles not available)

Clark, Slim: COWBOY SONGS   *Remington   Rem. 1017   10"*
(song titles not available)

Clauson, William: CONCERT ("*World-Famed Folk Songs Recorded 'Live' at Wellington Town Hall by the New Zealand Broadcasting Service*") (*12—guitar*)   *Capitol   T-10158   12"   (1957)*

115	Cindy	691	Streets of Laredo
281	Greensleeves		Out After Ale
369	John Henry		La Malaguena (in Spanish)
	I Know an Old Lady		Brian O'Linn
232	The Frog and the Mouse		Sinner Man
	La Bamba (in Spanish)	375	Johnny Sands

Clauson, William: FOLK SONGS (*21—guitar*)   *RCA Victor   LPM 1286   12"   (1956)*

434	Lil' Liza Jane	115	Cindy
440	Turtle Dove		Irish Love Song (Would God I
	All through the Night		Were a Tender Apple Blos-
	The Garden Where the Praties		som)
	Grow		Sippin' Cider
	Ladies' Man		John Grumlie
482	Cockles and Mussels (Molly		The Ash Grove
	Malone)	369	John Henry
614	Rogers, the Miller		The Bold Fisherman
	Three Jovial Hunstmen		The Rumpling of Your Gown-O
	Red Rosy Bush	51	Black Is the Color
	Sinner Man	232	The Frog and the Mouse
			Skye Boat Song

Clayton, Paul: AMERICAN BROADSIDE BALLADS IN POPULAR TRADITION (*—guitar*)   *Folkways   FA 2378   12"   (1958)*
(song titles not available)

Clayton, Paul: BAY STATE BALLADS (*14—guitar*)   *Folkways FA 2106 (FP47/2)   10"*

	Cape Cod Girls	24	The Bailiff's Daughter of Isling-
	Huzza for Commodore Rogers		ton
	The Ocean Rover	681	Springfield Mountain
57	Blow the Man Down		The Old Soldier
	Come All Ye Shipmates		Polly Van
799	Whiskey Johnny		The Embargo
	The Seaman's Grave	22	Bachelor's Hall
			Around the Ingals Blazing

Clayton, Paul: BLOODY BALLADS (*British and American Murder Ballads*) (*18*)   *Riverside   RLP 12-615   12"*

563	Pearl Bryan		Rose Connoley
547	The Banks of the Ohio		Jellon Grame
682	Stackolee	545	Omie Wise
744	The Two Brothers		The Suncook Town Tragedy
	The Brookfield Murder		Poor Ellen Smith

476 The Miller's Boy   731 Tom Dula
     Delia   188 Edward
588 Pretty Polly   Lula Viers
141 The Cruel Mother
     John Hollin

Clayton, Paul: BOBBY BURNS' MERRY MUSES OF CALEDONIA (25)
            Elektra   EKL-155   12"   (1958)

Nine Inch Will Please a Lady   Know Ye Not Our Bess
Our Jock's Broke Yesterday   Who the Devil Can Hinder the
How Can I Keep My Maiden-   Wind to Blow
  head?   Auntie Jean
Who Will Mow Me Now?   Hole to Hide It in
Johnnie Scott   Muirland Meg
John Anderson My Jo   No Hair on It
Tommie Makes My Tail Toddle   Cooper of Dundee
Tweedmouth Town   Duncan Davison
Would You Do That?   Lassie Gathering Nuts
Ellibanks   Thrusting of It
Beware of the Ripples   My Bonnie Highland Lad
Duncan Macleerie   Patriarch
Can You Labour Lea

Clayton, Paul: BRITISH BROADSIDE BALLADS IN POPULAR TRADI-
            TION (*19—guitar*)   *Folkways   FW 8708   12"*

482 When Cockle Shells Make Sil-   The Bold Fisherman
       ver Bells   Brian O'Lynn
     Pleasant and Delightful   148 The Dark-Eyed Sailor
     Three Maidens to Milking Did   Jim, the Carter's Lad
       Go   239 Geordie
 70 The Bonny Bunch of Roses   The Sweet Primroses
     The Bold Thrasher   Green Room
     My Grandmother   Herchard of Taunton Dene
     The Lost Lady Found   206 The False-Hearted Knight
     When Pat Came Over the Hill   341 The Indian Lass
     The Oyster Girl

Clayton, Paul: CONCERT OF BRITISH AND AMERICAN FOLKSONGS
            (*—guitar*)   *Riverside   RLP 12-836   12"   (1958)*
            (song titles not available)

Clayton, Paul: CUMBERLAND MOUNTAIN FOLKSONGS (*14—guitar, dul-
            cimer*)   *Folkways   FA 2007   10"*

     The Hunting Gamblers   Once I Courted a Pretty Little
447 Lord Bateman   Girl
     Floyd Collins   Spotty and Dudie
     Mush Todin   Kathy Fiscus
304 The House Carpenter   Tom Wilson
     Sugar Baby   Walk
588 Pretty Polly and False William   Cold Winter's Night
                                      712 Texas Rangers

Clayton, Paul: DULCIMER SONGS AND SOLOS   *Folkways*   *FA 2382*
12"   (1958)
(song titles not available)

Clayton, Paul: FOC'SLE SONGS AND SHANTIES (*20—with the Foc'sle
Singers*)   *Folkways*   *FA 2429*   12"   (1959)

	Ratcliffe Highway	218	Fire Down Below
611	Rio Grande		A Hundred Years Ago
	Haul on the Bowline	642	Santy Anno
	Maggie May		Captain Nipper
293	Haul Away Joe	290	Hangin' Johnny
372	Do My Johnny Booker	32	Banks of the Sacramento
	Roll the Cotton Down		Won't You Go My Way
	Haul Boys Haul	211	Goodbye Fare Thee Well
	Leave Her Johnny		All Bound to Go
	Paddy Lay Back		The Black Ball Line

Clayton, Paul: FOLK SONGS AND BALLADS OF VIRGINIA (*12—guitar*)
Folkways   *FA 2110* (*FP47/3*)   10"

595	Railroad Bill	213	The Farmer's Curst Wife
	In the Pines		Harvey Logan
238	Gambling Man	398	Lady Margaret
	Wild Rover	230	Frankie
	Bill Dooley		If I Had a Bottle of Rum
	Talt Hall	451	Lord Randal

Clayton, Paul: FOLKWAYS-VIKING RECORD OF FOLK BALLADS (*from*
The Viking Book of Folk Ballads of the English-Speaking World)
(*15—guitar*)   *Folkways*   *FA 2310*   12"

74	Botany Bay	24	Bailiff's Daughter of Islington
156	The Derby Ram		The Dying Stockman
181	Dupree	404	The Lass of Roch Royal
	Lilliburlero		Avondale's Mine Disaster
496	Naomi Wise	108	The Cherry Tree Carol
746	The Two Sisters		The Baffled Knight
384	Katherine Jaffray		The Sea Captain
	The Great Silkie of Sule Skerry		

Clayton, Paul: TIMBER-R-R! (*Folksongs and Ballads of the Lumberjack*) (15)
Riverside   *RLP 12-648*   12"

456	The Lumberman's Alphabet		The Rackets Around Blue
355	The Jam on Gerry's Rock		Mountain Lake
420	The Little Brown Bulls	97	Canaday
	The Hanging Limb	23	The Backwoodsman
358	James Whalen	453	The Lost Jimmy Whalen
817	The Wild Mustard River		Peter Amberly
	The Banks of the Little Eau Plaine		Harry Bail
350	Jack Haggerty and the Flat River Girl		The Jolly Shanty Boys

Clayton, Paul: UNHOLY MATRIMONY (*12—guitar, banjo*)   *Elektra*
       EKL-147   12″   (*1958*)

Stay Away from the Girls		The Charleston Merchant
The Wooden Legged Parson		Life on the Installment Plan
Will the Weaver		The Dumb Wife
Mother-in-Law Song	353	Jack the Sailor
323 I Wish I Was Single Again	213	The Farmer's Nagging Wife
The Old Wife Who Wanted Spruncin'		The Dirty Wife

Clayton, Paul: WANTED FOR MURDER (*American Folksongs of Outlaws and Desperadoes*) (*16*)   *Riverside*   RLP 12-640   12″

361 Jesse James	46	Billy the Kid
Cole Younger	89	Bully of the Town
Charles Guiteau		Sidney Allen
Duncan and Brady		Claude Allen
Kenny Wagner		Bad Lee Brown
811 Wild Bill Jones	641	Sam Bass
Quantrell		Coon-Can Game
Ella Speed		Zeb Turney's Girl

Clayton, Paul: WATERS OF TYNE (*English North Country Songs*) (*14—guitar*)   *Stinson*   SLP #70   10″

Waters of Tyne	279	Willow Tree
44 Billy Boy		Blaydon Races
Collier's Rant		Ca' Hawkie
Keel Row		Maa Bonny Lad
Lambton Worm		Heh You Seen Wor Jimmy
When This Old Hat Was New	34	Banks of the Dee
Geordie Hinny		
Cushie Butterfield		

Clayton, Paul: WHALING AND SAILING SONGS FROM THE DAYS OF MOBY DICK (*20—guitar*)   *Tradition*   TLP 1005   12″   (*1956*)

The Maid of Amsterdam		The Dying Sailor to His Shipmates
Paddy Doyle's Boots		
Spanish Ladies	689	Old Stormalong
605 Ranzo	637	Sally Brown
471 The Mermaid		Saturday Night at Sea
376 Johnny's Gone to Hilo		Admiral Benbow
655 Shenandoah		Round the Corner
Go Down You Blood Red Roses	280	Greenland Whale Fisheries
742 The Turkish Revelee		Boney Was a Warrior
The Girls Around Cape Horn		Lady Franklin's Lament
	642	Santy Anna

Clayton, Paul: WHALING SONGS AND BALLADS (*14—guitar*)   *Stinson*   SLP #69   10″

Blow Ye Winds	Desolation
A Fitting Out	The Coast of Peru
Whale to the Starboard	Ye Men of Renown

The Sailor's Grave
In Days of Old
The Sailorman's Alphabet
The Bark Gay Head

280   The Greenland Fishery
618   Rolling Home
        Off to Sea Once More
        The Wings of a Goney

Cooper, Clarence: GOIN' DOWN THE ROAD (9—guitar)   Elektra
EKL-27   10"

636   St. James Infirmary
        Water-boy
193   Erie Canal
677   Motherless Child
        Old Kentucky

101   Careless Love
        Go Where I Send You
        Darlin'
254   Goin' Down the Road Feelin'
        Bad

Cotton, Elizabeth: NEGRO FOLK SONGS AND TUNES (14—guitar, banjo)
Folkways   FG 3526   12"   (1958)

        Wilson Rag
        Freight Train
254   Goin' Down the Road Feeling
        Bad
        I Don't Love Nobody
        Ain't Got No Honey Baby Now
        Honey Babe Your Papa Cares
        for You
        Vastopol

533   Here Old Rattler
        Sun Done Gone
        Oh Babe It Ain't No Lie
        Sweet Bye and Bye
        Spanish Flang Dang
        When I Get Home
        What a Friend We Have in
        Jesus

Creswell, Grace: TRAGIC BALLADS (12—autoharp, guitar)   Rebel Records
411   12"   (1959)

451   Lord Randall
        Ra Re
152   Queen Jane
        Rose Condoley
188   Edward
        Mary Hamilton

727   The Three Ravens
        Red Bud's Blood
        George Campbell
369   John Henry
285   Gypsy Davey
        Scarborough Fair

Cruz, Señor Alonzo: MEXICAN LOVE SONGS, by the BLIND TROUBA-
DOUR OF OAXACA (13—guitar)   Cook Laboratories   5019   12"

        Doce Cascabeles (riding song)
        Small Girl, Full of Fire
        Pretty Bird—Do Me a Favor
        Far Away from My Land of
        Sunshine
        From Her Window She Bids Me
        Sing
        Again to Have Your Kisses

        Bright Morning Star
        Who Will It Be Who Will Love
        Me?
        The Girls in San Marcos
        Susanna Is Pretty
        Green Eyes
        Bewitching Rose
        La Llorona

Cuevas, Lolita: HAITIAN FOLK SONGS (8—guitar by Frantz Casseus)
Folkways   FW 6811 (FP811)   10"   (1953)

        Haiti
        Chouchounne
        Harvest Song
        Nan Guinan

        Lullaby
        Angelique, O
        Little Bird
        Sobo

Darling, Erik: (FOLKSONGS) (*13—banjo*)   *Elektra   EKL-154*

Salty Dog
In the Evening
J. C. Holmes
Cumberland Mountain Bear   65
    Chase
Oh What a Beautiful City
588   Pretty Polly
Paul and Silas

Hard Luck Blues
Banjo Medley
Swannanoa Tunnel
Boll Weevil
Let Me Fly
Candy Man

Davis, Blind Gary: THE SINGING REVEREND (*8—mouth harp acc. Sonny
        Terry*)   *Stinson   SLP #56   10"*

I Can't Make the Journey by
    Myself
Oh, What a Beautiful City
Jesus Met the Woman at the
    Well

You've Got to Move
Bad Company Brought Me Here
Motherless Children
Say No to the Devil
Death Is Riding Every Day

Davis, Ellabelle: RECITAL OF NEGRO SPIRITUALS (*9—piano, orch.*)
        London   LS 182   10"   (1950)

504   Nobody Knows the Trouble I've
        Seen
    Good News
    On Ma Journey   568
    I'm Travelling to the Grave   784

My Soul's Been Anchored in the
    Lord
I Stood on de Ribber Ob Jordan
Plenty Good Room
Were You There?
Oh What a Beautiful City

Decormier, Bob and Louise: BALLADS AND FOLKSONGS (*10—guitar*)
        Stinson   SLP #68   10"

Hi Ro Jerum
Walkin' and A-Talkin'
My Old Man   144
232   Missy Mouse
    Par un Matin

Sam Hall
Buffalo Boy
Cuckoo
French Partisan Song
Far from My Darlin'

Decormier, Bob and Louise: CATSKILL MOUNTAIN FOLK SONGS (*10—
        guitar*)   *Stinson   SLP #72   10"*

I Walked the Road Again   224
My Love Is Like a Dewdrop
The Knickerbocker Line
The Bonny Laboring Boy
Will You Go Out West
The Rock Island Line

The Foggy Dew
The Cordwood Cutter
Last Winter Was a Hard One
Friends and Neighbors

Decormier, Bob and Louise: SONGS CHILDREN SING IN ITALY (*sung in
        English and Italian*) (*16*)   *Judson Records   J-3025   12"*

The Band in the Square
One Day My Mother Went to
    Market
The Ball Keeps on Rolling
The Scissors Grinder

The Spider and the Cricket
The Ambassadors
Mira la Don Don Della
Bella Bimba
Come Little Children

My Castle
Run Little Pony
Ring-a-Ring-Around-O
Big Peas, Little Peas

Mother Villiana
The Goat
The Doll

DEEP SEA BALLADS and SOD BUSTER BALLADS   *Commodore*
Com. DL-30002   12"
(song titles not available)

Deller, Alfred: THE HOLLY AND THE IVY (*Christmas Carols of Old England*)
(23—*lute, recorder*)   *Vanguard*   *VRS-499*   12"   (1956)

Pat-a-pan
We Three Kings of Orient Are
I Saw Three Ships Come Sailing
It Came Upon the Midnight
  Clear
Good King Wenceslas
Once in Royal David's City
Rocking
The First Nowell
God Rest Ye Merry Gentlemen
Wither's Rocking Hymn
Silent Night

Wassail Song
Boar's Head Carol
Song of the Nuns of Chester
Past Three O'Clock
Lullay My Liking
Adam Lay Ybounden
Herrick's Carol
Angelus ad Virginem
The Holly and the Ivy
O Little One Sweet
Winter Rose
In Dulce Jubilo

Deller, Alfred: THE THREE RAVENS, English Folk Songs   (17—*lute*)
Vanguard   *VRS-479*   12"

727 Three Ravens
144 The Cuckoo
     How Should I Your True Love   36
       Know   763
     Sweet Nightingale
     I Will Give My Love an Apple
     The Oak and the Ash
253 Go from My Window
     King Henry   281

Coventry Carol
Wind and the Rain, Heigh Ho!
Barbara Allen
Waly, Waly
Down in Yon Forest
Matthew, Mark, Luke & John
A Toye
The Tailor and the Mouse
Greensleaves

Deller, Alfred: WRAGGLE TAGGLE GYPSIES (14—*lute, guitar*)
Vanguard   *VRS-1001*   12"

451 Lord Randall
     Sweet Jane
     Wraggle Taggle Gypsies
232 Frog and the Mouse
     Seeds of Love
     Flowers in the Valley
     Near London Town

804 O Who's Going to Shoe Your
       Pretty Little Foot
     Searching for Lambs
     Sweet England
     Blow Away the Morning Dew
     Dabbling in the Dew
     Strawberry Fair
     Just As the Tide Was Flowing

Donnegan, Lonnie: AN ENGLISHMAN SINGS AMERICAN FOLK SONGS
(11)   *Mercury*   MG20229   12"

760 Wabash Cannonball
     How Long, How Long Blues

825 The Wreck of the Old 97
     Ramblin' Man

230 Frankie and Johnny   I Shall Not Be Moved

230	Frankie and Johnny		I Shall Not Be Moved
	Don't You Rock Me Daddy-O		I'm Alabammy Bound
	Nobody's Child	595	Railroad Bill
			Old Riley

Driftwood, Jimmy: * NEWLY DISCOVERED EARLY AMERICAN FOLK
    SONGS (*11—guitar, bass, "picking bow"*)   *RCA Victor*   *LPM-1635*
                        12"   (*1958*)

	Battle of New Orleans		Pretty Mary
	Unfortunate Man		Sailor Man
	Fair Rosamond's Bower		Zelma Lee
675	Soldier's Joy	602	Rattlesnake Song
	Country Boy	526	Old Joe Clark
	I'm Too Young to Marry		

Dunbar, Max: SONGS AND BALLADS OF THE SCOTTISH WARS (1290-
    1745)   (*17—guitar*)   *Folkways*   *FW 3006*   *12"*

	Gude Wallace	The Wee, Wee German Lairdie
451	Lord Randal	Will Ye Go to Sheriffmuir?
	The Battle of Otterbourne	Bonnie George Campbell
	The Battle of Harlow	Kinmont Willie
	The Flowers o' the Forest	Awa', Whigs, Awa'
	The Bonny Earl of Moray	Bonnie Dundee
	Hughie Graham	Three Good Fellows
	The Bonnie House of Airlie	Johnnie Cope
	The Battle of Bothwell Bridge	

Duncan, Todd: SPIRITUALS   *Allegro*   *ALG-3022*   *12"*
       (song titles not available)

Dyer-Bennet, Richard: BALLADS   *Remington*   *Rem. 199-34*   *12"*
       (song titles not available)

Dyer-Bennet, Richard: BALLADS (*6—guitar*)   *Stinson*   *SLP # 35*   *10"*

36	Barbara Allen	369	John Henry
318	I Once Loved a Girl		Gently Johnny My Jingalo
727	The Three Ravens		Spanish Is a Loving Tongue

Dyer-Bennet, Richard: CONCERT (*10—guitar*)   *Stinson*   *SLP #61*   *10"*

	Phyllis and Her Mother	Jan Hinnerk
516	Old Bangum	The Three Rogues
508	Oh No John	Lincolnshire Poachers
	The Leprechaun	Cockle Shells
451	Lord Randall	
	The Ghost of Basel	

    * In mid-1959, RCA Victor released a new Jimmy Driftwood record (LPM
1994) titled JIMMY DRIFTWOOD AND THE WILDERNESS ROAD.

Dyer-Bennet, Richard: (FOLK SONGS) (9—guitar)   Decca   DLP 5046
                                        10"   (1949)

159	The Devil and the Farmer's Wife	695	Swapping Song
	Eggs and Marrowbone		The Old Maid
261	The Willow Tree		Early One Morning
758	Villikens and His Dinah	281	Greensleeves
			Oh Sally My Dear

Dyer-Bennet, Richard: MORE SONGS BY THE 20th CENTURY MINSTREL
            (12—guitar)   Stinson   SLP #60   10"

	The Three Tailors	The Lass from the Low Country
	Song of Reproach	The Charlestown Merchant
119	Colorado Trail	Moonrise
593	Quaker Lover	Secret Love
	Come All Ye	Blue Mountain Lake
	Where to?	Early One Morning

Dyer-Bennet, Richard: (SONGS) (16—guitar)   Dyer-Bennet   RD-B 1
                                    12"   (1955)

	Oft in the Stilly Night	14	So We'll Go No More A-Roving
	Molly Brannigan		Phyllis and Her Mother
	Down by the Sally Gardens		The Joys of Love
	The Bold Fenian Men	569	I'm a Poor Boy
	Three Fishers		Pull Off Your Old Coat
	The Bonnie Earl of Morey	172	Down in the Valley
	Fine Flowers in the Valley		Pedro
	The Vicar of Bray	170	The Lonesome Valley

Dyer-Bennet, Richard: (SONGS) (13—guitar)   Dyer-Bennet   DYB 2000
                                    12"   (1956?)

803	Cock Robin	24	The Bailiff's Daughter of Isling-
	Blow the Candles Out		ton
	Corn Rigs Are Bonnie		Veillée de Noël
	The Garden Where the Praties Grow		Jan Hinnerk
			Woman! Go Home
	Cockleshells		Eggs and Marrowbone
	The Beggarman	742	The Turkish Reverie
	Two Maids Went Milking		

Dyer-Bennet, Richard: (SONGS) (13—guitar) Dyer-Bennet DYB 3000 12"

	The Lady's Policy	399	The Lady Who Loved a Swine
165	Dinah and Villikens		Lilli Burlero
	Fain Would I Wed		The Beloved Kitten
	Willie Taylor	695	The Swapping Song
	Charlie Is My Darling	304	The House Carpenter
	Spottlied Auf Napoleons Rück-	250	Go Down, Moses
	zug Aus Russland 1812		
	The Lass from the Low Country		

Dyer-Bennet, Richard: (SONGS) (*14–guitar*)   *Dyer-Bennet   RD-B 4*
12″   (1957)

	A May Day Carol	727	The Three Ra'ens
	The Rising of the Moon		Song of Reproach
	The Kerry Recruit		Jag vill ga vall
	Searching for Lambs		The Three Tailors
	The Bonnets of Bonnie Dundee		The Swagman
	The Spanish Lady in Dublin	224	The Foggy, Foggy Dew
	City	228	The Fox
		175	Drill, Ye Tarriers, Drill

Dyer-Bennet, Richard: (SONGS) (*12–guitar*)   *Dyer-Bennet   DYB 5000*
12″   (1958)

281	Greensleeves	260	Golden Vanity
451	Lord Randal	593	Quaker Lover
	Westryn Wind	369	John Henry
	Venezuela		Brothers
	Spanish Is the Lovin' Tongue	319	I Ride an Old Paint
36	Barbara Allen		
	White Lily		

Dyer-Bennet, Richard: SONGS WITH YOUNG PEOPLE IN MIND
(*17–guitar*)   *Dyer-Bennet   DYB 6000*   12″   (1958)

	Leprechaun		The Keeper Did a Shooting Go
	Piper of Dundee		Little Pigs
	Three Jolly Rogues of Lynn	233	Frog Went a-Courting
	John Peel	252	Go Tell Aunt Rhodie
	The Tailor and the Mouse	554	One Morning in May
	Come All Ye	746	Two Sisters
273	Green Corn	724	Three Crows
	Hole in the Bottom of the Sea	516	Old Bangum
	Buckeye Jim		

Dyer-Bennet, Richard: THE 20th CENTURY MINSTREL (*11–guitar*)
Stinson   SLP #2   10″

	Blow the Candles Out	As I Was Going to Ballynure
	Venezuela	Westron Wynde
232	The Frog and the Mouse	John Peel
	Little Pigs	Brigg Fair
482	Molly Malone	Eddystone Light
	Two Maidens Went Milking	
	One Day	

Elliott, Jack: JACK TAKES THE FLOOR (*10–banjo, guitar*)   *Topic Records*
10 T 15   10″   (1958)

	San Francisco Bay	268	Grey Goose
	Ol' Riley		Mule Skinner's Blues
65	Boll Weevil	166	Dink Song
	Bed Bug Blues		Cocaine
	New York Town		
	Black Baby		

Elliott, Jack and Derroll Adams: THE RAMBLING BOYS (*10—banjo, guitar*)
Topic Records   10 T 14   10″   (1958)

599	Rich and Rambling Boys	186	East Virginia Blues
88	Buffalo Skinners		The Old Bachelor
	Wish I Was a Rock		Danville Girl
685	State of Arkansas	356	The Death of Mr. Garfield
	Mother's Not Dead		Roll on Buddy

English, Logan: THE DAYS OF '49 (*Songs of the Gold Rush*) (*13—guitar*)
Folkways   FH 5255   12″

790	What Was Your Name in the States		Life in California
			I Often Think of Writing Home
631	Sacramento	151	The Days of '49
	A Ripping Trip		He's the Man for Me
696	Sweet Betsy from Pike		Clementine
	Crossing the Plains		California Bloomer
	Prospecting Dream		Sacramento Gals

English, Logan: GAMBLING SONGS (*15—guitar*)   Riverside
RLP 12-643   12″

627	The Roving Gambler	352	Jack O' Diamonds
	The Texas Gambler	368	John Hardy
	My Father Was a Gambler		My True Love Is a Gambler
688	Stewball	682	Stackerlee
	The California Gambler	420	Little Brown Bulls
	Duncan and Brady		The Coon-Can Game
	Spotty and Doodie		A Hearty Good Fellow
	I Got Mine		

English, Logan: KENTUCKY BALLADS (*12—guitar*)   Folkways
FA 2136   10″

516	Bangum and the Boar	Bruton Town
186	East Virginia	Old Doc Jones
149	Little Cory	Love Henry
	Bold Robington's Courtship	The Lady and the Glove
811	Wild Bill Jones	Durant Jail
758	William and Dinah	
	A Railroader for Me	

Ennis, Seamus: THE BONNY BUNCH OF ROSES (*19—Uileann pipes, tin whistle*)   Tradition   TLP 1013   12″

	The Little Bench of Rushes		First House in Connaught
	The Kerry Recruit		Slow Pipe Tune
	Copperplate Reel		Thrush in the Straw
213	Farmer's Curst Wife	777	Wealthy Squire
	Fairy Boy		Hogan's Favorite
	Cuckoo's Hornpipe		Connaught Man's Rambles
70	Bonny Bunch of Roses		When the Cock Crows
	Woman's Lament in Battle		It Is Day
	Lark in the Morning		Marrowbones
	Will You Come with Me Over the Mountains		

Eskin, Sam: SHANTY MEN (*Songs of the Sailormen and Lumbermen*)
(*10—guitar*)   Folkways   FA 2019 (*FP 19*)   10″

650	Shanty-man's Life		Heave Away
	River Driver's Song		Boney
420	The Little Brown Bulls	732	Down to Hilo
611	The Rio Grande		The Sailor Loves Paddy Doyle
	Bulgine Run		A Hundred Years Ago

Eskin, Sam: SONGS OF ALL TIMES (*13—guitar*)   Cook Laboratories
1020   10″

803	Who Killed Cock Robin?	276	Green Grow the Lilacs
	The Tailor and the Crow	712	Texas Rangers
	My Children Are Laughing Be-		Cryderville Jail
	hind My Back	369	John Henry
617	Roll the Old Chariot	238	The Gambler
	You Can Dig My Grave	213	The Farmer's Curst Wife
465	Mary and Martha		The 24th of February

Faier, Billy: THE ART OF THE FIVE-STRING BANJO (*16*)   Riverside
RLP 12-813   12″

	The Rakes of Mallow		Lute Song for Five-String Banjo
	H'Kotsrim		Farewell Blues
273	Green Corn		Dance of a Spanish Fly
	Irish Medley		Three Jolly Rogues
	Yugoslav Kolo		Sailor's Hornpipe
298	High Barbary		The Wren Song
	Spanish Fandango		Greek Dance
	The Last of Callahan	156	The Darby Ram

Faye, Frances: SINGS FOLK SONGS (—orch.)   Bethlehem   BCP 6017
12″   (*1957*)
(song titles not available)

Ferrier, Kathleen: FOLK SONGS (*18—piano*) *   London   5411   (LS 538
and LS 48 combined)   12″

	Ye Banks and Braes		I Will Walk with My Love
	Now Sleeps the Crimson Petal		Have You Seen but a Whyte
	Over the Mountains		Lillie Grow
	Drink to Me Only with Thine		The Stuttering Lovers
	Eyes		My Bonny Lad
	The Fair House of Joy		The Keel Row
763	O Waly, Waly		Blow the Wind Southerly
	I Have a Bonnet Trimmed with		Willow, Willow
	Blue		Down by the Sally Gardens
44	My Boy Willie		The Lover's Curse
	I Know Where I'm Going		

* This is the only recorded collection of folksongs listed in "Critics' Choice 1948-1957—A Ten Year Survey," compiled by George Jelinek in the *Saturday Review*, June 28, 1958. (About 150 recordings were listed in all.)

Ford, "Tennessee" Ernie: SPIRITUALS (*12—orch., chorus*)
Capitol   T 818   12"

Just a Closer Walk with Thee	I Know the Lord Laid His
I Want to Be Ready	Hands on Me
Take My Hand, Precious Lord	He'll Understand and Say Well
Stand by Me	Done
When God Dips His Love in 773	Wayfaring Pilgrim
My Heart 784	Were You There?
Get on Board, Little Children	Peace in the Valley
Noah Found Grace in the Eyes	
of the Lord	

Ford, "Tennessee" Ernie: THIS LUSTY LAND (*12*)
Capitol   Cap T-700   12"

369 John Henry	804 Who Will Shoe Your Pretty
737 Trouble in Mind	Little Foot
Gaily the Troubadour	313 I Gave My Love a Cherry
The Last Letter	706 Nine Pound Hammer
Dark As a Dungeon	Chicken Road
209 False Hearted Girl	627 The Rovin' Gambler
	In the Pines

Foster, Pat (and Dick Weissman): DOCUMENTARY TALKING BLUES
(*14—banjo, guitar*)   Counterpoint   CPT-550
(song titles not available)

Foster, Pat (with Dick Weissman): GOLD IN CALIFORNIA (*Songs of the '49 Gold Rush*) (*13*)   Riverside   RLP 12-654   12"

Far California	The Fools of '49
696 Sweet Betsy from Pike	California Boy
Then Hurrah for Home	Striking a Lead
Sweet Jane	A Rival of the Greenhorn
Oh, California	The Miners' Meeting
Windham	182 The Dying Californian
790 What Was Your Name in the	
States	

Fuller, Jesse: FRISCO BOUND (*8—guitar*)   Cavalier   Cav 5006
10"   (*1955*)

Leavin' Memphis, Frisco Bound	Motherless Children
Got a Date, at Half Past Eight	As Long As I Can Feel the Spirit
Hump in My Back	8 Amazing Grace
Flavor in My Cream	Hark from the Tomb

Fuller, Jesse: WORK SONGS, BLUES, SPIRITUALS (*10—guitar, harmonica, kazoo, drums, fotdella*)   Good Time Jazz   L-12031   12"   (*1958*)

706 Take This Hammer	By and By
413 Linin' Up the Track	Fingerbuster
I'm Gonna Meet My Lovin' 682	Stagolee
Mother	99 Years
Tiger Rag	Hesitation Blues
Memphis Boogie	

Fuller, Jesse: WORKING ON THE RAILROAD (*6—guitar*)   *World Song*
    EG-10-027   10"

Railroad Work Song
413 Lining Up the Tracks
369 John Henry
Railroad Blues

San Francisco Bay Blues
Hangin' Round a Skin Game

Gainer, Patrick: FOLK SONGS OF THE ALLEGHENY MOUNTAINS
    (*16—rebec or dulcimer*)   *Folk Heritage Recording*   DB 2122-3   12"

	The Dear Companion	674	Soldier, Will You Marry Me?
374	Johnny Randal (Lord Randal)	588	Pretty Polly
188	Edward		What Shall I Give to Thee
108	The Cherry Tree Carol		The Rebec (instr.)
36	Barbara Allen	213	The Farmer's Curst Wife
194	On Erin's Green Shore	283	The Groundhog Song
	The Rejected Lover	115	Cindy
	A Few More Years	680	Sourwood Mountain

Galvin, Patrick: IRISH DRINKING SONGS (*16"*)   *Riverside*
    RLP 12-604   12"

A Sup of Good Whiskey
Mush Mush
Lanigan's Ball
Toast to Ireland
The Rakes of Mallow
The Cruiskeen Lawn
Garryowen
Mick McGilligan's Daughter
Finnegan's Wake

262 The Real Old Mountain Dew
Eyed Reilly
Barry of Macroom
484 The Moonshiner
Flowing Bumpers
Master McGrath
The Parting Glass

Galvin, Patrick: IRISH HUMOR SONGS (*14—banjo, guitar*)   *Riverside*
    RLP 12-616   12"

Lanty Leary
The Irish Rover
Brian O'Linn
Bold Thady Quill
The Balbally Farmer
The Peeler and the Goat
Square-Toed Boots

Song of the Taxes
Haste to the Wedding
The Mountjoy Hotel
Football Crazy
King Billy
The Cork Leg
The Humor Is on Me Now

Galvin, Patrick: IRISH LOVE SONGS (*15*)   *Riverside*   RLP 12-608   12"

I Know Where I'm Going
My Love Came to Dublin
97 Canada Iho
Brian Og and Molly Ban
The Bonny Boy
The Banks of the Roses
The Wind That Shakes the
    Barley
'Tis Pretty to Be in Ballinderry

The Maid of the Sweet Brown
    Knowe
663 Shule Aroon
I Know My Love
The Green Bushes
The Lark in the Clear Air
The Jackets of Green
The Royal Blackbird

Galvin, Patrick: IRISH REBEL SONGS, Vol. I (*10—guitar, banjo*)   *Stinson*
SLP #83   10"

The Rising of the Moon
Boulavogue
The Croppy Boy
Kelly from Killane
The Boys of Wexford

The Men of the West
Henry Joy McCracken
Dunlavin Green
The Memory of the Dead
Bold Robert Emmet

Galvin, Patrick: IRISH REBEL SONGS, Vol. II (*9—guitar, banjo*)   *Stinson*
SLP #84   10"

O'Donnell Abu
Clare's Dragoons
A Nation Once Again
The Fair at Turloughmore
The Bold Fenian Men

The Fenian Man o' War
God Save Ireland
The Smashing of the Van
Come to the Bower

Galvin, Patrick: IRISH REBEL BALLADS, Vol. III (*10—banjo, guitar*)
Stinson   SLP #85   10"

My Old Howth Gun
Bachelor's Walk
The Tri-Color Ribbon
676   The Soldier's Song
Lonely Banna Strand

224   The Foggy Dew
387   Kevin Barry
Whack Fol the Diddle
Song of Terence McSwiney
Johnson's Motor Car

Galvin, Patrick: IRISH STREET SONGS (*14*)   *Riverside*   RLP 12-613   12"

Courting in the Kitchen
455   The Lowlands of Holland
The Limerick Rake
The Dublin Murder Ballad
Donnelly and Cooper
The Old Orange Flute
757   Van Dieman's Land
The Hackler from Grouse Hall

Whiskey in the Jar
The Rocks of Baun
Boston City
The Enniskillen Dragoon
Johnny, I Hardly Knew Ye
481   Young Molly Ban

Gardell, Tony: A-ROVING WITH TONY GARDELL (*21 sea chanties*)
Cavalier   CVLP-6005   12"   (*1958*)
(song titles not available)

Gary, Sam: SPIRITUALS AND WORKSONGS   *Transition*
TRLP F 1   (*1956*)
(song titles not available)

Gibson, Bob: CARNEGIE CONCERT (*15*)   *Riverside*   RLP 12-816   12"

Sail Away, Lady
Alberta
Push Boat
193   The Erie Canal
370   John Riley
There Once Was a Poor Young
    Man
792   When I Was Single
You Must Come in at the Door

Michael, Row the Boat Ashore
Marry a Texas Girl
Day-O
Go Down to Bimini
Wheel-a Matilda
Good News
Mighty Day

Gibson, Bob: FOLKSONGS OF OHIO (*10—banjo, guitar*)   *Stinson*
SLP #76   10″

	Down in Sky Town	Over in the Meadow
	Katey Morey	Workin' on a Pushboat
721	There Was an Old Woman	216 Father Grumble
	Ohio River	[3 others]

Gibson, Bob: I COME FOR TO SING (*16*)   *Riverside   RLP 12-806   12″*

369	John Henry	175	Drill, Ye Tarriers
	Dance, Boatman, Dance		I'm Gonna Leave Old Texas
	Abilene	424	Mattie Groves
	Katie Morey		The Squirrel
453	Lost Jimmie Whelan		I Come for to Sing
	Ol' Bill	412	The Lily of the West
	To Morrow	681	Springfield Mountain
706	Take This Hammer		
	Money Is King		

Gibson, Bob: OFFBEAT FOLK SONGS (*18—banjo*)   *Riverside*
RLP 12-802   12″

	Noah	The Pig and the Inebriate
	Mighty Day	Bahaman Lullaby
	Snake Cure	A Maid Went to Dublin
303	The Horse Named Bill	Block Island Reel
	Pretty Boy	The Rejected Lover
	What Are Little Folks Made of	Delia
	Linstead Market	282 Greenwood Side
	The Abdication	Lula Girl
	Chickens	Andalucian Dance

Gilkyson, Terry: FOLK SONGS (*9—guitar*)   *Decca   DL 5263   10″   (1950)*

	I Know Where I'm Going	129	Cottoneyed Joe
51	Black Is the Color	44	Billy Boy
360	Jennie Jenkins	53	Blackeyed Susie
627	Roving Gambler	65	Boll Weevil
138	The Story of the Creation		

Gilkyson, Terry: GOLDEN MINUTES OF FOLK MUSIC (*8—guitar*)
Decca   DL-5457   10″

	Golden Minute	Sparrow Grass and Brown Bread
	Mackerel Fleet	Man About Town
285	Gypsy Davey	Lonesome Rider
	Tom Jack	Wait by the Willow

Gilmer, Julia Ann: CADS, BLACKGUARDS AND FALSE TRUE-LOVES
(*14*)   *ABC Paramount   ABC 168   12″*

418	The Little Black Mustache	562	Paper of Pins
335	I'm Sad and I'm Lonely	120	Come All Ye Fair and Tender
590	Pretty Saro		Ladies
253	Go 'Way from My Window	195	Ev'ry Night When the Sun Goes
36	Barbara Allen		Down

451   Lord Randall   281   Greensleeves
      Robin Adair   Wildwood Flower
674   Soldier, Soldier   101   Careless Love

Ginandes, Shep: AMERICAN FOLKSONGS FOR CHILDREN (10—guitar)
                  Elektra   EKL-7   10"   (1953)
719   There Was a Little Tree   804   Who Will Shoe My Little Foot
      I Went Up on the Mountain Top   233   Froggie Went A-Courting
483   The Monkey's Wedding   Oh, But I Won't Have Him
 44   Billie Boy   283   Ground Hog
310   I Bought Me a Cat   The Mare

Ginandes, Shep: BRITISH TRADITIONAL BALLADS IN AMERICA
                  (6—guitar)   Elektra   EKL-4   10"
261   The Golden Willow Tree   451   Lord Randall (Welsh Version)
141   The Cruel Mother   447   Lord Bateman
452   Lord Thomas and Fair Elinore   188   Edward

Ginandes, Shep: FRENCH TRADITIONAL SONGS (11—guitar)   Elektra
                  EKL-9   10"   (1953)
      Chevaliers de la Table Ronde   Les Moines de Saint Bernardin
      V'l'a l'Bon Vent   Le Joueur de Luth
      J'fais Pipi   Ne Pleure Pas, Jeannette
      Jeanneton   Ma Femme Est Morte
      Chanson de Corsaire   Complainte de Mandrin
      Près de la Fontaine

Ginandes, Shep: SINGS FOLKSONGS (16—guitar)   Elektra   EKL-133
                  12"   (1958)
 59   Bolakins   V'la le Bon Vent
744   The Two Brothers   Brizhki
      Miss Bailey   Trois Bateliers
808   The Wife of Usher's Well   Der Rebbe Elimelech
      The Anarchistic Garret   Le Joli Matelot
424   Mattie Groves   Las Mananitas
      Le Cantonnier   395   La Claire Fontaine
      En el Salón   J'fais Pipi

Gitter, Dean: GHOST BALLADS (12)   Riverside   RLP 12-636   12"
      Anne Boleyn   The Suffolk Miracle
      The Phantom Stagecoach   Miss Bailey's Ghost
672   Skin and Bones   The Reaper's Ghost
755   The Unquiet Grave   The Lady Gay
      Finnegan's Wake   453   Lost Jimmie Whelan
703   Sweet William's Ghost
      The Flying Dutchman

Glazer, Joe: SONGS OF JOE HILL (11—guitar)   Folkways
                  FA 2039 (FP39)   10"
      Scissor Bill   The Tramp
103   Casey Jones   Preacher and the Slave
      Mr. Block   There Is Power in the Union

Pie in the Sky
The Rebel Girl
We Will Sing One Song

Joe Hill
Joe Hill's Last Will

Glazer, Tom: OLDEN BALLADS (10–guitar) [and] Dyer-Bennet, Richard: OLDEN BALLADS (8–piano) *Mercury* MG 20007 12"

Glazer:		Dyer-Bennet:	
747	Twelve Days of Christmas	260	The Golden Vanity
	The Sheeling Song		The Lincolnshire Poacher
308	Hush Little Baby	156	The Derby Ram
	Sixteen Come Sunday		Swag Man
281	Green Sleeves	789	What Shall We Do with a
763	Waly Waly		Drunken Sailor?
	Uncle Reuben	304	The House Carpenter
	Blow the Candles Out		The Charleston Merchant
53	Black-Eyed Susie		Hullabaloo Belay
253	Go 'Way from My Window		

Gooding, Cynthia: FAITHFUL LOVERS AND OTHER PHENOMENA (14–guitar, banjo) *Elektra* EKL-107 12"

24	The Bailiff's Daughter		Great Selchie of Shule Skerry
	Lass of the Low Countrie		Lilliburlero
156	The Derby Ram		Down by the Seashore
	My Young Love Said to Me	240	George Collins
	The Dear Companion	496	Naomi Wise
	Lady's Policy	763	Waly, Waly
	All My Trials	108	The Cherry Tree Carol

Gooding, Cynthia: ITALIAN FOLK SONGS (16–guitar) *Elektra* EKL-17 10"

Quanto Spunta lu Sole
M'affaccio alla Finestra
Sul Capello
Non Ti Ricordi
Tenete l'Occhio Nero
Bella Ragazza
Tre Amoru
Peschi Fiorenti

O, Balis Tu, Pieri
Sul Ponte di Bassano
Fior di Bombace
Nina
Ses Tu Benedeta
El Avvelenato
Chitarra Fiorentina
Canto del Carcerato

Gooding, Cynthia: MEXICAN FOLKSONGS (11–guitar) *Elektra* EKL-8 10" (1953)

La Bamba
La Llorona
Lucrecia
El Palo Verde
La Voltereta
El Arreo

Rosita Alvirez
Román Castillo
El Tecolote
General Felipe Angeles
Que Linda Está la Mañana

Gooding, Cynthia: QUEEN OF HEARTS (*Early English Folksongs*) (15–guitar) *Elektra* EKL-131 12"

The Four Marys
I Gave My Love an Apple

746 The Two Sisters
    The Queen of Hearts

Through the Groves
O, Mother, Go and Make My Bed
My Only Jo and Dearie, O
Queen Eleanor's Confession
455 The Lowlands of Holland

Once I Had a Sweetheart
The Green Bushes
Strawberry Fair
The Banks of Green Willow
The Sprig of Thyme
The May-Day Carol

Gooding, Cynthia: THE QUEEN OF HEARTS (*English Folksongs*)
(*12—guitar*)   *Elektra   EKL-11   10"*

The Queen of Hearts
Through the Groves
O, Mother, Go and Make My Bed
My Only Joe and Dearie, O
Queen Eleanor's Confession

455 The Lowlands of Holland
Once I Had a Sweetheart
The Green Bushes
Strawberry Fair
The Banks of Green Willow
The Sprig of Thyme
The May-Day Carol

Gooding, Cynthia: TURKISH AND SPANISH FOLKSONGS (*13—guitar*)
Elektra   EKL-6   10"

Sakarya (Cavalry Song)
Ankaranin Tasina Bak (Prisoners' Chant)
Eminem (Courting Song)
Kâtip (Love Song)
Al Koyun (Shepherd Chant)
Yashi Meral (Mountain Song)

Donde Vas Rey Alfonsito
Tres Moricas
Anda Diciendo
Conde Olinos
Ay, un Galan
Eres Alta y Delgada
La Molinera

Gooding, Cynthia: TURKISH, SPANISH AND MEXICAN FOLKSONGS
(*18—guitar*)   *Elektra   EKL-128   12"*

Sakarya (Cavalry Song)
Ankaranin Tasina Bak (Prisoners' Chant)
Eminem Kâtip
Yashi Meral
Donde Vas Rey Alfonsito
Tres Moricas
Anda Diciendo
Conde Olinos
Eres Alta y Delgada

La Molinera
La Bamba
La Llorona
La Voltereta
Rosita Alvirez
Román Castillo
El Tecolote
General Felipe Angeles
Que Linda Está la Mañana

Gooding, Cynthia and Theodore Bikel: A YOUNG MAN AND A MAID
(*Love Songs of Many Lands*) (*17*)   *Elektra   EKL-109   12"*

Where Does It Lead
Coplas
Parle Moi
Ro'e Vero'a
281 Greensleeves
Hej Pada Pada
Ma Belle
Well Met Pretty Maid

691 Laredo
Sur la Route
A Meidl in di Yoren
As I Roved Out
Mi Jacalito
384 Katherine Jaffrey
La Ballade du Chercheur d'Or
Western Wind
Proschay

Greenway, John: AMERICAN INDUSTRIAL FOLKSONGS (18)   *Riverside*
RLP 12-607   12″

There Is Power in a Union	Hard Times in Coleman's Mines
I Am a Union Woman	A Weaver's Life Is Like an
Hard Times in the Mill	Engine
Dark As a Dungeon	Union Burying Ground
Oh, My God, Those 'Taters	Too Old to Work
The Death of Harry Simms	Dreadful Memories
Farther Along	Mother Jones
Monkey Ward Can't Make a	Chief Aderholt
Monkey Out of Me	Ludlow Massacre
What Shall We Do for the Strik-	Down on Robert's Farm
ing Seamen?	

Greenway, John: THE GREAT AMERICAN BUM (*Hobo and Migratory Worker's Songs*) (19)   *Riverside*   RLP 12-619   12″

	The Great American Bum	41 Big Rock Candy Mountain
	Portland County Jail	Hard Travelin'
	All Around the Water Tank	Dying Hobo
760	The Wabash Cannonball	Jay Gould's Daughter
	Ramblin'	The Lehigh Valley
	The Mild Mannered Man	Tramp, Tramp, Tramp
	Hobo Bill's Last Ride	Acres of Clams
	Bonneville Dam	Hallelujah, I'm a Bum
254	Going Down the Road	The Hobo's Lullaby
	Mysteries of a Hobo's Life	

Grimes, Anne: BALLADS OF OHIO (*20—dulcimer*)
Folkways   FH 5217   12″

	Pleasant Ohio	The Underground Railroad
	Battle of Point Pleasant	My Station's Gonna Be Changed
	Logan's Lament	O Ho! the Copperheads
404	Lass of Roch Royal	The Dying Volunteer
	St. Clair's Defeat	Ohio Guards
	Portsmouth Fellows	Ohio River Blues
	Christ in the Garden	Up on the Housetops
213	The Farmer's Curst Wife	520 Old Dan Tucker
	Girls of Ohio	Boatman's Dance
7	Alphabet Song	
	Darling Nelly Gray	

Guthrie, Woody: SONGS TO GROW ON (*for Mother and Child*) (*Composed, played and sung by W. Guthrie*) (*12—drum, guitar, rattle, tambourine*)
Folkways   FC 7015 (FP715)   10″

480	Mole in the Ground	Little Bat
	Elephant Don't Sleep	Story of the Frog
	The Little Black Bull	Bear Hunt
265	Good Bye Old Paint	226 The Fox
	As I Went Down to Darby	440 Turtle Dove
	Keeper Went A-Hunting	517 Old Blue

Guthrie, Woody: TALKING DUST BOWL (7—guitar)   Folkways
        FA-2011 (FP11)   10"

So Long, It's Been Good to   Blowing Down This Road Feel-
    Know You   ing Bad
Dust Storm Disaster   Dust Bowl Refugee
Talking Dust Bowl Blues   Tom Joad
Dust Can't Kill Me

Guthrie, Woody and Cisco Houston: COWBOY SONGS (8—guitar)   Stinson
        SLP-32   10"

113 Chisholm Trail   238 Gambling Man
 46 Billy the Kid   604 Red River Valley
805 Whoopie Ti Yi Yo   361 Jesse James
     Philadelphia Lawyer
     Ride Around Little Dogies

Guthrie, Woody and Cisco Houston: FOLK SONGS, Vol. I (8—guitar)
        Stinson   SLP #44   10"

285 Gypsy Davy   1 Ain't Gonna Be Treated This
569 Poor Boy   Way
     More Pretty Gals Than One   369 John Henry
     Pretty Boy Floyd   Ranger's Command
                                    88 Buffalo Skinners

Guthrie, Woody and Cisco Houston: MORE SONGS (8—guitar)   Stinson
        SLP #53   10"

     Foggy Mountain Top   90   Bury Me Beneath the Willow
     Take a Whiff on Me   Columbus Stockade
145 Cumberland Gap   260 The Golden Vanity
     Johnny Hard   Badman Lee Brown

Hall, Dickson: OUTLAWS OF THE OLD WEST (12)   MGM   3263   12"

     Joaquin Murietta   Doc Holliday
361 Jesse James   John Wesley Hardin
     Black Bart   641 Sam Bass
     Belle Starr   The Clantons and McLowrys
     The Dalton Brothers   Chief Sitting Bull
 46 Billy the Kid
     Johnny Ringo

Hayes, Roland: CHRISTMAS CAROLS OF THE NATIONS (13—piano)
        Vanguard   VRS-7016   10"

Sleep My Little One   O Come All Ye Faithful
D'Où Viens-Tu, Bergère   Der Heilige Joseph Singt
'Twas in the Moon of Winter-   The Glory Manger
    time   Three Wise Men to Jerusalem
Wiegenlied   Came
O Elijah, Prophet Great   Go Tell It on the Mountain
King Herod and the Cock   Stille Nacht, Heilige Nacht
The First Noël

Hayes, Roland: LIFE OF CHRIST IN FOLK SONG (13—piano)   *Vanguard*
VRS-462   12"   (1954)

Prepare Me One Body	568 Plenty Good Room
Three Wise Men to Jerusalem	The Last Supper
Came	Who Betrayed My Lord?
Lit'l Boy	They Led My Lord Away
Live a-Humble	295 He Never Said a Mumberlin
They Raised Poor Lazarus	Word
Hear the Lambs a-Cryin'	Did You Hear When Jesus Rose?
	784 Were You There?

Hayes, Roland: MY SONGS, AFRAMERICAN RELIGIOUS FOLK-SONGS
(17—piano)   *Vanguard*   VRS-494   12"

I'm Make Me a Man	You Must Come In By and
Let My People Go!	Through the Lamb
155 Deep River	686 Steal Away
422 Little David Play on Your Harp	Going Up to Heaven
179 Dry Bones	You're Tired, Child
Give-A Way, Jordan	Lord, Is This Heaven
Two Wings	163 Didn't My Lord Deliver Daniel?
A Witness	336 I'm Troubled
In-A Dat Mornin'	Heaven

Hayes, Roland: RECITAL (24—piano) A440 *Records* AC-1203 12" (1953)
(song titles not available)

Hemsworth, Wade: CANADIAN NORTHWOODS BALLADS (8—guitar)
Folkways   FW 6821 (FP821)   10"

Ye Girls of Old Ontario	355 Jam at Gerry's Rocks
The Wild Goose	Voilà le Bon Vent
Peter Rambly	The Shining Birch Tree
The Bride's Lament	Enoyons d'l'Avant

Hillel and Aviva: * LAND OF MILK AND HONEY (16) (Israeli Songs)
Riverside   RLP 12-803   12"

To the Spring	My Field
My Beloved Is from the Vine-	Not Day and Not Night
yards of Ain-Gedi	The Field in the Valley
The Shepherd's Pipe	Who Comes to Meet Me?
On the Mountains	David Among the Roses
The Cowboys from Lachish	Shepherd's Song
Twilight	The Sheep Bells
Caravan in the Mountains	She Drives Me Crazy
The Land of Milk and Honey	

* In 1959, Elektra issued A CONCERT WITH HILLEL AND AVIVA
(EKL-171).

Hilton, L. M.: MORMON FOLK SONGS (12)   *Folkways*
                    FA 2036 (FP 36)   10"

Hand Cart Song
Whoa Ha! Buck and Jerry Boy
Sago Lily
Sea Gulls and Crickets
Echo Canyon Song
Zack the Mormon Engineer

O Babylon!
Come Ye Saints
292 Hard Times Come Again No
    More
Round the Camp Fire
Courage to Say No
What's the Use of Repining

Hinton, Sam: A FAMILY TREE OF FOLK SONGS (20—*guitar*)   *Decca*
                    DL 8418   12"

The Red Herring
The Herring Song
The Old Sow
The Carrion Crow
The Farmer and the Crow
663 Shule Agra
Johnny Has Gone for a Soldier
Dis cum Bibble
Clear the Track
455 Lowlands (English)
Lowlands (American)

115 Cindy
Jim the Roper
Willy the Weeper
715 Lonesome Valley
Where Is Old Elijah?
Crucifixion
Hi Ho Jerum
The Piper o' Dundee
Talking Dustbowl Blues

Hinton, Sam: THE REAL McCOY (*Irish Folk Songs*) (20—*guitar*)   *Decca*
                    DL-8579   12"

The Wren
We Have Brought the Summer
    In
The Fox's Conversation
An Maidrin Ruadh
Rinnce Pilib an Cheoil
Lilliburlero
The Old Man Rockin' the Cradle
Arthur McBride
The Smashing of the Ban
Cruiskeen Lawn

262 The Real Old Mountain Dew
The Son of a Gambolier
The Eagle's Whistle
Balinderry
The Shepherd's Lamb
Father O'Flynn
The Famine Song
She Said the Same to Me
Paddy on the Railroad
No Irish Need Apply

Hinton, Sam: SINGING ACROSS THE LAND (21—*guitar*)   *Decca*
                    DL 8108   12"

230 Frankie and Johnny
Gambler's Blues
900 Miles
Bryan O'Lynn
213 Farmer's Curst Wife
558 Our Goodman
280 Greenland Fishery
Jolly Old Roger
375 Johnny Sands
681 Springfield Mountain
Old Boastun Was Dead

Tell Old Bill
Travelin' Man Blues
Doney Gal
Echo Canyon
Night Herder's Song
Sierra Peaks
Barnyard Song
Buffalo Boy
283 Ground Hog
526 Old Joe Clark

Holt, Will: SONGS AND BALLADS (9–*guitar*)   *Stinson   SLP 64   10"*
Bye-Bye   588   Pretty Polly
The Ash Grove   The Haying Song
Three Jovial Huntsmen   The Lass of Galilee
691 The Streets of Laredo
Miss Bailey's Ghost
Kesailta

Holt, Will: WORLD OF WILL HOLT (12–*guitar*)   *Coral   CRL 57114*
                    12"   (1957)
M.T.A.   Wraggle Taggle Gypsies
Easy Rider   Lazy Afternoon
Raspberries, Strawberries   Delia Gone
715 Lonesome Valley   283 Ground Hog
Two Calypsos   Clementine
Riflemen of Bennington   Daddy Roll 'Em

House, Wallace: BALLADS OF THE REVOLUTION (1767-1775) (11–*lute*)
        Folkways   FH 2151 (FP48/1)   10"
The World Turned Upside   Yankee Doodle
Down   How Happy the Soldier
The Liberty Song   Death of Warren
Free America   Pennsylvania Song
What Court Hath Old England   Bunker Hill
Maryland Resolves   34   Banks of the Dee

House, Wallace: BALLADS OF THE REVOLUTION (1776-1781) (8–*lute*)
        Folkways   FH 2152 (FP48/2)   10"
The Dying Sergeant   The Yankee Man of War
The British Light Infantry   (Mad) Anthony Wayne
Chester   Sergeant Champe
The Toast   Cornwallis Burgoyned

House, Wallace: BALLADS OF THE WAR OF 1812, Vol. I (13–*lute*)
        Folkways   FA 2163 (FP48/3)   10"
Hail! Columbia   Come All Ye Canadians
Eighth Day of November   Constitution and Guerriere
Song of the Vermonters   Hornet and Peacock
Johnny Has Gone for a Soldier   Shannon and Chespeake
Jefferson and Liberty   Perry's Victory
Benny Havens   James Bird
O! Hey Betty Martin

House, Wallace: BALLADS OF THE WAR OF 1812, Vol. 2 (12–*lute*)
        Folkways   FA 2164 (FP48/4)   10"
Charge the Can Cheerily!   676 The Soldier's Song
Ye Parliaments of England   306 Hunters of Kentucky
Battle of Stonnington   Jackson Campaign Song
Our Patriotic Diggers   Harrison Campaign Song
Star Spangled Banner   Old England Forty Years Ago
The Yankee Volunteers   Hail African Band!

House, Wallace: ENGLISH FOLK SONGS (*Sung in dialect, from 16 counties*) (*16—guitar*)   *Folkways*   FW 6823 (*FP823*)   *10"*

I'm Seventeen Cum Sunday
On Ilkley Moor
The Lover's Departure
The Poachers of Lincolnshire
Old Farmer Buck
Because I Were Shy
Young Herchard o' Taunton   156
Dean
Tally Ho! My Fine Sportsmen

Gently Johnny, My Jingalo
The Eddystone Light
Turmut Hoeing
Jack Hall
Be Kind to Me Dowter
The Barkshire Tragedy
The Derby Tup
Jan's Courtship

House, Wallace: ROBIN HOOD BALLADS (*10—lute*)   *Folkways*
FW 6839 (*FP839*)   *10"*

True Tale of Robin Hood
Robin Hood and Little John
Curtail Fryer
The Tanner
The Ranger

Three Squires
Maid Marian
Jolly Pinder
Morris
Death and Burial

House, Wallace: SONGS OF THE IRISH REBELLION OF 1798 (*12—lute*)
Folkways   FW 3002   *12"*

Bold McDermott Roe
The Shan Van Vocht
The Rising of the Moon
Dunlavin Green
Father Murphy
Sweet Country Wexford

The Bold Belfast Shoemaker
General Munroe
Billy Byrne of Ballymanus
The Rambler from Clare
The Wearing of the Green
Bold Robert Emmet

Houston, Cisco: COWBOY BALLADS (*9—guitar*)   *Folkways*
FA 2022 (*FP22*)   *10"*   (*1952*)

113   Chisholm Trail
162   Diamond Joe
319   I Ride an Old Paint
423   Little Joe, the Wrangler
183   The Dying Cowboy

688   Stewball
737   Trouble in My Mind
696   Sweet Betsy from Pike
        Tying a Knot in the Devil's Tail

Houston, Cisco: FOLK SONGS (*13—guitar*)   *Folkways*   FA 2346
12"   (*1958*)

Pat Works on the Railway
Blowing Down That Old Dusty
    Road
175   Drill, Ye Tarriers, Drill
        Dobie Bill
238   Rambling Gambling Man
842   The Zebra Dun
        Old Reilly

Old Howard
Make Me a Bed Right Down on
    Your Floor
65   The Boll Weevil
474   The Midnight Special
636   St. James Infirmary
        Great July Jones

Houston, Cisco: HARD TRAVELIN' (*11—guitar*)   *Folkways*
FA 2042 (FP42)   10"

Hard Travelin'
682   Stagolee
The John B. Sails
The Frozen Logger
440   Turtle Dove
True Love on My Mind

166   Dink's Song
Hound Dog
285   Gypsy Dave
Intoxicated Rat
The Girl in the Wood

Houston, Cisco: 900 MILES AND OTHER RAILROAD BALLADS
(*11—guitar*)   *Folkways*   FA 2013 (FP 13)   10"

900 Miles
825   Wreck of the 97
Great American Bum
238   The Gambler
Worried Man Blues
Getting-Up Holler

Hobo Bill
The Brave Engineer
The Rambler
595   Railroad Bill
569   Poor Boy

Houston, Cisco and Bill Bender: TRADITIONAL SONGS OF THE OLD
WEST (*8—guitar*)   *Stinson*   SLP #37   10"

367   Joe Bowers
Outlaw Horse
46   Billy the Kid
Drunken Rat
Windy Bill

735   Trail to Mexico
Bald Faced Steer
Tying a Knot in the Devil's Tail

Huntington, E. G.: FOLK SONGS OF MARTHA'S VINEYARD (*14—guitar*)
Folkways   FA 2032   10"

The Garden Where the Sham-
peens Grow
Gunpowder Tea
The Old Arm Chair
The Fit Comes on Me Now
580   Pop Goes the Weasel
36   Scarlet Town
Bow and Balance to Me

57   Blow the Man Down
Blow Ye Winds
Uncle Sam and Johnny Bull
Cross Over Jordan
Tarpaulin Jacket
Round Cape Horn
The Bold Privateer

Hurd, Peter: SINGS RANCHERA SONGS (*14—guitar*) (*Texts in Spanish
with English translation*)   *Folkways*   FA 2204 (FP 604)   10"   (1957)

El Pavito Real
La Calandria (The Lark)
Siete Leguas (Seven Leagues)
La Palomita Callejera (Little
Dove of the Streets)
El Toro Bravo (The Wild Bull)
El Palo Verde (The Palo Verde
Tree)
El Sombrerito (The Little Hat)
Las Chaparreras (The Chapar-
reras)

Los Barandales del Puente (The
Balustrade of the Bridge)
Corrido del Norte (Ballad of the
North)
El Jabali (The Wild Boar)
Fué en el Africa Lejana (It
Was in Far-off Africa)
El Corrido de Cananea (The
Ballad of Cananea)
Traígo Mi Cuarenta y Cinco (I
Carry My Forty-Five)

Isaacson, Dan: BALLADS (13—guitar)   Cornell   CRS-10021   10"   (1954)

	Washington Square Blues		Nine Hundred Miles
	Rising Sun Blues		What Folks Are Made of
138	The Creation		Zhankoye
	Young Women	313	I Gave My Love a Cherry
	Berta Lee	195	Every Night When the Sun
	Four Nights Drunk		Goes In
	With Her Head Tucked Under-	53	Black Eyed Susie
	neath Her Arm		

Ives, Burl: HISTORICAL AMERICA IN SONG
Burl Ives RECORDINGS for ENCYCLOPAEDIA BRITANNICA FILMS
Six 12" records

Ives, Burl: SONGS OF THE COLONIES (19)   Encyclopaedia Britannica Films
EBF Album I

	Confess Jehovah	51	Black Is the Color
	Mother Goose Songs		The Squire's Son
425	Little Mohee	608	The Riddle Song
	The Tailor and the Mouse	224	Foggy, Foggy Dew
36	Barbara Allen	228	The Fox
452	Lord Thomas	79	Brennan on the Moor
	Robin He Married	44	Billy Boy
451	Lord Randall		Queen Jane
	The Bold Soldier	440	Turtle Dove
188	Edward		

Ives, Burl: SONGS OF THE REVOLUTION (21)   Encyclopaedia Britannica
Films   EBF Album II

	The Escape of John Webb		Johnny Has Gone for a Soldier
	I Know Where I'm Going		Yankee Doodle
	My Days Have Been So Won-		Riflemen's Song at Bennington
	drous Free		The Battle of the Kegs
546	On Springfield Mountain		Ballad of Saratoga
	Chester		Cornwallis Country Dance
	What a Court Hath Old Eng-		Sir Peter Parker
	land		Yankee Man o' War
	Ballad of the Tea Party	673	Skip-to-my-Lou
	The Boston Tea Tax	101	Careless Love
	White Cockade	773	Wayfaring Stranger
	Free America		

Ives, Burl: SONGS OF NORTH AND SOUTH (24)   Encyclopaedia Britannica
Films   EBF Album III

	Ye Parliaments of England	520	Old Dan Tucker
	The Constitution and the Guer-	58	Blue Tail Fly
	riere		The Abolitionist Hymn
	Patriotic Diggers		Nicodemus
306	Hunters of Kentucky		Old Abe Lincoln
	The Hornet and the Peacock		All Quiet Along the Potomac
	Hey Betty Martin		Tonight

	John Brown	386	Kemo-Kimo
	Dixie		Beautiful Dreamer
	Bonnie Blue Flag	504	Nobody Knows the Trouble I've
	Goober Peas		Seen
	The Battle of Bull Run		Burying Ground
	Johnny Comes Marching Home	784	Were You There When They
	Lorena		Crucified My Lord

Ives, Burl: SONGS OF THE SEA (18)   *Encyclopaedia Britannica Films*
EBF *Album IV*

260	Golden Vanity	631	Sacramento
298	High Barbaree		Crocodile Song
	Maid of Amsterdam		Early in the Morning
	Henry Martin		Boston Come All Ye
	Hullabaloo Belay	293	Haul Away Joe
57	Blow the Man Down		Venezuela
	Blow Ye Winds	655	Shenandoah
	Away Rio	193	Erie Canal
787	The Whale		Eddystone Light

Ives, Burl: SONGS OF THE FRONTIER (18)   *Encyclopaedia Britannica*
Films   EBF *Album V*

560	Ox-Driving Song	627	Roving Gambler
696	Sweet Betsy from Pike	113	Chisholm Trail
174	Dreary Black Hills	531	Old Paint
	Peter Gray	246	Git Along Little Dogies
669	Sioux Indians	839	Young Man Who Wouldn't Hoe
367	Joe Bowers		Corn
790	What Was Your Name in the		I've Got No Use for Women
	States		The Hand-Cart Song
87	Buffalo Gals		Brigham Young
402	Greer County Bachelor		

Ives, Burl: SONGS OF EXPANDING AMERICA (21)   *Encyclopaedia Britan-*
nica Films   EBF *Album VI*

691	Streets of Laredo	680	Sourwood Mountain
46	Billy the Kid	129	Cotton-Eye Joe
368	John Hardy	134	Cowboy's Dream
361	Jesse James		Life Is Like a Mountain Rail-
175	Drill Ye Terriers		road
	Blue Mountain Lake	569	Poor Boy
	Patrick on the Railroad	517	Old Blue
	The Dying Hogger	474	Midnight Special
369	John Henry	41	Big Rock Candy Mountain
172	Down in the Valley	65	The Boll Weevil
792	When I Was Single		St. John's River

Ives, Burl: AUSTRALIAN FOLK SONGS (12—*guitar*) (*from his tour of*
Australia in 1952)   Decca   DL 8749   12"

	Wild Rover No More		Across the Western Plains I
	Click Go the Shears		Must Wander
812	The Wild Colonial Boy		Waltzing Matilda
	Nautical Yarn		

Oh, the Springtime, It Brings on   74   Botany Bay
   the Shearing   The Old Bullock Dray
The Station Cock   The Stockman's Last Bed
The Dying Stockman

Ives, Burl: BALLADS AND FOLK SONGS, Vol. I (*12—guitar*)   *Decca*
              DL 5080   10"   (1949)

	Dublin City	228	The Fox
	Cockle Shells	436	Lolly-Too-Dum
520	Old Dan Tucker	19	Aunt Rhody
193	The Erie Canal		Saturday Night
	The Eddystone Light		Wake Nicodemus
	Hullabaloo-Belay		
	Venezuela		

Ives, Burl: BALLADS AND FOLK SONGS, Vol. 2 (*9—guitar*)   *Decca*
              DL 5013   10"   (1949)

440	Turtle Dove	569	Po' Boy
161	The Devil's Nine Questions	335	I'm Sad and I'm Lonely
	No Wood Fire	172	Down in the Valley
709	Ten Thousand Miles	135	Cowboy's Lament
	My Good Old Man		

Ives, Burl: BALLADS, FOLK AND COUNTRY SONGS, Vol. 3 (*9—guitar*)
          Decca   DL 5093   10"   (1949)

	Roger Young		I'm Thinking Tonight of My
224	Foggy, Foggy Dew		Blue Eyes
41	Big Rock Candy Mountain	752	Old Uncle Ned
58	Blue Tail Fly		On the Grand Canyon Line
254	I'm Goin' Down the Road		
	It Makes No Difference Now		

Ives, Burl: CAPTAIN BURL IVES' ARK (*17*)   *Decca   DL 8587   12"*

	The Squirrel		Monkey and the Elephant
	Look at the Little Kitty Kat		Old Doctor Wango Tango
	Bango and His Baboon Drum	695	Swap Song
	Horace the Horse		Old Moby Dick
	Bear on the Ball		My Old Coon Dog
	Whistling Rabbit		Missouri Mule
	Ducks		Bird Courting Song
	Tenor Doodle-Doo	283	Ground Hog
	Bestiary		

Ives, Burl: CHILDREN'S FAVORITES (*7*)   *Columbia   CL-2570   10"*

	Little White Duck	233	Mr. Froggie Went A-Courtin'
	Lollipop Tree		Donut Song
	Little Engine That Could		Two Little Owls
			Fooba Wooba John

Ives, Burl: CHRISTMAS DAY IN THE MORNING (7)
Decca   DL 5428   10"

646   The Seven Joys of Mary
       What Child Is This
       There Were Three Ships
       King Herod and the Cock

Down in Yon Forest
The Friendly Beasts
307   Jesus Ahatonia (Huron Indian Carol)

Ives, Burl: CHRISTMAS EVE WITH IVES (11—guitar)   Decca   DL8391
12"   (1958)

       Silent Night
       There Were Three Ships
       Friendly Beasts
       Oh, Little Town of Bethlehem
       What Child Is This
307   Jesus Ahatonia

747   Twelve Days of Christmas
646   Seven Joys of Mary
       It Came Upon the Midnight Clear
       Down in Yon Forest
       King Herod and the Cock

Ives, Burl: CORONATION CONCERT (14—guitar)   Decca   DL 8080   12"

159   Devil and the Farmer
       St. John's River
41   Big Rock Candy Mountain
230   Frankie and Johnny
58   Blue Tail Fly
       Henry Martin
436   Lolly-Too-Dum
       Rodger Young

233   Mr. Froggie
       Cod Liver Oil
763   Waly, Waly
71   Bonnie Wee Lassie
       Venezuela
       How Now Shepherd

Ives, Burl: DOWN TO THE SEA IN SHIPS (18—guitar)
Decca   DL 8245   12"

353   Jack Was Every Inch a Sailor
642   Santy Anna
       You New York Girls
       Sailor's Grave
260   Golden Vanity
       Leave Her, Johnny, Leave Her
       Eddystone Light
       Go Down You Red Red Roses
618   Rolling Home
       Blow Ye Winds

       Hullabaloo Belay
       Wrap Me Up in My Tarpaulin Jacket
293   Haul Away, Joe
       Away Rio
       Ben Backstay
689   Stormalong
178   Drunken Sailor
       Highland Laddie

Ives, Burl: FOLK SONGS DRAMATIC AND HUMOROUS (10)   Decca
DL 5467   10"

246   Git Along Little Dogies
       From Here On Up the Hills
         Don't Get Any Higher
260   The Golden Vanity
308   Hush Little Baby
       I Know an Old Lady
       Goober Peas

516   Old Bangham
       Killigrew's Soiree
325   I Wonder As I Wander
       Tibby Dunbar

Ives, Burl: IN THE QUIET OF THE NIGHT (*16—guitar*)   *Decca*
DL 8247   12"

335	I'm Sad and I'm Lonely		No Wood Fire
308	Hush Little Baby		Tibby Dunbar
440	Turtle Dove	135	Cowboy's Lament
224	Foggy, Foggy Dew	246	Git Along Little Dogies
161	Devil's Nine Questions	172	Down in the Valley
500	Hear the Nightingale Sing		Saturday Night
709	Ten Thousand Miles		From Here On Up the Hills
569	Po' Boy		Don't Get Any Higher
	Cockle Shells		

Ives, Burl: MEN (*15—guitar*)   *Decca   DL 8125   12"*

	Locktender's Lament		Waltzing Matilda
560	Ox Driver's Song		Wild Rover
	Bold Soldier	230	Frankie and Johnny
	Young Married Man		The Deceiver
	Sad Man's Story		Sailor's Return
	Harlem Men		Prisoner's Return
	Western Settler	792	When I Was Single
		369	John Henry

Ives, Burl: MORE FOLKSONGS (*11—guitar*)   *Columbia   CL 6144*
10"   (*1950*)

	Robin, He Married	588	Pretty Polly
	Lavender Cowboy		Green Broom
517	Old Blue	298	High Barbaree
	Ballanderie		I've Got No Use for Women
	Baby Did You Hear	531	Old Paint
	Pueblo Girl		

Ives, Burl: THE RETURN OF THE WAYFARING STRANGER (*9—guitar*)
Columbia   CL 6058   10"   (1949)

546	On Springfield Mountain	119	Colorado Trail
425	Little Mohee	627	Roving Gambler
	Troubadour Song	368	John Hardy
451	Lord Randall	159	The Devil and the Farmer
71	Bonnie Wee Lassie		

Ives, Burl: SINGS FOR FUN (*14—guitar*)   *Decca   DL 8248   12"*

228	The Fox	65	Boll Weevil
	Three Jolly Huntsmen		Let's Go Hunting
193	Erie Canal		Goober Peas
	My Good Old Man	252	Go Tell Aunt Rhody
520	Old Dan Tucker		Killigrew's Soiree
	Wooly Boogie Bee	41	Big Rock Candy Mountain
58	Blue Tail Fly	254	I'm Goin' Down the Road

Ives, Burl: SINGS SONGS FOR ALL AGES (*16—guitar*)   *Columbia*
CL 980   12"

	Little White Duck	268 Grey Goose
	Lollipop Tree	787 Whale
	Little Engine That Could	Buckeye Jim
233	Mr. Froggie Went A-Courtin'	Sow Took the Measles
	Donut Song	The Goat
	Two Little Owls	Mr. Rabbit
	Fooba Wooba John	Tailor and the Mouse
	Old Witch, Old Witch	Mother Goose Song

Ives, Burl: SONGS OF IRELAND (*14—guitar*)   *Decca   DL-8444   12"*

	Maid of the Sweet Brown Knowe	Nell Flaherty's Drake
	Three Lovely Lasses from Ban-	The Wandering of Old Angus
	nion	Paddy and the Whale
79	Brennan on the Moor	On Board the Kangaroo
482	Molly Malone	Gils of Coleraine
	Women Is Angels	The Ould Orange Flute
	Kilgary Mountain	Mrs. McGrath
	Come Back Paddy Reilly	

Ives, Burl: THE WAYFARING STRANGER (*12—guitar*)   *Columbia*
CL 6109   10"

	Wee Cooper o' Fife	129	Cotton-Eyed Joe
608	Riddle Song	696	Sweet Betsy from Pike
	Tam Pierce	551	On Top of Old Smoky
	Peter Gray		I Know Where I'm Going
149	Darlin' Cory		I Know My Love
	Leather-Winged Bat	135	Cowboy's Lament

Ives, Burl: THE WAYFARING STRANGER (*10—guitar*)   *Stinson*
SLP 1   12"

579	Poor Wayfaring Stranger	58	The Blue Tail Fly
	Buckeyed Jim	79	Brennan on the Moor
224	The Foggy, Foggy Dew		The Bold Soldier
228	The Fox		The Sow Took the Measles
	Henry Martin	51	Black Is the Color

Ives, Burl: THE WAYFARING STRANGER (*26—guitar*)   *Columbia*
CL 628   12"

	Leather-winged Bat		Peter Gray
129	Cotton-Eyed Joe	149	Darlin' Cory
696	Sweet Betsy from Pike	368	John Hardy
551	On Top of Old Smoky	119	Colorado Trail
	I Know Where I'm Going	627	Roving Gambler
	I Know My Love	71	Bonnie Wee Lassie
135	Cowboy's Lament	159	The Devil and the Farmer
	Wee Cooper o' Fife	546	On Springfield Mountain
608	Riddle Song	425	Little Mohee
	Tam Pierce		Troubadour Song

Robin He Married
Lavender Cowboy
Green Broom

298 High Barbaree
I've Got No Use for Women
531 Old Paint

Ives, Burl: WOMEN: FOLK SONGS ABOUT THE FAIR SEX (8)   *Decca*
DL 5490   10"

434 Liza Jane
36 Barbara Allen
The Woman and the Chivalrous
Shark

The Wealthy Old Maid (War-
ranty Deed)
My Pretty Little Miss
160 Devilish Mary
482 Molly Malone
Nellie McNess

Ives, Burl: WOMEN (*12–guitar*)   *Decca*   DL 8246   12"

The Woman and the Chivalrous
Shark
Nellie McNess
My Pretty Little Miss
36 Barbara Allen
482 Molly Malone
Wealthy Old Maid

160 Devilish Mary
434 Liza Jane
Venezuela
436 Lolly-Too-Dum
Dublin City
I Know an Old Lady

Jacobs, Freddy: SWINGIN' FOLK TUNES (*12–orchestra*)   *Westminster*
WP 6087   12"

How Long
Uncle Reuben
608 Riddle Song
51 Black Is the Color of My True
Love's Hair
Row Lilly Lilly Row
Rockin' Bird
Come Along Susie

474 Midnight Special
Leather-Wing Bat
233 Froggie Went A-Courtin'
101 Careless Love
Venezuela

Jarrett, Merrick: THE OLD CHISHOLM TRAIL (*16–guitar*)   *Riverside*
RLP 12-631   12"   (1956)

518 The Old Chisholm Trail
796 When the Work's All Done This
Fall
134 The Cowboy's Dream
The Railroad Corral
High Chin Bob
576 I'm a Poor Lonesome Cowboy
The Cowboys' Dance Song
Cowboy Jack

245 The Gal I Left Behind Me
Roy Bean
423 Little Joe the Wrangler
The Lone Star Trail
690 The Strawberry Roan
Arizona Boys and Girls
Utah Carroll
All Day on the Prairie

Jefferson, Blind Lemon: CLASSIC FOLK-BLUES (*12*)   *Riverside*
RLP 12-125   12"

That Growling Baby Blues
Pneumonia Blues
Oil Well Blues
Long Lasting Loving
Tin Cup Blues
Mean Jumper Blues

Rising High Water Blues
Teddy Bear Blues
Bad Luck Blues
Big Night Blues
Peach Orchard Mama
Sunshine Special

Jefferson, Blind Lemon: FOLK BLUES (*8—guitar*)   *Riverside*
Riv. 1014   10"

Shuckin' Sugar Blues	Southern Woman Blues
Broke and Hungry	That Black Snake Moan #2
Lonesome House Blues	Balky Mule Blues
352 Jack o' Diamonds Blues	
Mosquito Moan	

Jemison, Eugene: SOLOMON VALLEY BALLADS (*9—guitar*)   *Folkways*
FA 2023 (FP-23)   10"   (1954)

709	Ten Thousand Miles Away	Girls, Quit Your Rowdy Ways
509	The Ocean Burial	The Old Elm Tree
	Crossing the Plains	Come All Ye Merry Hunters
	Fair Forella	201 Fair Charlotte
	The Bachelor's Complaint	

JOHNSON, BLIND WILLIE: His Story. (*Told, annotated and documented by Samuel B. Charters in Louisiana and Texas*) (8)   *Folkways   FG 3585   12"*

If I Had My Way	Dark Was the Night
Nobody's Fault but Mine	Match Box Blues
Jesus Is Coming Soon	It's a Good Little Thing
Mother's Children Have a Hard Time	Little Woman You're So Sweet

Kazee, Buell H.: HIS SONGS AND MUSIC (*Recorded by G. Bluestein*)
(*18—banjo*)   *Folkways   FS 3810   12"*

186	East Virginia	145	Cumberland Gap
92	Butcher's Boy	803	Cock Robin
	Dance Around My Pretty Little Miss	523	Old Grey Mare
		8	Amazing Grace
762	Wagoner's Lad		When Moses
227	Yellow Pups (Fox Chase)		My Christian Friends
368	John Hardy		Bread of Heaven
369	John Henry		Eternity
484	The Moonshiner	801	The White Pilgrim
149	Darling Corey		

Kines, Tom: OF MAIDS AND MISTRESSES (*16*)   *Elektra   EKL-137*
12"   (1958)

Peg O' Ramsay	There Was an Oul' Woman in Our Town
Corydon and Phyllis	
Elsie Marley	Banks of the Virgie-O
The Cumberland Lass	Star of the County Down
The Merchant and the Fiddler's Wife	Ye Maidens of Ontario
	Searching for Lambs
A Maid Goin' to Comber	The Shepherd's Daughter
The Brisk Young Widow	Jezebel Carol
The Palatine's Daughter	Kitty of Coleraine

Kossoy Sisters, The: BOWLING GREEN and other Folksongs from the Southern Mountains (*14—guitar, banjo acc. by Erik Darling*)   *Tradition*
TLP 1018   12″   (1956)

	Bowling Green		417	Little Birdie
156	The Darby Ram		331	I Never Will Marry
	In the Pines			I'll Fly Away
	Poor Ellen Smith			The Banks of the Ohio
667	Single Girl		762	The Wagoner's Lad
791	What Will We Do with the			Willie Moore
	Baby O			Engine 143
	Down in a Willow Garden			

Kraber, Tony: SONGS OF THE OLD CHISHOLM TRAIL   *Mercury*
MG-20003   10″   (1950)
(song titles not available)

Kraber, Tony: SONGS OF THE CHISHOLM TRAIL   *Mercury*
MG-20008   12″
(song titles not available)

Labrecque, Jacques: CANADIAN FOLKSONGS (*Chansons Populaires du
Canada*) (12)   *London*   LB-957   10″   (1954)

Gorloton Glin Glon
Quand J'Étais Chez Mon Père
L'Escaquette
C'est la Belle Françoise
La Fontaine Est Profonde
Genticorum

Le 25 de Mai
Quand un Gendarme Rit
Wing Tra La La
De Paris à La Rochelle
Cecilia
Le Petit Cordonnier

Labrecque, Jacques: FOLK SONGS OF FRENCH CANADA (23)   *Folkways*
FG 3560   12″

395	À la Claire Fontaine		Les Jeunes Filles à Marier
	Sur le Bord de la Seine		La Vieille Galante
	En Revenant des Noces		Dans la Cour du Palais
	À Paris	6	Au Chant de l'Alouette
	Sur le Petit Pont		La Fontaine Est Profonde
	Nous Vid'rons la Bouteille		La Perdriole
	Genticorum		Monsieur le Curé
	Le Roi Loys		Les Mentries
	La Prisonnière à la Tour		Je L'ai Vu Voler
	Les Trois Beaux Canards		Laquelle Marierons-Nous
	Au Bois du Rossignolet		La Petite Hirondelle
	Baum Bodi Baum		Avoine

Langstaff, John: SINGS FOLKSONGS AND BALLADS (*16—piano*)
Tradition   TLP 1009   12″

763	O Waly Waly		213	Farmer's Curst Wife
	Sir Patrick Spens		415	Lord Randal
	All 'Round My Hat			John Barleycorn
141	The Cruel Mother			She's Like the Swallow

370 John Riley   44 Billy Boy
     Carrion Crow   Croodin Doo
608 Riddle Song   Lover's Tasks
     Crawfish Man   Green Wedding

Lea, Terrea: AND HER SINGING GUITAR (15—guitar)   ABC-Paramount
               ABC-161   12"

    The Lass from the Low Country   715 Lonesome Valley
228 The Fox   Henry Martin
655 Shenandoah   Lavender Blue
    How Should I Your True Love   Little Wee Croodin' Doo
     Know?   Fare Thee Well, Oh Honey
    Wake Up, Jacob   The Jolly Farmer
120 Come All Ye Fair and Tender 677 Sometimes I Feel Like a Moth-
     Ladies   erless Child
    Sinner Man
    Ballynure Ballad

Lea, Terrea: FOLK SONGS AND BALLADS (16—guitar)   Hifirecord
              R404   12" LP

    Mary Hamilton   465 Mary and Martha
742 The Turkish Revery   The Chivalrous Shark
335 I'm Sad and I'm Lonely   Red Rosy Bush
    Gently Johnny My Jingalo   19 Aunt Rhody
    If'n I Was Your True Love   325 I Wonder As I Wander
    Kate Kearney   My Boy Willie
440 Turtle Dove   Scarlet Ribbons
                    Billy Barlowe
                    All the Pretty Little Horses

LEADBELLY MEMORIAL: VOLUME I (8—guitar)   Stinson SLP #17 10"

342 Good Night Irene   369 John Henry
    Good Morning Blues   Rock Island Line
    On a Monday   Ain't You Glad
    Old Riley   How Long

LEADBELLY MEMORIAL: VOLUME II (16—guitar, piano, concertina)
              Stinson   SLP #19

    Meeting at the Building   Fiddler's Dream
828 Yellow Gal   Noted Rider
    Talking Preacher   Burrow Love and Go
    We Shall Walk Through the   Line 'Em
     Valley   Bring Me Li'l Water, Silvy
    Cow, Cow, Yicky Yicky Yea   Julie Ann Johnson
    Out on the Western Plains   368 John Hardy
273 Green Corn   Whoa Back, Buck
    Big Fat Woman

LEADBELLY MEMORIAL: VOLUME III (*11—guitar*)
Stinson   SLP #48   10"

268	The Grey Goose	Blind Lemon
	Red Cross Store Blues	Leadbelly's Dance
	Ham and Eggs	Alberta
	Red River	In the Evening When the Sun
50	Black Girl	Goes Down
	You Don't Miss Your Water Blues	Digging My Potatoes

LEADBELLY MEMORIAL: VOLUME IV (*13—guitar*) Stinson SLP #51 10"

65	The Boll Weevil		Looky, Looky Yonder
	Ain't Going Down to the Well No Mo'		Black Betty
			Yellow Woman's Door Bells
251	Go Down Old Hannah		Poor Howard
230	Frankie and Albert	273	Green Corn
	Fannin Street		The Gallis Pole
	The Bourgeois Blues		De Kalb Woman

Leadbelly: MORE PLAY-PARTY SONGS (*14—guitar*) Stinson SLP #41 10"

	More Yet		What Are Little Boys Made of
	How Old Are You		Polly, Polly, Wee
274	Green Grass Growing All Around	673	Skip to My Lou
	Little Sally Walker		It's Almost Day
	Red Bird		Don't Mind the Weather
	Ha Ha This-A Way		How Do You Know
	All for You		Little Children's Blues

Leadbelly: PLAY-PARTY SONGS (*6—guitar*)   Stinson   SLP #39   10"

673	Skip to My Lou	Red Bird
	You Can't Lose-A Me, Cholly	Ha Ha This-A Way
	Sally Walker	It's Almost Day

LEAD BELLY'S LAST SESSIONS, Vol. 1   *Folkways   FA 2941 (FP241)*
2-12" *records*
"*Recorded by Frederic Ramsey, Jr. . . . Contains 52 selections: blues, hollers, spirituals, work songs, women blues, popular songs, etc. [Titles not given] Lead Belly relates personal experiences and associations of his life and his songs.*"
—*Quoted from the Folkways catalogue, Spring, 1958.*

LEAD BELLY'S LAST SESSIONS, Vol. 2   *Folkways   FA 2942 (FP242)*
2-12" *records*
"*Recorded by Frederic Ramsey, Jr. . . . 42 selections (2 hours of playing time) with Leadbelly singing, narrating, and playing his famous 12-string guitar.*" [*Titles not given*]—*Quoted from the Folkways catalogue, Spring, 1958.*

LEADBELLY'S LEGACY, Vol. 3: "Earliest Known Commercial Recordings"
(7)   *Folkways   FA 2024 (FP 24)   10"*

Ft. Worth and Dallas Blues	560	Ox Driving Song
Black Snake Moan		Daddy I'm Coming Back to You
Roberta		See See Rider
		Pigmeat

LEADBELLY'S LEGACY, Vol. 4: EASY RIDER (9—*guitar*)   *Folkways*
FA 2034 (FP 34)   10"

There's a Man Goin' Round 381	Jim Crow
Taking Names	Army Life
Easy Rider	Red Bird
Line 'Em	Hitler Song
T. B. Blues	Bourgeois Blues

Ledbetter, Huddie (Leadbelly): ROCK ISLAND LINE (*Leadbelly Legacy*
Vol. 2) (*12—guitar*)   *Folkways*   FA 2014 (FP 14)   10"

	Cotton Song	Old Riley
	Ha Ha This Way	Duncan and Brady
	Sukey Jump	Pigmeat
50	Black Girl	662 Shorty George
	Rock Island Line	Bottle Love and Go
	On a Monday	Blind Lemon

Ledbetter, Huddie (Leadbelly): TAKE THIS HAMMER (*Huddie Ledbetter
Memorial, Vol. 1*) (*15—guitar, piano, concertina, harmonica*)   *Folkways*
FA 2004 (FP 4)   10"   (1950)

Reels and Blues:		Work Songs and Spirituals:	
273	Green Corn	268	Gray Goose
828	Yellow Gal	564	Pick a Bale of Cotton
	You Can't Lose Me, Cholly	706	Take This Hammer
	Laura		Bring Me a Little Water, Silvy
	Good Morning Blues		Moaning
	Leaving Blues		Meeting at the Building
	Big Fat Woman		We Shall Walk Through the Valley
		342	Irene

Lloyd, A. L.: AUSTRALIAN BUSH SONGS (14)   *Riverside*
RLP 12-606   12"

Eubalong	The Lime-Juice Tub
The Cockies of Bungaree	The Maryborough Miner
Brisbane Ladies	The Drover's Dream
The Road to Gundagai	The Banks of the Condamine
The Castlereagh River	Bluey Brink
The Lachlan Tigers	Click Go the Shears
Bold Jack Donohue	812 The Wild Colonial Boy

Lloyd, A. L.: ENGLISH DRINKING SONGS (14)   *Riverside*
RLP 12-618   12"

156	The Darby Ram	Three Drunken Huntsmen
224	The Foggy Dew	All for Me Grog
	Maggie May	The Drunken Maidens
794	When Johnson's Ale Was New	625 Rosin the Beau
	The Butcher and the Chamber-	The Farmer's Servant
	maid	John Barleycorn
	A Jug of Punch	A Jug of This
	The Parson and the Maid	

Lloyd, A. L.: ENGLISH STREET SONGS (11) *Riverside RLP 12-614 12"*

341 The Indian Lass
    Died for Love
    The Unfortunate Rake
  70 The Bonny Bunch of Roses
    The Grand Conversation on Napoleon
    The Girl with the Box on Her Head

148 The Dark-Eyed Sailor
351 Jackie Monroe
    The Bloody Gardener
    The Cockfight
    The Oxford Tragedy

Lloyd, A. L.: THE FOGGY DEW and other Traditional English Love Songs (14—*concertina by Alf Edwards*) *Tradition TLP 1016 12"*

224 The Foggy Dew
    The Seven Gypsies
    The Maid's Lament
    The Husband with No Courage in Him
    The Trees They Do Grow High
440 Turtle Dove
    Brigg Fair

144 The Cuckoo
    The Isle of Cloy
800 Daughter, Daughter, Whistle
    Reynardine
674 The Soldier and the Maid
    The Maid on the Shore
    The Bird in the Bush

Lloyd, A. L. and Ewan MacColl: BLOW BOYS BLOW (16) *Songs of the Sea, Acc. concertina* (*Alf Edwards*), *guitar, banjo, mandolin* (*Ralph Rinzer*), *and guitar* (*Steve Benbow*). *Tradition TLP 1026 12"*

    Paddy Doyle
    Wild Goose Shanty
    The Handsome Cabin Boy
  56 Blow, Boys, Blow
799 Whiskey Johnny
    Paddy West
    Haul on the Bowline
    Row Bullies Row

    While Cruising Round Yarmouth
820 Old Billy Riley
    South Australia
    Whup Jamboree
    The Banks of Newfoundland
    Do Me Ama
    Jack Tar
    A Hundred Years Ago

Lloyd, A. L. and Ewan MacColl: HAUL ON THE BOWLIN' (11—*concertina*) *Stinson SLP #80 10"*

    Haul on the Bowlin'
    Row, Bullies, Row
    The Coast of Peru
    The Black Ball Line
    The Ship in Distress
    The Gauger

  57 Blow the Man Down
    Do Me Ama
642 Santy Ana
223 The Flying Cloud
    A Hundred Years Ago

Lloyd, A. L. and Ewan MacColl: OFF TO SEA ONCE MORE (13—*concertina*) *Stinson SLP #81 10"*

    Blood Roses
757 Van Dieman's Land
280 The Greenland Whale Fishery
    Paddy Doyle
    Johnny Todd
    Lord Franklin

605 Reuben Ranzo
    Sally Racket
    The Cruel Ship's Captain
    Handsome Cabin Boy
    The Dreadnaught
    Off to Sea Once More
689 Stormalong

Lloyd, A. L. and Ewan MacColl: THAR SHE BLOWS! (16) (*Whaling Ballads and Songs*)   *Riverside   RLP 12-635   12"*

Sperm Whale Fishery	605	Reuben Ranzo
Blood Red Roses		The Bonny Ship
Farewell to Tarwathie		The Diamond
The Eclipse		The Cruel Ship's Captain
The Cold Coast of Greenland		Off to Sea Once More
The Twenty-Third of March		Heave Away, My Johnny
The Coast of Peru		Paddy and the Whale
We'll Rant and We'll Roar		Greenland Bound

Lomax, Alan: TEXAS FOLK SONGS (16—*banjo, guitar, harmonica*)   *Tradition   TLP 1029   12"   (1958)*

369	My Little John Henry		Long Summer Days
	All the Pretty Little Horses		Eadie
	The Wild Rippling Water		Black Betty
	I'm Bound to Follow the Long-	602	Rattlesnake
	horn Cows	641	Sam Bass
	Ain't No More Cane on This	450	Lord Lovell
	Brazis		Billy Barlow
183	The Dying Cowboy	238	Rambling Gambler
	The Rich Old Lady		Godamighty Drag

Lomax, John A., Jr.: SINGS AMERICAN FOLKSONGS (20)   *Folkways   FG 3508   12"*

711	The Texian Boys		Long John
	I'm All Out and Down		Tin Maker Man
474	The Midnight Special	88	The Buffalo Skinners
	All the Baby Chickens in the		Louisiana Gal
	Garden		Hay Making Song
	The Cocaine Song	444	Long Time Ago
	The Factory Girl	369	John Henry
636	The St. James Infirmary	630	Rye Whiskey
805	Whoopee Ti Yi Yo, Git Along	564	Pick a Bale of Cotton
	Little Dogies	245	The Gal I Left Behind Me
	Tee Roo	265	Good Bye, Old Paint

Lunsford, Bascom Lamar: MINSTREL OF THE APPALACHIANS (13)   *Riverside   RLP 12-645   12"*

361	Poor Jesse James		Sundown
	Go to Italy		Fly Around, My Blue-Eyed Girl
	The Merry Golden Tree	52	Black Jack Davy
	I Shall Not Be Moved	779	Weeping Willow Tree
156	The Derby Ram	705	Swing Low, Chariot
527	The Old Man from the North		The Sailor on the Deep Blue
	Country		Sea
	The Miller's Will		

Lunsford, Bascom Lamar: SMOKY MOUNTAIN BALLADS (8–banjo)
Folkways   FA 2040 (FP40)   10"

	Swannanoa Tunnel	547	On the Banks of the Ohio
356	Mr. Garfield	681	Springfield Mountain
360	Jinnie Jenkins	152	The Death of Queen Jane
	Little Margaret	480	Mole in the Ground

Luther, Frank: GET ALONG LITTLE DOGIES, etc. (22)   Decca   DL-5035
10"   (1950)

246	Get Along Little Dogies	842	The Zebra Dun
	Cowboy's Gettin' Up Holler	269	Great Grandad
245	The Gal I Left Behind Me		Great Grandma
518	The Old Chisholm Trail	735	Trail to Mexico
	The Big Corral	276	Green Grow the Lilacs
	Cowboy Dance	302	Home on the Range
531	A-Ridin' Old Paint and Leadin'		The Bronco Buster
	Old Dan	690	The Strawberry Roan
600	Range of the Buffalo	712	War Song of the Texas Rangers
669	Sioux Indians	428	Little Old Sod Shanty on the
265	Goodbye Old Paint		Plain
	Cowboy's Meditation	604	Red River Valley

Luther, Frank and Zora Layman: SONGS OF THE NORTH AND SOUTH
(1861-65) (35 songs)   Decca   DL 8093   12"

North:
Battle Cry of Freedom
Marching Along
We Are Coming, Father Abraham, 300,000 More
Grafted into the Army
Hard Crackers Come Again No More
Tenting Tonight on the Old Camp Ground
Just Before the Battle, Mother
Just After the Battle
When Johnny Comes Marching Home Again
Brother Tell Me of the Battle
Dying Volunteer
Vacant Chair
Tramp, Tramp, Tramp
Oh, Wrap the Flag Around Me, Boys
Sleeping for the Flag
Battle Hymn of the Republic

Columbia the Gem of the Ocean
Faded Coat of Blue

South:
Bonnie Blue Flag
Cheer Boys Cheer
Maryland, My Maryland
Lorena
Eating Goober Peas
Here's Your Mule
All Quiet Along the Potomac Tonight
Ever of Thee I'm Fondly Dreaming
Rose of Alabama
Bonnie Eloise
A Life on the Vicksburg Bluff
Lilly Dale
When This Cruel War Is Over
Who Will Care for Mother Now?
Stonewall Jackson's Way
Cavaliers of Dixie
Stonewall Jackson's Requiem

Lynch, Christopher: THE MINSTREL BOY (9)   Columbia   ML 2016   10"

The Minstrel Boy
The Garden Where the Praties Grow

The Rose of Tralee
The Palatine's Daughter
A Little Bit of Heaven

A Ballynure Ballad
When Irish Eyes Are Smiling

The Young May Moon
You'd Better Ask Me

MacColl, Ewan: BAD LADS AND HARD CASES (*British Ballads of Crime and Criminals*) (16)   *Riverside   RLP 12-632   12″*

Turpin Hero   757 Van Dieman's Land
Spence Broughton   Hard Case
The Bonnie Banks of Airdire   Treadmill Song
Whiskey in the Jar   Ivor
Go Down You Murderer   Bill Brown
Ballad of Bentley and Craig   The Banks of the Royal Canal
The Black Velvet Band   Gilderoy
Superintendent Barratt
Barratty, Parratty

MacColl, Ewan: BARRACK ROOM BALLADS (*11—banjo, guitars, harmonica, by Peggy Seeger, Jimmy MacGregor, and John Cole*)   *Topic Records   10 T26   10″   (1958)*

Join the British Army   633 Young Trooper Cut Down in
Any Complaints   His Prime
Wadi Maktilla   Seven Years in the Sand
Second Front Song   Farewell to Sicily
When This Ruddy War Is Over   D-Day Dodgers
Bless 'Em All   Browned Off

MacColl, Ewan: BLESS 'EM ALL and Other British Soldiers' Songs (18)   *Riverside   RLP 12-642   12″*

Bless 'Em All   Seven Years in the Sand
Tell Me Boys, Have You Any   Join the British Army
  Complaints   When This Ruddy War Is Over
The Dying Soldier   The Second Front Song
The Ballad of Wadi Maktilla   Browned Off
633 The Trooper Cut Down in His   McKaffery
  Prime   The Fortress Song
Hand Me Down My Petticoat   The D Day Dodgers
All You Maidens Sweet and Kind   On the Move
Columbo   The Ghost Army of Korea

MacColl, Ewan: BRITISH INDUSTRIAL FOLK SONGS (*11—guitar*)   *Stinson   SLP #79   10″*

Poor Paddy Works on the Rail-   The Coal Owner and the Pit-
  way   man's Wife
The Gresford Disaster   The Iron Horse
The Four Loom Weaver   The Blantyre Explosion
I'm Champion at Keeping 'Em   The Wark of the Weavers
  Rolling   Four Pence a Day
The Collier Laddie   Cosher Bailey's Engine

MacColl, Ewan: SCOTS DRINKING SONGS (19)   *Riverside*
RLP 12-605   12"

We're a Jolly Fu'
The Calton Weaver
When She Came Ben She Bobbit
The Laird of the Dainty Doon
  Bye
Blow the Candle Out
Donald Blue
The Brewer Laddie
We're Gaily Yet
A Wee Drappie o't
The Cuckoo's Nest
Green Grow the Rashes, O

The Day We Went to Rothesay
The Bonnie Wee Lassie Who
  Never Said No
The Muckin' o' Geordie's Byre
Jock Hawk's Adventures in
  Glasgow
The Brisk Young Lad
I Wish That You Were Dead,
  Guidman
The Wind Blew the Bonnie Las-
  sie's Plaidie Awa'
Andro and His Cutty Gun

MacColl, Ewan: SCOTS FOLK SONGS (17)   *Riverside*   RLP 12-609   12"

The Barnyards o' Delgaty
Roy's Wife of Aldivalloch
The Reel o' Stumpie, O
Davie Faa
Tail Toddle
Charlie, O Charlie
Nicky Tams
The Wee, Wee German Lairdie
Friendless Mary

Johnnie Lad
Kissin's No Sin
Maggie Lauder
The Highland Muster Roll
The Wars o' Germany
Johnnie Cope
Lassie wi' the Yellow Coatie
The Bonnie Lass o' Fyvie

MacColl, Ewan: SCOTS STREET SONGS (15)   *Riverside*   RLP 12-612   12"

To the Begging I Will Go
The Brewer's Daughter
Fitba' Crazy   651
The Lion's Den
Jamie Raeburn's Farewell
92 The Butcher Boy
70 The Bonnie Bunch of Roses   757
35 The Banks of Sweet Dundee
Miss Brown

Cock o' the Midden
My Last Farewell to Stirling
The Sheffield Apprentice
Come All Ye Tramps and
  Hawkers
MacPherson's Lament
Van Dieman's Land

MacColl, Ewan and A. L. Lloyd: CHAMPIONS AND SPORTING BLADES
(*British Songs of Sporting and Gambling*) (14)   *Riverside*   RLP 12-652   12"

Card Playing Song   63 Reynard the Fox
The Bold Gambling Boy   671 Skewball
Gaelic Football Creeping Jane   The Turpin-Sugar Ray Fight
Morrissey and the Russian Sailor   The Football Match
The Cock Fight   Govan Pool-Room Song
The Sporting Races of Galway   Heenan and Sayers
Old Bob Ridley

MacColl, Ewan and Peggy Seeger: CLASSIC SCOTS BALLADS (16—guitar)
Tradition   TLP 1015   12"

	The Gairdener Chyld			Aikendrum
	Johnny Lad			The Wren She Lies in Care's Bed
191	The Elfin Knight			My Jo Janet
	Hughie Grame		674	The Trooper and the Maid
	I Loved a Lass			Moneymusk Lads
452	Lord Thomas and Fair Annie			Hunting-tower
	Glasgow Peggy		208	The False Lover Won Back
	The Mormond Braes		33	Banks of the Nile

MacColl, Ewan and Peggy Seeger: MATCHING SONGS OF THE BRITISH
ISLES AND AMERICA (16)   Riverside   RLP 12-637   12"

	The Sweet Kumadee		260	The Golden Vanity
	His Old Gray Beard Kept Wag-			
	gin'		72	Overshoes and Leggins
286	The Gypsy Laddie		52	The Black Jack Davy
651	The Sheffield Apprentice			I Was Brought Up in Cornwall
	There Was a Puggie in a Well		233	Froggie Went A-Courtin'
632	My Sailor Boy		699	Sweet William
	The Fishes Song			The Fish of the Sea
	Scarborough Fair		96	The Cambric Shirt

MacColl, Ewan and Peggy Seeger: SHUTTLE AND CAGE (12—banjo, guitar)
Topic Records   10-T13   10"   (1958)

The Wark of the Weavers

The Blantyre Explosion

Moses of the Mail

Fourpence a Day

Champion at Keeping Them
Rolling

The Four Loom Weaver

The Plodder Seam

Cosher Bailey's Engine

The Gresford Disaster

Cannilly, Cannilly

The Coalowner and the Pit-
man's Wife

Poor Paddy Works on the Railroad

McCurdy, Ed: THE BALLAD RECORD (20—guitar)   Riverside   RLP 12-601
12"   (1955)

	Sir Patrick Spens		298	High Barbary
727	The Three Ravens		79	Brennan on the Moor
745	The Twa Corbies			William Glen
243	Get Up and Bar the Door		92	The Butcher Boy
	Son Davie, Son Davie			The Poor and Single Sailor
755	The Unquiet Grave		681	Springfield Mountain (2)
	The Bitter Withy		369	John Henry
	Crow Song		97	Canada-I-O
52	Black Jack Davie		496	Naomi Wise
516	Old Bangum			

McCurdy, Ed: A BALLAD SINGER'S CHOICE (19—banjo and guitar by
Erik Darling)   Tradition   TLP 1003   12"

119	Colorado Trail		695	Swapping Song
	Bird's Courtship		36	Barbara Allen
276	Green Grow the Lilacs		440	Little Turtle Dove

174   Dreary Black Hills
319   I Ride an Old Paint
590   Pretty Saro
308   Hush Little Baby
      Lovely Ohio
      Back Bay Hill
      To the West

      Dear Evelina
      A Great Big Sea Hove in Long
         Beach
      Peter Gray
      Lukey's Boat
      Come to the Bower
      Star of Logy Bay

McCurdy, Ed: BARROOM BALLADS (*Sung and Declaimed*) (*14*) (*Assisted by Erik Darling*)   Riverside   *RLP 12-807   12"*

      My Darling Clementine
      A Persian Kitty
      The Baggage Coach Ahead
      The Face on the Barroom Floor
556   The Orphan Girl
      Liquor and Longevity
103   Casey Jones
      Abdul the Bul-Bul Amir

      Handsome Harry
      The Letter Edged in Black
      When a Fellow Begins to Get
         Bald
412   The Lily of the West
      A Poor Unfortunate
      A Fireman's Life

McCurdy, Ed: BLOOD, BOOZE 'N BONES (*17—guitar, banjo*)   Elektra   *EKP-108   12"*

149   Darlin' Cory
      Josie
      The Dublin Murder Ballad
      Four Nights Drunk
135   Cowboy's Lament
484   Kentucky Moonshiner
      No More Booze
      Farewell to Grog
      Portland County Jail
      Banks of the Ohio

368   John Hardy
      The Pig and the Inebriate
682   Stackerlee
401   Lamkins
      Yo Ho Ho
      Lulu
      The Drunkard's Doom

McCurdy, Ed: CHILDREN'S SONGS (*22—banjo and guitar by Billy Faier*)   Tradition   *TLP 1027   12"*   (*1958*)

 44   Billy Boy
      My Bonny Lies Over the Ocean
      S-m-i-l-e
      Tree in the Hole
233   Froggy Went A-Courting
513   O Suzanna
353   Jack Was Every Inch a Sailor
      O Dear What Can the Matter Be
386   Keemo Kimo
      Twinkle Twinkle Little Star
      I Had a Little Rooster

      One Man Went to Mow
      "Sing," Said the Mother
542   The Old Woman and the Pig
      A Hole in the Bucket
      The Little Black Bull
      Three Fishermen
      I Wish I Was
      I Had a Horse
264   Good Bye, My Lover, Good Bye
      Mr. Rabbit
      The Noble Duke of York

McCurdy, Ed: THE FOLK SINGER (*12—guitar*)   Dawn   *DLP 1127   12"*

101   Careless Love
 51   Black Is the Color
      Riders in the Sky
129   Cotton-Eyed Joe

 53   Pretty Little Black-Eyed Susie
      It Takes a Worried Man to Sing
         a Worried Song
      Ballad of the Frank Slide

Squid Jiggin' Ground	319 Ride an Old Paint
Western Wind	Lavender Cowboy
	Lukey's Boat

McCurdy, Ed: FRANKIE AND JOHNNIE   *By-Line Records   By-Line 1   10"*
(song titles not available)

McCurdy, Ed: SIN SONGS, Pro and Con (*14—guitar*)   *Elektra   EKL-24   10"*

The Jolly Boatsman	841 Young People Who Delight in
How Happy Is She	Sin
I Once Had Virtue	Poor Polly, the Mad Girl
The Gambler's Song	John Adkin's Farewell
The Good Boy's Song	Gambling on the Sabbath Day
262 Good Old Mountain Dew	An Address for All Concerning
630 Rye Whiskey	Death
729 Tobacco Is an Indian Weed	
Three Pretty Fair Maids	

McCurdy, Ed: SIN SONGS—Pro and Con (*18—guitar*)   *Elektra   EKL-124   12"*

Ballad of a Young Man	841 Young People Who Delight in
627 The Roving Gambler	Sin
The Jolly Boatsman	Poor Polly, the Mad Girl
How Happy Is She	John Adkin's Farewell
I Once Had Virtue	Gambling on the Sabbath Day
The Gambler's Song	An Address for All Concerning
The Good Boy's Song	Death
262 Good Old Mountain Dew	She Plays the Game
630 Rye Whiskey	234 Frozen Charlotte
729 Tobacco Is an Indian Weed	
Three Pretty Fair Maids	

McCurdy, Ed: SONGS OF THE OLD WEST (*13—guitar, banjo*)   *Elektra
EKL-112   12"*

631 Sacramento	685 State of Arkansas
Hoosen Johnny	361 Jesse James
269 Great-Grandad	134 The Cowboy's Dream
735 Trail to Mexico	428 Little Old Sod Shanty
Sally, Let Your Bangs Hang	Brown-Eyed Lee
Down	Chuck a Little Hell
88 Buffalo Skinners	183 The Dying Cowboy

McCurdy, Ed: * WHEN DALLIANCE WAS IN FLOWER (*17—guitar*)
(*With Erik Darling, banjo, and Alan Arkin, recorder*)   *Elektra   EKL-110   12"*

Go Bring Me a Lass	Two Maidens Went Milking
The Trooper	One Day
A Young Man and a Maid	A Lusty Young Smith
A Wanton Trick	Tom and Doll
There Was a Knight	A Riddle

* In 1959, Elektra issued a McCurdy record (EKL-170) titled SON OF
DALLIANCE.

A Maiden Did A-Bathing Go
The Jolly Tinker
Old Fumbler
The Three Travelers

Kitt Hath Lost Her Key
To a Lady
The Four Able Physicians
Sylvia the Fair

McCurdy, Ed: WHEN DALLIANCE WAS IN FLOWER, Vol. 2 (16—harpsichord, banjo, guitar, recorder)   Elektra   EKL-140   12"   (1958)

Uptails All
Tottingham Frolic
A Young Man
A Tradesman
A Tenement to Let
Young Strephen and Phillis
The Playhouse Saint
A Virgin's Meditation
The Jolly Miller

My Thing Is My Own
A Lady So Frolic and Gay
Would You Have a Young
  Virgin?
Of Chloe and Celia
The Jolly Pedlar's Pretty Thing
Phillis
To Bed to Me

McCurdy, Ed (Singer) and Michael Kane (Narrator): THE LEGEND OF
ROBIN HOOD (11)   Riverside   RLP 12-810   12"

Robin Hood's Birth
Robin Hood and the 15 Foresters
Robin Hood and Little John
Robin Hood Rescues Will Stutt-
  ley
Robin Hood and Maid Marian
Robin Hood and the Butcher

Robin Hood's Golden Prize
Robin Hood and the Prince of
  Aragon
Robin Hood and the Pedlar
Robin Hood and the Golden
  Arrow
Robin Hood's Death

McFerrin, Robert: DEEP RIVER, and Other Classic Negro Spirituals (14)
Riverside   RLP 12-812   12"

196 Ev'ry Time I Feel de Spirit
     Fix Me, Jesus
     His Name So Sweet
     I'm Gonter Tell God All o' My
       Troubles
705 Swing Low, Sweet Chariot
     A City Called Heaven
     Ain't Got Time to Die

     Here's One
     Let Us Break Bread Together
155 Deep River
     I Got to Lie Down
     Oh, Glory
     Witness
610 Ride On, King Jesus

McGhee, Brownie: BLUES (8—guitar)   Folkways   FA 2030 (FP 30/2)   10"

     Sporting Life
     Good Morning Blues
101 Careless Love Blues
     Betty and Dupree

     Move to Kansas City
     Worried Mind
     Pawnshop Blues
     Me and Sonny

McGhee, Brownie and Sonny Terry: SONGS (13—guitar, harmonica, acc.
drums by Gene Moore)   Folkways   FA 2327   12"

     Better Day
     Confusion
     Dark Road
369 John Henry
     Make a Little Money
     Old Jabo
     If You Lose Your Money

     Guitar Highway
     Heart in Sorrow
     Preachin' the Blues
     Can't Help Myself
     Best of Friends
     Boogie Baby

McGhee, Brownie and Sonny Terry: SONGS (*13—guitar, harmonica, and drums*)   *Topic Records*   *12 T29   12"   (1958)*

Better Day	Guitar Highway
Confusion	Heart in Sorrow
Dark Road	Preachin' the Blues
369 John Henry	Can't Help Myself
Let Me Make a Little Money	Best of Friends
Old Jabo	I Love You, Baby
If You Lose Your Money	

McNeil, Brownie: FOLKSONGS (*11—guitar*)   *Sonic Records   B-16847-8*   *12"   (1957)*

691	Streets of Laredo	228	The Fox Is on the Town
742	The Turkey Reveille	36	Barbara Allen
	Mary Hamilton	402	The Lane County Bachelor
735	The Trail to Mexico	162	Diamond Joe
	Jalisco No Te Rajes		Cuatro Milpas
807	The Wide Missouri		

Marais, Josef: SONGS OF MANY LANDS (*10—guitar*)   *Decca   DL-5106   10"*

Johnny with the Bandy Legs	252	Go Tell Aunt Rhody
I Hashe		The Sheep Are Coming
Waltzing Matilda		Down the Road
The Cherries		Besides the Windmill
When a Little Farm We Keep		
The Bouquet		

Marais, Josef: SOUTH AFRICAN VELD (*9—guitar*)   *Decca   DL 5014   10"*

Stelenbasch Boys	Brandy, Leave Me Alone
Taute Kobe	Here I Am
Stay Polly Stay	Sarie Marais
Pack Your Things and Trek	Henrietta's Wedding
Fereira	

Marais, Josef and Miranda: AFRICAN SUITE and SONGS OF SPIRIT AND HUMOR (*17—guitar*)   *Decca   DL 9047   12"*

War Chant		In the Boer Homestead
Hunger Chant		Everywhere
Riches Bring Sorrow		Sitting in Jail
Birthday Song		But the Cat Came Back
Stellenbosse Boys	729	Tobacco
Old Transvaal		Lilliburlero
There Comes Oompy Kahli		Eleven Little Froggies
Isibili		Unfortunate Miss Bailey
Awake		

Marais, Josef and Miranda: BALLADS OF LONG AGO (*12—With the Pardo Ancient Instrument Ensemble*)   *Columbia Masterworks   ML 4894   12"*

Chow Willy	A Messenger of Love
The Laird of Cockpen	A Legend of St. Nicholas
In Egypt	The Dilly Song

The Rumble Drum
Mother Mary Is Rocking Her
    Child
Berg Op Zoom

The Sheep under the Snow
The Welcome
The Silver Fleet

Marais, Josef and Miranda: BALLADS OF MANY LANDS (8)   *Decca*
    DL-5268   10"

How Lovely Cooks the Meat   228   The Fox
The Crickets   Floating Down the Stream
The Flocks, the Flocks   The Ratcatcher's Daughter
Riding Down from Bangor
The Grindstone Man

Marais and Miranda: CHRISTMAS WITH MARAIS AND MIRANDA (16)
    Decca   DL 9030   12"

108   The Cherry Tree Carol   Christmas Tree
       (England)   See There Comes the Steamboat
       Lullaby to a Doll (Africa)   Santa Claus
       The Angelus (France)   Won't You Come In
       Live Happily   Hogmanay Night
       Pilgrimage to Bethlehem   Today Is Sylvester
       Lord Jesus Has a Garden   Fife and Drum
       Let Us Sing of Christmas   Let Rich and Poor Rejoice
       African Carol   Today

Marais, Josef and Miranda: SONGS (8–*guitar*)   *Columbia*
    CL-6225 (FL 9542)   10"

Around the Corner   Bulu the Zulu
Mountain Is Far   Umbira Melody
Cecilia   Jonathan
Beau Reynolds   Frances, Oh Frances

Marais, Josef: SONGS FROM THE VELD, Vol. 2 (10–*band*)   *Decca*
    DL-5083   10"

Marching to Pretoria   "Ai Ai" the Pied Crow Cry
My Heart Is So Sad   As the Sun Goes Down
There's the Cape-Cart   Jan Pieriewiet
Meisiesfontein   There Comes Alibama
Siembamba   Train to Kimberly

MARAIS AND MIRANDA IN PERSON (15–*guitar*)   (*Recorded at Fullerton*
    Hall, Chicago, Feb. 2, 1955)   *Decca   DL 9026   12"   (1955)*

       Henrietta's Wedding   Little Marguerite
       Farewell to Belashaney   Wo-Yele-Yele Pale Sarah
       I Wonder When I Shall Be   The Grindstone Man
           Married   As the Sun Goes Down
526   Old Joe Clarke   Here Am I
       Rooster Chick   Siembamba
       The Small Husband   The Cherries
       Pastorale

MARAIS AND MIRANDA IN PERSON (*17—guitar*)   (*Recorded at Fullerton Hall, Chicago, Feb. 7, 1955*)   *Decca*   *DL 9027*   *12"*   (*1955*)

There's the Cape-Cart	Till the Queen Bee Arrive,
The Bouquet	Honey Hive Cannot Thrive
If Mama Strikes Me Down	Johnny with the Bandy Legs
The Crickets	Meisiesfontein
Ihashe	Auntie Mina's Cooking the Sirup
Farmer of Brienz	Polly, Polly
The Scorned Lover 139	Going Down to Cripple Creek
Ah Goote Noodle Soup	When That I Was a Tiny Little
The Angler's Song	Boy
Bid Me but Live	

Marais, Josef and Miranda: SOUTH AFRICAN FOLK SONGS (*8—guitar*)   *Columbia*   *CL 6226*   *10"*

Sarie Marais	Pity the Poor Patat
Ma Says, Pa Says	Animal Cries
When It Rains	Oh Brandy Leave Me Alone
Train to Kimberley	Sugarbush

Marais, Josef and Miranda: SUNDOWN SONGS (*16*)   *Decca*   *DL 8711*   *12"*   (*1958*)

Hali Ho!	One Day I Went A-Riding
Cloak of Night	Down to Niagara
Distant Mountain Peak	Running Water
Whistle and I'll Come to You	My Boat Is Drifting
We Travel the Highlands	Misery Must Have an Ending
Sitting by the Bright Firelight	You Can Make Fricadel
Snake Baked a Hoe-Cake	Silver Moon Sailing
Two Thousand Miles to Go	I'll Soon Be Starting on My Way

Marshall, Herta: TO YOU WITH LOVE: AMERICAN FOLK SONGS FOR WOMEN (*12—guitar*)   *Folkways*   *FA 2333*   *12"*   (*1957*)

590	Pretty Saro	804	Who's Gonna Shoe Your Pretty
608	Riddle Song		Little Foot
	Shady Grove		South Coast
	Buttermilk Hill	331	I Never Will Marry
	When I Lay Down and Die Do	211	Fare Thee Well
	Die	440	Turtle Dove
120	Come All Ye Fair and Tender		Willow Garden
	Ladies		

Matthews, Inez: SPIRITUALS (*21—piano*)   (*Great New Voices of Today, Vol. 6*)   *Period Records*   *SLP 580*   *12"*

'Round About de Mountain	Crucifixion
Hear de Lambs a Cryin'	Balm in Gilead
Litl' Boy	His Name So Sweet
Talk About a Chile	Fix Me, Jesus
Lord, I Didn't Know	I'm Goin' to Tell God All My
New-Born Again	Troubles
Gonna Ride Up in de Chariot	Po' Pilgrim

You're Tired, Chile
Live a Humble
301 Hold On
They Led My Lord Away
Witness

You Mus' Come in by an' thro'
    de Lamb
266 De Gospel Train
568 Plenty Good Room

Mills, Alan: CHRISTMAS SONGS OF MANY LANDS (25—guitar)
        Folkways   FC 7750   12"

The Angel Gabriel
No Room in the Inn
King Herod and the Cock
The Friendly Beasts
Bring a Torch
Shepherdess
Oh Tell Me
307 The Huron Carol
Rise Up Shepherd and Follow
Mother Mary
What Is the Matter?
Mary Had a Baby
The Wrenix Boy's Song

Little Bitty Baby
Joseph Dearest
O' Christmas Tree
As Lately We Watched
Haidom-Haidom
Gently, the Maiden
I Am So Happy
The Simple Birth
Fum-Fum-Fum
Bagpiper's Carol
Saint Basil
Come and Sing

Mills, Alan: FOLK SONGS FOR YOUNG FOLK, Vol. 1 (13—guitar)
        Folkways   FC 7021 (FP721)   10"

7 Alphabet Song
553 One More River
Mistress Bond
803 Who Killed Cock Robin?
The Bird's Ball
The Barnyard Song
Three Little Pigs

The Carrion Crow
The Tailor and the Mouse
233 The Frog He Would A-Wooing
    Go
The Mallard
Little Bingo
I Know an Old Lady Who
    Swallowed a Fly

Mills, Alan: FOLK SONGS FOR YOUNG FOLK, Vol. 2 (16—guitar)
        Folkways   FC 7022 (FP722)   10"

The Climate
Little Ship
Robin Sat on a Cherry Tree
Old Dumpty Moore
233 Frog Went A-Courting
63 Bold Reynard the Fox
525 The Old Hen Cackled
Robin's Last Will

Ten Little Chickadees
Wee Cock Sparra'
The Bull-Dog and the Bull-Frog
Goat Song
Old Woman and the Pedlar
580 Pop Goes the Weasel
156 Darby Ram
Down in Demarara

Mills, Alan: FOLK SONGS OF FRENCH CANADA (13—guitar)   Folkways
        FW 6929 (FP29)   10"   (1952)

395 À la Claire Fontaine
Isabeau s'y Promène
C'est la Belle Françoise
Monsieur le Curé
Ah! Si Mon Moine Voulait
    Danser!
Mon Père y m'a Marié

Les Raftsmen
Youpe! Youpe! sur la Rivière!
C'est l'Aviron
M'en Allant à la Chasse
Vive la Canadienne
Je Sais Bien Quelque Chose
Un Canadien Errant

Mills, Alan: FOLK SONGS OF NEWFOUNDLAND * (12—guitar)
      Folkways   FW 6831 (FP831)   10"   (1953)

Killigrew's Soiree	A Great Big Sea Hove in Long
Tickle Cove Pond	Beach
As I Roved Out 353	Jack Was Every Inch a Sailor
Time to Be Made a Wife	Lukey's Boat
It's the Boy That Builds the	The Squid-Jiggin' Ground
Boat	Two Jinkers
The Badger Drive	Anti-Confederation Song

Mills, Alan: FRENCH FOLK SONGS FOR CHILDREN (20—guitar)
      Folkways   FC 7208 (FP 708)   10"   (1953)
      (Counterpart to FC 7018—these in French)

Sur le Pont d'Avignon	Quand P'tit Jean Revint du Bois
Ah! Qui Marierons-nous?	Ma Mère M'envoie-t-au Marché
Monte sur un Éléphant 6	Alouette
La Poulette Grise 192	En Roulant ma Boule
Y a un Rat	Il Était un Petit Navire
Michaud Est Tombé	Il Était une Bergère
Le Petit Prince	L'Apprenti Pastouriau
Savez-Vous Planter des Choux?	Mariann' S'en Va-t-au Moulin
J'ai Perdu le "Do" de Ma	À la Volette
Clarinette	Marlbrough S'en Va-t-en Guerre
Meunier Tu Dors	

Mills, Alan: FRENCH FOLK SONGS FOR CHILDREN SUNG IN ENGLISH
      (20—guitar)   Folkways   FC 7018   10"

On the Bridge of Avignon 6	Alouette
Oh Who Will Marry?	Roll the Ball
On an Elephant	The Little Ship
The Grey Hen	There Was a Shepherd Maiden
A Mouse	The Apprentice Shepherd
Michaud, the Little Prince	Mary Anne Went to the Mill
Can You Plant Cabbages?	A la Volette
The "Do" of My Clarinet	Oh, Marlborough's Gone
Three Ducks	a-Warring!
Jean Went thru' the Woods	
Mother Sent Me to the Market	

Mills, Alan: MORE SONGS TO GROW ON (21—guitar)   Folkways
      FC (FP709)   10"

Hah, This Way	We Wish You a Merry
Up in a Balloon	Christmas
How Old Are You	The Beasts Carol
Raisins and Almonds	May Day Carol
724 Three Craw	The New River Train
Trip a Trop a Tronjes	

* Reissued in 1959, with additions, as a 12" (FW 8771).

319   I Ride Old Paint
       The Big Corral
219   Haul Away Joe
       Donkey Riding
       Two in the Middle
       Little Lady from Baltimore

612   Risselty Rosselty
       The Bold Fisherman
       There Was an Old Man
       We Whooped and We Hollered
434   Liza Jane

Mills, Alan: "O, CANADA," A History of Canada in Folk Songs (*Research by Edith Fowke*) (*26—guitar, drum*) *Folkways   FW 3001   12"   (1956*)

The French Period:
Eskimo Chant
Iroquois Lullaby
Vive les Matelots! (Long Live
    the Sailors)
À Saint-Malo, Beau Port de Mer
307   The Huron Carol
       Petit Rocher (Little Rock)
       Tenaquich Tenaga Quich'ka

The British Take Over:
La Courte Paille (The Short
    Straw)
Bold Wolfe, The Siege of
    Quebec
Le Sergeant
Come All Ye Bold Canadians
    (War of 1812)
The Chesapeake and the
    Shannon

Un Canadien Errant (A
    Wandering Canadian)

Confederation:
Anti-Fenian Song
No More Auction Block for Me
Anti-Confederation Song
Pork, Beans, and Hard-Tack
The Maple Leaf Forever
O, Canada!
La Rose Blanche (The White
    Rose)
The Franklin Expedition
    (1845-7)
428   The Little Old Sod Shanty
91   Bury Me Not on the Lone
       Prairie
       Old Grandma
       Saskatchewan
       When the Ice Worms Nest
       Again

Mills, Alan and The Shanty Boys: SONGS OF THE SEA (*32—guitar*) *Folkways   FA 2312   12"*

611   Rio Grande
293   Haul Away Joe
637   Sally Brown
       Chee'ly Men
372   Johnny Boker
       Paddy Doyle
       Dead Horse
       Salt Horse
14   A-Roving
732   Tom's Gone to Hilo
376   Johnny Come Down to Hilo
709   Ten Thousand Miles Away
655   Shenandoah
44   Billy Boy
455   Lowland
178   Drunken Sailor

56   Blow Boys Blow
57   Blow the Man Down
       Clear the Track
       Can't You Dance the Polka?
444   A Long Time Ago
       New Bedford Whalers
218   Fire Down Below
       The Sailor's Grave
       Boney Was a Warrior
642   Santy Anna
       The Chesapeake & Shannon
       Home Dearie
       Goodbye, Fare Ye Well
       Hilo Somebody
       Galloping Randy Dandy
       Leave Her Johnny

Moore, Geoffrey: SONGS OF THOMAS MOORE (*Irish Melodies*) (*15—Irish harp*)   *Judson Records*   J-3021   12"

The Minstrel Boy	Bendermeer's Stream
The Origin of the Harp	Oft in the Stilly Night
She Is Far from the Land	The Harp That Once through
Oh, 'Tis Sweet to Think	Tara's Halls
As Vanquished Erin	'Tis the Last Rose of Summer
Believe Me If All Those	Eveleen's Bower
Endearing Young Charms	Tho the Last Glimpse of Erin
The Meeting of the Waters	Love's Young Dream
Oh Arranmore, Loved	
Arranmore	

Moser, Artus: NORTH CAROLINA BALLADS (*11—dulcimer, guitar*)   *Folkways*   FA 2112 (FP40/2)   10"

680	Sourwood Mountain	206	The False Knight upon the
	Swannanoa Town		Road
	The Old Man over the Hill	145	Cumberland Gap
523	Old Grey Mare	451	Lord Randal
746	The Two Sisters		Poor Ellen Smith
	Wildwood Flower		Sweet Rivers

Murai, Jean: MAMA, I WANT A HUSBAND (*10—accordion, flute, drum, mandolin, guitar*)   *Stinson*   SLP #75   10"

800	Whistle, Daughter, Whistle	La Vayom V'Lo Vaylayla
	La Palomita	Mon Père M'a Donné un Mari
	Voszhe Vilstu	La Gitana
	Caro Mama Io Sono Malata	Old Woman's Courtship
	Pack She Back to She Ma	La Llorona

Niles, John Jacob: AMERICAN FOLK AND GAMBLING SONGS (*18*)   *RCA Camden*   CAL-219   12"

746	The Two Sisters	352	Jack O'Diamonds
542	The Old Woman and the Pig	627	The Roving Gambler
233	The Frog Went Courting		Gambler Don't Lose Your Place
	The Carrion Crow		at God's Right Hand
188	Edward		The Gambler's Lullaby
291	The Hangman		The Gambling Song of the Big
	I'm in the Notion Now		Sandy River
213	The Farmer's Cursed Wife		My Little Black Star
	The Three Little Hunters		American Street
803	Who Killed Cock Robin?		Field and Jailhouse Cries

Niles, John Jacob: AMERICAN FOLK SONGS (*14—dulcimer*)   *RCA Camden*   CAL-245   12"

831	You Got to Cross That	253	Go 'Way from My Window
	Lonesome Valley	554	One Morning in May
	Lass from the Low Countree	808	The Wife of Usher's Well
51	Black Is the Color of My True	152	Death of Queen Jane
	Love's Hair	424	Little Mattie Groves

286 Gypsy Laddie
425 My Little Mohee
325 I Wonder As I Wander Out
     under the Sky
     Lulle Lullay

646 Seven Joys of Mary
36   Ballad of Barbery Ellen

Niles, John Jacob: AMERICAN FOLK LOVE SONGS (9—dulcimer)
                 Boone-Tolliver   BTR-22   10"

425 Little Mohee
     Lass From the Low Country
144 Cuckoo
253 Go 'Way from My Window
51   Black Is My True Love's Hair

763 Waly, Waly
     Rosy Peach
440 Turtle Dove
     I'm Goin' Away

Niles, John Jacob: BALLADS   Boone-Tolliver   BTR-23   10"
              (song titles not available)

Niles, John Jacob: I WONDER AS I WANDER (18—dulcimer)   Tradition
                 TLP-1023   12"   (1957)

     Waken Little Shepherd
     Jesus, Jesus
233 Frog Went Courtin'
425 Little Mohee
     Sea Witch
     Irish Girl
253 Go 'Way from My Window
     In That Lovely Far-off City
     Lass from the Low Countree
369 John Henry

445 Look Down That Lonesome
     Road
325 I Wonder As I Wander
     When Jesus Lived in Galilee
     Lulle, Lullay
51   Black Is the Color of My True
     Love's Hair
     Venezuela
     I Had a Cat
     I'm Going Away

Niles, John Jacob: 50th ANNIVERSARY ALBUM (13—dulcimer)
                 RCA Camden   CAL-330   12"

144 The Cuckoo
447 Lord Bateman and the Turkish
     Lady
365 Jimmy Randal
     John of Hazel Green
     Carol of the Birds
442 That Lonesome Road
369 John Henry

809 The Wife Wrapt in the
     Wether's Skin
140 The Cruel Brother
     Down in Yon Forest
481 Molly Vaughn
     Mary Hamilton
     Earl Brand

Nye, Hermes: ANGLO-AMERICAN FOLK SONGS (10—guitar)   Folkways
                 FA 2037   (FP 37)   10"

     King Arthur Had Three Sons
     Saint Valentine's Day
     A North Country Maid
     Earl Murray
     Earl Richard

280 Greenland Fishery
     John Peel
471 The Mermaid
     The Herring
24   Bailiff's Daughter

Nye, Hermes: BALLADS AND RELIQUES (*Early English ballads of Francis James Child and Thomas Percy*)   (*19—guitar*)   *Folkways*   FA 2305   12"

	Robin Hood's Golden Prize	243	Get Up and Bar the Door
	Rob Roy		Clerk Saunders
	Queen Eleanor's Confession	703	Sweet William's Ghost
	Binnorie	452	Lord Thomas and Fair Elinor
727	The Three Ravens		The Queen's Maries
	The Lament of the Border		Lizzie Lindsay
	Widow		Glenlogie
	Whittingham Fair	763	Waly, Waly
	Sir Patrick Spens		Thomas the Rhymer
	Outlandish Knight		King O'Love

Nye, Hermes: BALLADS OF THE CIVIL WAR, Vol. 1 (*10—guitar*)
Folkways   FA 2187   (*FP48/7*)   10"

	Abolition Hymn		Lincoln and Liberty
150	Davy Crockett		All Quiet Along the Potomac
642	Santa Anna		Goober Peas
	Battle Hymn of the Republic		Lorena
	Bonnie Blue Flag		Longstreet's Rangers

Nye, Hermes: BALLADS OF THE CIVIL WAR, Vol. 2 (*10—guitar*)
Folkways   FA 2188   (*FP48/8*)   10"

145	Cumberland Gap		Manassas Rebel
105	Charleston Jail		When Johnny Comes Marching
	When This Cruel War Is Over		Home
	Old Soldier	263	Rebel Soldier
	Abe Lincoln		Cumberland Ship
	The Alabama		

Nye, Hermes: TEXAS FOLK SONGS (*13—guitar*)   *Folkways*   FA 2128
(*FP47/1*)   10"

	The Devil Made Texas	65	The Boll Weevil
	Bonnie and Clyde		Bucking Bronco
	Bad Brahma Bull	162	Diamond Joe
8	Amazing Grace	641	Sam Bass
88	The Buffalo Skinners		Toolle's Death
662	Shorty George		Corrido de Kansas
			Louisana Gals

O'Bryant, Joan: AMERICAN BALLADS AND FOLKSONGS (*16—guitar*)
Folkways   FA 2338   12"

667	Single Girl	385	Keep Your Hand on the Plow
	The Stern Old Bachelor		A Sailor's Life
	Life Is a Toil		The Maiden of the Plains
	The Promised Land		A Soldier's Wife
304	The House Carpenter's Wife		Marble Town
735	The Trail to Mexico	712	The Texas Rangers
412	The Lily of the West		Tom Sherman's Barroom
144	The Cuckoo		
	I'm on My Way		

O'Bryant, Joan: FOLKSONGS AND BALLADS OF KANSAS (*12–guitar*)
Folkways   FA 2134   10"

	Girls Quit Your Rowdy Ways	383	Kansas Boys
92	Butcher Boy		Old Limpy
127	Bill		In Kansas
842	Zebra Dun	481	Molly Bann
	Sweet William Died		Quantrill
447	Lord Batesman	517	Old Blue

[Felius] Odetta: ODETTA AT THE GATE OF HORN (*15–guitar and bass*)
Tradition   TLP-1025   12"

155	Deep River	237	The Gallows Pole
474	The Midnight Special	228	The Fox
706	Take This Hammer		Sail Away Ladies
112	Chilly Winds	455	Lowlands
	He's Got the Whole World in		Maybe She Go
	His Hand		Timber
	The Lass from the Low	281	Green Sleeves
	Countree	160	Devilish Mary
			All the Pretty Little Horses

ODETTA AND LARRY (*13*)   *Fantasy Records   3252   12"*

369	John Henry	320	I Was Born About 10,000 Years
	Old Cotton Fields at Home		Ago
	The Frozen Logger		The Car–Car Song
	Run, Come See Jerusalem		No More Cane on the Brazos
517	Old Blue		Pay Day at Coal Creek
	Water Boy		I've Been 'Buked and I've Been
642	Santy Ana		Scorned

ODETTA SINGS BALLADS AND BLUES (*18*)   *Tradition   TLP-1010   12"*

642	Santy Anno	352	Jack O'Diamonds
	If I Had a Ribbon Bow		'Buked and Scorned
	Muleskinner Blues		Easy Rider
10	Another Man Done Gone		Deep Blue Sea
379	Joshua		Oh Freedom
	Hound Dog Bay at the Moon		God's Gonna Cut You Down
	Glory, Glory		I'm on My Way
2	Alabama Bound		
	Been in the Pen		
	Shame and Scandal		

O'Hara, Mary: * SONGS OF ERIN (*18*)   *London   LL 1572   12"*

The Weaving Song	She Moved thro' the Fair
The Quiet Land of Erin	The Spanish Lady
I Wish I Had the Shepherd's	Eileen Aroon
Lamb	The Spinning Wheel
The Bonnie Boy	Dileen–O Dehmnhs
Aililiu Na Ganhna	Danny Boy

* In 1959, London issued LOVE SONGS OF IRELAND (LL 1784).

I Have a Bonnet Trimmed with
   Blue
Castle of Dromore
Next Market Day

My Lagan Love
Ceol An Phibrough
Fili Fili A Runo
The Ballynure Ballad

O'Hara, Mary: SONGS OF IRELAND (*18—Irish harp*)   *Tradition*
               TLP 1024   12"   (*1958*)

Haigh Didil Dum
Carraig Donn
The Frog Song
Óró Mo Bhaidin
Jackets Green
Seoladh Na Ngamhna
Wexford Mummer's Song
Farewell, but Whenever
The Leprauchan
Na Leanbhai I Mbeithil

Sliabh Na Mban
The Gartan Mother's Lullaby
Down by the Glenside
Maidrin Ruadh
Silent O Moyle or The Song of
   Fionnuala
Dia Luain Dia Mairt
The Famine Song
She Didn't Dance

Okun, Milt: ADIRONDACK FOLK SONGS AND BALLADS (*10—guitar*)
               Stinson   SLP #82   10"

	The Belle of Long Lake	215	The Fatal Wedding
	The Lass of Glenshee	285	The Gypsy Davy
151	The Days of '49		Bert La Fontaine's Packard
	Come to the Fair		The Banks of Champlain
	The Good Old Days		
	Dolan's Ass		

Okun, Milt: AMERICA'S BEST LOVED FOLK SONGS (*16-guitar*)
            Baton Records, Inc.   BL 1203   12"

369	John Henry	228	The Fox
551	On Top of Old Smoky		Rock Island Line
608	The Riddle Song (I Gave My	103	Casey Jones
	Love a Cherry)	768	Wanderin'
342	Good Night Irene	673	Skip to My Lou
58	Blue Tail Fly	308	Hush Little Baby
115	Cindy	655	Shenandoah
696	Sweet Betsy from Pike		
41	Big Rock Candy Mountain		
	Old Woman Who Swallowed a		
	Fly		

Okun, Milt: EVERY INCH A SAILOR—FO'C'SLE SONGS AND SHANTIES
      (*15—guitar*)   *Stinson*   SLP 65   10"

353	Jack Was Every Inch a Sailor	280	Greeland Fisheries
218	Fire Down Below		Round the Corner, Sally
	Mainsail Haul		Can't You Dance the Polka
	Gloucester Girls	290	Hanging Johnny
	Bold McCarty		Jack Tar
	Sailor's Grave	732	Tommy's Gone to Hilo
471	The Mermaid		Ship Rambolee
	Boney		

Okun, Milt: I SING OF CANADA (12—guitar, banjo) Stinson SLP #71 10"

	Donkey Riding	Smoky Mountain Bill
	Trinity Cake	A-Rishima, Tishima, Tee
	She's Like the Swallow	Un Canadien Errant
	J'ai Perdu le Do	A Gay Spanish Maid
650	The Shantyman's Life	Catch A-Hold This One
	La Poulette Grise	Vive la Canadienne

Okun, Milt: MERRY DITTIES (Folk Songs of Love and Play) (14)   Riverside
RLP 12-603   12"

14	A-Roving		Early One Morning
	Lavender's Blue		Puttin' on the Style
	The Bold Grenadier		Captain Walker's Courtship
	Unfortunate Miss Bailey		Katey Morey
	The Trooper and the Tailor	44	Billy Boy
	Jackie Rover	323	I Wish I Was Single Again
	The Little Scotch Girl		Won't You Sit with Me Awhile

Okun, Milt and Ellen Stekert: TRADITIONAL AMERICAN LOVE SONGS
(17)   Riverside   RLP 12-634   12"

	Must I Go Bound	562	Paper of Pins
	She's Like the Swallow		Trouble
663	Shule Aroo	224	The Foggy Dew
96	The Cambric Shirt		The Brazos River
	The Lass from the Low Country		Spanish Is the Loving Tongue
	Poor Lolette	195	Every Night When the Sun
804	Who Will Shoe?		Goes In
	The Lass of Glenshee		Red Rosy Bush
	He Took Me by the Hand	502	No, John, No

Olsen, Dorothy: I KNOW WHERE I'M GOING (12)   RCA Victor
LPM-1606   12"   (1958)

	Innismore		Marrowbones
	Hi-Ro-Je-Rum		Spanish Is the Loving Tongue
	I Know Where I'm Going		Brian O'Lynn
	Must I Go Bound		Give Me Your Hand
385	Keep Your Hand on the Plow	763	Cockle Shells and Silver Bells
	Crawfish Man		Somebody's Tall and Handsome

Paley, Tom: FOLK SONGS FROM THE SOUTHERN APPALACHIANS
(16—banjo, guitar)   Elektra   EKL-12   10"   (1953)

649	Shady Grove	522	Old Grey Goose
	The Miller's Song		Wildwood Flower
	The Lord by the Northern Sea		Jackaro
359	The Jealous Lover		O'Sullivan Mor (banjo)
	Deep Water	526	Old Joe Clark (banjo)
	Little Maggie	221	Flop-Eared Mule (banjo)
	Girl on the Greenbriar Shore		White Cockade (banjo)
	Coal Creek March (banjo)		Buck Dancers' Choice (guitar)

Peacock, Ken: SONGS AND BALLADS OF NEWFOUNDLAND (13)
                    Folkways   FG 3505   12"

802	Who Is at My Window		Brown Flour 1926
	Weeping?		Green Shores of Fogo
	Bonnie Banks of the Virgie-O		Lonely Waterloo
	Bill Wiseman	175	Drill Ye Heroes, Drill
292	Hard Times	358	Jimmy Whalen
	The Loss of the Eliza		I'll Be Seventeen Come Sunday
	Woman from Dover		

Ramsay, Obray: BANJO SONGS OF THE BLUE RIDGE AND GREAT
                    SMOKIES (14)   Riverside   RLP 12-649   12"

599	The Rambling Boy		God Gave Noah the Rainbow
	Keep on the Sunny Side		Sign
	Polly Put the Kettle On	661	Shortenin' Bread
	Little Margaret		Wildwood Flower
	I Am a Pilgrim	491	My Lord, What a Morning
139	Cripple Creek	442	Lonesome Road Blues
	Down by the Sea Shore	779	Weeping Willow
	Song of the French Broad River		

Reed, Dock and Vera Hall: SPIRITUALS (10)   (Recorded in Alabama by
        Harold Courlander)   Folkways   FA 2038   (FP38)   10"

	I'm Going Home on the Morn-	Job Job
	ing Train	What Month Was Jesus Born
	My God Ain't No Lying Man	Somebody's Talking about Jesus
	Where the Sun Will Never Go	Death Is Awful
	Down	I'm Climbing Up the Hills of
737	Troubled Lord I'm Troubled	Mt. Zion
	Look How They Done My Lord	

Reed, Susan: FOLK SONGS (9—Irish harp, zither)   Columbia Masterworks
                    ML 54368   12"   (1958)

696	Sweet Betsy from Pike	482	Molly Malone
440	Turtle Dove	211	Fare Thee Well
	Next Market Day		(obverse side contains 7 SONGS
608	The Riddle Song		OF THE AUVERGNE—not
842	The Zebra Dun		listed here)
	Gentle Johnny, My Jingalo		
	My Lagan Love		

Reed, Susan: [FOLK SONGS] (19—zither, Irish harp)
                    Elektra   EKL-116   12"

51	Black Is the Color	253	Go Away from My Window
	The Old Woman		A Mighty Ship
335	I'm Sad and I'm Lonely		Mother, I Would Marry
175	Drill, Ye Terriers	36	Barbara Allen
281	Greensleeves		Michie Banjo

Zelime
Gué, Gué
The Soldier and the Lady
482 Molly Malone
Three White Gulls

Venezuela
If I Had a Ribbon Bow
Miss Bailey
Danny Boy

Reed, Susan: I KNOW MY LOVE (*11—Irish harp, zither*)　*RCA Victor*
LXA-3019　10"

I Know My Love (Irish Folk
Song)
The Three Gulls (Italian Folk
Song)
211 Fare Thee Well
253 Go 'Way from My Window
(Carolina Folk Song)
482 Molly Malone (Old Irish Folk
Song)
451 Lord Randall (English-Scottish
Ballad)

A Mighty Ship (Norwegian Folk
Song)
360 Jennie Jenkins (Scottish Folk
Song)
Danny Boy (Old Irish Air)
My Love Is Like a Red, Red
Rose (Old English Folk Song)
The Soldier and the Lady (Old
English Folk Song)

Reed, Susan: OLD AIRS FROM IRELAND, SCOTLAND AND ENGLAND
(*13—zither, Irish harp*)　*Elektra*　*EKL-26*　10"　(1954)

At the Foot of Yonders Moun-
tain
The Pretty Girl Milking Her
Cow
The Leprechaun
He Moved through the Fair
Bendemeer's Stream
Irish Famine Song

Wraggle Taggle Gypsies
Seventeen Come Sunday
224 The Foggy Dew
I Know My Love
Must I Go Bound
The Boreens of Derry
763 Wailie, Wailie

Reed, Susan: SINGS OLD AIRS (*16—zither, Irish harp*)
Elektra　*EKL-126*　12"

260 The Golden Vanity
19 Aunt Rhody
The Pretty Girl Milking Her
Cow
Must I Go Bound
The Leprechaun
He Moved through the Fair
Bendemeer's Stream
Irish Famine Song

213 Devil and the Farmer's Wife
Wraggle Taggle Gypsies
Seventeen Come Sunday
I Know My Love
224 The Foggy Dew
At the Foot of Yonders Moun-
tain
763 Wailie, Wailie
The Boreens of Derry

Ritchie, Jean: FIELD TRIP (*21—dulcimer*)　*Collector Limited Ed.*
CLE 1201　12"　(1956)

588 Pretty Polly
On the Banks of Red Roses
The Cuckoo's Nest
144 The Cuckoo
Bog Down in the Valley-O
Tree in the Valley-O

36 Barbara Allen
36 Barbara Allyn
36 Barbara Ellen
233 Froggie Went A-Courting
233 Uncle Frog Went Out to Ride
Orange and Lemon

497	Needle's Eye	67	Bonaparte's Retreat
	A Maid in Her Father's Garden		Derry Gaol
585	A Pretty Fair Miss	291	The Hangman Song
67	Bonaparte's Retreat	101	When My Apron It Hung Low
		101	Careless Love

Ritchie, Jean: KENTUCKY MOUNTAIN SONGS (16—dulcimer)   *Elektra*
EKL-25   10"   (1954)

	Cedar Swamp		O Sister Phoebe
505	Nottamun Town		False Sir John
291	The Hangman Song	649	Shady Grove
	Old King Cole	389	Killy Kranky
673	Skip to My Lou	440	Lonesome Dove
22	Bachelor's Hall	542	Old Woman and Pig
245	The Girl I Left Behind	432	The Little Sparrow
	Jemmy Taylor-O	255	Goin' to Boston

Ritchie, Jean: [KENTUCKY MOUNTAIN SONGS] (21—dulcimer and guitar)
Elektra   EKL-125   12"

	Cedar Swamp	144	Cuckoo (Version 1)
505	Nottamun Town	144	Cuckoo (Version 2)
291	The Hangman Song	51	Black Is the Color
	O Sister Phoebe	542	Old Woman and Her Pig
	False Sir John	432	Little Sparrow
	O Love Is Teasin'	255	Goin' to Boston
	Old Virginny		
672	Skin and Bones		**Dulcimer pieces:**
22	Bachelor's Hall	649	Shady Grove
	Little Devils		Old King Cole
389	Killy Kranky	674	Skip to My Lou
	Jemmy Taylor-O		

Ritchie, Jean: RITCHIE FAMILY OF KENTUCKY, THE   *Folkways*
FA-2316   12"   (1958)
(song titles not available)

Ritchie, Jean: SATURDAY NIGHT AND SUNDAY TOO (20—dulcimer, fiddle,
banjo)   *Riverside*   RLP 12-620   12"

	Side 1 (*Saturday Night*)		Side 2 (*Sunday*)
	Betty Larkin		Been a Long Time a-Travelling
	Two Dukes A-Rovin'		The Day Is Past and Gone
791	Baby-O		Father Get Ready
279	Green Grows the Willow Tree		Guide Me, O Thou Great
	Susan Girl		Jehovah
	Dear Companion		I've Got a Mother
	Huntin' the Buck		Sing to Me of Heaven
398	Lady Margaret		Hiram Hubbard
	Charlie		God Bless Them Moonshiners
	Hop Up My Ladies	649	Shady Grove
			Lullaby Medley

Ritchie, Jean: SINGING FAMILY OF THE CUMBERLANDS (10) (*Songs and Folktales of a Famous Mountain Family*)   Riverside   RLP 12-653   12"

Song Titles:

	A Twelvemonth More Has
755 The Unquiet Grave	Rolled Around
202 Fair Ellen	Gonna See My True Love
Oh, Father Won't You Come	176 Awake, Awake, You Drowsy
Wondrous Love	Sleeper
Old Tyler	Sweet Bye and Bye
	144 The Cuckoo

(NOTE: Folktales not listed here)

Ritchie, Jean: SONGS FROM KENTUCKY (17—*dulcimer*)   Westminster
        WP-6037   12"   (1956)

526	Old Joe Clark	721	There Was an Old Woman
674	Oh, Soldier, Soldier	554	One Morning in May
	Gentle Fair Jenny		Jackero
741	The Turkish Lady		Little Devils
233	Froggie Went A-Courting	588	Pretty Polly
22	Bachelor's Hall		Jubilee
667	Single Girl	114	Christ Was Born in Bethlehem
36	Barbry Ellen	680	Sourwood Mountain
308	Hush Little Baby		

Ritchie, Jean: SOUTHERN MOUNTAIN CHILDREN'S SONGS AND
    GAMES (18—*dulcimer, guitar*)   Folkways   FC 7054 (FC754)   12"

	Jenny, Put the Kettle On	695	The Swapping Song
	Go In and Out the Window		Old King Cole
	The Old Soup Gourd	528	The Old Man in the Woods
	Among the Little White Daisies	537	Old Shoe Boots
638	Sally Goodin	680	Sourwood Mountain
	Fiddle-I-Fee		Green Gravels
	Old Bald Eagle		Mammy Had an Old Goose
	Two Dukes A-Riding	803	Who Killed Cock Robin?
	Kitty Alone		
	Love Somebody		

Ritchie, Jean: TRADITIONAL SONGS OF HER KENTUCKY MOUNTAIN
    FAMILY (16—*dulcimer*)   Elektra   EKLP-2   10"   (1952)

	O Love Is Teasin'		Jubilee
51	Black Is the Color		My Boy Willie
	A Short Life of Trouble	308	Hush Little Baby
554	One Morning in May (Version 1)	285	The Gypsum Davy
554	One Morning in May (Version 2)	144	Cuckoo (Version 1)
	Old Virginny	144	Cuckoo (Version 2)
672	Skin and Bones	149	Little Cory
	The Little Devils		Keep Your Garden Clean

Ritchie, Jean and Oscar Brand: COURTING SONGS (12—*dulcimer, banjo, guitar, fiddle*)   Elektra   EKL-22   10"   (1954)

	Hey, Little Boy		My Love Is a Rider
	I Wonder When I Shall Be	407	Lazy John
	Married		Aunt Sal's Song

383 Kansas Boys
     The Keys of Canterbury
839 A Young Man Who Wouldn't
     Hoe Corn
299 Hog Drovers

     My Good Old Man
562 Paper of Pins
502 No, Sir

Ritchie, Jean and Oscar Brand: RIDDLE ME THIS (16) (*Courting and
     Riddle Songs*)   Riverside   RLP 12-646   12"

674 Soldier, Soldier
     My Good Old Man
360 Jennie Jenkins
608 The Riddle Song
562 Paper of Pins
     Pretty Li'l Reckless Boy
803 Who Killed Cock Robin
 44 Billy Boy

 96 The Cambric Shirt
     The Deaf Woman's Courtship
     I Will Give My Love an Apple
     Marching across the Green Grass
     Riddle Me This
     What Are Little Boys Made of
     Madam, Will You Walk
     Big Glass Doll

Ritchie, Jean and Tony Kraber: BALLADS IN COLONIAL AMERICA
          New Records   NRLP-2005   10"
          (song titles not available)

Roberts, Robin: FOLK AND TRADITIONAL LOVE SONGS (10—*guitar,
          dulcimer*)   Stinson   SLP #77   10"

     She Moved through the Fair
     As He Walked Down by the
       River
436 Lolly Toodum
     Dabbling in the Dew
     I Lost My Love
     Lay the Lilly Oh

440 Turtle Dove
590 Pretty Saro
     Johnson Boys
     The Old Maid

Roberts, Robin: IRISH STREET SONGS (13—*guitar*)   Stinson   SLP #63
               10"   (1955)

     The Old Man Rocking the
       Cradle
     The Tri-Colored Ribbon
     Molly Brannigan
     When Pat Comes Over the Hill
     Eileen Aroon
     Mrs. McGrath

663 Shule Aroon
     The Banks of the Roses
     Kelly of Killarne
     The Garden Where the Praties
       Grow
     Brian O'Linn
     Cuc-a-Nandy
224 The Foggy Dew

Roberts, Robin: TRADITIONAL FOLK SONGS AND BALLADS (21—*guitar,
          dulcimer*)   Stinson   SLP 77   12"   (1958)

     Johnson's Boys
590 Pretty Saro
     Hard Ain't It Hard
144 Cuckoo
436 Lolly Toodum
440 Turtle Dove

120 Come All You Fair and Tender
       Ladies
335 Sad and Lonely
     As He Walked Down by the
       River

680   Sourwood Mountain
       Lay the Lilly Oh
       I Lost My Love
       The Old Maid
       Dabbling in the Dew
       Down by the Sally Garden
       Green Broom

674   Soldier, Soldier
       Pu'ing Bracken
763   Cockle Shells
       Love Is Kind
       She Moved through the Fair

Robertson, Jeannie: SONGS OF A SCOTS TINKER LADY (13)   *Riverside*
                        RLP 12-633   12"

       What a Voice
       When I Was Noo But Sweet
          Sixteen
       Roy's Wife of Aldivalloch
253   Go Away from My Window
       Lord Lovat
 83   The Broken Token

 92   The Butcher Boy
       MacCrimmon's Lament
       The Overgate
286   The Gypsy Laddie
       The Bonnie Wee Lassie That
          Never Said No
       The Four Maries
 79   Brennan on the Moor

Robertson, Walt: AMERICAN NORTHWEST BALLADS (8–*guitar*)
                  Folkways   FA 2046 (FP 46)   10"

768   Wandering
       Puget Sound
       Life Is a Toil
       The Frozen Logger

       I Have Led a Good Life
       The Portland County Jail
       The Sow Took the Measles
 42   Bile Them Cabbage Down

Robeson, Paul: SPIRITUALS (8–*piano*) *Columbia ML 4105 12" (1949)* ?

250   Go Down Moses
       Balm in Gilead
       By an' By
077   Sometimes I Feel Like a Mother-
          less Child

369   John Henry
       Water Boy
504   Nobody Knows de Trouble I've
          Seen
379   Joshua Fit de Battle of Jericho

    [Other side of record, Popular Favorites, not listed here—no folksongs]

Robeson, Paul: [SPIRITUALS AND FOLKSONGS] (13–*piano, chorus &*
                  orchestra)   *Vanguard   VRS-9037   12"*

       Water Boy
655   Shenandoah
       Jerusalem
       Londonderry Air
677   Sometimes I Feel Like a Mother-
          less Child
       Get On Board, Little Children

155   Deep River
       John Brown's Body
       The House I Live In
       Loch Lomond
       Drink to Me Only with Thine
          Eyes
379   Joshua Fought the Battle of
          Jericho

Robeson, Paul: SWING LOW, SWEET CHARIOT: Traditional songs arr. by
       Lawrence Brown (16–*piano*)   *Columbia   ML 2038   10"   (1949)*

705   Swing Low, Sweet Chariot
196   Ev'ry Time I Feel de Spirit
       I Got a Home in Dat Rock

       O Gimme Your Han'
       No More Auction Block
       Great Gittin' Up Mornin'

	Hear de Lam's A-Cryin'	722	Hammer Song
	Goin' to Ride Up in de Chariot		Dere's a Man Goin' 'Round
	I'll Hear de Trumpet		I Know de Lord
197	Ezekiel Saw de Wheel	248	Git On Board, Little Chillen
579	Poor Wayfarin' Stranger	422	Lil' David

Rodgers, Jimmie: SINGS FOLK SONGS (*12—guitar*)   *Roulette   R-25042*
12″   (*1958*)

	Bo Diddley	674	Soldier, Won't You Marry Me?
608	The Riddle Song	451	Lord Randal
434	Liza	226	The Fox and the Goose
	I Love a Lassie	51	Black Is the Color
	The Crocodile Song	233	Froggy Went A-Courtin'
	Waltzing Matilda		Gotta Lotta Tunes in My Guitar

Ross, Bob: TO YOU WITH LOVE: AMERICAN FOLK SONGS FOR MEN
(*18 guitar*)   *Folkways   FA 2334   12″   (1957)*

51	Black Is the Color	551	On Top of Old Smoky
	Venezuela		I'm Gonna Marry
440	Turtle Dove		Mary, My Beloved
281	Green Sleeves	253	Go 'Way from My Window
	Spanish Is the Loving Tongue	165	Dinah and Villikins
604	Red River Valley	224	Foggy Dew
172	Down in the Valley	101	Careless Love
608	Riddle Song		Sugar Bush
	Laura		
	Drink to Me Only		

Rubin, Ruth: JEWISH CHILDREN'S SONGS AND GAMES (*12*) (*banjo,*
Pete Seeger)   *Folkways   FC 7224 (FC 724)   10″*

Michalku	Du Maydeleh Du Fines
By Dem Shteti	Oksn, Beker Lid
Yomi, Yomi, Tons, Tons	Homnstashn
Lomir Zich Ibberbetn	Shayn Bin Ich, Shayn, Bin Ich,
Amoi Iz Geven a Myseh	Shayn
Kesteleh	A Genayveh
Shpits-Boydim	

Rubin, Ruth: JEWISH FOLK SONGS (*17 Yiddish and Israeli Songs*)   *Oriole*
Records Vol. III   12″   (1954)

Gitare	Fishelech Koyfn
Sheltn, Shelt Ich Dem Tog	Beker Lid
Papir Iz Doch Vays	Dortn, Dortn Ibern Vasserl
Bay Dem Shtetl	Yafim Halelot
Ale Vasserlech	Zemmer Lach
Tonts, Tonts Antkegn Mir	Se Ug'di
Molad'ti	Zirmu Galim
Shir Ha-Hagana	Shir Ha-Avoda
Viglid	

Rubin, Ruth: YIDDISH LOVE SONGS (18)   *Riverside   RLP 12-647   12″*

Play for Me
Guitar
I Vow to You
Mother, Why Do You Torment
   Me?
To Buy Some Fish
I Am in Love
Two Little Turtle Doves
I Curse the Day
Where Have You Been?

If You Love Me
You Are Leaving Me
All the Rivulets
Tumbalalayka
Paper Is White
Listen, Little Maiden
At Parting
On the Sea
Silent, the Starry Night

Runge, John: CONCERT OF ENGLISH FOLK SONGS, A (18)   *Riverside
   RLP 12-814   12″*

Little Sir William
Old Daddy Fox
Poor Old Horse
224   The Foggy Dew
Turmut Hoein'
399   The Lady and the Swine
I Will Give My Love an Apple
Sucking Cider through a Straw

239   Geordie
Joe, the Carrier Lad
Sylvie
724   The Three Crows
471   The Mermaid
The Water Is Wide
Barley Mow
94   The Clucking Hen
674   Soldier, Soldier
Star, News, Standard

Runge, John: TRADITIONAL ENGLISH FOLK SONGS (21–guitar)
   Stinson   SLP-88   12″   (1958)

239   Geordie
The Oyster Girl
I Will Give My Love an Apple
Joe the Carrier Lad
Sylvie
The Lincolnshire Poacher
Poor Old Horse
Early One Morning
Turmut Hoein'
51   Black Is the Color of My True-
   Love's Hair
The Plymouth Maid's Lament
The Tailor and the Mouse

451   Lord Rendall
The Barley Mow
Topsy-Turvey Land
724   There Were Three Crows
Counting Sheep
The Mouse, the Frog and the
   Little Red Hen
Michael Finnegan
The Pigtail
Oh the Oak and the Ash

Sandburg, Carl: THE AMERICAN SONGBAG (15–guitar)   *Lyrichord
   LL-4   10″*

297   He's Gone Away
65   Boll Weevil Song
101   Careless Love
Mama Have You Heard the
   News
Saddle Song
In de Vinter Time
Man Goin' Roun'

303   The Horse Named Bill
Sam Hall
Moanish Lady
224   Foggy, Foggy Dew
324   I Wish I Was a Little Bird
335   I'm Sad and I'm Lonely
Cigarettes Will Spoil Yer Life
Jay Gould's Daughter

Sandburg, The Great Carl: * BALLADS AND SONGS (17—*guitar*)   *Lyrichord*

LL 66   12"

	The Good Boy	303	The Horse Named Bill
65	Boll Weevil Song		Jay Gould's Daughter
101	Careless Love	297	He's Gone Away
	In de Vinter Time	103	Casey Jones
	Moanish Lady!	319	I Ride an Old Paint
224	Foggy, Foggy Dew		Man Goin' Roun'
324	I Wish I Was a Little Bird	237	Gallows Song
335	I'm Sad and I'm Lonely		
	Cigarettes Will Spoil Yer Life		
	We'll Roll Back the Prices		

Schlamme, Martha: FOLK SONGS OF MANY LANDS (10)   *Vanguard*

7012   10"

Gizratech (Israeli)	248	Get on Board Little Children
Die Vogelhochzeit (Austrian)		(American)
Broiges, Yoshke Fuhrt Awek		No More Auction Block for Me
(Yiddish)		(American)
Paal Paa Haugen (Norwegian)		A Soulcake (English)
Harvest Dance (Russian)		Johnny, I Hardly Know You
I'm Going to Get Married (Nova		(Irish)
Scotian)		

Schlamme, Martha: FOLK SONGS OF MANY LANDS (16)   *Vanguard*

VRS-9019   12"

Die Vogelhochzeit (Austria)		Yoshke Fuhrt Awek (Jewish)
Broiges (Jewish)		Gizratech (Israel)
Roe Ve Roa (Israel)		Paal Paa Haugen (Norway)
Two Shepherd Songs (Israel)		A Soulcake (England)
La Petit Jeanneton (Swiss)		Buffalo Boy (U.S.)
I'm Going to Get Married (Nova		No More (U.S.)
Scotia)		Johnny I Hardly Know You
Just Like the Swallow (New-		(Ireland)
foundland)	248	Get on Board (U.S.)
Harvest Dance (Russia)		

Schlamme, Martha: GERMAN FOLK SONGS (12—*banjo & recorder by Pete*

Seeger)   *Folkways*   FW 6843 (FP 843)   10"   (1954)

Wenn Alle Bruennlein Fliessen	Ufm Berge, Da Geht der Wind
Da Drobn am Bergal	Bei Mondenschein
Rosestock Holderbluet	Yodel Song
Es Geht Eine Dunkle Wolk	Der Schwere Traum
Herein	Die Dedanken Sind Frei
Dat du Min Leevsten Bist	Muss I Denn?
Es Burebuebli	

* In 1959, Columbia issued a Sandburg record: FLAT ROCK BALLADS (ML 5339).

Schlamme, Martha: JEWISH FOLK SONGS (*16—orch.*)   *Vanguard*
                VRS-9011   12"   (*1947*)

Mal Komashmo Lon
Shein bin ich Shein
Tum-balalayka
Die Mesinke
Sug mir du shein Meidele
Dire-Gelt
A pintele
Oy, Dorta, Dorta, Ibern Vaser

Freilath
Partizaner Lid
Zog Nit Keynmol
Zhankoye
Til in Veldele
Chanuke, O Chanuke
Geh ich mir Spatzieren
Die Machetunem gehen

Scott, Tom: SING OF AMERICA, Gems of American Folklore (*12—guitar*)
                Coral   CRL 56056   10"   (*1952*)

	The Story of Twelve	680	Sourwood Mountain
369	John Henry	224	Foggy, Foggy Dew
	Scudda Hoo	644	Set Down Servant
233	Froggie Went A-Courtin'		Two Wings
293	Haul Away Joe	44	Billy Boy
674	Soldier Will You Marry Me	608	Riddle Song

Scott, Tom and Will Rogers, Jr.: GREAT AMERICAN FOLK HEROES (7)
                Judson Records   J-3013   12"

	Wild Bill Hickok	369	John Henry
689	Old Stormy		Paul Bunyan
641	Sam Bass		Rip Van Winkle
361	Jesse James		

Seeger, Peggy: [FOLKSONGS] (*8—banjo and guitar*)   *Topic Records*
                10 T 9   (*1958*)

160	Devilish Mary	120	Come All Ye Fair and Tender
145	Cumberland Gap		Ladies
331	I Never Will Marry	808	The Wife of Usher's Well
	The Lady of Carlisle		
	The Fair Maid by the Shore		
	The Deer Song		

Seeger, Peggy: ANIMAL FOLK SONGS FOR CHILDREN (*17*)   *Folkways*
                FC 7051   10"

	Little Brown Dog	517	Oh, Blue
598	The Big Sheep (The Ram of		The Deer Song (The Sally
	Darby)		Buck)
805	Riding Round the Cattle	725	And We Hunted, and We
	(Whoop-ti-yddle-um-yea)		Hunted (Three Jolly Welsh-
	The Old Cow Died (Sail		men)
	Around)		Peep Squirrel
	Raccoon and Possum		A Squirrel Is a Pretty Thing
	Little Lap-Dog Lullaby (Come		Snake Baked a Hoecake
	Up, Horsey)		Old Lady Goose
	Jack, Can I Ride? (See the Ele-		My Old Hen's Good Old Hen
	phant Jump the Fence)		(Chuck Old Hen)
	Daddy Shot a Bear		Of All the Beast-es (I'd Rather
			Be a Panther)

Seeger, Peggy: FOLK SONGS OF COURTING AND COMPLAINT (11–
banjo, guitar)   Folkways   FA 2049 (FP49)   10"

800	Whistle, Daughter, Whistle	762	The Wagoner's Lad
792	When I Was Single	443	Long Lonesome Road
304	The House Carpenter		The Old Maid
	When First Unto This Country		Leatherwing Bat
	All of Her Answers	92	The Butcher's Boy
839	Young Man Who Wouldn't Hoe		
	Corn		

Seeger, Peggy, Barbara, and Penny: AMERICAN FOLK SONGS FOR
CHRISTMAS (18)   Folkways   FC 7053   10"

In the Morning When I Rise		Bright Morning Stars Are Rising
Oh, Watch the Stars		Rise Up Shepherd and Follow
Shine Like a Star in the Morning	108	Joseph and Mary (The Cherry Tree Carol)
Oh, Mary and the Baby		Mary Had a Baby
Sweet Lamb	362	Jesus Born in Bethlea
Babe of Bethlehem		January, February (The Last Month of the Year)
Cradle Hymn		
Ain't That a Rockin' All Night		Poor Little Jesus
Sing Hallelu		The Angel Band
		The Twelve Apostles

Seeger, Pete: AMERICAN BALLADS (14–banjo, guitar)   Folkways
FA-2319   12"

588	Pretty Polly	260	The Golden Vanity
	The Three Butchers	285	Gypsy Davy
369	John Henry	213	The Farmer's Curst Wife
	Jay Gould's Daughter		Down in Carlisle
826	The Titanic Disaster	636	St. James Hospital
204	Fair Margaret and Sweet William	361	Jesse James
		36	Barbara Allen
368	John Hardy		

Seeger, Pete: AMERICAN FAVORITE BALLADS (17–banjo, guitar)
Folkways   FA-2320   12"   (1957)

172	Down in the Valley	87	Buffalo Gals
512	Mary Don't You Weep		Cielito Lindo
58	The Blue Tail Fly	762	The Wagoner's Lad
	So Long, It's Been Good to Know You	230	Frankie and Johnny
760	Wabash Cannon Ball	551	On Top of Old Smoky
673	Skip to My Lou	41	Rock Candy Mountain
825	Wreck of the 97		Yankee Doodle
520	Old Dan Tucker	391	I Ride an Old Paint
		302	Home on the Range

Seeger, Pete: AMERICAN FAVORITE BALLADS, Vol. II (18–banjo, guitar)
Folkways   FA 2321   12"   (1958)

513 Oh, Susanna!
608 The Riddle Song
     Beautiful City
     Sally Ann
     House of the Rising Sun
655 Shenandoah
474 Midnight Special
101 Careless Love
     Hard Travelling

569 Poor Boy
50   Black Girl
2   Alabama Bound
682 Stagolee
51   Black Is the Color
252 Go Tell Aunt Rhody
     The Water Is Wide
228 The Fox
     The Keeper and the Doe

Seeger, Pete: AMERICAN FOLK SONGS FOR CHILDREN (11–banjo)
Folkways   FC 7001 (FP701)   10"   (1953)

363 Jim Along Josie
     There Was a Man and He Was
       Mad
     Clap Your Hands
654 She'll Be Coming 'Round the
       Mountain

     All Around the Kitchen
     Billy Barlow
75   Bought Me a Cat
366 Jim Crack Corn
     Train Is A-Coming
     This Old Man
233 Frog Went A-Courting

Seeger, Pete: AMERICAN INDUSTRIAL BALLADS (24–banjo)   Folkways
FH 5251   12"

     Peg and Awl
     The Blind Fiddler
88   The Buffalo Skinners
     Eight Hour Day
292 Hard Times in the Mill
     Roll Down the Line
     Hayseed Like Me
     The Farmer Is the Man
     Come All You Hardy Miners
     He Lies in the American Land
103 Casey Jones
     Let Them Wear Their Watches
       Fine

     Weave Room Blues
     Seven Cent Cotton
     Mill Mother's Lament
     Fare Ye Well, Old Ely Branch
     Beans, Bacon and Gravy
     Death of Harry Simms
     Winnsboro Cotton Mill Blues
     Ballad of Barney Graham
     My Children Are Seven in
       Number
     Raggedy
     Pittsburgh Town
     Sixty Per Cent

SEEGER, PETE, AT CARNEGIE HALL WITH SONNY TERRY (18–banjo,
guitar, harmonica)   Folkways   FA 2412   12"   (1958)

     The Bells
     Ladies Auxiliary
564 Pick a Bale of Cotton
     I Know an Old Lady Who Swal-
       lowed a Fly
     Twelve Gates to the City
     Coal Creek March
227 Fox Chase
     Right on That Shore
     Rohzinkes mit Mandlen

     In Tarrytown
     Kum Ba Yah
     Cleano and Ladies Auxiliary
     Reuben James
692 Study War No More
     Passing Through
     Pay Day at Coal Creek
     Buddy Won't You Roll Down
       the Line
13   Arkansas Traveler

Seeger, Pete: BIRDS, BEASTS, BUGS AND LITTLE FISHES (*11–banjo*)
Folkways   FC 7010 (F 710)   10"

	Baa, Baa, Black Sheep		Doggies
283	Ground Hog		The Little Rooster
	Come All You Young Sailor Men	233	Frog Went A-Courting
	Alligator Hedgehog		I Know an Old Lady
	Teensy, Weensy Spider		
268	Grey Goose		
	Mister Rabbit		

Seeger, Pete: CONCERT (*17–banjo, guitar, recorder*)   Stinson   #57
2-10"   LP's

304	The House Carpenter		Winnsboro Cotton Mill Blues
280	Greenland Fisheries		Paddy Works on the Railway
	I Had a Wife		Long John
	Oh, Hard Is the Fortune	251	Go Down Old Hannah
	Oh, You Can Give Marriage a		The Road to Eilat
	Whirl		Money Is King
	Ariran		Kisses Sweeter Than Wine
	(Four Recorder Melodies)		In the Evening When the Sun
	Die Gedanken Sind Frei		Goes Down
	Bayeza		

Seeger, Peter: DARLING COREY (*16–banjo*)   Folkways   Fa 2003
(FP 3)   10"   (1950)

370	John Riley		**Banjo Pieces:**
612	Risselty-Rosselty	139	Cripple Creek
160	Devilish Mary	526	Old Joe Clark
	Come All Fair Maids	326	Ida Red
186	East Virginia Blues		My Blue-Eyed Gal
	I Had a Wife	355	Jam on Jerry's Rocks
	Skillet Good and Greasy		Penny's Farm
149	Darling Corey		Danville Girl
		246	Git Along Little Dogies

Seeger, Pete: FRONTIER BALLADS, Vol. 1 (*15–banjo*)   Folkways
FA 2175   (FP48/5)   10"

211	Fare You Well	367	Joe Bowers
	Polly		Wake Up Jacob
	No Irish Need Apply	145	Cumberland Gap
	Johnny Gray	193	Erie Canal
	Greer County Bachelor	57	Blow the Man Down
	Cowboy Yodel	560	Ox Driver's Song
735	The Trail to Mexico	711	The Texian Boys
		669	Sioux Indians

Seeger, Pete: FRONTIER BALLADS, Vol. 2 (*13–banjo*)   Folkways
FA 2176   (FP48/6)   10"

283	Ground Hog	526	Joe Clark
	Blue Mountain Lake		Mule in the Mine
	Paddy Works on the Railways		Holler
839	Wouldn't Hoe Corn	13	Arkansas Traveler

792   When I Was Single   630   Rye Whiskey
      Wondrous Love   773   Wayfaring Stranger
      Play Party

Seeger, Pete: GAZETTE, Vol. I, No. 1 (*20—banjo, guitar*)   *Folkways*
                    FN 2501   12″   (*1958*)
      Pretty Boy Floyd   Roll on Columbia
      Banks of Marble   Reuben James
      TVA Song   Then We'll Have Peace
      Martian Love Song   The Scaler
      42 Kids   Newspapermen
685   State of Arkansas   Talking Atom
      Declaration of Independence   Battle of Maxton Field
      Teachers' Blues   Doctor Freud
      The Wild West   There Is Mean Things
      Demi Song   Happening in This Land
      Ballad of Sherman Wu

Seeger, Pete: LOVE SONGS FOR FRIENDS AND FOES (*19—banjo, guitar
      chalil*)   *Folkways   FA 2453*   (*FP85/3*)   *12″*
      Open the Door   Kisses Sweeter Than Wine
      I'll Sing Me a Love-Song   Chalil Melody
      The Trip We Took Over the   Little Girl See through My
        Mountain   Window
      She Moved through the Fair   Strangest Dream
      Sally My Dear   Listen Mr. Bilbo
502   No, Sir, No!   Autherine
      Stranger's Blues   706   The Hammer Song
      I'm Gonna Walk and Talk with   River of My People
        Jesus   Ink Is Black
      Over the Hills   The Happy Whistler

PETE SEEGER SAMPLER (*12—banjo*)   *Folkways   FA 2043*   (*FP43*)   *10″*
      I'm on My Way   Hush! Tara, Tara
      Hey Lolly Lolly Lo   I Was Born in 1894
      Suliram   Deep Blue Sea
379   Joshua Fit the Battle of Jericho   Spanish Folk Song
376   Johnny Comes Down to Hilo   Dig My Grave
      Putting on the Style   Delia's Gone
      (Italian folksong: Christmas)

Seeger, Pete: WITH VOICES TOGETHER WE SING (*14—banjo*)   *Folkways*
                    FA 2452   (*FP85/2*)   *12″*
      Deep Blue Sea   691   Streets of Laredo
612   Risselty, Rosselty   Brandy Leave Me Alone
      Equinoxial   Didn't Old John
      Oleanna   Michael Row the Boat
      Chanukah   Senzenina
      What Month Was Jesus Born In   Wimoweh
      Que Bonita Bandera   Wasn't That a Time

Seeger, Pete and Frank Hamilton: NONESUCH AND OTHER FOLK TUNES
(14—harmonica, flute, recorder, mandolin, guitar, banjo, 12-string guitar, and
voices)   Folkways   FA 2439   12″   (1959)

Rye Straw
Ragtime Annie
I Know My Love
Lady Gay
Blues   451
Nonesuch
Singing in the Country
Chaconne

Ituri Tune
My Home's Across the Smoky
  Mountains
Pretty Little Widder
Lord Randall
Battle of New Orleans
Meadowlands

Sellers, Brother John: BLUES AND FOLKSONGS (15—piano, harmonica,
guitar, trumpet, bass, drums)   Vanguard   VRS-9036   12″

352   Jack of Diamonds
    Down by the Riverside
    I Love You Baby
    Every Day I Have the Blues
    Two Little Fishes
442   Lonesome Road
369   John Henry
    Sally Go Round the Sunshine

65   Boll Weevil
    Great Day
504   Nobody Knows the Trouble I've
    Seen
    Farewell Work Life
    Let Us Run
    Doretha Boogie
    When I've Been Drinking

Sellers, Brother John, and Sonny Terry: BLUES AND FOLK SONGS
(10—harmonica, guitar)   Vanguard   VRS-7022   10″

352   Jack of Diamonds
    I Love You, Baby
    Sally Go Round the Sunshine
    Every Day I Have the Blues
504   Nobody Knows the Trouble I've
    Seen

    Let Us Run
    I've Been Lonesome, I've Been
    Worried
    When I've Been Drinking
442   Lonesome Road
    Great Day

Silvera, Dick: FOLK SONGS, BALLADS, BLUES, WORK SONGS
(19—guitar, banjo by Dick Weissman)   Stinson   SLP-87   12″   (1958)

Skinner, Skinner
Pay Me My Money Down
Ninety-Six Miles from
  Birmingham
I'm Working My Way Back
  Home
Ragged Levee
Going Down the River
Drinkin' of the Wine
Come Love and Go with Me
Alberta Let Your Hair Hang
  Low
Whoa Mule

642   Sandy Anna
    I Gotta Lay in Yonder
    Graveyard
290   Hangin' Johnny
    When I'm Gone to Come No
    More
    Long John
    Make More Room
    Shilo Brown
    Heaven Doors Goin' to Be
    Closed
    Man Going Round Taking
    Names

Silverman, Jerry: FOLK BLUES, Vol. 1 (*12—guitar*)   *Audio-Video*
              A-V 101   12"   (*1958*)
737 Trouble in Mind   Buddy Bolden's Blues
     Talking Dust Bowl Blues   The Long-Line Skinner Blues
     Alberta, Let Your Hair Hang   Pay Day at Coal Creek
       Low   How Long?
     Number 12 Train   Things About Comin' My Way
     Marryin' Blue Yodel   Darlin'
     Been in the Pen So Long

Stafford, Jo: AMERICAN FOLK SONGS (*7—orchestra*)   *Capitol   H-75   10"*
579 Poor Wayfaring Stranger   325 I Wonder As I Wander
297 He's Gone Away   Red Rosey Bush
 51 Black Is the Color   36 Barbara Allen
500 The Nightingale

Steele, Pete: BANJO TUNES AND SONGS (*16—banjo*)   (*Recorded and
     edited by Ed Kahn*)   Folkways   FS 3828   12"   (*1958*)
     Ellen Smith   The War Is A-Raging for
417 Little Birdie   Johnny
649 Shady Grove   Coal Creek March
292 Hard Times   Last Payday at Coal Creek
     Goin' Around This World   326 Ida Red
     Baby Mine   588 Pretty Polly
186 East Virginia   The Scolding Wife
144 The Cuckoo   304 The House Carpenter
     The Train Is A-Pulling the
       Crooked Hill

Stekert, Ellen: OZARK MOUNTAIN FOLKSONGS Vol. 1 (*8—guitar*)
                  Stinson   SLP 49   10"
     Down by the Sea Shore   800 Whistle, Daughter, Whistle
     Grandma's Advice   Wildwood Flower
549 On the Banks of the Sweet   Putting on the Style
       Dundee   102 Caroline of Edinborough Town
216 Father Grumble

Stekert, Ellen: SONGS OF A NEW YORK LUMBERJACK (*18—guitar*)
                  Folkways   FA 2354   12"
     Bounding the U.S.   228 The Fox
     The Hills of Glenshee   The Cumberland and the
     The Western Pioneers   Merrimac
746 The Two Sisters   The Singular Dream
     Johnny Troy   400 Lake of Ponchartrain
     Poor Old Anthony Rolly   The Black Cook
     Pat Murphy of the Irish Brigade   Abe Lincoln Went to
     The Drummer Boy   Washington
     The Trouble Down at   The Shanty Boy and the
       Homestead   Farmer's Son
                                        The Raftman's Song
                                   359 The Jealous Lover

Stracke, Win: AMERICANA *(12—guitar by Richard Pick)*   *Bally*
Bal-12013   12"   (1957)

	Paul Bunyan's Manistee	667 Single Girl
	No Irish Need Apply	Duncan and Brady
768	Wanderin'	Acres of Clams
	Debate: Cold Water Versus Rye	Venezuela
	Whiskey	119 The Colorado Trail
41	Big Rock Candy Mountain	Ladies' Man
166	Dink's Song	

Stracke, Win: GOLDEN TREASURY OF SONGS AMERICA SINGS
(with Arthur Norman Chorus)   (22)   *Golden Records*
GLP:31   12"   (1958)

520	Old Dan Tucker	87	Buffalo Gals
53	Black Eyed Susie	19	Aunt Rhody
680	Sourwood Mountain		Paddy Works on the Railway
655	Shenandoah		Elanoy
	Un Deux Trois	611	Rio Grande
103	Casey Jones	308	Hush Little Baby
175	Drill Ye Tarriers	65	Boll Weevil
369	John Henry	576	Poor Lonesome Cowboy
564	Pick a Bale of Cotton	115	Cindy
193	The E-r-i-e Canal		Leather Winged Bat
386	Kemo Kimo		One More Day

Summers, Andrew Rowan: CHRISTMAS CAROLS *(6—dulcimer)*   *Folkways*
FA 2002   10"

Hark, the Herald Angels Sing	Silent Night
Lully, Lullay Thou Tiny Little	God Rest You Merry
Child	Gentlemen
O Come All Ye Faithful	Good King Wenceslas

Summers, Andrew Rowan: "THE FALSE LADYE" *(6—dulcimer)*   *Folkways*
FA 2044   (FP44)   10"

The Ballad of Lady Hamilton	763	Waly, Waly
The False Ladye	44	Billy Boy
Willie of Hazel Green	746	The Two Sisters

Summers, Andrew Rowan: HYMNS AND CAROLS, *Early American Folksongs*
(7—dulcimer)   *Folkways*   FA 2361   (FP61)   12"

	Wondrous Love	108	Cherry Tree Carol No. 2
	Land of Pleasure		The Babe of Bethlehem
296	The Hebrew Children		
	Garden Hymn		
	Boundless Mercy		

Summers, Andrew Rowan: THE LADY GAY *(7—dulcimer)*   *Folkways*
FA 2041   (FP41)   10"

108	The Cherry Tree Carol	237	The Hangman's Tree
	The Lady Gay	744	Two Brothers
516	Old Bangum		Early One Morning
36	Barbara Allen		

Summers, Andrew Rowan: SEEDS OF LOVE (6–dulcimer) *Folkways*
FA 2021 (FP21) 10"

The Seeds of Love		Hares on the Mountain
My Mother Chose My Husband	213	The Farmer's Curst Wife
Plaint for My Lost Youth	508	O, No, John!

Summers, Andrew Rowan: SINGS [BALLADS] (9–dulcimer) *Folkways*
FA 2348 12"

	I Will Give My Love an Apple	655	Shenandoah
152	The Death of Queen Jane		Full Moon
	Blackbirds and Thrushes		O Death Rock Me Asleep
727	The Three Ravens	452	Lord Thomas and Fair Ellender
226	Old Mr. Fox		

Summers, Andrew Rowan: THE UNQUIET GRAVE, *American Tragic Ballads*
(8–dulcimer) *Folkways* FA 2364 (FP 64) 12" (1952)

755	The Unquiet Grave	140	The Cruel Brother
	Searching for Lambs	239	Geordie
589	Pretty Sally		At the Foot of Yonders Mountain
738	The True Lover's Farewell	304	The House Carpenter

Sykes, Paul: GREAT AMERICAN FOLK SONGS (12) *Crown*
CLP-5057 12"

58	Blue Tail Fly	19	Aunt Rhody
	I Know an Old Woman	224	Foggy Foggy Dew
520	Old Dan Tucker		Venezuela
551	On Top of Old Smoky	592	The Prison Song
41	Big Rock Candy Mountain	319	I Ride an Old Paint
	Hullabaloo Belay	342	Goodnight Irene

Temple, Pick: FOLK SONGS OF THE PEOPLE (8–guitar) RCA "X"
LXA-3022 10"

	Down, Down, Down	369	John Henry
320	I Was Born 10,000 Years Ago		Colley's Run-I-O
	I Had a Bird	375	Johnny Sands
	Sal on the Erie Canal		The Runaway Logger Train

Terry, Sonny: CITY BLUES (10–harmonica, with guitar by Alec Stewart)
Elektra EKL-15 10"

Chain the Lock on My Door	Custard Pie
Little Annie	Kansas City
Louise Blues	Late One Saturday Evening
Down in the Bottom Blues	Old Woman Blues
Baby, Baby Blues	Hard Luck Blues

Terry, Sonny: FOLK BLUES (8–mouth harp, guitar) *Elektra*
EKL-14 10" (1954)

227	The Fox Chase	369	John Henry
	Talking About the Blues		Mama Told Me
	Goodbye Leadbelly		Moaning and Mourning Blues
604	Red River		In the Evening

Terry, Sonny: HARMONICA AND VOCAL SOLOS (8)   *Folkways*
                FA 2035   (FP 35)   10"

Alcoholic Blues	661 Shortnin' Bread
Women's Blues	Stomp
Lost John	Hollers
Fine False	
Beautiful City	

SONNY TERRY AND HIS MOUTH HARP (8—*harmonica*)   *Stinson*
                SLP #55   10"

Greyhound Bus Blues	Don't You Hear Me Calling You
She Is a Sweet Woman	Blues
South Bound Express	Tell Me Little Woman
You Don't Want Me Blues	Silver Fox Chase
Worried and Lonesome Blues	

Terry, Sonny: and His "MOUTH-HARP" (14)   *Riverside*   RLP 12-644   12"

In the Evening	Custard Pie
Kansas City	I Woke Up This Mornin'
369 John Henry	Old Woman Blues
227 The Fox Chase	Talkin' about the Blues
Louise Blues	Chain the Lock on My Door
604 Red River	Moanin' and Mournin'
Goodbye, Leadbelly	Baby, Baby

Todd, Dylan: LOVE SONGS, OLD AND NEW (15)   *Judson Records*
                J-3010   12"   (1958)

Aura Lee	604 Red River Valley
281 Greensleeves	51 Black Is the Color
Passing By	Mo Mary
My Love's an Arbutus	276 Green Grow the Lilacs
Unchained Melody	763 Waly, Waly
A Border Affair	Autumn's Going
To Celia	Early One Morning
Troubadour's Song	

Traubel, Helen: NEGRO SPIRITUALS and BALLADS (6—*orch.*)   *Columbia*
                ML-4221   12"

705 Swing Low, Sweet Chariot	250 Go Down Moses
784 Were You There?	504 Nobody Knows de Trouble I've
155 Deep River	Seen
686 Steal Away	(Popular ballads, titles not listed—6)

Travis, Merle: BACK HOME (12—*guitar*)   *Capitol*   T 891   12"   (1957)

708 Nine Pound Hammer	581 Possum Up a 'Simmon Tree
That's All	I Am a Pilgrim
369 John Henry	Over by Number Nine
730 John Bolin	36 Barbara Allen
Muskrat	Lost John
Dark As a Dungeon	Sixteen Tons

Van Wey, Adelaide: ALL DAY SINGIN', Louisiana and Smoky Mountain
Ballads (9—guitar, zither)   Folkways   FA 2009   (FP 9)   10″   (1950)

All Day Singin'
The Cheat
Birdie
The Blackbird and the Crow
Tan Patate—La Tchuite (When
   Your Potato's Done It's Time
   to Eat It)

Fais Do Do (Go to Sleep)
En Avant Granadie (Forward
   March Grenadiers)
Mon Cher Sabin
Gue, Gue, Solingaie (Sweep the
   Dreampath Clear)

Van Wey, Adelaide: CREOLE SONGS AND STREET CRIES OF NEW
ORLEANS (11—zither)   Folkways   FA 2202   (FP602)   10″

Remon
Lu-Lu-Lu
Salangadou
Aine, De, Toue
Fais Do Do
Mon Cher Sabin

Momzell Zizi
Jacques
Compere La Pain
Tan' Siro E Dou
Maison Denise

Vincent, Jenny Wells: SPANISH-AMERICAN CHILDREN'S SONGS
(10—guitar, accordion) (Sung in both Spanish and English)
Cantemos Records Amerecord ALP-102 10″ (1957)

Mi Gallo Tuerto (My One-Eyed Rooster)
Canto de Cuna (Cradle Song)
Mi Chacra (My Farm)
Las Mananitas (Morning Serenades)
A La Puerta del Cielo (At the Gate of Heaven)
El Zapatero (The Shoemaker)
El Quelele (The White Hawk)
El Coqui (The Frog)
Tecolote de Guadana (The Owl of Guadana)
Don Simon

WANDERIN' WITH STAN WILSON (7—guitar)   Cavalier   Cav 5505   10″

768   Wanderin'
      Baltimore Oriole
298   High Barbaree

224   Foggy Foggy Dew
      Woman with the Rollin' Pin
      Bridge
36   Barbara Allen

WANDERIN' WITH STAN WILSON (10—guitar)   Cavalier   Cav 6002   10″

768   Wanderin'
230   Frankie and Johnnie
      Venezuela
369   John Henry
36   Barbara Allen
      Tongue Tied Baby

224   Foggy Foggy Dew
      King Edward Eighth
      Bing Crosby
      High Noon

Warfield, William: DEEP RIVER (6—symphony)   Columbia   AAL 32   10″

155   Deep River
      Water Boy
      Without a Song
      Mah Lindy Lou

Jeanie with the Light Brown
   Hair
Dusty Road

Warfield, William: OLD AMERICAN SONGS and FIVE SEA CHANTIES
(10—piano)   Columbia   ML 2206   10"

	The Boatman's Dance	611	Rio Grande
	The Dodger		Blow Ye Winds
444	Long Time Ago		Across the Western Ocean
	Simple Gifts		Mobile Bay
310	I Bought Me a Cat	655	Shenandoah

Warner, Frank: AMERICAN FOLK SONGS AND BALLADS (10—banjo)
Elektra   EKLP-3   10"   (1952)

385	Keep Your Hand on the Plow	151	The Days of Forty-Nine
	Hold My Hand, Lord Jesus		Gilgarry Mountain
450	Lord Lovel		Blue Mountain Lake
	Battle of Bull Run	731	Tom Dooley
263	The Unreconstructed Rebel		
	He's Got the Whole World in His Hand		

Warner, Frank: SONGS AND BALLADS OF AMERICA'S WARS (13—banjo,
guitar)   Elektra   EKL-13   10"   (1954)

	Felix the Soldier		Perry's Victory
	The Press Gang Soldier		The Battle-Cry of Freedom
	The Ballad of Montcalm and Wolfe		The Twenty-Third
			Virginia's Bloody Soil
	Doodle Dandy		The Southern Girl's Reply
	Paul Jones	263	An Old Unreconstructed
	The British Soldier		The Bonnie Blue Flag

West, Harry and Jeanie: GOSPEL SONGS (16)   Folkways   FA 2357   12"

	When Our Lord Shall Come Again		The Man of Galilee
			Oh, Hide You in the Blood
	Matthew Twenty-Four	8	Amazing Grace
	What Are They Doing in Heaven Today		Preach the Gospel
			Only One Step More
	Sweet Bye and Bye		Thirty Pieces of Silver
	Walking My Lord Up Calvary's Hill		The Sea of Life
			I'm Gonna Let It Shine
	He'll Set Your Fields on Fire		I'm Only on a Journey Here
	Campin' in Canaan's Land		

West, Harry and Jeanie: MORE SOUTHERN MOUNTAIN FOLK SONGS
(10—guitar, banjo, mandolin)   Stinson   SLP 74   10"

649	Shady Grove		Cryin' Holy
	Wildwood Flower		Gypsy Girl
	Katy Cline	586	Pretty Little Pink
186	East Virginia	29	Bangham and the Boar
	Walkin' in My Sleep		Katy Dear

West, Harry and Jeanie: SMOKY MOUNTAIN BALLADS (17)   *Esoteric*
ES-545   12"

	Sing Song Kitty		Bringing in the Georgia Mail
599	Rambling Boy		Little Red Shoes
	Watermelon on the Vine	588	Pretty Polly
430	The Little Rosewood Casket		Working on a Building
52	Black Jack Davie	440	Lonesome Dove
	Mother's Only Sleeping		Where the Soul Never Dies
336	I'm Troubled, I'm Troubled	36	Barbara Allen
	Goodbye Maggie	798	Where Are You Going, Alice?
	Handsome Molly		

West, Harry and Jeanie: SOUTHERN MOUNTAIN FOLK SONGS (*10—guitar,*
banjo, mandolin)   *Stinson*   *SLP 36*   *10"*

	Red Rockin' Chair		Old Reuben
374	Jimmy Randall		George Collins
	Little Birdie		Little Maggie
	Down in a Willow Garden		Nellie Cropsey
	The Old Arm Chair		Drifting Too Far from the Shore

West, Lucretia: SPIRITUALS (*18—piano*)   *Westminster*   *WP-6063*
12"   (1957)

	Weepin' Mary	130	Couldn't Hear Nobody Pray
539	Ol' Time Religion	677	Sometimes I Feel Like a Mother-
	I Want Jesus to Walk with Me		less Child
610	Ride On, King Jesus	4	All God's Chillun Got Wings
	De Blin' Man Stood on de Road		Peter, Go Ring Dem Bells
196	Ev'ry Time I Feel de Spirit		Wade in de Water
504	Nobody Knows de Trouble I've		Let Us Break Bread Together
	Seen	615	Roll, Jordan, Roll
	We Are Clim'in' Jacob's Ladder	422	Lil'le David Play on Yo' Harp
266	De Gospel Train		
	Sinner, Please Don't Let Dis		
	Harves Pass		

White, Josh: [BALLADS AND BLUES] (*16—guitar*)   *Decca*   *DL 8665*   12"

313	I Gave My Love a Cherry	369	John Henry
482	Molly Malone		Nobody Knows You When
274	Green Grass Growing All		You're Down and Out
	Around		Evil-Hearted Man
	The Lass with the Delicate Air		Jelly, Jelly
	Strange Fruit		Sometime
451	Lord Randall, My Son	230	Frankie and Johnny
	Watercress		Black Water Blues
	Waltzing Matilda		Josh and Bill Blues

White, Josh: BALLADS AND BLUES (8—*guitar*) Vol. I   *Decca*   *DL 5082*
10"   (1949)

313   I Gave My Love a Cherry
    Evil Hearted Man
    Nobody Knows You When You
      Are Down and Out
230   Frankie and Johnny
    The Lass with the Delicate Air

369   John Henry
    Someday
    Strange Fruit

White, Josh: CHAIN GANG SONGS (10—*guitar, with vocal quartet, bass, and*
drums)   *Elektra*   *EKL-158*   12"   (1958)

737   Trouble
    'Twas on a Monday
    Going Home, Boys
    Nine Foot Shovel
    Crying Who? Crying You
    Dip Your Fingers in the Water

536   The Old Ship of Zion
    Mary Had a Baby
196   Every Time I Feel the Spirit
    Did You Ever Love a Woman

White, Josh: JOSH AT MIDNIGHT (12)   (*with Sam Gary and Al Hall*)
Elektra   *EKL-102*   12"

636   St. James Infirmary
597   Raise a Rukus
    Scandalize My Name
    Jesus Gonna Make Up My Dyin'
      Bed
    Timber
    Jelly, Jelly
    One Meat Ball

379   Joshua Fit the Battle of Jericho
    Don't Lie Buddy
    Number Twelve Train
    Peter
    Takin' Names

White, Josh: JOSH WHITE COMES A-VISITING   *Period*   *SLP 1115*
10"   (1956)
(song titles not available)

White, Josh: SINGS [FOLKSONGS] (*guitar*)   *Mercury*   *MG-25014*
10"   (1949)
(song titles not available)

White, Josh: JOSH [SINGS BLUES] (12—*guitar, with bass by Al Hall and*
drums by Sonny Greer)   *Elektra*   *EKL-114*   12"

474   Midnight Special
    Miss Otis Regrets
    Halleleu
    Woman Sure Is a Curious Critter
    Prison Bound Blues
    Gloomy Sunday

    Ball and Chain Blues
    One for My Baby
    Jim Crow Train
    Told My Captain
    So Soon in the Mornin'
    Bury My Body

White, Josh: A JOSH WHITE PROGRAM (*12—guitar*)   *London*   *LL 1147*
(*LPB-338*)   *10"*

	Call Me Darling		Apples, Peaches, and Cherries
	Like a Natural Man		Take a Gal Like You
	The Lass with the Delicate Air		Waltzing Matilda
36	Barbara Allen	442	Lonesome Road
224	Foggy Foggy Dew	482	Molly Malone
	I'm Gonna Move to the Outskirts of Town	295	He Never Said a Mumbling Word

White, Josh: THE JOSH WHITE STORIES (Vol. 1) (*12—guitar*)   *ABC Paramount   ABC-124   12"*

65	Boll Weevil	129	Cotton-Eyed Joe
	Water Cress		Nobody Knows You When You're Down and Out
	What You Gonna Do		When I Lay Down and Die Do
	I'm a Mean Mistreater		Die
230	Frankie and Johnny		
	House of the Rising Sun	292	Hard Times Blues
181	Dupree	295	He Never Said a Mumblin' Word

White, Josh: THE JOSH WHITE STORIES (Vol. 2) (*12—guitar*)   *ABC Paramount   ABC-166   12"*

	Good Morning Blues	Two Little Fishes and Five Loaves of Bread
268	The Gray Goose	
	You Won't Let Me Go	I Know Moonlight
	Don't Smoke in Bed	Red River
737	Trouble in Mind	I Had a Woman
677	Sometimes I Feel Like a Motherless Child	Fine and Mellow
		Strange Fruit

White, Josh: JOSH WHITE'S BLUES (*10—guitar*) *Mercury MG20203 12"*

	How Long How Long Blues		I Had to Stoop to Conquer You
101	Careless Love		Baby
	Oh Lula		I Know How to Do It
	St. Louis Blues	166	Dink's Blues
	Kansas City Blues		Mint Julep
			Good Morning Blues

White, Josh: SINGS (*8—guitar*)   *Stinson   SLP #15   10"*

	One Meat Ball		Well, Well, Well
	Motherless Children		T. B. Blues
636	St. James Infirmary	379	Joshua Fit the Battle of Jericho
101	Careless Love		
	Outskirts of Town		

White, Josh: SINGS THE BLUES (*9—guitar*)   *Stinson   SLP #14   10"*

	Baby, Baby		Mean Mistreatin' Woman
181	Dupree		When I Lay Down and Die Do
	Miss Otis Regrets		Die
211	Fare Thee Well		I Got a Head Like a Rock
	No. 12 Train	129	Cotton Eyed Joe

White, Josh: THE STORY OF JOHN HENRY and BALLADS, BLUES AND
OTHER SONGS (8)   *Elektra*   *EKL-701*   *2-10" LP's*

THE STORY OF JOHN		BALLADS, etc.
HENRY complete on one 10"	50	Black Girl
LP		Free and Equal Blues
		Live the Life
		Sam Hall
		Where Were You, Baby
		Delia's Gone
		Run, Mona, Run
		You Don't Know My Mind

White, Josh: 25th ANNIVERSARY ALBUM (*guitar*)   *Elektra   EKL-123   12"*

Side 1:		**Side 2:**
Story of John Henry	50	Black Girl
musical narrative specially		Free and Equal Blues
prepared by Josh White		Live the Life
		Sam Hall
		Where Were You Baby
		Delia's Gone
		Run, Mona, Run
		You Don't Know My Mind

White, Kitty: KITTY WHITE SINGS [FOLKSONGS] (*12*)   *Mercury*
MG20183   12"

680	Sourwood Mountain	211	Fare Thee Well
	Leather Winged Bat		Chicken Road
	If I Had a Ribbon Bow		Dark As a Dungeon
709	Ten Thousand Miles	579	Poor Wayfaring Stranger
727	Three Ravens		Hammer Man
	West Wind		
	Love Is Like a Mountain		

Wilder, Dick: PIRATE SONGS AND BALLADS (*9—guitar*)   *Elektra*
EKL-18   10"   (1954)

	The Bold Princess Royal	99	Captain Kidd
	The Romantic Pirate		The Female Smuggler
	Henry Martyn		Bold Manning
	The Female Warrior	298	High Barbaree
		223	The Flying Cloud

Williams, Betty Vaiden: FOLK SONGS AND BALLADS OF NORTH CARO-
LINA (*17—autoharp*)   *Vanguard   VRS-9028   12"*

436	Lolly too dum		Vandy, Vandy
763	Wailee Wailee		The Lass from the Low Countree
	One Day As I Wandered	440	Turtle Dove
51	Black Is the Color	253	Go 'Way from My Window
804	Who's Going to Shoe My Pretty	313	I Gave My Love a Cherry
	Little Foot		

I Wonder When I Shall Be Married	773 Wayfaring Stranger
607 The Rich Old Lady	My Old Man
Young Hunting	71 Bonnie Wee Lassie
	36 Barbara Allen

Williams, Camilla: SPIRITUALS (8—piano)   M-G-M Records   E-156   10"

301 Hold On	Talk About a Child
City Called Heaven	On Ma Journey
Poor Me	His Name So Sweet
When I've Done	Oh, What a Beautiful City

Wilson, Stan: BALLADS AND CALYPSO (12—guitar)   Verve
MG V-2019   12"

Walter Winchell	The Old Lady Who Swallowed
228 The Fox	a Fly
Blow the Candles Out	The Cry of the Wild Goose
Sixteen Come Sunday	One for My Baby (and One
Potato	More for the Road)
When I Lay This Body Down	Kitch
Tol' My Cap'n	They Call the Wind Maria

Wilson, Stan: CALYPSO (11—guitar)   Verve   MG V-2051   12"

Mary Ann	Don't Stop the Carnival
Run, Come See Jerusalem	Boombay
Sloop, John B.	Pound Your Plantain in the
My Name Is Morgan but It	Mortar
Ain't J.P.	You Don't Need Glasses to See
Jane, Jane, Jane	Waikiki Farewell
Delia Gone	

Wilson, Stan: FOLK SONGS (12—guitar)   Verve   MG V-2076   12"

Miner's Lament (Coal So Black —Ore So Gray)	108 Cherry Tree Carol
Eight Babies	Marching to Pretoria
The Old Woman	270 Ship Titanic
Adieu Fulard, Adieu Madra	John the Revelator
Night Rider	Lili Marlene
Galveston Flood	The Hawaiian Wedding Song

Wilson, Stan: LEISURE TIME (12—guitar)   Cavalier   Cav 6003   12"

636 St. James Infirmary	451 Lord Randall
Ugly Woman	Bridge
Evil-Hearted Man	Woman with the Rolling Pin
Lowland Sea	You Girls
Donkey City	Baltimore Oriole
281 Greensleeves	
Waltzing Matilda	

Wood, Hally: AMERICAN FOLKSONGS OF SADNESS AND MELANCHOLY (11—Guitar)   Elektra   EKL-10   10"   (1953)

House of the Rising Sun	590 Pretty Saro
When I Was a Young Girl	Burns and His Highland Mary

    O Lovely Appearance of Death   435   Locks and Bolts
    Death Come Creeping   My Dearest Dear
588   Pretty Polly   King's Highway
                                          O Daddy Be Gay

Wood, Hally: TEXAS FOLK SONGS *(14–guitar, banjo)*   *Stinson*
                       SLP #73   *10"*

    Sugar Babe   131   Courting Case
    O Freedom   Come and Go with Me
    Worried Blues   Love Henry
792   When I Was Single   8   Amazing Grace
    B'lieve I'll Call the Captain   Santa Claus Blues
    Farther Along   Red Apple Juice
636   St. James Hospital   Glory Hallelujah

Yarbrough, Glenn: COME AND SIT BY MY SIDE *(14–guitar)*   *Tradition*
                       TLP 1019   *12"*

604   Red River Valley   569   Poor Boy
    Dark As a Dungeon   Capitol Ship
368   John Hardy   The Tailor and the Mouse
    Lonesome Valley   Suspiros del Chanchamayo
547   Banks of the Ohio   Old Maid's Song
    All Round My Hat   Come Again
    My Mule Sal
    Waltzing Matilda

Yarbrough, Glenn: HERE WE GO, BABY *(15–guitar)*   *Elektra*   *EKL-135*
                       12"   *(1958)*

    Rich Gal, Poor Gal   440   Turtle Dove
    Spanish Is a Loving Tongue   264   Goodbye My Lover
    Hey, Jim Along   553   One More River
    Johnny I Hardly Knew You   Sailor's Grave
    All My Sorrows   Wasn't That a Mighty Day
    Hard Ain't It Hard   House of the Rising Sun
    All Through the Night   This Land Is Your Land
    Here We Go, Baby

CHAPTER 20

Long-Playing Records of Choral or Other Groups, Instrumentals, etc.

THE preliminary discussion given in Chapter 19 applies to the present chapter and is therefore not repeated here. The one point to be added pertains to the method of alphabetizing. Here the records are listed alphabetically according to the over-all record title and not by singers. For example, the beginning of a listing will read, *Folk Songs of the New World*, or *Instrumental Music of the Southern Appalachians*, or *Riverside Folksong Sampler*. If appropriate, then the performing group is named after the title, and other data are set down in proper order.

AFRO-AMERICAN BLUES AND GAME SONGS (25)   *Lib. of Cong. Music Div.   AAFS L 4   12"*

	I Don't Mind the Weather	227	Fox Chase
162	Diamond Joe		All Hid?
	Joe the Grinder		Little Girl, Little Girl
10	Another Man Done Gone		Pullin' the Skiff
65	Boll Weevil Blues		Old Uncle Rabbit
	Two White Horses		Sea Lion Woman
	Country Rag		Ain't Gonna Ring No More
662	Shorty George	661	Shortnin' Bread
	Blues		Poor Little Johnny
	Country Blues		Go to Sleep
336	I Be's Troubled	624	Rosie
	Lost John		Run, Nigger, Run
	Gon' Knock John Booker to the Low Ground		
586			

AFRO-AMERICAN SPIRITUALS, WORK SONGS, AND BALLADS (17)
Lib. of Cong. Music Div.   AAFS L 3   12"

Trouble So Hard
Choose Your Seat and Set Down
Handwriting on the Wall
498 The New Buryin' Ground
408 Lead Me to the Rock
The Blood-Strained Banders
Run Old Jeremiah
Ain't No More Cane on This Brazos
Long Hot Summer Days

445 Look Down That Long, Lonesome Road
Long John
Jumpin' Judy (2)
624 Rosie
I'm Going to Leland
268 The Grey Goose
369 John Henry

AMERICAN BANJO SCRUGGS STYLE (Tunes and songs from southeast coast states) (12)   Folkways   FA 2314   12"

369 John Henry
442 Lonesome Road Blues
139 Cripple Creek
254 Going Down the Road
Sally Anne
638 Sally Goodin

344 Irish Washerwoman
740 Turkey in the Straw
129 Cotton-Eye Joe
Train 45
115 Cindy
283 Ground Hog

AMERICAN BANJO TUNES AND SONGS WITH THE STONEMAN FAMILY AND VARIANTS OF BANJO PICKING WITH SUTPHIN, FOREACRE AND DICKENS, Recorded by Michael Seeger (21)   Folkways FA 2315   12"

Say Darling
Black Dog Blues
When the Springtime Comes
Stoney's Waltz
499 The New River Train
The Hallelujah Side
145 Cumberland Gap
John Brown
42 Bile Them Cabbage Down
825 The Wreck of the 97

442 Lonesome Road Blues
Little Sadie
Late Last Night
Frankie Was a Good Girl
I Met a Handsome Lady
369 John Henry
The Cruel War
The Golden Pen
13 The Arkansas Traveler
A Rose in Grandma's Garden
Lost John

AMERICAN CHILDREN SING CHRISTMAS CAROLS (sung by five children's choirs of New York) (24)   Westminster   WP-6026   12"   (1956)

Joy to the World (English)
Noardil se Kristus Pan (Czech)
Stille Nacht (German)
Voces Varias (Spanish)
Hark! The Herald Angels Sing (English)
Les Anges dans Nos Campagnes (French)
Vesela Koleda (Czech)

Las Velitas de Navidad (Spanish)
The First Noel (English)
O Du Fröhliche (German)
Nesem Vam Noviny (Czech)
Il Est Né, le Divin Enfant (French)
God Rest You Merry Gentlemen (English)

Chtic aby spal (Czech)
Am Weihnachtsbaum (German)
Good King Wenceslas (English)
Sel bych rád k Beltemu (Czech)
O Come All Ye Faithful (English and German)

Weihnachtsglocken (German)
Deck the Halls (English)
El Niño Jesús (Spanish)
Noël Nouvelet (French)
Coventry Carol (English)
Co to Znamená (Czech)

AMERICAN FOLK DANCE, by Eva Decker and Harley Luse (10)
Imperial   FD-102   10"

Decker:

759   Virginia Reel
Spanish Waltz
Boston Two Step
Oxford Minuet
Fireman's Dance

Luse:

Spanish Circle
Glow-worm
129   Cotton-Eyed Joe
Veleta Waltz
California Schottische

AMERICAN FOLK SONGS SUNG BY THE SEEGERS (Peggy, Barbara, and
Michael, with notes by Charles Seeger) (12—autoharp, banjo, mandolin,
fiddle, guitar)   Folkways   FA 2005   10"

Old Molly Hare
When I First Came to This
Land
Jane
606   The Rich Irish Lady
My Home's Across the Smoky
Mountain

Freight Train Blues
The Wedding Dress Song
202   Fair Ellender
Five Times Five
The Kicking Mule
Dance to Your Daddy
Goodbye Little Bonnie

AMERICAN FOLK TALES AND SONGS: Told by Richard Chase and sung
by Jean Ritchie and Paul Clayton (15)   Tradition   TLP 1011   12"

435   Locks and Bolts
The Snakebit Hoehandle
522   The Old Grey Goose Is Dead
The Big Toe
Wondrous Love
695   Swapping Song
Hickory Toothpick

608   Riddle Song
Gambling Suitor
That's Once
Bashful Courtship
Split Dog
Deaf Woman's Courtship
Man in the Kraut Tub
161   Devil's Questions

AMERICAN SEA SONGS AND SHANTIES (I), Ed. D. B. M. Emrich, sung
by Richard Maitland, Noble B. Brown, Captain Leighton Robinson (11)
Lib. of Cong. Music Div.   AAFS L 26   12"   (1939-51)

Maitland:

Haul the Bowline
178   The Drunken Sailor
14   A-Roving, or The Amsterdam
Maid
Paddy, Get Back
Heave Away
Paddy Doyle

Brown:

56   Blow, Boys, Blow
605   Reuben Ranzo

Robinson:

The Sailor's Alphabet
The Dead Horse, or Poor Old
Man
372   Johnny Boker

AMERICAN SEA SONGS AND SHANTIES (II), *Ed. D. M. Emrich, sung by John M. Hunt, Noble B. Brown, Richard Maitland, Captain Leighton Robinson, as shantymen, with Alex Barr, Arthur Brodeur, and Leighton McKenzie (10)   Lib. of Cong. Music Div.   AAFS L 27   12"* (1939-46)

Hunt:

794   When Jones's Ale Was New

Brown:

57   Blow the Man Down

Maitland:

57   Blow the Man Down, II
       So Handy, Me Boys, So Handy

444   A Long Time Ago

Robinson:

611   Rio Grande
799   Whisky Johnny
       Roll the Cotton Down
618   Rollin' Home
       Homeward Bound

AMERICAN SQUARE DANCE GROUP: RUNNING SET AND LONG-WAYS DANCES (*Margot Mayo, Leader*) (20)   *Decca   DL 8012   12"*

       Hog-Eyed Sally
638   Sally Goodin
       Turkey Buzzard
       Sugar in the Gourd
       Old Granny Hare
526   Old Joe Clark
675   Soldier's Joy
       Sugar in My Coffee
409   Leather Britches
680   Sourwood Mountain
       Pigtown Fling

       Money Musk
       Boston Fancy
       Hull's Victory
       Tempest
       Fireman's Dance
759   Virginia Reel
740   Turkey in the Straw
       John Brown's Body
       Thady You Gander

ANGLO-AMERICAN BALLADS (10)   *Lib. of Cong. Music Div.*
                              AAFS L 7   12"

261   The Golden Willow Tree
599   The Rambling Boy
744   The Two Brothers
       The Four Marys
746   The Two Sisters

452   Lord Thomas and Fair Ellender
59   Bolakins (Lamkin)
726   The Three Babes
       Sanford Barney
       Claude Allen

ANGLO-AMERICAN BALLADS (15)   *Lib. of Cong. Music Div.*
                              AAFS L 1   12"

304   The House Carpenter
213   The Farmer's Curst Wife
285   The Gypsy Davy
36   Barbara Allen
588   Pretty Polly, I
588   Pretty Polly, II
       The Rich Old Farmer

161   The Devil's Nine Questions
       It Makes a Long Time Man
          Feel Bad
       O Lord Don't 'Low Me to Beat
          'Em
554   One Morning in May
420   The Little Brown Bulls
669   The Sioux Indians
       Lady of Carlisle

ANGLO-AMERICAN SHANTIES, LYRIC SONGS, DANCE TUNES AND SPIRITUALS (21)   *Lib. of Cong. Music Div.   AAFS L 2   12"*

637	Sally Brown	190	The Eighth of January
	Haul Away My Rosy	638	Sally Goodin
	Pay Day at Coal Creek	115	Cindy
	The Little Dove	526	Old Joe Clark
709	Ten Thousand Miles	112	Chilly Winds
674	Soldier, Won't You Marry Me?	139	Cripple Creek
	Fod		Coal Creek March
616	Roll on the Ground	369	John Henry
	The Last of Callahan		The Train
	The Ways of the World		
	Glory in the Meeting House		
	Grub Springs		

ANGLO-AMERICAN SONGS AND BALLADS (14)   *Lib. of Cong. Music Div.   AAFS L 12   12"*

447	Lord Bateman	619	Rolly Trudum
561	Expert Town (The Oxford Girl)	736	The Tree in the Wood
496	Naomi Wise	680	Sourwood Mountain
188	Edward	156	The Darby Ram
	My Parents Raised Me Tenderly		The Widow's Old Broom
233	Froggie Went A-Courting	558	Our Goodman
7	The Singing Alphabet	699	Sweet William

ANGLO-AMERICAN SONGS AND BALLADS (13)   *Lib. of Cong. Music Div.   AAFS L 14   12"*

36	Barbara Allen	538	Old Smoky
108	The Cherry Tree Carol	160	Devilish Mary
229	Frank James, The Roving	149	Darling Cory
	Gambler (Boston Burglar)		Fiddle-I-Fee
102	Caroline of Edinboro' Town	45	Billy Grimes
834	Young Charlotte	216	Father Grumble
352	Jack of Diamonds	127	Common Bill

ANGLO-AMERICAN SONGS AND BALLADS (18)   *Lib. of Cong. Music Div.   AAFS L 20   12"*

139	Cripple Creek	505	Nottingham Fair
	Git Along Down to Town	675	The Soldier's Joy
	Kicking Mule		Give the Fiddler a Dram
	A Railroader for Me		Black Mountain Blues
428	Little Old Sod Shanty	183	The Dying Cowboy
	Good Old Campbell		Red Whiskey
361	Jesse James	246	Little Dogies
	Baa, Baa, Black Sheep		My Sweetheart's a Cowboy
	Blue-Eyed Girl		
	The Cruel War Is Raging		

ANGLO-AMERICAN SONGS AND BALLADS (22)   *Lib. of Cong. Music Div.   AAFS L 21   12"*

680	Sourwood Mountain	658	Shoo Fly
	Do, Little Bobby, Do		Sandy River

	Grey Eagle	206	The False Knight upon the Road
	Bonaparte's Retreat		On a Bright and Summer's
	There's More Pretty Girls Than		Morning
	One	455	The Lowlands of Holland
480	I Wish I Was a Mole in the	82	The Broken Token
	Ground	152	Death of Queen Jane
	Heavy-Loaded Freight Train		Jackie's Gone A-Sailing
	Shout, Little Lulu	699	Sweet William
	The Loss of the "New		Buffalo Boy
	Columbia"		The Barnyard
	The Wild Barbaree		My Grandmother Green

ANTHOLOGY OF AMERICAN FOLK MUSIC: BALLADS, Anglo-American, Part 1 (*Ed. Harry Smith; various singers and instruments*) (*27*)   *Folkways   FA 2951   (FP251)   2-12" records   (1952)*
". . . makes use of documentary phonograph records to demonstrate the many segments that make up rural American culture."
—From the catalogue (Folkways), Spring, 1958

	Henry Lee	826	When That Great Ship Went
	Fatal Flower Garden		Down (Titanic)
304	The House Carpenter	824	Engine one-forty-three (C & O
	Drunkards Special		Wreck)
543	Old Lady and the Devil		Got the Farm Land Blues
92	The Butchers Boy	545	Ommie Wise
762	The Wagoners Lad		My Name Is John Johanna
392	King Kong Kitchie Kitchie		Bandit Cole Younger
	Ki-me-o		Charles Guiteau
537	Old Shoes and Leggins	368	John Hardy
	Willie Moore	682	Stackalee
	Lazy Farmer Boy		White House Blues
	Peg and Awl	230	Frankie
369	Gonna Die with My Hammer in	103	Kassie Jones (Casey Jones)
	My Hand		Down on Penny's Farm
		65	Mississippi Boweavil Blues

ANTHOLOGY OF AMERICAN FOLK MUSIC: SECULAR AND RELIGIOUS, Part 2 (*Ed. Harry Smith; various singers and instruments*) (*29*)   *Folkways   FA 2952   (FP252)   2-12" records   (1952)*

	Sail Away Lady		Oh Death
	The Wild Wagoner		Rocky Road
	Wake Up Jacob		Present Joys
	La Danseuse		This Song of Love
	Georgia Stomp		Judgment
	Brilliancy Medley		Better Things
	Indian War Whoop		Laid My Burden Down
	Old Country Stomp		John the Baptist
517	Old Dog Blue	179	Dry Bones
	Saut Crapaud		John the Revelator
	Arcadian One Step		Little Moses
	Home Sweet Home		Shine on Me
	Newport Blues		50 Miles of Elbow Room
	Moonshiners Blues		In the Battlefield
	Born Again		

ANTHOLOGY OF AMERICAN FOLK MUSIC: AMERICAN BALLADS,
Part 3 (*Ed. Harry Smith; various singers and instruments*) (28)
Folkways   FA 2953   (FP253)   2-12" records   (1952)

144   The Coo Coo Bird
186   East Virginia
     Minglewood Blues
554   One Morning in May
     James Alley
     Sugar Baby
480   I Wish I Was a Mole
     Mountaineer's Courtship
     Merchant's Daughter
     Bob Lee Junior
667   Single Girl
     Le Vieux Soulard
     Rabbit Foot Blues
     Expressman Blues

Poor Boy Blues
Feather Bed
Country Blues
99 Year Blues
Prison Cell Blues
Two White Horses
C'est Si Triste
Down Plank Road
Spike Driver Blues
K. C. Moan
Train on the Island
Lone Star Trail
Fishing Blues
Roll Down the Line

AUTHENTIC SQUARE DANCES, *Bill Wimberley et al.* (8—*orch.*)
Mercury   MG 20262   12"

     Ragtime Annie
42   Boil Them Cabbage Down
110   Chicken Reel
     Black Mountain Rag

13   Arkansas Traveler
     Devil's Dream
710   Tennessee Wagoner
     Liberty

BADMEN AND HEROES, *Ed McCurdy, Jack Elliott and Oscar Brand*
(10—*guitar*)   *Elektra   EKL-16   10"   (1955)*

99   Captain Kidd
104   Charles Guiteau
361   Jesse James
46   Billy the Kid
     Quantrell

64   Robin Hood and the Bold
     Pedlar
     Bold Turpin
     Pretty Boy Floyd
364   Jim Fisk
361   Jesse James

BADMEN AND HEROES AND PIRATE SONGS, *Sung by Ed McCurdy,
Oscar Brand, Jack Elliott, and Dick Wilder* (16—*guitars*)   *Elektra
EKL-129   12"*

104   Charles Guiteau
361   Jesse James
46   Billy the Kid
     Quantrell
     Bold Turpin
     Pretty Boy Floyd
364   Jim Fisk
64   Robin Hood and the Bold Pedlar
     The Bold Princess Royal

The Romantic Pirate
Henry Martyn
The Female Warrior
99   Captain Kidd
The Female Smuggler
Bold Manning
298   High Barbaree

BAHAMAN SONGS, FRENCH BALLADS AND DANCE TUNES, SPANISH
RELIGIOUS SONGS AND GAME SONGS (19)   *Lib. of Cong. Music
Div.   AAFS L 5   12"*

     Dig My Grave
37   Round the Bay of Mexico
     Bowline

Sail, Gal
Hallie Rock
Bimini Gal

Le Plus Jeune des Trois
Sept Ans sur Mer
Les Clefs de la Prison
Petite-Fille à Albert Moreau
Acadian Waltz
Acadian Blues
O Chère 'Tite Fille

Joe Ferail
Songs from Los Pastores
Songs from El Nino Perdido
El Tecolote
La Batalla del Ojo de Agua
Mexican Children's Games

BALLAD HUNTER, THE: *Lectures on American Folk Music with Musical Illustrations by John A. Lomax* (5 LP records in 10 parts)

Part I. CHEYENNE: *Songs from the range and the hill country* (8)

Part II. BLUES AND HOLLERS: *"Being Lonesome" songs* (8)
Lib. of Cong. Music Div.   AAFS L 49   12"

Part I:		Part II:	
174	Dreary Black Hills		Red River Blues
265	Good-bye Old Paint		Wasn't I Lucky
361	Jesse James (2 versions)	10	Another Man Done Gone
79	Brennan on the Moor		I'm Gwine to Texas
355	The Jam on Gerry's Rocks		Prison Blues
699	Sioux Indians		Mule Skinners' Hollers
91	Bury Me Not on the Lone Prairie		Country Rag
			Two White Horses

Part III. CHISHOLM TRAIL: *Cowboy songs along the famous old cattle trail* (7)

Part IV. ROCK ISLAND LINE: *Woodcutters' songs and songs of prisons* (4)
Lib. of Cong. Music Div.   AAFS L 50   12"

Part III:		Part IV:	
735	Trail to Mexico		The Rock Island Line
113	Chisholm Trail (2)		Jumpin' Judy
805	Whoopee Ti Yi Yo, Git Along Little Dogies (2)	369	John Henry
101	Careless Love		It Makes a Long Time Man Feel Bad
	Factory Girl		

Part V. TWO SAILORS: *Sea shanties and canal boat ballads* (6)

Part VI. BOLL WEEVIL: *Songs about the little bug that challenged King Cotton* (7)
Lib. of Cong. Music Div.   AAFS L 51   12"

Part V:		Part VI:	
	Old Woman Under the Hill	65	Boll Weevil (7)
293	Haul Away My Rosy		
794	When Jones's Ale Was New		
	Trip on the Canal		
	Dark-Eyed Canaler		
36	Barbara Allen		

Part VII. SPIRITUALS: *Religion through songs of the Southern Negroes* (8)

Part VIII. RAILROAD SONGS: *Work songs for rail tamping and track laying* (8)

Lib. of Cong. Music Div.   AAFS L 52   12"

Part VII:

498   The New Buryin' Ground
       Jesus My God, I Know His
          Name
       Choose Your Seat and Set Down
677   Sometimes I Feel Like a
          Motherless Child
408   Lead Me to the Rock
       The Blood-Strained Banders
       If I Got My Ticket, Lord
       God Don't Like, No No

Part VIII:

Can't You Line 'Em?
Track Laying Holler
Wake Up Call
Track Calling
The Dallas Railway
No More, My Lord
Steel Laying Holler
Pauline

Part IX. JORDAN AND JUBILEE: *Songs from Livingston, Alabama* (9)

Part X. SUGARLAND, TEXAS: *Convict songs from a Texas prison* (6)

Lib. of Cong. Music Div.   AAFS L 53   12"

Part IX:

The Blood Done Sign My Name
Soon One Morning
Gonna Walk Around in Jordan
Tell the News
Jubilee
Steamboat Landing Holler
Dog Caught a Hog
Sermon on Job
Job, Job

Part X:

564   Pick a Bale of Cotton
       Dat's All Right, Honey
       The Geese and the Goats
268   The Gray Goose
369   Little John Henry
662   Shorty George

BALLAD OF OKLAHOMA, *10-inch LP recording for the Oklahoma 50th Anniversary Celebration (1907-1957), distributed by Red Plains Trading Post, Ltd. Narration by John Doremus and songs by Bob Duncan and the Surrey Singers of Oklahoma University. Dulcimer music by Mrs. Flora Belle "Granny" Ramsey.* (7)

[Limited Gold Seal Edition, mfd. by RCA Victor]

576   Poor Lonesome Cowboy
119   The Colorado Trail
428   My Little Sod Shanty on the
          Plains

 53   Black-Eyed Susie
       Sandy Land
673   Skip-to-My-Lou
       The Dicky Bird Was Singing

BALLADS OF CARELESS LOVE   *Cornell   10050   10"*

(song titles not available)

BANJO SONGS OF THE SOUTHERN MOUNTAINS (*Field recordings—performers: Obray Ramsey, Henry Gentry, George Pegram, Walter Parham, Harry and Jeanie West, Aunt Samantha Bumgarner*) (*17—banjo*) *Riverside   RLP 12-610   12"*

	Little Maggie		Poor Little Ellen
139	Cripple Creek		Fly Around, My Pretty Little
	Keep My Skillet Good and		Miss
	Greasy	13	Arkansas Traveler
	Old Reuben	73	The Boston Burglar
101	Careless Love	262	Good Old Mountain Dew
369	John Henry		Lost John
	Way Down on the Island	588	Pretty Polly
176	Awake, Awake, Ye Drowsy		Finger Ring
	Sleepers	145	Cumberland Gap

BANJOS, BANJOS, AND MORE BANJOS! *Dick Weissman, Billy Faier, and Eric Weissberg* (*17*)   *Judson Records   J-3017   12"*

	Buck Dancer's Choice		Cape Cod Blues
417	Little Birdie		Hard, Ain't It Hard
	Glory, Glory		Red Wing
526	Old Joe Clark		You Can Dig My Grave
112	Chilly Winds	680	Sourwood Mountain
	East Tennessee Blues		900 Miles
	Shout Lulu	139	Cripple Creek
	Pigtown Fling		Blue Goose
	A Day in the Kentucky		
	Mountains		

BINORIE VARIATIONS: HORNPIPE AND CHANTEY, *by Tom Scott, performed by the Vienna Orchestra, F. Charles Adler, conducting. Composers Recordings   CRI-104   12"*
(Based on "The Twa Sisters," Child ballad No. 10)

BOUND FOR GLORY. *Songs and Story by Woody Guthrie. Edited by Millard Lampell. Told by Will Geer.* (*11*)   *Folkways   FA 2481   (FP78/1)   12"*

682	Stagolee	There's a Better World
	(Children's Songs—titles not	A-Coming
	given)	This Is Your Land
	Vigilante Man	Fishing (Talking Blues)
	Do Re Mi	Reuben James
	Pastures of Plenty	Jesus Christ
	Grand Coulee Dam	

BRITISH-AMERICAN BALLADS OF NEW ENGLAND (*Done by six singers —two women, four men*) (*Accompanying explanatory notes*) (*8*) *Flanders Ballad Collection   12" LP   (1953)   (Middlebury College, Middlebury, Vermont)*

	King John and the Bishop	21	Babylon: Bonnie Banks of
	Robin Hood and the Three		Fordie
	Squires	213	The Farmer's Curst Wife
24	The Bailiff's Daughter of	808	The Wife of Usher's Well
	Islington	447	Lord Bateman
		188	Edward

CAJUN SONGS FROM LOUISIANA (14)   Folkways   FE 4438
(FP438)   12"

Gabriel
Les Maringouins
Cinquante Soud
La Fille
Valse de Church Point
Johnny Kane Dance
J'ai Passé Dessou' l'Pommier

Jolie Blonde
Fleur de la Jeunesse
Les Filles de Vermillon
Le Papier D'Éping'
J'ai Passé Devant Ta Porte
Danser Colinda
La Noce à Joséphine

CANADIAN FOLK SONGS, Edited with Notes by Marius Barbeau. (Vol. VIII:
The Columbia Library of Folk and Primitive Music, Compiled and
Edited by Alan Lomax) (39—various singers and instruments)   Columbia
SL-211   12"

Iroquois Indian:

The Rain Dance, Part 1 (Indian
ritual song)
The Rain Dance, Part 2
The Fish Dance (Song)
The Corn Dance (Thanksgiving
ritual song)
Nigahnegao (Little-Water)
(Song of condolence)
Gacowa (A stomp dance)
False Faces

French Canadian:

Ce Sont les Filles de St. Con-
stant
Malbrouck S'en Va-t-en Guerre
192   En Roulant Ma Boule (While
Rolling My Ball)
Je M'en Fus à Sa Porte (I Went
to Her Doorstep)
Charmante Bergère, en Gardant
Ton Troupeau
395   À la Claire Fontaine (In the
Clear Fountain)
Je Pars Demain pour les Hauts
d'Ottawa
Par un Bon Matin, J'Me Suis
Levé
Le Reel Gaspésien (harmonica)
Le Reel Canadien

Buvons, Mes Amis
Breakdown Annoncé
Bonjour, Jolie Bergère

**English Songs — Newfoundland
and Nova Scotia:**

The Banks of the Vergie-O, or
The Bonnie Banks of Fordie
(Child 14)
141   The Cruel Mother (Child 20)
The Carrion Crow
Daniel Monroe
The Foreman Jerry Ryan
The Feller from Fortune
My Name, It's Delaney
Strathspey (fiddle tune)
Milling Frolic Song
Charlie Yackam
Milling Frolic Song (No. 2)
Scots Reels (fiddle)

Northwest Indians:

Headdress Song
Medicine Song
Gambling Song

Caribou Eskimo Songs:

The Fingers (Magic Song)
Piherk for Hunting
Piherk for the Dead
Aagnerk (Magic Song)

CAROL SINGING AT KINGSWAY HALL (12)   London   LL 1147   12"

Hark! the Herald Angels Sing
Silent Night, Holy Night
Angels We Have Heard on High
As with Gladness Men of Old
O Little Town of Bethlehem
The First Nowell

O Come, All Ye Faithful
Away in a Manger
While Shepherds Watched
Angels from the Realms of Glory
God Rest Ye Merry, Gentlemen
Good King Wenceslas

CAROLS BY THE BACH CHOIR (7)   *London*   *LPS-263*   10″

While Shepherds Watched	Ding! Dong! Merrily on High
Good King Wenceslas	The First Nowell
Silent Night, Holy Night	God Rest Ye Merry, Gentlemen
Hark! the Herald Angels Sing	

CAROLS BY THE BACH CHOIR AND WESTMINSTER ABBEY CHOIR (14)   *London*   *LL 1095*   12″

O Come, All Ye Faithful	While Shepherds Watched
Whence Is That Goodly Fragrance	Good King Wenceslas
	Silent Night, Holy Night
Come, Rock the Cradle for Him	Hark! the Herald Angels Sing
The Holly and the Ivy	Ding! Dong! Merrily on High
Lullay My Liking	The First Nowell
See Amid the Winter Snow	God Rest Ye Merry, Gentlemen
In Dulci Jubilo	

CEREMONY OF CAROLS, A (*Benjamin Britten*), *Robert Shaw Chorale of Women's Voices* (12)   *RCA Victor*   *LM-1008*   12″

Procession	This Little Babe
Welcum Yole	Interlude
There Is No Rose	In Freezing Winter Night
That Yonge Child	Spring Carol
Balulalew	Dee Gracias
As Dew in Aprille	Recession

(Reverse side has Mass in G by Poulenc)

CHAIN GANG: VOLUME I (*Woody Guthrie, Sonny Terry, Alek Stewart*) (6)   *Stinson*   *SLP #7*   10″

Chain Gang Blues	Rock Me Momma
Cornbread, Meat and Molasses	Chain Gang Special
682 Stackolee	
Long John	

CHAIN GANG: VOLUME II (*Woody Guthrie, Sonny Terry, Alek Stewart*) (6)   *Stinson*   *SLP #8*   10″

Red River	564 Pick a Bale of Cotton
Ham and Eggs	It Takes a Chain Gang Man
Betty and Dupree	Lost John

CHICAGO MOB SCENE: A Folk Song Jam Session (16)   *Riverside* *RLP 12-641*   12″

Talkin' Nothin' Blues	151 The Days of '49
Ain't A-Goin' to Work Tomorrow	Banana Boat Song
	Tin Can Blues
Mama Don't 'Low	Get Away Ol' Man
How'll I Make It Blues	Life Is a Trail
399 The Old Woman Who Loved a Swine	Square Dance
	Handsome Molly
900 Miles	Mob Blues
144 The Cockoo	Ol' Kimball

CHILDREN'S GAME SONGS OF FRENCH CANADA (Recorded in Montreal) (19) Folksongs FC 7214 (FP714) 10"

395   À la Claire Fontaine!
Ah! Tu Danses Bien, Madeleine!
Trois Canards
Salade, Salade
Là-haut, sur Montagne
Belle Pomme d'Or
Trois Fois Passera
La Pêche aux Moules
Les Gars de Lochmine
Le P'tit Moulin sur la Rivière

Promenons-nous dans le Bois
Allo, Monsieur
Nous N'irons Plus au Bois
J'ai un Beau Château
Le P'tit Avocat
J'ai Tant Dansé, J'ai Tant Sauté
Un Éléphant, Ça Trompe
Le Jeu de la Corde
Bal Chez Boule

CHRISTMAS CAROLS, by Leroy Anderson Orchestra (28) Decca DL 8193 12"

Joy to the World
Deck the Hall with Boughs of Holly
God Rest Ye Merry Gentlemen
Good King Wenceslas
Hark! The Herald Angels Sing
First Nowell
Silent Night
Jingle Bells
O Come, All Ye Faithful
O Little Town of Bethlehem
O Sanctissima
While by My Sheep
Bring a Torch, Jeannette, Isabella
From Heaven High I Come to You

It Came Upon the Midnight Clear
We Three Kings of Orient Are
Patapan
Away in a Manger
Wassail Song
Lo, How a Rose E'er Blooming
O Come, Little Children
In Dulci Jubilo
Angels in Our Fields Abiding
Pastores a Belen
O Come, O Come, Emmanuel
I Saw Three Ships
Coventry Carol
March of the Kings

CHRISTMAS CAROLS (Lyn Murray Singers) (8) Columbia ML-4081 12"

Adeste Fideles
Silent Night, Holy Night
Joy to the World
Oh, Little Town of Bethlehem
The First Nowell

Hark! The Herald Angels Sing
It Came Upon the Midnight Clear
God Rest Ye Merry Gentlemen

CHRISTMAS CAROLS (Mount Holyoke College Glee Club) (11) and CHRISTMAS CAROLS (Celebrity Quartette) (6—organ) Columbia ML 4231 12"

Holyoke:
Sing We Noel
Yuletide Is Here
In Dulci Jubilo
Holy Day Holly
Wake, Nightingale

Carol of the Nuns of Saint Mary
Touro-Louro-Louro
O'er Her Child
Jacques, Come Here
Carol of the Birds
Patapan

Celebrity:
O Come All Ye Faithful
Hark, The Herald Angels Sing
Away in a Manger

The First Nowell
Christians Awake!
The Coventry Carol

CHRISTMAS CAROLS (*St. Luke's Choristers*) (*9*)   *Capitol*   *H-9000*   *10"*

Adeste Fideles
It Came Upon a Midnight Clear
Oh Little Town of Bethlehem
Deck the Hall
Christmas Eve Is Here

Hark the Herald Angels Sing
First Noel
Silent Night
Away in a Manger

CHRISTMAS CAROLS, Vol 1 (*Randolph Singers*) (*19*)   *Westminster*
WP-6022   *12"*

Silent Night
O Little Town of Bethlehem
God Rest You Merry, Gentlemen
What Child Is This? (Green-
  sleeves)
The First Noel
Bring a Torch, Jeannette
Lo, How a Rose E'er Blooming
Angels We Have Heard on High
Oh Come, All Ye Faithful
Let Carols Ring (Swedish)

Hush, O Heaven (Tyrolean)
Patapan (Burgundian)
Virgin's Cradle Hymn (English)
Carol of the Bells (Ukrainian)
Quid Petis, O Fili? (English)
Shepherds, Tell Me (French)
Quickly, My Friends (Proven-
  çal)
Lullay My Liking (English)
Saint Staffan (Swedish)

CHRISTMAS CAROLS, Vol. 2 (*Randolph Singers*) (*20*)   *Westminster*
WP-6023   *12"*

We Wish You a Merry Christmas
It Came Upon the Midnight
  Clear
Good King Wenceslas
We Three Kings of Orient Are
Away in a Manger
Hark! The Herald Angels Sing
The Coventry Carol
The Boar's Head Carol
Joy to the World
Cantique de Noël

747

325

Deck the Halls
Cradled in a Manger
Sing We Noel Once More
How Far It Is to Bethlehem
The Twelve Days of Christmas
Jesus, Jesus, Rest Your Head
O Come, O Come, Emmanuel
Fum! Fum! Fum!
I Wonder As I Wander
Wassail Song

CHRISTMAS HYMNS AND CAROLS, Robert Shaw Chorale (*20*)   *RCA*
Victor   *LM-1112*   *12"*

Oh Little Town of Bethlehem
Silent Night
We Three Kings
Hark the Herald Angels Sing
First Noel
Adeste Fideles
Away in a Manger
God Rest Ye Merry, Gentlemen
Joy to the World
It Came Upon a Midnight Clear

325

Angels We Have Heard on High
O Come, O Come, Emanuel
Coventry Carol
Carol of the Bells
I Wonder As I Wander
Lo, How a Rose E'er Blooming
Go Tell It on the Mountain
Wassail Song
Deck the Hall
Echo Hymn

CHRISTMAS HYMNS AND CAROLS, Vol. I (*Robert Shaw Chorale*) (25)
RCA Victor   LM-2139   12"

O Come All Ye Faithful
First Nowell
O Little Town of Bethlehem
O Come Emanuel
Away in a Manger
Silent Night   325
Joy to the World
It Came Upon the Midnight
Clear
Angels We Have Heard on High
Christmas Hymn
Lo, How a Rose E'er Blooming
Hark, The Herald Angels Sing
Bring a Torch, Jeanette, Isabella

Deck the Halls with Boughs of
Holly
God Rest Ye Merry, Gentlemen
My Dancing Day
We Three Kings
I Wonder As I Wander
Patapan
Coventry Carol
I Sing of a Maiden
Shepherd's Carol
Go, Tell It on the Mountain
Carol of the Bells
Wassail Song

CHRISTMAS HYMNS AND CAROLS, Vol. II (*Robert Shaw Chorale*) (26)
RCA Victor   LM-1711   12"

I Saw Three Ships
O Tannenbaum
Allons, Gay, Gay Bergères
The Holly and the Ivy
Fum, Fum, Fum
Hacia Belén Va un Borrilo
Ya Viene la Vieja
La Virgen Lava Pañales
108   The Cherry Tree Carol
Mary Had a Baby
How Unto Bethlehem
747   The Twelve Days of Christmas
Christ Was Born on Christmas
Day
Here, 'mid the Ass and Oxen
Mild

Break Forth, O Beauteous, Heav-
enly Light
So Blest a Sight
A Virgin Unspotted
Good King Wenceslas
The Boar's Head Carol
How Far Is It to Bethlehem
March of the Kings
Touro-Louro-Louro
Carol of the Birds
O Magnum Mysterium
What Child Is This
Masters in This Hall

COUNTRY DANCE MUSIC, WASHBOARD BAND (*7—washboard, banjo,
harmonica, guitar, bass*)   Folkways   FA 2201 (FP601)   10"

115   Cindy
Bottle Up and Go
139   Cripple Creek
369   John Henry

526   Old Joe Clark
673   Skip to My Lou
273   Green Corn

COURTIN'S A PLEASURE and FOLKSONGS FROM THE SOUTHERN
APPALACHIANS, *sung by Jean Ritchie, Oscar Brand and Tom Paley*
(21)   Elektra   EKL-122   12"

Hey, Little Boy
I Wonder When I Shall Be Mar-
ried
Keys of Canterbury

839   Young Man Who Wouldn't Hoe
Corn
299   Hog Drovers
407   Lazy John

383   Kansas Boys
      My Good Old Man
562   Paper of Pins
502   No, Sir
649   Shady Grove
      The Miller's Song
522   Old Grey Goose
      Jackaro

      Girl on the Greenbriar Shore
      Little Maggie
      Banjo pieces:
      Coal Creek March
      O'Sullivan Mor
526   Old Joe Clark
      White Cockade
221   Flop-Eared Mule

COWBOY DANCES (*Lloyd Shaw*) (*14—orch.*)   *Decca*
               DL 9003   12"   (*1950*)

245   The Girl I Left Behind
675   Soldier's Joy
 13   Arkansas Traveler
      Devil's Dream
710   Tennessee Wagoner
      Durang's Hornpipe
      Nellie Bly

      Four and Twenty
      White Cockade
      Four White Horses
      Honest John
      Chichester
      I Wonder
      Romping Molly

COWBOY SONG FAVORITES, *by Foy Willing, Riders of the Purple Sage
and Red River Dave* (*12*)   *Allegro Royale-1594*   12"

      Tumbling Tumbleweeds
      Cool Water
302   Home on the Range
604   Red River Valley
      The Last Roundup
 91   Bury Me Not on the Lone Prairie

654   She'll Be Coming Round the
         Mountain
      Mexicali Rose
 58   The Blue Tail Fly
518   The Old Chisholm Trail
352   Jack o' Diamonds
 41   The Big Rock Candy Mountain

COWBOY SONGS, BALLADS AND CATTLE CALLS FROM TEXAS (*Ed.
Duncan B. M. Emrich; sung by L. Parker Temple, John A. Lomax, Jess
Morris, Sloan Matthews, Johnny Prude, J. M. Waddell, Harry Stephens*)
(*13*)   *Lib. of Cong. Music Div.*   AAFS L 28   12"   (*1941-48*)

      Colley's Run-I-O (guitar)
         (Temple)
 88   The Buffalo Skinners (Lomax)
265   Goodbye, Old Paint (I) (fiddle)
         (Morris)
265   Goodbye, Old Paint (II) (Mat-
         thews)
712   The Texas Rangers (Matthews)
      Cattle Calls (Matthews)
      The Cowboy's Life Is a Very
         Dreary Life (Matthews)

842   The Zebra Dun (Waddell)
174   The Dreary Black Hills
         (Stephens)
      The Night-Herding Song
         (Stephens)
183   The Dying Cowboy (Matthews)
691   The Streets of Laredo (Prude)
      The Dying Ranger (Prude)

DEEP RIVER AND OTHER SPIRITUALS, *Robert Shaw Chorale* (*16*)
         RCA Victor   LM-2247   12"   (*1958*)

155   Deep River
705   Swing Low, Sweet Chariot
163   Didn't My Lord Deliver Daniel
196   Every Time I Feel the Spirit
      I Wanna Be Ready

722   This Ol' Hammer
      This Little Light o' Mine
      Who Is That Yonder?
      Lord, If I Got My Ticket,
      Soon One Mornin'

There Is a Balm in Gilead   179 Dry Bones
Soon-a Will Be Done   644 Set Down, Servant
491 My Lord, What a Morning
Ain'-a That Good News

EARLY AMERICAN PSALMODY, *Margaret Dodd Singers (8)   New A'A'O*
Records, Inc.   NRLP 2007   10"
Old Hundred (Ps. 100)   London (Ps. 19)
Windsor (Ps. 16)   York (Ps. 66)
Ten Commandments (Ps. 6)   Pater Noster (Ps. 85)
Hallelujah (Ps. 128)   Old 113th (Ps. 115)

ELEKTRA NEW FOLK SAMPLER *(18)   Elektra EKL-SMP-2 12" (1956)*
Josie   Must I Go Bound
Déclaration Paysanne   Mangwani Mpulele
193 Erie Canal   137 Crawdad Song
Coplas   Moulin de la Galette
64 Robin Hood and the Bold Pedlar 156 Darby Ram
Ptsach Bazemer   Au Clair de la Lune
505 Nottamun Town   Keys of Canterbury
Bella Regazza   My Ain House
369 John Henry
Sevillanas

ENGLISH AND SCOTTISH POPULAR BALLADS, THE. *Sung by Ewan
MacColl and A. L. Lloyd Vol. 1 (9)   Riverside   RLP-12-621   12"*
(1956)
451 Lord Randal (12)   746 Minnorie (10)
213 The Devil and the Ploughman   (The Twa Sisters)
(278) (The Farmer's Curst   Hind Horn (17)
Wife)   558 Our Goodman (274)
The Laird o' Drum (236)   755 The Unquiet Grave (78)
Herod and the Cock (55)
(The Carnal and the Crane)
Thomas Rhymer (37)

ENGLISH AND SCOTTISH POPULAR BALLADS, THE. *Sung by Ewan
MacColl and A. L. Lloyd Vol. 1 (9)   Riverside   RLP-12-622   12"*
(1956)
Eppie Morrie (223)   243 Get Up and Bar the Door (275)
Sir Hugh (155)   397 The Outlandish Knight (4)
(The Jew's Daughter)   (Lady Isabel and the Elf-
The Shepherd Lad (112)   Knight)
(The Baffled Knight)   The Bonnie Hoose o' Airlie (199)
Robin Hood and the Tanner   The Rantin Laddie (240)
(126)
Richie Story (232)

ENGLISH AND SCOTTISH POPULAR BALLADS, THE. *Sung by Ewan MacColl and A. L. Lloyd Vol. 2 (8)   Riverside   RLP-12-623   12"* (1956)

The Broomfield Hill (43)
458 The Prickly Bush (95)
(The Maid Freed from the Gallows)
Johnnie o' Breadisley (114) (Johnie Cock)
240 George Collins (85) (Lady Alice)

The Trooper and the Maid (299)
809 The Cooper o' Fife (277) (The Wife Wrapt in Wether's Skin)
204 Fair Margaret and Sweet William (74)
Glasgow Peggie (228)

ENGLISH AND SCOTTISH POPULAR BALLADS, THE. *Sung by Ewan MacColl and A. L. Lloyd Vol. 2 (10)   Riverside   RLP-12-624   12"* (1956)

The Broom of Cowdenknowes (217)
The Keach in the Creel (281)
239 Georgie (209) (Geordie)
The Jolly Beggar (279)
447 Lord Bateman (53) (Young Beichan)
The Knight and the Shepherd's Daughter (110)

68 Bawbee Allen (84) (Bonny Barbara Allen)
64 Robin Hood and the Bold Pedlar (132)
188 My Son David (13) (Edward)
Sir Patrick Spens (58)

ENGLISH AND SCOTTISH POPULAR BALLADS, THE. *Sung by Ewan MacColl and A. L. Lloyd Vol. 3 (8)   Riverside   RLP-12-625   12"* (1956)

The Battle of Harlaw (163)
84 The Dover Sailor (295) (The Brown Girl)
Amang the Blue Flowers and the Yellow (25) (Willie's Lyke-Wake)
260 The Golden Vanity (286)

184 The Douglas Tragedy (7) (Earl Brand)
The Dowie Dens o' Yarrow (214) (The Braes o' Yarrow)
Robin Hood and the Bishop of Hereford (114)
The Gairdner Child (219) (The Gardner)

ENGLISH AND SCOTTISH POPULAR BALLADS, THE. *Sung by Ewan MacColl and A. L. Lloyd Vol. 3 (10)   Riverside   RLP-12-626   12"* (1956)

Gil Morice (83) (Child Maurice)
The Crafty Farmer (283)
286 Gipsies-O (200) (The Gypsy Laddie)
401 Long Lankin (93) (Lamkin)
The Beggar Laddie (280)
Rob Roy (225)

108 The Cherry Tree (54) (The Cherry-Tree Carol)
The Heir o' Lynne (267) (The Heir of Linne)
Lang Johnnie More (251)
Hughie the Graeme (191)

ENGLISH AND SCOTTISH POPULAR BALLADS, THE. *Sung by Ewan MacColl and A. L. Lloyd Vol. 4 (9)   Riverside   RLP-12-627   12"* (1956)

	Jock the Leg (282)	404 Lord Gregory (76)
	(Jock the Leg and the Merry Merchant)	(The Lass of Roch Royal)
146	The Daemon Lover (243)	The Bonnie Earl o' Murray (181)
	The Earl of Aboyne (235)	Clyde's Water (216)
191	Scarborough Fair (2)	(The Mother's Malison)
	(The Elfin Knight)	The Lover's Ghost (248)
		(The Grey Cock)
		Henry Martin (250)

ENGLISH AND SCOTTISH POPULAR BALLADS, THE. *Sung by Ewan MacColl and A. L. Lloyd Vol. 4 (9)   Riverside   RLP-12-628   12"* (1956)

The Burning o' Auchendoun (183) (Willie Macintosh)
The Banks of Green Willow (24) (Bonnie Annie)
Bessie Bell and Mary Gray (201)
670 Bold Sir Rylas (18) (Sir Lionel)
100 Captain Wedderburn's Courtship (46)

Captain Ward and the Rainbow (287)
Dives and Lazarus (56)
452 Lord Thomas and Fair Eleanor (73) (Lord Thomas and Fair Annet)
141 The Cruel Mother (20)

GREAT BRITISH BALLADS (Supplement to THE ENGLISH AND SCOTTISH POPULAR BALLADS) (*Sung by Ewan MacColl and A. L. Lloyd Vol. 5 (10)   Riverside   RLP-12-629   12"   (1956)*)

The Bitter Withy
Lang A-Growing
78 The Bramble Briar
The Seven Virgins
Down in Yon Forest

The Blind Beggar's Daughter of Bethnal Green
The Bold Fisherman
Six Dukes Went A-Fishing
The Holy Well
660 The Shooting of His Dear

FAVORITE COWBOY SONGS, *by Sons of the Pioneers (25)   RCA Victor LPM-1130   12"*

Press Along to the Big Corral Wind
Bunkhouse Bugle Boy
La Borachita
Timber Trail
Happy Cowboy
Tumbling Tumbleweeds
302 Home on the Range
135 Cowboy's Lament
Pajarillo Barrenquero
So Long to the Red River Valley
Come and Get It
Curly Joe from Idaho
Carry Me Back to the Lone Prairie

The Everlasting Hills of Oklahoma
134 Cowboy's Dream
Along the Santa Fe Trail
Cool Water
The Last Round-Up
Far Away Stomp
604 Red River Valley
696 Sweet Betsy from Pike
Slow Moving Cattle
Texas Stomp
Yellow Rose of Texas

FAVORITE SPIRITUALS, *sung by The Ames Brothers (8)   Coral*
CRL 56050   10"

179	Dry Bones	379	Joshua Fit de Battle of Jericho
155	Deep River	250	Go Down Moses
	Shadrack		Blind Barnabas
705	Swing Low Sweet Chariot		Who Built the Ark

FAVORITE SPIRITUALS, *sung by The Golden Gate Quartet (12)*
RCA Victor   CAL 308   12"

196   Every Time I Feel the Spirit
    He Said He Would Calm the
    Ocean
    Hide Me in Thy Bosom
    What a Time
    Our Father
    I'm a Pilgrim
    I Looked Down the Road and I
    Wondered

When They Ring the Golden
    Bells
You'd Better Mind
Job
Gabriel Blows His Horn
Jonah in the Whale

FESTIVAL OF CAROLS (*Westminster Abbey Choir*) (7)   *London*
LPS-267   10"

O Come, All Ye Faithful
Whence Is That Goodly Fra-
    grance
Come, Rock the Cradle for Him

The Holly and the Ivy
Lullay My Liking
See Amid the Winter Snow
In Dulci Jubilo

FIRESIDE TREASURY OF FOLK SONGS, THE (*15–chorus, orch.*)
Golden Records   A198:17   12"   (1957)

740	Turkey in the Straw	348	I've Been Working on the Rail-
551	On Top of Old Smoky		road
	De Camptown Races		Clementine
276	Green Grow the Lilacs	57	Blow the Man Down
513	Oh, Susanna!		Dixie
	A Mighty Fortress Is Our God		Stand Up, Stand Up, for Jesus
	Battle Hymn of the Republic		Rock of Ages
58	The Blue Tail Fly		The Star-Spangled Banner

FISK JUBILEE SINGERS, *John W. Work, Director (11)   Folkways*
FA 2372 (FP72)   12"

312   I Couldn't Hear Nobody Pray
    O the Rocks and the Mountains
    Rockin' Jerusalem
    When I Was Sinkin' Down
    You May Bury Me in the East
    The Angels Done Bowed Down
    Done Made My Vow to the
    Lord

I'm A-Rollin' through an
    Unfriendly World
Lord, I'm Out Here on Your
    World
784   Were You There
    Great Camp Meeting

FOLK FAVORITES, Vol. 1   *Chicago-Int'l   Chi. CRC-1   10"*
(song titles not available)

FOLK FAVORITES, Vol. 2   *Chicago-Int'l*   *Chi. CRC-3*   *10"*
(song titles not available)

FOLK FAVORITES, Vol. 3   *Chicago Int'l*   *Chi. CRC-4*   *10"*
(song titles not available)

FOLK MUSIC FESTIVALS: THE INTERNATIONAL MUSICAL
  EISTEDDFOD, *at Llangollen, North Wales, 1952* (35)
      Westminster   WF 12009   2-12" records

Vol. I:

Hymn: Llanfair
England: Bacup Coconut Dance
England: Summer Is Icumen in
England: The Herald (Elgar)
England: Grenoside Sword
  Dance
England: Psalm 23 (Schubert)
Scotland: Entry with Pipes, and
  Jig Fergus McIvor
Wales: Betty My Love
Wales: Carol, Trymder
Ukraine: Hahilky, Easter Dance
Ukraine: The Grey Cuckoo
  Callas
Ukraine: Khorovidm Village
  Green Dance
Italy: Serenata del Burtuli
France: Stick Dance from Ven-
  dée
Ireland: Hornpipe
Sweden: Little Karen
Holland: Skote Tyre

Vol. II:

England: Contraponto Bestiale
U.S.A.: Contraponto Bestiale
Italy: Contraponto Bestiale
Germany: Sauerland Quadrille
  and Kreuzkonig Dance
Germany: Vorspruch (Distler)
Austria: Holzhacker Polka
Austria: Stille Nacht (Gruber)
Austria: Zu Regensburg
Serbia: Bachelor's Dance
Spain: Wedding Dance from
  Ibiza
Spain: Three Christmas Songs
  from Ibiza
Spain: Tenebrae factae sunt
  (Victoria)
Penillion: Hedduch, Poem of
  Peace
Spain: Erotazaia
Spain: Sevillana
Austria: Die Wassermuhle
Serbia: Warrior's Dance
Spain: Ama Begira Zazu

FOLK MUSIC FROM NOVA SCOTIA, *Recorded by H. Creighton (Sixteen
singers in "songs ranging from Child ballads to lumbermen songs and
songs of the sea.")* (25) *Folkways   FM 4006 (P1006)   12"   (1956)*

Mo Dhachaidh (My Home)
Captain Conrod
New Year's and Children's Verse
  in German   206
The Welcome Table
Micmac Indian War Dance Song
  & Indian War Song
Acadian Lullaby
Un Matin Je Me Lève
Chanson d'un Soldat
Acadian Dance Tune

Old Tune Played on the Mouth
  Organ
Rain, Rain, the Wind Does Blow
The False Knight Upon the Road
Chin Music
Lady Gowrie
Moose and Bear Calls
I'm Going to Get Married
The Red Mantle
His Jacket Was Blue
The Gay Spanish Maid

Sea Chanties:

Sally Around the Corner O
611   Rio Grande

Leave Her, Johnny, Leave Her
Goodbye, Fare You Well
Hangman Johnny
Haul the Alabama Bowline

FOLK MUSIC FOR PEOPLE WHO HATE FOLK MUSIC: *Herb Strauss*
(with acc. by Mundell Lowe and his friends) *(12)   Judson Records*
J-3003   12"

Rumbaling
Marie
Aura Lee
La Jesucita
Spanish Is the Loving Tongue
Come My Pretty Lady

Water Boy
Perhaps
Raisins and Almonds
655   Story of Shenandoah
When
709   Ten Thousand Miles

FOLK SINGERS: *Gene Austin, Vernon Dalhart, and Jimmie Rodgers* *(6)*
RCA Popular Collector's Issue   LPT 6   10"

Carolina Moon (Austin—orch.)
592   The Prisoner's Song (Dalhart—
         viola, guitar)
825   Wreck of the Old 97 (Dalhart—
         harmonica, guitar)

Blue Yodel: T for Texas
   (Rodgers—guitar)
Away Out on the Mountain
   (Rodgers—guitar)
Ramona (Austin—orch.)

FOLKSONGS, *by Howard University Choir   Key Records   Key 12   10"*
(song titles not available)

FOLK SONGS FOR BABIES, SMALL CHILDREN, PARENTS AND BABY
SITTERS, *by The Babysitters   Vanguard   VRS-9042   12"   (1958)*
(song titles not available)

FOLK SONGS FOR CAMP, *sung by The Wagoners* *(17)   Folkways*
FC 7030 (FP730)   10"

Train Is A-Coming
Who Did Swallow Jonah
Nous Sommes à la Musicale
Sail Away Ladies
On Ilkla Moor Baht Hat
Good News
My Little Rooster
617   Roll the Old Chariot Along
Children, Go Where I Send Thee

137   Crawdad Hole
37   Round the Bay of Mexico
Saraspunda
Az Der Rebbe
680   Sourwood Mountain
637   Sally Brown
Chairs to Mend
Run Come See

FOLK SONGS FOR YOUNG AND OLD: *Mechau Family* *(13—guitar)*
Stinson   SLP #47   10"

When I Lay Me Down and Die
Ribbon Bow
763   Walie
800   Whistle, Daughter, Whistle
Walking on the Green Grass
Lass from the Low Country
Johnny Has Gone for a Soldier
Six Little Mice

53   Black Eyed Suzy
269   Great Grandad
Hound Dog
Hard, Ain't It Hard
127   Common Bill

FOLK SONGS OF FOUR CONTINENTS: *Pete Seeger and Song Swappers* (9)
Folkways   FW 6911 (FP911)   10"

Silvy
Si Mon Moine
280 The Greenland Whalers
Mi Caballo Blanco (Chile)
Oleanna (Norway)

Bonuwa Yo (Liberia)
Raaupati Ram (India)
Hey, Daroma (Israel)
Bimini Gal (Bahamas)

FOLK SONGS OF THE FRONTIER: *Roger Wagner Chorale (13–guitar, banjo, harmonica)   Capitol   P-8332   12"*

302 Home on the Range
     Night-Herding Song
     Snag-Tooth Sal
 91 O, Bury Me Not on the Lone
     Prairie
276 Green Grow the Lilacs
518 The Old Chisholm Trail
265 Goodby, Old Paint

805 Whoopee-Ti-Yi-Yo (Git Along
     Little Dogies)
735 The Trail to Mexico
576 I'm a Poor Lonesome Cowboy
 88 The Buffalo Skinners
423 Little Joe, the Wrangler
     Curtains of Night

FOLK SONGS OF THE NEW WORLD: *Roger Wagner Chorale (13–guitar, banjo, harmonica)   Capitol   P-8324   12"*

 51 Black Is the Color
348 I've Been Working on the Rail-
     road
773 Wayfaring Stranger
115 Cindy
325 I Wonder As I Wander
551 On Top of Old Smoky
691 Streets of Laredo (The Cow-
     boy's Lament)

677 Sometimes I Feel Like a Moth-
     erless Child
655 Shenandoah
673 Skip to Mah Lou
297 He's Gone Away
178 Drunken Sailor
 58 Blue Tail Fly

FOLKSAY: VOLUME I (*Pete Seeger, Leadbelly, Cisco Houston, Bess Lomax, Woody Guthrie, Baldwin Hawes, Josh White, Blind Sonny Terry, Alex Stewart*) (8)   *Stinson   SLP #5   10"*

Glory
Poor Lazarus
668 It Was Sad When That Great
     Ship Went Down
900 Miles

804 Who's Gonna Shoe Your Pretty
     Little Feet
115 Cindy
     Don't Lie, Buddy
     Mule Skinner Blues

FOLKSAY: VOLUME II (*Leadbelly, Woody Guthrie, Cisco Houston, Blind Sonny Terry, Bob Carey, Roger Sprung, Eric Darling*) (8)   *Stinson   SLP #6   10"*

  2 Alabama Bound
 37 Round the Bay of Mexico
731 Tom Dooley
160 Devilish Mary

474 Midnight Special
     Sportin' Life Blues
137 Crawdad Song
597 Raise a Rukus

FOLKSAY: VOLUME III (*Woody Guthrie, Cisco Houston, Pete Seeger, Leadbelly, Blind Sonny Terry, Josh White*) (8)   Stinson   SLP #9   10"

828 Yellow Gal
     Hard Traveling
627 The Roving Gambler
     Lost John

103 Casey Jones
     Railroad Whistle
     I've a Pretty Flower
42   Bile Dem Cabbage Down

FOLKSAY: VOLUME IV (*Pete Seeger, Woody Guthrie, Leadbelly, Cisco Houston, Ernie Lieberman*) (8)   Stinson   SLP #11   10"

655 Shenandoah
     Cumberland Mountain Bear
     Chase
688 Stewball
     Sowing on the Mountain
     Bennington Rifleman

169 Down in the Willow Garden
     T for Texas
139 Cri͟ple Creek

FOLKSAY: VOLUME V (*Cisco Houston, Pete Seeger, Woody Guthrie, Hally Wood, Leadbelly, Frank Warner, Sonny Terry*) (9)   Stinson   SLP #12   10"

120 Come All You Fair and Tender
     Ladies
706 Take This Hammer
     Hobo Bill

252 Go Tell Aunt Rhody
     Teeroo
     Johnson Boys
     The Rover
     House of the Rising Sun
538 Old Smokey

FOLKSAY: VOLUME VI (*Tom Glazer, Pete Seeger, Woody Guthrie, Cisco Houston, Frank Warner, Leadbelly, Ernie Lieberman, Gary Davis, Sonny Terry*) (10)   Stinson   SLP #13   10"

172 Down in the Valley
233 Froggy Went A-Courting
839 Young Man Who Wouldn't Hoe
     Corn
     Corn Bread Rough
     Jolly Roving Tar

691 Streets of Laredo
674 Soldier, Soldier
224 The Foggy Dew
193 Erie Canal
     When the Train Comes Along

FOLKSONGS WITH THE FOLKSMITHS (16)   Folkways
                    FA 2407   12"

     We've Got Some Singing to Do
     Hava Na Shira
369 John Henry
251 Old Hannah
     Glory Be to the New Born King
     Come Up Horsey
     Three White Gulls
     Amen (Mary Had a Baby)
     Oh Sinner Man

301 Hold On (Keep Your Hand on
        the Plow)
     Kum Ba Yah
     Wade in the Water
     Run to Jesus
     Hey Langor
     Tina
     All Night Long

FOLLOW THE DRINKING GOURD, *Michael LaRue and the Drinking Gourd Singers* in AMERICAN NEGRO SLAVE SONGS (*13*) *Esoteric ES-560 12"*

369	John Henry		March On
	Look Over Yonder		Voo-Doo American
	Hush, Somebody's Calling My	597	Raise a Ruckus
	Name		Driving Steel
	Hey Everybody	301	Hold On
	You Gonna Reap		Follow the Drinking Gourd
10	Another Man Done Gone		
	I'm Packing Up		

FROZEN LOGGER, etc.   *Chicago-Int'l   Chi. CRC-2   10"*

(song titles not available)

GATEWAY SINGERS AT THE HUNGRY I, THE (*15*)   *Decca DL 8671   12"*   (*1958*)

	This Little Light of Mine	627	Roving Gambler
569	Poor Boy	193	The Erie Canal
	Oleanna		Deep Blue Sea
301	Hold On		Roll Down the Line
	The Sinking of the Reuben	211	Fare Thee Well
	James		Three Israeli Folk Dances
228	The Fox		
	The Ballad of Sigmund Freud		

GET ON BOARD: *The Folkmasters* (*6—harmonica, guitar*)   *Folkways FA 2028 (FP28)   10"*

474	Midnight Special		Mamma Blues No. 2
564	Pick a Bale		Man Is Nothing but a Fool
	I'm in His Care	597	Raise a Ruckus

GOLDEN GATE SPIRITUALS, *Golden Gate Quartet* (*8*)   *Columbia CL 6102   10"*   (*1950*)

	No Restricted Signs	Jezebel
379	Joshua Fit de Battle of Jericho	Blind Barnabus
705	Swing Down, Chariot	Wade in the Water
	God's Gonna Cut You Down	I Will Be Home Again

GOSPEL SONGS, *The Missionary Quintet* (*Recorded in Nassau, Bahamas*) (*9—no acc.*)   *Folkways   FW 6824* (*FP824*)   *10"*   (*1953*)

179	Dry Bones	249	Give Me That Old Time Religion
	On This Side of Jordan	163	My Lord Did Deliver
	In That New Jerusalem		I Got a Home in That Rock
	Let the Church Roll On		Jesus on My Mind
			Climbing Up the Mountain

HOUR OF IRISH BALLADS, AN   *Record Corp. of America Royale #1439   12"*

(song titles not available)

INSTRUMENTAL MUSIC OF THE SOUTHERN APPALACHIANS (*Performers: Hobart Smith, Mrs. Etta Baker, Boone Reid, Mrs. Edd Presnell, Richard Chase, Lacey Phillips*) (*20—banjo, fiddle, dulcimer, harmonica, guitar*) *Tradition* *TLP 1007* *12"* (*1956*)

139	Cripple Creek (fiddle)	680	Sourwood Mountain (banjo)
	Pateroller (banjo)	595	Railroad Bill (guitar)
	One Dime Blues (guitar)	673	Skip to My Lou (harmonica)
254	Goin' Down the Road Feeling	675	Soldier's Joy (banjo)
	Bad		Molly Brooks (harmonica)
8	Amazing Grace (dulcimer)	588	Pretty Polly (fiddle)
245	The Girl I Left Behind Me		Johnson Boys (banjo)
	(harmonica)	369	John Henry (guitar)
	Marching Jaybird (banjo)		Drunken Hiccups (fiddle)
	John Brown's Dream (fiddle)	649	Shady Grove (dulcimer)
638	Sally Goodin (dulcimer)	89	Bully of the Town (guitar)

IRISH FESTIVAL SINGERS, *Album 1* (*12*)   *Angel*   *Ang. 65016*   *12"*

Palatine's Daughter
Danny Boy
Spanish Lady
I Have a Bonnet Trimmed with
Blue

Norah O'Neale
Stuttering Lovers
Star of County Down
Padraic
(titles incomplete)

IRISH FESTIVAL SINGERS, *Album 2* (*15*)   *Angel*   *Ang. 65025*   *12"*

Bold Fenian Men
Battle Hymn
She Is Far from the Land
Lullaby
Sea Wrack
Wake Feast
Lane o' Thrushes
Harp That Once thro' Tara's
Halls

Ireland
A Soft Day
O Breathe Not His Name
Father O'Flynn
Lough Scheelin
Last Rose of Summer
Meeting of the Waters

IRISH FOLK SONGS: *The McNulty Family* (*12*)   *Colonial*
Col-LP-121   *12"*

Likeable Lovable Leitrim Lad
Three Leaf Shamrock from
Glenor
O'Hara from Tara MacNamara
Martha the Flower of Sweet
Strabane
Somewhere in Ireland
My Auld Skellara Hat

Bedelia
Ann Carawath—Hornpipe
When I Mowed Pat Murphy's
Meadow
Off to Philadelphia
Green on the Green
Dora My Darling

JEWISH YOUNG FOLKSINGERS, THE (*10*)   *Stinson*   *SLP #67*   *10"*

Oy A Liebe
Rozhinkes Mit Mandlen
In A Shtetl
S'Falt A Shmei
Dire Gelt

La Carmagnole
En Mi Viejo San Juan
163 Didn't My Lord Deliver Daniel
Frankie Slide
Hava Na Gila

JIMMY CRACK CORN, *Bill Hayes and The Buckle Busters* (*13*)
                Kapp Records   KL-1106   12"   (*1958*)

58	Blue Tail Fly	The Bum Song
41	Big Rock Candy Mountain	655 Across the Shenandoah
	The Roving Kind	768 Wanderin'
	Little White Duck	Barbary Ann
	Wimoweh	I Know Where I'm Goin'
254	Goin' Down the Road	Patsy-Ory-Ory-Ay
	Dance with a Dolly	

LISTEN TO THE STORY (*American Ballads*)   Coral   CLP 59001   10"
                (song titles not available)

LITHUANIAN FOLK SONGS IN THE UNITED STATES (*Recorded by Dr. Jonas Balys*)   *Folkways*   FM 4009 (*P1009*)   12"   (*1936-50*)
        Choral Rounds, Dance Songs, Weddings Songs,
                Love Songs, Ballads
            (No individual titles given)

LONESOME TRAIN (*Norman Corwin Production*)   Decca   DL-5054   10"
        "A Musical Legend About the Martyrdom of Abraham Lincoln"
                (No individual titles given)

LONESOME VALLEY, *Pete Seeger* et al. (*9—banjo, mandolin, guitars*)
            Folkways   FA 2010 (*FP10*)   10"   (*1951*)

172	Down in the Valley	551 On Top of Old Smoky
599	The Rambler	53 Black-Eyed Suzie
	Arthritis Blues	133 Cowboy Waltz
573	Polly Wolly Doodle All Day	Sowing on the Mountain
	Lonesome Traveler	

MORMON TABERNACLE CHOIR SINGS CHRISTMAS CAROLS (*15*)
            Columbia   ML-5222   12"

Joy to the World	What Child Is This?
When Jesus Was a Little Child	Beautiful Saviour
Away in a Manger	Carol of the Nativity
A Boy Is Born	Tell Us, Shepherd Maids
There Shall a Star from Jacob	Holy City
O Come, O Come Emmanuel	I Heard the Bells
Far, Far Away on Judea's Plains	Silent Night
O Holy Night	

MOUNTAIN MUSIC, BLUEGRASS STYLE (*12—authentic bluegrass bands*)
    Recorded by Mike Seeger   *Folkways*   FA 2318   12"   (*1959*)

Short Life of Trouble	Ain't Nobody Gonna Miss Me
Katy Cline	When I'm Gone
Philadelphia Lawyer	Little Willie
	Whitehouse Blues

706   Nine Pound Hammer
       All the Good Times Have
           Passed and Gone

499   New River Train
       Feast Here Tonight
42   Bile Dem Cabbage Down
       Snow Dove

MUSIC BOX OF CHRISTMAS CAROLS, *The Welch Chorale with Music Boxes from the Bornand Collection* (22)   *Vanguard   VRS 428   12"*

Joy to the World
The First Noel
Sing We Noel
Hark the Herald Angels Sing
It Came Upon a Midnight Clear
O Tannenbaum
Carol of the Advent
Chimes of Trinity
Good King Wenceslas
Jingle Bells
Little Town of Bethlehem

281   Greensleeves
       A-Rocking All Night
       Adeste Fideles
       Auld Lang Syne
       Lute Book Lullaby
       Ave Maria
       King Herod
       Once Mary Would Go
           Wandering
       Silent Night
       O Sanctissima
       Song of the Birds

MUSIC FOR MOONSHINERS, *by Laurel River Valley Boys* (12) *Judson Records   J-3031   12"*

       Roll in My Sweet Baby's Arms
262   Good Old Mountain Dew
       Tennessee Blues
442   Lonesome Road Blues
525   Old Hen Cackle
369   John Henry
       Dance All Night with a Bottle in
           Your Hand

499   New River Train
145   Cumberland Gap
       Train 45
680   Sourwood Mountain
708   Nine Pound Hammer

MUSIC FROM THE SOUTH: Vol. I, COUNTRY BRASS BANDS   *Folkways FA 2650 (FP650)   12"*

(Mostly not folksongs)

(NOTE: There are a number of other volumes in this series, not listed here, recorded by Frederic Ramsey, Jr., on a Guggenheim Fellowship in 1954.)

NEGRO FOLK MUSIC OF ALABAMA, Vol. I: Secular (14)   *Ethnic Folkways Library   FE 4417 (P417)   12"   (1951)*

Mama Don't Tear My Clothes
    (mouth harp)
Southern Pacific (mouth harp)
Black Woman (field blues)
Kansas City Blue (vocal–guitar)
Salty Dog Blues (vocal–guitar,
    tub)
I'm Goin' Up North (ring game)
Little Sally Walker (ring game)
See See Rider (ring game)

Mama's Goin' to Buy Him a
    Little Lap Dog (lullaby)
Soon As My Back's Turned
    (lullaby)
She Done Got Ugly (work song)
10   Now Your Man Done Gone
    (work song)
Field Calls (hollers)
Brer Rabbit and the Alligator
    (story)

NEGRO FOLK MUSIC OF ALABAMA, Vol. II: Religious (*Recorded by Harold Courlander*) (*11*)   Ethnic Folkways Library   FE 4418 (P418)   12"
(1951)

Trampin' Trampin' (Dock Reed)	Free at Last (Reed and Hall)
Dead and Gone (Dock Reed	Jonah (story and song)
and Vera Hall)	Low Down Death Right Easy
Abraham and Lot (sermon)	Jesus Goin' to Make Up My
Rock Chair, I Told You to Rock	Dyin' Bed (Reed)
I Wonder Where My Brother	Prayer (Reed and Hall)
Gone	Move Members Move

NEGRO FOLK MUSIC OF ALABAMA, Vol. III (*Recorded by Harold Courlander*)   Folkways   FE 4471 (P471)   12"
(songs, tales, and sermonizing)

NEGRO FOLK MUSIC OF ALABAMA, Vol. IV (*Recorded by Harold Courlander*)   Folkways   FE 4472 (P472)
(sermonizing and spirituals)

NEGRO FOLK MUSIC OF ALABAMA, Vol. V (*Recorded by Harold Courlander*) (*6*)   Folkways   FE 4473 (P473)   12"

Where the Sun Will Never Go	737 Troubled
Down	What Month Was Jesus Born in
My God Ain't No Lyin' Man	Job, Job
I'm Goin' Home on the Morning	
Train	

NEGRO FOLK MUSIC OF ALABAMA, Vol. VI (*Recorded by Harold Courlander*)   Folkways   FE 4474 (P474)   12"
(games and songs—work songs, chain-gang songs, etc.)

NEGRO PRISON CAMP WORK SONGS (*10*)   Folkways
FE 4475 (P475)   12"   (1951)

Let Your Hammer Ring	Lost John
Here Rattler Here	You Got to Hurry
Chopping in the New Ground	I Need More Power
Mighty Bright Light	We Need Another Witness
251 Go Down Old Hannah	
Grizzly Bear	

NEGRO PRISON SONGS FROM THE MISSISSIPPI STATE PENITEN-
TIARY, *Collected by Alan Lomax* (*7*)   Tradition   TLP 1020   12"
(1947)

Murder's Home	682 Stackerlee
Black Woman	Prison Blues
Old Dollar Mamie	(and others)
Tangle Eye Blues	
How I Got in the Penitentiary	
(interview)	

NEGRO RELIGIOUS SONGS AND SERVICES (15)   *Lib. of Cong. Music Div.*   *AAFS L 10   12"*

Do Lord, Remember Me
House Done Built Without
  Hands
Oh, the Lamb of God, the Lord
  Done Sanctified Me
We Are Almost Down to the
  Shore
Shine Like a Star in the Morning
Ain't No Grave Can Hold My   686
  Body Down

Down on Me
Certainly, Lord
The Man of Calvary
Wasn't That a Mighty Storm
Holy Babe
Meet Me in Jerusalem
When I Lay My Burden Down
In New Jerusalem
Steal Away

NEGRO WORK SONGS AND CALLS (15)   *Lib. of Cong. Music Div.*   *AAFS L 8   12"*

Unloading Rails
Tamping Ties
Heaving the Lead Line   533
Mississippi Sounding Calls   251
Arwhoolie (Cornfield Holler)
Quittin' Time Songs
Mealtime Call
Possum Was an Evil Thing   734

Come On, Boys and Let's Go to
  Huntin'
Old Rattler
Go Down, Old Hannah
Hammer Ring
Roll 'Im on Down
The Rock Island Line
Track-Lining Song

NIGHT IN IRELAND, Vol. 1, *by the McNulty Family* (12)   *Copley Records*   *Cop. 610   12"*   (1958)

Good-Bye I'm on My Way to
  Dear Old Dublin Bay
Let Mr. Maguire Sit Down
John Mitchell
Exile of Cork   194
Leather Away with the Wattle
O Polka
Miss Fogarty's Christmas Cake

Mother Malone
They Sailed Away from Dublin
  Bay
Jacket's Green
Erin's Green Shore
Mother's Love Is a Blessing
I Don't Care If I Do

NIGHT IN IRELAND, Vol. 2, *by the McNulty Family* (12)   *Copley Records*   *Cop. 611   12"*   (1958)

Along the Rocky Road to Dublin
When You Look in the Heart of
  a Shamrock
Susie O'Malley
Homes of Donegal
Stack of Wheat Hornpipe
Darling Girl from Clare

McNamara from Mayo
Boys from the County Armagh
Hills of Knock-na-Shee
Fair Roscommon Polka
Queenstown Harbor
Tipperary Daisy

NOVA SCOTIA FOLK MUSIC FROM CAPE BRETON, *recorded by Diane Hamilton* (16—guitar, fiddle, bass)   *Elektra   EKL-23   10"*

The 79th Farewell to Gibraltar
My Ain House
The Sailor's Love Song
Lullaby

Mouth Music
Marquis of Huntley
The Shean Truibbas

233   Mr. Frog Went A-Courtin'
      Though I Sailed in My
      Ignorance
      Oh, Birdie Tell
      Haste to the Wedding
      Speed the Plow

675   Soldier's Joy
      My Young Maid
      In the Glen Where I Was
      Young
      121st Psalm

NURSERY SONGS, by Gene Kelly and quartet (16—orch.)   Columbia
                 JL 8001   10"   (1949?)

      Jack and Jill
437   London Bridge
      Three Little Kittens
  7   Alphabet Song
      Sing a Song of Sixpence
      Mary Had a Little Lamb
      Little Boy Blue
580   Pop! Goes the Weasel
      Farmer in the Dell

      Ten Little Indians
      See Saw Margery Daw
 44   Billy Boy
      Little Bo-Peep
      Hickory Dickory Dock
      Pussy Cat
      Mulberry Bush

OFF-BEAT FOLK SONGS (The Shanty Boys) (15—guitars, banjo, washtub,
            bass)   Elektra   EKL-142   12"   (1958)

      Dance Boatman
      Puttin' on the Style
197   Ezekiel
      Home in That Rock
      Oxtail Rag-out
767   Walking Cane
      Away Rio
      Shuckin' the Corn

      Sweet Potato
      Johnson Boys
605   Rubin Ranzo
      Oh Mona
474   Midnight Special
      Out After Beer
      Crying Holy

OLD HARP SINGERS, Hymns, Anthems, Fuguing Songs sung in Shape Note
            Tradition (8)   Folkways   FA 2356   12"

      Wondrous Love
      Morning Trumpet
      Northfield
      Pleasant Hill

      Whitestone
      Hightower
      Liberty
      Edom

OUR SINGING HERITAGE, Vol. I (Peggy Seeger, Paul Clayton, Pat Foster,
      George Pegram) (18)   Elektra   EKL-151   12"   (1958)

      Jack Went A-Sailing
690   Strawberry Roan
607   Rich Old Lady
427   Little Old Log Cabin in the
      Lane
      Gypsy Lover
792   When I Was Single
      Roll On Buddy
304   House Carpenter
      Nobody Knows You When
      You're Down and Out

804   Who's Gonna Shoe Your Pretty
      Little Foot
      Goodbye Little Bonnie Goodbye
      Mary What You Call That
      Pretty Little Baby
400   Lakes of Ponchartrain
233   Froggie Went A-Courting
370   John Riley
      Johnny Runkins
      Yellow Rose of Texas
      Love Henry

OUR SINGING HERITAGE, Vol. II   *Elektra*   *EKL-152*   *12"*
(song titles not available)

OUR SINGING HERITAGE, Vol. III (*Songs collected and arranged by Frank
Warner*) (*19—banjo by Billy Faier*)   *Elektra   EKL-153   12"*   (*1958*)

The Jolly Tinker	The Jolly Roving Tar
Hi Rinky Dum	'Frisco
Lynchburg Town	52 Blackjack Davy
Dan Doo	Bony on the Isle of St. Helena
Johnson Boys	Bay of Biscayo
Jump Her Juberju	Bold Dickie and Bold Archie
Jamie Judge	Raccoon
Lewiston Falls	Fresh Peanuts
We're Coming Idaho	Victory
Fod	

PICKIN' AND BLOWIN': *George Pegram* (*banjo*) *and Walter Parham*
(*mouth harp*) (*18*)   *Riverside   RLP 12-650   12"*

533	Old Rattler	526	Old Joe Clark
825	The Wreck of the Old 97		Downfall of Paris
	Lost John		Will the Circle Be Unbroken
	Georgia Buck		Listen to the Mocking Bird
94	Cackling Hen		Johnson's Old Gray Mule
680	Sourwood Mountain	110	Chicken Reel
	Wildwood Flower	740	Turkey in the Straw
172	Down in the Valley		Foggy Mountain Top
	Fly Around My Pretty Little		
	Miss		
	Roll On Buddy		

PLAY AND DANCE SONGS AND TUNES (*26*)   *Lib. of Cong. Music Div.*
AAFS L 9   12"

	Little Rosa Lee		O, Fly Around, My Pretty Little
	Haste to the Wedding		Miss
	Off She Goes	675	Soldier's Joy
	Jig (medley)		We're Goin' Around the
344	Irish Washerwoman		Mountain
	Pigtown Fling		Old Lady Sittin' in the Dining
	Devil's Dream		Room
	Nancy's Fancy		Satisfied
	Old Blue Sow	42	Bile Dem Cabbage Down
	Where'd You Get You Whiskey	245	The Girl I Left Behind Me
	Pore Little Mary Settin' in the		Devil's Dream
	Corner		Mississippi Sawyer
638	Sally Goodin (2)	3	All Around the Maypole
637	Old Sally Brown		Sissy in the Barn
	Gwan Roun', Rabbit		

POPULAR SQUARE DANCE MUSIC *(Tommy Jackson)* *(12)*   **Dot**
                    DLP-3015   12"

259 Golden Slippers
13   Arkansas Traveler
42   Boil Them Cabbage Down
     Chinese Breakdown
675 Soldier's Joy
221 Flop-Eared Mule
     Fiddlin' Rag

Mississippi Sawyer
Bill Cheatham
Lead Out
Uncle Joe
Ragtime Annie

PROMISED LAND, *A Treasury of American Folk Music from All Four Corners of the Land (The Welch Chorale) (19)*   *Lyrichord   LL 64   12"*

     Promised Land
     Charlottown
655 Shenandoah
     Cousin Jedediah
362 Jesus Born in Bethlea
     Nelly Bly
515 Ol' Ark's A-Moverin'
513 Oh! Susanna
579 Poor Wayfarin' Stranger

512 O Mary, Don't You Weep!
     I Have a Mother
434 Li'l Liza Jane
438 The Lone Prairie
     Lamentation Over Boston
     Gonna Ride Up in the Chariot
     Bethlehem
705 Swing Low, Sweet Chariot
784 Were You There?
686 Steal Away

PUTTIN' ON THE STYLE, *by The Gateway Singers (13—orch.)*   *Decca*
                    DL 8413   12"   (1957)

     Puttin' on the Style
     Fair Maid
     Monaco
     Sally Don't You Grieve
     Bury Me in My Overalls
     Run, Come See Jerusalem

320 I Was Born About 10,000 Years
       Ago
     Rock Island Line
474 Midnight Special
     Come to the Dance
     True Love
     Tumbalalaika
197 Ezekiel Saw the Wheel

RIVERSIDE FOLKSONG SAMPLER *(20—banjo, guitar, concertina, harmonica, dulcimer, fiddle)*   *Riverside   S-2   12"   (1956)*

     Chickens (Bob Gibson)
563 Pearl Bryan (Paul Clayton)
     She Moves through the Fair
       (Margaret Barry)
     The Carlton Weaver (Ewan
       MacColl)
760 The Wabash Cannonball (John
       Greenway)
     A Sup of Good Whiskey (Patrick
       Galvin)
727 The Three Ravens (Ed
       McCurdy)
     The Lime Juice Tub (A. L.
       Lloyd)
     Little Maggie (Obray Ramsey)
     Early One Morning (Milt Okun)

421 Little Brown Jug (Oscar Brand
       and Erik Darling)
649 Shady Grove (Jean Ritchie)
     I Went Up on the Mountain
       (Artus Moser)
156 The Darby Ram (A. L. Lloyd)
451 Lord Randall (Ewan MacColl)
     Football Crazy (Patrick Galvin)
518 The Old Chisholm Trail
       (Merrick Jarrett)
292 Hard Times in the Mill (John
       Greenway)
     To the Begging I Will Go
       (Ewan MacColl)
     Blow Gabriel (The Rev. Gary
       Davis)

RUN COME HEAR, *by The Folk Singers* (*15*)   *Elektra*   *EKL-157*   *12"*
(*1958*)

Poor Howard	385	Keep Your Hand on That Plow
Peter Gray		Pay Me My Money Down
Silvy		By'm By
Hullabaloo		Little Maggie
Peat Bog Soldiers		Brown Eyes
Deep Blue Sea		Banuwa
Michael Row the Boat Ashore		Room Enough
Hole in the Bottom of the Sea		

SACRED HARP SINGING (*19*)   *Lib. of Cong. Music Div.*
AAFS L 11   *12"*

Windham	Ballstown
Mear	Edom
Wondrous Love	Fillmore
Lover of the Lord	Sardis
Montgomery	Mission
Northfield	Vain World Adieu
Mount Zion	Heavenly Vision
Milford	David's Lamentation
Stratfield	Sherburne
Evening Shade	

SHIVAREE! *A New Presentation of Folk Music* (*Oscar Brand, Jean Ritchie, Harry and Jeanie West, Tom Paley*) (*19*)   *Esoteric*   *ES-538*   *12"*

139	Cripple Creek	323	I Wish I Was Single Again
213	A Farmer's Wife	616	Roll on the Ground
	The Good Peanuts		The Blackest Crow
42	Bile Them Cabbage Down	160	Devilish Mary
526	Joe Clarke		Ain't Gonna Work Tomorrow
	Pretty Little Willow	595	Railroad Bill
90	Bury Me Beneath the Willow	44	My Billy Boy
	Down the Old Plank Road	13	Arkansas Traveller
161	The Devil's Nine Questions	597	Raise a Ruckus Tonight
661	Shortnin' Bread		

SING OUT, SWEET LAND! (*Selections by the Original Cast*) (*17*)   *Decca*
DL-8023   *12"*

	As I Was Going Along	230	Frankie and Johnny
	Where?	627	The Roving Gambler
41	Big Rock Candy Mountain		Hammer Ring
58	Blue Tail Fly		Watermelon Cry
254	I'm Goin' Down the Road		Trouble, Trouble
425	Little Mohee		Basement Blues
768	Wanderin'	103	Casey Jones
	I Have Been a Good Boy		More Than These
163	Didn't My Lord Deliver Daniel		

SONGS AND BALLADS OF AMERICAN HISTORY and of the ASSASSINA-
TION OF PRESIDENTS (*Ed. Duncan B. M. Emrich; sung by Judge
Learned W. Hand, Captain Pearl R. Nye, Warde H. Ford, Mrs. Minta
Morgan, Bascom Lamar Lunsford*) (*11*)   Lib. of Cong. Music Div.
AAFS L 29   12"

The Iron Merrimac (Hand)
The Battle of Antietam Creek
(Ford)
The Southern Soldier (Morgan)
Washington the Great (Morgan)
Zolgotz (Lunsford—banjo)
356 Mr. Garfield (Lunsford—banjo)

104 Charles Guiteau (Lunsford)
Booth Killed Lincoln (Lunsford)
Booth Killed Lincoln (Lunsford
—fiddle tune)
The Cumberland's Crew (Nye)
Phil Sheridan (Hand)

SONGS AND BALLADS OF THE ANTHRACITE MINERS (*14*)
Lib. of Cong. Music Div.   AAFS L 16   12"

Down, Down, Down
The Avondale Mine Disaster
Me Johnny Mitchell Man
Boys on the Hill
On Johnny Mitchell's Train
Rolling on the Rye Grass
The Old Miner's Refrain
When the Breaker Starts Up
Full Time

John J. Curtis
A Celebrated Workingman
Union Man
The Miner's Doom
Down in a Coal Mine
The Shoofly

SONGS AND DANCES OF QUEBEC (*Instrumental and vocal*) (*10*)
Folkways   FW 6951 (*FP951*)   10"

Danse Carrée
Reel de Rinouski
Son Voile Qui Voilait
Reel Canadien
Grand Chapeau

La Petite Vache Noire
Le Violin en Discorde
Danse Deuxième Set
Le Bastringue
Potpourri

SONGS FROM CAPE BRETON ISLAND, *Recorded by Sidney Robertson
Cowell* (*various singers*) (*13*)   Folkways   FE 4450 (*P450*)   12"
(*1955*)

("This album is devoted to Gaelic songs which survive in Nova Scotia.
Included are milling (waulking) songs, love songs, sailors' songs, nostalgia
songs and examples of Gaelic pipes.")

He Mo Leannan (Hey, My
Darling)
Mo H-Ingheann Dhonn (My
Brown-Haired Maiden)
La-La, Lo, La Luadhadh (With
Water, with Milling)
An Seoladair Curanta (The
Steadfast Mariner)

'n Uair Nighidh Tu (When You
Wash)
A' Challuinn (New Year's Day)
Gaol an T-Seoladair (The
Sailor's Sweetheart)
Moladh Na Lanndaidh (In
Praise of Islay)
's A' Righinn thu dhe Shogh
(Thou Art Princess of Cheer)

Mo Run, Mo Nighean Dhonn
Bhoidheach (My Love, My
Pretty Brown-Haired Girl)
Lan I de Dh'ainneadh (She Is
Full of Patience)

Flowers of the Forest (bagpipes)
I'll Get a Soldier for a Shilling
(bagpipes)

SONGS OF FRENCH CANADA, *Recorded by Laura Boulton, Samuel Gesser,*
Carmen Roy and M. Asch (25)   *Folkways   FE 4482   12"   (1957)*

Son Voile Qui Volait
Chanson Mensonge
Tous les Gens du Plaisir
Je Suis Amoureux
Reel (harmonica, 7 spoons)
C'était une Vieille Salope
Pis Ote-Toe Donc
Reel (harmonica, spoons)
Le Mariage Anglais
La Passion de Jésus-Christ
Je M'ai Fait une Jolie Maîtresse
Un Petit Peu d'Amour Mesdames
Ram'nez Vos Moutons
Belle, Tu N'as Plus d'Amitié
pour Moi

Derrière Chez-Nous, y a-t'un
Champ d'pois
Galop de la Malbaie
Royal David
The "Brandy" (jig)
J'ai Fait une Maîtresse
Corbleur, Sambleur, Marion
Au Long de la Mer Jolie
Fiddle Dance
Le Miracle du Nouveau-Né
Bidou
Prince Eugène

SONGS OF THE GOLDEN WEST and **SONGS OF THE DEEP SOUTH,** *by*
The Hollywood Soundstage Chorus (12)   *Somerset Records   Album*
P-1500   12"

Songs of the Golden West:
302 Home on the Range
805 Yippe Vi-Yi-Yo
619 Streets of Laredo
 91 Bury Me Not on the Lone Prairie
604 Red River Valley
     Darlin' Clementine

Songs of the Deep South:
In the Evening by the Moonlight
Old Black Joe
John Brown's Body
Dixie
Old Folks at Home
My Old Kentucky Home

SONGS OF THE MORMONS and **SONGS AND BALLADS OF THE WEST**
(13)   *Lib. of Cong. Music Div.   AAFS L 30   12"*

Mormons:
On the Road to California (or
The Buffalo Bull Fight)
The Handcart Song
Echo Canyon
St. George
Tittery-Ire-Aye
The Utah Iron Horse

West:
621 Root Hog or Die
684 Starving to Death on a Govern-
     ment Claim
     Freighting from Wilcox to Globe
     Custer's Last Charge
     The Brazos River
367 Joe Bowers
641 Sam Bass

SONGS OF THE RAILROAD, *by Merrill Jay Singers   Cabot Records*
CAB-503   12"   (1957)

760 Wabash Cannonball
825 Wreck of the Old 97
369 John Henry
103 Casey Jones

348 I've Been Working on the Rail-
     road
     Where D'Ya Work-a John?
     (and others)

SONGS OF THE SMOKY MOUNTAINS, *Roy Acuff and His Smoky Mountain Boys (8)   Columbia   HL 9004   10″   (1950)*

Wreck on the Highway	760 Wabash Cannon Ball
Fire Ball Mail	Freight Train Blues
The Precious Jewel	Wait for the Light to Shine
Pins and Needles	Low and Lonely

SONGS OF THE SOUTH, *by Norman Luboff Choir (15)   Columbia CL 860   12″*

My Old Kentucky Home	51 Black Is the Color of My True
317 I Must Walk That Lonesome	Love's Hair
Valley	27 The Ballad of the Boll Weevil
Sweet Lorena	Dixie
Salangadou	Tender Love
504 Nobody Knows the Trouble I've	172 Down in the Valley
Seen	705 Swing Low, Sweet Chariot
386 Kemo Kimo	Un-Deux-Trois
155 Deep River	
Carry Me Back to Old Virginny	

SONGS OF THE WEST, *by Norman Luboff Choir (12)   Columbia CL 657   12″*

91 Bury Me Not on the Lone Prairie	302 Home on the Range
518 The Old Chisholm Trail	604 Red River Valley
805 Whoopie Ti Yi Yo	Doney Gal
Tumbling Tumbleweeds	119 Colorado Trail
319 I Ride an Old Paint	Night Herding Song
Cool Water	691 Streets of Laredo

SONGS TO GROW ON *(School Days), American Folksongs sung by Pete Seeger, Charity Bailey, Adelaide VanWey, Lead Belly, Cisco Houston (13)   Folkways   FC 7020 (FP20)   10″*

By 'm By	255 Going to Boston
Mail Boat	218 Fire Down Below
Cape Cod Shanty	673 Skip to My Lou
Rock Island Line	252 Tell Aunt Rhodie
479 Mocking Bird	Brass Wagon
137 Crawdad Hole	268 Grey Goose
Night Herding Song	

SONGS TO GROW ON *(This Is My Land, Vol. 3) (10)   Folkways FC 7027 (FP27)   10″*

Jerry Oil the Car	517 Old Blue
456 Lumbermen's Alphabet	Cumberland Deer Chase
461 Hoe Corn	Old Man
Miss Alido	Miner's Song
293 Haul Away Joe	
Bonneville Dam	

SOUTHERN MOUNTAIN FOLKSONGS AND BALLADS *(Field Recordings)*
(Performers: Obray Ramsey, Henry Gentry, George Pegram, Walter Parham, Harry and Jeanie West) (18)   Riverside   RLP 12-617   12"

	Bonny Blue Eyes	394	Knoxville Girl
708	Nine Pound Hammer		I Am a Pilgrim
73	The Boston Burglar	104	Charles Guiteau
227	Mountain Fox Chase	480	Mole in the Ground
547	Banks of the Ohio		Wild Bill Jones
160	Devilish Mary		Pickin' and Blowin'
	Jim Gunter and the Steer	108	The Cherry Tree Carol
	The Sailor on the Deep Blue Sea	551	On Top of Old Smoky
90	Bury Me Beneath the Willow		
	I Went Up on the Mountain		

SOUTHERN MOUNTAIN HOEDOWNS *(Woody Guthrie, Cisco Houston, Sonny Terry, Alec Stewart, etc.) (8)   Stinson   SLP #54   10"*

87	Buffalo Gals	526	Joe Clark
520	Old Dan Tucker	326	Ida Red
	Salty Dog Breakdown		Hoe Cakes Baking
638	Sally Gooden		Fiddle Breakdown

SPANISH AND MEXICAN FOLK MUSIC OF NEW MEXICO, *Recorded by J. D. Robb   Folkways   FE 4426 (P426)   12"*

Includes Huapangos Entriega de Novias, La Luna Se Va Metiendo, El Zapatero, Jesusita Cuna, Corrido de Elena, and others; matachinas, corridos, and decimos. (No titles given)

SPIRITUALS, Vol. 1, *Camp Meetin' Choir   Mercury   MG-25083   10"*
(song titles not available)

SPIRITUALS, Vol. 2, *Camp Meetin' Choir   Mercury   MG-25084   10"*
(song titles not available)

SPIRITUALS: *Graham Jackson Choir (16)   Westminster   WP-6048   12"*

155	Deep River	705	Swing Low, Sweet Chariot
	Certainly Lord	250	Go Down, Moses
196	Every Time I Feel de Spirit		Guide My Feet
692	Ain't Gonna War No More	686	Steal Away
130	Couldn't Hear Nobody Pray	422	Li'l David
	Trampin'		Bye and Bye
379	Joshua Fit de Battle of Jericho		Jacob's Ladder
	I'm So Glad Trouble Don't Last		
	Always		
	Heaven		

SPIRITUALS, *by Howard University Choir* (18)   *RCA Victor   LM-2126*
12″   (1957)

Let Us Break Bread Together
196 Every Time I Feel the Spirit
Done Made My Vow
130 Couldn't Hear Nobody Pray
414 Listen to the Lambs
My Soul Is Anchored in the Lord
There Is a Balm in Gilead
Lord I Want to Be a Christian
This Little Light o' Mine

504 Nobody Know the Trouble I See
491 My Lord What a Mornin'
705 Swing Low, Sweet Chariot
Good News
Glory Manger
Ain'a That Good News
Go Tell It on the Mountain
Rockin' Jerusalem
784 Were You There

SPIRITUALS: *Selah Jubilee Quartet*   *Remington   RLP-1023   10″*
(song titles not available)

SPIRITUALS: *Tuskegee Institute Choir* (15)   *Westminster*
XWN-18080   12″

197 Ezekiel Saw de Wheel
312 I Couldn't Hear Nobody Pray
There Is a Balm in Gilead
I've Been 'Buked
196 Ev'ry Time I Feel the Spirit
414 Listen to the Lambs
Mary Had a Baby
784 Were You There

155 Deep River
Hail Mary!
Behold the Star
I Want to Be Ready
Ain'a That Good News
King Jesus Is A-Listening
Rockin' Jerusalem

SQUARE DANCE TONIGHT! *Tommy Jackson* (16)   *Dot   DLP-3085   12″*

Down Yonder
Alabama Jubilee
Hamilton County Breakdown
Camptown Races
Don't Let the Deal Go Down
Crazy Creek
Hoedown Polka
103 Casey Jones

415 Listen to the Mockingbird
Tangle Weed
434 Little Liza Jane
Tomahawk
Dill Pickles
Cherokee Shuffle
Busy Fingers
Polk County Breakdown

SQUARE DANCES, *The Haystackers* (8)   *London   APB-1008   10″*

94 The Cacklin' Hen
Climbin' Up the Golden Stairs
673 Skip to My Lou

513 Oh Susanna
Tennessee Breakdown
Haste to the Wedding
344 The Irish Washerwoman
680 Sourwood Mountain

SQUARE DANCES, *by the Pinetoppers*   *Coral   CRL-56200   10″*
(song titles not available)

SQUARE DANCES (*Piute Pete and His Country Cousins*) (8)   *Folkways*
FA 2001 (FPI)   10"

87	Buffalo Gals	604	Red River Valley
	Steam Boat		Looby Loo
	Shoo Fly		Step Right Back
	Ricketts Hornpipe		Duck for Oyster

SQUARE DANCES (*with calls*) (*Carson Robinson*) (7—*orch.*)   *Columbia*
CL 6029   10"   (1949)?

	The First Two Ladies Cross	581	'Possum in the 'Simmon Tree
	Over	513	Oh! Susanna
	Darling Nelly Gray	421	Little Brown Jug
	Buffalo Boy Go 'Round the Out-		
	side		
	Dive for the Oyster		

SQUARE DANCES WITH CALLS, *Carson Robinson, etc.* (8)   *MGM Records*
E 557   10"

	Hook and a Whirl	Pokeberry Promenade
	Head Couple Separate	Lady Round the Lady
	Bob's Favorite	The Devil's Britches
796	When the Work's All Done This	The Maverick
	Fall	

SQUARE DANCES, with calls, *by Carson Robinson, etc.* (*14*)   *RCA Victor*
LPM-1238   12"

	Spanish Cavaliers	126	Comin' Round the Mountain
344	Irish Washerwoman		Paddy Dear
	Jingle Bells	740	Turkey in the Straw
259	Golden Slippers	580	Pop Goes the Weasel
513	Oh! Susanna		The Girl Behind Me
	Captain Jinks		Blackberry Quadrille
	Triple Right and Left Four		
	Solomon Levi		

SQUARE DANCES, *by Woodhull's Old-Tyme Masters* (*12*)   *RCA Victor*
CAL-220   12"

513	Oh! Susanna	580	Pop Goes the Weasel
	Captain Jinks		The Wearin' of the Green
	The Girl Behind Me		Triple Right and Left Four
	Blackberry Quadrille	675	Soldier's Joy
344	The Irish Washerwoman		Pony Boy
	Bloom on the Sage		Ann Green

SQUARE DANCES (*without calls*) *Guy Lombardo and His Royal Canadians*
(*24*)   *Decca   DL 5277   10"*

740	Turkey in the Straw	288	Hand Me Down My Walkin'
	Fiddler's Dream		Cane
654	She'll Be Comin' Round the		Fire in the Mountain
	Mountain		

39 The Bear Went Over the
    Mountain
759 Virginia Reel
264 Goodbye My Lover, Goodbye
675 Soldier's Joy
87 Buffalo Gals
673 Skip to My Lou
245 The Girl I Left Behind Me
    Fisher's Hornpipe
110 Chicken Reel

526 Old Joe Clark
421 Little Brown Jug
326 Ida Red
580 Pop Goes the Weasel
13 Arkansas Traveler
259 O Dem Golden Slippers
520 Old Dan Tucker
680 Sourwood Mountain
    Devil's Dream
    Nellie Bly

STORY OF THE AMERICAN REVOLUTION, *Sung by Bill Bonyun, Dr. J. A. Scott, Chorus, with accompaniments by Mattatuck Drum and Fife Band* (22) *Heirloom Records* HL-502 12" (1958)

The Old Lady Who Lived Over
the Sea
What a Court Hath Old England
The Irishman's Epistle
The Dying British Sergeant
Sullivan's Island (Sir Peter
Parker)
The Battle of Trenton
The Fate of John Burgoyne
Come Out Ye Continentalers
Sir Henry Clinton's Invitation to
the Refugees
Yankee Doodle's Expedition to
Rhode Island

Johnny Has Gone for a Soldier
John Paulding and the Spy
Cornwallis' Surrender
Yankee Doodle
To the Commons
To the Ladies
Riflemen of Bennington
How Stands the Glass Around?
The Battle of the Kegs
Paul Jones' Victory
Cornwallis Country Dance
The World Turned Upside
Down

SWING LOW, *dePaur Infantry Chorus* (6—unacc.) *Columbia* AL 45
10" (1953)

705 Swing Low, Sweet Chariot
    In Dat Great Gittin'-up Mornin'
504 Nobody Knows de Trouble I've
    Seen

Who Built de Ark?
I Want Jesus to Walk wid Me
Soon Ah Will Be Done

SWING YOUR PARTNER (*Square Dances*) (8—band) *Columbia*
HL 9009 10"

13 Arkansas Traveler
675 Soldiers Joy
    Walkin' Up Town
    My Love Is But a Lassie O
    Mississippi Sawyer

638 Sallie Goodin
761 Wagoner
    Light Foot Bill

TERRY'S, SONNY, WASHBOARD BAND (8) *Folkways*
FA 2006 (FP 6) 10"

The Woman Is Killin' Me
Diggin' My Potatoes
Wine-Headed Woman
Louise

Baby Changed the Lock on the
Door
Custard Pie Blues
Crazy Man Blues
Sonny's Jump

TRADITION FOLK SAMPLER (14)   *Tradition   TSP-1   12"*

The Bird's Courtship (McCurdy)
O'Donnell Aboo (Clancy Broth-
ers and Makem)
369 John Henry (Baker)
Rodenos (Flamenco)
Dark As a Dungeon (Yarbrough)
Ha-Na-Ava-Ba-Ba-Not
(Hillel and Aviva)
320 I Was Born About Ten Thou-
sand Years Ago (Brand)
Keel Row (Cameron)

The Gambling Suitor (Ritchie
and Clayton)
The Hearse Song (Davies)
376 Johnny's Gone to Hilo (Clayton)
Johnny Lad (MacColl)
The Fairy Boy (Ennis)
Spiritual Trilogy (Odetta):
Oh, Freedom
Come and Go with Me
I'm on My Way

VOICES OF HAITI (*Recorded near Croix-Des-Missions and Petionville in
Haiti, by Maya Deren*) (9)   *Elektra   EKL-5   10"*

Creole O Voudoun (Yanvalou
Beat)
Ayizan Marché (Zepaules)
Signalé Agwé Arroyo (Yanvalou)
Ibo Lélé (Ibo)

Nago Jaco Colocoto (Nago
Crabiné)
Miro Miba (Petro)
Zulie Banda (Banda)
Ghede Nimbo (Mahi)
Pó Drapeaux (Congo Mazonne)

WAGON WHEELS (*Arr. M. Gould*), *by Morton Gould and His Orchestra* (9)
Columbia   ML 4858   12"

High Noon
Wagon Wheels
Riders in the Sky
302 Home on the Range
The Last Roundup

551 On Top of Old Smoky
I'm an Old Cowhand
Tennessee Waltz
Buckaroo Blues

WAYFARERS, THE (17)   *RCA Victor   LPM 1213   12"*

Landlord Fill the Flowing Bowl
Hammsi
436 Lolly Too Dum
When the Sun Goes Down
308 Hush Little Baby
Ah, Si Mon Moine
773 Wayfaring Stranger
531 Old Paint
112 Chilly Winds

172 Down in the Valley
Lass from the Low Countree
Mr. McGuire
La Vaquilla
Waltzing Matilda
Linstead Market
El Venadito
Zemerlach

WEAVERS, THE: FOLK SONGS OF AMERICA AND OTHER LANDS (8)
Decca   DL-5285   10"

Tzena, Tzena
The Frozen Logger
I Know Where I'm Going
Drinking Gourd
Around the World

149 Darling Corey
308 Hush Little Baby
Easy Rider Blues

WEAVERS AT CARNEGIE HALL, THE (20)   Vanguard   VRS-9010
12″   (1957)

149 Darling Corey
    Pay Me My Money Down
    Rock Island Line
    Wimoweh
    Suliram (I'll Be There)
    Lonesome Traveller
    Woody's Rag and 900 Miles
    Follow the Drinking Gourd
795 When the Saints Go Marching
    In
308 Hush Little Baby

342 Goodnight Irene
    Kisses Sweeter Than Wine
281 Greensleeves
    Around the World
    Venga Jaleo
    Shalom Chaverim
    I Know Where I'm Going
    Sixteen Tons
    I've Got a Name in That Rock
    Go Where I Send Thee

WEAVERS AT HOME, THE (17)   Vanguard   VRS-9024   12″   (1958)

This Land Is Your Land
Wild Goose Grasses (In Tarry-
    town)
Meet the Johnson Boys
Tina
Come Little Donkey
All Night Long
Every Night
91 Bury Me
Empty Pockets Blues

642 Aweigh, Santy Ano
19 Aunt Rhodie
    Eres Alta
    Kum Bachura
    You Old Fool
474 Let the Midnight Special
    Almost Done
    Howard's Dead and Gone

WEAVERS ON TOUR, THE * (21—banjo, guitars, recorder)   Vanguard
VRS-9013   12″

Tzena, Tzena
So Long
Michael Row the Boat
Fi-Li-Mi-oo-Re-Ay
Clementine
I Don't Want to Get Adjusted
744 Two Brothers
Wasn't That a Time
Go Tell It on the Mountain
Santa Claus Is Coming
We Wish You a Merry Christmas

538 Old Smoky
65 Boll Weevil
175 Drill Ye Tarriers, Drill
    Over the Hills
    Frozen Logger
    John B.
    Ragaputi
    My Y' Malel
    Poor Little Jesus

WOLF RIVER SONGS, Recorded and Annotated by Sidney Robertson Cowell, in Wisconsin, Wyoming, and California (17—unacc.)   Folkways Monograph Series   FW 4001 (P 1001)   12″   (1956)

420 The Little Brown Bulls
    We Are Anchored by the Road-
    side, Jim
840 Foreman Monroe
    The Keith & Hiles Line

812 The Wild Colonial Boy
    Land of Pleasure
    Andrew Batan

* In 1959, Vanguard issued THE WEAVERS TRAVELING ON (VRS 9043), and Decca issued THE BEST OF THE WEAVERS (DL 8893).

223 The Flying Cloud
     The Wreck of the Lady Sher-
       brooke
588 Pretty Polly
453 The Lost Jimmie Whalen
     River Driver's Song
     Nightingales of Spring

79   Brennan on the Moor
455 The Lowlands Low
837 Young Johnny
     Sinking of the Cumberland

WORK SONGS AND SPIRITUALS, *dePaur's Infantry Chorus* (9)   *Columbia*
ML 2119   10"

Water Boy
Great Gawd A'mighty
Honor, Honor
Take My Mother Home
Jerry

Tol' My Cap'n
Sweet Little Jesus Boy
His Name So Sweet
414 Listen to the Lambs

WORLD FESTIVAL OF FOLK SONG AND FOLK DANCE (UNESCO)
(*Second World Festival of the International Folk Music Council, held in
Biarritz and Pamplona, 1953*) (27)   *Westminster   WF 12008   12"*

Side 1:

France: Jabadao (Brittany dance-song)
Spain: Chanson de Fête Basque (pipe and drum)
Spain: Bolero; Jota del U y el Doxte (guitars, etc.)
Norway: Vestlandsspringar Dance (fiddle)
Spain: Jota (group of dances)
Spain: Men's Stick Dance (pipe and drum)
Finland: Sjalaskuttan (wedding dance—violin)
Finland: Rihmarulla
Italy: La Corrente della Società (accordions)
Japan: Kazoo Uta (koto)   Japan: Sakura (dance)
Yugoslavia: Poscoica; Bunjevacko Kolo
Switzerland: Alphorn Trio; Yodels; Dance
England: Shooting; Morris Dance; Sword Dance
Scotland: Sword Dance (bagpipes)
Northern Ireland: Two-Handed Reel

Side 2:

Germany: Yodels from Bavaria
United States: The Cuckoo; Goodbye Girls, I'm Going to Boston
       (Jean Ritchie with dulcimer)
Netherlands: Donder in't hoot (dance)
Spain: Arku Dantza; Txakarranku (pipe and drums)
Spain: Sevillanas (guitars and bandurrias)
Indonesia: Gamelan music, by Indonesian dancers
Turkey: Hos Bilezik; Kastamani Davel Oyun
Irish Republic: Io Fada O Bhaile (Gaelic song)
Irish Republic: Reel (Uillean pipes)
Sweden: Traskodans (solo dance)
France: L'Escloupette (cabrettes and accordion)
France: Satan Dantza (Dance of the Satans)
Yugoslavia: Shkupetari (zurla and drum)
Yugoslavia: Two-part chorus and dance

WORLD OF FOLK DANCES, THE (Series) (*Michael Herman's Folk Dance Orchestra*)   *RCA Victor   6-12" records*

Series 1:	HAPPY FOLK DANCES	LPM-1620
Series 2:	FESTIVAL FOLK DANCES	LPM-1621
Series 3:	FOLK DANCES FOR ALL AGES	LPM-1622
Series 4:	ALL-PURPOSE FOLK DANCES	LPM-1623
Series 5:	FOLK DANCES FOR FUN	LPM-1624
Series 6:	FIRST FOLK DANCES	LPM-1625

(Folk dances from many countries of the world, with booklets giving patterns and maneuvers for performers.)

Index of Names
and Subjects

A

Abbey Theatre Players, 189, 190
Abramson, Robert, 48
Acadian Bicentennial, 216
Acadian folksongs, 312
accordion, 249, 261-62
Adams, Derrol S., 25, 29, 510
Adams, James Barton, 292
Adams, Ramon F., 413
Adirondack Folk Song and Dance Festival, 182, 445
Adler, Larry, 254
African Bantu folksongs, 154
Afro-American folk music, 317, 360, 586, 587
Alfred Deller Consort, 79
All-Florida Folk Festival, 36, 174, 445
Allen, G. N., 136
Allen, Lewis, 197
Allen, William Francis, 318
Allison, John, 25, 29-30, 488
Almanac Singers, The, 111
American folk music, 87, 127, 144, 154, 279
Amburgey, Jethro, 258
American ballads, 84, 300, 307, 322, 499, 500, 507, 523, 526, 543, 555, 567, 569, 570, 576, 579, 581, 582, 584, 592, 593, 594, 620
American Folklore Society, 200, 272, 300, 393, 433, 436
American Folk Singers, The, 30
American Folk Song Society, 445
American-Indian music, 16
American Negro folksongs, 16, 31, 60-61, 77, 109, 110, 113, 174, 176, 185, 299, 313, 329, 504, 613, 614

American Negro hymns, 195
American Negro slave songs, 610
American Negro Theatre, 39
American Negro worksongs, 195
American Society of Composers, Authors, & Publishers (ASCAP), 52, 61
American Square Dance Group, 236, 589
American white spirituals, 192, 283-86
Ames Brothers, 605
Ames, Russell, 426-27
Anderson, Marian, 109, 241, 242, 488, 489
Anderson, Pink, 242, 489
Andrews, Edward D., 371-72
Anglo-American ballads, 35, 589, 590
Anglo-American folksongs, 554, 590
Annual Folk Festival (Renfro, Kentucky), 148, 443
Annual Record Music Award, 95
Antoine, LeRoy, 391
Apel, Willi, 264
Appalachian folksongs, 279
Archer, Frances, 25, 30-31, 489
Archer and Gile, 25, 30-31, 489
Archive of American Folk Song, Library of Congress (see Library of Congress Archive of American Folk Song)
Archive of Midwest Folklore, 180
Archive of Songs (Arkansas Folklore Society), 78
Arizona Folklore Collection, 186
Arkansas Folklore Society, 36, 53, 56, 78, 89, 119, 135, 395, 434, 437, 444
Arkin, Alan, 25, 31-32, 489
Armstrong, M. F., 372
Armstrong, Sarah Gray, 311
army songs, 321, 541
Arnold, Byron, 5, 307

631

Arnold, Eddy, 490
art song, defined, 6
Art Morrow Singers, The, 33, 160
Arthur Norman Chorus, The, 575
ASCAP, 52, 61
Asch Records, 42, 84, 119, 228
Ashley, Clifford, 430
Atcher, Bob, 242, 490
Australian bush songs, 143, 537
Australian folksongs, 527
Austrian folkways, 135, 137, 236
autoharp, 44, 46, 184, 190, 228, 249, 256

B

Babysitters, The, 607
Bach Choir, The, 597
Badger State Folklore Society, 216, 440
Bailey, Jay, 25, 32
Baillargeon, Hélène, 25, 32-33, 490
Bair, Fred, 25, 33-34
Balanchine, George, 16
Balfour, Nemonie, 262
Ball, E. C., 25, 34-35
Ball, Orra, 25, 34-35
ballads
    American, 84, 300, 307, 322
    American Negro, 315
    Anglo-American, 35
    British, 84, 149, 150, 154, 156, 157, 219,
        238, 277, 279, 300, 307, 309, 322
    Canadian, 160, 275-77, 521
    Child, 180, 277, 281, 282, 283, 301, 302,
        303, 306, 308, 309, 310, 315, 323-24,
        327
    collections of, 275-392
    cowboy, 80, 152, 154, 251, 292-93, 308
    definition of, 5
    French Canadian, 275-77
    recordings of, 495, 499, 500, 507, 523,
        526, 543, 547, 555, 567, 569, 570,
        576, 579, 581, 582, 584, 592, 593,
        594, 620
Ballanta, Nicholas G. J., 345
Ballard, Elizabeth Flanders, 282
ballet, based on folklore, 15-16
Balys, Dr. Jonas, 612
banjo, 63, 250-51, 252, 253, 256, 258,
    261, 263, 308
banjo tunes and songs, 308, 511, 559,
    574, 587, 595
Bantock, Granville, 342-43
Barbeau, Marius, 5, 33, 185, 187, 273,
    275-77, 279, 304, 336, 340
Barker, Horton, 25, 35, 394
Barnes, Bobby (Henry), 25, 35-36, 256
Barnes, George, 119
Barry, Margaret, 25, 36-37, 143, 491
Barry, Phillips, 272, 273, 274, 277-78,
    279, 282
Bartholomew, M., 265
Bartusek, Libushka, 337
Baum, Paul F., 278
Bayard, Samuel P., 265, 311
Beck, Earl Clifton, 312, 320, 390
Beckman, Gertrude Wheeler, 83

Beers, Evelyne (Mrs. Fiddler), 25, 30,
    37-39, 232
Beers, Robert (Fiddler Beers), 25, 30,
    37-39, 62, 159, 232, 265
Beethoven, Ludwig Von, 261
Belafonte, Harry, 25, 39-41, 112, 491,
    492
Belden, Henry M., 279, 301, 436
Beltona Records, 181
Bender, Bill (William, Jr.), 25, 41-42,
    492, 525
Benét, Stephen Vincent, 251
Benjamin, Arthur, 173
Bennett, Marjorie, 492
Benton, Jessie, 25, 42, 120
Benton, Thomas Hart, 12, 15, 25, 42, 120,
    252, 253, 254, 265, 294, 411
Bernstein, Leonard, 204
Berry, Cecilia Ray, 337
Best, Dick, 353
Bikel, Theodore, 25, 43, 492, 493, 518
Bixler, Helen, 243
Black, Eleanora, 372
Blegen, Theodore C., 377
blues, 55, 111, 219, 225
    defined, 5
    folk, 238
    recordings of, 492, 497, 546, 573, 581,
        582, 583, 593
Bluestein, G., 533
Boette, Marie, 25, 43-44
Boguslav, Raphael, 242, 493
Bolton, Dorothy G., 342
Bone, David W., 363
Boni, Margaret Bradford, 110, 203, 334
Bonyun, Bill, 25, 44-45, 67, 494
Bonyun, Gene, 494
Boone-Tolliver Records, 178
Boswell, George W., 25, 45-46, 52, 394
Botkin, B. A., 30, 203, 299, 416, 420, 424,
    427, 428, 438
Bourinot, Arthur, 276
Bowles, Michael, 332
Bowmar Records, 63
Boyer, Walter C., 319
Boyle, Hal, 136-37
Boyle, Mary Ella M., 25, 46, 256
Bradford, Roark, 14, 419
Brand, Oscar, 8, 25, 46-48, 85, 194, 213,
    353, 494, 495, 496, 562, 592, 600
Breton, Max, 155
Brewster, Paul G., 279, 302
Brill, Marty, 242, 496
Briscoe, Mrs. Mary (High), 25, 48-49,
    113
British ballads, 84, 149, 150, 154, 156,
    157, 219, 238, 277, 279, 300, 307,
    309, 322, 501, 516, 595
British folksongs, 78, 117, 154, 294-96,
    308, 541
Britten, Benjamin, 15, 597
Britton, George, 242, 497
Brockway, Howard, 340
Brodis, John Benson, 497
Bronson, Bertrand Harris, 296, 323
Brooklyn Academy of Music, 209
Brooks, John B., 242

Broonzy, Big Bill (William Lee), 25, 49-50, 212, 218, 219, 250, 497, 498
Brown, Frank Clyde, 9, 230, 273, 278-80, 438
Brown, George, 282, 283
Brown, Lawrence, 332
Brunswick Records, 129
Bryan, Charles Faulkner, 15, 25, 45, 50-52, 70, 102, 215, 256, 257, 260, 266, 327
Buchanan, Annabel Morris, 236, 335, 440, 442, 443
Buckle Busters, The, 611
Buckley, Bruce, 25, 52-53, 112, 217, 498
Buffington, Albert F., 319
Burget, Frederic, 337
Burnett, W. H., 25, 53-54
Buschmann, Fredrich, 253
Byrne, Jerry, 25, 54

C

Cahn, Rolf, 25, 54-55
Cain, Noble, 218
Cajun folksongs, 312
Caldwell, Erskine, 11
California Folklore Society, 434
calypso, 238, 584
Cambiaire, Pierre C., 367
Cameron, Isla, 25, 55, 143, 498
Camp Meetin' Choir, 623, 624
Campa, Arthur Leon, 322
Campbell, Booth, 25, 55-56
Campbell, Gerard, 242, 498
Campbell, John C., 426
Campbell, Olive Dame, 294
Canadian ballads, 160, 275-77, 521
Canadian folksongs, 32, 187, 188, 206, 534, 596
Canadian Records, 152
Cansler, Loman, 25, 52, 57, 499
Cantemos Records, 243
Capitol Records, 105, 140
Caribbean folksongs, 40
Carmen Records, 202
Carmer, Carl, 326, 355, 438
Carmer, Elizabeth Black, 326
Carr, R. V., 292
Carrière, Joseph Médard, 337, 338
Cartier, Jacques, 188
Casseus, Frantz, 504
Chagall, Marc, 299
Chalmers, Keith, 25, 57-58
Chambers, H. A., 357
Chaney, Brainerd, 51
chanteys, 5, 195
Chapman, Arthur, 292
Chappell, Louis W., 309, 419
Charles, Lee, 499
Charters, Samuel B., 533
Chase, Dorothy, 25, 58-59
Chase, Richard, 361, 378, 588
Chassidic songs, 200
Chatham, John H. 314
Chickering, Geraldine Jencks, 9, 303
Child, Francis James, 3, 143, 271, 274, 279, 324

Child (Francis James) collection of ballads, 180, 277, 281, 282, 283, 301, 302, 303, 306, 308, 309, 310, 315, 323-24, 327, 555
Child, Marilyn, 499
children's songs, 322, 327-28, 516, 568, 570
Christmas songs, 328, 520, 569, 575, 587, 598, 599
Churchill, Stuart, 25, 59-60, 209
Clancy, Liam, 65, 181
Clark, Badger, 292
Clark, Edgar Rogie, 25, 60-61, 102, 394, 499
Clark, Keith, 25, 61-62, 499
Clauson, William, 25, 62-63, 500
Clayborn, Garland K., 25, 63-64
Clayborn, James R., 25, 63-64
Clayton, Paul, 25, 52, 64-65, 394, 500, 501, 502, 503
Clough, Francis F., 485
Cobos, Rubén, 25, 65-66
Coffin, Tristran P., 400-01
Colby, Fred W., 25, 66
Colcord, Joanna C., 316, 319
Cole, John, 541
Coleman, Satis N., 354
collections
  of ballads, 275-392
  of folksongs, 275-392
Collector Limited Editions Records, 194
Colorado Folklore Society, 435
Colorado Springs Fine Arts Center, 96
Coltman, Bob (Robert), 25, 67, 208
Columbia Records, 50, 116, 125, 140, 145, 155, 190, 221, 234
Combs, Josiah H., 306
comic songs, 312, 322
Community Drama Group (Florida), 58
Concert Hall Society Records, 84
concertina, 262
Connelly, Marc, 14
Continental songs, 84
Cook Laboratories, Inc., 87
Cooney, Barbara, 327, 328, 330
Cooper, Clarence, 242, 504
Cooperative Recreation Service, Delaware, Ohio, 365
Copeland, Dave, 25, 67-68
Copland, Aaron, 15, 17
Coral Records, 119, 210
Corbin, Alice, 250
Corelli, 16
Cornell Recording Society, 122, 217
Cornett, Banjo Bill, 25, 68-69, 251
cornstalk fiddle, 263
Corralaires, The, 159
Corwin, Norman, 47
Cotton, Elizabeth, 504
Council for the Daniel Boone Folk Arts Festival, 238
Council of the Southern Mountains, 257
Counterpoint Records, 89, 231
Country Dancers Festival, Healdsburg, Cal., 446
country-style songs, 6, 285, 497, 600
Courlander, Harold, 311, 559

courting songs, 279, 562, 563, 600
Covarrubias, Miguel, 331
cowboy songs, 80, 152, 154, 251, 292-93, 308, 500, 520, 524, 601
Cowell, Sidney Robertson, 239, 243, 400, 628
Cox, Harry, 149
Cox, John Harrington, 5, 10, 252, 265, 279, 310, 369-70, 390, 439-40
Craven, Thomas, 265
Creighton, Helen, 273, 279, 280-81, 336
Creole folksongs, 174, 175, 228, 312, 578
Creswell, Grace, 25, 69-70, 247, 504
Crisp, Rufus, 25, 70
Croy, Homer, 6, 7, 11
Cruz, Alonzo, 504
Cub Records, 228
Cuevas, Lolita, 242, 504
Cullinan, Ralph, 189, 190
Cuming, G. J., 485
Cunha, A. R., 385

D

Dagel, Kathy, 25, 73-74
Dane, Barbara (Spillman), 25, 74-75
Danufsky, Dr. Philip G., 25, 75-76
Darling, Erik, 25, 76, 111, 494, 505, 534, 543, 544
Davidson, Donald, 45, 51, 283
Davidson, Levette J., 405
Davis, Arthur Kyle, Jr., 10, 279, 322, 404, 439
Davis, Ellabelle, 505
Davis, Reverend Gary, 25, 76-77, 231, 489, 505
Davis, Mary Jo, 77-78
Davis, Oliva Lenore, 78
Davis, Thomas Morris, 25, 77-78
Davis, Mrs. Thomas Morris (Lula Smith), 25, 77-78
Davis, T. M., family, 77-78, 248
Day, Doris, 78
Dean, M. C., 368
Dean-Smith, Margaret, 274, 405
Decca Records, 60, 84, 111, 112, 116, 119, 125, 129, 145, 150, 155, 181, 197, 234, 240, 265
Decker, Eva, 588
De Cormier, Bob, 242, 505
De Cormier, Louise, 242, 505
Dehr, Rich, 25, 78-79
Delaware Folklore Society, 435
Delius, Frederick, 16
Deller, Alfred, 25, 79-80, 143, 506
De Mille, Agnes, 47
de Montigny, Louvigny, 340
Denson Brothers, 286
Deren, Maya, 627
Deschamps, Mrs. L. F. (see Ritchie, May)
Desprez, Frank, 292
Dett, R. Nathaniel, 343-44
Deutsch, Leonhard, 358
Devall, Dick, 25, 80, 248
d'Harcourt, Marguerite, 304
d'Harcourt, Raoul, 304
Diard, Marion, 25, 80-81, 229

Dick, Everett, 425
Disc Records, 84, 119, 140, 197, 231, 238
Dobie, J. Frank, 162, 389-90, 405, 439
Doerflinger, William, 239, 316-17
Dolmetsch, Arnold, 263
Dolph, Edward Arthur, 321
Donnegan, Lonnie, 242, 506
Dorson, Richard M., 396-97
Downes, Olin, 356-57
drama, use of folksongs in, 13-15
Drama Workshop (New York), 39
Driftwood, Jimmy, 26, 164-65, 507
drinking songs, 279, 312, 494
drum, 249, 263
dulcimer, 44, 52, 99, 100, 101, 132, 141, 176, 177, 178, 184, 189, 191, 194, 201, 202, 215, 221, 222, 226, 249, 254, 256-61, 266, 293
Dunbar, Max, 242, 507
Duncan, Bob, 25, 52, 81-82, 84, 105, 444
Duncan, Reverend J. B., 274
Duncan, Todd, 109, 507
D'Urfey, Thomas, 117
Dvořák, Anton, 16, 360
Dyer-Bennet, Richard, 25, 44, 83-84, 105, 117, 126, 227, 250, 260, 344, 394, 507, 508, 509

E

Eakins, Thomas, 13
Eaton, Allen H., 252, 260, 263, 265, 266, 417-18
Eckstrom, Fannie Hardy, 277, 312
Eddy, Mary O., 302
Edmonds, Randolph, 14
Egner, Philip, 321
Elektra Records, 32, 65, 76, 85, 88, 89, 92, 93, 106, 108, 111, 112, 116, 120, 152, 185, 190, 234, 241
Elizabethan ballads, 128
Elliot, Bill (William Byron), 26, 84-85
Elliot, Jack, 26, 85-86, 105, 509, 510, 592
Elliot, June, 26, 85-86, 105
Elson, Louis C., 337
Emberson, Frances G., 293
Emrich, Duncan, 80, 243, 588, 589
Encyclopaedia Britannica Films, 125
England, Paul, 275
English, Logan, 242, 510
English ballads, 84, 149, 150, 154, 156, 157, 219, 238, 277, 279, 300, 307, 309, 322
English Folk Dance and Song Society, 144
English folksongs, 78, 80, 117, 154, 294-96, 308
Ennis, Seumas, 242, 510
Eskin, Sam, 25, 86-87, 105, 241, 247, 394, 511
Ewen, David, 423, 426

F

Faier, Billy (William David), 26, 87-88, 511
Farwell, Arthur, 339

Faulk, John Henry, 239
Faulk collection, 239
Faye, Frances, 511
Federation of Music Clubs, 236
Felius, Odetta, 242, 556
Felton, Harold W., 365
Ferrier, Kathleen, 511
Ficker Records, 30
fiddle, 249, 251-53, 256, 261, 263, 293
fiddle tunes, 45-46, 308, 317
Fiddler Beers and Mrs. Fiddler (see Beers, Robert and Evelyne)
Fife, Austin and Alta, 424
Filiatrault, Roger, 26, 187, 188, 202 (see also Quatuor Alouette, Le)
Finger, Charles J., 370-71
Fisher, Miles Mark, 421
Fisher, William Arms, 352
Fisk Jubilee Singers, 272
five-stringer (five-string banjo), 251
F-L Music Company, 232
flamenco, 55
Flanders, Helen Hartness, 273, 279, 282-83, 439
    Collection of Ballads and Folksongs, 65, 282 ff., 436, 437
Flemish folksongs, 154
Fletcher, John Gould, 434
Florida Folk Festival, 110, 114, 222, 243
Flowers, Robert E. Lee, 26, 88-89
flute, 263
Folk and Square Dance Festivals, Lincoln, Neb., 446
Folk Dance Festival, Oakland, Cal., 446
Folk Festival, Asheville, North Carolina, 210
Folk Festival, Louisiana, 216
Folk Festival, North Carolina, 220, 232
folk festivals, 440 ff.
folklore societies, 433 ff.
Folkmasters, The, 610
Folk Music Research for Wyoming, 236
folk opera, 14-15
folk operetta, 129
Folk Singers, The, 76, 619
Folksmiths, The, 112
folksongs, 451-84
    Acadian, 312
    African Bantu, 154
    Afro-American, 317, 360
    American, 87, 127, 144, 154, 279
    American-Negro, 16, 31, 60-61, 77, 109, 110, 174, 176, 195, 299, 313, 329
    Australian bush, 143
    Austrian, 135, 137, 236
    British, 78, 117, 154, 277, 279, 294-96, 308
    Canadian, 32, 187, 188, 206, 534, 596
    Caribbean, 40
    Christmas, 328
    collections of, 275-392
    Creole, 174, 175, 228, 312
    definition of, 4-6
    French, 154, 272
    French-Canadian, 187, 188, 215, 275-77, 303
    Hebrew, 40, 200, 324

Newfoundland, 185, 206
New Mexican, 66, 250
Ozark, 293-94
    religious, 283-87
    resurgence of, 4-5
    titles, list of, 451-84
    traditional, 5
Folk-Song Society of the Northeast, 436, 437
Folkways Records, 53, 57, 65, 92, 94, 105, 111, 112, 116, 118, 119, 120, 121, 137, 140, 161, 170, 179, 185, 197, 198, 201, 211, 221, 225, 228, 234, 243
Ford, Ira W., 323
Ford, "Tennessee" Ernie, 241, 242, 512
Forli, Melozzo da, 267
Fortier, Achille, 359
Foster, Pat, 26, 89, 512
Foster, Stephen, 222
fotdella, 90
four-string tenor banjo, 251
Fowke, Edith Fulton, 10, 94, 126, 171, 206, 243, 336, 337, 552
Fox, Lillian M., 265
Frankel, Emily, 117
Fraser, Norman, 406, 485
Frederick, Carl, 263
French, John C., 314
French-Canadian folksongs, 187, 188, 215, 490, 550
    collections of, 275-77
French folk dances, 92
French folksongs, 154, 272
French harp, 253, 265
Friedman, Albert B., 325
Frost, Robert, 282
Frothingham, Robert, 386
Fuller, Jesse, 26, 88-90, 105, 512, 513
Fuson, Harvey H., 304

G

Gaelic songs, 180
Gagnon, Ernest, 272, 276, 305
Gainer, Dr. Patrick W., 26, 52, 90-91, 102, 266, 513
Galvin, Patrick, 242, 513, 514
gambling songs, 279, 553
Gard, Wayne, 10, 414
Gardell, Tony, 514
Gardner, Emelyn Elizabeth, 9, 303
Garrison, Lucy McKim, 318
Gary, Sam, 514
Gay, John, 14
Geer, Will, 196
Geiringer, Karl, 263, 264, 265, 267
Geller, James A., 367
German folksongs, 54
Gerould, Gordon Hall, 412
Gershwin, George, 15
Gibbon, J. Murray, 333, 340
Gibson, Bob, 26, 62, 91-92, 110, 514, 515
Gideon, Miriam, 117
Gilbert, Ronnie, 111
Gile, Beverly, 26, 30-31, 489
Gilkyson, Terry, 242, 515

Gilmer, Julia Ann, 242, 515
Ginandes, Dr. Shep, 26, 92-93, 516
Giorgione, 267
Gitter, Dean, 242, 516
Glazer, Joe, 26, 93-94, 105, 298, 516
Glazer, Tom, 26, 94-95, 517
Golden, Peter, 96, 105
Golden, Terry, 26, 95-97, 105
Golden Gate Quartet, The, 234, 605, 610
Gooding, Cynthia, 26, 97-98, 229, 517, 518
Goossens, Eugene, 51
Gordon, Hally Wood, 339
Gordon, Robert Winslow, 147, 307
Gorman, Michael, 37
gospel singing, 76, 77, 111, 130
Goss, John, 160
Gould, Morton, 17, 627
Gray, Roland P., 383-84
Grohe, Herman C., 255
Greenleaf, Elizabeth Bristol, 301, 336
Greenway, John, 104, 241-42, 298, 519
Greer, Dr. I. G., 26, 29, 37, 98-99, 232, 247, 394
Greer, Mrs. I. G. (Willie Spainhour), 26, 37, 98-99, 232, 260
Gregory, Frosia, 26, 99-100, 110, 256
Gregory, Paul, 40
Grieg, Gavin, 274
Griffin, Mrs. G. A., 308
Grimes, Anne, 26, 52, 100-02, 248, 261, 263, 265, 266, 394, 519
Grise, Dr. George C., 26, 102-03
Guffey, Sol, 141
Guion, David, 17
guitar, 249-59, 252, 253, 258, 261
    records of, 535
Guthrie, Annette, 232
Guthrie, Woody, 26, 85, 89, 103-04, 105, 106, 111, 118, 126, 140, 196, 213, 231, 232, 298, 361, 413-14, 519, 520, 595

H

Habimah Seminary of Actors (Israel), 43
Hague, Albert, 333
Hague, Eleanor, 250, 264, 387
Hall, Dickenson, 242
Hall, Kenneth Martin, 26, 107
Hall, Vera, 559
Halpert, Herbert, 429
Hals, Frans, 267
Hamilton, Diane, 65, 615
Hamilton, Frank, 26, 108, 135, 573
Hammerstein, Oscar, II, 14
Hammontree, Doney, 26, 108-09, 248
Handy, W. C., 264, 331, 357, 391
Hanford, James Holly, 302
harmonica, 249, 253-54, 261
harp, 249, 262
harpsichord, 248
Harrington, John, 310
Harris, Roy, 17, 70
Harrison, Ruthann, 177
Hart, Weldon, 178

Hartlan, Enos, 281
Hartlan, Richard, 281
Hawes, Bess Lomax, 58, 135, 156
Hayden, Palmer, 12
Hayes, Bill, 611
Hayes, Roland, 26, 109-10, 520, 521
Haynes, Valerie, 26, 110, 256
Hays, Lee, 26, 110-11
Haystackers, The, 624
Haywood, Charles, 10, 16, 93, 243, 401
Healy, Arthur, 283
Heath, Gordon, 55
Hebrew folksongs, 40, 200, 324
Helen Hartness Flanders Ballad collection, 65, 282 ff. (see also Flanders, Helen Hartness)
Hellerman, Fred, 26, 111-12, 496
Hemsworth, Wade, 242, 521
Henry, Mellinger E., 10, 306, 321, 401
Herzog, George, 278, 408
Hesse, Albert A., 255, 265
Heywood, Charles, 106
Hickerson, Joe, 26, 52, 53, 112-13
Hicks, Nathan, 230, 259
Higginson, T. W., 377
High, Fred, 26, 113, 136, 377-78
Higley, Brewster, Dr., 6, 7
hillbilly music, 7, 91, 149
Hillbilly Homecoming, 102
Hille, Waldemar, 378
Hillel and Aviva, 242, 521
Hillhouse, Mrs. Cora, 26, 114
Hilton, Lavoli M., 26, 114-15, 394, 522
Hindemith, Paul, 51
Hinkle, Lewis, 258
Hinton, Sam, 26, 52, 115-16, 262, 522
H.M.V. Records (London), 55, 150, 195
Hoey, Elizabeth Wilkes, 336, 337
Holbrook, Stewart H., 418
Holland, Lori, 26, 116
Holt, Will, 26, 116-17, 136, 523
Hoosier Folklore Society, 434
horns, 263
Horton, Lewis Henry, 129
House, Wallace, 26, 79, 117-18, 523, 524
Houston, Gil "Cisco," 26, 104, 118-19, 520, 524, 525
Hudson, Arthur Palmer, 279, 308, 370, 436
Hulbert, A. B., 264, 416-17
Hull House Camp, 57
Hunkins, Eusebia Simpson, 15
Hunter, Max, 26, 119-20
Huntington, E. Gale, 26, 120-21
Huntington, Emily, 26, 120-21
Hurd, Peter, 26, 109, 121-22, 525
Hurston, Zora Neale, 420
Huston, John, 13, 370
Hustvedt, S. B., 274, 411

I

Illinois Folklore Society, 435
Indiana University Archives of Folk and Primitive Music, 393
Indian dance festivals, 446

industrial folksongs, 519, 570
international balladeers and folksingers, 43, 62, 80, 98, 208, 229
International Catalogue of Recorded Folk Music, 11
International Council of Negro Folklore, 61
International Folk Music Council, 11, 144
International Folk Music Festivals (Venice, Edinburgh), 47, 148, 168, 442
International Service of Radio-Canada, 33
Irish ballads, 78
Irish folksongs, 40, 96, 154, 181, 190, 195, 303
Irish harp, 181, 262
Irish harp-lute, 184
Irish street singer, 36
Isaacson, Dan, 26, 122, 526
Israeli folksongs, 75-76, 243, 324
Italian folk music, 261
Ives, Burl, 26, 42, 59, 100, 102, 105, 110, 111, 118, 122-26, 136, 137, 142, 173, 190, 196, 218, 227, 231, 332-33, 351, 428-29, 526, 527, 528, 529, 530, 531, 532

J

Jackson, Aunt Molly, 298
Jackson, George Pullen, 10, 45, 51, 52, 273, 279, 283-87, 327, 429-30
Jackson, Graham, 623
Jackson, Mahalia, 40, 213
Jacob, Jules, 26, 187 (see also Quatuor Alouette, Le)
Jacobs, Freddy, 242, 532
Jaffe, Joe, 213
James, Thelma G., 393
Jansen, William Hugh, 393
Jarrett, Merrick, 532
Jefferson, Blind Lemon, 233, 234, 335, 532
Jefferson, Thomas, 251
Jemison, Gene (Eugene), 26, 75, 127-28, 533
Jenkins, Gordon, 119
Jessye, Eva A., 376
Jewish folksongs, 299, 324-25
Johnson, Guy B., 313, 314
Johnson, J. Rosamond, 332, 344
Johnson, James Weldon, 331, 352
Johnston, Richard, 10, 336, 337
Joint Committee on Folk Arts, 307
Jones, Spike, 263
Jordan, Philip D., 355-56
Jubilee Singers, 329
Jubileers, The, 30
Judson Records, 225, 231

K

Kagan, Michael, 493
Kagen, Sergius, 173

Kahn, Ed, 574
Kane, Michael, 546
Kansas Folklore Society, 435
Kapp, Paul, 212
Karpeles, Maud, 11, 260, 295, 336, 414
Kazee, Buell Hilton, 26, 128-30, 533
kazoo, 90, 263
Kelley, Daniel E., 6
Kelly, Gene, 616
Kennedy, Charles O'Brien, 390
Kennedy, R. Emmet, 341, 362
Kentucky ballads, 235
Kentucky Folk Festival, 141
Kentucky Folklore Society, 435
Kershaw, Karl, 69
Keynote Records, 30, 84
khalil, 43 (see also recorder)
Kincaid, Bradley, 26, 130-31, 235, 375-76
Kines, Tom, 242, 533
King, Marty (Martha Bennett), 26, 131-32
King, Stanton H., 375
Kinscella, Hazel G., 372
Kittredge, George Lyman, 272, 274, 289
Knibbs, H. H., 292
Knott, Sarah Gertrude, 236, 442, 445
Koch, William, 263
Koehn, Willa Mae Kelly, 322
Kolb, Sylvia, 391
Kornfeld, Barry, 26, 76, 77, 132-33
Korson, George G., 265, 273, 279, 287-89
Kossoy, Ellen, 26, 133
Kossoy Sisters, The, 534
Kraber, Tony, 196, 534, 563
Krehbiel, H. E., 338, 339, 360
Kukler, Adolph, 26, 37, 134-35, 137
Kukler, Mrs. Adolph (Augusta Marie Holzer), 26, 37, 134-35, 137
Kunitz, Charlene (Charlene Robbins), 26, 135-36
Kyne, Peter B., 321

L

La Berge, Colbert, 79
Labor Arts Records, 94, 105
labor songs, 93, 94
Labrecque, Jacques, 242, 534
Lacombe, Gilbert, 33, 161
Laine, Frankie, 78
Lair, John, 384
La Liberté, Alfred, 33
Lamarre, Émile, 25, 187 (see also Quatuor Alouette, Le)
Lane, Lawrence, 218
Langstaff, John, 138
Larkin, Margaret, 352-53
Latter-day Saints songs, 114
Laurel River Valley Boys, 613
Laws, G. Malcom, Jr., 399, 407
Lea, Terrea, 242, 535
Leach, MacEdward, 152, 300
Leadbelly (see Ledbetter, Huddie)
Ledbetter, Huddie (Leadbelly), 26, 64, 111, 118, 139-40, 145, 170, 189, 196, 212, 231, 262, 335, 535, 536, 537

Ledford, Homer, 259, 266
Lee, Archie, 26, 141-42, 260
Lee, Charles, 242
Lee, Katie, 26, 142
Leighton, Clare, 278
Lengyel, Cornel, 380-81
Library of Congress Archive of American Folk Song, 9, 10, 54, 56, 65, 70, 99, 101, 108, 109, 115-16, 140, 144-45, 146, 147, 150, 153, 163, 186, 194, 196, 216, 220, 221, 223, 224, 228, 230, 234, 247, 249, 254, 261, 292, 307, 331, 402-03, 485
lieder singing, 109, 154, 217
Lillie, Gordon W., Major (Pawnee Bill), 73
Linscott, Eloise H., 264, 309
Lipkin, Arthur Bennett, 51
Lismer, Arthur, 276
List, George, 393
Lloyd, A. L., 26, 143-44, 149, 537, 538, 542, 602, 603, 604
Lloyd, Norman, 203, 334
Lochlainn, Colm O., 373
Loggins, Vernon, 242, 243
Lomax, Alan, 10, 11, 26, 48, 52, 76, 129, 140, 143, 144-45, 170, 184, 194, 195, 203, 211, 236, 239, 240, 264, 279, 289, 291, 322, 339, 400, 539
Lomax, John A., 6, 10, 11, 80, 105, 139, 140, 144, 146, 171, 239, 240, 272, 273, 279, 289-93, 322, 410, 439, 539, 593
Lombardo, Guy, 625
London Records, 234
"lonesome tunes," Southern, 31
Long, Mrs. Maud, 26, 145-46
Longstaff, John, 26, 138, 534
Loudermilk, Romaine H., 26, 146-47
Louisiana ballads, 228
Louisiana Folklore Society, 184, 436
"Louisiana Lady" (see Nickerson, Camille Lucie)
love songs, 305, 554
Ludekens, Fred, 13
lullabies, 279, 312
lumberjack songs, 308
Lummis, C. F., 292
Lumpkin, Ben Gray, 4, 11, 42, 404-05, 485
Lund, Engel, 207
Lunsford, Bascom Lamar, 26, 147-49, 220, 251, 356, 443-44, 539, 540
lute, 63, 79, 189, 262
Luther, Frank, 241, 242, 330, 540
Lynch, Christopher, 540

M

McCarthy, Patrick, 178
MacColl, Ewan, 26, 55, 143, 149-50, 538, 541, 542, 543, 602, 603, 604
McCord, May Kennedy, 26, 150-51
McCrady, John, 13
McCurdy, Ed, 26, 76, 85, 100, 126, 151-52, 543, 544, 545, 546, 592

MacDowell, Edward, 16
McDowell, Lucien L., 368, 384
McFerrin, Robert, 242, 546
McGhee, Brownie, 546, 547
McGill, Josephine, 338
McIlhenny, E. A., 331
Mackenzie, W. Roy, 105, 300-01, 330, 336, 423-24
Maclean, Calum, 181
MacLeish, Archibald, 292
Macmillan, Ernest, 333
McMullen, Mildred M., 379
McNeil, Brownie, 26, 52, 102, 152-54, 547
McNulty Family, The, 611
madrigals, 79, 80
Majestic Records, 79
mandolin, 63, 249, 258, 261, 265
Mansfield, Grace Y., 301
Marais, Josef, 26, 154-56, 171, 232, 250, 547, 548, 549 (see also Marais and Miranda)
Marais and Miranda, 26, 30, 37, 154-56, 232, 547, 548, 549
Marchand, Charles, 187
Marcotte, Jean (Cleveland), 26, 156
Marcotte, Will (Wilfred D.), 26, 156
marriage folksongs, 305
Marsh, J. B. T., 388
Marshall, Herta, 549
Marston, Annie Viola, 277
Matthews, Inez, 109, 549
Maxwell, Elsa, 125
Mayo, Margot, 236, 589
Mechau, Dorik, 26, 157-59
Mechau, Duna, 26, 157-59
Mechau, Michael, 26, 157-59
Mechau, Paula (Paula Ralska), 26, 156-59, 171
Mechau, Vonni, 26, 157-59
Mechem, Kirke, 6, 388
medieval songs, 83
mental therapy, folksinging and, 36
Mercury Records, 50, 84, 197, 234
Merrick, Jarrett, 26, 126-27
Mesta, Perle, 125
Mexican-American folksongs, 228, 229
Mexican ballads, 152-53
Mexican Folklore Society, 437
Mexican ranchero songs, 154
Michigan Folklore Society, 436
Mickelsen, Erik, 26, 159
Milburn, George, 373
Milhaud, Darius, 16
Miller, Albert (see Mills, Alan)
Miller, Mitch, 190
Mills, Alan, 26, 33, 126, 159-61, 326, 490, 550, 551, 552
Milton, L. M., 248
Minnesota Folk Festival of Nations, 446
minstrel songs, 131
Miracle Records, 213
Miranda (Mrs. Joseph Marais), 26, 154-56, 171, 232, 547, 548, 549 (see also Marais and Miranda)
Missionary Quintet, The, 610
Mississippi Folklore Society, 436

Missouri Folklore Society, 9, 301, 302, 436
Mitchell, Merlin P., 26, 161-62
Mobley, Pleaz W., 26, 162-63
Modern Language Association, 200
Montigny, Louvignyde, 340-41
Moon, Jacob Robert, 26, 163-64, 232
Moon, Winnifred Minter, 26, 163-64, 232
Moore, Frank, 383
Moore, Geoffrey, 553
Mormon folksongs, 114, 115, 424
Morris, Dr. Alton, 5, 114, 308
Morris, Jimmy (Jimmy Driftwood), 26, 164-65
Morris, Mary Ella (see Bayle, Mary Ella M.)
Morrison, Absie S., 26, 165-66
Morrow, Arthur, 326
Morton, Ferdinand (Jelly Roll), 145
Moser, Artus Monroe, 26, 166-68, 553
Mountain Dance and Folk Festival (North Carolina), 148, 442, 443
Mountain Festival, Asheville, North Carolina, 101
Mountain Folk Festival, Berea, Ky., 445
mountain songs, 228, 328-29
mournful songs, 312
mouth organs, 253
Murai, Jean, 26, 168, 229, 262, 263, 553
Murray, Carmen (Carmen Harriette Himmaugh), 26, 30, 37, 169-70, 232
Murray, Lynn, 119
Murray, Philip Jesse "Jim" (Jr.), 26, 30, 37, 169-70
Musée National du Canada (see National Museum [Ottawa])
musical compositions, based on folksongs, 16-18
Musicraft Records, 140
Myers, Susanna, 338

N

National Federation of Music Clubs, 216
National Folk Festival, 443
National Folk Festival, Oklahoma City, 32, 39, 62, 101, 102, 113, 141, 151, 175, 188, 216, 226, 227, 229, 235, 236
National Folk Festival, St. Louis, 56, 442, 443
National Folk Festival Association of America, 441-42
National Museum (Ottawa), 33, 277
Neal, Ruth, 26, 173-74
Nebraska Folklore and Ethnology Group, 437
Neely, Charles, 389
Negro ballads, 315
Negro chanteys, 195
Negro folklore, in symphonies, 16
Negro folk music, 60-61, 239, 250, 299, 313, 315, 329
Negro folksinging, 77, 176
Negro slave songs, 610
Negro spirituals, 31, 109, 110, 113, 222, 228, 272, 546, 601

Negro stories, 14
Negro theater, 14
Newell, William Wells, 310
New England Folk Festival, 445
New England folksongs, 279, 312
Newfoundland folksongs, 185, 206, 301
New Hampshire Folk Festival, 117
New Mexican folksongs, 66, 250, 322
New Mexico Folklore Society, 434-35, 437
New Mexico Folk Singers, The, 66
New York City Ballet Company, 16
New York Folklore Society, 230, 437
New York Latin-American Folk Group, 168
Nicholas, Louis, 52, 71
Nickerson, Camille Lucie ("Louisiana Lady"), 26, 174-75
Niles, Abbe, 331
Niles, John Jacob, 26, 29, 42, 52, 64, 79, 102, 118, 128, 169, 175-78, 201, 202, 259, 266, 354, 383, 553, 554
Norman Luboff Choir, 622
North Carolina Folklore Society, 438
North Carolina folksongs, 279
North Carolina State Fair Folk Festival, 148
Nova Scotia ballads, 300
nursery songs, 308, 309
Nye, Hermes, 26, 178, 554, 555

O

Oberndorfer, Anne, 334
Oberndorfer, Marx, 334
O'Brien, Oscar, 187, 188, 333
O'Bryant, Joan, 27, 179-80, 555
occupational songs, 55
Odum, Howard W., 313, 314, 424
O'Flynn, Anna C., 337
O'Hara, Geoffrey, 333
O'Hara, Mary, 27, 143, 180-81, 556
Ohio Federation of Music Clubs, 101
Ohio Folklore Archive, 101
Ohio Folklore Society, 438
Ohio Valley Research Project, 101
Ohioana Library, 101
Oklahoma Folklore Society, 438
Oklahoma University Lecture and Entertainment Bureau, 82
Okun, Beth Griffin, 182
Okun, Milt T., 27, 181-82, 445, 557, 558
Oldfather, Charles H., Jr., 27, 182-83
Old Fiddlers' Contest, Athens, Tex., 446
Old Harp Singers, The, 51
Old Town School of Folk Music, 108, 219
Olney, Marguerite, 282
Olsen, Dorothy, 242, 558
O'Neal, Charles, 155
O'Neill, Capt. Francis, 418
orchestral suites, based on folksongs, 16
Oriole Records, 201
Oster, Dr. Harry, 27, 183-84, 202
O'Sullivan, Donal, 418

outlaw and criminal songs, 309
Owens, William A., 250, 264, 322, 388-89
Ozark Folk Festival, 32, 36, 39, 56, 63, 74, 78, 81, 82, 85, 89, 113, 119, 134-35, 151, 159, 165, 180, 214, 226, 444
Ozark folklore, 226
Ozark Folklore Society, 162, 434
Ozark folksongs, 267, 293-94

P

painting, based on folklore, 12-13, 15
Paley, Tom, 27, 184-85, 558
Pardo, Lily, 154
Parrish, Lydia, 317
party songs, 307, 308
Paskman, Dailey, 371
Pawnee Bill (Major Gordon W. Lillie), 73
Payant, Lee, 55
Peacock, Kenneth, 25, 185, 559
Peattie, Roderick, 201, 266, 417
Pelley, Farrell, 190
Pennington, John B., 27, 186
Pennsylvania Dutch Folk Festival, 438, 444
Pennsylvania German Folklore Society, 438
Percy, Thomas, 271, 555
Period Records, 234
Perry, Lawrence, 16
Persons, Simmons, 341
Peterson, Clara G., 366
Phelps, William Lyon, 292
Philadelphia Orchestra Children's Concerts, 95
piano and folksongs, 248
piano compositions, based on folksongs, 16
Pick, Richard, 575
Pierce, Norman E., 105
Pike, Gustavus D., 374
Pinetoppers, The, 624
pioneer ballads, 55, 197, 308
pirate songs, 312, 592
political songs, 93, 94
popular song, defined, 6
Post, Ruth, 200, 324
Pound, Louise, 3, 11, 279, 297, 299, 403, 423, 437
Powell, Dr. Desmond, 27, 105, 186
Powell, John, 17
Procter Brothers, 367-68
protest songs, 94, 104, 298
psaltery, 38, 249, 254, 265
psychiatric therapy, use of folksongs in, 47
Putnam, Herbert, 292
Putnam, John F., 257

Q

Quatuor Alouette, Le, 27, 187-88, 202 (see also Filiatrault, Roger; Jacob, Jules; Lamarre, Emile; Trottier, André)

R

Raine, James Walt, 419-20
Ralska, Paula (see Mechau, Paula)
Ramsey, Frederic, Jr., 536
Randolph, Vance, 5, 8, 9, 10, 56, 109, 150-51, 252, 253, 261, 265, 273, 279, 293-94, 415, 417, 422, 423, 429, 434
rattle, 249, 263
Rayburn, Otto Ernest, 151, 226, 252, 421-22, 444
RCA Victor Records, 30, 50, 60, 63, 80, 140, 161, 166, 178, 190, 202, 206, 213, 243
rebec, 44
recorder, 43, 249, 262-63
Reed, Dock, 559
Reed, Jared, 27, 189
Reed, Susan, 27, 110, 189, 190, 559, 560
religious folksongs, 114, 279, 283-87, 299, 300, 305, 308, 310, 313, 317
Rettenberg, Milton, 339
Richardson, Ethel P., 328
Richmond, Edson W., 298
Richmond, Vivian, 135
Rickaby, Franz, 303
Ridings, Sam P., 414
Riggs, Lynn, 14, 79
Ritchie, Abigail (Hall), 27, 191, 193
Ritchie, Balis, 27, 191, 193
Ritchie, Edna, 27, 192
Ritchie, Jason (Uncle Jason), 27, 191, 192, 202
Ritchie, Jean (Jean Ritchie Pickow), 10, 27, 52, 105, 191, 193-94, 202, 240, 248, 256, 339, 356, 425, 561, 562
Ritchie, Jewel (Mrs. Robinson), 27, 192
Ritchie, May (May Ritchie Deschamps), 27, 191, 202
Ritchie, Una, 27, 191, 192
Ritchies, The Singing, 27, 190-93, 339
Riverside Records, 37, 65, 77, 88, 89, 92, 108, 112, 120, 143, 149, 150, 152, 201, 225, 231
Roast, Walter, 281
Robb, John Donald, 121, 339, 437
Robbins, Charlene (see Kunitz, Charlene)
Roberts, Robin, 27, 195, 563
Robertson, Jeannie, 149, 242, 564
Robertson, Walt, 242, 564
Robeson, Paul, 109, 234, 241, 242, 340, 564
Robins, John D., 281
Robinson, Earl, 27, 62, 196-97, 203
Robinson, Frank V., 27, 198
Robinson, Julie, 41
Rodgers, Jimmie, 565
Rodgers, Richard, 14
Rogers, Will, Jr., 568
Ross, Bob, 27, 198-99, 565
Roth, Herbert, 27, 199
Rubin, Ruth, 27, 52, 199-201, 324, 565, 566
Rufty, Hilton, 327
Runge, John, 242, 566
Rupp, Franz, 488

Russian folksongs, 116, 213
Ryder, Mark, 117

S

Saber, Rubyan, 48
Sachs, Curt, 264, 265, 266, 267
Saint-Laurent, François, 304
Salazar, Marcelo, 98
Saletan, Anthony (Tony), 27, 204-05
Salt, Waldo, 197
samisen, 44
Sampson, George, 274
Sandburg, Carl, 10, 27, 29, 42, 64, 109, 142, 184, 189, 198, 205-06, 218, 241, 242, 243, 273, 329, 334, 566, 567
Sapir, Edward, 5, 276
Sargent, Helen Child, 274
satirical songs, 279, 312
Scammell, Arthur R., 27, 206-07, 248
Scandinavian ballads, 300
Scarborough, Dorothy, 315, 318
Schick, Lawrence, 321
Schirmer's American Folk-Song Series, 10, 176, 177, 273, 345-51
Schlamme, Martha, 27, 108, 207-08, 567, 568
Scholander, Sven, 83, 262
Scholes, Percy A., 264, 266, 267
Schwarzer, Franz, 255
Scott, Edgar C., Jr., 265
Scott, Joy Pride, 210
Scott, Molly, 27, 208
Scott, Tom (Thomas Jefferson), 27, 208-10, 243, 352, 568
Scott, Sir Walter, 271
Scottish ballads, 149, 157, 238
Scottish folksongs, 154, 303, 308
sea songs, 294, 308, 309, 312
Sear, Dave, 496
Sebastian, John, 254
Seeger, Barbara, 569, 588
Seeger, Charles, 260, 266, 283, 290, 588
Seeger, Peggy, 541, 543, 568, 569, 588
Seeger, Penny, 569
Seeger, Pete, 27, 32, 42, 62, 70, 76, 88, 111, 135, 140, 169, 184, 210-12, 213, 225, 229, 231, 250, 251, 263, 264, 267, 565, 567, 569, 570, 571, 572, 573, 588
Seeger, Ruth Crawford, 248, 290, 292, 327, 328, 330
Segovia, Andres, 227, 250
Selah Jubilee Quartet, The, 624
Sellers, Brother John, 27, 212-13, 573
Seminar on American Culture (Cooperstown, N. Y.), 200
Senior, Doreen, 281
Settlers, The, 53, 112, 217
Shanty Boys, The, 616
Sharp, Cecil James, 3, 5, 8, 11, 76, 191, 260, 266, 273, 279, 294-96, 304, 330, 336, 415-16
Shaw, Lloyd, 342, 415, 601
Shaw, Robert, 51, 601
Shay, Frank, 361-62, 373-74, 375, 376

Shepperd, Mary Earley, 414
Sherwin, Sterling, 343, 386
Sheton, Robert, 181
Shinhan, Jan Philip, 279
Shoemaker, Floyd C., 293
Shoemaker, Henry W., 257, 262, 313, 314
Shoolman, Regina Lenore, 276
Shriner, Herb, 47
Siegmeister, Elie, 17, 124, 354-55, 359, 366
Sierra Folk Singers, The, 108
Silber, Irwin, 340
Silver Strike Jubilee (Arkansas), 36
Silvera, Dick, 573
Silverman, Jerry, 27, 213-14, 335, 574
Sires, Ina, 355
Sloane, Irving, 48
Slovakian folksongs, 236
Smith, C. Alphonso, 99, 323, 438
Smith, C. Fox, 363
Smith, Dennis, 281
Smith, Fred, 27, 214
Smith, Harry, 591
Smith, Reed, 327, 386
Smith, Winifred, 27, 214-15
Smoky Mountain ballads, 228
Smyth, Mary Winslow, 277, 312
Smythe, Augustine T., 364
Society for the Classical Guitar, 106, 128
soldier songs, 321
Sonenfield, Irwin, 117
Sonic Records, 153, 154
Sons of the Pioneers, 604
Sordoni, Alberta, 339
Sound Studios Records, 94, 105
South African folksongs, 154
South American folksongs, 40
South Carolina Folklore Society, 435, 439
South Carolina Negro Folksong Guild, 439
Southeastern Folklore Society, 435, 439
Southern Illinois Folk Festival, 62
Southwest folksongs, 279
Spaeth, Sigmund, 190, 328, 362, 371, 380, 392
Spanish folksongs, 66, 135
Spanish guitar, 58
Spanish Music Center (New York City), 63
Spanish-American folksongs, 228, 229, 250
Spiller, Robert E., 243
spiritual folksongs, 15, 248, 279
spirituals, 5, 10, 15, 55, 289
    Negro, 285-87
    white, 192, 283-86, 590
square dances, 589, 592
Square Dance Tournament, Steamboat Springs, Colo., 446
Stafford, Jo, 78, 241, 242, 574
Starr, Mary Agnes, 27, 215-17
Starr, Morton Hull, 217
Steck, Pete, 574
Steinbeck, John, 253, 254
Stekert, Ellen, 27, 52, 53, 112, 217, 558, 574

Steuben glass, 18-20, 22
Stewart, Alec, 225
Still, William Grant, 16, 358
Stinson Records, 42, 65, 77, 117, 119, 136, 140, 143, 150, 171, 182, 195, 217, 225, 231, 234
Stone, Eleanor, 27, 217-18
Stout, Earl J., 369
Stracke, Win, 27, 108, 218-19, 575
Stradivari violin, 248, 251
Strangways, A. H. Fox, 414
Stringfield, Lamar, 16
Stringham, Edwin John, 326
Sturgill, Virgil L., 27, 219
Summers, Andrew Rowan, 27, 221, 243, 575, 576
Swan, Howard, 420-21
Swedish folksongs, 154, 205
Sweeney, Joe, 251
Swiss folksongs, 154
Sykes, Paul, 576
symphonies, based on folksongs, 16

T

Taggart, Joel, 233
talking blues, 197
Talley, Thomas W., 313
Tanglewood Festival, 213
Tarriers, The, 31, 76
Tarwater, Rebecca (Rebecca Tarwater Hicks), 27, 221-22
Tate Family, The Charles, 27, 222, 243
Tate, Annie Lee, 222
Tate, Arthur Lee, 222
Tate, Charles, 222, 243
Tate, Charles, Jr., 222
Tate, James, 222
Tate, Minnie Lee, 222
Tate, Sarah Lee, 222
Tate, William, 222
Taylor, Archer, 279
Taylor, Harrison, 67
Temple, Pick (Lafayette Parker Temple), 27, 222-24, 243, 576
Tennessee Folklore Society, 45, 52, 257, 439
Terkel, Studs, 218, 498
Terry, Sonny (Blind Sonny Terry), 27, 213, 225, 546, 547, 573, 576, 577
Texas ballads, 161
Texas Federation of Music Clubs, 36
Texas folk music, 250
Texas Folklore Society, 153, 154, 179, 322, 439
Theatre Guild, 15
Thériac-Caney, Joséphine, 338
Thomas, James Edward (Uncle Eddie), 202, 258, 266
Thomas, Jean, 366, 412, 427
Thomas, Millard, 40
Thompson, Harold W., 10, 122, 183, 289, 315, 413, 438
Thompson, Stith, 279, 380
Thomsen, Paul S., 27, 225-26
Thorpe, Jack, 272, 385

Todd, Dylan, 577
Topic Records, 37, 143, 150
Torre, Rey de la, 83, 117
Tradition Records, 55, 65, 88, 112, 143, 150, 181, 241
Traubel, Helen, 577
travel songs, 305
Travis, Merle, 577
Trottier, André, 27, 187 (see also Quatuor Alouette, Le)
Tuamdha, Sean Og O, 180-81
Tyler, Ruth H., 27, 226-27, 256

U

Underwood, Pierson, 16
union songs, 94, 104
University of Arkansas Folklore Archives, 109, 113, 119, 186, 214, 227, 434, 444
University of Arkansas Folklore Society, 214
Untermeyer, Louis, 243
urban life, effect on folksinging, 3
Usher, Alex (Alexandra MacNutt Usher), 27, 227

V

Vanguard Records, 32, 79, 111, 112, 207, 212, 213, 225, 237
Van Stone, Mary, 264, 356
Van Wey, Adelaide, 27, 227-28, 578
Vermont Archive of Folk Songs, 282, 283
Vermont Commission on Country Life, 283
Vermont Folklore Society, 439
Vinaver, Chemjo, 299
Vincent, Jenny Wells (Deborah Jeannette Hill), 27, 228-29, 262, 578
violin, 251, 252
Virginia Folk-Lore Society, 322, 323, 439
Vocalion Records, 129
Voice of America, 106, 164, 170
Vollmer, Lulu, 192
Vox Records, 84
voyageur songs, 216

W

Walker, William, 15, 386-87, 441
Wallace, Henry, 211
Warfield, William, 109, 241, 242, 578, 579
Waring, Fred, 209
war songs, 305, 308, 309, 321, 322
Warner, Frank, 27, 44, 229-30, 243, 251, 437, 579
Washboard Band, The, 600
Washington Folklore Society, 439
Water, Edward N., 290
Wattle Records, 143, 150
Weavers, The, 76, 110, 111, 112, 211, 627-28
Weill, Kurt, 15, 160, 198

Weissman, Dick, 27, 230, 512, 573
Welk, Lawrence, 225
Wells, Evelyn K., 10, 274, 413
Wendell, Barrett, 289
West, Harry, 27, 30, 37, 232, 233, 579, 580
West, Jeanie, 27, 30, 37, 232-33, 579, 580
Westminster Abbey Choir, 597
West Virginia Folk Festival, 91
West Virginia Folk-Lore Society, 310, 439
Western ballad, 239
Western Folklore Festival, 444
Western songs, 6, 236, 239, 304
Wetmore, S., 265
Whall, W. B., 381-82
Wheeler, Mary, 215, 344, 387
whistles, 263
White, B. F., 286
White, Josh, 5, 27, 111, 126, 140, 196, 213, 232-35, 243, 250, 335, 580, 581, 582, 583
White, Kitty, 242, 583
White, Newman Ivey, 5, 278, 298
white spirituals, 192, 283-86
White Top Mountain Folk Festival, 35, 221, 443
Whitfield, Irène Thérèse, 262, 312
Whiting, Bartlett Jere, 279
Whitmire, Ross C., 27, 29, 235-36
Whitmire, Mrs. Ross C. (Alice M. Gideon), 27, 235-36
Wiggens, Ella May, 298
Wilder, Dick, 27, 236-37, 583
Wilder, Jack, 592
Wilgus, D. K., 410
Willan, Healey, 275, 340
Williams, Betty Vaiden, 27, 236, 583
Williams, Camilla, 109, 242, 584
Williams, Cratis, 27, 237-38
Williams, Spencer, 250

Willing, Fay, 601
Wills, Charlie, 149
Wilson, Edward A., 363
Wilson, George P., 279, 415
Wilson, Stan, 27, 238-39, 584
Wimberley, Bill, 592
Winterich, John T., 375
Wolford, Leah Jackson, 379
Wood, Hally, 27, 52, 239-40, 243, 248, 585
Wood, Theodore, Jr., 27, 240
Woods, George B., 274
Worcester Festival Children's Concerts, 95
Work, John W., 250, 329, 416
work songs, 94, 195, 197, 222, 225, 279, 299, 308
World Festival of Folk Dance and Song, 194
Wyeth, N. C., 121
Wyman, Loraine, 340, 358

Y

Yarbrough, Glenn, 27, 240-41, 499, 584
Yiddish folksongs, 116, 168, 200-01, 213, 324, 565, 566
Yoder, Don, 319
Young People's Records, Inc., 95
Young, Susie Carr, 277
Young, Victor, 119

Z

Zeitlin, David, 27, 241
Zeitlin, Jacob, 241
zither, 36, 44, 135, 184, 190, 215, 228, 235, 249, 254-56, 261, 265

Title Index

TO BOOK ONE AND BOOK TWO

Unless otherwise indicated, titles between quotation marks denote songs, those in italics are either books or compilations of songs.

A

Abe Lincoln in Illinois, play, 79
"Adventures in Folk Song," recordings, 132
Adventures of a Ballad Hunter (Lomax), 10, 105, 410
African Heartbeat (Marais & O'Neal), opera, 155
"African Trek," radio program, 155
Afro-American Folksongs (Krehbiel), 360
Afro-American Symphony (Still), 16
Ah, Wilderness!, play, 124
Alan Mills Book of Folk Songs and Ballads, The, 161, 326
Allan's Lone Star Ballads, 360-61
Alouette! (Barbeau), 275
Always the Young Strangers (Sandburg), 242, 243
"Amazing Grace" (Bryan), 51
America Sings (Carmer), 326
American Anthology of Old-World Ballads (Smith), 327
American Balladry from British Broadsides (Laws), 399
American Ballads and Folk Songs (Lomax & Lomax), 289
American Ballads and Songs (Pound), 11, 297-98
American Ballad Singers (Siegmeister), 17
American Country Dances (Schirmer's American Folk-Song Series), 347-48
American-English Folk-Songs (Sharp), 330
American-English Folk-Songs from the Southern Appalachian Mountains (Schirmer's American Folk-Song Series), 349
American Folk Lore (Niles), recordings, 178

American Folk Music for High School and Other Choral Groups (Bryan & Jackson), 52, 327
American Folksong (Guthrie), 361
American Folk Song and Folk Lore (Lomax & Cowell), 400
American Folk Songs for Children (Seeger), 327
American Folk Songs for Children in Home, School and Nursery School (Seeger), 327-28
American Folk Songs for Christmas (Seeger), 328
American Folk-Songs for Young Singers (Schirmer's American Folk-Song Series), 350
American Folksongs of Sadness and Melancholy (Wood), recording, 243
American Folksongs of Protest (Greenway), 104, 298
"American Folk-Song Series" (Schirmer), 10, 176, 177, 273, 345-51
American Folk Tales and Songs (Chase), 361
"American Folkways" series, 11, 421-22
American Mountain Songs (Richardson), 328
American Negro Folk-Songs (White), 5, 298-99
American Negro Songs (Work), 264, 329
American Play-Party Song, with a Collection of Oklahoma Texts and Tunes, The (Botkin), 299
Americans and Their Songs (Luther), 330
American Sea Songs and Chanteys from the Days of Iron Men and Wooden Ships (Shay), 361-62
American Songbag, The (Sandburg), 10, 198, 206, 329-30
"America's Music" (Win Stracke), radio program, 219

Amigos Cantando (Cooperative Recreation Service, Delaware, Ohio), 364
Analytical Index to the Journal of American Folklore, An (Coffin), 400-01
And Hear My Banjo Play (Pete Seeger), motion picture, 211
"Angel with Lute" (Forli), painting, 267
Anglo-American Ballads (Nye), recording, 179
Anglo-American Ballad Study Book, The (Schirmer's American Folk-Song Series), 350
Anglo-American Carol Study Book, The (Schirmer's American Folk-Song Series), 351
Anglo-American Folksong Scholarship Since 1898 (Wilgus), 410-11
Animal Folk Songs (Seeger), 264
Animal Folk Songs for Children (Seeger), 330-31
Another Sheaf of White Spirituals (Jackson), 283-84
Anthology of Jewish Music (Vinaver), 299
Appalachia, Variations on an Old Slave Song (Delius), symphonic composition, 16
Appalachian Spring (Copland), symphonic composition, 15
"Arkansas Traveler" (Seeger), 211
Arkansas Traveler (Guion), symphonic composition, 17
"A-Roving," 320
Artist in America, An (Benton), 253, 265, 411
"Arts of the South" (Benton), painting, 253
"Arts of the West" (Benton), painting, 253
Autoharp Accompaniments to Old Favorite Songs (Fox), 265

B

Ballad Book, The (Leach), 152, 300
Ballad Books and Ballad Men (Hustvedt), 274, 411
"Ballad Collecting in the Cumberlands" (Clayton), 65
"Ballad for Americans" (Robinson), 196
Ballad Makin' in the Mountains of Kentucky (Thomas), 412
Ballad of Tradition, The (Gerould), 412
Ballad Tree, The (Wells), 10, 274, 413
Ballads and Sea Songs from Nova Scotia (Mackenzie), 300-01
Ballads and Sea Songs of Newfoundland (Greenleaf), 301
Ballads and Songs (Belden), 301-02
Ballads and Songs (Missouri Folklore Society), 9
Ballads and Songs from Ohio (Eddy), 302
Ballads and Songs of Indiana (Brewster), 302-03
Ballads and Songs of Southern Michigan (Gardner & Chickering), 9, 303

Ballads and Songs of the Shanty-Boy (Rickaby), 303-04
Ballads, Carols, and Tragic Legends from the Southern Appalachian Mountains (Schirmer's American Folk-Song Series), 349
Ballads for Ballots (Joe Glazer), recording, 105
Ballads for Sectarians (Joe Glazer), recording, 105
Ballads, Love-Songs, and Tragic Legends from the Southern Appalachian Mountains (Schirmer's American Folk-Song Series), 349
Ballads Migrant in New England (Flanders & Olney), 282
Ballads of LaSalle County, Illinois (Clark), recording, 61
Ballads of the Civil War (Nye), recording, 179
Ballads of the Kentucky Highlands (Fuson), 304
"Banjo Blues" (Williams), 250
"Barbara Allen," 123, 130, 192, 277, 302, 310, 316, 319
"Barbary Ellen," 176
Barber Shop Ballads (Spaeth), 362
Barber Shop Ballads and How to Sing Them (Spaeth), 362
"Bawdy Songs and Backroom Ballads" (Brand), recordings, 48
Bayou Ballads (Schirmer's American Folk-Song Series), 345
Beech Mountain Folk-Songs and Ballads (Schirmer's American Folk-Song Series), 348
Befo' de War Spirituals (McIlhenny), 331
Beauties of Harmony, 285
Beggar's Opera, The (Gay), 14
Bell Witch, The (Bryan), folk cantata, 51
"Bergère aux champs, La," 277
Best of the American Cowboy, The (Adams), 413
Bibliography for the Study of American Folk-Songs with Many Titles of Folk-Songs from Other Lands, A (Henry), 401
Bibliography of French-Canadian and French Folk Music, A, 216
Bibliography of North American Folklore and Folksong, A (Haywood), 10, 16, 401-02
Big Lake (Riggs), play, 14
"Bile Dem Cabbage Down," 79
Billy the Kid (Copland), orchestral composition, 15
Binorie Variations (Tom Scott), orchestral composition, 209
Birmingham Suite (Bryan), orchestral composition, 51
Black Bard, The, A Review of Negro Folk Music (Clark), 61
Black Cameos (Kennedy), 362
"Black-Eyed Susie," 211
Black Is the Color of My True Love's Hair (Niles), orchestral composition, 178

"Black Jack Davy," 78, 232
"Blind-Man's Buff," 311
Blow High, Blow Low (Wilson), 363
"Blow the Man Down," 276, 301, 320
Blow the Man Down (Harris), orchestral composition, 17
Blues, An Anthology (Handy), 331
Body, Boots and Britches (Thompson), 10, 413
"Bonny Barbara Allan," 301
"Bonyparte," 15
Book of American Negro Spirituals, The (Johnson), 331-32
Book of Shanties, A (Smith), 363
Bound for Glory (Guthrie), 103-04, 105, 413-14
Boys from Syracuse, The, play, 124
Bright Road, motion picture, 40
British Ballads from Maine (Barry), 277
British Traditional Ballad in North America, The (Coffin), 402
"Broadway Open House" (McNeil), radio program, 153
"Bronze Book Series" (Whitmire), 235
Brown, Frank C., Collection of North Carolina Folklore, 9, 278
"Brown Girl, The," 192
Buffalo Country (Duncan), 82, 105
"Buffalo Gals," 211
"Buffalo Skinners," 93, 162
Bulletin of the Folk-Song Society of the Northeast, 278
Burl Ives Irish Songs, 332
Burl Ives Song Book, The, 136, 332-33
Burl Ives' Tale of America, 136
"Bury Me Not on the Lone Prairie," 162
"Butcher's Boy, The," 129

C

Cabins in the Laurel (Sheppard), 414
California, motion picture, 197
"Camera Three," television program, 152
Canadian Folk Songs (Fowke & Johnston), 10
Canadian Folk Songs (Gibbon), 333
Canadian Song Book, The (Macmillan), 333
"Captain Kidd," 320
Capstan Bars (Bone), 363-64
"Careless Love," 180
Carl Sandburg's New American Songbag, 334
Carmen Jones, motion picture, 40
Carolina Low-Country, The (Smythe, et al.), 364
"Casey Jones," 211
"Casey Jones," as portrayed by Ludekens, 13
Cat on a Hot Tin Roof (Williams), play, 125
Cavalcade of American Song, 196
Cavalleria Rusticana, 227
Cecil Sharp (Strangways & Karpeles), 414
Century of Progress in American Song (Oberndorfer), 334

Chansons Canadiennes (Barbeau), 275
Chansons Folkloriques Françaises du Canada (d'Harcourt), 304-05
Chansons Populaires du Canada (Gagnon), 272, 276, 305-06
"Charlottown" (Bryan), 51
Check-List of Recorded Songs in the Archive of American Folk Song to July, 1940 (Library of Congress), 247, 249, 402-03
"Cherry Tree, The," 177
"Chevrolet Teletheatre," 210
Child Ballads from the Southern Highlands (Cratis Williams), recording, 238
Chisholm Trail, The (Gard), 10, 414
Chisholm Trail, The (Ridings), 414
Christian Harmony, 285
Coal Dust on the Fiddle (Korson), 287
Colored Sacred Harp, 286
"Columbia World Library of Folk and Primitive Music, The," 195
Come All Ye Bold Miners (Lloyd), 143
Come A Singing! Canadian Folk-Songs (Barbeau, Lismer, Bourinot), 276
"Come Sing with Me" (Cahn), radio program, 55
"Concert Champêtre" (Giorgione), painting, 267
Concise Oxford Dictionary of Music, The (Scholes), 264, 266
Copper Sun (Clark), 61
Corn Country (Croy), 11
Country Songs of Vermont (Schirmer's American Folk-Song Series), 349
Courting Songs, motion picture, 194
Cowboy Ballads (Houston), recording, 119
Cowboy Dances (Shaw), 415
Cowboy Jamboree: Western Songs and Lore (Felton), 365
Cowboy Lore (Allen), 365-66
"Cowboy Singing" (Eakins), painting, 13
"Cowboy's Lament, The," 290
Cowboy Songs (Lomax), 272
Cowboy Songs and Other Frontier Ballads (Lomax), 11, 144, 146, 289-90
Creole Songs of New Orleans (Peterson), 366
Cumberland Concerto (Harris), 17
Cumberland Interlude, 1790 (Bryan), orchestral composition, 51
Current Biography, 243

D

"Dance Drama Duo," 117
"Danville Girl," 211
Darker America (Still), symphonic poem, 16
"Darling Cora," 129
Darling Corie (Siegmeister-Allan), 366
"Darling Cory," 211
Dark of the Moon (Seeger), play, 211
Deepsea Shanties (Guthrie), recording, 104
"Derby Ram," 320
Devil's Ditties (Thomas), 366

Devil's Pretty Daughter and Other Ozark Folk Tales, The (Randolph), 429
Devil Take Her, The (Benjamin), opera, 173
Dicky Bird Was Singing, The (Duncan), 82
Down-East Spirituals and Others (Jackson), 284-85
Down in the Holler. A Gallery of Ozark Folk Speech (Randolph & Wilson), 415
Down in the Valley (Weill), folk opera, 15, 160, 197
"Down in the Willow Garden," 232
"Down in Yon Forest," 177
"Drunkard's Lone Child, The," 127
"Drunken Sailor," 294, 320
Dustbowl Ballads (Guthrie), recording, 104
"Dying Californian, The," 316
"Dying Cowboy, The," 15, 105, 290, 301

E

East Tennessee and Western Virginia Mountain Ballads (Cambiaire), 367
"East Virginia," 129
"East Virginia Blues," 232
Encyclopaedia Britannica, The, 243
English and Scottish Ballads, The (Child), 274
English and Scottish Popular Ballads, The (Child), 143, 271
English Folk-Chanteys (Sharp), 294
English Folk Song: Some Conclusions (Sharp), 11, 415-16
English Folk Songs (House), recording, 118
English Folk Songs from the Southern Appalachians (Sharp), 5, 266, 294-96
English Poetry and Prose of the Romantic Movement (Wood), 274
"E-ri-ee Canal," 210
"Evening Shade," 51

F

Faith Is the Victory (Kazee), 130
Famous Songs and Their Stories (Geller), 367
Fanfare and Cantilena (Tom Scott), orchestral composition, 209
"Fiddle Tunes and Rockin' Chair Songs" (The Beers), 37
Field Trip (Ritchie & Pickow), recording, 194
Fifteen Shaker Songs (Schirmer's American Folk-Song Series), 350
Finder, The, play, 227
Fireside Book of Folk Songs (Boni), 110, 203, 334-35
Fishermen's Ballads and Songs of the Sea (Procter Brothers), 367-68
Flying Cloud (Dean), 368
"Foggy Foggy Dew, The," 123-24, 209
Folk Ballad and Carol (Niles), 201

Folk Ballads from North Carolina (Frank C. Brown Collection of North Carolina Folklore), 279
Folk Blues (Silverman), collection and recording, 213, 214, 335
Folk Dances of Tennessee (McDowell), 368
Folk Hymns of America (Buchanan), 335
Folklore from Iowa (Stout), 369
Folk Music in America (Barry), 278
Folk Music of the United States and Latin America (Library of Congress), 403
Folk-Say (Botkin), 416
Folksay (Guthrie), recording, 104
Folk Song Chapbook (Kingston), 369
"Folk Song Festival" (Brand), radio program, 47, 213
Folk Song Hit Parade (Faier), 88
Folk-Song of Nebraska and the Central West, A Syllabus (Pound), 403-04
Folk Song of the American Negro (Work), 416
Folk Songs du Midi des États-Unis (Combs), 306
"Folk Songs for Children," film series, 136
Folk Songs for Singing (Scott & Scott), 210
"Folk Songs for Young Folk," radio program, 160
Folk Songs from Newfoundland (Karpeles), 336
Folk Songs from North Carolina (Frank C. Brown Collection of North Carolina Folklore), 279
Folk-Songs from the Kentucky Highland (Schirmer's American Folk-Song Series), 345
Folk Songs from the Southern Highlands (Henry), 306, 321
Folk-Songs Mainly from West Virginia (Cox), 369-70
Folksongs of Alabama (Arnold), 5, 9, 307
Folk-Songs of America (Gordon), 307-08
Folk Songs of Canada (Fowke), 126, 171, 243, 336-37
Folksongs of Florida (Morris), 5, 308
Folk Songs of French Canada (Barbeau-Sapir), 5, 276
Folk Songs of Many Nations (Elson), 337
Folksongs of Mississippi and Their Background (Hudson), 308-09
Folk Songs of Old New England (Linscott), 264, 309
Folk-Songs of Old Quebec (Barbeau), 276
Folk Songs of Old Vincennes (O'Flynn et al.), 337-38
Folk Songs of the Canadian Maritimes and Newfoundland (McCurdy), recording, 152
Folk-Songs of the Four Seasons (Myers), 338
Folk-Songs of the Kentucky Mountains (McGill), 338-39

Folk Songs of the People (Temple), recording, 243
Folk-Songs of the Roanoke and the Albemarle (Chappell), 309-10
Folk-Songs of the South (Cox), 5, 265, 310
Folk-Songs of the West and South (Farwell), 339
Folk-Songs of Virginia (Davis), 404
Folksongs on Records (Lumpkin), 4, 11, 404-05, 485
"Folksongs with Marion Diard," television series, 81
Folk Song Symphony (Harris), 17
Folk Song: U.S.A. (Lomax and Lomax), 11, 264, 290-91
Folk Tunes from Mississippi (Hudson-Herzog), 370
"Ford Foundation Transcribed Series," 95
Forty-Three Years for Uncle Sam (High), 113
Forty-Niners (Hulbert), 264, 416-17
Fourteen Children's Songs (Rubin), recording, 201
Frank C. Brown Collection of North Carolina Folklore, 9, 278
"Frankie and Johnny," 13, 106, 211
Frankie and Johnny (Huston), 13, 370
French Traditional Songs (Ginandes), recording, 93
"Frog a-Wooing, A," 276
"Frog's Courtship, The," 279
Frog Went A-Courtin' (Langstaff), 138
"Frog Went Courtin'," 177
From an Ozark Holler. Stories of Ozark Mountain Folk (Randolph), 417
From the Black Belt (Still), melodic suite, 16
From the New World (Dvořák), symphony, 16
From the Sacred Harp (Tom Scott), orchestral composition, 209
From Where the Pattern Grew (Una Ritchie), pageant, 192
Frontier Ballads (Finger), 370-71
Funk & Wagnalls Standard Dictionary of Folklore, Mythology, and Legend, 417

G

Games and Rhymes, Beliefs and Customs, Riddles, Proverbs, Speech, Tales and Legends (Frank C. Brown Collection of North Carolina Folklore), 279
Games and Songs of American Children (Newell), 310-11
Garland of Green Mountain Song, A (Flanders), 282
Garland of Mountain Song, A (Jean Ritchie), 202, 203, 240, 339
"Gentlemen, Be Seated" (Paskman & Spaeth), 371
Giants in the Land (Robinson), motion picture, 197
"Gift to Be Simple, The," 15

Gift to Be Simple, The (Andrews), 371-72
"Girls, Quit Your Rowdy Ways," 180
"Git Along Little Dogies," 15
Glidden Tour, The, motion picture, 108
"God's Goin' to Trouble the Waters," 144
"Gold Rush" (Brand), television program, 47
Gold Rush Song Book, The (Black & Robertson), 372
"Golden Vanity, The," 277
"Good-by Old Paint," 15
"Good Night Ladies," 16
"Good Old Rebel," 56
"Go Tell Aunt Rhody," 74
"Go 'Way from My Window," 94, 177
Grapes of Wrath, The (Steinbeck), 253, 265
"Great Gildersleeve," radio program, 142
Great Smokies and the Blue Ridge, The (Peattie), 201, 266, 417
Green Grow the Lilacs (Riggs), play, 14, 79
"Green Lilac Hill," 119
Green Pastures, The (Connelly), play, 14
"Grey Goose," 211
"Ground Hog," 211
Guide to American Folklore, A (Davidson), 405
Guide to English Folk Song Collections, A (Dean-Smith), 274, 405
Guide to Life and Literature of the Southwest (Dobie), 405-06
"Guy Is a Guy, A" (Brand), 47
"Gypsy Davy, The," 319

H

Haiti Singing (Courlander), 311
"Halls of Ivy, The," radio program, 142
Hampton and Its Students (Armstrong & Ludlow), 372
Handicrafts of New England (Eaton), 263
Handicrafts of the Southern Highlands (Eaton), 265, 266, 417-18
Hands That Built America, motion picture, 45
Handy Play Party Book (Cooperative Recreation Service, Delaware, Ohio), 365
"Happy Is the Miller," 311
Happy Page, The, play, 227
Hard Travelin' (Houston), recording, 119
Harvard Dictionary of Music (Apel), 264
"Haul Away, Joe," 320
Hesperian Harp, 286
Highways and Byways (Whitmire), 235
Hill Country Tunes (Bayard), 265, 311
Hispanic Folk Songs of New Mexico (Robb), 339-40
"Historical America in Song" (Ives), recordings, 125
"History of Indiana" (Benton), mural, 252

History of Musical Instruments, The (Sachs), 264, 266
History Sings (Kinscella), 372
Hobo's Hornbook, The (Milburn), 373
"Hobo's Last Ride, The," 129
Holy Old Mackinaw: A Natural History of the American Lumberjack (Holbrook), 418
"Home on the Range" (Higley & Kelley), 6, 73, 290
origin of, 6-7
Story of (Mechem), 388
Home on the Range (Gould), orchestral composition, 17
Home on the Range (Guion), orchestral composition, 17
"Hop-Scotch," 311
"Hop Up, My Ladies," 15
Hornpipe and Chantey (Scott), orchestral composition, 209
"House Carpenter, The," 319
House I Live In, The, motion picture, 197
How to Play the 5-String Banjo (Seeger), 70, 210, 264
"Hunters of Kentucky, The," 316
"Hymns of All Churches," radio program, 218

I

"I Come for to Sing," radio program, 219
"If He'd Be a Buckaroo by His Trade," 15
"I Have a Mother in the Heavens" (Bryan), 51
I Hear America: Literature in the United States Since 1900 (Loggins), 242, 243
I Married an Angel, play, 124
"I'm Going Home," 318
"I'm on My Way" (Gershwin), 15
Indian Suite (MacDowell), 16
"In Kansas," 180
International Catalogue of Recorded Folk Music (Fraser), 406, 485
International Who Is Who in Music, 170, 171, 201, 202
Irish Folk Music (O'Neill), 418
Irish Folk Music and Song (O'Sullivan), 418-19
Irish Street Ballads (Lochlainn), 373
Irish Street Songs (Roberts), recording, 195
Iron Men and Wooden Ships (Shay), 373-74
It Happened in the Ozarks (High), 113
"I Wonder As I Wander," 177
"I Wouldn't Marry," 279

J

"Jack o' Diamonds," 290
"Jealous Lover, The," 279
"Jealous Lover of Lone Green Valley" (Benton), painting, 12
"Jennie Jenkins," 211
"Jerusalem," 51
"Jesse James," 205, 211, 242, 290

"Jester, The" (Hals), painting, 267
"Jimmy Randall," 232
"Joe Bowers," 162
"Joe Hill" (Robinson), 203
"John Hardy," 79, 129, 310
"John Henry," 79, 211
"John Henry," a portrayal by Hayden, 13
John Henry (Bradford), play, 14, 234, 419
John Henry: A Folk-Lore Study (Chappell), 419
John Henry Legend, The (E. R. Clark), recording, 61
John Henry Suite (Gragson), 17
John Henry: Tracking Down a Negro Legend (Johnson), 419
John Jacob Niles Suite (Hart), 178
Journal of American Folklore, 10, 278
Jubilee Singers and Their Campaign for Twenty Thousand Dollars, The (Pike), 274, 374
Jubilee Songs: Complete, 374

K

Kaintuck' (Still), tone poem, 16
"Katy Cline," 232
"Keep Your Hand on the Plow," 14
Kentucky Harmony, 285
"Kevin Barry," 93-94
King's Book of Chanties, 375
"Kisses Sweeter Than Wine" (Hellerman), 112
"Kraft Music Hall," television program, 189

L

"Lady Alice," 279
"Lady Isabel and the Elf-Knight," 323
Lamentation (Niles), oratorio, 177
Land of Cotton, The (Edmonds), play, 14
Land of Saddle Bags: A Study of the Mountain People of Appalachia, The (Raine), 419-20
"Lass of Mohee," 301, 320
Last Leaves of Traditional Ballads and Ballad Airs (Grieg), 274
Lay My Burden Down: A Folk History of Slavery (Botkin), 420
"Leavin' fo' de Promis' Lan' " (Gershwin), 15
Let's Sing a Little (Mills), recording, 161
Lift Every Voice (Silber), 340
"Listening Post," radio program, 95
List of American Folksongs Currently Available on Records, A (Library of Congress), 4, 11, 125, 407
Literary History of the United States, A (Spiller, *et. al.*), 243
Little Black Sambo (Edna Ritchie), operetta, 192
"Little Black Train," 15
Little Book of Carols (Cooperative Recreation Service, Delaware, Ohio), 365

"Little Dogies," 105
"Little Mohee, The," 129
Log Cabin Ballads (Still), orchestral composition, 16
"Lonesome Dove," 15
"Lonesome Road" (Benton), painting, 12
Lonesome Train, The, motion picture, 197
Lonesome Tunes: Folk Songs from the Kentucky Mountains (Wyman), 340
"Lonesome Valley, The," 318
Look Away (Cooperative Recreation Service, Delaware, Ohio), 365
"Lord Bateman," 78, 277
"Lord Randall," 78, 232, 277
"Lord Thomas and Fair Annet," 279
Lore of the Lumber Camps (Beck), 312
Louisiana French Folk Songs (Whitfield), 312
Lover's Melodies (Balis Ritchie), 191

M

Mademoiselle from Armentieres (Winterich), 375
Maine Woods Songster, The (Barry), 278
"Marble Town," 180
Mary the Rose (Niles), cantata, 177
"Ma Says, Pa Says," 171
"Meaning of America, The," radio program, 219
Mechau Balladeers, recording, 171
Mellows (Kennedy), 341
"Merry Lute Player" (Hals), painting, 267
"Methodist Pie," 94
Mexican Border Ballads and Other Lore (Boatright), 171
"Minstrel's History of the U.S.A., A," concert program, 219
Minstrels of the Mine Patch (Korson), 287
Minstrelsy of Maine (Eckstrom & Smyth), 312-13
Minstrelsy of the Scottish Border, The (Scott), 271
"Misery Moon the Hoo-dooed Coon," 123
Missouri Harmony, 285
"Mister Rabbit," 211
Modern American Poetry (Untermeyer), 243
Modern Art: The Men, the Movements, the Meaning (Craven), 265
"Monitor," radio program, 184, 227, 243
More Mellows (Kennedy), 341-42
More Pious Friends and Drunken Companions (Shay), 375
More Songs of the Hill-Folk (Schirmer's American Folk-Song Series), 348
Mountain Minstrelsy of Pennsylvania (Shoemaker), 266, 313
Mountain Songs of North Carolina (Schirmer's American Folk-Song Series), 265, 345-46
"Mountain Whippoorwill, The" (Benét), 251
Mules and Men (Hurston), 420

Musical Instruments (Geiringer), 264, 265-66, 267
"Music from America," radio program, 164
Music in the Southwest (Swan), 420-21
Music of the Ballads, The (Frank C. Brown Collection of North Carolina Folklore), 279
"Music of the Streets," radio program, 149
My Favorite Mountain Ballads and Old-time Songs (Kincaid), 137, 375-76
"My Man's Gone Now" (Gershwin), 15
My Pious Friends and Drunken Companions (Shay), 376
My Spirituals (Jessye), 376
"My Sweetheart's a Cowboy," 105
"My Western Home," 7

N

"Name That Tune," television program, 135
"National Farm and Home Hour," radio program, 226
Native American Balladry, A Descriptive Study and Bibliographical Syllabus (Laws), 407-08
"Needle's Eye, The," 311
Negro and His Songs, The (Odum & Johnson), 313
Negro Folk Rhymes (Talley), 313
Negro Folk-Songs (Schirmer's American Folk-Song Series), 346
Negro Folk Songs As Sung by Lead Belly (Lomax & Lomax), 139, 170, 291-92
Negro Sings a New Heaven, The (Grissom), 376-77
Negro Slave Songs in the United States (Fisher), 421
"*Negro Spirituals*" (Higginson), 377
Negro Workaday Songs (Odum & Johnson), 314
New Green Mountain Songster, The (Flanders, Ballard, Brown, Barry), 274, 282
Night with Belafonte, A, show, 40
900 Miles and Other Railroad Songs (Houston), recording, 119
"Nobody Knows the Trouble I've Had," 318
North Pennsylvania Minstrelsy (Shoemaker), 314
Norwegian Emigrant Songs and Ballads (Blegen-Ruud), 377
Notes on Virginia (Jefferson), 251
Nursery Songs from the Appalachian Mountains (Sharp), 342

O

"Oats, Pease, Beans, and Barley Grows," 311
"Oh Dem Golden Slippers," 16
"Oh Doctor Jesus" (Gershwin), 15
"Oh I Can't Sit Down" (Gershwin), 15
Ohio Valley Ballads (Buckley), recording, 53

Oklahoma! (Rodgers & Hammerstein), musical play, 14
Old Bangum Would A-Hunting Go (Brand), 47
"Old Chisholm Trail," 15, 162
"Old Dog Tray," 316
"Old Grandad," 15
"Old Gray Mare," 211
"Old Joe Clark" (Bryan), 51-52
"Old Mackenzie Trail, The" (Lomax), 292
Old, Old Folk Songs (High), 113, 377-78
"Old Paint," 162
Old Songs and Singing Games (Chase), 378
Old Songs Hymnal (Bolton), 342
Old World Ballads in America (Summers), recording, 221
Ol' Man Adam an' His Chillun (Bradford), 14
"Omnibus," television program, 117
On Christmas Day in the Morning (Langstaff), 138
One Hundred English Folk Songs (Sharp), 11
One Hundred Folksongs of All Nations (Bantock), 342-43
On the Trail of Negro Folk-Songs (Scarborough), 315
"On Top of Old Smoky," 6
Opus Americana No. 2 (Milhaud), ballet suite, 16
Ordre de Bon-temps, L' (Montigny), 340-41
Our Singing Country (Lomax & Lomax), 289, 292
"Out Where the West Begins" (Chapman), 292
Over in the Meadow (Langstaff), 138
Ozark Country (Rayburn), 421-22
Ozark Folksongs (Randolph), 5, 9, 109, 150-51, 265, 293-94
Ozark Guide (Rayburn), 226
Ozark Mountain Folks (Randolph), 265, 422
Ozarks: An American Survival of Primitive Society (Randolph), 423
Ozark Set (Siegmeister), orchestral composition, 17
Ozark Superstitions (Randolph), 10, 422

P

Paint Your Wagon, musical play, 189
Panorama of American Popular Music (Ewen), 423
Papa Pompino (King), play, 131
Paul Bunyan (Britten), opera, 15
"Pease Porridge Hot," 311
Pennsylvania Songs and Legends (Korson), 288
People's Song Book, The (Hille, et. al.), 378
"People's Songs Library," 111
Personal Choice (McColl), 150
Peter Peter Pumpkin Eater (King), play, 131

"Philco Studio One," television program, 189
Phonolog. The All-in-One Record Catalog, 408
Pills to Purge Melancholy (Holt), recording, 117
Pioneer Songs (Daughters of Utah Pioneers), 378
Pioneer Songster, A (Thompson), 315-16
"Plainte du coureur de bois, La," 277
Play-Party in Indiana, The (Wolford), 379
Poetic Origins and the Ballad (Pound), 423
Porgy and Bess (Gershwin), folk opera, 15
Prairie Sings, The. Northwest Kansas Folksongs (McMullen), 379
"Prentice Boy, The," 316
"Pretty Polly," 211, 319
Primitives, The (Riggs), play, 14
Prizefighter (King), play, 131
"Promised Land," 51
"Pussy Wants a Corner," 311
Put's Golden Songster, 379-80

Q

Quest of the Ballad, The (Mackenzie), 105, 423-24

R

"Railroad Hour, The," radio program, 142
Railroad Songs of Yesterday (Sherwin-McClintock), 343
Rainbow Round My Shoulder (Odum), 424
"Ramblin' Gamblin' Man," 119
Read 'em and Weep (Spaeth), 380
"Red River Valley," 16, 211
"Red Rockin' Chair," 232
"Red Whiskey," 105
"Religious Folksong in America" (Chalmers), recital program, 58
Religious Folk-Songs of the Negro As Sung at Hampton Institute (Dett), 343-44
Reliques of Ancient English Poetry (Percy), 271
"Renaud, Lisette," 277
Research in Primitive and Folk Music in the United States (Herzog), 408
"Reuben Ranzo," 301
Rhapsody for the Merry Month of May (Niles), choral work, 177
Richard Dyer-Bennet, The 20th-Century Minstrel. A Collection of 20 Songs and Ballads, 344
"Ring Around the Rosie," 311
"Rio Grand," 294
"Rock Island Line," 129
Rodeo (Copland), orchestral composition, 15
Roll and Go (Colcord), 316
Rolling Along in Song (Johnson), 344
"Rolling River," 301
"Rollin' Stone," 239

"Roll Jordan, Roll," 318
Romance of Rosy Ridge, motion picture, 197
Romance of Scarlet Gulch, play, 79
Romancero du Canada (Barbeau), 277
Roosevelt Story, The, motion picture, 197
Round the Levee (Thompson), 380
Roustabout Songs (Wheeler), 215, 344
"Rovin' Gambler, The," 177
"Roving Bachelor, The," 316
"Roving Cowboy, The," 129
"Roving Gambler," 93
Royal Journey, motion picture, 207
"Runaway Logging Train, The" (Temple), 224
"Rye Wiskey," 162

S

Sacred Harp, 51, 248
Saint Helena Island Spirituals (Ballanta-Taylor), 345
Saints of Sage and Saddle (Fife), 424
"Sally Brown," 294
Sandhog (Robinson & Salt), folk opera, 197
"San Francisco Blues" (Fuller), 90
San Francisco Songster, 1849-1939, A (Lengyel), 380-81
"Santy Anna," 301
Schirmer's American Folk-Song Series, 10, 176, 177, 273, 345-51
Scotland Sings (McColl), 150
Search, The, motion picture, 56, 78, 109
Sea Songs and Shanties (Whall), 381-82
Sea Songs of Sailing, Whaling, and Fishing (Ives), 137, 351
Second Book of Negro Spirituals (Johnson), 352
"See Me Cross the Water" (Bryan), 51
Series of Old American Songs (Brown University), 382
"Seven Joys of Mary, The," 169
Seven Kentucky Mountain Songs (Schirmer's American Folk-Song Series), 346
Seven Negro Exaltations (Schirmer's American Folk-Song Series), 346
Seventy Negro Spirituals (Fisher), 352
"Shanadar" (Shenandoah), 294
Shanty Book, The. Parts I, II, *Sailor Shanties*, 382-83
Shantymen and Shantyboys (Doerflinger), 240, 316-17
Shape-Note Study Book, The (Schirmer's American Folk-Song Series), 351
"Shenandoah," 6, 320
Shuttle and Cage (McColl), 150
Sidewalks of America (Botkin), 424
"Sierry Peaks," 157
"Silent Night," 6
Sing for Your Supper, play, 196
Singin' Billy (Bryan), opera, 15, 51
Singing Cowboy (Larkin), 352-53
Singing Family of the Cumberlands (Ritchie), 10, 105, 202, 256, 425
Singing Holidays: The Calendar in Folksong (Brand), 47, 353

Singing Soldiers (Niles), 175-76, 383
Sing, Man, Sing, musical drama, 40
Sing of America (Scott & Scott), 210, 352
Sing Out, Sweet Land (Siegmeister), play, 17, 124
"Sis Joe," 15
"Skip—to-M'Lou" (Bryan), 51
Slave Songs of the Georgia Sea Islands (Parrish), 317-18
Slave Songs of the United States (Allen, Ware, Garrison), 274, 318
Smoky, motion picture, 124
Smoky Mountain (Hunkins), orchestral composition, 15
Smoky Mountain Ballads (van Wey), 228
Snow Queen, The (King), play, 131
Social Harp, 286
Sodbuster Ballads (Guthrie), recording, 104
Sod-House Frontier, The (Dick), 425
Solomon Valley Ballads (Jemison), recording, 128
Song Catcher in the Southern Mountains (Scarborough), 318-19
Song Fest (Best), 353
Songs Along the Mahantongo (Boyer, Buffington, Yoder), 319
Songs and Ballads from Nova Scotia (Creighton), 280-81
Songs and Ballads of the American Revolution (Moore), 383
Songs and Ballads of the Anthracite Miner (Korson), 265, 288-89
Songs and Ballads of the Maine Lumberjacks (Gray), 383-84
Songs for Wee Folk (Reed), recording, 190
Songs from the Hills of Vermont (Schirmer's American Folk-Song Series), 346-47
Songs from the Old Camp Ground (McDowell), 384
Songs Lincoln Loved (Lair), 384
Songs My Mother Never Taught Me (Niles), 176, 354
Songs of All Time (Cooperative Recreation Service, Delaware, Ohio), 365
Songs of America (Ewen), 426
Songs of American Folks (Coleman & Bregman), 354
Songs of American Sailormen (Colcord), 319-20
"Songs of Canada" ("Songs Chez Nous"), radio program, 160
Songs of Early America (Siegmeister), 354-55
Songs of Expanding America (Ives), recording, 136
Songs of Hawaii (Cunha), 385
Songs of Joe Hill (Joe Glazer), recording, 105
Songs of North and South (Ives), recording, 136
Songs of the Cattle Trail and Cow Camp (Lomax), 292-93
Songs of the Colonies (Ives), recording, 136

Songs of the Cowboys (Thorpe), 272, 385

Songs of the Frontier (Ives), recording, 136

Songs of the Gold Miners (Sherwin & Katzman), 386

Songs of the Hill-Folk (Schirmer's American Folk-Song Series), 348

Songs of the Michigan Lumberjacks (Beck), 312, 320

Songs of the Open Range (Sires), 355

Songs of the Revolution (Ives), recording, 136

Songs of the Rivers of America (Carmer), 355

Songs of the Sea (Ives), recording, 136

Songs of the Sea and Sailors' Chanteys: An Anthology (Frothingham), 386

Songs of the Wobblies (Joe Glazer), recording, 105

Songs of Work and Freedom (Glazer & Fowke), 94

Songs of Yesterday (Jordan & Kessler), 355-56

Songs Sung in the Southern Appalachians (Henry), 321

"Sound off!" Soldier Songs from the Revolution to World War II (Dolph), 321

"Sound off!" Soldier Songs from Yankee Doodle to Parley Voo (Dolph), 321

"Sounds of Our Times," recording series, 87

"Sourwood Mountain," 15

"Sourwood Mountain" (Benton), painting, 12, 253

Sourwood Mountain (Underwood & Perry), ballet suite, 16

South Carolina Ballads (Smith), 386

Southern and Western Pocket Harmonist, 286

Southern Folklore Quarterly, 278

Southern Harmony, The, 285

Southern Harmony, and Musical Companion, The (Walker), 15, 386-87

Southern Highlander and His Homeland, The (Campbell), 426

Spanish-American Folk-Songs (Hague), 264, 387

Spanish Folk-Poetry in New Mexico (Campa), 322

Spanish Folk Songs of New Mexico (VanStone), 264, 356

Spanish Songs of Old California (Schirmer's American Folk-Song Series), 347

Spiritual Folk-Songs of Early America (Jackson), 284, 285

Square Dance, ballet suite, 16

"Squid Jiggin' Ground" (Scammell), 206

"Steal Away to Jesus" (Edmonds), 14

Steamboatin' Days (Wheeler), 215, 387

Sticks in the Knapsack and other Ozark Folk Tales (Randolph), 429

"Stormalong," 320

Story of American Folk Song, The (Ames), 426-27

Story of "Home on the Range," The (Mechem), 388

Story of the Jubilee Singers, with Their Songs, The (Marsh), 388

Story of the Sacred Harp, 1844-1944, The (Jackson), 285-86

Strangers in this World (Bryan), musical folk play, 51

"Streets of Laredo," 162

"Sugarbush," 171

Suite in Southern Mountains (Stringfield), 16

"Summertime" (Gershwin), 15

Sump'n Like Wings (Riggs), play, 14

Sun Shines Bright, The (Thomas), 427

Sun-Up (Vollmer), play, 192

Swapping Song Book, The (Ritchie), 356

Sweet Freedom's Song (Cooperative Recreation Service, Delaware, Ohio), 365

Sweet Land of Liberty, motion picture, 95

"Sweet Little Boy Jesus," 177

Swing and Turn: Texas Play-Party Games (Owens), 388-89

"Swing Low Sweet Chariot" (McCrady), painting, 13

T

Take This Hammer (Leadbelly), recording, 170

Tales and Songs of Southern Illinois (Neely), 389

Talking Turtle and other Folk Tales (Randolph), 429

"Telephone Spotlight on Missouri," television series, 82

"Telephone Spotlight on Texas," television series, 82

Ten Christmas Carols from the Southern Appalachian Mountains (Schirmer's American Folk-Song Series), 348

Tender Land, The (Copland), opera, 15

Terry Golden Album, recording, 106

Texas and Southwestern Lore (Dobie), 389-90

Texas Folk Songs (Nye), recording, 179

Texas Folk Songs (Owens), 264, 322

Texas Li'l' Darlin', musical play, 189

"Theatre Guild on the Air," radio program, 95

"There Was a Tree Stood in the Ground," 311

They Knew Paul Bunyan (Beck), 390

30 and 1 Folk Songs from the Southern Mountains (Lunsford & Stringfield), 356

Thirty-six South Carolina Spirituals (Schirmer's American Folk-Song Series), 347

This Is the Army (Berlin), musical play, 124

"This Land of Song," television series, 136

Three for Tonight (Gregory), musical show, 40

"Three Lovely Ducks," 276
"Three Ravens, The," 323
Time Out of War, A, motion picture, 108
Tom Benton's Saturday Night, recording, 265
"Tom Glazer's Ballad Box," radio program, 95
Tony Beaver (Marais & Breton), folk opera, 155, 171
Town Crier, The, motion picture, 197
Traditional Ballads, Mainly from West Virginia (Cox), 390
Traditional Ballads of Virginia (Davis), 322-23
Traditional Music of America (Ford), 323
Traditional Songs from Nova Scotia (Creighton), 281
Traditional Tunes of the Child Ballads, The (Bronson), 323-24
"Trail to Mexico, The," 73, 162
"Train to Kimberley," 171
Treasury of American Ballads: Gay, Naughty, and Classic, A (Kennedy), 390-91
Treasury of American Folklore, A (Botkin), 427
Treasury of American Song, A (Downes & Siegmeister), 356-57
Treasury of Folk Songs, A (Kolb), 391
Treasury of Jewish Folksong, A (Rubin), 200, 324-25
Treasury of Negro Spirituals, The (Chambers), 357
Treasury of New England Folklore, A (Botkin), 427-28
Treasury of Railroad Folklore, A (Botkin & Harlow), 428
Treasury of Southern Folklore, A (Botkin), 428
Treasury of the Blues, A (Handy), 264, 357
Treasury of the World's Finest Folk Song, A (Deutsch), 358
Treasury of Western Folklore, A (Botkin), 428
"Troubadours de By-Town," 187
"True Story," radio program, 95
Turkey in the Straw (Guion), orchestral composition, 17
"Turkish Lady," 301
"Turkish Reveler," 78
"21-inch Classroom-Music, Grade 2," television series, 205
20,000 Leagues Under the Sea (Clauson), recording, 63
"TV Workshop," 95
Twelve Negro Spirituals (Still), 358
Twenty Kentucky Mountain Songs (Wyman), 358

U

Union Harmony, 285
Unsung Americans Sung (Handy), 391
"U. S. Steel Hour," television program, 137

V

"Venus and the Lute Player" (Titian), painting, 267
Vermont Chap Book (Flanders), 283
Vermont Folk-Songs and Ballads (Flanders & Brown), 283
Viking Book of Folk Ballads of the English-Speaking World, The (Friedman), 325
Vingt-et-Une Chansons Canadiennes (Fortier, *et. al.*), 359
"Virginia Reel," 311
"Voice of America," radio program, 47
Voice of Haiti, The (Antoine), 391
"Voici le printemps," 277

W

Walk in the Sun, A, motion picture, 197
"Water Boy" (Edmonds), 14
Wayfaring Stranger (Ives), 105, 123, 124, 136, 428-29
'Way Up on Old Smoky (Siegmeister-Wheeler), 359
We Always Lie to Strangers. Tall Tales from the Ozarks (Randolph), 429
Weep Some More, My Lady (Spaeth), 392
"Wellsprings of America," radio series, 145
Western Symphony, ballet suite, 16
"We the People," radio program, 95
When Johnny Comes Marching Home (Harris), orchestral composition, 17
When We Grow Up, motion picture, 197
"Whiskey Johnny," 211, 320
White and Negro Spirituals, Their Life Span and Kinship (Jackson), 286-87
White Pilgrim, The (Kazee & Horton), play, 129
White Spirituals in the Southern Uplands (Jackson), 10, 285, 429-30
White Spiritual Symphony (Bryan), 51
Who Blowed Up the Church House? and other Ozark Folk Tales (Randolph), 429
Who's Who in Music, 236
Will Holt Concert, A, recording, 117
Will the Mail Train Run Tonight, play, 79
"Wondrous Love," 51
Work and Sing (Siegmeister), 359
Work and Sing, An International Songbook (Cooperative Recreation Service, Delaware, Ohio), 365
World Library of Folk and Primitive Music, A, recordings, 145
World's Encyclopaedia of Recorded Music, The (Clough & Cuming), 485
"Wreck of the Old 97" (Benton), painting, 12

Y

Yankee Whaler, The (Ashley), 430
"You Got to Cross That Lonesome Valley," 177
"Young Charlotte," 301
"Young Johnnie," 78

Index of
Long-Playing
Records

LISTED IN BOOK THREE

A

Absolute Nonsense (Brand), 494
Actor's Holiday, An (Bikel), 492
Adirondack Folk Songs and Ballads (Okun), 557
African Suite (Marais-Miranda), 547
Afro-American Blues and Game Songs, 586
Afro-American Spirituals, Work Songs, and Ballads, 587
All Day Singin' (Van Wey), 578
American Ballads (Smith), 592
American Ballads and Folksongs (O'Bryant), 555
American Banjo Scruggs Style, 587
American Banjo Tunes and Songs (Michael Seeger), 587
American Children Sing Christmas Carols, 587
American Drinking Songs (Brand), 494
American Favorite Ballads, I (Seeger), 569
American Favorite Ballads, II (Seeger), 570
American Folk and Gambling Songs (Niles), 553
American Folk Dance (Decker-Luse), 588
American Folk Love Songs (Niles), 554
American Folk Songs (Niles), 553
American Folk Songs (Stafford), 574
American Folk Songs and Ballads (Warner), 579
American Folk Songs for Children (Seeger), 570
American Folk Songs for Christmas (Peggy, Barbara, and Penny Seeger), 569

American Folk Songs Sung by the Seegers (Seeger), 588
American Folksongs for Children (Ginandes), 516
American Folksongs of Sadness and Melancholy (Wood), 584
American Folk Tales and Songs (Chase), 588
American Industrial Ballads (P. Seeger), 570
American Industrial Folk Songs (Greenway), 519
American Negro Slave Songs, 610
American Northwest Ballads (W. Robertson), 564
American Revolution, Story of the (Bill Bonyun), 626
American Song Bag, The (Sandburg), 566
American Square Dance Group (Mayo), 589
American Tragic Ballads (Summers), 576
Americana (Stracke), 575
America's Best Loved Folk Songs (Okun), 557
And Her Singing Guitar (Lea), 535
Anglo-American Ballads, 589
Anglo-American Folk Songs (Nye), 554
Anglo-American Shanties, Lyric Songs, Dance Tunes, and Spirituals, 590
Anglo-American Songs and Ballads, 590
Animal Folk Songs for Children (Seeger), 568
Anthology of American Folk Music, 591, 592
Anthracite Miners, Songs and Ballads of the, 620
A-Roving with Tony Gardell (Gardell), 514

655

Art of the Five-String Banjo (Faier), 511
Assassination of Presidents, 620
Australian Bush Songs (Lloyd), 537
Australian Folk Songs (Ives), 527
Authentic Square Dances (Wimberley), 592

B

Back Home (Travis), 577
Backroom Ballads (Brand), 495
Bad Lads and Hard Cases (MacColl), 541
Badmen and Heroes (McCurdy-Elliott-Brand-Wilder), 592
Badmen and Heroes and Pirate Songs (McCurdy-Brand-Elliott-Wilder), 592
Bahaman Songs, 592
Ballad Hunter, The (Lomax), 593
Ballad of Oklahoma, 594
Ballad Record, The (McCurdy), 543
Ballad Singer's Choice, A (McCurdy), 543
Ballads (Dyer-Bennet), 507
Ballads (Isaacson), 526
Ballads (Niles), 554
Ballads and Blues (White), 581, 582
Ballads and Calypso (Wilson), 584
Ballads and Folksongs, I, II (Ives), 528
Ballads and Reliques (Nye), 555
Ballads and Songs (Sandburg), 567
Ballads, Blues and Other Songs (White), 583
Ballads, Folk, and Country Songs (Ives), 528
Ballads of Careless Love, 594
Ballads of the Civil War, I and II (Nye), 555
Ballads of LaSalle County, Illinois (Clark), 499
Ballads of Long Ago (Marais-Miranda), 547
Ballads of Many Lands (Marais-Miranda), 548
Ballads of Ohio (Grimes), 519
Ballads of the Revolution (House), 523
Ballads of the War of 1812, I and II (House), 523
Banjos, Banjos, and More Banjos! (Weissman-Faier-Weissberg), 595
Banjo Songs of the Blue Ridge and Great Smokies (Ramsay), 559
Banjo Songs of the Southern Mountains, 595
Banjo Tunes and Songs (Steele), 574
Barrack Room Ballads (MacColl), 541
Barroom Ballads (McCurdy), 544
Bawdy Sea Shanties (Brand), 496
Bawdy Songs and Backroom Ballads (Brand), 495
Bay State Ballads (Clayton), 500
Belafonte Sings the Blues (Belafonte), 492
Big Bill's Blues (Broonzy), 497

Birds, Beasts, Bugs and Little Fishes (Seeger), 571
Binorie Variations: Hornpipe and Chantey (Scott), 595
Bless 'Em All (MacColl), 541
Blood, Booze 'n Bones (McCurdy), 544
Bloody Ballads (Clayton), 500
Blow Boys, Blow (Lloyd-MacColl), 538
Blues (Belafonte), 492
Blues (Broonzy), 497
Blues (McGhee), 546
Blues and Folk Songs (Sellers), 573
Blues and Hollers (Lomax), 593
Blues Concert (Broonzy), 497
Bobby Burns' Merry Muses of Caledonia (Clayton), 501
Boll Weevil (Lomax), 593
Bonny Bunch of Roses, The (Ennis), 510
Bound for Glory (Guthrie), 595
Bowling Green and Other Folksongs from the Southern Mountains (Kossoy), 534
Bravo Bikel (Bikel), 493
British-American Ballads of New England, 595
British Broadside Ballads in Popular Tradition (Clayton), 501
British Industrial Folk Songs (MacColl), 541
British Traditional Ballads in America (Ginandes), 516

C

Cads, Blackguards and False True-Loves (Gilmer), 515
Cajun Songs from Louisiana, 596
Calypso (Belafonte), 491
Calypso (Wilson), 584
Canadian Folk Songs (Barbeau), 596
Canadian Folk Songs (Labrecque), 534
Canadian Northwoods Ballads (Hemsworth), 521
Captain Burl Ives' Ark (Ives), 528
Caribou Eskimo Songs, 596
Carnegie Concert (Gibson), 514
Carol Singing at Kingsway Hall, 596
Carolina Street Ballads, 489
Carols by the Bach Choir, 597
Catskill Mountain Folk Songs (Decormier), 505
Celebrity Quartette, 598
Ceremony of Carols, A (Britten), 597
Chain Gang: Volumes I and II (Guthrie-Terry-Stewart), 597
Chain Gang Songs (White), 581
Champions and Sporting Blades (MacColl-Lloyd), 542
Chants de Noel of French Canada (Baillargeon), 490
Cheyenne (Lomax), 593
Chicago Mob Scene, 597
Children's Favorites (Ives), 528
Children's Game Songs of French Canada, 598

Children's Songs (McCurdy), 544
Christmas Carols (Summers), 575
Christmas Carols, 598, 599
Christmas Carols of the Nations (Hayes), 520
Christmas Day in the Morning (Ives), 529
Christmas Eve with Ives (Ives), 529
Christmas Hymns and Carols (Shaw Chorale), 599, 600
Christmas Songs of Many Lands (Mills), 550
Christmas with Marais and Miranda (Marais-Miranda), 548
City Blues (Terry), 576
Classic Folk Blues (Jefferson), 532
Classic Scots Ballads (MacColl-Seeger), 543
Come and Sit by My Side (Yarbrough), 585
Community Concert (Archer-Gile), 489
Concert (Clauson), 500
Concert (Dyer-Bennet), 507
Concert (Seeger, Pete), 571
Concert of British and American Folksongs (Clayton), 501
Concert of English Folk Songs (Runge), 566
Concert with Hillel and Aviva (Hillel-Aviva), 521
Coronation Concert (Ives), 529
Country Blues (Broonzy), 497
Country Dance Music, 600
Courting and Riddle Songs (Ritchie-Brand), 562
Courting Songs (Ritchie-Brand), 563
Courting Songs (Ritchie-Kraber), 563
Courtin's a Pleasure (Ritchie-Brand-Paley), 600
Cowboy Ballads (Houston), 524
Cowboy Dances (Shaw), 601
Cowboy Song Favorites (Willing), 601
Cowboy Songs (Clark), 500
Cowboy Songs (Guthrie-Houston), 520
Cowboy Songs, Ballads and Cattle Calls from Texas, 601
Creole Songs and Street Cries of New Orleans (Van Wey), 578
Cumberland Mountain Folksongs (Clayton), 501

D

Darling Corey (Seeger), 571
Days of '49, The (English), 510
Deep River (Warfield), 578
Deep River and Other Classic Negro Spirituals (McFerrin), 546
Deep River and Other Spirituals (Shaw), 601
Documentary Talking Blues (Foster-Weissman), 512
Down to the Sea in Ships (Ives), 529
Duet Songs of French Canada (Baillargeon-Mills), 490
Dulcimer Songs and Solos (Clayton), 502

E

Early American Folksongs (Atcher), 490
Early American Psalmody (Margaret Dodd Singers), 602
Early English Ballads (Child-Percy), 555
Elektra New Folk Sampler, 602
English and American Folksongs (Child-Yarbrough), 499
English and Scottish Popular Ballads (MacColl-Lloyd), 602, 603, 604
English Drinking Songs (Lloyd), 537
English Folk Songs (House), 524
English Songs, 596
English Street Songs (Lloyd), 538
Englishman Sings American Folk Songs, An (Donnegan), 506
Ethnic Folkways Library, 613
Evening with Belafonte, An (Belafonte), 492
Every Inch a Sailor (Okun), 557

F

Faithful Lovers and Other Phenomena (Gooding), 517
False Ladye, The (Summers), 575
Family Tree of Folk Songs, A (Hinton), 522
Favorite Cowboy Songs (Sons of the Pioneers), 604
Favorite Spirituals, 605
Festival of Carols, 605
Field Trip (Ritchie), 561
Fiftieth Anniversary Album (Niles), 554
Fireside Treasury of Folk Songs, 605
Fisk Jubilee Singers, 605
Five Sea Chanties (Warfield), 579
Flat Rock Ballads (Sandburg), 567
Foc'sle Singers, 502
Foc'sle Songs and Shanties (Clayton), 502
Foc'sle Songs and Shanties (Okun), 557
Foggy Dew, The (Lloyd), 538
Folk and Traditional Love Songs (Roberts), 563
Folk Blues (Broonzy), 498
Folk Blues (Jefferson), 533
Folk Blues (Silverman), 574
Folk Blues (Terry), 576
Folk Favorites, 605, 606
Folk Jazz U.S.A. (Brooks), 497
Folk Music for People Who Hate Folk Music (Strauss), 607
Folk Music from Nova Scotia (Creighton), 606
Folksay, I-VI, 608
Folk Singer, The (McCurdy), 544
Folk Song from the South Appalachians (Paley), 558
Folk Songs (Clauson), 500
Folk Songs (Ferrier), 511
Folk Songs (Gilkyson), 515
Folk Songs (Guthrie-Houston), 520
Folk Songs (Houston), 524

Folk Songs (Reed), 559
Folk Songs (Seeger), 568
Folk Songs (Wilson), 584
Folk Songs and Ballads (Lea), 535
Folk Songs and Ballads of North Carolina (Williams), 583
Folk Songs and Ballads of Virginia (Clayton), 502
Folk Songs, Ballads, Blues, Work Songs (Silvera), 573
Folk Songs Dramatic and Humorous (Ives), 529
Folk Songs for Babies, Small Children, Parents and Baby Sitters (The Babysitters), 607
Folk Songs for Young Folk, Vol. I, II (Mills), 550
Folk Songs from Far Corners (Archer-Gile), 489
Folk Songs of Courting and Complaint (Seeger), 569
Folk Songs of French Canada (Labrecque), 534
Folk Songs of French Canada (Mills), 550
Folk Songs of Love and Play (Okun), 558
Folk Songs of Many Lands (Schlamme), 567
Folk Songs of Martha's Vineyard (Huntington), 525
Folk Songs of Newfoundland (Mills), 551
Folk Songs of the Allegheny Mountains (Gainer), 513
Folk Songs of the New World, 586
Folk Songs of the People (Temple), 576
Folksongs (Arkin), 489
Folksongs (Darling), 505
Folksongs (Howard University Choir), 607
Folksongs (McNeil), 547
Folksongs and Ballads of Kansas (O'Bryant), 556
Folksongs for Camp (Wagoners), 607
Folksongs for Young and Old (Mechau Family), 607
Folksongs from the Southern Appalachians, 600
Folksongs of Four Continents (Seeger-Song Swappers), 608
Folksongs of Israel (Bikel), 493
Folksongs of Israel (Bikel-Kagan), 493
Folksongs of Ohio (Gibson), 515
Folksongs of the Frontier (Wagner Chorale), 608
Folksongs of the New World (Wagner Chorale), 608
Folksongs with the Folksmiths, 609
Folkways-Viking Record of Folk Ballads (Clayton), 502
Follow the Drinking Gourd (LaRue-Drinking Gourd Singers), 610
Frankie and Johnnie (McCurdy), 545
French Ballads and Dance Tunes, 592
French Folk Songs for Children (Mills), 551

French Folksongs for Children Sung in English (Mills), 551
French Traditional Songs (Ginandes), 516
Frisco Bound (Fuller), 512
Frontier Ballads, I, II (Seeger), 571
Frontier Ballads and Cowboy Songs (Bender), 492
Frozen Logger, 610

G

Gambling Songs (English), 510
Gateway Singers at the Hungry I, The, 610
Gazette (Seeger), 572
Gems of American Folklore (Scott), 568
German Folk Songs (Schlamme), 567
Get Along Little Dogies, etc. (Luther), 540
Get on Board (Folkmasters), 610
Ghost Ballads (Gitter), 516
G.I. American Army Songs (Brand), 496
Goin' Down the Road (Cooper), 504
Gold in California (Foster-Weissman), 512
Golden Gate Spirituals (Golden Gate Quartet), 610
Golden Minutes of Folk Music (Gilkyson), 515
Golden Treasury of Songs America Sings (Stracke), 575
Gospel Songs (Missionary Quintet), 610
Gospel Songs (West), 579
Great American Bum, The (Greenway), 519
Great American Folk Heroes (Scott-Rogers), 568
Great American Folk Songs (Sykes), 576
Great New York Voices of Today, Vol. 6, 549

H

Haitian Folk Songs (Cuevas), 504
Hard Travelin' (Houston), 525
Harlem Street Spirituals (Anderson-Davis), 489
Harmonica and Vocal Solos (Terry), 577
Harry Belafonte at Carnegie Hall (Belafonte), 492
Haul on the Bowlin' (Lloyd-MacColl), 538
Here We Go Baby (Yarbrough), 585
Heroes, Heroines & Mishaps (Allison), 488
His Songs and Music (Kazee), 533
His Story (Broonzy), 498
Historical America in Song (Ives), 526
History of Canada in Folk Songs (Fowke), 552
Holly and the Ivy, The (Deller), 506
Howard University Choir, 607
Hymns and Carols (Summers), 575

I

I Come for to Sing (Gibson), 515
I Know My Love (Reed), 560
I Know Where I'm Going (Olsen), 558
I Sing of Canada (Okun), 558
I Wonder As I Wander (Niles), 554
In the Quiet of the Night (Ives), 530
Instrumental Music of the Southern Appalachians, 586, 611
Irish Ballads, 610
Irish Drinking Songs, 513
Irish Festival Singers, 611
Irish Humor Songs (Galvin), 513
Irish Love Songs (Galvin), 513
Irish Melodies (Moore), 553
Irish Rebel Ballads (Galvin), 514
Irish Rebel Songs, I and II (Galvin), 514
Irish Street Songs (Galvin), 514
Irish Street Songs (Roberts), 563
Italian Folk Songs (Gooding), 517

J

Jack Takes the Floor (Elliott), 509
Jewish Children's Songs and Games (Rubin), 565
Jewish Folk Songs (Rubin), 565
Jewish Folk Songs (Schlamme), 568
Jewish Folksongs (Bikel), 493
Jewish Young Folksingers, The, 612
Jimmy Crack Corn (Hayes–Buckle Busters), 611
Johnson, Blind Willie: His Story (Charters), 533
Jordan and Jubilee (Lomax), 594
Josh at Midnight (White), 581
Josh White Comes a-Visiting (White), 581
Josh White Program, A (White), 582
Josh White Stories, I, II, The (White), 582
Josh White's Blues (White), 582

K

Kentucky Ballads (English), 510
Kentucky Mountain Songs (Ritchie), 561
Kitty White Sings (White), 583

L

Lady Gay, The (Summers), 575
Land of Milk and Honey (Hillel and Aviva), 521
Laughing America (Brand-Hellerman), 496
Leadbelly Memorial, Vol. I-II, 535; Vol. III-IV, 536
Leadbelly's Last Sessions, Vol. 1-2, 536
Leadbelly's Legacy, Vol. 3, 536; Vol. 4, 537
Legend of John Henry (Clark), 499

Legend of Robin Hood, The (McCurdy-Kane), 546
Leisure Time (Wilson), 584
Leroy Anderson Orchestra, 598
Life of Christ in Folk Song (Hayes), 521
Listen to the Story, 612
Lithuanian Folk Songs in the U.S. (Balys), 612
Lonesome Train, 612
Lonesome Valley (Seeger), 612
Louisiana and Smoky Mountain Ballads (Van Wey), 578
Love Is a Gentle Thing (Belafonte), 492
Love Songs for Friends and Foes (Seeger), 572
Love Songs of Ireland (O'Hara), 556
Love Songs, Old and New (Todd), 577
Lyn Murray Singers, 598

M

Mama I Want a Husband (Murai), 553
Marais and Miranda in Person (Marais-Miranda), 548, 549
"Mark Twain" and Other Folk Favorites (Belafonte), 491
Matching Songs of the British Isles and America (MacColl-Seeger), 543
Men (Ives), 530
Merry Ditties (Okun), 558
Mexican Folksongs (Gooding), 517
Mexican Love Songs (Cruz), 504
Minstrel Boy, The (Lynch), 540
Minstrel of the Appalachians (Lunsford), 539
Missouri Folk Songs (Cansler), 499
More Folksongs (Ives), 530
More Play-Party Songs (Leadbelly), 536
More Songs (Guthrie-Houston), 520
More Songs by the 20th Century Minstrel (Dyer-Bennet), 508
More Songs to Grow On (Mills), 551
More Southern Mountain Folk Songs (West), 579
Mormon Folk Songs (Hilton), 522
Mormon Tabernacle Choir Sings Christmas Carols, 612
Mount Holyoke College Glee Club, 598
Mountain Music, Bluegrass Style (M. Seeger), 612
Music Box of Christmas Carols (Welch Chorale), 613
Music for Moonshiners, 613
Music from the South: Country Brass Bands (Ramsey), 613
My Songs (Hayes), 521

N

Negro Folk Music of Alabama, 613, 614
Negro Folk Songs and Tunes (Cotton), 504
Negro Prison Camp Work Songs, 614
Negro Prison Songs, Mississippi Penitentiary (Lomax), 614

Negro Religious Songs and Services, 615
Negro Spirituals and Ballads (Traubel), 577
Negro Work Songs and Calls, 615
Newly Discovered Early American Folk Songs (Driftwood), 507
Night in Ireland (McNulty), 615
900 Miles and Other Railroad Ballads (Houston), 525
North Carolina Ballads (Moser), 553
Nova Scotia Folk Music from Cape Breton (Hamilton), 615
Nursery Songs (Kelly), 616

O

O, Canada (Mills), 552
Odetta and Larry (Odetta), 556
Odetta at the Gate of Horn (Odetta), 556
Odetta Sings Ballads and Blues (Odetta), 556
Of Maids and Mistresses (Kines), 533
Off to Sea Once More (Lloyd-MacColl), 538
Off-Beat Folk Songs (Shanty Boys), 616
Offbeat Folk Songs (Gibson), 515
Ohio Valley Ballads (Buckley), 498
Old Airs from Ireland, Scotland, and England (Reed), 560
Old American Songs (Warfield), 579
Old Chisholm Trail, The (Jarrett), 532
Old Harp Singers, 616
Olden Ballads (T. Glazer–Dyer-Bennett), 517
Once Over Lightly (Arkin), 489
Our Singing Heritage, 616, 617
Outlaws of the Old West (Hall), 520
Ozark Mountain Folksongs, I (Stekert), 574

P

Pardo Ancient Instrument Ensemble, 547
Pennsylvania Dutch Folk Songs (Britton), 497
Pete Seeger Sampler (Seeger), 572
Pickin' and Blowin' (Pegram-Parham), 617
Pie in the Sky (Brand), 496
Pirate Songs and Ballads (Wilder), 583
Play and Dance Songs and Tunes, 617
Play Party Songs (Leadbelly), 536
Popular Square Dance Music (Jackson), 618
Presenting the Belafonte Singers (Belafonte), 492
Promised Land (Welch Chorale), 618
Puttin' on the Style (Gateway Singers), 618

Q

Queen of Hearts (Gooding), 517

R

Railroad Songs (Lomax), 594
Rambling Boys, The (Elliott-Adams), 510
Randolph Singers, 599
Real McCoy, The (Hinton), 522
Recital (Hayes), 521
Recital of Negro Spirituals (Davis), 505
Recordings for Encyclopaedia Britannica Films (Ives), 526
Return of the Wayfaring Stranger (Ives), 530
Riddle Me This (Ritchie-Brand), 562
Ritchie Family of Kentucky, The (Ritchie), 561
Riverside Folksong Sampler, 586, 618
Robert Shaw Chorale of Women's Voices, 597
Robin Hood Ballads (House), 524
Rock Island Line (Ledbetter), 537
Rock Island Line (Lomax), 593
Roving Balladeer, The (Brill), 496
Run Come Hear (Folk Singers), 619

S

Sacred Harp Singing, 619
St. Luke's Choristers, 599
Saturday Night and Sunday Too (Ritchie), 561
Scots Folk Songs (MacColl), 542
Scots Street Songs (MacColl), 542
Seeds of Love (Summers), 576
Shanty Boys, The, 552
Shanty Men (Eskin), 511
Shivaree, 619
Shuttle and Cage (MacColl-Seeger), 543
Sin Songs, pro and con (McCurdy), 545
Sing a Song of Childhood (Bennet-King), 492
Sing of America (Scott), 568
Sing Out, Sweet Land!, 619
Singing Across the Land (Hinton), 522
Singing Family of the Cumberlands (Ritchie), 562
Singing Reverend, The (Davis), 505
Sings (Broonzy), 498
Sings (White), 582
Sings (Ballads) (Summers), 576
Sings (Blues) (Broonzy), 498
Sings American Folksongs (J. Lomax), 539
Sings and Josh White Comes A-Visiting (Broonzy), 498
Sings Eleven Great Spirituals (Anderson), 488
Sings Folk Songs (Faye), 511
Sings Folksongs (Ginandes), 516
Sings Folk Songs (Rodgers), 565
Sings Folk Songs and Ballads (Langstaff), 534
Sings for All Ages (Ives), 531
Sings for Fun (Ives), 530
Sings His Favorites (Belafonte), 491
Sings of the Caribbean (Belafonte), 492
Sings Old Airs (Reed), 560

Sings Ranchera Songs (Hurd), 525
Sings Spirituals, 488, 489
Sings the Blues (White), 582
Smoky Mountain Ballads (Lunsford), 540
Smoky Mountain Ballads (West), 580
Solomon Valley Ballads (Jemison), 533
Son of Dalliance (McCurdy), 545
Songs (Dyer-Bennet), 508, 509
Songs (Marais-Miranda), 548
Songs (McGhee-Terry), 546, 547
Songs and Ballads (Holt), 523
Songs and Ballads of American History, 620
Songs and Ballads of America's Wars (Warner), 579
Songs and Ballads of Newfoundland (Peacock), 559
Songs and Ballads of the Scottish Wars (Dunbar), 507
Songs and Ballads of the West, 621
Songs and Dances of Quebec, 620
Songs Children Sing in Italy (Decormier), 505
Songs from a Village Garret (Boguslav), 493
Songs from Cape Breton Island (Cowell), 620
Songs from Kentucky (Ritchie), 562
Songs from the Veld (Marais), 548
Songs of a New York Lumberjack (Stekert), 574
Songs of a Scot Tinker Lady (Robertson), 564
Songs of Acadia (Baillargeon-Mills), 491
Songs of All Times (Eskin), 511
Songs of an Irish Tinker Lady (Barry), 491
Songs of Erin (O'Hara), 556
Songs of Expanding America (Ives), 527
Songs of French Canada, 621
Songs of Ireland (Ives), 531
Songs of Ireland (O'Hara), 557
Songs of Joe Hill (J. Glazer), 516
Songs of Many Lands (Marais), 547
Songs of North and South (Ives), 526
Songs of the Chisholm Trail (Kraber), 534
Songs of the Colonies (Ives), 526
Songs of the Deep South, 621
Songs of the Frontier (Ives), 527
Songs of the Golden West, 621
Songs of the Irish Rebellion of 1798 (House), 524
Songs of the Mormons, 621
Songs of the Old Chisholm Trail (Kraber), 534
Songs of the Old West (McCurdy), 545
Songs of the Railroad (Merrill Gay Singers), 621
Songs of the Revolution (Ives), 526
Songs of the Saddle (Atcher), 490
Songs of the Sea (Ives), 527
Songs of the Sea (Mills-Shanty), 552
Songs of the Smoky Mountains, 622
Songs of the South (Luboff), 622
Songs of the West (Luboff), 622

Songs of Thomas Moore (Moore), 553
Songs to Grow On (Guthrie), 519
Songs to Grow On (Seeger), 622
Songs with Young People in Mind (Dyer-Bennet), 509
Sonny Terry and His Mouth Harp (Terry), 577
South African Folk Songs (Marais-Miranda), 549
South African Veld (Marais), 547
Southern Mountain Children's Songs and Games (Ritchie), 562
Southern Mountain Folk Songs (West), 580
Southern Mountain Folksongs and Ballads, 623
Southern Mountain Hoedowns, 623
Spanish-American Children's Songs (Vincent), 578
Spanish and Mexican Folk Music of New Mexico (Robb), 623
Spanish Religious Songs and Game Songs, 592
Spirituals, 623, 624
Spirituals (Duncan), 507
Spirituals (Ford), 512
Spirituals (Lomax), 594
Spirituals (Matthews), 549
Spirituals (Reed-Hall), 559
Spirituals (Robeson), 564
Spirituals (West), 580
Spirituals (Williams), 584
Spirituals and Folksongs (Robeson), 564
Spirituals and Work Songs (Gary), 514
Square Dance Tonight (Jackson), 624
Square Dances, 624, 625
Story of John Henry (White), 583
Sundown Songs (Marais-Miranda), 549
Swing Low (De Paur Infantry Chorus), 626
Swing Low, Sweet Chariot (Charles), 499
Swing Low, Sweet Chariot (Robeson), 564
Swing Your Partners, 626
Swingin' Folk Tunes (Jacobs), 532

T

Take This Hammer (Ledbetter), 537
Talking Dust Bowl (Guthrie), 520
Terry's, Sonny, Washboard Band, 626
Texas Folk Songs (Lomax), 539
Texas Folk Songs (Nye), 555
Texas Folk Songs (Wood), 585
Thar She Blows! (Lloyd-MacColl), 539
This Is My Land, 622
This Lusty Land (Ford), 512
Three Ravens, The (Deller), 506
Through Bushes and Briars (Cameron), 498
Timber-r-r! (Clayton), 502
To You with Love (Marshall), 549
To You with Love (Ross), 565
Tradition Folk Sampler, 627
Traditional American Love Songs (Okun-Stekert), 558

Traditional English Folksongs (Runge), 566
Traditional Folk Songs and Ballads (Roberts), 563
Traditional Songs of Her Kentucky Mountain Family (Ritchie), 562
Traditional Songs of the Old West (Houston-Bender), 525
Tragic Ballads (Creswell), 504
Turkish and Spanish Folksongs (Gooding), 518
Turkish, Spanish and Mexican Folk Songs (Gooding), 518
Twentieth Century Minstrel, The (Dyer-Bennet), 509
Twenty-fifth Anniversary Album (White), 583
Two Sailors (Lomax), 593

U

Unholy Matrimony (Clayton), 503
Unquiet Grave, The (Summers), 576

V

Voices of Haiti (Maya Deren), 627

W

Wagon Wheels (Gould), 627
Wanderin' (Arnold), 490
Wanderin' with Stan Wilson, 578
Wandering Minstrel, The (Campbell), 498
Wanted for Murder (Clayton), 503

Waters of Tyne (Clayton), 503
Wayfarers, The, 627
Wayfaring Stranger, The (Ives), 531
Weavers, Best of the, 628
Weavers, The: Folksongs of America and Other Lands, 627
Weavers at Carnegie Hall, The, 628
Weavers at Home, The, 628
Weavers on Tour, The, 628
Weavers Traveling On, The, 628
Whaling and Sailing Songs from the Days of Moby Dick (Clayton), 503
Whaling Songs and Ballads (Clayton), 503
When Dalliance Was in Flower (McCurdy), 545, 546
Who Built America? (Bonyun), 494
With Voices Together We Sing (Seeger), 572
Wolf River Songs (Cowell), 628
Women (Ives), 532
Women: Folk Songs about the Fair Sex (Ives), 532
Work Songs, Blues, Spirituals (Fuller), 512
Working on the Railroad (Fuller), 513
World Festival of Folk Song and Folk Dance, 629
World of Folk Dances, The (Herman), 630
World of Will Holt (Holt), 523
Wraggle Taggle Gypsies (Deller), 506

Y

Yankee Legend (Bonyun), 494
Yiddish and Israeli Songs (Rubin), 565
Yiddish Love Songs (Rubin), 566